FROMMER'S

COMPREHENSIVE TRAVEL GUIDE

COLORADO

2ND EDITION

by Don and Barbara Laine
with John Gottberg

PRENTICE HALL TRAVEL

NEW YORK • LONDON • TORONTO • SYDNEY • TOKYO • SINGAPORE

FROMMER BOOKS
Published by Prentice Hall General Reference
15 Columbus Circle
New York, NY 10023

ISBN 0-671-86654-0
ISSN 1053-2463

Design by Robert Bull Design
Maps by Geografix Inc.

FROMMER'S EDITORIAL STAFF
Editorial Director: Marilyn Wood
Editorial Manager/Senior Editor: Alice Fellows
Senior Editors: Lisa Renaud, Sara Hinsey Raveret
Editors: Charlotte Allstrom, Thomas F. Hirsch, Peter Katucki, Theodore Stavrou
Assistant Editors: Margaret Bowen, Christopher Hollander, Alice Thompson, Ian Wilker
Editorial Assistants: Gretchen Henderson, Douglas Stallings
Managing Editor: Leanne Coupe

Special Sales
Bulk purchases (10+ copies) of Frommer's Travel Guides are available to corporations at special discounts. The Special Sales Department can produce custom editions to be used as premiums and/or for sales promotions to suit individual needs. Existing editions can be produced with custom cover imprints such as a corporate logo. For more information write to: Special Sales, Prentice Hall Travel, 15 Columbus Circle, New York, NY 10023.

CONTENTS

LIST OF MAPS

INVITATION TO THE READERS

In researching this book, we have come across many wonderful establishments, the best of which we have included here. We are sure that many of you will also come across appealing hotels, inns, restaurants, guest houses, shops, and attractions. Please don't keep them to yourself. Share your experiences, especially if you want to comment on places that have been included in this edition that have changed for the worse. You can address your letters to:

Don and Barbara Laine
Frommer's Colorado
c/o Prentice Hall Travel
15 Columbus Circle
New York, NY 10023

A DISCLAIMER

Readers are advised that prices fluctuate in the course of time, and travel information changes under the impact of the varied and volatile factors that affect the travel industry. Neither the author nor the publisher can be held responsible for the experiences of readers while traveling. Readers are invited to write to the publisher with ideas, comments, and suggestions for future editions.

SAFETY ADVISORY

Whenever you're traveling in an unfamiliar city or country, stay alert. Be aware of your immediate surroundings. Wear a money belt and keep a close eye on your possessions. Be particularly careful with cameras, purses, and wallets, all favorite targets of thieves and pickpockets.

CHAPTER 1

GETTING TO KNOW COLORADO

**1. GEOGRAPHY &
PEOPLE**

- **DID YOU KNOW . . . ?**

2. HISTORY

- **DATELINE**

**3. SPORTS &
RECREATION**

**4. RECOMMENDED
BOOKS**

Colorado is the heartland of the Rocky Mountains, the backbone of North America. With
more than 50 peaks that soar above 14,000 feet, it is
the most highly elevated state in the United States,
and perhaps the most spectacular. The Rockies—
with their evergreen and aspen forests, their racing
streams and rivers, their wealth of wildlife—are
perfect for recreation throughout the year, from
summer hiking and rafting to winter skiing.

But Colorado is not *only* the mountains. It is also
the wheat and corn fields of the vast eastern prairies,
the high plateau country of the west, and the modern, sophisticated cities of the Front
Range.

Take the time to see the sights of cosmopolitan Denver, the "Mile High City";
Colorado Springs, home of the U.S. Air Force Academy and U.S. Olympic Training
Center; and the university towns of Boulder and Fort Collins. Indulge in luxury hotels,
gourmet cuisine, and year-round recreation at thriving resort communities such as
Aspen, Vail, and Steamboat Springs. Ride the narrow-gauge steam trains and relive the
mining-boom days in rejuvenated towns such as Durango, Georgetown, and Cripple
Creek, straight out of the Old West but alive with 20th-century verve. Immerse
yourself in the natural and human-made wonders of national parks and monuments
such as Mesa Verde, Rocky Mountain, Great Sand Dunes, Dinosaur, Black Canyon of
the Gunnison, and Bent's Old Fort, each with its own unique fascination.

Get to know Colorado's people. Meet the hotelier in Denver and the cowboy in
Craig, the ski instructor in Crested Butte and the Hispanic farmer in San Luis.

Come to Colorado for the seasons. Whatever you do, don't stay indoors. Enos
Mills, an early 20th-century environmentalist who was the driving force behind the
creation of Rocky Mountain National Park, said that a knowledge of nature is the
basis of wisdom. In other words, get out and get smart. That's the essence of
Colorado.

1. GEOGRAPHY & PEOPLE

First-time visitors traveling to Colorado may be awed by the looming wall of the
Rocky Mountains. They come into sight a good 100 miles away, soon after drivers
cross the state boundary with Kansas. East of the Rockies, a 5,000-foot peak is
considered high; yet Colorado alone has 1,143 mountains above 10,000 feet,
including 53 over 14,000! Highest of all is Mount Elbert at 14,433 feet. The ridge of
the Continental Divide zigzags more or less through the center of the 104,000-square-
mile state.

Thanks to territorial legislators of the last century, Colorado is an almost-perfect
rectangle, measuring some 385 miles east to west and 275 miles north to south. Its
basic topography can be visualized by dividing the state into vertical thirds: The
eastern third is plains, the midsection is high mountains, and the western third is mesa
land.

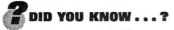
DID YOU KNOW . . . ?

- Four Corners Monument near Towaoc is the only place in America where visitors can stand in four states—Colorado, New Mexico, Arizona, and Utah—at once.
- Butch Cassidy robbed his first bank, in Telluride, in 1880.
- The key collection at the Baldpate Inn near Estes Park could unlock Hitler's desk, Mozart's wine cellar, Fort Knox, and Westminster Abbey.
- Colorado contains 75% of all land in the continental U.S. above 10,000 feet in elevation.
- The world's largest natural mineral hot-spring swimming pool is at Glenwood Springs.
- Pictographs found near Springfield, in the southeast, date from the 5th century A.D. and may be Celtic in origin.
- Denver gets more days of sunshine a year than San Diego or Miami.
- The world's highest automobile tunnel, the Eisenhower Tunnel, crosses the Continental Divide at 11,000 feet.
- The two largest known dinosaur skeletons on earth were uncovered south of Grand Junction in the 1970s.

That's a broad simplification, of course. The central Rockies, though they cover six times the mountain area of Switzerland, are not a single vast highland but are composed of a series of high ranges running in roughly north-south directions. The spectacular San Juans separate the southwestern corner from the rest of Colorado, with the result that it is culturally more akin to the Southwest than to the Rocky Mountains.

The westward-flowing Colorado River system dominates the western part of the state, with tributary networks including the Gunnison, Dolores, and Yampa-Green rivers. East of the divide, the primary river systems are the South Platte, the Arkansas, and the Rio Grande, all flowing toward the Gulf of Mexico. Particularly in eastern Colorado, but also in the west, the rivers are not broad bodies of water like the Ohio or Columbia, or even like the Allegheny or Willamette. They are streams heavy with spring and summer snowmelt, and during much of the year, they are reduced on the dry prairies to mere trickles by the heavy demands of farm and ranch irrigation. Besides agricultural use, they are a prime wildlife habitat and a tremendous outdoor recreational resource.

The forested mountains are essential to retaining the precious water for the lowlands. Eleven national forests comprise 15 million acres of land, and there are 8 million acres controlled by the Bureau of Land Management also open for public recreational use. Another half million acres are within national parks, monuments, and recreation areas under the administration of the National Park Service. Besides all this, the state operates more than 40 state parks and recreation areas.

Colorado's name, Spanish for "red," derives from the state's red soil and rocks. Some of the sandstone agglomerates have become attractions in their own rights, such as the Red Rocks Amphitheatre west of Denver and the startling Garden of the Gods State Park in Colorado Springs.

Of Colorado's 3.3 million people, some 80% live along the "Front Range," the I-25 corridor, where the plains meet the mountains. Denver, the state capital, has a population close to 500,000, with another million in the metropolitan area. Colorado Springs has the second largest population with about 280,000 residents, followed by Pueblo (99,000), Boulder (83,000), Fort Collins (88,000), and Greeley (61,000).

DATELINE

- **12,000 B.C.**
  First inhabitants include Folsom Man.
- **3,000 B.C.**
  Prehistoric farming communities.
  (continues)

2. HISTORY

The history of Colorado is a testimony to the human ability to adapt to and flourish in a difficult environment. This land of high mountains and limited water continues to challenge its inhabitants even today.

Archeologists say the earliest inhabitants of Colorado

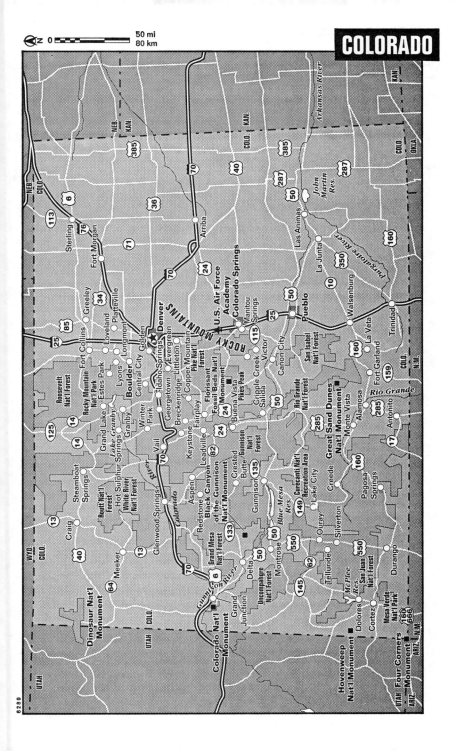

COLORADO

50 mi
80 km

6289

migrated from the Bering Land Bridge about 12,000 B.C. Weapon points discovered in Folsom, New Mexico, just southeast of modern Trinidad, Colorado, established for the first time that prehistoric peoples hunted now-extinct mammals such as woolly mammoths. Stable farming settlements, evidenced by the remains of domestically grown maize, date from about 3,000 B.C.

Around the beginning of the Christian Era, the early Anasazi people lived in shallow rock shelters, or pit houses, in the region of modern Durango. One of America's best-known Pre-Columbian civilizations, they left behind distinctive basketwork. By about A.D. 700, Anasazi culture had expanded into elaborate cliff villages throughout what is now known as the Four Corners Region (where Colorado, New Mexico, Arizona, and Utah come together). Remnants of the cliff dwellers' culture, which was at its peak around A.D. 1000, are best observed at Mesa Verde National Park in southwestern Colorado.

By the time Spanish conquistadores, the first European visitors, arrived in the mid-16th century, the Anasazi had long since departed. Their cliff dwellings were abandoned around the 13th century for unknown reasons. In the Anasazis' place were two major nomadic Native American cultures: the mountain dwellers of the west, primarily Utes, and the plains tribes of the east, principally Arapahoe, Cheyenne, and Comanche.

EXPLORATION & SETTLEMENT

Spanish colonists, having established settlements at Santa Fe, Taos, and other upper Rio Grande locations in the 16th and 17th centuries, didn't find Colorado's San Luis Valley attractive for colonization. Not only was there a lack of financial and military support from the Spanish crown, but the fierce, freedom-loving Comanches and Utes wouldn't be roped into a servile hacienda life.

Nevertheless, the Spanish still held title to southern and western Colorado in 1803, when U.S. president Thomas Jefferson paid $15 million to buy the vast Louisiana Territory from Napoleon. The tract included the lion's share of modern Colorado, to the sources of the Arkansas and Platte rivers near the Continental Divide.

To explore the hinterlands, Jefferson commissioned a company of 16 soldiers, led by Capt. Zebulon Pike. Pike and his party left St. Louis in June 1806. By the end of November, they were camped at the foot of the landmark mountain that today bears the captain's name: Pikes Peak. They continued west until they were arrested by Spanish soldiers for trespassing on the Rio Grande. In July 1807, after being taken to Santa Fe for questioning and to Chihuahua, Mexico, for jailing, Pike and his men were released to American authorities.

Pike's eyewitness account of previously inaccessible Santa Fe was of major interest to Americans. When Mexico won its independence from Spain in 1821 and dropped the ban against trade with other countries, William Becknell led a pack train from St. Louis to Santa Fe and sold his wares for seven times their original cost. Becknell returned the following year, establishing the Santa Fe Trail.

To mesh the growing Santa Fe trade with eastern demands for Rocky Mountain furs, Bent's Fort was built on the Arkansas River (near modern La Junta) between 1828 and 1832 by brothers William and Charles Bent and their partner, Ceran St. Vrain. In 1838 a second outpost, Fort St. Vrain, was built on the South Platte River east of modern Denver. A road linked the two with Fort Laramie on the North Platte.

Many of the furs were provided by "mountain men," self-reliant adventurers including Kit Carson, Jim Bridger, Lucien Maxwell, and Tom Fitzpatrick. Making their livings mainly as trappers and guides, these men forged a mutual understanding with the Native American tribes and became legends in their own times.

The fur boom collapsed around 1840. By that time, Missouri Sen. Thomas Hart Benton was pushing his doctrine of "Manifest Destiny." Benton believed that control of the West Coast would wrest the fabled trade with Asia from the British and other European powers.

Americans had been generally apathetic to western expansion ever since an 1820 expedition led by Maj. Stephen Long had labeled the high plains of eastern Colorado "the great American desert." In 1842, in hopes of reversing public opinion, Benton sent his son-in-law, Lt. John Charles Frémont, to map the Oregon Trail from the Missouri River up the North Platte to the Continental Divide. Frémont was so taken by the country that he returned in 1843 to plot a new route. Employing Carson and other mountain men as his guides and hunters, he took his party across the Continental Divide to Oregon, south through the Sierra Nevada to the Mojave Desert and back across Utah and Colorado to Bent's Fort. In the fall of 1844, after 18 months and 5,000 miles of traveling, they returned to St. Louis. Jessie Benton Frémont wrote and published the expedition's story based on her husband's letters and journals, and it caused great excitement among the American public. The Mormon migration to Utah and the rush of easterners to the Columbia River country were almost direct consequences of John Frémont's expedition and Jessie Frémont's hyperbole. (It enhanced John's fame, as well: 12 years later, in 1856, he narrowly lost the U.S. presidential election to Democrat James Buchanan.)

Meanwhile, Texas had declared its independence from Mexico in 1844. Within three years President James Polk had found an excuse to invade Mexican territory. In the summer of 1847, Gen. Stephen Kearny and an army of 1,700 men paused at Bent's Fort en route to Santa Fe, which they conquered in August without a shot being fired. From there, Kearny marched west to California, which he took in December. The treaty of Guadalupe Hidalgo, on February 2, 1848, set the U.S.–Mexico frontier close to its present boundary. (A small piece of Arizona and New Mexico was added in 1853.)

Modern Colorado was split between the territories of Utah (in 1850), which extended from the California border to the Continental Divide; New Mexico (in 1850), including Bent's Fort and the southeast; Kansas (in 1854), from the divide east to Missouri; and Nebraska (in 1854), including the South Platte Valley of the northeast.

DATELINE

Utes obtain treaties guaranteeing 16 million acres of western Colorado land.

- **1864** Hundreds of innocent Cheyennes killed in Sand Creek Massacre; University of Denver becomes Colorado's first institution of higher education.
- **1870** Kansas City–Denver rail line completed; agricultural commune of Greeley established by Nathan Meeker; Colorado State University opens.
- **1871** Gen. William Palmer founds Colorado Springs.
- **1876** Colorado becomes 38th state.
- **1877** University of Colorado opens in Boulder.
- **1878** Little Pittsburg silver strike launches Leadville mining boom, Colorado's greatest.
- **1879** Milk Creek Massacre by Ute warriors leads to tribe's removal to reservations.
- **1890** Sherman Silver Purchase Act; gold discovered at Cripple Creek, leading to state's biggest gold rush.
- **1893** Women win right to vote; silver industry collapses following repeal of Sherman Silver Purchase Act.

(continues)

DATELINE

• **1901–07** President Theodore Roosevelt sets aside 16 million acres of national forest land in Colorado.

• **1906** U.S. Mint built in Denver.

• **1913** Wolf Creek Pass highway is first to cross Continental Divide in Colorado.

• **1915** Rocky Mountain National Park established.

• **1934** Direct Denver–San Francisco rail travel begins; Taylor Grazing Act ends homesteading.

• **1941–45** World War II establishes Colorado as military center.

• **1947** Aspen's first chair lift begins operation.

• **1948–58** Uranium "rush" sweeps western slope.

• **1955** Environmentalists prevent construction of Echo Park Dam in Dinosaur National Monument.

• **1988** Sen. Gary Hart, a frontrunner for the Democratic presidential nomination, withdraws from race after a scandal.

• **1991** Denver awarded major-league baseball franchise (the Rockies) in 1993, making it the 15th U.S. city with three major professional sports.

Arapahoe County was among those created within the Kansas Territory, extending over 150 miles east from the Continental Divide to the 103rd meridian. It was populated almost exclusively by plains tribes until 1858, when gold seekers discovered flakes of the precious metal in sands near the junction of Cherry Creek and the South Platte. General William Larimer established Denver adjacent to the site, naming it after Kansas governor James Denver.

The Cherry Creek strike was literally a flash in the gold-seeker's pan, but strikes in the nearby mountains in early 1859 were much more significant: at Clear Creek, near what would become Idaho Springs; and in a quartz vein at Gregory Gulch, which led to the founding of Central City. When word got back East that summer, 50,000 pioneers vowed to reach "Pikes Peak or Bust."

THE TERRITORY

Abraham Lincoln was elected president in November 1860. Congress, then dominated by Republicans eager to please the wealthy gold-mine owners, created the Colorado Territory on February 28, 1861. The new territory absorbed neighboring sections of Utah, Nebraska, and New Mexico to fill out the boundaries that the state still has today.

Lincoln's Homestead Act of 1862 brought much of the public domain into private ownership, and led to the platting of Front Range townships, starting with Denver in 1861.

Controlling the Native American peoples was a priority of the territorial government. A treaty negotiated by Tom Fitzpatrick at Fort Laramie in 1851 had guaranteed the entire Pikes Peak region to the nomadic plains tribes, but that had been made moot by the rush of settlers in the late 1850s. The Fort Wise Treaty of 1861 exchanged the Pikes Peak territory for five million fertile acres of Arkansas Valley land, north of modern La Junta. But when the Arapahoes and Cheyennes continued to roam their old hunting grounds, conflict was inevitable. Frequent rumors and rare instances of hostility against settlers gave the Colorado cavalry sufficient reason to attack a peaceful settlement of Cheyennes—flying Old Glory and a white flag—in November 1864. About 200 Cheyennes, two-thirds of them women and children, were killed in what has become known as the Sand Creek Massacre.

The Cheyennes and Arapahoes vowed revenge and launched a campaign to drive whites from their ancient hunting grounds. Their biggest triumph was the destruction of the town of Julesburg in 1865. But the cavalry, bolstered by returning Civil War veterans, managed to force the two tribes into reservations in Indian Territory (now Oklahoma) using the Medicine Lodge Creek Treaty of October 1867. The cavalry suppressed the few remaining renegades with victories over the Cheyennes near Wray (1868) and Sterling (1869).

Mining was at a standstill in 1864 when William Gilpin, who had served as the first territorial governor from 1861 to 1862, bought the million-acre Sangre de Cristo grant embracing the San Luis Valley. Intending to sell parcels to

European investors on speculation, he hired Brown University chemistry professor Nathaniel Hill to evaluate its mineral wealth.

Hill saw greater potential for the Central City area—if he could develop a smelting process to reduce its gold, silver, and copper ores to concentrates. After a transatlantic research trip to Wales and discussions with a Cornish metallurgist, he opened a smelter in Black Hawk in 1867. It was an immediate success. It not only attracted investment from the East but set the stage for the large-scale spread of mining throughout Colorado in years to come.

When the first transcontinental railroad was completed in 1866, the Union Pacific went through Cheyenne, 100 miles north of Denver. Such entrepreneurs as William Loveland, the founder of Golden—a town 14 miles west of Denver that shared the territorial capital until 1867—promoted a rail link with Cheyenne. Finally, former Gov. John Evans (1862–65) and banker Jerome Chaffee hired Gen. William J. Palmer, director of the Kansas Pacific Railroad, to build a Kansas City–Denver railroad. It was completed in 1870.

Water and land issues also were an important focus. The territorial and federal legislatures in 1866 passed what was called the Colorado Doctrine of prior appropriation, later adopted throughout the Rockies. It held that during times of near drought, when a stream's low flow didn't provide sufficient water for every farm along its route, priority for beneficial use was given on a seniority basis to the first persons to file a claim to a farm along that stream.

One of the most important developments in Colorado agriculture was conceived not in Denver, but in New York. *New York Tribune* editor Horace Greeley sent his farm columnist, Utopian idealist Nathan Meeker, to establish an agrarian prairie commune to be known as Union Colony in 1870. Meeker recruited more than 200 pioneers from all walks of life, purchased a tract on the Cache la Poudre River from Evans's and Chaffee's Denver Pacific Railroad, and called his community Greeley in honor of his patron.

The potentially fertile soil needed irrigation to be productive. Colonist E. S. Nettleton devised a canal system that revolutionized high-altitude agriculture. A series of long ditches ran parallel to the Cache la Poudre but fell at a more gradual rate than the river, irrigating many thousands of acres of barren land.

Farther east, the prairie grasses provided fine grazing for herds of longhorn cattle. The largest livestock empire was that of John Wesley Iliff, who bought 2,000 longhorns at $10 a head in 1867, sold them for $35 a head, and soon became a millionaire with 650,000 acres of land in northern Colorado. He brought the public domain into private ownership by reversing the intent of the Homestead Act, as his employees signed their land over to him in a sort of neofeudal autocracy. To assure his empire's security, he stationed armed foremen at all nine of his ranches.

Other stockmen imitated Iliff's success. But numerous factors led to the cattle industry's rapid demise. As more and more longhorns populated the plains, competing with sheep for the prairie grasses, their price rose dramatically. Barbed wire, invented in 1874, soon surrounded farms and railroad tracks, further diminishing the animals' range. Soon they were branded as disease carriers and banished from Colorado entirely.

STATEHOOD

Colorado had already begun moving in the direction of statehood during the Civil War years but it wasn't until August 1, 1876, that Colorado became the 38th state. Coming less than a month after the United States' 100th birthday, it was natural that Colorado should become known as "the Centennial State." John Routt was elected the first governor.

The state's new constitution gave the vote to African Americans, but not to women, despite the strong efforts of the Colorado Women's Suffrage Association. This was mildly surprising: The feminist movement was particularly strong in the state. Since Julia Holmes had donned "bloomers" to climb Pikes Peak in 1858, women had played an active if behind-the-scenes role in Colorado's growth. The suffragettes finally succeeded in winning the vote in 1893, three years after Wyoming became the first state to offer universal suffrage.

At the time of statehood, most of Colorado's vast western region was still occupied by some 3,500 mountain and plateau dwellers of a half-dozen Ute tribes. Unlike the plains tribes, their early relations with white explorers and settlers had been peaceful and unpressured. Their great Chief Ouray, leader of the Uncompahgre Ute tribe of the Southwest, had negotiated treaties in 1863 and 1868 that guaranteed them 16 million acres, or most of western Colorado. In 1873, Ouray agreed to sell the United States one-fourth of that acreage in the mineral-rich San Juan Mountains in exchange for hunting rights and $25,000 in annual annuities.

But a mining boom that began in 1878 led to a flurry of intrusions into Ute territory and stirred up a "Utes Must Go!" sentiment fueled by editorials in the *Denver Tribune*. Tension grew until, in September 1879, Greeley founder Nathan Meeker (then a Native American agent), cavalry Maj. Thomas Thornburgh, and 20 other men were killed in the Milk Creek Massacre near the modern-day town of Meeker. The incident convinced the U.S. Senate that the safety of Americans was more important than appeasing the tribes. The Utes were moved in 1880 to small reserves in southwestern Colorado and Utah. Their vacated lands were opened to settlement in 1882.

The Milk Creek Massacre is remembered for the rescue of Thornburgh's surviving but besieged troops by the African American Company D of the Ninth Cavalry. Their action was considered a turning point toward better white-black relations during an especially difficult period.

THE MINING BOOM

On April 28, 1878, when August Rische and George Hook hit a vein of silver carbonate 27 feet deep on Fryer Hill in Leadville the real mining boom began. They called their strike the Little Pittsburg.

Perhaps the stir over the strike wouldn't have been so great had not Rische and Hook eight days earlier traded one-third interest in whatever they found for a basket of groceries from storekeeper Horace Tabor, the mayor of Leadville and a shrewd entrepreneur. Tabor was well acquainted with the Colorado "law of apex," which said that if an ore-bearing vein surfaced on a man's claim, he could follow it wherever it led, even out of his claim and through the claims of others. Within a few months, Hook and Rische sold out; Senator Chaffee and financier David Moffat bought in; and the Little Pittsburg Consolidated Mining Company was earning $8,000 a day.

Tabor, a legend in Colorado, typifies the "rags-to-riches" success story of a common working-class man. A native Vermonter, he had mortgaged his Kansas homestead in 1859 and moved west to the mountains, where he had been a postmaster and storekeeper in several hamlets before Leadville. He was 46 when the Little Pittsburg strike was made. By 50, he was the state's richest man and its Republican lieutenant governor. His love affair and marriage to Elizabeth "Baby Doe" McCourt, a young divorcée for whom he left his assiduous wife, Augusta, became both a national scandal and the subject of numerous books, even an opera.

The Leadville strike was the greatest of many claims that led to the peopling of the

---

IMPRESSIONS

I spent a night in a silver mine. I dined with the men down there. . . . Poems every one of them. A complete democracy underground. I find people less rough and coarse in such places. There is no chance for roughness. The revolver is their book of etiquette.
—OSCAR WILDE, *quoted in the Morning Herald,* 1882.

Colorado Rockies. The construction of towns and transportation of mineral wealth was made easier by the narrow-gauge Denver & Rio Grande Railroad. This network was the brainchild of Gen. William Palmer, who had founded the resort of Colorado Springs in 1871 after leaving the Kansas Pacific Railroad directorship. Pueblo, Alamosa, Leadville, Durango, Silverton, Grand Junction, and other communities were linked to Denver by various D&RG spur routes by 1882.

But trouble loomed. Silver was being produced faster than the market could absorb it, causing an unstable partnership in the silver-and-gold exchange upon which the U.S. monetary system was based. The limited commitment of the Sherman Silver Purchase Act of 1890 forced the Treasury Department to pay more for silver than it was worth on world markets. When the act was repealed in 1893, the Colorado silver industry collapsed. Every silver mine and smelter in the state closed down. Thousands lost their jobs, and many resorted to crime and violence to get food for their families. Even Horace Tabor found himself penniless.

But while silver's value was on the wane, gold's was rising. In the fall of 1890, a cowboy named Bob Womack found gold in Cripple Creek as it flowed through a cow pasture on the southwestern slope of Pikes Peak. He sold his so-called El Paso Lode to Winfield Scott Stratton, a carpenter and amateur geologist. Stratton's mine earned him a tidy profit of $6 million by 1899, when he sold it to an English company for another $11 million. Cripple Creek turned out to be the richest goldfield ever discovered, ultimately producing $500 million in gold.

Unlike the flamboyant Tabor, Stratton was an introvert and a neurotic. His fortune was twice the size of Tabor's, and it grew daily as the deflation of silver's value boosted that of gold. But he invested most of it back in Cripple Creek, searching for a fabulous mother lode that he never found. Ultimately, by the early 1900s, overproduction of gold began to drive the price of the metal back down, just as had happened to silver.

ENVIRONMENTALISM & TOURISM

Exploration of Colorado had not ceased with Frémont's epic journey of 1843–44. In 1867 and 1868, natural scientist John Wesley Powell, a Civil War veteran with an amputated arm, scaled several of Colorado's 14,000-foot peaks. In 1869 and again in 1871–72, he led descents of the Green and Colorado rivers, becoming the first to travel through Arizona's Grand Canyon. His writings both as an explorer, and subsequently as director of the U.S. Geological Survey, influenced many later environmentalists.

Similarly influential was Ferdinand Hayden's *Atlas of Colorado,* produced in 1877 and still regarded as a leading authority on Colorado topography.

But modern Colorado environmentalism really began in September 1900, when Theodore Roosevelt made his first visit to the state as the Republican vice-presidential nominee. Soon after Roosevelt acceded to the presidency in September 1901, after the assassination of President McKinley, he began to declare more and larger chunks of the Rockies as forest reserves. Then he removed them from the jurisdiction of the Department of the Interior and placed them in the Department of Agriculture, under the aegis of the U.S. Forest Service. By 1907, when an act of Congress forbade the president from creating any new reserves by proclamation, nearly one-fourth of Colorado was national forest land—16 million acres in 18 forests.

Another project that reached fruition during the Teddy Roosevelt administration was the establishment of Mesa Verde National Park in 1906. The cliff dwellings and artifacts had been discovered by surveyors for mapmaker Hayden in the 1870s, but vandals and souvenir hunters were soon helping themselves. A feminist group, the Cliff Dwellers Association, arranged to lease the lands from the Ute tribes, who held title to them, and successfully lobbied for the park's creation.

Tourism grew hand-in-hand with the setting aside of public lands. Eastern tourists had been visiting Colorado since the 1870s, when Palmer founded his Colorado

Springs resort and made the mountains accessible via his Denver & Rio Grande Railroad.

Estes Park was among the first resort towns to emerge in the 20th century, spurred by the visit in 1903 by Freelan Stanley. With his brother Francis, Freelan had invented the Stanley Steamer, a kerosene-powered automobile, in Boston in 1899. Freelan Stanley freighted one of his vehicles to Denver and drove the 40 miles via Longmont to Estes Park in less than two hours, a remarkable speed at the time. Finding the climate conducive to his recovery from tuberculosis, he returned in 1907 with a fleet of a dozen Stanley Steamers and set up a shuttle service to Estes Park from Denver. Two years later, having made extensive real-estate purchases, he built the Stanley Hotel, still a hilltop landmark today.

Stanley developed a friendship with Enos Mills, a young innkeeper whose property was more a workshop for students of wildlife than a business. A devotee of conservationist John Muir, Mills believed tourists should spend their Colorado vacations in the natural environment, camping and hiking. As Mills gained national stature as a nature writer and lecturer, he urged that the national forest land around Longs Peak, outside of Estes Park, be redesignated as a national park. In January 1915, the 400-square-mile Rocky Mountain National Park was created by President Woodrow Wilson; today it is one of America's leading tourist attractions, with more than two million visitors each year.

THE MODERN ERA

World War I affected Colorado in much the same way it did the rest of the country. Some 43,000 Coloradans served in the armed forces, 1,000 of them dying. Back home, dry-land wheat farmers and sugar-beet producers made large profits. On the western slope, there was a small boom in the rare metal vanadium, a uranium ore derivative used in hardening steel.

The 1920s saw the growth of highways and the completion of the Moffat Tunnel, a 6.2-mile passageway beneath the Continental Divide that (in 1934) led to the long-sought direct Denver–San Francisco rail connection. Of more tragic note was the worst flood in Colorado history. Pueblo was devastated when the Arkansas River overflowed its banks on June 1, 1921: 100 people were killed, and damage exceeded $16 million. The disaster led to the passage by the state legislature of a bill for flood control.

The Great Depression of the 1930s was a difficult time for many Coloradans, but it had positive consequences. The federal government raised the price of gold from $20 to $35 an ounce, reviving Cripple Creek and other stagnant mining towns. The Civilian Conservation Corps built roads and trails in the mountains. The Works Progress Administration employed tens of thousands in positions from construction to the arts. The Agricultural Adjustment Administration supported the farming communities. And the state's first Department of Public Welfare was created.

In 1934 the Taylor Grazing Act ended homesteading and initiated a schedule of fees for use of unoccupied public lands by ranchers, miners, and others. The federal act, which applied throughout the American West, provided the basis for the Bureau of Land Management, established in 1946.

World War II attracted many of the defense installations that are now an integral part of the Colorado economy. Colorado Springs is also the site of the $200-million U.S. Air Force Academy, authorized by Congress in 1954 and opened to cadets in 1958.

The war was also indirectly responsible for the other single greatest boon to Colorado's late 20th-century economy—the ski industry. Soldiers in the 10th Mountain Division, on leave from Camp Hale before heading off to fight in the Italian Alps, often crossed Independence Pass to relax in the lower altitude and milder climate of the 19th-century silver-mining village of Aspen. They tested their skiing skills against the slopes of Ajax Mountain, using a frightening boat-on-a-rope conveyance to climb the hill.

In 1945, Walter and Elizabeth Paepcke—he the founder of the Container Corporation of America, she a devoted conservationist—moved to Aspen and established the Aspen Company as a property investment firm. Skiing was already popular in New England and the Midwest, but had few devotees in the Rockies. (There was a famous ski jump at Steamboat Springs and smaller hills around Denver, Colorado Springs, and Leadville.) Paepcke bought a 3-mile chair lift, the longest and fastest in the world at the time, and had it ready for operation by January 1947. Soon, easterners were flocking to Aspen—and the rest is ski history. Paepcke soon established a summer music festival, the Aspen Institute for Humanistic Studies, and the Aspen Health Center to round out the town as a year-round resort.

3. SPORTS & RECREATION

SPECTATOR SPORTS   Denver is a mecca for professional sports, with major-league football (the Broncos), basketball (the Nuggets), soccer (the Foxes), and baseball (the Rockies of the National League). Area football fans also thrive on college sports; in fact, Colorado's three largest universities—Colorado (Boulder), Colorado State (Fort Collins), and Air Force Academy (Colorado Springs)—all won bowl titles in early 1991. In addition, the largest indoor rodeo in the United States is held as part of the National Western Stock Show in Denver in January.

OUTDOOR SPORTS   While 50,000 people might attend a football game on a given Saturday, hundreds of thousands of others enjoy the state's outdoor wonderland.

Two-thirds of the Colorado Rockies are within national forests, making them ideal for backpacking, camping, and other pursuits. More than 400 public campgrounds are maintained in the forests. Rocky Mountain National Park and an ample handful of designated wilderness areas around Pikes Peak, Mount Evans, the San Juan Mountains, and near Steamboat Springs, Glenwood Springs, and Vail, offer true backcountry experiences.

Fishing   For anglers, many cold-water species live in the mountains, including seven kinds of trout (native cutthroat, rainbow, brown, brook, lake, kokanee, and whitefish), walleye, yellow perch, northern pike, tiger muskie, and bluegill. Warm-water sport fish (especially in eastern Colorado and in large rivers) include catfish, crappie, and bass—largemouth, smallmouth, white, and wiper.

The season is year-round, except in certain specified waters. A 25¢ additional charge will be added to each license fee for search and rescue operations in the state. A 1-year license costs $20 for an adult nonresident (15 and over), $20 for a resident; 5-day licenses are $18 and 1-day licenses $5 for nonresidents and residents alike. Children under 15 are restricted to half the daily bag limit without a license. For general information on fishing, call 303/291-7533, or for up-to-date fishing reports, call 303/291-7534.

Hunting   Hunting license fees depend upon the animal being sought. A 25¢ additional charge will be added to each license fee for search and rescue operations in the state. An annual small-game license is $40 for nonresidents, $15 for residents. Big-game licenses vary in cost from $150 for nonresidents, $20 for residents, for deer or antelope, to $1,000 for nonresidents, $200 for residents, for moose. Elk, mountain lion, bear, mountain goat, and bighorn sheep are also game of renown. Colorado has the largest elk herd in North America; elk licenses cost $250 for nonresidents, $30 for residents. Anyone born in 1949 or later must display a hunter-education course card or certificate before they will be issued a license.

The main rifle-hunting season begins in early October and continues until mid-December each year. Dates vary by region and species. This season is preceded by a 6-week archery-hunting season (mid-August to late September) and a 10-day muzzle-loading-rifle season.

For information on big game, call 303/291-7529; small game, 303/291-7546; upland game birds, 303/291-7547; and waterfowl, 303/291-7548.

Boating   White-water rafting has become one of Colorado's most popular sports. The towns of Salida and Buena Vista, both located on the upper Arkansas River, have become known as rafting capitals.

Less excitable boating enthusiasts find lakes and rivers all over the state, from the world's highest anchorage at Grand Lake to waterskiing on various reservoirs on the eastern plains. Large craft take to Shadow Mountain, Granby, Dillon, Blue Mesa, and other reservoirs. Navajo State Recreation Area in the southwest gives access to a 35-mile-long reservoir straddling the New Mexico border.

Bicycling   Bicycling is popular everywhere, especially around Denver and Boulder. Maps and information on bike routes are available from the Colorado Department of Transportation, 4201 E. Arkansas Ave., Room 235, Denver, CO 80222 (tel. 303/757-9011).

Rockhounding   Rockhounding is carried on in various areas for recovery of semiprecious gemstones and petrified woods that take a high polish. Chalcedony varieties of quartz are widespread throughout the state. Agatized fossil bones that can be cut and polished are also found. Gemstones include beryl, topaz, phenacite, and aquamarine. Gold is found in every major mining area, and there is also silver, lead, copper, zinc, molybdenum, and uranium. Gold panning is a popular pastime. Information is available from the Geology Museum at the Colorado School of Mines, 1500 Illinois St., Golden, CO 80401 (tel. 303/273-3823).

Skiing   The most popular winter sport, of course, is skiing, dealt with extensively in subsequent chapters on individual resorts. You can telephone for ski conditions throughout Colorado by calling 831-7669.

SOURCES OF RECREATIONAL INFORMATION   Recreational information sources in Colorado include:

Colorado Association of Campgrounds, Cabins, and Lodges (commercial properties), 5101 Pennsylvania Ave., Boulder, CO 80303 (tel. 303/499-9343). A directory is available by mail.

Colorado State Parks (state parks, boating, R.V., and snowmobile regulations), 618 State Centennial Building, 1313 Sherman St., Denver, CO 80203 (tel. 303/866-3437).

Colorado Division of Wildlife (hunting and fishing regulations), 6060 Broadway, Denver, CO 80216 (tel. 303/297-1192 or 291-7529, for a recording that gives seasons and regulations). There are regional offices at 317 W. Prospect Ave., Fort Collins, CO 80522 (tel. 303/484-2836); 2126 N. Weber St., Colorado Springs, CO 80907 (tel. 719/473-2945); 711 Independent Ave., Grand Junction, CO 81505 (tel. 303/248-7175); and 2300 S. Townsend Ave., Montrose, CO 81401 (tel. 303/249-3431).

Colorado Geological Survey, 1313 Sherman St., Suite 715, Denver, CO 80203 (tel. 303/866-2611).

Colorado Outfitters Association, P.O. Box 440021, Aurora, CO 80044 (tel. 303/368-4731).

Colorado Llama Outfitters and Guides Association, 30361 Rainbow Hills Rd., Golden, CO 80401 (tel. 303/526-0092 or 800/462-8234).

U.S. Bureau of Land Management, 2850 Youngfield St., Lakewood, CO 80215 (tel. 303/239-3600).

U.S. Fish and Wildlife Service, P.O. Box 25486, Federal Center, Denver, CO 80225 (tel. 303/236-7904).

U.S. Forest Service, Rocky Mountain Region, P.O. Box 25127, Lakewood, CO 80225 (tel. 303/236-9431).

U.S. Geological Survey (topographical maps), P.O. Box 25046, Federal Center, Mail Stop 504, Denver, CO 80225 (tel. 303/236-5829).

U.S. National Park Service, P.O. Box 25287, Denver, CO 80225 (tel. 303/969-2000).

4. RECOMMENDED BOOKS

Because so much of Colorado's appeal involves its fascinating history, a bit of prevacation reading can enhance your trip. A good, relatively short book to start with is *Colorado: A History* (New York: W. W. Norton, 1984) by Marshall Sprague. Real history buffs may prefer the longer, more detailed *A Colorado History* (Boulder: Pruett, 1988) by Carl Ubbelohde and others. Those who enjoy long novels will want to get their hands on James Michener's 1,000-page *Centennial* (New York: Random House, 1974).

Robert G. Athearn's *The Coloradans* (Albuquerque: University of New Mexico, 1982) describes the personalities of those who helped shape the state. People driving through Colorado will enjoy James McTighe's *Roadside History of Colorado* (Boulder: Johnson Books, 1989) and Halka Chronic's *Roadside Geology of Colorado* (Denver: Mountain Press, 1980). For lighter reading, try *Eccentric Colorado* (Boulder: Pruett, 1985), by Kenneth Jessen, which contains 32 true stories of some of Colorado's stranger bits of history, including tales of a streetcar-riding horse, con artists, geniuses, alien invaders, and Colorado's famous cannibal, Alferd Packer.

Books are available mail order from the state's largest bookstore, a tourist attraction in its own right, the Tattered Cover, at 2955 E. First Ave., Denver, CO 80206 (tel. 303/322-7727 or toll free 800/833-9327). Another good source for Colorado books is the smaller, and somewhat more personal, Chinook Bookstore, at 210 N. Tejon St., Colorado Springs, CO 80903 (tel. 719/635-1195 or toll free 800/999-1195).

CHAPTER 2

PLANNING A TRIP TO COLORADO

I t's important to spend some time preparing for any journey, including a trip to Colorado. This chapter offers a variety of planning tools, including information on when to go, how to get there, how to get around once you're there, and some suggested itineraries.

1. INFORMATION

Start at the **Colorado Tourism Board,** 1625 Broadway, Suite 1700, Denver, CO 80202 (tel. 303/592-5410 or 800/433-2656). Request a "Vacation Kit" containing the official state vacation guide, map, events guide, and related information.

Other good advance information sources are **American Youth Hostels,** P.O. Box 2370, Boulder, CO 80306 (tel. 303/442-1166); the **Colorado Hotel and Lodging Association,** 999 18th St., Suite 1240, Denver, CO 80202 (tel. 303/297-8335 or toll free 800/777-6880 for a central reservation service); **Colorado Restaurant Association,** 899 Logan St., Suite 300, Denver, CO 80203 (tel. 303/830-2972); **Colorado Dude & Guest Ranch Association,** P.O. Box 300, Tabernash, CO 80478 (tel. 303/887-3128); **Colorado Council on the Arts & Humanities,** 750 Pennsylvania St., Denver, CO 80203 (tel. 303/894-2617); **Colorado Historical Society,** 1300 Broadway, Denver, CO 80203 (tel. 303/866-3682); **U.S. Forest Service Regional Headquarters,** P.O. Box 25127, Lakewood, CO 80225 (tel. 303/236-9431); and the **National Park Service Regional Headquarters,** P.O. Box 25287, Denver, CO 80225 (tel. 303/969-2000).

The tourist councils of the various cities and regions are listed in the appropriate chapters in this book.

2. WHEN TO GO

To hear a Coloradan tell it, the state has three seasons: winter, summer, and fall. Spring comes and goes so quickly: one day, usually in April, the sun has broken through and the snow is melting fast.

Along the Front Range, including Denver and Colorado Springs, summers are hot and dry, evenings pleasantly mild. Relative humidity is very low, and temperatures seldom rise above the 90s. Evenings start to get cooler by mid-September, but even as late as November days can as easily be warm as they can be crisp. Winters are, surprisingly, warmer and less snowy than those of the Great Lakes or New England; golf courses, in fact, remain open year-round! Denver boasts more than 300 sunny days a year, with more annual hours of sun than San Diego or Miami Beach.

Most of the state is considered semiarid. The prairies average about 16 inches of precipitation annually; the Front Range, 14 inches; the western slope, only about 8 inches. The rain, when it falls, is commonly a short deluge: a summer afternoon thunderstorm.

COLORADO
CALENDAR OF EVENTS

JANUARY

✪ *ASPEN/SNOWMASS WINTERSKOL* *This 5-day event includes a parade, fireworks, torchlight ski descent, freestyle skiing and ice-skating competition, skydiving, and more.* **Where:** *Aspen.* **When:** *3rd week.*

☐ **Ullrfest,** Breckenridge. A week-long festival in honor of Ullr, Norse god of snow. Parade, fireworks, torchlight display, ski competitions. 3rd week.

✪ *COWBOY DOWNHILL* *Professional rodeo cowboys tame a slalom course, lasso a resort employee, and saddle a horse before crossing the finish line.* **Where:** *Steamboat Springs.* **When:** *2nd weekend.*

FEBRUARY

☐ **Steamboat Springs Winter Carnival,** Steamboat Springs. The longest continuously observed winter carnival west of the Mississippi River includes a week of downhill and cross-country ski races, jumping, broomball, and "ski joring" street events. 1st full week.

☐ **Loveland Valentine Remailing Program,** Loveland. More than 250,000 valentines are remailed from Loveland. February 14.

☐ **Estes Park Cup,** Estes Park. Annual dog weight-pull competition.

MARCH

☐ **Crane Festival,** Monte Vista. Whooping and sandhill cranes returning to the San Luis Valley for the spring are welcomed by bus tours, wildlife art exhibits, and evening lectures by naturalists. Mid-March.

☐ **Easter Sunrise Service, Garden of the Gods,** Colorado Springs. Easter Sunday.

☐ **Winter Quarters,** La Junta. Life during the mid-19th-century fur-trading era at Bent's Old Fort is reenacted for four days and three nights.

APRIL

☐ **Flauschink,** Crested Butte. Winter is "flushed" out and spring/summer greeted with a parade of polka music and a coronation ball. 1st or 2nd weekend.

☐ **Mountain Man Rendezvous,** Kit Carson. Dressed in period costumes, mountain men engage in a black powder shoot, cooking, craft-making of the 19th century. Usually the 3rd weekend.

MAY

☐ **Bolder Boulder,** Boulder. More than 35,000 runners compete in a 10-kilometer marathon through the streets of Boulder. Memorial Day.

☐ **Telluride Mountain Film Festival,** Telluride. A festival of mountain and adventure films. Late May.

☐ **Territory Days,** Colorado Springs. The Old Colorado City historic district hosts a carnival, games, contests, and a prestatehood gunfight.

☐ **Iron Horse Bicycle Classic,** Durango. Mountain bikers race the Durango & Silverton Railroad from Durango to Silverton. Memorial Day weekend.

JUNE

✪ *FIBARK FESTIVAL   North America's longest and oldest downriver kayak race is the focus of a 4-day festival. It includes live entertainment, foot and boat races, a parade, carnival rides, arts and crafts. **Where:** Salida. **When:** Mid-June.*

☐ **Telluride Bluegrass Festival,** Telluride. Country and acoustic music are also performed at this 4-day festival, founded in 1974. Third full weekend of June.

☐ **Springspree,** Colorado Springs. Downtown merchants and restaurateurs close their doors and move outdoors for two days. Late June.

JULY

☐ **Independence Day.** Parades, barbecues, fireworks, and other celebrations throughout the state. July 4.

☐ **Pikes Peak Auto Hill Climb,** Colorado Springs. This "race to the clouds," held annually since 1916, takes drivers to the top of 14,110-foot Pikes Peak. July 4.

☐ **Brush Rodeo,** Brush. The world's largest amateur rodeo, with more than 400 participants, includes all the traditional rodeo events, plus wild cow milking, a parade, footrace, dance, and fireworks. Early July.

☐ **Colorado Shakespeare Festival,** Boulder. Considered one of the top three Shakespeare festivals in the country, held in an open-air theater. June to August.

✪ *COLORADO STATE MINING CHAMPIONSHIP   Entrants from six states compete in old-style hand steeling, hand mucking, spike driving, and newer methods of machine drilling and machine mucking. **Where:** Creede. **When:** July 4 weekend.*

✪ *HIGH COUNTRY FOLK LIFE FESTIVAL   American heritage celebration. Dulcimer and fiddle-playing contests, storytellers, folk art, crafts demonstrations. **Where:** Buena Vista. **When:** Mid-July.*

☐ **Last Trial of Alferd Packer,** Lake City. Western State College students reenact the trial of Packer, Colorado's most nefarious cannibal, in the courtroom where his trial took place. Early July.

☐ **Skookum Day,** Fort Collins. Blacksmiths, craftspeople, and others demonstrate traditional crafts and trades in a day of historical re-creations.

AUGUST

☐ **Boom Days,** Leadville. Parade, carnival, street fair, live entertainment, food booths, mine-drilling competition. The highlight is a 22-mile pack-burro race. 1st weekend.

☐ **Rocky Mountain Wine and Food Festival,** Winter Park. Colorado's finest chefs and many of America's best-known vintners offer their creations to benefit the National Sports Center for the Disabled. 3rd weekend.

⊘ *COLORADO STATE FAIR National professional rodeo, carnival rides, food booths, industrial displays, horse shows, animal exhibits, and entertainment by top-name performers. **Where:** Pueblo. **When:** Mid-August through Labor Day.*

☐ **Pikes Peak Marathon,** Manitou Springs. Runners race up and down 14,110-foot Pikes Peak via the Barr Trail. 4th weekend.
☐ **Telluride Jazz Festival,** Telluride. 1st full weekend.

SEPTEMBER

☐ **West Fest,** Copper Mountain. Music, art, and culture of the traditional American West are featured. Country-and-western performer Michael Martin Murphey ("Wildfire") is the annual headliner, supported by cowboy poets, a mountain man rendezvous, artists, and craftspeople, as well as Native American weavers and dancers. Labor Day weekend.
☐ **Steamboat Vintage Auto Race & Concours d'Elégance,** Steamboat Springs. More than 200 classic cars in a mountain course; vintage aircraft fly-in; rodeo series finals. Labor Day weekend.
☐ **Meeker Classic Championship Sheepdog Trial,** Meeker. Sheepdogs corral flocks of sheep in timed competition. Dogs from across the nation compete. Weekend after Labor Day.
☐ **Vail Fest,** Vail. An Oktoberfest-style weekend with street entertainment, yodeling contest, 5km and 10km runs, dancing, games, and sing-alongs. 2nd weekend.
☐ **Colorfest,** Durango and vicinity. Dozens of events focusing on fall colors. September and October.

OCTOBER

☐ **Cross Orchards Apple Jubilee,** Grand Junction. A good old-fashioned apple festival during harvest time. Early October.
☐ **Oktoberfest,** Brush. Polkas, food, crafts, and an antique auto show are highlights of this family fun day, with free admission. Early October.
☐ **Western Arts, Film, and Cowboy Poetry Gathering,** Durango. Historical lectures, demonstrations, art, poetry, and film are featured. Late September to early October.

NOVEMBER

☐ **Christmas Card Lane,** Buena Vista. Giant Christmas cards from local merchants line Highway 24 at both ends of town. Thanksgiving through New Year's Day.

DECEMBER

☐ **Celebration of Lights,** Vail. Month-long festival of music and holiday celebrations. Former President and Mrs. Gerald Ford, Vail residents, light the town Christmas Tree. Fireworks erupt at midnight on New Year's Eve.
☐ **Royal Gorge Bridge Christmas Celebration,** Cañon City. There are hay rides across the bridge, caroling performances, free cider, thousands of lights, and free evening admission. All month.
☐ **Christmas Tree Mountain Lighting,** Salida. All month.
☐ **Carousel and Old Town Christmas,** Burlington. All month.
☐ **Posada,** Pueblo. A processional with a living nativity.

DENVER
CALENDAR OF EVENTS

JANUARY

○ *NATIONAL WESTERN STOCK SHOW AND RODEO* The world's largest livestock show and indoor rodeo, beginning with a parade through downtown Denver. There are 23 rodeo performances, a trade exposition, western food and crafts booths, and livestock auctions. *Where:* Denver Coliseum/National Western Complex. *When:* 2nd and 3rd weeks of January. *How:* Tickets $5 to $14; write 4655 Humboldt St., Denver, CO 80216 (tel. 303/295-1660).

MARCH

☐ **Saint Patrick's Day.** The second largest Irish holiday parade in the United States features floats, marching bands, and more than 5,000 horses. March 17.
☐ **Pow Wow.** More than 700 Native American dancers and musicians, representing some 70 tribes from 22 states, gather for this annual event. Arts and crafts are sold.

APRIL

☐ **Opera Colorado,** Boettcher Concert Hall. Late April through mid-May.

MAY

☐ **Cinco de Mayo Celebration,** Santa Fe Drive. May 5.

JUNE

☐ **Cherry Blossom Festival,** Sakura Square. Japanese food bazaar at Buddhist Temple, performances, demonstrations, arts and crafts. 2nd weekend.

○ *COLORADO RENAISSANCE FESTIVAL* Sixteenth-century England outdoor fair. *Where:* Larkspur. *When:* June and July weekends and holidays.

JULY

☐ **Independence Day.** Parades, fireworks, concerts. July 4.
☐ **Colorado Indian Market.** Jewelers, painters, potters, weavers, sculptors, dancers, musicians, and others from more than 90 Native American tribes hold their market at Currigan Exhibition Hall. 2nd weekend.

SEPTEMBER

☐ **A Taste Of Colorado.** Billed as "a festival of mountain and plain," this is Denver's largest celebration, with an annual attendance of about 500,000. Local restaurants serve house specialties; there are also crafts exhibits and free concerts from top-name acts. Labor Day weekend.
☐ **Larimer Square Oktoberfest.** Three-week festival re-creates Munich's famous beerfest. Three weekends in late September and early October.

OCTOBER

☐ **Denver International Film Festival.** 2nd through 3rd Thursday.
☐ **Great American Beer Festival.** Hundreds of American beers. Mid-October.

DECEMBER

☐ **World's Largest Christmas Lighting Display.** The Denver City and County Building is illuminated by 20,000 red, green, blue, and yellow floodlights.

3. HEALTH, INSURANCE & OTHER CONCERNS

HEALTH

Colorado's elevation—about two-thirds of the state is more than a mile above sea level—translates to less oxygen and lower humidity. This creates a unique set of problems for short-term visitors.

Get plenty of rest, avoid large meals, and drink plenty of nonalcoholic fluids, especially water. As you climb into the mountains, be wary of acute mountain sickness, which is characterized in its early stages by headaches, shortness of breath, appetite loss and/or nausea, tingling in the fingers or toes, and lethargy and insomnia. Ordinarily, it requires no treatment, or can be treated with aspirin and a slower pace. If it persists or worsens, descend to a lower altitude.

Less common but more serious is high altitude pulmonary edema, which results in a cough with congestion, shortness of breath, and possibly mental changes from lack of oxygen. It looks and feels like pneumonia. Those suffering from this problem should consult a doctor to receive oxygen and go to a lower elevation.

Individuals with heart or respiratory problems should consult their home physicians before planning trips to the Colorado mountains. Those in generally good health need not take any special precautions, but can ease the transition to high elevations by changing altitude gradually. For instance, spend a night or two in Burlington (elevation 4,163 feet) before going to Denver (elevation 5,280 feet); or spend at least two or three nights in Colorado Springs (elevation 6,012 feet) before even thinking about driving or taking the cog railway to the top of Pikes Peak (elevation 14,110 feet).

Lowlanders can also help their bodies adjust to higher elevations by taking it easy for their first few days in the mountains, cutting down on cigarettes and alcohol, and avoiding sleeping pills and other drugs. There is a drug, Diamox R, that can be taken to help prevent altitude problems, and relieve the symptoms if they occur. You should consult medical professionals about its use.

Because the sun's rays are more direct in the thinner atmosphere, they cause sunburn more quickly. Their potential for skin damage increases when they reflect off snow. Use a good sunblock.

Any time of year, keep yourself warm and your clothing dry. Hypothermia is most threatening in winter, but is not unheard of in the middle of a cold summer night.

INSURANCE

Before starting your trip to Colorado, peruse your medical insurance policy to be certain you're covered when away from home. If you are not, buy a traveler's policy, available at banks, travel agencies, and automobile clubs. Coverage offered by many companies is relatively inexpensive. Besides medical assistance, including hospitalization and surgery, it should include the cost of an accident or death, loss or theft of baggage, costs of trip cancellation, and guaranteed bail in the event of a lawsuit or other legal difficulties.

SAFETY PRECAUTIONS

While there are many reasons to visit Colorado, among those most often cited are its historic sites and magnificent outdoor activities. While these are wonderful reasons to visit, they are also the factors that can ruin a vacation if you're not careful.

When visiting historic sites, such as ghost towns, gold mines, and railroads, keep in mind that these were probably built more than 100 years ago, at a time when safety standards were extremely lax, if they existed at all. Never enter abandoned buildings, mines, or railroad equipment on your own. When you're visiting commercially operated historic tourist attractions, use common sense and don't be afraid to ask questions.

Walkways in mines are often uneven, poorly lit, and sometimes slippery, caused by seeping groundwater that can also stain your clothing with its high iron content. When entering old buildings, be prepared for steep, narrow stairways, creaky floors, and low ceilings and doorways. Steam trains are a wonderful experience as long as you remember that steam is very hot, and that oil and grease will ruin your clothing. You never, never want to be in the way of any rolling railroad equipment.

When heading into the great outdoors, keep in mind that injuries often occur when people fail to follow instructions. Believe the signs that tell you to stay on established ski trails, to hike only in designated areas and carry rain gear, to always wear a life jacket when rafting, and to wear a helmet when bicycling. Mountain weather can be very fickle, and many of the most beautiful spots are in remote areas. Be prepared for extreme changes in temperature at any time of year, and watch out for summer afternoon thunderstorms that can leave you drenched and shivering in a matter of minutes. If you have any doubts when you're in Colorado, ask the U.S. Forest Service, the Bureau of Land Management, the police, or people at local sporting goods stores.

4. WHAT TO PACK

It's impossible to offer this advice too often: *Travel as light as possible.*

Except perhaps for underwear and socks, carry no more than three changes of clothing. Ideally, you shouldn't have more than one suitcase and a small bag of essentials that fits neatly under an airplane seat or in the upper rack of a train or bus.

Be sure to pack a sweater and/or a rainproof jacket. Even in summer, it can get cold at night. You'll want shorts and a swimsuit (for hotel pools or mountain lakes) in the summer, and several layers of warm clothing, including gloves and wool hat, in winter. You won't need a coat and tie or an evening dress unless you're in the state on business or plan dinner at one of the handful of very elegant restaurants in Colorado. Certainly, formal wear is rarely seen in resort communities. No matter what your plans, a good pair of walking shoes is essential.

A few other easily forgotten items that could prove priceless during your stay: (1) a travel alarm clock, so as not to be at the mercy of your hotel for wake-up calls; (2) a Swiss army knife, which has a multitude of uses, from bottle opener to screwdriver for ski bindings; (3) a magnifying glass to read the small print on maps; and (4) a small first-aid kit (containing an antibiotic ointment, bandages, aspirin, soap, a thermometer, motion-sickness pills, and required medications).

5. TIPS FOR THE DISABLED, SENIORS & STUDENTS

FOR THE DISABLED

The **Information Center for Individuals with Disabilities,** Fort Point Place, 27-43 Wormwood St., Boston, MA 02210 (tel. 617/727-5540), provides travel assistance and can also recommend tour operators; and **Mobility International USA,** Box 3551, Eugene, OR 97403 (tel. 503/343-1284), charges a small annual fee and provides travel information for those with disabilities.

Amtrak will, with 24 hours' notice, provide porter service, special seating, and a substantial discount (tel. toll free 800/USA-RAIL). If you're traveling with a companion, **Greyhound** will carry you both for a single fare (tel. toll free 800/231-2222 or for a Spanish speaking operator, toll free 800/531-5332).

An organized tour package can make life on the road much easier, and one well-established firm that specializes in travel for the disabled is **Evergreen Travel Service/Wings on Wheels Tours,** 4114 198th St., Suite 13, Lynnwood, WA 98036 (tel. 206/776-1184 or toll free 800/435-2288).

FOR SENIORS

Nearly all major U.S. hotel and motel chains now offer a **senior citizen's discount,** and you should be sure to ask for the reduction *when you make the reservation*—there may be restrictions during peak days—and be sure to carry proof of your age (driver's license, passport, etc.) when you check in. Among those chains that offer the best discounts are **Marriott Hotels** (tel. toll free 800/228-9290) for those 62 and over and **La Quinta Inns** (tel. toll free 800/531-5900) for ages 52 and over. You can save sightseeing dollars if you are 62 or over by picking up a **Golden Age Passport** from any federally operated park, recreation area, or monument. **Elderhostel,** 80 Boylston St., Boston, MA 02116 (tel. 617/426-7788) also provides stimulating vacations at moderate prices for those over 60, with a balanced mix of learning, field trips, and free time for sightseeing. If you fancy organized tours, **AARP Travel Service** (see below) puts together terrific packages at moderate rates and **Saga International Holidays,** 120 Boylston St., Boston, MA 02116 (tel. toll free 800/343-0273), arranges tours for single travelers over 60.

Membership in the following senior organizations also offers a wide variety of travel benefits: The **American Association of Retired Persons (AARP),** 601 E. St. NW, Washington, DC 20049 (tel. 202/434-2277); and the **National Council of Senior Citizens,** 925 15th St. NW, Washington, DC 20005 (tel. 202/347-8800).

Major sightseeing attractions and entertainments also often offer senior discounts—*be sure to ask when you buy your ticket.*

FOR STUDENTS

Before setting out, use your high school or college ID to obtain an International Student Identity Card from the **Council on International Educational Exchange (CIEE),** 205 E. 42nd St., New York, NY 10017 (tel. toll free 800/GET-ANID), or 312 Sutter St., Rm. 407, San Francisco, CA 94108 (tel. 415/421-3473). It will entitle you to several student discounts, although not as many as in many foreign countries. For economical accommodations, as well as a great way to meet other traveling students, join **Hostelling International–American Youth Hostels,** Box 37613, Washington, DC 20013-7613 (tel. 202/783-6161); for $8, or free with membership, they'll send a directory of all U.S. and Canadian hostels. One of the leading student travel tour operators is **Contiki Holidays,** 1432 E. Katella Ave., Anaheim, CA 92805 (tel. 800/466-0610), for ages 18 through 35. Remember, too, to *always* ask about student **discount** tickets to attractions.

6. GETTING THERE

BY PLANE Denver's International Airport—the seventh busiest in the United States with approximately 1,400 flights each day—maintains a toll-free information line: 800/AIR-2-DEN. This line offers information on flight schedules and connections, parking, ground transportation, current weather conditions, even local accommodations.

Airlines The "official" carrier for Colorado, and the one with the greatest number of connections to and from the state, is **Continental** (tel. 800/525-0280). The airline offers more than 140 nonstops to Denver from cities across the United

States. It also serves Colorado Springs and Grand Junction, and its feeder line, **Continental Express,** visits numerous other Colorado towns and resorts.

Denver is also served by **America West** (tel. 800/247-5692), **American** (tel. 800/433-7300), **Delta** (tel. 800/221-1212), **Trans World** (tel. 800/221-2000), **United** (tel. 800/241-6522), **USAir** (tel. 800/428-4322), eight foreign carriers, and several regional airlines.

Fares   The least expensive domestic airfares usually require advance purchase of three, seven, or fourteen days, and Saturday night stay-over, or some other requirements. These fares go by such names as Max-Saver, Super-Saver, or APEX, depending on airline. Other categories of tickets include first class, standard coach, and business class.

It is virtually impossible to get a low-cost air ticket to Denver during the height of ski season, with the Christmas holidays and Presidents' Weekend in February being particularly hectic.

Flights from the U.K.   At press time **British Airways** (tel. 081/897-4000 in London) was not offering direct flights from London to Denver, though direct flights may be offered in 1994. Travelers from the United Kingdom can take British Airways flights to such cities as Philadelphia and Chicago and make connecting flights with United Airlines to Denver.

Getting to & from the Airport   Bus, taxi, and shuttle services are provided between Denver International Airport and downtown Denver, and most major car-rental companies have outlets at the airport. In addition, various companies offer shuttles to other communities in the state, particularly the closer ski resorts. Call the airport's toll free **information** line, 800-AIR-2-DEN, for local phone numbers of specific airlines and other airport services.

BY TRAIN   **Amtrak** has two routes through Colorado. The *Zephyr,* which links San Francisco and Chicago, travels each direction three times daily. It passes through Grand Junction, Glenwood Springs, Kremmling, Winter Park, Denver, Fort Morgan, Sterling, and Julesburg en route to Omaha, Nebr. Inquire at Union Station, 707 17th St., Denver, CO 80202 (tel. 303/534-2812 or 800/872-7245).

The *Southwest Chief,* which runs once daily in each direction between Los Angeles and Chicago, travels from Albuquerque, N.Mex., via Trinidad, La Junta, and Lamar before crossing the southeastern Colorado border into Kansas. Inquiries can be directed to Amtrak, First Street and Colorado Avenue, La Junta, CO 81050 (tel. 719/384-2275).

You can get a copy of Amtrak's National Timetable from any Amtrak station, from travel agents, or by contacting Amtrak, 400 N. Capitol St. NW, Washington, DC 20001 (tel. 800/USA-RAIL).

BY BUS   **Greyhound** (tel. 303/292-6111) has an extensive network that reaches nearly every corner of the state, with daily connections nearly everywhere. **TNM&O Coaches** (Texas, New Mexico & Oklahoma Coaches; tel. 806/763-5389) covers much of the southern part of the state, including some communities that Greyhound does not visit.

BY CAR   Some 1,000 miles of interstate highways form a star on the map of Colorado, with its centerpoint at Denver. I-25 crosses the state from south to north, extending from New Mexico to Wyoming; over its 300 miles, it transits nearly every major city of the Front Range, including Pueblo, Colorado Springs, and Fort Collins. I-70 crosses from west to east, extending from Utah to Kansas, a distance of about 450 miles; it enters Colorado near Grand Junction, passes through Glenwood Springs, Vail, and Denver, and exits just east of Burlington. I-76 is an additional 190-mile spur that begins in Denver and extends northeast to Nebraska, joining I-80 just beyond Julesburg.

Visitors entering Colorado from the southwest may take U.S. 160 (from Flagstaff, Ariz.) or U.S. 550 (from Farmington, N.Mex.). Both routes enter the state near Durango.

The approximate mileage to Denver from various cities around the United States and Canada are shown in the accompanying map.

COLORADO DRIVING TIMES & DISTANCES

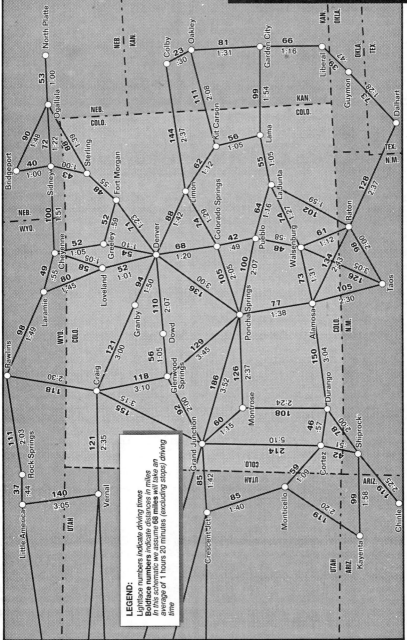

LEGEND:
Lightface numbers indicate driving times
Boldface numbers indicate distances in miles
In this schematic we assume **68 miles** will take an average of 1 hours 20 minutes (excluding stops) driving time

PACKAGE TOURS

Among the operators offering tours to and within Colorado are the following:
   Discover Colorado Tours, 2401 E. St., Suite 204, Golden, CO 80401 (tel. 303/277-0129). Personalized individual and group scenic tours.
   Gray Line, 5855 E. 56th Ave., Denver, CO 80022 (tel. 303/289-2841). Provides tours to gambling locations, Rocky Mountain National Park, and historic sites.
   National Reservations Network, 11072 N. Colo. 9 (P.O. Box 3670), Breckenridge, CO 80424 (tel. 303/453-9237 or 800/525-8583). Specializes in summer and winter resort vacations.
   Organizers Etc., 7373 S. Alton Way, Suite B-100, Englewood, CO 80112 (tel. 303/771-1178 or 800/283-2754). Sports and recreation packages for individuals and groups.

7. GETTING AROUND

BY PLANE   The leading in-state commuter network is **Continental Express** (tel. 800/525-0280), which connects Denver with Aspen, Durango, Gunnison, Montrose, Steamboat Springs, and Telluride. **Mesa Airlines** (tel. 800/637-2247) also flies to numerous smaller towns around Colorado.

BY TRAIN   Amtrak's *Zephyr* is a convenient way to cross the state. It runs east to west (Julesburg–Denver–Grand Junction) and west to east three times daily in each direction. This route avoids the I-90 corridor between Glenwood Springs and Denver, and thus fails to serve such resorts as Vail and Breckenridge. It does, however, make a stop in Winter Park, making that the only ski resort in Colorado with direct rail service. For information, check at Union Station, 707 17th St., Denver, CO 80202 (tel. 303/892-1442, or 800/872-7245). On winter weekends, the *Rio Grande Ski Train* plies the same route from Denver. Inquire at 555 17th St., Denver, CO 80202 (tel. 303/296-4754).
   Numerous **scenic railroads,** including a handful of narrow-gauge operations, are found throughout the state. Information on all can be obtained from Colorado Scenic Rails Association, 17155 W. 44th Ave. (P.O. Box 641), Golden, CO 80402 (tel. 800/866-3690). They include the Leadville Colorado and Southern Railroad, the Limon Twilight Limited, and the Wyoming and Colorado Scenic Railroad; five narrow-gauge railroads (the Black Hawk and Central City, the Cripple Creek/Victor, the Cumbres & Toltec, the Durango-Silverton, and the Georgetown Loop); and two more specifically serving tourists, the Manitou and Pikes Peak Cog Railway and the Royal Gorge Scenic Railway.

BY BUS   Every sizable town in the state is accessible by either **Greyhound** (tel. 303/292-6111) or **TNM&O Coaches** (Texas, New Mexico & Oklahoma Coaches; tel. 806/763-5389).

BY CAR   Visitors who plan to drive their own car to and around Colorado should give their vehicle a thorough road check before starting out. The high elevation and changeable weather conditions can create special problems for an engine, and it can be life threatening to be stranded in the heat or cold with a vehicle that does not run. Check your lights, windshield wipers, horn, tires, battery, drive belts, fluid levels, alignment, and other possible trouble spots.
   Make sure your driver's license, vehicle registration, safety-inspection sticker, and auto-club membership (if you have one) are valid. Check with your auto insurance agency to make sure you're covered when out of state, and/or when driving a rental car. *You must carry proof of insurance.*
   Unless otherwise posted, the speed limit on open roads is 55 m.p.h. (90kmph).

Minimum age for drivers is 16. Safety belts are required for drivers and all front-seat passengers age 4 and over; children under 4 must use approved child seats.

Colorado law allows drivers to make a right turn at a red signal, after coming to a complete stop, unless posted otherwise. Colorado law requires that seat belts and child restraints be used at all times.

Gas is readily available at service stations throughout the state. All prices are subject to the same fluctuations as elsewhere in the United States. Anticipate much higher prices in mountain resort communities and remember that mountain driving decreases mileage considerably.

An **official state highway map** is distributed by the Colorado Tourism Board. Otherwise, you can get one from bookstores, or (if you're a member) from the American Automobile Association (AAA).

You can get **information on road conditions** from the Colorado State Patrol. For highways within two hours of Denver, call 303/639-1111; for major roads throughout the state, call 303/639-1234.

Winter Road Closings Two notable Colorado highways are closed in winter. U.S. 34, the Trail Ridge Road through Rocky Mountain National Park, is the highest continuous highway in the world, crossing the Continental Divide at 12,183 feet. Colorado 82, over Independence Pass (elevation 12,095 feet) east of Aspen, is the main route between Denver and Aspen in the summer months. In addition, the Mount Evans Road (Colo. 103 and Colo. 5) from Idaho Springs (35 miles west of Denver) to the 14,264-foot summit of Mount Evans is the highest paved road in North America; it's open June to September only. The world's highest tunnel at 11,000 feet, the Eisenhower Tunnel, carries I-70 beneath Loveland Pass year-round.

Snow tires or chains are often required when roads are snow covered or icy, or during winter storms. Motorists planning travel over unimproved high-elevation roads at any time of year should inquire locally about conditions before attempting them.

Information For additional information on driving in Colorado, contact the Colorado State Patrol, 700 Kipling St., Denver, CO 80215 (tel. 303/239-4518); or the Colorado Department of Transportation, 4201 E. Arkansas Ave., Denver, CO 80222 (tel. 303/757-9228). If you're planning to use a four-wheel-drive or off-road vehicle, you can communicate with the Colorado Association of Four-Wheel Drive Clubs, P.O. Box 1413, Wheat Ridge, CO 80034 (tel. 303/321-1266).

Road Emergencies In case of an accident or road emergency, contact the state patrol. American Automobile Association members can get free emergency road service wherever they are, 24 hours, by calling AAA's emergency number (tel. 800/336-4357). In Colorado, AAA headquarters is at 4100 E. Arkansas Ave., Denver, CO 80222 (tel. 303/753-8800 or 800/283-5222).

Rental Cars Car rentals are available in every sizable town and city in the state, always at the local airport, and usually also downtown. Widely represented agencies include **Alamo** (tel. 800/327-9633), **Avis** (tel. 800/331-1212), **Budget** (tel. 800/527-0700), **Dollar** (tel. 800/327-7607), **Hertz** (tel. 800/654-3131), **National** (tel. 800/227-7368), and **Thrifty** (tel. 800/FOR-CARS).

Major East-West Highways Besides **I-70** and **I-76**, major east-west highways are **Colo. 14**, linking Fort Collins with both Steamboat Springs and Sterling; **U.S. 40**, connecting Denver with Salt Lake City, Utah, via Steamboat Springs; **Colo. 82**, between Glenwood Springs, Aspen, and Independence Pass; **U.S. 24**, starting in the Vail Valley and proceeding through Leadville and Buena Vista to Colorado Springs and east; **U.S. 50**, which leads from Grand Junction to Montrose, Gunnison, Salida, Cañon City, Pueblo, and La Junta toward Wichita, Kans.; and **U.S. 160**, extending from Arizona through Durango and Alamosa to Walsenburg.

Major North-South Highways In addition to **I-25**, principal north-south highways are **U.S. 550**, which branches off from U.S. 50 in Montrose and transits Durango en route to Farmington, N. Mex.; **U.S. 285**, connecting Denver with Santa Fe, N.M., via Buena Vista, Salida, and Alamosa; **Colo. 9**, a straight shot from Breckenridge and Summit County to Cañon City; **Colo. 71**, which spans the eastern plains from Scottsbluff, Nebr., via Brush and Limon to Rocky Ford; and **U.S.**

385, which follows Colorado's eastern border from Julesburg through Burlington and Lamar all the way to Odessa, Tex.

BY BICYCLE Bicycling is popular everywhere. You'll see many long-distance travelers, both on touring and mountain bikes. Maps and information on bike routes are available from the Colorado Department of Transportation.

SUGGESTED ITINERARIES

IF YOU HAVE 1 WEEK

Day 1: Arrive in Denver, preferably late morning or early afternoon. Browse Larimer Square and the 16th Street Mall.

Day 2: In the morning, visit the Denver Art Museum, the Colorado History Museum, the U.S. Mint, and/or the State Capitol. After lunch, take the short drive to the university town of Boulder.

Day 3: Follow U.S. 36 to Estes Park, eastern gateway to Rocky Mountain National Park. From there, the spectacular Trail Ridge Road slips over the Continental Divide to Grand Lake, where you can camp or sleep under a more solid roof.

Day 4: Take U.S. 40 through the Winter Park resort community and over Berthoud Pass to Georgetown, one of the best preserved of Victorian mining towns. I-70 goes through the Eisenhower Tunnel to Frisco, where you can turn on Colo. 9 to charming Breckenridge.

Day 5: Colorado 9 runs southeast 100 miles in a near-straight line to Cañon City; see the magnificent Royal Gorge and the re-created western film town of Buckskin Joe. Proceed northeast to Colorado Springs for the evening.

Day 6: Spend a full day in Colorado Springs. Choose between the Pikes Peak Cog Railway, the U.S. Olympic Training Center, the Garden of the Gods, and other sights.

Day 7: Stop and visit the U.S. Air Force Academy on your way back to Denver, where your flight home awaits.

IF YOU HAVE 2 WEEKS

Days 1 and 2: Same as above.

Day 3: Take Canyon Boulevard (Colo. 119) west to Nederland, then follow the foothills north on Colo. 72 and Colo. 7 to Estes Park. Camp out or stay in cabins on the wilderness fringe.

Day 4: In the morning, enjoy spectacular Trail Ridge Road through Rocky Mountain National Park, across the Continental Divide to Grand Lake. After lunch, proceed south on U.S. 40 to Winter Park, Berthoud Pass, and Georgetown, one of the best-preserved Victorian mining towns.

Day 5: I-70 and Colo. 91 will take you uphill to Leadville, Colorado's 2-mile-high city. See the historic district and National Mining Hall of Fame, then continue across Independence Pass to the famed resort town of Aspen.

Day 6: Give yourself a day in Aspen, to shop, sightsee, hike, bike, or just enjoy the clean mountain air.

Day 7: Drive to Montrose. The route follows the Roaring Fork River west to Carbondale, turns south along Colo. 133 through the quaint historic village of Redstone, and transits Delta with its Fort Uncompahgre. Try to complete the 140-mile drive by midafternoon, leaving yourself a few hours to visit Black Canyon of the Gunnison National Monument.

Day 8: It's 98 miles via the "Million Dollar Highway," U.S. 550, to Durango. En route, between the memorable old mining towns of Ouray and Silverton, you'll cross Red Mountain Pass through the San Juan Mountains. Durango's historic district is one of Colorado's largest and best preserved.

Day 9: Visit the Anasazi cliff dwellings of Mesa Verde National Park, about 40 miles west of Durango.

Day 10: Get an early start for the 150-mile drive across Wolf Creek Pass on U.S. 160 to Alamosa. Spend part of the afternoon at eerie Great Sand Dunes National Monument, 30 miles northeast of Alamosa.

Day 11: Head north to the rafting capital of Salida, then east on U.S. 50 to Cañon City. See the Royal Gorge, the re-created Old West town of Buckskin Joe, and other sights.

Days 12 and 13: Two full days in Colorado Springs (see Day 6 in "If You Have 1 Week," above). A worthwhile side trip is to Cripple Creek, a wonderful 19th-century hillside mining town and venue of legalized gambling.

Day 14: See Day 7 in "If You Have 1 Week," above.

IF YOU HAVE 3 WEEKS

Day 1: Arrive in Denver, preferably late morning or early afternoon. Browse Larimer Square and the 16th Street Mall.

Day 2: Explore the State Capitol, U.S. Mint, Denver Art Museum, numerous other museums, and City Park.

Day 3: Enjoy a leisurely day in Boulder. Stroll the Pearl Street Mall and University of Colorado campus, or visit the Celestial Seasonings tea factory for a guided tour.

Day 4: Take Canyon Boulevard (Colo. 119) west to Nederland, then follow the foothills north on Colo. 72 and Colo. 7 to Estes Park. Camp out or stay in cabins on the wilderness fringe.

Day 5: Spend the day in Rocky Mountain National Park. Dawdle across the Continental Divide on the Trail Ridge Road and enjoy the sunset on Grand Lake.

Day 6: Take U.S. 40 south through the Winter Park resort community, over Berthoud Pass, to Georgetown, one of Colorado's best-preserved Victorian mining towns.

Day 7: Follow I-70 to Frisco, seat of Summit County, and detour on a 10-mile spur to Breckenridge. After lunch, return to I-70 and proceed west to Vail, considered America's most popular ski resort (and a booming summer resort as well).

Day 8: Take U.S. 24 south to Leadville, the state's highest city at over 10,000 feet elevation. See the historic district and National Mining Hall of Fame, then continue across Independence Pass to Aspen.

Day 9: Shop, sightsee, hike, bike, or just enjoy Aspen's clean mountain air.

Day 10: Drive to Montrose via Carbondale, the historic village of Redstone, Paonia, and Delta. Leave a few afternoon hours to visit Black Canyon of the Gunnison National Monument.

Day 11: The "Million Dollar Highway," U.S. 550 to Durango, passes through the picturesque historic mining towns of Ouray and Silverton and across Red Mountain Pass, an alpine locale worthy of Switzerland. You'll be in Durango three nights.

Day 12: Durango's historic district is one of Colorado's largest and best preserved, and its Durango & Silverton Narrow Gauge Railroad plies a magnificent route.

Day 13: This is a day of archeological discovery. Spend most of it at Mesa Verde National Park, some 40 miles west, or at Ute Mountain Park, south of Cortez. Hovenweep National Monument and other sites are in the Cortez area.

Day 14: It's 150 miles on U.S. 160 via Wolf Creek Pass to Alamosa. Spend the afternoon at seemingly misplaced Great Sand Dunes National Monument, 30 miles northeast of Alamosa.

Day 15: Continue east again on U.S. 160 to Walsenburg, then pick up Colo. 10 to La Junta. After lunch, visit Bent's Old Fort National Historic Site, the reconstructed hub of a trading empire in the 1830s and 1840s. Proceed to Pueblo for dinner.

Day 16: Browse Pueblo in the morning, including the Rosemount Victorian House Museum and the Greenway Raptor Center. Then take U.S. 50 west to Cañon City, the Royal Gorge, and the western theme village of Buckskin Joe.

Day 17: Weather and road conditions permitting, take the graded gravel Florence-Victor road north to Cripple Creek, a noted 19th-century hillside mining town and venue of legalized gambling. Then continue on Colo. 67 and U.S. 24 north and east to Colorado Springs for the next three nights.

Days 18 and 19: There's plenty to fill two days in Colorado Springs: the Manitou and Pikes Peak Cog Railway, U.S. Air Force Academy, U.S. Olympic Training

Center, Garden of the Gods rock formations, Cave of the Winds, museums, historic sites, and much more.

Day 20: Return to Denver for one last day. Complete your souvenir hunting at the Cherry Creek Shopping Center, or get out of town to historic Central City, the Coors Brewery at Golden, or Red Rocks Amphitheatre at Evergreen.

Day 21: Have a great flight home!

FAST FACTS *COLORADO*

American Express American Express Travel Agency, 555 17th St., Anaconda Tower, Denver (tel. 303/298-7100), offers full member services and currency exchange. Open Monday through Friday from 8:30am to 5pm. To report a lost card, call 800/528-4800. To report lost traveler's checks, call 800/221-7282.

Banks Banks are typically open Monday through Thursday from 10am to 3pm and on Friday from 10am to 6pm. Drive-up windows may be open later. Some may also be open on Saturday morning. Most branches have cash machines available 24 hours (call 800/THE-PLUS for the location nearest you). Colorado National Bank is the state's oldest, and has branches seemingly everywhere.

Business Hours In general, Monday through Friday from 9am to 5pm. Many stores are also open on Friday night and Saturday; those in major shopping malls have Sunday-afternoon hours as well.

Camera/Film Film of all kinds is widely available at camera stores throughout the state, and simple repairs can be handled in the major cities.

Drugstores You'll find 24-hour prescription services available at selected Walgreens Drug Stores around the state. Prices at Thrifty and Wal-Mart outlets might be somewhat less. If you're having trouble getting a prescription filled, call the nearest hospital pharmacy.

Electricity As throughout the United States, 110 to 115 volts, 60 cycles. AC.

Emergencies Throughout Colorado, the number to dial for police, fire, or medical emergencies is 911 or 0 for an operator.

Language You may hear a smattering of Spanish in the southern part of the state, but English is by far the dominant language spoken.

Liquor Laws The legal drinking age is 21. Except for 3.2% beer, sold in supermarkets, and convenience stores Monday through Sunday from 5am to midnight, alcoholic beverages must be purchased in liquor stores. These are open Monday through Saturday from 8am to midnight. Beverages may be served in licensed restaurants, lounges, and bars Monday through Saturday from 7am to 2am, Sunday from 8am to 2am, and Christmas Day from 8am to midnight, with the proper licenses.

Mail It takes two to three days for mail from major Colorado cities to reach other major American cities. Figure an extra day or two to/from smaller communities. Domestic postage for letters is 29¢ for the first ounce, 23¢ per additional ounce, and 19¢ for a postcard. Postage to most foreign countries is 50¢ per half ounce (it's 40¢ per ounce to Canada, 35¢ per ounce to Mexico). Buy stamps and send parcels from post offices in any city, town, or village. Major-city post offices are open Monday through Friday from 8am to 5pm and on Saturday from 9am to noon, with some 24-hour service available; smaller communities often have limited hours.

You can have mail sent to you in any city or town in Colorado. Have it addressed to you, c/o General Delivery, Main Post Office, Name of City and ZIP Code. The post office will hold it for one month. You must pick it up in person and show identification (a passport or valid picture driver's license will suffice).

Maps The official state highway map is published by the state Department of Highways and distributed free by the Colorado Tourism Board. Many local visitors bureaus and chambers of commerce publish maps of their cities or regions. The American Automobile Association (AAA) supplies detailed state and city maps free to members.

Newspapers/Magazines The state's two largest daily newspapers, both published in Denver, are the morning *Denver Post* and the afternoon *Rocky Mountain News*. Other cities and large towns, especially regional hubs, have daily newspapers, and many smaller towns publish weeklies. National newspapers like *USA Today* and the *Wall Street Journal* can be purchased in cities and major hotels.

Pets   Dogs, cats, and other small pets are accepted at many motels around the state, though not as universally in the larger cities. Some properties require owners to pay a damage deposit in advance.

Police   In emergency, dial 911 or 0 for operator. Police departments also have nonemergency lines; in Denver, for instance, call 303/575-3127.

Radio/TV   There are well over 100 AM and FM radio stations in Colorado, so if you have a car radio or other receiver, you'll never be far from the rest of the world. Denver has 10 television stations, including ABC, CBS, NBC, and PBS affiliates; Colorado Springs has five more; and other cities have their own stations. Cable or satellite service is available at most hotels.

Safety   Whenever you're traveling in an unfamiliar city or region, stay alert. Be aware of your immediate surroundings and keep a close eye on your possessions. Be especially careful with cameras, purses, and wallets, all favorite targets of thieves and pickpockets. Some travelers feel safest wearing a money belt.

Taxes   Colorado state sales tax is 3%. Each county tacks an additional local tax on top of that. Each county also charges a local hotel tax to support the tourism infrastructure and other industries.

Telephone/Fax   Colorado uses two telephone area codes. In most of the state, including Denver, the area code is 303. But the south-central and southeastern parts of the state—south and east from Leadville, including Colorado Springs—use area code 719.

Local calls are normally 25¢. Facsimiles can be transmitted by most major hotels at a nominal cost to guests, and at Kinko's outlets in major cities.

Time   Colorado is on mountain standard time (seven hours behind Greenwich mean time), one hour ahead of the West Coast and two hours behind the East Coast. Daylight saving time is in effect from April to October.

Tipping   A tip of 50¢ per bag is appropriate for hotel valets and airport porters. If you're staying longer than a night or two in a hotel or motel, tip about $1 per night for maid service. Restaurant servers should get 15% to 20% of your bill for service.

Water   You *can* drink the water everywhere but be cautious about lakes and streams when you're enjoying the great outdoors. The diarrhea-causing *giardia* parasite, primarily spread by livestock, has invaded many previously pristine bodies of water.

FOR FOREIGN VISITORS

All overseas visitors to the state of Colorado must first satisfy the entrance requirements for a visit to the United States. This chapter is designed to make your trip planning as uncomplicated as possible.

1. PREPARING FOR YOUR TRIP

NECESSARY DOCUMENTS

Most foreigners entering the United States must carry two documents: (1) a valid **passport,** expiring not less than six months prior to the scheduled end of their visit to the United States; and (2) a **tourist visa,** which can be obtained without charge at any American consulate. Exceptions are Canadian nationals, who must merely carry proof of residence, and British and Japanese nationals, who require a passport but no visa.

To obtain a visa, complete the visa application and submit a passport photo. Visa application forms are available from U.S. embassies and consulates as well as from airline offices and leading travel agencies. At most consulates it's an overnight process, though it can take longer during the busy summer period of June, July, and August. Those who apply by mail should enclose a large, self-addressed, stamped envelope, and expect a response in about two weeks.

In theory, a tourist visa (Visa B) is valid for single or multiple entries for a period of one year. In practice, the consulate that issues the visa uses its own discretion in granting length of stay. Applicants in good standing, who can supply the address of a relative, friend, or business acquaintance in the United States, are most likely to be granted longer stays. (American resident contacts are also useful in passing through customs quickly.)

MEDICAL REQUIREMENTS

New arrivals in the United States do not need any inoculations unless they are coming from, or have stopped over in, an area known to be suffering from an epidemic, especially cholera or yellow fever.

Anyone applying for an immigrant's visa must undergo a screening test for the AIDS-associated HIV virus, under a law passed in 1987. This test does not apply to tourists.

Any visitor with a medical condition that requires treatment with narcotics or other drugs, or with paraphernalia such as syringes, must carry a valid, signed prescription from a physician. This allays suspicions of drug smuggling by customs and other officials.

TRAVEL INSURANCE

Insurance for tourists is optional in the United States. Medical care is very costly, however, and every traveler is strongly advised to secure full insurance coverage before starting a trip.

For a relatively low premium, numerous specialized insurance companies will cover (1) loss or theft of baggage, (2) costs of trip cancellation, (3) guaranteed bail in the event of a lawsuit or other legal difficulties, (4) the cost of medical assistance (including surgery and hospitalization) in the event of sickness or injury, and (5) the cost of an accident, death, or repatriation. Travel agencies, automobile clubs, and banks are among those selling travel insurance packages at attractive rates.

2. GETTING TO & AROUND THE U.S.

By Plane   Nearly all major airlines, including those of the United States, Europe, Asia, Australia, and New Zealand, offer **APEX** (advance purchase excursion) fares that significantly reduce the cost of transoceanic air travel. This enables travelers to pick their dates and ports, but requires that they prepurchase their ticket, and meet minimum- and maximum-stay requirements—often 15 to 90 days. Season of travel and individual airline discounts also affect fares, but this is the most widely acknowledged means of cheap, flexible travel.

Some large airlines, including Delta, Eastern, Northwest, TWA, and United, have in the past offered foreign travelers special add-on discount fares under the name **Visit USA.** Though not currently available, they may be repeated in the future, and are worth asking a travel agent about. These tickets (which could be purchased overseas only) allowed unlimited travel between U.S. destinations at minimum rates for specified time periods, such as 21, 30, or 60 days. Short of bus or train travel, which can be inconvenient and time-consuming, this was the best way of traveling around the country at low cost.

By Train   Amtrak, the American rail system, offers a **USA Railpass** to non–U.S. citizens. Available only overseas, it allows unlimited stopovers during a 45-day period of validity. Fares vary according to the size of the region being traveled.

By Bus   Foreign students can obtain the **International Ameripass** for unlimited bus travel on Greyhound/Trailways throughout the United States and Canada. Available for 7 to 30 days, it can be purchased with a student ID and a passport in New York, Orlando, Miami, San Francisco, and Los Angeles.

By Car   Foreign visitors who plan to rent a car can visit an American Automobile Association (AAA) office to obtain a "touring permit," which validates a foreign driver's license.

For detailed information on travel by car, train, and bus, see "Getting Around" in Chapter 2.

FAST FACTS   **FOR THE FOREIGN TRAVELER**

Currency & Exchange   In the American monetary system, 100 cents (¢) equal 1 dollar ($1).

Foreign visitors accustomed to paper money of varied colors and sizes should look carefully at the U.S. "greenbacks"—all **bills** are green, and all are the same size regardless of value. Aside from the numbers, Americans often differentiate them by the portrait they bear: The $1 bill ("a buck") depicts George Washington; the seldom-seen $2, Thomas Jefferson; the $5, Abraham Lincoln; the $10, Alexander Hamilton; the $20, Andrew Jackson. Larger bills, including the $50 (Ulysses S. Grant) and the $100 (Benjamin Franklin), are not welcome in payment for small purchases.

There are six **coins,** four of them widely used: 1 cent ("penny," of brown copper), 5 cents ("nickel"), 10 cents ("dime"), and 25 cents ("quarter"). The 50-cent piece ("half dollar") is less widely circulated and $1 coins—including the older, large silver dollar and the newer, small Susan B. Anthony coin—are rare.

If they're *in U.S. dollars,* **traveler's checks** are easily cashed in payment for goods or services at most hotels, motels, restaurants, and large stores. If they're *in a foreign currency,* the best exchange rates are offered by major banks. However, the best course of action is not to bring any foreign currency; the foreign-exchange bureaus common in other countries are largely absent from U.S. cities.

The most widely used method of payment by travelers in the United States is **credit cards.** In Colorado, VISA (BarclayCard in Britain, Chargex in Canada) and MasterCard (EuroCard in Europe, Access in Britain, Diamond in Japan) are accepted almost everywhere. American Express is taken by most establishments; Diners Club and Carte Blanche, by a large number; Discover, by an increasing number. EnRoute and JCB, the Japanese Credit Bank card, are beginning to come into favor as well.

Use of this "plastic money" reduces the necessity to carry large sums of cash or traveler's checks. Credit cards are accepted almost everywhere, including a number of grocery stores. Credit cards can be used for a deposit on a car rental, as proof of identity (often preferred to a passport) when cashing a check, or as a "cash card" for withdrawing money from banks that accept them.

Customs & Immigration   U.S. Customs allows each adult visitor to import the following, duty free: (1) 1 liter of wine or hard liquor; (2) 1,000 cigarettes or 100 cigars (*not* from Cuba) or 3 pounds of smoking tobacco; and (3) $400 worth of gifts. The only restrictions are that the visitor must spend at least 72 hours in the United States, and must not have claimed the exemption on imported goods within the preceding six months. Importing food and plants is forbidden.

Foreign visitors may import or export up to $5,000 in U.S. or foreign currency, with no formalities. Larger amounts of money must be declared to Customs.

Visitors arriving by air, no matter what the port of entry, are well advised to be exceedingly patient and to resign themselves to a wait in the Customs and Immigration line. At busy times, especially when several overseas flights arrive within a few minutes of each other, it can take two or three hours just to get a passport stamped for arrival. Allow *plenty* of time for connections between international and domestic flights!

Border formalities by road or rail from Canada are relatively quick and easy.

Embassies & Consulates   Embassies in the United States for English-speaking foreign visitors include the **Australian Embassy,** 1601 Massachusetts Ave. NW, Washington, DC 20036 (tel. 202/797-3000); **Canadian Embassy,** 1746 Massachusetts Ave. NW, Washington, DC 20036 (tel. 202/785-1400); **Irish Embassy,** 2234 Massachusetts Ave. NW, Washington, DC 20008 (tel. 202/462-3939); **New Zealand Embassy,** 37 Observatory Circle NW, Washington, DC 20008 (tel. 202/328-4800); **U.K. Embassy,** 3100 Massachusetts Ave. NW, Washington, DC 20008 (tel. 202/462-1340). None of these countries has a consulate in Denver.

Emergencies   A single emergency telephone number, **911,** will put you in touch with police, ambulance, or fire department throughout most but not all of Colorado. You can also obtain emergency assistance by dialing 0 (zero) for an operator.

Legal Aid   Those accused of serious offenses are advised to say and do nothing before consulting an attorney. Under U.S. law, an arrested person is permitted one telephone call to a party of his or her choice: Call your embassy! If you are pulled up for a minor infraction, such as a traffic offense, never attempt to pay the fine directly to a police officer. You may wind up arrested on the much more serious charge of attempted bribery. Pay fines by mail or directly into the hands of the clerk of a court.

Safety   While tourist areas are generally safe, crime is on the increase everywhere, and U.S. urban areas tend to be less safe than those in Europe or Japan. Visitors should always stay alert. This is particularly true of large U.S. cities. Ask the local tourist office if you're in doubt about which neighborhoods are safe. Avoid deserted areas, especially at night.

Avoid carrying valuables on the street, and don't display expensive cameras or electronic equipment. Hold on to your pocketbook, and place your billfold in an inside pocket. Keep your possessions in sight in public places.

Hotels are open to the public, and in a large hotel, security may not be able to screen everyone from entering. Always lock your room door—don't assume that once inside your hotel you are automatically safe.

Safety while **driving** is particularly important. Ask you rental agency about personal safety, or ask for a brochure of traveler safety tips. Obtain written directions or a map showing how to get to your destination. If possible, arrive and depart during daylight hours. If you drive off a highway into a doubtful neighborhood, leave the area as quickly as you can.

Park in well-lighted, well-traveled areas if possible. Always keep your car doors locked, whether attended or unattended. Look around you before you get out of your car, and never leave any packages or valuables in sight. If someone attempts to rob you or steal your car, do *not* try to resist the thief/carjacker—report the incident to the police department immediately.

Taxes   In the United States, there is no VAT (Value-Added Tax) or other indirect tax at a national level. Colorado levies a 3% state tax on gross receipts, including hotel checks and shop purchases. Food is exempt. In addition, each city or county levies additional taxes, which vary greatly, to support the local tax base.

Telephone & Fax   Public telephone booths are easily found in cities like Denver and Colorado Springs, but may be more difficult to find in smaller towns. Stores and gas stations are your best bets. Hotels often add a per-call surcharge of up to 75¢ to your room bill, even though the standard charge for local calls is but 25¢.

Colorado has two **area codes:** 303 for Denver and the northern and western parts of the state; 719 for Colorado Springs and the south-central and southeastern regions.

For direct **overseas calls,** dial 011, followed by the country code (Australia, 61; Ireland, 353; New Zealand, 64; United Kingdom, 44; etc.), then the city code and the number of the person you are calling. For Canada and **long-distance** calls within the United States, dial 1 followed by the area code and the number you want. For reversed-charge or collect calls, and for person-to-person calls, dial 0 (zero) instead of 1, then follow the same procedure as above, and an operator will come on the line. For long-distance directory assistance, dial 1, the area code you need, then 555-1212.

Fax service (for instant facsimile transmission) can be provided by major hotels at a nominal charge, or by business service centers in most towns and cities.

Time   The United States is divided into six time zones. From east to west, they are: eastern standard time (EST, five hours behind Greenwich mean time), central standard time (CST), mountain standard time (MST), Pacific standard time (PST), Alaska standard time (AST), and Hawaii standard time (HST). Keep time zones in mind when traveling or telephoning long distances in the United States. For example, noon in New York City (EST) is 11am in Chicago (CST), 10am in Denver (MST), 9am in Los Angeles (PST), 8am in Anchorage (AST), and 7am in Honolulu (HST). Daylight saving time is in effect from the first Sunday in April through the last Saturday in October; this alters the clock so that sunrise and sunset are an hour later.

Toilets   Some foreign visitors complain that public restrooms are hard to find in the States. There are none on the streets, but most hotels, restaurants, bars, department stores, gasoline stations, museums, and other tourist attractions have them available. In a restaurant or bar, it's usually appropriate to order a cup of coffee or soft drink to qualify you as a customer.

Yellow Pages   There are two kinds of telephone directories available. The general directory is called the "white pages," and includes individuals and businesses alphabetically by name. The second directory, called *Yellow Pages,* lists all local services, businesses, and industries alphabetically by category, with an index in the back. Listings include not only the obvious, such as automobile repairs and drugstores (pharmacies), but also restaurants by cuisine and location, places of worship by religious denomination, and other information.

DENVER

It's no accident that Denver is called "the Mile High City." When you climb the State Capitol steps, you're precisely 5,280 feet above sea level.

It wasn't intended to be that way. In fact, it could not have been more purely coincidental.

Denver, you see, is a fluke of history, one of the few cities ever built by man that was not on an ocean, lake, or navigable river, or even on an existing road or railroad, at the time of its founding.

In the summer of 1858, a few flecks of gold were discovered by eager Georgia prospectors where Cherry Creek empties into the shallow South Platte River. A tent camp quickly sprang up on the site (the first permanent structure was a saloon). When militia Gen. William H. Larimer arrived in 1859, he claim-jumped the land on the east side of the Platte, laid out a city, and—hoping to gain political favors—named it after James Denver, governor of the Kansas Territory, of which this land was then a part. He didn't know that Denver had already resigned.

Larimer's wasn't the only settlement on the South Platte. Three others claimed equal predominance. But Larimer, a shrewd man, had a solution. For the price of a barrel of whiskey, he bought out the other founders, and the name Denver stuck.

Although the gold found in Denver was but a teaser for much larger strikes in the nearby mountains, the community grew as a shipping and trade center with a milder climate than the mining towns it served. A devastating fire in 1863, a deadly flash flood in 1864, and Native American tribal hostilities in the late 1860s created many hardships. But the establishment of rail links to the east and the influx of silver from the rich mines to the west kept Denver going. Leadville silver and Cripple Creek gold made it a showcase city in the late 19th and early 20th centuries. The U.S. Mint built here in 1906 established Denver as a banking and financial center.

In the years following World War II, it mushroomed to become the largest city between the Great Plains and the Pacific coast, with about 500,000 residents in Denver and over 1.8 million in the metropolitan area. Today, it's a sprawling city, extending from the Rocky Mountain foothills on the west, far into the plains on the south and east. Denver is noted for its dozens of tree-lined boulevards; its 200 city parks, comprising more than 20,000 acres; and its architecture, from Victorian to sleek contemporary.

1. ORIENTATION

ARRIVING

BY PLANE Scheduled to open in early 1994, the **Denver International Airport** is 24 miles northeast of downtown Denver, about a 35 to 45 minute drive. Covering 53 square miles, twice the size of New York's Manhattan Island, DIA boasts one of the tallest flight control towers in the world.

WHAT'S SPECIAL ABOUT DENVER

Architectural Highlights
- The State Capitol (1890–1908), a replica of the U.S. Capitol with a gold-plated dome.
- Brown Palace Hotel (1892), Frank Edbrooke's remarkable, triangular masterpiece.
- Larimer Square, Denver's oldest retail district, restored to its 19th-century spirit.

Museums
- Denver Art Museum, with the world's largest Native American art collection.
- Denver Museum of Natural History, exhibiting skeletons of dozens of prehistoric creatures found in Colorado.
- Museum of Western Art, offering paintings and sculptures by O'Keeffe, Remington, and Russell.
- Black America West Museum, which documents the lives of African American cowboys and pioneers.

Historical Sites
- Molly Brown House (1889), Victorian home of the "Unsinkable" heroine of the *Titanic* disaster.
- Buffalo Bill's Grave and Museum, honoring the famous frontier scout and Wild West showman.
- Pearce-McAllister Cottage (1899), with its upstairs doll and miniatures museum.

Industrial Tours
- The U.S. Mint, where more than five *billion* coins are produced yearly.
- Coors Brewing Company, the largest single brewing facility in the world.
- Hakushika Saké brewery, a new facility producing the national drink of Japan.

Events/Festivals
- National Western Stock Show & Rodeo, the world's largest cattle show and indoor rodeo, each January.

- A Taste of Colorado, where mountain and plain join for food and fun, Labor Day weekend.

For the Kids
- Elitch Gardens, the Rockies' largest amusement park.
- Children's Museum of Denver, a hands-on experience to delight children and adults.
- Tiny Town, the oldest kid-size village in the U.S.

Shopping
- Cherry Creek Shopping Center, the state's largest and most fashionable indoor mall.
- 16th Street Mall, a granite-paved pedestrian promenade that runs one mile through the heart of downtown.
- Tivoli Denver, a 19th-century brewery transformed into a dining/shopping center.

Parks
- City Park, 314 city-center acres that include a zoo, natural history museum, lakes and gardens, and golf course.
- Denver Botanic Gardens, impressive indoor-outdoor home to thousands of exotic and native plants.
- Denver Mountain Parks, encompassing 20,000 acres in the adjacent Rockies.

Natural Spectacles
- Red Rocks Amphitheatre, a 9,000-seat outdoor theater set between spectacular 400-foot red sandstone rocks.
- The silhouette of the Rocky Mountains seen from any city skyscraper at sunset.

The airport has 88 gates, five full-service runways, and expects to serve at least 34 million passengers annually.

Major Airlines serving Denver include American, America West, Continental,

Delta, GP Express, Great Lakes, Mexicana, Midwest Express, Northwest, Trans World, United, and USAir.

Regional and commuter airlines connect Denver with other points in the state; they include **Continental Express, Mesa Airlines,** and **United Express.**

For major airlines' national reservations phone numbers, see the "Getting There" section in Chapter 2. For other information, including local phone numbers for specific airlines and other airport services, call the Denver International Airport toll-free **information** line, 800/AIR-2-DEN.

Getting to & from Town Bus, taxi, and limousine services are provided between Denver International Airport and downtown Denver, and most major car-rental companies have outlets at the airport. Cost of a **city bus** ride from the airport to downtown Denver is $6, from the airport to Boulder costs $8. **Shuttle service** is available from the Airporter (321-3222), and there are also several **taxi** companies (see the "Getting Around" section, below), but fares from the new airport were not available at press time. Because there are no major hotels at Denver International Airport, travelers should check on the availability and cost of hotel shuttle service when making their reservations.

BY TRAIN **Amtrak,** 17th Street and Wynkoop Street (tel. 892-1442 or toll free 800/USA-RAIL), connects Denver with San Francisco and serves western Colorado from Denver to such points as Winter Park, Granby, Glenwood Springs, and Grand Junction. There are six arrivals and departures daily.

BY BUS **Greyhound,** 1055 19th St. (tel. 293-6555 or toll free 800/231-2222) is the major bus service in Colorado. There are about 60 daily arrivals and departures to towns, cities, and resort communities throughout the state.

BY CAR The principal highway routes into Denver are I-25 from the north (Fort Collins, Cheyenne) or south (Colorado Springs, Albuquerque); I-70 from the east (Burlington, Kansas City) and west (Grand Junction); and I-76 from the northeast (Sterling). If you're driving into Denver from Boulder, take U.S. 36; from Salida and southwest, U.S. 285.

TOURIST INFORMATION

The downtown tourist information office is at the **Denver Metro Convention and Visitors Bureau,** 225 W. Colfax Ave., Denver, CO 80202 (tel. 303/892-1505), across from the U.S. Mint. Ask for the "Official Visitors Guide," a 96-page booklet with a comprehensive listing of accommodations, restaurants, and all other visitor services in Denver and surrounding areas. The information center is open in summer, Monday through Saturday from 8am to 5pm and on Sunday from 10am to 2pm; in winter, Monday through Friday from 8am to 5pm and on Saturday from 9am to 1pm.

For visitors who run into difficulties of one kind or another, **Travelers Aid** has an office at 1245 E. Colfax Ave. (tel. 303/832-8194).

CITY LAYOUT

You can never truly get lost in Denver, as long as you remember that the mountains—almost always visible—are to the west. All the same, it can be perplexing to get around a city of half a million people. Denver has the added confusion of an older grid system, oriented northeast-southwest to parallel the South Platte River, surrounded by a newer north-south grid system.

MAIN ARTERIES & STREETS

It's probably easiest to get your bearings from Civic Center Park. From here, Colfax Avenue—U.S. 40—extends east and west as far as the eye can see. Ditto Broadway, which reaches north and south.

DOWNTOWN DENVER North of Colfax and west of Broadway is the center of downtown Denver, where the streets use the old grid pattern. **16th Street,** a mile-long pedestrian mall, cuts northwest off Broadway just above this intersection.

(Numbered streets parallel 16th to the northeast, all the way to 44th; and to the southwest, as far as 5th.) Intersecting the numbered streets at right angles are **Lawrence Street** (one way northeast) and **Larimer Street** (one way southwest), 12 and 13 blocks, respectively, from the Colfax–Broadway intersection.

I-25 skirts downtown Denver to the west, with access from Colfax or from **Speer Boulevard,** which winds diagonally along Cherry Creek past Larimer Square.

OUTSIDE DOWNTOWN   Outside the downtown sector, the pattern is a little less confusing. But keep in mind that the numbered *avenues* that parallel Colfax to the north and south (Colfax is equivalent to 15th Avenue) have nothing in common with the numbered *streets* of the downtown grid. In fact, any byway labeled an "avenue" runs east-west, never north-south.

FINDING AN ADDRESS

NORTH-SOUTH ARTERIES   The thoroughfare that divides avenues into "east" and "west" is Broadway which is one way south between 19th Street and I-25. Each block east or west adds 100 to the avenue address; thus a restaurant at 2115 E. 17th Ave. is a little over 21 blocks east of Broadway—just beyond Vine Street.

Main thoroughfares that parallel Broadway to the east include Downing Street (1200 block), York Street (2300 block; it becomes University Boulevard south of 6th), Colorado Boulevard (4000 block), Monaco Parkway (6500 block), and Quebec Street (7300 block). Colorado Boulevard (Colo. 2) is the most significant artery, intersecting I-25 on the south and I-70 on the north. North-south cross streets that parallel Broadway west of Broadway include Santa Fe Drive (U.S. 85; 1000 block); west of I-25 are Federal Boulevard (U.S. 287 North, site of the city's main sports arenas; 3000 block), and Sheridan Boulevard (Colo. 95; 5200 block), the boundary between Denver and Lakewood.

EAST-WEST ARTERIES   Denver streets are divided into "north" and "south" at Ellsworth Avenue, about 1½ miles south of Colfax. Ellsworth is a relatively minor street, but it's a convenient breaking point because it's just a block south of First Avenue. With addresses increasing by 100 per block, that puts an address like 1710 Downing Street at the corner of East 17th Avenue. First Avenue, Sixth Avenue, Colfax (1500 block), 26th Avenue, and Martin Luther King Jr. Boulevard Parkway (3200 block) are the principal east-west thoroughfares. There are no numbered avenues south of Ellsworth. Major east-west byways south of Ellsworth are Alameda Avenue (Colo. 26; 300 block), Mississippi Avenue (1100 block), Florida Avenue (1500 block), Evans Avenue (2100 block), Yale Avenue (2700 block), and Hampden Avenue (U.S. 285; 3500 block).

There are excellent Denver maps on the reverse side of the Official State Highway Map, and in the removable centerfold of the Denver Visitors Guide. Both are available free of charge from the Convention and Visitors Bureau (see "Tourist Information," above).

NEIGHBORHOODS IN BRIEF

Lower Downtown   Downtown Denver can be divided into three subdistricts. Lower Downtown ("LoDo") is the oldest part of the city. It extends northwesterly from Lawrence Street to Union Station and from the shops of Tivoli Denver northeast to 19th Street. No skyscrapers are permitted in this historic preservation district, most of which dates from the late 19th century.

Central Business District   This extends along 16th Street, 17th Street, and 18th Street between Lawrence Street and Broadway. Here, the ban on skyscrapers certainly does not apply!

Civic Center Park   This area is at the southeast end of 15th Street, where Broadway and Colfax Avenue meet. This 2-square-block oasis of green is surrounded by state and metropolitan government buildings, the Denver Art Museum, the Colorado History Museum, the U.S. Mint, and the public library.

Capitol Hill   Located just southeast of downtown and extending roughly from the State Capitol (Colfax and Lincoln) past the Governor's Mansion to East Sixth

Avenue, and from Broadway to Cheesman Park (on Franklin Street), is Capitol Hill. The area preserves a great many Victorian mansions from the mining-boom days of the late 19th and early 20th centuries, including the Molly Brown House and the Grant Humphreys Mansion. There are no old wooden buildings: After the disastrous fire of 1863, the government forbade the construction of wooden structures until after World War II.

Cherry Creek Home of Cherry Creek Shopping Center and Denver Country Club, this area extends north from East First Avenue to East Eighth and east from Downing Street to Steele Street. You'll find huge, ostentatious stone mansions here, especially around Circle Drive (southwest of Sixth and University)—this is where most of Denver's wealthiest families have lived for generations.

Historic Districts There are 17 recognized historic districts in Denver, including Capitol Hill, the Clements District (around 21st Street and Tremont Street, just east of downtown), and Ninth Street Park in Auraria (off Ninth Street and West Colfax Avenue). Historic Denver, 1330 17th St. (tel. 303/534-1858), offers walking-tour maps of several of these areas.

Glendale Denver fully surrounds little Glendale, an incorporated city in its own right. The center of a lively entertainment district, Glendale straddles Cherry Creek on South Colorado Boulevard south of East Alameda Avenue.

Tech Center At the southern end of the metropolitan area is Tech Center, along I-25 between Belleview Avenue and Arapahoe Road. In this district, about a 25-minute drive from downtown, there are eight technological centers, headquarters of several international and national companies, and a handful of upscale hotels heavily oriented to the business traveler.

2. GETTING AROUND

BY BUS The **Regional Transportation District (RTD)** (tel. 299-6000 or toll free 800/366-7433 for route and schedule information, 299-6700 for other business), calls itself "The Ride." It provides good service within Denver and its suburbs and outlying communities, including Boulder, Longmont, and Evergreen.

Local fares are $1 during peak hours (Monday through Friday from 6 to 9am and 4 to 6pm), 50¢ during off-peak hours. Exact change is required. Express fares start at $1.50; regional fares vary ($2.50 Denver-Boulder). Senior citizens pay only 15¢ off-peak, and children 5 and younger travel free.

The various routes have different schedules of frequency including time of last bus, which varies from 9pm to 1am. Maps of all routes are available at the RTD office, 1600 Blake St., Monday through Friday from 8:30am to 5pm; and at the Denver Metro CVB, 225 W. Colfax Ave.

Free buses run up and down the 16th Street Mall between the Civic Center and Market Street every 90 seconds.

A bargain for visitors is the **Cultural Connection Trolley** (tel. 299-6000), which runs daily, every half hour, with stops at Denver's most popular tourist stops, including the State Capitol, Denver Botanic Gardens, Denver Zoo, U.S. Mint, and almost all major downtown museums. Cost is $1 for a full-day pass, and detailed route information is available at the Denver Visitors Bureau.

BY TAXI The main services are **Yellow Cab** (tel. 777-7777), **Zone Cab** (tel. 444-8888), and **Metro Taxi** (tel. 333-3333). Taxis can be hailed on streets, though it's best to either call or wait at a taxi stand outside a major hotel.

BY CAR Visitors unfamiliar with the Denver traffic pattern may prefer to wait until they're ready to leave the city before renting a car. Rush-hour traffic, especially on I-25, is no fun, and most downtown hotels charge a sizable sum for parking.

For regulations and advice on driving in Colorado, see Chapter 2. The American Automobile Association (AAA) maintains an office in Denver at 4100 E. Arkansas Ave. (tel. 753-8800 or toll free 800/283-5222).

Parking Downtown parking-lot rates vary from 75¢ per half hour to $10 for all day. Rates climb with proximity to the 16th Street Mall and the central business district. Keep a handful of quarters, dimes, and nickels if you hope to use on-street parking meters.

Car Rentals Rental agencies in Denver, some with offices in or near downtown as well as at Denver International Airport, include **Alamo,** 7400 E. 41st Ave. (tel. 321-1176 or toll free 800/327-9633); **Avis,** 1900 Broadway (tel. 839-1280 or toll free 800/831-2847); **Budget,** 2150 Broadway (tel. 341-2277 or toll free 800/527-0700); **Dollar,** 7450 E. 29th Ave. (tel. 398-2323 or toll free 800/800-4000); **General** (tel. 790-9220 or toll free 800/327-7607); **Hertz,** 2001 Welton (tel. 297-9400 or toll free 800/654-3131); and **National** (tel. 770-9900 or toll free 800/227-7368).

Campers, travel trailers, and motor homes may be rented from **Cruise America,** 8950 N. Federal Blvd. (tel. 426-6699 or toll free 800/327-7778), or **Go Vacations of America,** 275 W. 43rd Ave. (tel. 480-0100).

For the traveler seeking true luxury, several limousine services operate from Denver. Among them are **Admiral Limousines,** 4120 Brighton Blvd. Unit 1-B (tel. 296-2003 or toll free 800/828-8680), and **Colorado Limousine Service,** 1304 Ogden St. (tel. 832-7155 or toll free 800/628-6655).

ON FOOT Downtown Denver is a pleasure to explore on foot. It's only a little over a mile from end to end, and the pedestrian mall on 16th Street makes the walk especially easy. Outside downtown, the metropolis stretches mile after mile in all directions. It's wise to take a bus or taxi.

FAST FACTS: *DENVER*

American Express The American Express Travel Agency is located in the Anaconda Tower at 555 17th St. (tel. 303/298-7100). Open Monday through Friday from 8:30am to 5pm. Full member services and currency exchange are offered. To report a lost card, call toll free 800/528-4800; to report lost traveler's checks, call toll free 800/221-7282.

Area Code The telephone area code in the Denver metropolitan area is 303.

Babysitters The YWCA of Metropolitan Denver has a year-round Child Care Information Network (tel. 825-7141) with free information on part-time and drop-in child-care services. In summer, the Summer Fun Day Camp, 7710 W. 35th Ave., Wheat Ridge (tel. 232-9191), is an excellent option. Concierges and front desks at leading hotels can also arrange child care.

Banks Leading banks include Colorado National Bank, 17th and Champa (tel. 892-4222); First Interstate Bank of Denver, 633 17th St., at California Street (tel. 293-2211); and the Women's Bank, 821 17th St. (tel. 293-2265). Money Express, 901 E. Colfax Ave. (tel. 830-CASH), offers 24-hour check cashing. Foreign currency is exchanged at Thomas Cook Currency Services, 1580 Court Place, downtown (tel. 571-0808).

Dentist For referrals, call Dial-4-Health (tel. 443-2584) or visit the Centre Dental Associates, 1600 Stout St., Suite 1370 (tel. 592-1133).

Doctor For referrals, call Dial-4-Health (tel. 443-2584) or St. Joseph Hospital's Med Search (tel. 866-8000). For emergency treatment, near downtown is St. Joseph Hospital, 1835 Franklin St. (tel. 837-7240).

Drugstores Reliable prescription services are available at Walgreen's Drug Stores, open 24 hours a day at 2000 E. Colfax Ave. at Race Street (tel. 331-0917).

Emergencies For police, fire, or medical emergencies, call 911. For Colorado State Patrol, call 239-4501. For the Poison Control Center, call 629-1123.

Eyeglasses At 999 18th St., at Curtis Street, Suite 146, the Visionary (tel. 298-9398) can handle all routine and emergency optical and eye-care needs in short order. Outside downtown, you can get 1-hour replacement of lost or broken glasses at Lenscrafter stores in major shopping malls.

Hairdressers/Barbers Downtown on the 16th Street Mall is Shear

Productions, Republic Plaza, 303 16th St. (tel. 592-4247). Near the Cherry Creek Shopping Center is Paul Garcia's, 3000 E. Third Ave. (tel. 333-5577). Both are full-service salons catering to men as well as women. Fantastic Sams has more than two dozen salons in the Denver metropolitan area, offering speedy, low-cost haircuts.

Hospitals Among Denver-area hospitals are St. Joseph's Hospital, 1835 Franklin St. (tel. 837-7240), just east of downtown; Rose Medical Center, 4567 E. Ninth St. (tel. 320-2455), east of Colorado Boulevard; Swedish Medical Center, 501 E. Hampden Ave. (tel. 788-6959), in Englewood; and St. Anthony's Hospital, 4231 W. 16th Ave. (tel. 629-3511), west of Mile High Stadium.

Information See "Orientation," above.

Laundry/Dry Cleaning Nearly every major hotel offers valet drop-off and pick-up service, but the charge can be steep. Colorado Lace is a reputable chain of dry cleaners with over 20 locations in the Denver metropolitan area. One-day dry cleaning service is available at La Petite Cleaners, 2314 Sixth Ave., at Josephine Street (tel. 377-7459).

Libraries The Denver Public Library, 1357 Broadway (tel. 640-8800, TDD information for persons with hearing impairments, call 640-8980), has its main facility adjacent to Civic Center Park, abutting downtown. There are branches throughout the metropolitan area. The main library has a fine collection on western history and art, and has copy machines and computers available (for a fee) for public use. A local or Colorado library card is required to check out material. Open Monday through Wednesday from 10am to 9pm, Thursday through Saturday from 10am to 5:30pm, and on Sunday from 1 to 5pm.

Lost Property Consult the city police (tel. 575-3127).

Maps Denver's largest map store is Maps Unlimited, 899 Broadway, at Ninth Street (tel. 623-4299 or toll free 800/456-8703).

Newspapers/Magazines The state's two largest daily newspapers are the morning *Denver Post,* a broadsheet, and the afternoon *Rocky Mountain News,* a tabloid. There's also a widely read weekly, *Westword,* known as much for its controversial jibes at local politicians as for its entertainment listings. Best of all, it's free from newsstands. National newspapers such as *USA Today* and the *Wall Street Journal* can be purchased on the streets and at major hotels.

Photographic Needs Robert Waxman Camera and Video, with supplies, equipment, photo processing, and repairs, has six Denver locations, including what is believed to be the biggest single-floor camera store in the world, at 15th Street and California (tel. 623-1155). For photo processing you might also visit the Pro Lab, 1200 W. Mississippi Ave. (tel. 744-6126) or Pallas Photo Labs, 700 Kalamath St. (tel. 893-0101).

Police In emergency, dial 911. For nonemergency needs, call 575-3127.

Post Office The Main Post Office is downtown at 920 20th St., open Monday through Friday from 9am to 5pm. Denver offers full postal services 24 hours a day at two other locations: Terminal Annex, 1595 Wynkoop St. (tel. 297-6801), next to the train station; and at the General Mail Facility, 7500 W. 53rd Place (tel. 297-6456).

Radio/TV Two dozen AM and FM radio stations in the Denver area cater to all musical, news, sports, and entertainment tastes. Among them are KOA (850 AM) for news and sports, KMJI (100.3 FM) for light rock, KRFX (103.5 FM) for classic rock "oldies," KWMX (1600 AM and 107.5 FM) for contemporary rock, KLMO (1060 AM) for country, and KVOD (99.5 FM) for classical music. Denver has 10 television stations; they include KCNC (Channel 4), the NBC affiliate; KMGH (Channel 7), the CBS affiliate; and KUSA (Channel 9), the ABC affiliate. Other major stations are KWGN (Channel 2), an independent; and KRMA, Channel 6, the PBS affiliate. Cable or satellite service is available at most hotels.

Safety Although Denver is generally a safe city, it is not crime free. Stay alert, be aware of your immediate surroundings, and keep a close eye on your possessions, especially cameras, purses, and wallets. The 16th Street Mall is seldom a problem, but even streetwise Denverites avoid late-night walks along certain sections of East Colfax Avenue, just several blocks away.

The Rape Assistance and Awareness Program (tel. 443-7300) operates a 24-hour hot line.

Shoe Repairs   Right on the 16th Street Mall is Shoe Biz, in Republic Plaza at 303 16th St. (tel. 893-9686). Shoes and boots are quickly repaired, often while you wait.

Taxes   Total sales tax in Denver is 7.3%. The tax is lower in some neighboring counties, including suburbs. The hotel tax in Denver, added to room charges to support the tourism infrastructure and other industries, is 4.7%, bringing the total tax on rooms to 12%.

Telephone/Fax   Local calls are normally 25¢. For directory assistance, dial 1-555-1212. Facsimiles can be transmitted by most major hotels at a nominal cost. For 24-hour FAX service, there are several Kinko's Copies outlets, including one at 2043 S. University Blvd. (tel. 778-8734).

Weather/Road/Ski Conditions   For a weather report, time, and temperature, call 337-2500. Road condition reports are available by calling 639-1111 for the area within a 2-hour drive of Denver. Call 639-1234 for statewide conditions. A recorded ski report can be reached at 831-SNOW.

3. ACCOMMODATIONS

Although most Denver properties do not change rates seasonally, as you'll find in other parts of Colorado, hotels that cater to business travelers, such as the luxurious Brown Palace and Warwick, offer substantial discounts on weekends, often as much as 50% lower than weeknights.

Rates listed here are the official, or "rack rates," and do not take into consideration any individual or group discounts. Discounts are often given to senior citizens, members of the military, employees of large corporations, and members of travel clubs or other organizations. Make a point of asking for a discount. Because the chain hotel's national reservation service is not allowed to offer special discounts, it is usually best to call the hotel directly to get the best rate.

Another way to save money on Denver lodging is to call the Mile High Adventure Club (tel. toll free 800/489-4888). It offers discounted rates at more than 30 hotels, plus discounts on a wide variety of activities, including bungee jumping, fishing, golf, skiing, theaters, and concerts.

In these listings, the following categories define price ranges: very expensive, over $150 per night double; expensive, $110 to $150; moderate, $75 to $110; inexpensive, $40 to $75; budget, less than $40 per night double. An additional 12% tax is levied onto all bills, and is not included in the rates.

DOWNTOWN

VERY EXPENSIVE

BROWN PALACE HOTEL, 321 17th St., Denver, CO 80202. Tel. 303/ 297-3111 or toll free 800/321-2599 in North America, 800/228-2917 in Colorado. Fax 303/293-9204. 205 rms, 25 suites. A/C TV TEL

$ Rates: $159–$199 single; $174–$214 double; $225–$675 suite. Weekend rates start at $89. AE, CB, DC, DISC, ER, JCB, MC, V. **Parking:** $12 per day.

The first open-atrium hotel in the U.S. opened in August 1892—and has never closed. This National Historic Landmark was the masterpiece of architect Frank Edbrooke, who designed it in Italian Renaissance style. Bounded by Broadway, 17th Street, and Tremont Place, the building is triangular in shape—though you'd never know it unless you looked down on it from a nearby office tower. A stained glass ceiling eight stories above the Victorian lobby allows the rich-wood

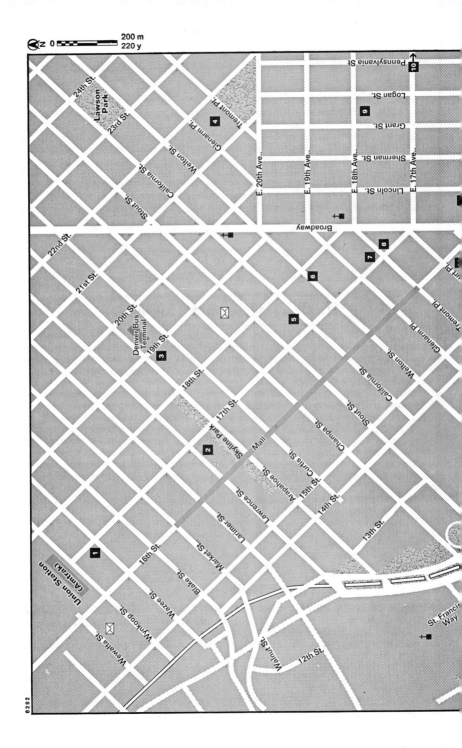

DENVER ACCOMMODATIONS

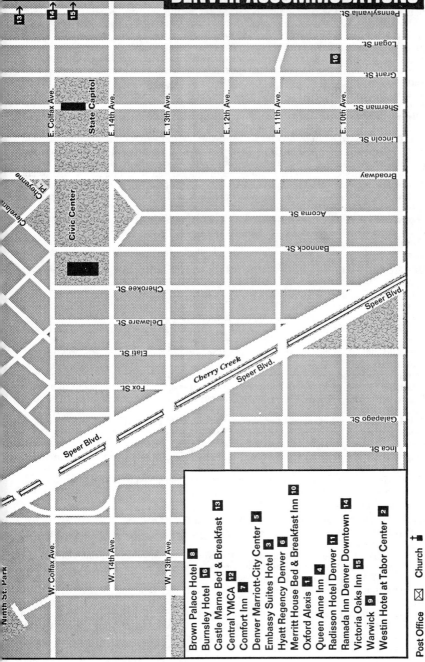

Pennsylvania St.

Logan St.

Grant St.

Sherman St.

Lincoln St.

Broadway

Acoma St.

Bannock St.

Cherokee St.

Delaware St.

Elati St.

Fox St.

Galapago St.

Inca St.

State Capitol

Civic Center

Cheyenne Pl.

Cleveland

Cherry Creek

Speer Blvd.

Speer Blvd.

Speer Blvd.

E. Colfax Ave.

E. 14th Ave.

E. 13th Ave.

E. 12th Ave.

E. 11th Ave.

E. 10th Ave.

W. Colfax Ave.

W. 14th Ave.

W. 13th Ave.

Ninth St. Park

13 **14** **15** **16**

Brown Palace Hotel **8**
Burnsley Hotel **16**
Castle Marne Bed & Breakfast **13**
Central YMCA **12**
Comfort Inn **7**
Denver Marriott-City Center **5**
Embassy Suites Hotel **3**
Hyatt Regency Denver **6**
Merritt House Bed & Breakfast Inn **10**
Oxford Alexis **1**
Queen Anne Inn **4**
Radisson Hotel Denver **11**
Ramada Inn Denver Downtown **14**
Victoria Oaks Inn **15**
Warwick **9**
Westin Hotel at Tabor Center **2**

Post Office ⊠   Church ✝

paneling and Mexican onyx to glow. Original grillwork surrounds the mezzanine, and a huge American flag is suspended in the center of the atrium. Dwight Eisenhower kept the Western White House at the Brown Palace during his presidency, 1953 to 1961. His Eisenhower Suite has rich masculine decor, integrity, and even a dent in the fireplace trim said to have been made by an errant golf ball!

Standard rooms come in different Victorian decors, from peaches to carmines to deep greens. Most have antique furnishings. Rooms have desks, remote-control TVs tucked away in armoires, and period prints on the walls. Local calls cost 50¢. (There's no access charge.) Oh, yes, the tap water's great: The Brown Palace has its own artesian wells!

Dining/Entertainment: Fine dining is in the Palace Arms (see "Dining," below). Ellyngton's serves breakfast ($3.75 to $10.50) and lunch (light grills and pastas, $7.25 to $10) daily from 7am to 2pm, and a Dom Perignon brunch on Sunday from 10:30am to 2:30pm. The Ship Tavern is open daily from 11am to 11pm for drinks and casual dining (steak and seafood, $7 to $21). Cocktails are served in the lobby and in Henry C's, a modern lounge adjoining Ellyngton's. The lobby also offers a Devonshire tea (with finger sandwiches, scones, and pastries) Monday to Saturday from 2 to 4:30pm for $8.50. Lunch is also served in the Brown Palace Club, for private members and hotel guests only.

Services: 24-hour room service, full concierge service, valet laundry, no-smoking rooms, turn down, robes, Crabtree and Evelyn amenities.

Facilities: United Airlines desk, jeweler, florist, hair salon for men and women, apparel shop, gift shop, newsstand; meeting facilities for up to 750.

DENVER MARRIOTT—CITY CENTER, 1701 California St., Denver, CO 80202. Tel. 303/297-1300 or toll free 800/228-9290. Fax 303/298-7474. 612 rms, 15 suites. A/C TV TEL

$ Rates: $135–$145 single; $155–$165 double; $270–$475 suite. Weekend rates $79 single or double. AE, MC, V. **Parking:** $12 per day.

This tall black tower in the center of the financial district is oriented more to the business traveler than to the vacationer. Its lobby, simple and elegant with heavy use of marble and glass, is relatively small for a major hotel. An escalator leads down to the restaurant and lounge.

Rooms have a king-size or two double beds, a table and chairs, a desk with a telephone (75¢ charge for local calls or long-distance access), a credenza with a color TV (and in-house movies), built-in radio, individual temperature control, and a full-mirror closet door.

Dining/Entertainment: Marjolaine's serves breakfast and lunch buffets and an international menu selection for dinner ($9.95 to $16.95). The lounge also serves light lunch fare.

Services: Room service, valet laundry, babysitting, no-smoking floors, upgraded concierge level.

Facilities: Guest laundry, games room, gift shop/newsstand; fitness center with Universal and free weights, aerobics classes, pool, Jacuzzi, men's and women's saunas; meeting facilities for up to 2,300 people.

HYATT REGENCY DENVER, 1750 Welton St., Denver, CO 80202. Tel. 303/295-1200 or toll free 800/233-1234. Fax 303/293-2565. 513 rms, 27 suites. A/C TV TEL

$ Rates: $140 single; $160 double; $310–$1,000 suite. Weekend rates $65 single or double. Children 18 and under stay free in parents' room. AE, CB, DC, DISC, JCB, MC, V. **Parking:** $10 per day.

The first thing visitors see when they enter the Hyatt is a pair of Belgian crystal chandeliers that seem to float on a mural of the sky painted on the lobby ceiling. It's a dramatic touch, but then, this is a dramatic property. The 26-story hotel is part of a four-building office-shopping-parking complex that also includes the 40-story Anaconda Tower. A glass-covered atrium links the quartet.

An art deco motif of light greens and mauves carries through the hotel to the guest rooms. There's a feeling of luxury here, with fabric wall coverings, long drapes, and marble-top oak dressers. Every room has soundproof windows that open, an individual thermostat, a well-lit desk, a color TV (in-room movies), direct-dial phones, an alarm clock, and an electric shoe polisher. Bathrooms are elaborate, with oversize bath towels, a scale, radio extension speakers, even a telephone.

Dining/Entertainment: McGuire's, for casual dining, is open Sunday through Thursday from 6am to midnight and on Friday and Saturday from 6am to 2am. Main dishes run $6.25 to $17.25, and there's a deli sandwich buffet Monday through Friday. Sky Court serves light meals and beverages daily from 11am to 4pm on the fourth-floor deck Memorial Day to Labor Day.

Services: Room service (during restaurant hours), valet laundry, half-hourly shuttle ($5 fee), no-smoking and concierge floors.

Facilities: Athletic club; rooftop swimming pool (open summers), tennis courts, and jogging track; gift shop; meeting facilities for 1,500.

WESTIN HOTEL AT TABOR CENTER, 1672 Lawrence St., Denver, CO 80202. Tel. 303/572-9100 or toll free 800/228-3000. Fax 303/572-7288. 407 rms, 13 suites. A/C MINIBAR TV TEL
$ Rates: $145–$165 single; $170–$190 double; $290–$1,050 suite. AE, CB, DC, DISC, MC, V. **Parking:** $8 per day self-park, $12 per day valet.

The focal point of the 2-square-block Tabor Center shopping-and-office complex, the 19-story Westin bridges the historical gap between the central business district and lower downtown. Its contemporary design incorporates architectural elements of nearby Victorian-era structures. The second-floor lobby, reached by an elevator or a long escalator, features three-dimensional murals and modern fountains against a sand-tone background. Marble, brass, and bird's-eye maple wood add elegance.

The well-lit, spacious guest rooms, 75% of which have king-size beds, are beautifully appointed and have 9-foot ceilings. Modern furnishings with English styling have black lacquer or tortoise-shell accents. Every room has a remote-control color TV (with pay movie channels), clock radio, and two phones—one on a full-size working desk. There's an 85¢ charge for local calls or long-distance access. The Executive Club on the hotel's top three floors has upgraded features and amenities, among them continental breakfast and afternoon cocktails and a resident concierge.

Dining/Entertainment: The award-winning Augusta is regarded by many as the finest hotel restaurant in Denver (see "Dining," below). A casual, contemporary bistro, the Tabor Grill serves three meals daily from 6am to 11pm. There's live entertainment nightly Monday through Saturday in the Lobby Lounge.

Services: 24-hour room service, valet laundry, no-smoking floors, rooms for the handicapped, turn down, complimentary shoeshine.

Facilities: Health club ($5 fee) with indoor/outdoor swimming pool, hot tub, sauna, exercise and weight room, and racquetball courts; meeting space for 500; gift shop; indoor connection to Tabor Center shopping arcade.

EXPENSIVE

EMBASSY SUITES HOTEL, Denver Place, 1881 Curtis St., Denver, CO 80202. Tel. 303/297-8888 or toll free 800/733-3366; 800/297-8888 in Colorado. Fax 303/298-1101. 337 suites. A/C MINIBAR TV TEL
$ Rates (including breakfast): $134 single; $144 double. AE, CB, DC, DISC, JCB, MC, V. **Parking:** $10 Mon–Fri, $7 Sat–Sun.

Every room in this modern building is either a one- or two-bedroom suite. The hotel, heavily geared toward long-term business travelers, occupies the bottom 19 stories of a 37-story structure (the top half is offices).

The interior makes use of mirrors and skylights to give it a bright, spacious appearance. Guest rooms also appear larger than they are, thanks again to mirrors. But the rooms are very comfortable: Decorated in shades of peach or teal, they have either a king-size or two double beds. (A second bedroom has just one double.) The remote-control TV is tucked away in an armoire, and each bedroom has a TV as well. There are telephones in the bedroom and in the parlor; local calls and access charges are 60¢. All rooms have small refrigerators, wet bars, coffeemakers, and clock radios.

Dining/Entertainment: The airy, gardenlike Plaza Café serves breakfast and lunch daily. Dinners ($9.50 to $15) are offered in Burgundy's, romantic with subdued lighting. The Club Deli is open daily from 8am to 8pm for snacks. There are two bars: the Piano Bar, open daily from 4pm to midnight, and the Mezzanine Bar, serving complimentary cocktails to hotel guests only, from 5 to 7pm nightly.

Services: Concierge, valet laundry, foreign-currency exchange, complimentary newspaper, 51% no-smoking rooms.

Facilities: Outdoor pool (open May to September), small 24-hour exercise room, sauna, whirlpool, meeting space for 350, gift shop.

OXFORD HOTEL, 1600 17th St., at Wazee St., Denver, CO 80202. Tel. 303/628-5400 or toll free 800/228-5838. Fax 303/628-5413. 79 rms, 2 suites. A/C TV TEL

$ Rates: $115–$150 single; $120–$160 double; $155–$275 suite. AE, CB, DC, DISC, MC, V. **Parking:** $10 per day, valet.

Along with the Brown Palace, this is one of the few hotels to have survived the sweeping land-clearing projects in Denver in the early 1980s. And like the Brown, it was designed by architect Frank Edbrooke a century ago. Behind a simple red sandstone facade, the interior of this lower downtown property boasts marble walls, carpeted floors, stained-glass windows, frescoes, and silver chandeliers, all of which were restored and exactly reproduced between 1979 and 1983, according to Edbrooke's original drawings. It is listed on the National Register of Historic Places.

Some 1,300 antique pieces were imported from England and France—armoires, Asian carpets, light fixtures, art deco chairs and tables, and bedsteads—to furnish the 81 large rooms fashioned during the restoration from the 200 original small rooms. No two are alike. Appointed in forest green or navy blue, they feature individual thermostats, hair dryers, dressing tables, large closets, and good amenities packages. Some rooms have canopied beds and fireplaces; most have stocked minibars. There's bedside lighting, but electrical outlets are limited. Local phone calls are 75¢.

Dining/Entertainment: McCormick's Fish and Oyster House (see "Dining," below) is open for three meals daily. The art deco Cruise Room Bar is open daily from 4:30 to 10pm. Its dinner menu is famous for Angus beefsteaks. The Corner Bar has enormous stained-glass panels on its back bar.

Services: 24-hour room service, valet laundry; downtown-area limousine service in 1937 Hudson; no-smoking and disabled-accessible rooms; complimentary afternoon sherry at 4pm in the lobby; complimentary morning paper and overnight shoeshine.

Facilities: Health club and salon ($7 fee) with Universal and free weights, aerobics classes, and steam room; meeting space for 120.

RADISSON HOTEL DENVER, 1550 Court Place, Denver, CO 80202. Tel. 303/893-3333 or toll free 800/333-3333. Fax 303/892-0521. 674 rms, 66 suites. A/C TV TEL

$ Rates: $120–$140 single; $140–$160 double; $250–$600 suite. Weekend rates available. AE, CB, DC, DISC, JCB, MC, V. **Parking:** $10 per day, underground.

Designed by renowned architect I. M. Pei, this 22-story hotel has a unique exterior of glass and crushed rock that sparkles with flecks of gold when the sun shines. The large lobby, one floor above street level, greets visitors with marble and stainless steel.

Guest rooms are furnished in distinctive contemporary American or traditional Queen Anne decor, with king- or queen-size beds, comfortable wing-back chairs, work areas, and armoires. Some have two bathrooms. Views from the upper floors of this centrally located hotel, right on the 16th Street Mall, are great, looking out on the city or toward the mountains.

Dining/Entertainment: Finnegan's Restaurant and Pub, decorated in Irish antiques, presents authentic Irish cuisine and live entertainment Tuesday through Saturday evenings. Open daily from 11am to 11pm, later for bar service, entrées cost from $5.95 to $16.95. Windows serves breakfast and lunch, with café-style dining daily from 6:30am to 2pm.

Services: Room service, valet laundry, disabled-accessible rooms, no-smoking floor, concierge service, business center with secretarial service, and on-site audiovisual service.

Facilities: Recently upgraded health club with weight room, steam room, sauna, and heated outdoor swimming pool (open year-round); over 70,000 square feet of meeting and exhibit space.

THE WARWICK, 1776 Grant St., at E. 18th Ave., Denver, CO 80203. Tel. 303/861-2000 or toll free 800/525-2888. Fax 303/832-0320. 145 rms, 49 suites. A/C TV TEL

$ Rates (including European style buffet breakfast): $135–$155 single; $145–$165 double; $170–$500 suite. Weekend rate $69–$75 single or double. Children under 18 stay free in parents' room. AE, CB, DC, DISC, JCB, MC, V. **Parking:** $5 per day, underground.

 One of four Warwicks in the United States (the others are in New York, San Francisco, and Seattle), this elegant midsize hotel is more characteristic of hostelries in Paris, where the corporate office is located. It's one of Denver's best bargains. The small but sophisticated lobby, in particular, has a European accent, with richly upholstered antique chairs and couches on marble floors.

Even standard rooms have a full private balcony, and all but a few have a refrigerator, wet bar, and dining table. Appointed in navy blue, forest green, or a muted rust tone, guest rooms have one king- or two queen-size beds, simple brass and mahogany furniture, antique hunting prints on the walls, cable TV in an armoire, clock radio, and telephone with two incoming lines—one for a modem connection. There's another phone in the bathroom. Local calls are 60¢.

Dining/Entertainment: The Liaison Restaurant and Lounge serves breakfast daily, lunch and dinner Monday through Friday. The fare is contemporary American, with the dinner menu changing monthly, though a Friday-night seafood buffet ($18.50) is a big draw. The lounge won a "Best of Denver" award for its hors d'oeuvres, served Monday through Friday from 4:30 to 7pm.

Services: 24-hour room service and concierge, valet laundry, courtesy limousine within a 5-mile radius, no-smoking rooms and rooms equipped for the disabled, complimentary newspaper; babysitting and secretarial services (fee).

Facilities: Rooftop swimming pool (seasonal), gift shop, meeting space for 300, complimentary membership at adjacent athletic club.

MODERATE

THE BURNSLEY HOTEL, 1000 Grant St., at E. 10th Ave., Denver, CO 80203. Tel. 303/830-1000, or toll free 800/231-3915. 85 suites. A/C TV TEL

$ Rates: $95–$135 single or double; $225 penthouse suite. Weekend packages available. AE, CB, DC, MC, V. **Parking:** Free in hotel garage.

This small, elegant hotel offers suites and only suites, and at very reasonable rates. All of the luxurious but comfortable units have private patio areas, in addition to separate living, bedroom, dining, and fully stocked kitchen areas. The hotel boasts fine furnishings and works of art, imported toiletries, cable television with HBO, and a swimming pool and fitness center. Full secretarial services are available.

CASTLE MARNE BED & BREAKFAST, 1572 Race St., Denver, CO 80206. Tel. 303/331-0621 or toll free 800/92-MARNE. Fax 303/331-0623. 7 rms, 2 suites (all with bath). A/C TEL

$ Rates (including breakfast): $80–$105 single; $95–$120 double; $140–$180 suite. AE, CB, DC, MC, V. **Parking:** Ample street parking.

This impressive stone mansion, built in 1889, and a National Historic Landmark, has a gorgeous circular stained-glass peacock window and ornate fireplaces. It got its name from an owner whose son fought in the World War I Battle of the Marne. Denver's first indoor bathroom is still in operation in the Van Cise Room; the

IMPRESSIONS

. . . cash! why they create it here.
—WALT WHITMAN, on Denver in *SPECIMEN DAYS, 1879*

plumbing has been upgraded, but the claw-foot tub and marble vanity are the same. The John T. Mason Suite is named for a past owner, the curator of the Museum of Natural History; it displays part of his butterfly collection. The Presidential Suite has three rooms, a tower sitting room, a private fireplace, and a Jacuzzi solarium behind French doors. Guests enjoy a gourmet breakfast and afternoon tea as well. The inn also has a games room, library, gift shop, and an office for business travelers' use. No smoking is permitted. Not suitable for children under 10.

MERRITT HOUSE BED & BREAKFAST INN, 941 E. 17th Ave., Denver, CO 80218. Tel. 303/861-5230. 10 rms (all with bath). A/C TV TEL
$ Rates (including breakfast): $80–$95 single; $90–$125 double. AE, MC, V.
Located right in the middle of "Restaurant Row" on East 17th Avenue at Ogden Street, the Merritt House is another historic home. A handsome oak stairway leads from the parlor to guest rooms, each individually decorated with Victorian antiques or reproductions such as Alexander Graham Bell–style telephones, lamps that would make Thomas Edison proud, and cable TV—here known as "electric vision." All have private bath; the few with Jacuzzis are higher priced than those with simple showers. The house also boasts a glass-enclosed porch and won the Colorado State Preservation Award in 1988. A hearty breakfast is served each morning. There is a desk in each room and a fax machine is available. Only children over 12 are accepted.

QUEEN ANNE BED AND BREAKFAST INN, 2147-51 Tremont Place, Denver, CO 80205. Tel. 303/296-6666 or toll free 800/432-4667. Fax 303/296-2151. 10 rms, 4 suites (all with bath). A/C TV TEL
$ Rates (including breakfast): $75–$125 single or double. $115–$145 suite. AE, DC, DISC, MC, V. **Parking:** Private lot.
★ A favorite of both business travelers and couples seeking a romantic getaway, the Queen Anne might be considered the perfect bed and breakfast in the perfect location. Actually two Victorian homes—one built by famed architect Frank Edbrooke in 1879, and the other built in 1886—each room or suite has a telephone with free local calls and a writing desk. Innkeeper Tom King also provides piped-in chamber music, fresh flowers, and fax services. The 10 double rooms in the 1879 Pierce house are all unique, decorated with period antiques. The four two-room suites in the adjacent 1886 Roberts house are each dedicated to a famous artist (Norman Rockwell, Frederic Remington, John Audubon, and Alexander Calder). The suites have deep soaking tubs, and the Remington suite has its own hot tub. Located in the Clements Historic District, the Queen Anne borders downtown Denver and is within easy walking distance of the State Capitol, 16th Street Mall, Convention Center, restaurants, theaters, and office buildings. Breakfast is an elaborate continental affair. Smoking and pets are not allowed.

INEXPENSIVE

COMFORT INN, 401 17th St., Denver, CO 80202. Tel. 303/296-0400 or toll free 800/237-7431. 229 rms (all with bath). A/C TV TEL
$ Rates (including continental breakfast): $59–$79 single or double. AE, CB, DC, MC, V. **Parking:** $7.50 per day.
This may be Denver's best value in a modern, comfortable downtown accommodation. A private walkway over Tremont Place connects the Comfort Inn to the mezzanine of the Brown Palace Hotel—by which it was once owned as an annex. Rooms were renovated in 1992. The higher rooms in this 22-story hotel have great views, but they tend to overheat on hot summer days in spite of the air-conditioning system, so a lower-level room is preferable. Guests are treated to a free cocktail party with hot hors d'oeuvres at 5pm daily.

LA QUINTA INN CENTRAL, 3500 W. Park Ave. (I-25, Exit 213), Denver, CO 80216. Tel. 303/458-1222 or toll free 800/531-5900. Fax 303/433-2248. 105 rooms (all with bath), 1 suite. A/C TV TEL
$ Rates (including continental breakfast): $50–$58 single or double; $59–$69 suite. AE, CB, DC, DISC, MC, V.

Ⓕ FROMMER'S COOL FOR KIDS:
HOTELS

Loews Giorgio Hotel (see p. 50) Kids get a coloring book, crayons, and animal crackers when they arrive; there's also a special children's menu in the Tuscany Restaurant.

Sheraton Inn Denver Airport (see page 50) Outdoor types can play volleyball, horseshoes, and other games in this hotel's 18,000-square-foot outdoor garden area.

Rooms at this clean, modern three-story motel have Southwest-style furnishings and two doubles or king-size beds. Some rooms have recliners and hookups for computer modems. Facilities include an in-house laundry, fax service, and a heated pool (open seasonally). Close to downtown and the train station, the hotel is next to a 24-hour Denny's Restaurant with a lounge. The La Quinta has disabled-accessible rooms. Pets are welcome.

RAMADA INN DENVER DOWNTOWN, 1150 E. Colfax Ave., Denver, CO 80218. Tel. 303/831-7700 or toll free 800/524-8603. Fax 303/894-9193. 146 rooms (all with bath). A/C TV TEL
$ Rates (including continental breakfast): $45–$55 single; $50–$62 double. Reduced weekend rates. AE, CB, DC, DISC, MC, V.
The brightly decorated rooms are reached from an interior corridor and open onto a courtyard with a large heated swimming pool, open seasonally. There's cable television with HBO, as well as a fax and Xerox service. Rooms for the disabled, as well as nonsmokers, are available. Pets are accepted.

VICTORIA OAKS INN, 1575 Race St., Denver, CO 80206. Tel. 303/355-1818. 9 rooms (1 with bath). A/C TEL
$ Rates (including continental breakfast): $45–$75 single; $55–$85 double. AE, MC, V.
A European-style bed and breakfast, this circa-1896 Victorian home with handsome oak floors and leaded-glass windows is in fact a favorite of European travelers. Eight upstairs rooms share three baths, and the one guest room on the main floor has a fireplace and private bath. The inn is centrally located and provides a continental breakfast of fruit, Danish, muffins, cereals, coffee, tea, and juice. Guests have kitchen and laundry privileges.

BUDGET

CENTRAL YMCA, 25 E. 16th Ave., Denver, CO 80202. Tel. 303/861-8300. 189 rms (30 with bath). A/C
$ Rates: $20–$27 single; $38–$40 double. MC, V.
Located just a block from the State Capitol, the Y offers clean, small, simple rooms—just big enough for a bed, a chair, and a dresser. Most share a bath down the hall; private baths are available. Overnight guests may use the Y's swimming pool, gymnasiums, sports courts, and workout rooms. Telephone is available.

OUTSIDE DOWNTOWN
EXPENSIVE

STOUFFER CONCOURSE HOTEL, 3801 Quebec St., Denver, CO 80207. Tel. 303/399-7500 or toll free 800/HOTELS-1. Fax 303/321-1966. 390 rms, 10 suites. A/C MINIBAR TV TEL
$ Rates: $130–$150 single; $140–$160 double; $195–$650 suite. AE, CB, DC, DISC, JCB, MC, V. **Parking:** Garage available.

Rated by Andrew Harper's *Hideaway Report* as the No. 1 airport hotel in the United States, the Stouffer Concourse is a white double pyramid 12 stories high with a 10-story atrium. Tropical palms and fig trees rise beneath the central skylight, with plants draping from the balconies. A phone beside the reception desk underscores the hotel's commitment to service: It's a direct line to a red phone on the general manager's desk!

Each spacious room is appointed in peach and lime. It has two queen-size beds or one king size, with an easy chair and ottoman, a desk with a telephone, a large vanity, an armoire, and a private balcony. Coffee and a morning newspaper are delivered with the wake-up call. Three concierge floors have upgraded amenities, including complimentary breakfast foods.

Dining/Entertainment: There's a piano in the Concorde Restaurant and Lounge, open daily from 6:30am to 11pm. Lunch entrées run $6.25 to $12.95; dinners—steaks and seafood in creative preparations—$12.25 to $19.50.

Services: 24-hour room service and concierge service, courtesy airport shuttle, no-smoking rooms and rooms equipped for the disabled; incoming faxes are free, outgoing faxes have reduced rates, and there's no operator-assistance surcharge on 800 or credit-card calls.

Facilities: Indoor and outdoor swimming pools, whirlpool, steam room, full exercise room; meeting facilities for 1,300.

LOEWS GIORGIO HOTEL, 4150 E. Mississippi Ave., Denver, CO 80222. Tel. 303/782-9300 or toll free 800/345-9172. Fax 303/758-6542. 178 rms, 19 suites. A/C TV TEL

$ Rates (including continental breakfast): $135–$170 single or double; $185–$350 suite. Weekend rate available. Children under 18 stay free in parents' room. AE, CB, DC, MC, V. **Parking:** Free.

Staying at Loews Giorgio is a little like taking a trip to Rome. Located just east of Colorado Boulevard and south of the community of Glendale, this is a black-steel and reflecting-glass tower on the outside—but inside, it's *bella Italia*. When it opened in 1987, the "ribbon" cut was a 20-foot strand of fettuccine. Columns are finished in faux marble and pillars are worked in faux wood grain. Renaissance-style murals and paintings look five centuries old.

Italian furnishings include exquisite king-size and double beds with rolltop headboards. There's a wide use of colors (especially peaches and reds), floral patterns, Italian silk wall coverings, and marble-top furnishings. All of the spacious rooms have at least three phones. The west-facing rooms have superb views of the Rocky Mountains.

Guests have health-club privileges at Cherry Creek Sporting Club and may request in-room exercise cycles. Business travelers have modem hookups in their rooms, plus use of a staffed business center. The top-rated Tuscany Restaurant serves three meals daily, with a menu that features the cuisine of Italy's Tuscany region. The Loews Georgio also offers all the usual services one expects in a top luxury hotel.

MODERATE

SHERATON INN DENVER AIRPORT, 3535 Quebec St., Denver, CO 80207. Tel. 303/333-7711 or toll free 800/328-2268. Fax 303/322-2262. 192 rooms, 4 suites. A/C TV TEL

$ Rates: $75–$95 single; $85–$105 double; $175–$295 suite. Weekend rate $69 single or double. Children under 18 stay free in parents' room. AE, CB, DC, DISC, ER, JCB, MC, V. **Parking:** Free.

Luxury guest rooms with views of the Rocky Mountains and downtown Denver are what you'll find at this eight-story hotel, along with an 18,000-square-foot outdoor garden area for summertime volleyball, horseshoes, or loafing. Rooms have two phones with call waiting and automated wake-up calls, clock radios, and remote cable TVs with HBO and pay-per-view movies. There are desks and either a king or two double beds. Suites have different themes: Southwestern, Oriental, Executive, or Traditional (with kitchen).

The hotel offers a full range of services, dining, and other facilities.

INEXPENSIVE

ON GOLDEN POND BED & BREAKFAST, 7831 Eldridge St., Arvada, CO 80005. Tel. 303/424-2296. 6 rms (all with bath). A/C
$ Rates (including breakfast): $40–$100 single or double. DISC, MC, V.
Ten acres of countryside surround this custom-built two-story brick home in the Rocky Mountain foothills 15 miles west of Denver. Verandas overlook a floating gazebo in a natural pond that attracts birds and other wildlife. Host Kathy Kula, a native of Germany, serves an extensive breakfast outdoors or indoors, and a *kaffeeklatsch* of coffee and pastries in the afternoon. Each guest room has a sliding glass door, which opens onto the veranda. Four of the rooms have private Jacuzzis; the Italianate Peacock Room has a king-size bed beneath a cathedral ceiling. All guests share a living room TV and fireplace and a swimming pool and outdoor hot tub.

THE HAMPTON INN, 3605 S. Wadsworth Blvd., Lakewood, CO 80235. Tel. 303/989-6900 or toll free 800/HAMPTON. 148 rms (all with bath). A/C TV TEL
$ Rates (including continental breakfast): $50–$60 single or double. AE, CB, DC, DISC, MC, V.
Located on the southwestern edge of the metropolitan area, just south of U.S. 285 on Colo. 121, this pleasant motel offers rapid access to the foothills communities west of Denver. The rooms are well lit and brightly decorated, and feature king-size or double beds and comfortable lounge chairs. There are nonsmoking floors and disabled-accessible rooms.

BUDGET

CAMERON MOTEL, 4500 E. Evans Ave. (I-25, Exit 203), Denver, CO 80222. Tel. 303/757-2100. Fax 303/757-0974. 33 rooms (all with bath), 2 suites. A/C TV TEL
$ Rates: $34 single; $38 double; $45 suite. AE, DISC, ER, MC, V.
A small mom-and-pop motel about 10 minutes from downtown, this motel is a clean, quiet alternative to some of the more expensive chains. Built in the 1940s, the property has been completely renovated. Rooms have glazed-brick interiors and remote control color cable TV's with 60 channels. Rooms with kitchens are available. Seventeen of the rooms have tub/shower combinations, and 18 rooms have only showers. Pets are accepted, at an extra charge of $5 each. Owners live on-site and their pride of ownership shows.

MOTEL 6, 6 W. 83rd Pl., Thornton, CO 80221. Tel. 303/429-1550 or 505/891-6161 for central reservations. 121 rms (all with bath). A/C TV TEL
$ Rates: $27 single; $33 double. AE, CB, DC, DISC, MC, V.
A no-frills accommodation, the Motel 6 has just enough amenities to make a night's stay comfortable. Rooms, though small, are clean; they have a phone and television; and there's even a swimming pool for summer afternoon dips. They have free local calls, HBO and ESPN, and have nonsmoking and disabled-accessible rooms. One small pet is allowed. This Motel 6 is located off I-25 at Exit 219, north of Denver. There are others in the metropolitan area at 10300 S. I-70 Frontage Rd., Wheat Ridge, CO 80033 (tel. 303/467-3172); at 480 Wadsworth Blvd., Denver, CO 80226 (tel. 303/232-4924); and near the airport at 12020 E. 39th Ave., Denver, CO 80239 (tel. 303/371-1980).

CAMPING

DELUX R.V. PARK, 5520 N. Federal Blvd., Denver, CO 80221. Tel. 303/433-0452. 29 sites.
$ Rates: $18 with hookups. No credit cards.
This campground, with shaded sites, hot showers, laundry, and full hookups, has the best Denver location for travelers who take their homes with them. It's convenient to buses and shopping and recreational facilities are nearby. Open year-round, the

campground is located five blocks north of I-70, Exit 272, on the east side of Federal Boulevard.

4. DINING

The categories below define a very expensive restaurant as one in which most dinner main courses are priced above $20; expensive, most dinner main courses $15 to $20; moderate, main courses $10 to $15; inexpensive, main courses $6 to $10; budget, main courses under $6.

DOWNTOWN

VERY EXPENSIVE

AUGUSTA, in the Westin Hotel at Tabor Center, 1672 Lawrence St. Tel. 572-9100.
    Cuisine: NEW AMERICAN. **Reservations:** Recommended.
$ Prices: Apeptizers $4.50–$9.50; main courses $6.50–$12 at lunch, $14.75–$26 at dinner. AE, CB, DC, DISC, MC, V.
    Open: Lunch Tues–Fri 11:30am–2pm; dinner Tues–Sat 5:30–10pm.
Considered by locals to be one of the best hotel restaurants in Denver, the Augusta offers great views of the city, art deco decor with black-marble walls, and an imaginative, exciting menu. Specialties include rotisseried prime rib, free-range chicken, and Long Island duckling. Other choices include veal, beef tenderloin, Colorado lamb, several pastas, and a variety of seafood dishes.

Especially inviting are the sauces used on the various entrées, such as raspberry barbecue sauce on the swordfish, sweet-and-sour coconut sauce on the salmon, and red-currant bourbon sauce on the duck breast.

CLIFF YOUNG'S, 700 E. 17th Ave. Tel. 831-8900.
    Cuisine: NEW AMERICAN. **Reservations:** Highly recommended.
$ Prices: Appetizers $8–$16; main courses $7.95–$14.95 at lunch, $22–$30 at dinner. AE, CB, DC, DISC, MC, V.
    Open: Lunch Mon–Fri 11am–2pm; dinner Sun–Thurs 6–10pm, Fri–Sat 6–11pm.
This is probably the one restaurant in the city that no one would argue if you labeled it "Denver's best." Spacious, elegant, dimly lit, it is sophisticated without being pretentious, like the ultimate upscale bistro. A classical pianist plays nightly and is joined by a violinist Wednesday through Sunday. Young, who has a master's degree in philosophy and is a published poet, has developed a foundation of loyal local customers since he opened his restaurant in 1984. "It's my sensitivity for people," he says. That, the impeccable service, and the superb cuisine.

The menu changes seasonally, but is likely to include rack of lamb with apricot mustard and brioche crust, filet mignon, duck in plum sauce, and pan-roasted quail. There are more than 300 selections in the wine cellar.

PALACE ARMS, in the Brown Palace Hotel, 321 17th St. Tel. 297-3111.
    Cuisine: INTERNATIONAL. **Reservations:** Recommended.
$ Prices: Appetizers $6–$23.50; main courses $7.75–$16 at lunch, $19–$29 at dinner. AE, CB, DC, DISC, JCB, MC, V.
    Open: Lunch Mon–Fri 11:30am–2pm; dinner nightly 6–10pm.
The Palace Arms is a Napoleonic museum. Napoleon's own dueling pistols are mounted just inside the doorway, and a pair of papier-mâché golden eagles are parade decorations from the great Frenchman's march to Notre Dame to crown himself emperor. Behind glass are a full set of French military band figures, carved from wood by an imprisoned dollmaker. Replicas of battle flags, rich leather banquettes, 19th-century hunting prints, and ornate mirrors lend a strong European atmosphere. The cuisine is an interesting combination of traditional American, new American,

classical French, and southwestern influences. Start with a fresh lobster enchilada or pasta torta of chicken mousseline; follow with a wild-rice soup (with brandied almond cream). For the main course try sautéed breast of ringneck pheasant, roast loin of veal with sweetbreads and zucchini caponata, or cannelloni of shrimp, lobster, scallops, and mussels. Flambés are a dessert specialty. The wine list is one of 42 around the world to receive the *Wine Spectator* magazine's award of excellence.

EXPENSIVE

THE BROKER RESTAURANT, 821 17th St., near Champa St. Tel. 292-5065.
　　Cuisine: STEAK/SEAFOOD. **Reservations:** Recommended.
$ **Prices:** Lunch $7.95–$14.95; dinner $15–$33. AE, CB, DC, MC, V.
　　Open: Lunch Mon–Fri 11am–2:30pm; dinner Sun–Thurs 5–10pm, Fri–Sat 5–10:30pm.
A huge vault in the basement of the old Denver National Bank building is the site of the Broker, fittingly located in the heart of the financial district. Diners enter through a circular 23-ton door and sit in cherry-wood booths once used by bank customers to inspect safety-deposit boxes. European antiques add to the Wall Street atmosphere.

　　Generous portions are an earmark of meals at the Broker. New York and porterhouse steaks, beef Wellington, Rocky Mountain trout, rack of lamb, roast duck, Alaskan king-crab legs and blackened catfish are just some of the house favorites. Nonmeat eaters are catered to with vegetarian pasta medley. A 24-ounce bowl of steamed Gulf shrimp precedes all main dishes and soup or salad, baked bread, vegetables, and dessert are included with all meals. Table-side preparation of Caesar salad and cherries jubilee is also offered. The mammoth wine list (67 pages long) includes everything from regional maps to winery addresses and is worth a visit in itself. Bottles run $14 to $2,000, the latter for a 1914 château Lafite Rothschild.

BUCKHORN EXCHANGE, 1000 Osage St., at W. 10th Ave. Tel. 534-9505.
　　Cuisine: ROCKY MOUNTAIN. **Reservations:** Recommended.
$ **Prices:** Appetizers $4.25–$8.25; main courses $5.50–$12.50 at lunch, $16–$29 at dinner. AE, CB, DC, DISC, MC, V.
　　Open: Lunch Mon–Fri 11:30am–3pm; dinner Sun–Thurs 5:30–10:30pm, Fri–Sat 5:30–11pm.
Denver's dining institution is located outside the downtown core, a few blocks south of the Ninth Street Historic District opposite the Rio Grande Railroad Yards. Founded in 1893 by Henry H. "Shorty Scout" Zietz—nicknamed by Sitting Bull and employed as a cowboy scout or hunting guide by such notables as Buffalo Bill and Theodore Roosevelt—it still occupies the same premises it did when Colorado Liquor License No. 1 was awarded. That certificate is still displayed over the 136-year-old hand-carved oak bar in the upstairs Victorian parlor and saloon. You'll have to search a bit to find it, though: Much more in evidence throughout the restaurant are 235 large animals (some heads, some full bodies) and more than 250 other taxidermy items, as well as a collection of 125 rare firearms.

　　Come to the Buckhorn to try Rocky Mountain oysters, smoked buffalo sausage, buffalo prime rib, elk steak, rabbit, pheasant, or alligator tail. If you're not the adventurous sort, you can also get steaks (a 24-oz. porterhouse), chops, ribs, or a catch of the day. Homemade bean soup comes with every meal, and dessert is old-fashioned apple pie or chocolate "moose."

DENVER BUFFALO COMPANY, 1109 Lincoln St. Tel. 832-0880.
　　Cuisine: AMERICAN/WESTERN. **Reservations:** Recommended for dinner.
$ **Prices:** Appetizers $4–$9; main courses $6–$12.50 at lunch, $14–$30 at dinner. DISC, MC, V.
　　Open: Lunch Mon–Sat 11am–2:30pm; dinner Mon–Thurs 5–9pm, Fri–Sat 5–10pm.
You can't miss this busy restaurant, bar, deli, art gallery, and trading post, with the big

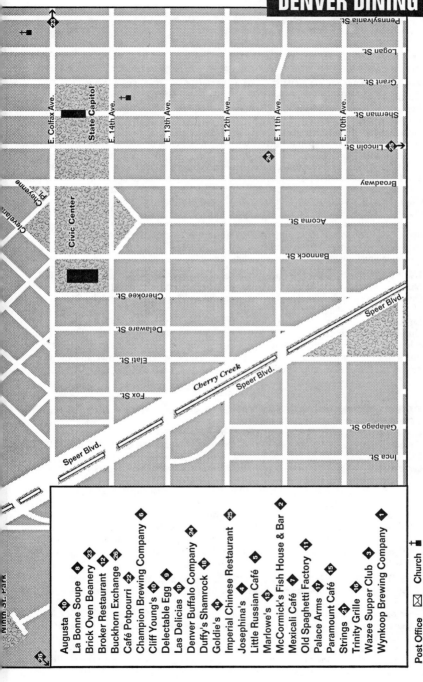

DENVER DINING

Augusta **10**
La Bonne Soupe **8**
Brick Oven Beanery **23**
Broker Restaurant **12**
Buckhorn Exchange **28**
Café Potpourri **22**
Champion Brewing Company **6**
Cliff Young's **40**
Delectable Egg **9**
Las Delicias **19**
Denver Buffalo Company **24**
Duffy's Shamrock **18**
Goldie's **14**
Imperial Chinese Restaurant **25**
Josephina's **4**
Little Russian Café **5**
Marlowe's **13**
McCormick's Fish House & Bar **2**
Mexicali Café **7**
Old Spaghetti Factory **11**
Palace Arms **17**
Paramount Café **15**
Strings **21**
Trinity Grille **16**
Wazee Supper Club **3**
Wynkoop Brewing Company **1**

Post Office ⊠ Church ✝■

bronze statue of a buffalo out front. The buffalo steaks, burgers, sausage, and even hot dogs come from the company's own Colorado ranch and are also available to take out or ship from the deli. For those not interested in buffalo, the restaurant offers seafood, poultry, and pasta dishes.

The bar is open all afternoon, serving a limited lunch menu, and there's live entertainment (country western, folk, or jazz) on Friday and Saturday nights.

STRINGS, 1700 Humboldt St., at E. 17th Ave. Tel. 831-7310.
   Cuisine: CASUAL CONTEMPORARY. **Reservations:** Recommended.
$ Prices: Appetizers $4.75–$8.25; main courses $6.25–$12 at lunch, $11.25–$25 at dinner. AE, CB, DC, MC, V.
   Open: Mon–Sat 11am–11pm, Sun 5–11pm.

Rated as Denver's No. 1 restaurant in which "to see and be seen," Strings welcomes guests in T-shirts as well as tuxedos. It's especially popular among the before- and after-theater crowds. A casual establishment on Restaurant Row, Strings has two levels of seating. Contemporary music albums and posters decorate the walls, and large flower arrangements contrast with the black-and-white color scheme.

Chef Noel Cunningham, a native of Dublin, Ireland, orients his menu around pastas and fresh seafood. He calls it California Irish cuisine, though there's a definite northern Italian influence as well. Go for the *penne bagutta* (with chicken, mushrooms, broccoli, and a spicy tomato-and-basil rustica sauce), Strings pasta (with asparagus and cream, champagne, and caviar), or duck breast rosé (charbroiled with wild rice, maple syrup, and a creamy date sauce).

TRINITY GRILLE, 1801 Broadway, at Tremont Place. Tel. 293-2288.
   Cuisine: STEAK/SEAFOOD. **Reservations:** Recommended.
$ Prices: Appetizers $4.50–$8; main courses $6.50–$12 at lunch, $11–$26 at dinner. AE, DC, MC, V.
   Open: Mon–Thurs 11am–10:30pm, Fri 11am–11pm, Sat 5:30–11pm.

Subdued elegance characterizes this fine restaurant, located opposite the Brown Palace Hotel and next door to the Museum of Western Art. In effect an upscale urban tavern, it boasts mahogany furnishings with brass trim, leaded-glass windows and tile floors, white linen tablecloths, and original artwork on the walls.

MODERATE

IMPERIAL CHINESE RESTAURANT, 1 Broadway, at First Ave. Tel. 698-2800.
   Cuisine: CHINESE. **Reservations:** Recommended.
$ Prices: Individual dishes $6–$15. Complete multicourse dinners $15–$25. AE, DC, MC, V.
   Open: Mon–Thurs 11am–10pm, Fri 11am–10:30pm, Sat noon–10:30pm, Sun 4–10pm.

Spicy Szechuan and Hunan, hearty Mandarin, and delicate Cantonese items are offered at this restaurant, named by *Westword* readers as the best Chinese establishment in Denver seven years running. A laughing Buddha and exquisite hand-carved wooden screens greet diners at the entrance, and inside, the mirrored ceiling and gold decor provide a regal atmosphere. You can't go wrong with anything here, but try the hot-and-sour soup, the sesame chicken, sweet-and-sour pork, or the Dungeness crab stir-fried with scallions and ginger. Seafood, in fact, is a specialty here.

JOSEPHINA'S RISTORANTE, 1433 Larimer St. Tel. 623-0166.
   Cuisine: ITALIAN. **Reservations:** Recommended most nights; not accepted Fri–Sat.
$ Prices: Appetizers $3.50–$6.75; main courses $8.95–$18.95. AE, DISC, MC, V.
   Open: Sun–Thurs 11am–11pm, Fri–Sat 11am–midnight. **Closed:** Thanksgiving and Christmas.

A Larimer Square institution, Josephina's invokes nostalgia for decades past. Posters, neon lights, and early to mid-20th-century advertising signs decorate the walls of the bar. A wall-size mural of flappers from the Roaring Twenties backs the bandstand (there's live rock or blues nightly). The adjacent dining room keeps the nostalgic feel, but it has carpets instead of a hardwood floor and white-linen service.

House specialties include fettuccine Josephina's (with chicken, tomatoes, and wine sauce), eggplant parmigiana, and rack of veal chop, prepared a different way daily. There's a wide selection of seafood and pasta, including seafood Josephina's (scampi, bay shrimp, mussels, scallops, and clams on fettuccine) and pasta *puttanesca* (with sun-dried tomatoes, olives, red pepper, and garlic).

Josephina's has a secluded, romantic restaurant at 17th Avenue and Downing Street (tel. 860-8011) and a festive patio restaurant at 7777 E. Hampden Ave., Aurora (tel. 750-4422).

LA BONNE SOUPE, 1512 Larimer St., Writer Sq. Tel. 595-9169.

Cuisine: FRENCH. **Reservations:** Recommended.

$ Prices: Appetizers $5.95–$7.95; main courses $5.25–$15.95 at lunch, $6.95–$17.95 at dinner. AE, CB, DC, MC, V.

Open: Mon–Thurs 11am–10pm, Fri–Sat 11am–11pm, Sun noon–9:30pm.

A faithful replica of a French sidewalk bistro, this casual restaurant combines a patio café atmosphere with indoor seating that looks out onto Writer Square mall. Owner Shep Brown created it with the memory of his native Paris fresh in mind.

As the name suggests, soups are a meal in themselves. French onion, asparagus, and lamb, mushroom, and barley are always available, as is a soup du jour. Fondues (cheese, bourguignonne, and chocolate) are crowd pleasers. The plats du jour include poulet chasseur, lasagne maison, and filet mignon au poivre.

THE LITTLE RUSSIAN CAFE, 1424 Larimer St. Tel. 595-8600.

Cuisine: RUSSIAN. **Reservations:** Recommended.

$ Prices: Appetizers $5–$8; main courses at lunch $6.50–$14, dinner $9–$16. AE, DC, DISC, JCB, MC, V.

Open: Lunch Mon–Sat 11am–2:30pm; dinner Sun–Thurs 5:30–10pm, Fri–Sat 5:30–11pm.

A quiet, romantic restaurant set back in a Larimer Square arcade, Leningrad native Eugene Valershteyn's café is a touch of the old country . . . with a generous dose of the new, as well. A uniformed mannequin plays the balalaika in a front window. Russian paintings and posters decorate the discreet, dimly lit dining room. There's also an outdoor patio.

Meals start with a shot of ice-cold vodka, followed by *yazyk* (spicy sliced beef tongue) or *vareniki* (potato-and-onion dumplings). They normally include a soup like *schi* (cabbage, carrots, and celery in beef broth) or borscht (the famous beet-rich concoction). Among the main dishes are *zharkoe* (a beef-and-mushroom casserole), *kurinyie kotlety* (garlic-flavored chicken cutlets), *nelma* (a fish, carrot, and cheese casserole), and, of course, beef à la Stroganoff.

MARLOWE'S, 16th St., at Glenarm St. Tel. 595-3700.

Cuisine: STEAK/SEAFOOD. **Reservations:** Recommended.

$ Prices: Appetizers $3.50–$13.50; main courses $5.95–$12.95 at lunch, $7.25–$18.95 at dinner. AE, CB, DC, MC, V.

Open: Mon–Thurs 11am–11pm, Fri 11am–midnight, Sat 5pm–midnight.

Once called by *Cosmopolitan* magazine "one of the 10 hottest restaurant-bars in the country," Marlowe's has two levels of plant-surrounded seating beneath a vaulted ceiling and an outdoor patio on the 16th Street Mall, where seating seems always to be at a premium. Occupying a corner of the 1891 Kittredge Building, listed in the National Register of Historic Places, it features an antique cherry-wood bar, granite pillars, and plenty of open space for mixing.

Many folks come here just for drinks and appetizers, like oysters Rockefeller, smoked trout, and rumaki (baked chicken livers). There's an extensive choice of salads. Full meals, with salad, bread, and vegetables, include a Chicago-style veal rib chop, filet, chicken marsala, Pacific salmon, and fish du jour.

MCCORMICK'S FISH AND OYSTER HOUSE, in the Oxford Hotel, 1659 Wazee St. Tel. 825-1107.

Ⓕ FROMMER'S COOL FOR KIDS:
RESTAURANTS

Casa Bonita *(see p. 62)* If the kids' attention isn't on the tacos, they'll be enthralled by puppet shows, high divers, a funhouse, and a video arcade.

The Old Spaghetti Factory *(see p. 59)* Dine inside an old trolley car, or take an adventure tour of the other fascinating turn-of-the-century antiques. And what child doesn't like spaghetti and spumoni?

Buckhorn Exchange *(see p. 53)* Every species of large game animal you might imagine is mounted on the walls of this century-old restaurant once frequented by Buffalo Bill and Teddy Roosevelt.

Brick Oven Beanery *(see p. 59)* Good, wholesome food and honest-to-gosh malted milks and ice-cream sodas appeal to the kid in all of us. They've even got peanut-butter-and-jelly sandwiches on the menu.

Cuisine: SEAFOOD. **Reservations:** Recommended.
$ **Prices:** Appetizers $2.95–$9.95; lunch and light dishes $3.50–$12.50; dinner $9.50–$21.95. AE, CB, DC, DISC, JCB, MC, V.
  Open: Breakfast Mon–Fri 6:30–10am; lunch Mon–Fri 11:30am–2:30pm; dinner Sun–Thurs 5–10pm, Fri–Sat 5–11pm; brunch Sat–Sun 7am–2pm.
Operating out of lower downtown's restored Oxford Alexis Hotel, an active part of city life since 1891, McCormick's is owned by the same seafood lovers who operate McCormick and Schmick's in Seattle and Jake's in Portland, Oregon. The restaurant maintains the turn-of-the-century theme with original stained-glass windows and skylights, oak booths, and a fine polished-wood bar.
  Seafood is flown in fresh daily, including Dungeness crab from Alaska, Goose Point oysters from Washington state, mussels from Maine, fresh yellowfin tuna from Hawaii, swordfish from California, rockfish from Oregon, and trout from Idaho.

INEXPENSIVE

CHAMPION BREWING COMPANY, 1442 Larimer Sq. Tel. 534-5444.
  Cuisine: AMERICAN. **Reservations:** Accepted.
$ **Prices:** Appetizers $1.50–$5.50; main courses $4–$10. AE, MC, V.
  Open: Daily 11am–2am.
"Home-style American grub" from around the country is what beer lovers eat here, while putting down schooners of Larimer lager or home-run ale, two of this brew pub's specialties. There are sandwiches, burgers, popcorn shrimp, chicken wings, and regional favorites such as Midwest VKV, southern fried chicken, and New England crab cakes. The outdoor patio fills up quickly in nice weather, and brewery tours are offered Saturdays from 1 to 3pm.

MEXICALI CAFE, 1453 Larimer St. Tel. 892-1444.
  Cuisine: MEXICAN. **Reservations:** For parties of six or more; not accepted Wed–Fri at lunch or Fri–Sat at dinner.
$ **Prices:** Appetizers $2.75–$6.95; main courses $5.25–$11.95. AE, DISC, MC, V.
  Open: Sun–Thurs 11am–10pm, Fri–Sat 11am–11pm.
The small burrito bar at the Larimer Square street entrance is misleading: The fiesta is at the bottom of the stairs. Mariachi music is piped through, and the bright orange-and-red decor may at first pop your eyes out. An orange 1947 Cadillac protrudes from one wall. The food is just as much fun: traditional foods like mesquite-roasted rellenos, fajita burritos, and Santa Fe trail hash; rotisserie-turned meats like chile-rubbed chicken (with green-chile pesto) or Baja camarónes (shrimp) in a spicy barbecue sauce.

THE OLD SPAGHETTI FACTORY, 1215 18th St., at Lawrence St. Tel. 295-1864.

Cuisine: ITALIAN. **Reservations:** For large parties only.
$ **Prices:** Main courses $4.25–$9.50. AE, MC, V.
Open: Lunch Mon–Fri 11:30am–2pm; dinner Mon–Thurs 5–10pm, Fri–Sat 5–11pm, Sun 4–10pm.

Cable cars have long since ceased to be a part of the Denver scene, but they live on in the historic Tramway Cable building, with its 195-foot chimney. One of the trolley cars, in fact, is so much a part of this restaurant that there's seating inside it! The cheerful atmosphere of Victorian relics is a great place for a plate of spaghetti, served with a choice of five different sauces. Every meal includes salad, fresh warm bread with garlic butter, beverage, and spumoni ice cream.

SFUZZI, 3000 E. First Ave., in Cherry Creek Mall. Tel. 321-4700.

Cuisine: ITALIAN. **Reservations:** Recommended.
$ **Prices:** Appetizers $3.25–$5.50; main courses $8.75–$11. AE, DC, MC, V.
Open: Lunch Mon–Sat 11am–4pm; dinner Mon–Wed 5:30–11pm, Thurs–Sat 5:30pm–midnight, Sun 5:30–10pm; brunch Sun 11am–3pm.

The "S" is silent and the food excellent. Along with the usual Italian standards, you'll find creative specialties such as Romano crusted chicken salad with roasted mushrooms. Even the pizzas are different, if that's what you're looking for, with caramelized onions and goat cheese included in the topping list. There are also Sfuzzi's in Dallas, Houston, New York, Boston, and several other locales around the country.

WYNKOOP BREWING COMPANY, 1634 18th St., at Wynkoop St. Tel. 297-2700.

Cuisine: INTERNATIONAL. **Reservations:** For large parties.
$ **Prices:** Appetizers $2.25–$5.25; lunch $3.95–$7.25; dinner $7.95–$13.95. AE, DISC, MC, V.
Open: Mon–Sat 11am–2am; Sun 11am–midnight; brewery tours Sat 1–5pm.

When the Wynkoop opened its doors in 1988 as Denver's first new brewery in more than 50 years, it started a minirevolution. Nearly a dozen other small private breweries have since opened in Colorado, but the Wynkoop sets the standard. Located in a renovated LoDo warehouse across from Union Station, the brewery-restaurant was the brainchild of a pair of laid-off geologists who found the road to commercial success not too rocky. Free tours of the brewery, which turns out a variety of brews, are offered on Saturday between 1 and 5pm.

The food served here is surprisingly good—shepherd's pie filled with Colorado lamb, mashed potatoes, and vegetable, Uncompahgre black-bean cakes with rice, Greek salad, marinated shark steak, lamb burger, and homemade apple-pecan sausage. There's a little of everything . . . and it all goes with beer.

BUDGET

BRICK OVEN BEANERY, 1007 E. Colfax Ave., at Ogden St. Tel. 860-0077.

Cuisine: AMERICAN.
$ **Prices:** $3.45–$6.95. AE, DISC, MC, V.
Open: Daily 11am–10pm.

There's nothing fancy about this restaurant. Meals are dished up from a cafeteria-style line, which often extends all the way to the door. That in itself should tell you something. Meats are rotisserie roasted, breads baked on the premises, salads and desserts homemade, malts and ice-cream sodas prepared 1950s style. Keeping in the mood, big band and swing music from the 1940s and 1950s plays in the background. And you can't argue with a leg of lamb dinner, a wild-rice meat loaf, or a half chicken with dressing and potatoes, salad and bread, for $6.

THE DELECTABLE EGG, 1642 Market St. Tel. 572-8146.

Cuisine: AMERICAN.

$ Prices: $2.95–$5.95. AE, DC, DISC, MC, V.
Open: Mon–Fri 6:30am–2pm, Sat–Sun 7am–2pm.

Every city should have a café like this one: eggs prepared 42 different ways, pancakes, waffles, and french toast . . . plus, for the after-11am lunch crowd, a variety of salads and sandwiches. You can get your eggs skillet fried, baked in a frittata, scrambled into pita pockets, smothered with chile or hollandaise, or any other way. About the only thing you can't get is a Denver omelet—here, it's called the "Mile High."

The Delectable Egg has a second downtown location at 16th Street and Court Place (tel. 892-5720).

DUFFY'S SHAMROCK, 1635 Court Place. Tel. 534-4935.
Cuisine: AMERICAN.
$ Prices: Breakfast $1.60–$4.50; lunch $3.50–$7; dinner $4.50–$11. AE, DC, MC, V.
Open: Mon–Fri 7am–2am, Sat 8am–2am, Sun 11am–2am.

In operation for more than three decades, this traditional Irish bar and restaurant with fast, cheerful service has been thriving since the late 1950s. It specializes in Irish coffees and imported Irish beers. Daily specials may include prime rib, barbecued beef, fried prawns, or a stuffed bell pepper in creole sauce. Sandwiches on every kind of bread are also offered: corned beef, Reuben, Braunschweiger, even a Dagwood. If you're still hungry after the sandwich, order the Duffy's special: hot raisin-and-custard pudding with blueberries, rice, and cream.

GOLDIE'S, 511 16th St., at Glenarm Place. Tel. 623-6007.
Cuisine: DELI.
$ Prices: $4–$6. AE, DC, MC, V.
Open: Mon–Sat 11am–4pm.

A New York–style deli wedged between Marlowe's and the Paramount Café in the historic Kittredge Building, Goldie's features imported and kosher foods, with an emphasis on sandwiches . . . to eat there or carry out on the 16th Street Mall. Consider the jive turkey, Toulouse la Tuna, a veggie or Italian sub, roast beef, ham and cheese, or the Bronx blintz.

LAS DELICIAS, 439 E. 19th Ave., at Pennsylvania St. Tel. 839-5675.
Cuisine: MEXICAN.
$ Prices: Main courses $5–$7. MC, V.
Open: Mon–Sat 8am–9pm, Sun 9am–9pm.

Las Delicias occupies half a dozen interconnected rooms, all faced in plain red brick. The restaurant is a favorite among Hispanic families, who come back again and again. The food is always served with chips and spicy salsa. Tamales, burritos, tacos, and other Mexican standbys are served, along with generous portions of carne asada and carne de puerco adovado. All dishes are served with plenty of fresh hot tortillas.

PARAMOUNT CAFE, 511 16th St. Tel. 893-2000.
Cuisine: AMERICAN.
$ Prices: $3.95–$6.95. AE, DC, MC, V.
Open: Mon–Thurs 11am–10:30pm, Fri–Sat 11am–11pm.

The former snack bar of Denver's historic Paramount Theatre, in the 1891 Kittredge Building on the 16th Street Mall, has been remodeled into one of the city's most popular restaurants. The atmosphere is lively and a bit noisy, with oldies and current pop music on the jukebox. Movie and rock star posters and photos cover the walls. There's a red vinyl soda fountain–style bar that serves a number of specialty drinks plus Paramount Rock and Roll Ale, specially brewed for the café. The menu features burgers, chicken sandwiches, large salads, and Tex-Mex fare. Leave room for the margarita pie.

THE WAZEE SUPPER CLUB, 600 15th St., at Wazee St. Tel. 623-9518.
Cuisine: PIZZA/SANDWICHES.
$ Prices: $3.10–$7.20, more for large pizzas. MC, V.
Open: Mon–Sat 11am–1am.

A former plumbing-supply store in lower downtown, the Wazee is a depression-era relic with a black-and-white tile floor and a bleached mahogany back bar. A hangout for jazz and pizza lovers (some say the pizza here is the best in the city), it also serves an array of sandwiches from kielbasa to corned beef, buffalo to ham and cheese. There are 13 beers on draft. Don't miss the dumbwaiter used to shuttle food and drinks to the mezzanine floor: It's a converted 1937 garage-door opener.

OUTSIDE DOWNTOWN

EXPENSIVE

THE FORT, 19192 Colo. 8, off W. Hampden Ave. (U.S. 285), Morrison. Tel. 697-4771.

Cuisine: ROCKY MOUNTAIN. **Reservations:** Recommended.

$ Prices: Appetizers $3.95–$12.95, main courses $11.75–$28.95. AE, CB, DC, MC, V.

Open: Dinner only, Mon–Fri 6–10pm, Sat 5–10pm, Sun 5–9pm. Special holiday hours.

There are many reasons to drive the 18 miles southwest from downtown Denver to visit the Fort. One is the atmosphere: The building is a full-scale reproduction of Bent's Fort, Colorado's first fur-trading post, hand-built adobe brick by adobe brick in 1962. The interior is equally authentic, and the staff are dressed as 19th-century Cheyenne–Native Americans. Another reason is owner Sam Arnold, a broadcast personality and master chef who opens champagne bottles with a tomahawk. He's had his menu translated into French, German, Spanish, Japanese, and braille.

But the best reason is the food. The Fort built its reputation on high-quality, low-cholesterol buffalo, of which it serves the largest variety and greatest quantity of any restaurant in the world. There's buffalo steak, buffalo tongue, broiled buffalo marrow bones, and even "buffalo eggs"—hard-boiled quail eggs wrapped in buffalo sausage, which he served to Bryant Gumbel and Jane Pauley of the "Today Show." Other house specialties are Taos trout, basted in a mint sauce and topped with bacon bits; "The Bowl of the Wife of Kit Carson," a spicy-hot chicken stew; broiled quail; and elk medallions with wild huckleberry sauce. Diehards can get beefsteak.

MODERATE

TRAIL DUST STEAK HOUSE, 7107 S. Clinton St., Tech Center, Englewood. Tel. 790-2420.

Cuisine: STEAK. **Reservations:** For large groups only.

$ Prices: Appetizers $3–$5; lunch $5–$12; dinner $8–$20. AE, DISC, MC, V.

Open: Lunch Mon–Fri 11am–2pm; dinner Mon–Thurs 5–11pm, Fri 5pm–midnight, Sat 4pm–midnight, Sun noon–10pm.

Country music lovers flock to the Trail Dust, which serves up live dance music along with mesquite-broiled steaks and ribs nightly. Steaks come in sizes from 9 to 50 ounces, and are served with salad, beans, and ranch bread. Chicken and fish are also available. The unusual decor is comprised of necktie tips—if you let them clip yours off, you'll get a free drink.

To reach the Trail Dust, exit I-25 south at Arapahoe Road, drive one block east, and turn onto Clinton Street. There's a second Trail Dust at the north end of Denver: 9101 Benton St., Westminster (tel. 427-1446), next to the Westminster Mall.

WHITE FENCE FARM, 6263 W. Jewell Ave., Lakewood. Tel. 935-5945.

Cuisine: AMERICAN. **Reservations:** Only for parties of 15 or more.

$ Prices: $8.95–$16.95. MC, V.

Open: Tues–Sat 5–9pm, Sun noon–8pm. **Closed:** January.

Locals come here for the family-style fried-chicken dinners—one-half chicken per person plus bowls of potatoes, corn fritters, coleslaw, and bean salad for $8.95. Other possibilities include T-bone steaks, deep fried shrimp, broiled whitefish filet, and liver and onions. There's a children's menu, and freshly baked pies.

In keeping with its family atmosphere, there's a children's playground, petting farm, carriage rides, old farm machinery, and a country store, all in a beautiful country setting 20 minutes from downtown Denver.

INEXPENSIVE

CASA BONITA, in the JCRS Shopping Center, 6715 W. Colfax Ave., Lakewood. Tel. 232-5115.
   Cuisine: MEXICAN/AMERICAN. **Reservations:** For large parties only.
$ **Prices:** Lunch or dinner $5.50–$8.50. AE, CB, DC, DISC, MC, V.
   Open: Daily 11am–9:30pm.
A west Denver landmark, this is more a theme park than a restaurant! A peach-colored Spanish cathedral-type bell tower greets visitors, who will find nonstop action inside: divers plummeting into a pool beside a 30-foot waterfall, puppet shows, a video arcade, Black Bart's Cave (a funhouse), and strolling mariachi bands. The food is served cafeteria style, which is truly an undertaking in a restaurant that seats 1,100! There's standard Mexican fare—enchiladas, tacos, tamales, and fajitas—along with country-fried steak, fried chicken, and fried fish. Hot sopaipillas, served at your table with honey, are delicious.

T-WA INN, 555 S. Federal Blvd., near W. Virginia Ave. Tel. 922-4584.
   Cuisine: VIETNAMESE.
$ **Prices:** Lunch $4.95–$11.95; dinner $6.95–$13.95. AE, CB, DISC, DC, MC, V.
   Open: Daily 11am–10pm.
Denver's first Vietnamese restaurant is still its best. The decor is simple but pleasant, with Viet folk songs providing atmospheric background. Try the egg rolls, with shrimp and crabmeat wrapped in rice paper; the hearty meat-and-noodle soups; the chicken salad; or the soft-shell crab. Vietnamese food, for the uninitiated, has similarities both to Thai and southern Chinese cooking.

BUDGET

HEALTHY HABITS, 865 S. Colorado Blvd. Tel. 733-2105.
   Cuisine: VEGETARIAN/DELI.
$ **Prices:** $5.95–$8.95. AE, MC, V.
   Open: Daily 11am–9pm.
Greater Denver's finest salads are found inside this unprepossessing cafeteria-style café just south of Exposition Street. The 70-item salad bar offers everything you'd expect, and more—like hearts of palm, artichoke hearts, avocados, herring, and chunks of tuna. Leave room for fresh fruit and a variety of pasta salads. The restaurant also has soup and pasta bars, and a fresh bakery section with wonderful cookies and muffins.
   They won the 1993 *Rocky Mountain News* Reader's Choice Awards for both Salad Bar and Health Food.

SPECIALTY DINING

Some of the establishments mentioned below are discussed in detail above.
   Local Favorites   For local favorites, don't miss the Buckhorn Exchange or the Fort, both serving Rocky Mountain cuisine.
   Hotel Dining   The best is at the Palace Arms in the Brown Palace Hotel, and the Augusta in the Westin Tabor Center, and the Liaison in the Warwick.
   Dining with a View   If you like a view with your meal, consider the Fort, in the foothills 18 miles west of Denver: In the evening, it's fun to watch the city lights.
   Dining Complexes   There are two dining complexes in downtown Denver: the Plaza Court Food Emporium, in Republic Plaza at 370 17th St., with fast-food outlets; and the Tabor Center Food Court, 1201 16th St., between Larimer Street and Lawrence Street, with 18 booths serving everything from felafel to egg foo yung.
   After Theater   The pre- and posttheater crowd appreciates the theatre café in the Galleria of the Denver Performing Arts Complex, 14th Street at Curtis Street (tel. 623-7733). Make reservations for dinner, then return after the performance for dessert and coffee and miss the traffic.
   Light Meals   Light, casual, and fast-food is readily found throughout the city. Personal favorites are La Bonne Soup, Duffy's Shamrock, and Healthy Habits.
   For Breakfast   Consider the Delectable Egg, Duffy's Shamrock,

McCormick's Fish House, or Las Delicias. You can get a great weekend brunch at McCormick's or at Ellyngton's in the Brown Palace Hotel.

Afternoon Tea   Denver's best bet for an afternoon Devonshire tea is the lobby of the Brown Palace Hotel.

Late-Night Dining   Night owls have slim pickings in Denver after about 11pm. One of the best bets is Bennigan's, with seven locations around the metropolitan area—including one at 1699 S. Colorado Blvd., just off I-25 (tel. 753-0272). There are two in Lakewood, two in Aurora, and one each in Westminster and Tech Center. The international menu is served Monday through Saturday until 2am and on Sunday to midnight.

After the bars close, try Jerusalem, 1890 E. Evans Ave. near the University of Denver (tel. 777-8828). An inexpensive Arabic café, it serves up huge portions of gyros and shish kebabs Monday through Friday until 4am and 24 hours on Saturday and Sunday.

Picnic Fare   My choice for picnic fare—especially if a picnic means people-watching on the 16th Street Mall—is Goldie's. Outside downtown, check out the Bagel Deli, with two locations, at 6217 E. 14th Ave., at Krameria Street (tel. 322-0350), and 6439 E. Hampden Ave., at Monaco Parkway (tel. 756-6667).

CHAPTER 5

WHAT TO SEE & DO IN DENVER

1. ATTRACTIONS
- **DID YOU KNOW . . . ?**
- **WALKING TOUR—DOWNTOWN DENVER**
2. SPORTS & RECREATION
3. SAVVY SHOPPING
4. EVENING ENTERTAINMENT
5. EASY EXCURSIONS FROM DENVER

Denver's focal point, from a tourist's point of view, is Civic Center Park where Colfax Avenue meets Broadway. Here are the State Capitol, the U.S. Mint, the Denver Art Museum, the Colorado Historical Museum, and other important sites. What's more, the Civic Center is at the southeast corner of the square mile of downtown, in which lie the Colorado Convention Center and the Denver Center for the Performing Arts, Larimer Square, Union Station, most major hotels, and, of course, the principal shopping district.

Denver, therefore, is a great place for walkers. But don't restrict yourself to the downtown hub: Many more attractions are a 10 minutes' drive away, with others spread throughout the metropolitan area.

1. ATTRACTIONS

SUGGESTED ITINERARIES

IF YOU HAVE 1 DAY Start at **Larimer Square,** Denver's birthplace. Have a casual breakfast in the **Market** and give yourself a self-guided walking tour of the historic sites. Then stroll the **16th Street pedestrian mall.** Your goal is the **State Capitol,** just across Broadway. En route, take a 1-block detour to have an early lunch or a cup of tea at the **Brown Palace Hotel.** After seeing the Capitol, explore other Civic Center sites, including the Denver Art Museum.

IF YOU HAVE 2 DAYS Spend your first day as suggested above.

On day 2, take a drive west. Venture into the old mining towns in the Rocky Mountain foothills—atmospheric communities like **Central City, Idaho Springs,** and **Georgetown.** En route, visit the **Red Rocks Amphitheatre** near Morrison. On your return, tour the **Coors Brewery** and **Hakushika Saké brewery** in Golden.

IF YOU HAVE 3 DAYS Spend your first two days as suggested above.

On day 3, enjoy more of Denver. The city has numerous historic homes, beautiful parks, attractive new shopping centers, and several highly touted museums. I recommend the **Denver Museum of Natural History,** the **Museum of Western Art,** and the **Black American West Museum.**

 **DID YOU KNOW . . . ?**

- Denver is exactly one mile high—the 15th step of the State Capitol Building is 5,280 feet above sea level.
- The first cheeseburger was grilled at Louis Ballast's Denver drive-in in 1944.
- Denver has the second-highest per capita number of college graduates of any major city in the U.S.
- Golda Meir, the former prime minister of Israel, attended North High School in Denver.
- The highest paved road in North America—to the top of 14,260-foot Mount Evans—is part of 20,000 acres of city parks.
- Douglas Fairbanks, the famous movie star of the 1920s and 1930s, was expelled from Denver's East High School.

IF YOU HAVE 5 DAYS OR MORE   Spend days 1 to 3 as suggested above.

On day 4, day-trip to nearby cities such as Colorado Springs, home of the Air Force Academy and the Pikes Peak Cog Railway, or Boulder and Fort Collins, both lively university towns.

For your fifth day, climb higher into the Rockies to resort communities like Estes Park, gateway to Rocky Mountain National Park, or Breckenridge and Vail, across the Continental Divide.

THE TOP ATTRACTIONS

DENVER ART MUSEUM, 100 W. 14th Pkwy., at Civic Center Park. Tel. 640-2793.

This 10-story, 28-sided structure has a million shimmering glass tiles covering its exterior. Inside is the largest and oldest collection of Native American art of any art museum in the United States, as well as a large collection of western art, and 35,000 other art objects in seven curatorial departments.

The Native American collection consists of 20,000 pieces from 150 tribes of North America, covering a time span of some 2,000 years and valued at more than $25 million. Works are arranged geographically in 10 areas covering 22,000 square feet. The collection is growing not only through the acquisition of historic pieces, but by the commissioning of contemporary Native American artists.

Other exhibits include major collections of African, oceanic, and early New World art, such as Pre-Columbian artifacts, Spanish colonial arts, some Spanish Peruvian works, and a group of southwestern *santos*. A solid representation of European artists includes works by Van Dyck, Tintoretto, Rubens, Veronese, Monet, Renoir, Matisse, Modigliani, Degas, Chagall, and Toulouse-Lautrec. There are period rooms of art in French Gothic, English Tudor, and Spanish baroque styles, and Asian works from China, Japan, and India. At the top of the gallery floors is an exhibit of textiles and costumes from around the world.

Guided tours are available, and performing-arts events are frequently scheduled—including jazz most Wednesdays from 5 to 8pm, when the working day is over. A gift shop has unusual replicas of certain treasures displayed and many books on art and southwestern lore. A restaurant has an open patio for warm-weather lunches.

Admission: $3 adults, $1.50 students and seniors, children under 6 free; free for everyone Sat.

Open: Tues–Sat 10am–5pm, Sun noon–5pm.

DENVER MUSEUM OF NATURAL HISTORY, City Park, 2001 Colorado Blvd. Tel. 322-7009 (reservations) or 370-6357 (information) or 370-8257 for the hearing impaired.

This rambling three-story museum is the fifth-largest natural history museum in the United States. Exquisitely fashioned human and animal figures in more than 90 dioramas depict life on earth in various eras on four continents.

The first floor has articulated skeletons of mammals 50 million years old and displays on ancient Old World cultures and prehistoric American peoples. The second floor has a butterfly exhibit and sections devoted to Colorado wildlife, North American bears and sea life, and Australian ecology. This floor also has rooms showing artifacts of early Native American tribes from Alaska to Florida. The third-floor exhibits include displays of South American wildlife and the habitats of Botswana, including a spectacular savanna diorama called "The Watering Hole."

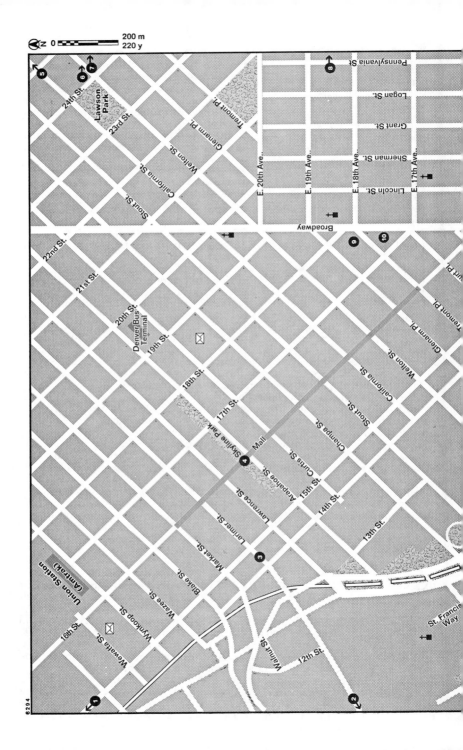

DENVER ATTRACTIONS

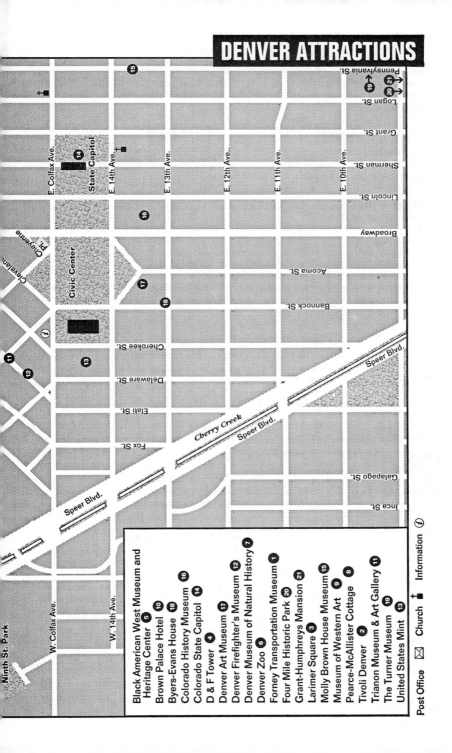

Ninth St. Park

W. Colfax Ave.

W. 14th Ave.

Speer Blvd.

Cherry Creek

Speer Blvd.

Speer Blvd.

E. Colfax Ave.

State Capitol

Civic Center

Pt. Cheyenne

Cleveland

E. 14th Ave.

E. 13th Ave.

E. 12th Ave.

E. 11th Ave.

E. 10th Ave.

Fox St.

Elati St.

Delaware St.

Cherokee St.

Bannock St.

Acoma St.

Broadway

Lincoln St.

Sherman St.

Grant St.

Logan St.

Pennsylvania St.

Inca St.

Galapago St.

Black American West Museum and
Heritage Center **5**
Brown Palace Hotel **10**
Byers-Evans House **18**
Colorado History Museum **16**
Colorado State Capitol **14**
D & F Tower **4**
Denver Art Museum **17**
Denver Firefighter's Museum **12**
Denver Museum of Natural History **7**
Denver Zoo **6**
Forney Transportation Museum **1**
Four Mile Historic Park **20**
Grant-Humphreys Mansion **21**
Larimer Square **3**
Molly Brown House Museum **15**
Museum of Western Art **9**
Pearce-McAllister Cottage **8**
Tivoli Denver **2**
Trianon Museum & Art Gallery **11**
The Turner Museum **19**
United States Mint **13**

Post Office ■   Church ⊠   Information ①

The new Hall of Life offers hands-on studies of genetics, the wonder of birth, human anatomy, the five senses, fitness, and nutrition. The Coors Hall of Minerals displays semiprecious gemstones and minerals of the Southwest, including the largest gold nugget ever found in Colorado: the 8½-pound Tom's Baby.

The museum also houses the **IMAX Theater** (tel. 370-6300), which presents science, nature, or technology/oriented films with sense-surround sound on a screen 4½ by 6½ *stories* in dimension; and the **Charles C. Gates Planetarium** (tel. 370-6351), which schedules frequent multimedia star programs and laser light shows.

Admission: Museum, $4.50 adults, $2.50 children under 13 and seniors; IMAX, $5 adults, $4 children and seniors; planetarium, $3.50 adults, $2.50 children and seniors; There are combination rates available.

Open: Daily 9am–5pm. **Closed:** Christmas Day.

UNITED STATES MINT, 320 W. Colfax Ave., at Cherokee St. Tel. 844-3582 or 844-3331.

The mint opened in 1863 and originally melted gold dust and nuggets into bars. In 1904 the office moved to the present site, and two years later began coinage operations in both gold and silver. Copper pennies began to be made a few years later. Silver dollars (containing 90% silver) were last manufactured in 1935; gold purchases were discontinued in 1968. In 1970 the coinage law changed and all silver was eliminated from dollars and half dollars: today they are made of a copper-nickel alloy.

Coins are made from prefabricated rolls of metal supplied by private dealers to the mint, which concentrates on the blanking function and on stamping the actual coins. The mint stamps more than five billion coins a year. A coin minted in Denver has a small *D* on it.

From the upstairs gallery, visitors watch coin metal stamped into coin blanks (both sides are stamped in a single stroke), then the coins are edge-rolled to make a raised rim. The next steps are inspection, weighing, counting, and bagging, before being stored in vaults to await shipment.

A visitor center has a machine that stamps blank coins, turning them into souvenir medals, and has various collectors' items in freshly minted coins on sale.

Admission: Free.

Open: 20-minute tours depart from the gate on Cherokee Street every half hour, Mon, Tues, Thurs, and Fri 8am–3pm, and Wed 9am–3pm.

COLORADO STATE CAPITOL, Broadway and E. Colfax Ave. Tel. 866-2604.

The building was built to survive 1,000 years. Constructed of granite from a Colorado quarry in 1886, the most salient feature is its gold dome, which rises 272 feet above the ground. The dome, first sheathed in copper, was replaced with 200 ounces of gold after a public outcry: Copper was not a Colorado product.

Murals depicting the history of water in the state adorn the walls of the first-floor rotunda. There is a fine view upward from here to the underside of the dome, a vertical distance of 180 feet. The rotunda, at the heart of the building, echoes the layout of the national Capitol in Washington, D.C. South of the rotunda is the governor's office, paneled in walnut and lighted by a massive chandelier.

Various levels of the interior of the capitol may interest visitors. The basement has hearing rooms open to the public. On the first floor, the west lobby has a case showing moon rocks and another displaying dolls in miniature ball gowns as worn by various governors' wives. To the right of the main lobby, the governor's reception room is open to the public. The second floor has main entrances to the House, Senate, and old Supreme Court chambers. Entrances to the public and visitor galleries for the House and Senate are on the third floor. The Colorado Hall of Fame is located near the top of the dome, with stained-glass portraits of Colorado pioneers. Views from the dome on clear days are spectacular.

Admission: Free.

Open: 30-minute tours are offered year-round (more frequently in summer), Mon–Fri 9:15am–3:30pm (dome is locked at 3:30pm).

LARIMER SQUARE, 1400 block of Larimer St. Tel. 534-2367.

This was where Denver began. Larimer Street between 14th Street and 15th Street comprised the entire community of Denver City in 1858, with false-front stores, hotels, and saloons to serve gold seekers and other pioneers. In the mid-1870s it was the main street of the city and the site of Denver's first post office, bank, theater, and streetcar line. But by the 1930s the street had declined so badly that it was a "skid row" of pawnshops, gin mills, and flophouses. It had an impending appointment with the wrecking ball until 1965, when the entire block was purchased by a group of investors with a strong interest in historic preservation.

The Larimer Square project became Denver's first major historic-preservation effort. All 16 of the block's commercial buildings, constructed in the 1870s and 1880s, were renovated, providing space for street-side retail shops, restaurants, and nightclubs, and upper-story offices. A series of inner courtyards and open spaces were created. The project reached its climax in 1973 when Larimer Square was added to the National Register of Historic Places.

A self-guided walking tour pamphlet is available at the Larimer Square information booth, on the southeast side of Larimer Street near 15th Street. To make an appointment for a free guided tour, call 534-2367.

MORE ATTRACTIONS
ARCHITECTURAL HIGHLIGHTS

BROWN PALACE HOTEL, 321 17th St., at Tremont Place. Tel. 297-3111.

✪ Designed in Italian Renaissance style by famed architect Frank Edbrooke, this was the first atrium lobby and the second fireproof building in the United States when it opened in August 1892. A National Historic Landmark, the building is triangular in shape and is built of Colorado red granite and Arizona sandstone. Native Rocky Mountain animals are carved into the sandstone medallions between the seventh-floor windows. Mexican onyx panels the lobby walls and white marble provides the flooring; elaborate cast-iron grillwork surrounds six tiers of balconies to the stained-glass ceiling high above the lobby. There's a remarkable Napoleonic collection in the Palace Arms restaurant; and the Ship Tavern was designed and decorated to resemble the interior of a ship.

Admission: Free.
Open: Daily 24 hours.

D & F TOWER, 16th and Arapahoe Sts.

This 325-foot structure is a replica of the campanile of St. Mark's Basilica in Venice, Italy. When it was erected in 1910, it was the third-tallest building in the United States and the tallest west of the Mississippi River. The tower is especially beautiful when viewed from the fountains at either end of Skyline Park, which runs for three blocks along Arapahoe Street. Not open to the public.

TIVOLI DENVER, 901 Larimer St. Tel. 629-8712.

A landmark brewery for 105 years, from 1864 to 1969, this historic building was saved from demolition and developed into a shopping and entertainment complex in 1985. It is crowned by a seven-story tower patterned after a Bavarian castle which was built in 1890 for storage of malt, barley, and hops. Two-story-high copper brewing kettles, a grain roll mill, and the powerhouse are among remnants left behind by the old brewery. Historic photos and beer-label reproductions are further reminders.

Admission: Free.
Open: Mon–Sat 10am–9pm, Sun noon–5pm.

HISTORIC BUILDINGS

BYERS-EVANS HOUSE, 1310 Bannock St. Tel. 620-4933.

William N. Byers, who built this elaborate Victorian home in 1883, was the founder of the *Rocky Mountain News*. In 1889, William Gray Evans, son of John Evans, Colorado's second territorial governor, purchased the house. Restored to its present appearance during the era of World War I, the house contains original Evans family furnishings. Guided tours include a film about the Byers and Evans families and describe the architecture of the house. It's located just behind the Denver Art Museum.

Adjacent to the Byers-Evans House, and included in the Byers-Evans admission fee, is the Denver History Museum, containing artifacts of early Denver life, from the gold rush to World War II. In addition to traditional museum exhibits, it contains interactive video displays on historical events and issues, facts and figures, biographies of early Denverites, and historic photos.

Admission: $2.50 adults, $2 seniors, $1 children 6–16, free for children under 6.
Open: Tues–Sun 11am–3pm. Closed Mon and state holidays.

GRANT-HUMPHREYS MANSION, 770 Pennsylvania St. Tel. 894-2505.

Colorado Gov. James Grant built this 30-room mansion in 1902, and oil industrialist Albert Humphreys purchased it in 1917. This is 15,000 square feet of beaux arts elegance, rich with period pieces. Tours can be guided or self-guided and are wheelchair accessible. Groups often rent the building for private parties.

Admission: $2 adults, $1 seniors and children 6–16, free for children under 6.
Open: Tues–Fri 10am–2pm. **Closed:** Major holidays.

MOLLY BROWN HOUSE MUSEUM, 1340 Pennsylvania St. Tel. 832-4092.

✪ The property of Historic Denver, Inc., the Molly Brown House Museum was designed by Denver architect William Lang and was built in 1889 of Colorado lava stone with sandstone trim. It was the residence from 1894 to 1932 of James and Margaret (Molly) Brown. The "unsinkable" Molly Brown became a national heroine in 1912 when the *Titanic* sank: she took charge of a group of immigrant women in a lifeboat and later raised money for their benefit. She was also the first preservationist of Denver, and in 1930 she bought the home of poet Eugene Field for the city.

Restored to its 1910 appearance, the Molly Brown House has a large collection of turn-of-the-century furnishings and art objects, many the former possessions of the Brown family. A carriage house at the rear of the house is also open to visitors.

Admission: $3 adults, $2 seniors over 65, $1.50 children 6–18, free for children under 6.
Open: Year-round Tues–Sat 10am–4pm, Sun noon–4pm; June–Aug, also Mon 10am–4pm. **Closed:** Major holidays.

PEARCE-McALLISTER COTTAGE, 1880 Gaylord St. Tel. 322-3704.

Whereas most of the historic homes in Denver are Victorian in architecture, this one is Dutch colonial revival. It was built in 1899 by Frederick J. Sterner for metallurgist Harold Pearce and his wife, Cara, who wanted an East Coast–style cottage. It was sold in 1907 to lawyer Henry McAllister, Jr., whose wife, Phebe, decorated the home in the popular colonial revival style of the 1920s. All the furnishings, down to books and tiny knickknacks, were bequeathed to the Colorado Historical Society, which used them to re-create the McAllisters' life-style. The house—located just west of City Park—also contains a gift shop and the **Denver Museum of Miniatures, Dolls, and Toys.**

Admission: $3 adults, $2 seniors and children 2–16, free for children under 2.
Open: Tues–Sat 10am–4pm, Sun 1–4pm.

MUSEUMS & GALLERIES

Museums

BLACK AMERICAN WEST MUSEUM AND HERITAGE CENTER, 3091 California St., at 31st St. Tel. 292-2566.

Nearly one-third of the cowboys in the Old West were black. Located in the heart of the Five Points neighborhood, this museum tells their story—along with the story of black doctors, teachers, miners, farmers, newspaper reporters, and state legislators. In fact, it's lodged in the Victorian home of Dr. Justina Ford, the first black female physician licensed to practice in Denver.

Paul Steward began collecting photographs, saddles, guns, clothing, and other artifacts as a hobby. Now the 35,000-item collection is acknowledged by the Smithsonian Institution for its great significance.

Admission: $2 adults, $1.50 seniors, 75¢ children 12–17, 50¢ children under 12. **Open:** Wed–Fri 10am–2pm, Sat noon–5pm, Sun 2–5pm. **Closed:** Major holidays.

COLORADO HISTORY MUSEUM, 1300 Broadway. Tel. 866-3682.

If this book's introductory section on history piqued your interest, this museum at the Civic Center is the place to come. The Colorado Historical Society's permanent exhibits include "The Colorado Chronicle," an 1800 to 1949 time line that incorporates biographical plaques and a remarkable collection of photographs, news clippings, and various paraphernalia. Dozens of dioramas portray various episodes in state history, from the medieval Anasazi cliff-dweller culture through early settlement, including an intricate re-creation of 19th-century Denver. There's a life-size display of early transportation and industry, including heavy mining equipment and exhibits of mining techniques.

The museum also has fascinating changing exhibits and an interesting gift shop, and offers a series of in-house lectures and statewide historical and archeological tours.

Admission: $3 adults, $1.50 seniors, students with an ID, and children 6–16, free for children under 6.
Open: Mon–Sat 10am–4:30pm, Sun noon–4:30pm.

FORNEY TRANSPORTATION MUSEUM, 1416 Platte St. Tel. 433-3643.

More than 100 antique and classic cars and trucks, plus some 350 other exhibits, fill a huge turn-of-the-century historic building and pour out onto the surrounding grounds. The collection includes a number of one-of-a-kind vehicles, including Amelia Earhart's "Gold Bug" roadster, a Rolls Royce that once belonged to Prince Aly Khan, and a 1909 French taxicab that transported World War I soldiers from Paris to the Battle of the Marne. Other displays include three locomotives, including the world's largest steam locomotive—Big Boy No.4005—and wagons, music boxes, historic fashions, farm equipment, and a model-train display.

The museum is housed (mostly) in the former City of Denver streetcar powerhouse building, built at the turn of the century. To reach it, take I-25 to Exit 211 (23rd Ave.) and go east on Water Street one-half mile.

Admission: $4 adults, $2 children 12–18, $1 children 5–11.
Open: May–Sept, Mon–Sat 9am–5pm, Sun 11am–5pm; Oct–Apr, Mon–Sat 10am–5pm, Sun 11am–5pm.

FOUR MILE HISTORIC PARK, 715 S. Forest St. Tel. 399-1859.

The oldest log home (1859) still standing in Denver is the centerpiece of a 14-acre living-history farm. Everything is authentic for the period 1859 to 1883—including the house (a former stagecoach stop), its furnishings, outbuildings, farm equipment, even the costumes of the volunteers. There are draft horses and chickens in the barn and crops in the garden. A "phased interpretive plan" depicts the guided evolution of pristine prairie to cultivated farm, with examples of stock ranching and dry-land and irrigated farming.

Several times a season, volunteers in period dress engage in chores from plowing and blacksmithing to quilting and cooking.

The park is four miles southeast of downtown Denver, on the east side of Glendale at Exposition Avenue.

Admission: $3 adults, $1.50 seniors and children 6–15, free for children under 6.
Open: Apr–Sept, Wed–Sun 10am–4pm (last tour at 3pm); also 3rd weekend of Oct (Halloween event) and 2nd weekend of Dec (Holiday Open House). **Closed:** Oct–Mar.

Galleries

MUSEUM OF WESTERN ART, 1727 Tremont Place. Tel. 296-1880.

This museum occupies a three-story Victorian brick house that was originally

Denver's most notorious brothel and gambling casino. Among the 125 paintings and sculptures are classic western scenes by Frederic Remington and Charles Russell, landscapes by Albert Bierstadt and Thomas Moran, and works by 20th-century painters. The gift shop sells hard-to-find art books and prints.

Admission: $3 adults, $2 seniors and students, free for children under 7.

Open: Tues–Sat 10am–4:30pm.

TRIANON MUSEUM AND ART GALLERY, 335 14th St., at Tremont Place. Tel. 623-0739.

A museum gallery where everything is available for sale to serious collectors, the Trianon has a beautiful collection of 16th-, 17th-, and 18th-century European works—paintings, sculptures, furniture, crystal, porcelain, silver, and bronzes. There are also some Asian treasures and a fine gun collection.

Admission: $1 adults and students, free for children under 12.

Open: Mon–Sat 10am–4pm.

THE TURNER MUSEUM, 773 Downing St. Tel. 832-0924.

The Capitol Hill home of Douglas and Linda Graham houses one of the outstanding private art collections in the United States. Permanent exhibitions include watercolors and engravings of impressionist J. M. W. Turner and numerous land-scapes by Thomas Moran, whose work helped inspire the National Park Service. About 3,000 other works are shown on a revolving basis.

The Grahams serve three gourmet meals daily, by reservation: breakfast ($10), lunch ($12), and a candlelit dinner ($25). There are also regular classical music recitals. In 1992, *Westword* designated the museum "The Best Place to Eat While Viewing Art."

Admission: $7.50, including a 30-minute personalized tour.

Open: Mon–Fri 2–5pm, Sun noon–5pm, and by appointment.

MUSEUM OF OUTDOOR ARTS, 7600 E. Orchard Rd., #160N, Engle-wood. Tel. 741-3609.

Fifty pieces of artwork, both sculpture and paintings, are set throughout the Greenwood Plaza business park, about 15 minutes south of downtown Denver, at the site of Fiddler's Green Amphitheatre. Call ahead to arrange a guided tour, or obtain a self-guided tour map and stroll among the artworks at your own pace. It's also a good place for a picnic.

Admission: Free; guided tours, by appointment, $3 adults, $1 children 17 and under.

Open: Daily 8am–7pm.

NEIGHBORHOODS

FAR EAST CENTER, Federal Blvd., between W. Alameda and W. Missis-sippi Aves.

Denver's Asian community is focused along this strip, which burgeoned in the aftermath of the Vietnam War to accommodate throngs of Southeast Asian refugees, especially Thais and Vietnamese. Look for authentic restaurants, bakeries, groceries, gift shops, and clothing stores. The Far East Center building at Federal and Alameda is built in Japanese pagoda style.

FIVE POINTS, 20th to 38th Sts., northeast of downtown.

The "five points" actually meet at 23rd Street and Broadway, but the cultural and commercial hub of Denver's African American community covers a much larger area and incorporates four historic districts. Restaurants offer the likes of soul food, barbecued ribs, and Caribbean cuisine, while jazz and blues musicians and contempo-rary dance troupes perform in theaters and nightclubs. The Black American West Museum and Heritage Center is also in this neighborhood.

LA ALMA/LINCOLN PARK, Santa Fe Dr., between W. Colfax and W. Sixth Aves.

Hispanic culture, art, food, and entertainment predominate along this strip, notable for its southwestern character and architecture. There are numerous restaurants, art galleries, and crafts shops. Denver's annual Cinco de Mayo celebration takes place here each May.

LOWER DOWNTOWN, Wynkoop St. to Market St. and 20th St. to Speer Blvd.

Twenty-two square blocks surrounding the Union Station contain numerous National Historic Landmarks and refurbished turn-of-the-century warehouses. Restaurants, galleries, antiques stores, and at least one outstanding hotel (the Oxford Hotel) operate in this district. See "Orientation" in Chapter 4, above.

UPTOWN, Broadway to York St. (City Park) and E. Colfax Ave. to E. 23rd Ave.

Denver's oldest residential neighborhood is best known today for two things: It's bisected by 17th Avenue's "Restaurant Row" (see "Dining," in Chapter 4) and several of its classic Victorian and Queen Anne–style homes have been converted to bed-and-breakfasts (see "Accommodations," in Chapter 4).

PARKS & GARDENS

BARR LAKE STATE PARK, 13401 Picadilly Rd., Brighton. Tel. 659-6005 or 659-1160.

About 25 miles northeast of Denver via I-76, this wildlife sanctuary of 2,500 acres comprises a prairie reservoir and surrounding wetlands. Motors are not allowed, but you can sail, paddle, or row, as well as fish. A 9-mile hiking and biking trail that circles the lake is popular in winter with snowshoers and cross-country skiers. A boardwalk from the nature center at the south parking lot leads to a good view of a heron rookery. Bird blinds along this trail offer wildlife observation and photography. Two picnic areas have tables and grills; there's a commercial campground opposite the park entrance.

Admission: $3 per vehicle.

CASTLEWOOD CANYON STATE PARK, 2989 S. State Highway, Franktown. Tel. 688-5242.

Steep canyons, a meandering stream, a waterfall, lush vegetation, and considerable wildlife bless this small park. The remains of Castlewood Canyon Dam can be seen; built for irrigation in 1890, it collapsed in 1933 and killed two people. The park, 30 miles south of Denver on Douglas County Road 51 east of Castle Rock, has picnic facilities and hiking trails.

Admission: $3 per vehicle.

CHATFIELD STATE RECREATION AREA, 11500 N. Roxborough Park Rd., Littleton. Tel. 791-7275.

Just 8 miles south of downtown Denver via U.S. 85, this park occupies 5,600 acres of prairie against a backdrop of the steeply rising Rocky Mountains. Chatfield Reservoir has a 26-mile shoreline that invites swimming, boating, fishing, and other water sports. The area also has 18 miles of paved bicycle trails, plus hiking and horseback-riding paths. In winter, there's ice fishing and cross-country skiing.

An observation area on the south side of the park offers a view of a 27-acre nature-study grove, closed during nesting season because of its heron rookery. The park also has a model-airplane field, complete with paved runways and a hot-air balloon launching pad.

There are 193 pull-through campsites with showers, laundry, and dump station. Various sites offer picnicking facilities.

Admission: $3 per vehicle; camping fee $7–$10 daily.

CHERRY CREEK STATE RECREATION AREA, 4201 S. Parker Rd., Aurora. Tel. 690-1166. For camping reservations, call toll free 800/678-2267. In Denver, call 470-1144.

Because Cherry Creek, the central attraction of the park, used to flood Denver, Cherry Creek Dam was built in 1950. The resulting 880-acre reservoir has become a mecca for 1.5 million visitors a year. Located at the southeast Denver city limits off Parker Road and I-225, the park has 3,900 acres of grounds.

Water sports include swimming, waterskiing, boating, and fishing. There's a nature trail, dog-training area, rifle range, pistol range, and trap-shooting area. Six miles of paved bicycle paths and 10 miles of bridle trails circle the reservoir (horse rentals are offered). Rangers guide walks on a 1½-mile nature trail and offer evening programs in an amphitheater. There's even a prairie dog colony with a special observation area. Winter-sports enthusiasts enjoy skating, ice fishing, and ice boating.

The park's 102 campsites include showers, laundry, and dump station, but no water or electrical hookups. Many lakeshore sites have picnic tables with grills.

Admission: $4 per vehicle; camping fee $7–$10 daily.

CITY PARK, E. 17th to E. 26th Ave., between York St. and Colorado Blvd.

Denver's largest urban park covers 314 acres—96 square blocks—on the east side of Uptown. Established in 1881, and still containing Victorian touches, it includes two lakes (with boat rentals), athletic fields, playgrounds, tennis courts, picnic areas, even an 18-hole municipal golf course. In the summertime there are band concerts in the park. It's also the site of both the Denver Zoo and the Denver Museum of Natural History, with its planetarium and IMAX Theater.

Admission: Free for park, although the zoo, museum, golf course, and other sites charge independently.

Open: Daily 24 hours.

DENVER BOTANIC GARDENS, 1005 York St. Tel. 331-4000 or 331-4010 (24-hour recording).

These outstanding 20-acre outdoor and indoor gardens display plants native to the desert, plains, mountain foothills, and alpine zones; there's also a traditional Japanese garden, scripture garden (tying plants to biblical history), herb garden, home demonstration garden, water garden, and "wingsong" garden to attract songbirds.

Even in the cold of winter, the dome-shaped, concrete-and-Plexiglas Boettcher Memorial Conservatory houses 800 species of tropical and subtropical plants. Huge, colorful orchids and bromeliads share space with a collection of plants used for foods, fibers, dyes, building materials, and medicines. The Botanic Gardens also include a gift shop, library, and auditorium. Adjoining the gardens to the west is 20-square-block Cheesman Park.

Admission: May–Sept, $4 adults, $2 seniors and children 6–15; Oct–Apr, $3 adults, $1.50 seniors, $1 children; free for children under 6.

Open: Daily 9am–4:45pm. **Closed:** Christmas and New Year's days.

DENVER MOUNTAIN PARKS, Department of Parks and Recreation, 1445 Cleveland Place. Tel. 575-2227.

Land in the mountains near Denver was acquired and set aside for recreational use by the city at the beginning of the 20th century. The 18 mountain parks are great places for hiking, picnicking, birdwatching, golfing, or lazing in the grass and sun.

The largest, Genesee Park, is 20 miles west of Denver off I-70; its 2,400 acres contain playgrounds, picnic areas with fireplaces, a softball field, a scenic overlook, and an elk and buffalo enclosure. Among the others are Daniels Park, 23 miles south of Denver via County Line Road and County Road 29, with similar facilities on 1,000 acres; and Dedisse Park, 2 miles west of Evergreen on Colo. 74, which has picnic facilities and a golf course. Echo Lake Park and Red Rocks Park are discussed later in this chapter (see "Easy Excursions from Denver"). The Winter Park ski resort, also a Denver park, has extensive coverage in Chapter 9, "The Northern Rockies."

DENVER ZOO, City Park, 23rd Ave. and Steele St. Tel. 331-4110.

Four hundred species of animals, nearly 1,300, live in this very spacious zoological park. Feeding times are posted near the zoo entrance so you can time your visit to see the animals at their most active. The Bear Mountain exhibit, when it was built in 1918, was the first animal exhibit in the United States to be constructed of simulated concrete rockwork. At the other end of the time line, Northern Shores (1991) allows underwater viewing of polar bears and sea lions; Tropical Discovery (1994) re-creates an entire tropical ecosystem under glass, complete with leopards and crocodiles, piranhas and king cobras. Exotic waterfowl inhabit several ponds, and 300 avians live in Bird World, which includes a hummingbird forest and a tropical aviary. The feline house was remodeled in 1993.

A miniature train circles Children's Zoo near the zoo's west entrance. The rubber-tired Zooliner tours all zoo paths spring through fall. Full meals are served at the Hungry Elephant, a zoo cafeteria with outdoor eating area. Many visitors bring picnic lunches and eat them on the expansive lawns.

Admission: $6 adults, $4 seniors and children 4–13 (accompanied by an adult), free for children 3 and under.

Open: Summer, daily 9am–6pm; winter, daily 10am–5pm. (Hours change with daylight saving time.)

ROCKY MOUNTAIN ARSENAL, Havana St. and E. 72nd Ave. Tel. 289-0132.

Once a place where the federal government manufactured chemical weapons such as mustard and chlorine gases, later the site of insecticide production, the Rocky Mountain Arsenal is now an environmental success story. Covering 27 square miles of open grasslands and wetlands north of Stapleton Airport, the RMA is home to deer, coyotes, various small mammals and reptiles, and thousands of birds—including (in winter) an estimated 100 bald eagles, making this one of the largest eagle nesting grounds in the lower 48 states.

There's a small information center and bald eagle viewing station on the site. Tours of wildlife resources and of waste-disposal cleanup operations are offered by the co-custodians, the U.S. Army and U.S. Fish and Wildlife Service.

Admission: Free.

Open: Daytime hours; tours by advance appointment.

WASHINGTON PARK, S. Downing to S. Franklin Sts. and E. Virginia to E. Louisiana Aves.

Named for its replica of George Washington's flower gardens at Mount Vernon, this 155-acre park also encompasses two lakes (Smith and Grasmere).

Admission: Free.

Open: Daily 24 hours.

COOL FOR KIDS

Denver abounds with activities geared for children, and the listings below will appeal to young travelers of any age. In addition, some sights listed in the previous sections provide fun for the entire family. These include the Colorado History Museum, the Denver Art Museum, the Denver Museum of Natural History, the Denver Zoo, Four Mile Historic Park, and the U.S. Mint.

BIG FUN, 920 S. Monaco Pkwy., 1½ blocks south of Leetsdale Dr. Tel. 329-8957.

Denver's largest indoor play park for children 2 to 12, there are gigantic play structures for climbing, sliding, and running, including the Alpine Wave and Turtle Racers.

Admission: Weekdays $5.50 children 2–12; weekends $6.50 children 2–12; at all times, $2.95 children under 2, free admission for adults.

Open: Mon–Thurs 10am–8pm, Fri–Sat 10am–9pm, Sun 11am–7pm.

CELEBRITY SPORTS CENTER, 888 S. Colorado Blvd. Tel. 757-3321.

Older children are happy to spend the entire day at the 150,000-square-foot facility, built in 1960 by Walt Disney himself. Three five- and six-story water slides encircle part of the building. There's also an Olympic-size indoor swimming pool, 80 bowling lanes, three arcade rooms with more than 300 video games and pinball machines, and numerous other activities. There are also two restaurants and a snack bar, as well as a bowling pro shop and a tavern for kids over 21. Younger children must be supervised, but child care is offered at no charge.

Admission: Free; attractions charge individually. (In summer an all day pass is available for $7.)

Open: Sun–Thurs 8:30am–midnight, Fri–Sat 8:30am–2am.

CHILDREN'S MUSEUM, 2121 Crescent Dr. Tel. 433-7444.
This is Denver's best hands-on experience. Children can assume the roles of shoppers and checkout clerks at a miniature Safeway supermarket, become news commentators at a mini-TV studio, experience what it feels like to be physically disabled in various ways, or even explore bedtime fears. Then they can make a totem pole, get their faces painted, try a flight simulator, or check out the pinhole camera. The most popular exhibit is the ballroom, where a sea of 80,000 plastic balls await. The newest addition is a gigantic plastic mountain used for year-round ski lessons. Exhibits change frequently, and special events are scheduled throughout the year.
Admission: $3 adults; $4 children; $1.50 seniors over 60; free for children under 2. Free admission Friday evenings.
Open: Tues–Sun 10am–5pm, plus Fri 5:30–8pm for Friday Night Live. **Directions:** Take Exit 211 (23rd Avenue) east off I-25; turn right on Seventh Street, and again on Crescent Drive.

ELITCH GARDENS, 4620 W. 38th Ave. at Tennyson St. Tel. 455-4771.
Established in 1889, this traditional amusement park offers something for everyone. For the kids, there are two wooden roller coasters, including "The Twister," rated Number 3 in the world, and a steel-loop coaster. There's also a 1925 carousel, a log-flume ride, 16 other major rides, a miniature golf course, a 53-lane Skee Ball casino, and Miniature Madness, a child/adult participation area with kiddie rides, a maze, suspension bridges, and an outdoor children's theater. Adults enjoy the park's elaborate flower gardens, its regular outdoor concerts, and the oldest summer-stock theater in the United States. There are a dozen restaurants and snack bars in the park.
Admission: Gate admission Mon–Fri with unlimited rides, $13 adults and children over 52 inches, $13 children under 52 inches, $10.50 children 3 and under; gate admission only, $7.50, free for children 3 and under (individual ride tickets can be purchased inside); admission is higher on Sat–Sun.
Open: Mid-Apr to May, Sat–Sun 10am–8pm; June–Labor Day, daily 10am–8pm.

FUNPLEX, 9670 W. Coal Mine Ave., at Kipling St., Littleton. Tel. 972-4344.
A huge entertainment mall on the south end of Denver, Funplex offers two miniature golf courses, 40 bowling lanes, the Starport roller-dance rink, a large video arcade, a special Kids Korner for the under-8 set only, an A&W Restaurant, and more.
Admission: Varies by activity, $2.50–$3.75 (discount packages available for more than one activity).
Open: Memorial Day–Labor Day, daily 11am–10pm; winter, daily 3:30–10pm. Skating Wed–Sun only; bowling closes at midnight.

KIDSPORT, Denver International Airport. Tel. 433-7444.
The Children's Museum operates KidsPort, a discovery center at the airport. It has hands-on educational and recreational exhibits on geography, world travel, and health; a horizontal rock-climbing wall; a "ballroom"; a play space for infants; and a gift shop.
Admission: $1 adults, $2 children, free for kids under 2.
Open: Daily 9am–7pm.

LAKESIDE AMUSEMENT PARK, I-70 and Sheridan Blvd. Tel. 477-1621.
Denver's newer amusement park (it dates from 1910) has 27 major rides, including three roller coasters: the Cyclone, Dragon, and Wild Chipmunk. There's also a 15-ride Kiddie Playland, Crystal Palace, and miniature golf course.
Admission: Gate admission, 75¢; unlimited rides, $6.95 Mon–Fri, $7.95 Sat–Sun and holidays.
Open: May, Sat–Sun and holidays noon–11pm; June–Labor Day, Mon–Fri 6–11pm, Sat–Sun and holidays noon–11pm (Kiddie Playland, Mon–Fri 1–10pm, Sat–Sun and holidays noon–10pm). **Closed:** Labor Day–Apr.

TINY TOWN, 6249 S. Turkey Creek Rd. Tel. 790-9393.

The oldest kid-size village in America is just 30 minutes west of downtown Denver in the Rockies foothills. More than 80 buildings, all built at one-sixth scale, and a working railroad attract more than 60,000 visitors a year. The community was built in 1915 as a stagecoach stop and has come back "from the dead" four times, after a fire and three floods. There's a snack bar and gift shop.

Admission: $2 adults, $1 children under 12; train $1.
Open: Memorial Day–Sept, daily 10am–5pm; May and Oct weekends 10am–4pm. **Closed:** Winter. **Directions:** Drive west on U.S. 285 (Hampden Avenue) and watch for the signs in Turkey Creek Canyon.

WATER WORLD, 90th Ave. at Pecos St., Federal Heights. Tel. 427-SURF.

The largest publicly owned water park in the United States is this complex at the north end of the Denver metropolitan area. The park has pools with oceanlike waves, river rapids for inner-tubing, twisting water slides, a small children's play area, and other attractions—22 in all.

Admission: $13.50 adults, $12.50 children 4–12, free for seniors and children 3 and under.
Open: Memorial Day–Labor Day, Sat–Tues and Thurs 10am–6pm, Wed and Fri 10am–9pm. **Closed:** Winter. **Directions:** Take the Thornton exit (84th Avenue) off I-25 north.

WALKING TOUR — DOWNTOWN DENVER

Start: Denver Information Center, Civic Center Park.
Finish: State Capitol, Civic Center Park.
Time: 2 to 8 hours, depending on how much time you spend shopping, eating, and sightseeing.
Best Times: Any Tuesday through Friday in late spring.

Start your tour of the downtown area at the Denver Information Center of the Denver Metro Convention & Visitors Bureau, opposite Civic Center Park on West Colfax Avenue at 14th Street. After collecting information about the city, cross to:

1. **Civic Center Park,** a 2-square-block oasis featuring a Greek amphitheater, fountains, statues, flower gardens, and 30 different species of trees—two of which (it is said) were originally planted by Abraham Lincoln at his Illinois home.
   Overlooking the park on its east side is the State Capitol. On its south side, from east to west, are the:
2. **Colorado History Museum,** a staircaselike building with exhibits that make the state's colorful history come to life; the Denver Public Library; and the:
3. **Denver Art Museum.** Designed by Gio Pointi of Milan, Italy, the art museum is a 28-sided, 10-story structure that resembles a medieval fortress with a skin of over a million tiny glass tiles. Inside are 35,000 works of art, including the renowned American Indian collection.
   On the west side of Civic Center Park is the:
4. **City and County Building,** decorated in spectacular fashion with a rainbow of colored lights during the Christmas season.
   A block farther west is the:
5. **U.S. Mint.** Modeled in the Italian Renaissance style, the building resembles the Palazzo Riccardi in Florence. Over 60,000 cubic feet of granite and 1,000 tons of steel went into its construction in 1904.
   Cross back over Colfax to the information center, then turn diagonally northwest up 14th Street. Four blocks ahead, on the left, is the:
6. **Colorado Convention Center,** with its impressive, five-story, steplike white facade. Opened in June 1990, the million-square-foot building contains a 7-acre exhibit room and the largest ballroom between Chicago and L.A.

It's another two blocks up 14th to the:

7. **Denver Center for the Performing Arts,** covering four square blocks between 14th Street and Cherry Creek, Champa Street and Arapahoe Street. The complex is entered under a block-long, 80-foot-high glass archway. The center includes seven theaters, the nation's first symphony hall in the round, the world's only voice-research laboratory, even a smoking solar fountain. Free tours are offered even when there's no performance scheduled.

Two more blocks up 14th past the arts center is:

8. **Larimer Square,** Denver's oldest commercial district. The 18 restored turn-of-the-century Victorian buildings contain more than 30 shops and a dozen restaurants and clubs. Colorful awnings, hanging flower baskets, and quiet open courtyards accent the square, once home to such notables as Buffalo Bill Cody and Bat Masterson. Horse-drawn-carriage rides originate here for trips up the 16th Street Mall or through lower downtown. A new addition to Larimer Square is the Champion Brewing Company, with its unmistakable "Home Run Chewing Gum" wall mural.

A walkway at the east corner of Larimer and 15th leads through:

9. **Writer Square,** another shopping-and-dining complex with quaint gas lamps, brick walkways, and outdoor cafés.

At 16th Street, cross to the:

10. **Tabor Center,** a glass-enclosed shopping complex of 70 shops on three levels. In effect a 2-block-long greenhouse (with the Westin Hotel rising out of its midst), the Tabor Center was developed by the Rouse Company, the same firm responsible for Boston's Faneuil Hall, New York's South Street Seaport, and Baltimore's Harborplace.

The Tabor Center is anchored at its east end by the:

11. **D & F Tower,** a city landmark patterned after the campanile of St. Mark's Basilica in Venice, Italy, in 1910. Here, begin a leisurely stroll down the:

12. **16th Street Mall,** with the State Capitol building in the southeast distance as your directional beacon. The $76-million pedestrian path is the finest people-watching spot in the city, from street entertainers to lunching office workers to travelers like yourself. Built of red and gray granite, it is lined with 200 red oak trees, a dozen fountains, festive banners, and a lighting system straight out of *Star Wars*—not to mention the outdoor cafés, restored Victorian buildings, modern skyscrapers, and hundreds of shops, restaurants, and department stores. Through it run sleek European-built shuttle buses, offering free transportation up and down the mall as often as every 90 seconds.

You'll walk seven blocks down 16th Street from the Tabor Center before reaching Tremont Place. Turn left, go one block farther, and across the street, on your right, you'll see the:

13. **Brown Palace Hotel.** One of the most beautiful grande-dame hotels in the United States, it was built in 1892 and features a nine-story atrium lobby topped by a Tiffany stained-glass ceiling. Step into the lobby for a look-see before continuing across Broadway on East 17th Avenue. Go two blocks to Sherman Street, turn right, and proceed two blocks south on Sherman to East Colfax Avenue.

You're back overlooking Civic Center Park, but this time, you're at the:

14. **State Capitol.** If you stand on the 13th step on the west side of the building, you're exactly 5,280 feet—one mile—above sea level. Architects modeled the Colorado capitol after the U.S. Capitol building in Washington, D.C., and used the world's entire supply of rare rose onyx in its interior wainscoting. A winding, 93-step staircase leads to an open-air viewing deck beneath the capitol dome, with a sunny-day panorama from Pikes Peak to the Wyoming border.

ORGANIZED TOURS

Half- and full-day bus tours of Denver and the nearby Rockies are offered by the ubiquitous **Gray Line,** P.O. Box 38667, Denver, CO 80238 (tel. 303/289-2841). A 6-hour tour, leaving the Denver Bus Center at 19th Street and Curtis Street, at 9am,

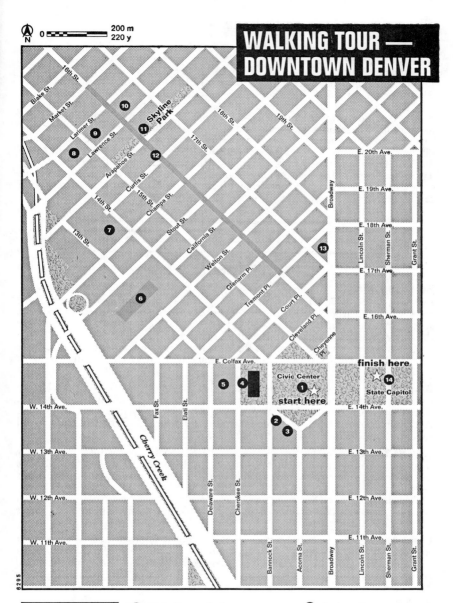

0 ⊨═══ 200 m
220 y

N

Blake St.
16th St.
Market St.
Larimer St.
Lawrence St.
Arapahoe St.
Curtis St.
14th St.
15th St.
Champa St.
13th St.
Stout St.
California St.
Welton St.
Glenarm Pl.
Tremont Pl.
Court Pl.
Cleveland Pl.
Cheyenne Pl.
Skyline Park
17th St.
18th St.
19th St.
Broadway
E. 20th Ave.
E. 19th Ave.
E. 18th Ave.
Lincoln St.
Sherman St.
Grant St.
E. 17th Ave.
E. 16th Ave.
E. Colfax Ave.
Civic Center
start here
finish here
State Capitol
W. 14th Ave.
Fox St.
Elati St.
E. 14th Ave.
W. 13th Ave.
Cherry Creek
Delaware St.
Cherokee St.
E. 13th Ave.
W. 12th Ave.
E. 12th Ave.
W. 11th Ave.
Bannock St.
Acoma St.
Broadway
Lincoln St.
Sherman St.
Grant St.
E. 11th Ave.

6295

Denver
COLORADO

1 Civic Center Park
2 Colorado History Museum
3 Denver Art Museum
4 City and County Building
5 U.S. Mint
6 Colorado Convention Center
7 Denver Center for the Performing Arts
8 Larimer Square
9 Writer Square
10 Tabor Center
11 D & F Tower
12 16th Street Mall
13 Brown Palace Hotel
14 State Capitol

takes in Denver, Red Rocks Park, Buffalo Bill's Grave, and old foothills mining towns. It costs $30 per person.

Highly recommended is the 10-hour Rocky Mountain National Park tour, offered June to September, that takes travelers over the 12,183-foot summit of the park's Trail Ridge Road. Cost is $36. Rates for children are lower.

Back-road mountain tours departing from Denver to remote areas, reached on half- and full-day trips by four-wheel-drive vehicles, show visitors ghost towns, old mining camps, historic wagon trails, and other historic sites. Star treks on mountaintops at night can be arranged, as well as overnight camping and fishing trips. One firm offering these trips year-round is **Best Mountain Tours by the Mountain Men,** 3003 S. Macon Circle, Aurora (tel. 750-5200). Destinations and daily availability vary. Typical rates are $30 per person for a 4½-hour tour, $50 for an all-day summer tour. Customized tour prices are considerably higher. The Mountain Men also provide private charters to the gambling casinos and the ski resorts.

2. SPORTS & RECREATION

SPECTATOR SPORTS

AUTO RACING Bandimere Speedway, 3051 S. Rooney Rd., Morrison (tel. 697-6001 or 697-4870 for a 24-hour recording), is the place to go for drag racing, with races scheduled from April through September. There are special events for high school students, motorcycles, pickup trucks, street cars, and sports cars, plus car shows, swap meets, and even volleyball tournaments.

Colorado National Speedway, at the I-25, Exit 232, 20 minutes north of Denver (tel. 665-4173), has NASCAR Winston Racing and RMMRA Midgets Saturday nights April through September.

BASEBALL The Colorado Rockies, which began life as a National League expansion team in 1993, has taken over the Colorado sports scene with a vengeance. The team is playing at Mile High Stadium, home of the Denver Broncos football team, until its own Coors Field is completed in 1995. For information and tickets, call ROCKIES (tel. 762-5437 or toll free 800/388-7625).

BASKETBALL The Denver Nuggets of the National Basketball Association play their home games at McNichols Sports Arena, 1635 Bryant St. (tel. 893-DUNK). There are 41 home games a year between November and April, with playoffs continuing into June. Ticket prices range from $8.50 to $25.

The University of Denver (tel. 871-2336) plays a competitive college basketball schedule from late November to March, in addition to women's gymnastics, men's hockey, and other sports.

FOOTBALL The Denver Broncos of the National Football League make their home at Mile High Stadium, 1900 Eliot St. (tel. 433-7466), part of a sports complex reached at Exit 210B of I-25. Single seats cost $19 to $30, but home games are sold out months in advance. Tickets go on sale the third week of July, so call early. Your best bet may be to find someone hawking tickets outside the stadium entrance on game day.

You'll have better luck getting into a college game. The University of Colorado Buffaloes in Boulder play in the Big Eight Conference. For ticket information, call 492-8337. Other top college football teams in the area are at Colorado State University in Fort Collins and the Air Force Academy in Colorado Springs.

GREYHOUND RACING The Mile High Greyhound Park, East 62nd Avenue and Colorado Boulevard, Commerce City (tel. 288-1591), has pari-mutuel dog races June to December, Monday through Saturday at 8pm and on Monday, Wednesday, and Saturday at 1pm. Admission is $1; reserved clubhouse seats are $3. When the local dog-racing season ends, offtrack betting from other Colorado greyhound tracks continues.

HORSE RACING Arapahoe Park, 26000 E. Quincy Ave. (tel. 690-2400), has pari-mutuel horse racing from May to September, Fridays, Saturdays, Sundays, and holidays at 1pm, with offtrack betting from other tracks the rest of the year. General admission costs $1; with seats in the dining areas from $3 to $5.

RODEO The National Western Stock Show and Rodeo is held the second and third weeks of January at the Denver Coliseum, 4701 Marion St., and the National Western Complex, at Brighton Boulevard and I-70. With more than $400,000 in prize money, it's considered to be one of the world's richest rodeos. Call 303/295-1660 for a schedule of events and ticket information.

RECREATION

Denver's proximity to the Rocky Mountains makes it possible to spend a day skiing, snowmobiling, horseback riding, hiking, river running, sailing, fishing, hunting, mountain climbing, or rockhounding—and be back in the city by nightfall. There are over 200 miles of jogging and bicycle paths, 100 or more free tennis courts, and over three dozen public golf courses. The city also boasts the world's largest sporting-goods store: Gart Brothers Sports Castle, on Broadway at 10th Avenue (tel. 861-1122). There are 30 other Gart Brothers outlets around the Denver area.

Campsites are easily reached from Denver, as are sites suitable for hang gliding and hot-air ballooning. Campers enjoy many parts of the state, where half the land is in the public domain. Sailing is popular within the city at Sloans Lake and in Washington Park, and the Platte River is clear for many miles of river running in rafts, kayaks, and canoes.

The state and federal agencies, listed in Chapter 1, "Sports & Recreation," can help you with various aspects of outdoor recreation.

BALLOONING You can't beat a hot-air balloon ride for viewing the magnificent Rocky Mountain scenery. Looney Balloons (tel. 979-9476) offers sunrise flights year-round, or you might also try Aero-Cruise Balloon Adventures (tel. 469-1234). Life Cycle Balloon School, Ltd. (tel. 759-3907), offers champagne flights for two.

BICYCLING Denver is crisscrossed everywhere by paved bicycle paths, including a 10-mile stretch along the bank of the South Platte River and along Cherry Creek beside Speer Boulevard. All told, the city has 85 miles of off-road trails for bikers and runners. Bike paths link the city's 205 parks, and many city streets are marked with bike lanes. In all, the city has more than 130 miles of designated bike paths and lanes. Maps and information on bike routes in and beyond the Denver area are available from the Colorado Department of Highways, 4201 E. Arkansas Ave., Room 235, Denver (tel. 757-9313).

Two Wheel Tours, P.O. Box 2655, Littleton (tel. 303/798-4601 or toll free 800/343-8940), offers half- and full-day bicycle tours of Denver, Vail, Mount Evans, and other Rocky Mountain destinations. Tours include breakfast, lunch, and hotel pick up and drop-off.

BOATING Within the Denver city limits, Sloans Lake (West 17th Avenue from Newton Street to Sheridan Boulevard) is a popular spot for punting. More serious boaters enjoy the powerboat marinas at Cherry Creek State Recreation Area, 4201 S. Parker Rd., Aurora (tel. 690-1166), 11 miles from downtown off I-225, and Chatfield State Recreation Area, 11500 N. Roxborough Park Rd., Littleton (tel. 303/794-8508), 16 miles south of downtown Denver off U.S. 85; and the facilities at Barr Lake State Park, 13401 Picadilly Rd., Brighton (tel. 659-6005), 21 miles northeast of downtown via I-76. Motors aren't permitted on Barr Lake, so it's especially enjoyed by sailors and board sailors.

For information on other boating opportunities, consult the Colorado State Parks, the National Park Service, or the U.S. Forest Service. (See Chapter 1, "Sports & Recreation," for addresses and telephone numbers.)

BOWLING Two of Denver's biggest bowling centers are the Celebrity Sports Center, 888 S. Colorado Blvd. (tel. 757-3321), with 80 lanes and automatic scoring, open daily from 8:30am to midnight; and the Funplex, 9670 W. Coal Mine Ave.,

Littleton (tel. 972-8111), with 40 lanes, open daily from 3:30pm to midnight (in summer, 11am to midnight).

FISHING   A couple of good bets in the metropolitan area are Chatfield Reservoir, with trout, bass, and panfish, and Cherry Creek Reservoir, which boasts trout, walleye pike, bass, and crappie (see the addresses under "Boating," above). In all, there are more than 7,100 miles of streams and over 2,000 reservoirs and lakes in Colorado: for information, consult the Colorado Division of Parks and Outdoor Recreation; the Colorado Division of Wildlife; or the U.S. Fish and Wildlife Service. For information on licenses, see Chapter 1, "Sports & Recreation."

A couple of sporting goods stores that can provide more detailed information are Uncle Milty's Tackle Box, 4811 S. Broadway, Englewood (tel. 789-3775), especially for local lakes and streams; and Flyfisher Ltd., 252 Clayton St. (tel. 322-5014), particularly for higher mountain lakes and streams.

Flyfishing Services, Inc. (tel. 979-3077), offers half- and full-day fishing trips within two hours of Denver, including transportation.

GOLF   You'll often hear it said throughout the Front Range that you can play golf at least 320 days a year—that the sun always seems to be shining, and even when it snows, what little sticks melts quickly. With the resultant demand, the city of Denver operates seven municipal golf courses (for information on any of them, call the Denver Department of Parks and Recreation, tel. 964-2563): the City Park Golf Course, East 25th Avenue and York Street (tel. 295-4420); Evergreen Golf Course, Evergreen (tel. 674-4128); Harvard Golf Course (par 3), East Iliff Avenue and South Clarkson Street (tel. 698-4078); Kennedy Golf Course, 10500 E. Hampden Ave. (tel. 751-0311); Overland Golf Course, South Santa Fe Drive and Jewell Avenue (tel. 698-4975); Wellshire Golf Course, 3333 S. Colorado Blvd. (tel. 692-5636); and Willis Case Golf Course, West 50th Avenue and Vrain Street (tel. 458-4877). Greens fees for nonresidents at city courses are $16 for 18 holes, $10 for 9 holes, and $6 for the par-3 Harvard course.

There are many more privately owned golf clubs and country clubs in the greater Denver area, many of which offer reciprocal memberships with clubs in other cities. Probably the best known is the exclusive Castle Pines Golf Club (tel. 688-6000) at Castle Rock, midway between Denver and Colorado Springs off I-25; it's the site each August of a major PGA tournament.

For information on private clubs and other golf information, contact the following: Colorado Golf Association, 5655 S. Yosemite St., Suite 101, Englewood, CO 80111 (tel. 303/779-4563); or Colorado Golf Resort Association, 2110 S. Ash, Denver 80222 (tel. 303/699-4653).

HIKING/BACKPACKING   The newly created Colorado Trail is a hiking, horse, and mountain-biking route winding 500 miles from Denver to Durango. Opened in 1988, it took 15 years to create with volunteer labor. For information, write P.O. Box 260876, Lakewood, CO 80226 (tel. 303/526-0809).

For hikes specific to the Denver area, contact the city Department of Parks and Recreation (tel. 964-2500) for information on the 18 Denver Mountain Parks. Nearby state parks well known for their hiking trails are Roxborough State Park, 10 miles south of Littleton (tel. 973-3959), and Golden Gate State Park, 16 miles northwest of Golden (tel. 592-1502). Or contact any of the following state or federal agencies: Colorado Division of Parks and Outdoor Recreation, Colorado Division of Wildlife, National Park Service, U.S. Bureau of Land Management, and U.S. Forest Service. For topographic maps, consult either the Colorado Geological Survey or the U.S. Geological Survey. (See Chapter 1, "Sports & Recreation.")

HORSEBACK RIDING   Horse enthusiasts can find a mount at Stockton's Plum Creek Stables, 7479 W. Titan Rd., Littleton (tel. 791-1966), near Chatfield Reservoir 15 miles south of downtown. Guided rides, by appointment only, are $12 per hour; children must be at least 7. Stockton's also offers hayrides, barbecue picnics, and wintertime sleighrides.

Detailed information on longer trips can be obtained from the Colorado Outfitters Association; see Chapter 1, "Sports & Recreation."

HUNTING   There's no hunting in the immediate Denver area, but opportunities abound in the foothills and plains. For information, consult the Colorado Division of Wildlife, Colorado Outfitters Association, or U.S. Fish and Wildlife Service. (See Chapter 1, "Sports & Recreation.")

OFF-ROAD VEHICLES   The best source of information is the Colorado Assocation of Four-Wheel Drive Clubs, P.O. Box 1413, Wheat Ridge, CO 80034 (tel. 303/343-0646). The Colorado Division of Parks and Outdoor Recreation, U.S. Bureau of Land Management, and U.S. Forest Service can also offer suggestions. (See Chapter 1, "Sports & Recreation.")

RECREATION CENTERS   The Denver Department of Parks and Recreation (tel. 964-2500) operates 30 rec centers around the city. Daily guest passes are available at many of them, at a price of $4 for adult nonresidents and $2 for anyone 17 or younger. Facilities may include basketball courts, indoor or outdoor swimming pools, weight rooms, and fitness classes. The following may be most convenient for out-of-town visitors: Eisenhower Recreation Center, 4300 E. Dartmouth Ave. (tel. 692-5650), with an outdoor pool; Martin Luther King, Jr., Recreation Center, 3880 Newport St. (tel. 331-4034), with an indoor pool and racquetball; 20th Street Recreation Center, 1011 20th St., between Arapahoe Street and Curtis Street (tel. 295-4430), with an indoor pool; and Washington Park Recreation Center, 701 S. Franklin St. (tel. 698-4962), with an indoor pool.

Major private athletic clubs in downtown Denver include the Athletic Club at Denver Place, 1849 Curtis St. (tel. 294-9494), with an indoor pool, gymnasium, indoor track, squash and racquetball courts, weight and exercise room, cardiovascular equipment, aerobics classes, and massage; and the International Athletic Center, 1630 Welton St. (tel. 623-2100), with a major weight and cardiovascular training center, regular aerobics classes, and racquetball and squash courts.

RIVER RAFTING   No one seriously rafts the South Platte through Denver (though there *is* a human-made kayak chute in downtown Denver). But the river is rafted nearer its source, along with many other rivers around the state during the mid-May to Labor Day season. Among rafting companies with headquarters in the Denver area are:

Whitewater Encounters, 1422 S. Chambers Circle, Aurora, CO 80012 (tel. 303/751-0161 or toll free 800/530-8362). Rates are $33 to $59 for half-day or full-day trips on the Arkansas River.

For more information on rafting, contact the Colorado River Outfitters Association, P.O. Box 1662, Buena Vista, CO 81211 (tel. 303/369-4632).

SKIING   The nearest ski resorts to Denver are Eldora Mountain Resort, 45 miles west via Boulder (tel. 440-8700); Loveland Basin and Valley, 56 miles west via I-70 (tel. 571-5580); and Winter Park, 73 miles west via I-70 and U.S. 40 (tel. 892-0961). Eldora and Winter Park boast nordic as well as alpine terrain. All areas are discussed in detail in subsequent chapters of this book.

Full information on skiing in the state can be obtained from Colorado Ski Country USA, 1560 Broadway, Suite 1440, Denver, CO 80202 (tel. 837-0793), or the Colorado Cross Country Ski Association, Box 1336, Winter Park, CO 80482 (tel. toll free 800/869-4560).

Some useful Denver telephone numbers for skiers: ski-area information (tel. 831-7669), weather report (tel. 398-3964), road conditions (tel. 639-1111).

SWIMMING   If your hotel doesn't have a pool, visit a recreation center or athletic club (see above).

TENNIS   The Denver Department of Parks and Recreation (tel. 964-2500) manages 139 tennis courts, 49 of them lit for night play. The most popular are in City Park, Berkeley Park, Green Valley Park, Washington Park, and Sloan Lake Park. For more information on tennis, contact the Colorado Tennis Association, 1201 S. Parker Rd., Suite 200, Denver (tel. 695-4116).

3. SAVVY SHOPPING

THE SHOPPING SCENE

Most Denver visitors who are afoot concentrate their shopping along the 16th Street Mall and adjacent areas—including Larimer Square, the Shops at Tabor Center, Writer Square, and (just slightly farther away) Tivoli Denver.

For those with a vehicle, there are many more options, first and foremost of which is the huge Cherry Creek Shopping Center south of downtown. There are many more suburban shopping malls, as well.

Business hours vary from store to store and from shopping center to shopping center. In general, it's safe to say that shops will be open Monday through Friday from 10am to 9pm, on Saturday from 10am to 6pm, and on Sunday from noon to 5pm.

SHOPPING A TO Z

ANTIQUES

ANTIQUE GUILD, 1298 S. Broadway. Tel. 722-3359.
More than 250 dealers under one roof make this an antiques hunter's dream. You'll find fine European hardwood furniture, American primitive and pine furniture, china, glassware, stained glass, textiles, prints, objects in art deco and art nouveau styles, and much more. Open seven days a week.

ARTS & CRAFTS

CORE NEW ART SPACE, 1412 Wazee St. Tel. 571-4831.
This lower downtown cooperative gallery features very contemporary, avant-garde, and "cutting-edge" art. Open Thursday, Saturday, and Sunday from noon to 5pm, and Friday from noon to 10pm.

DENVER COOPERATIVE ARTS CENTER, 720 E. 18th Ave. Tel. 839-9439.
Located uptown near Restaurant Row, the co-op offers a representation of many area artists at highly reasonable prices.

GALLERY ONE, 1512 Larimer St. Tel. 629-5005.
Paintings, graphics, and sculptures by internationally recognized artists are offered at Writer Square. Open Monday through Saturday from 10am to 9pm and on Sunday from noon to 5pm. Also in Cherry Creek North Shopping Center.

NATIVE AMERICAN TRADING COMPANY, 1301 Bannock St. Tel. 534-0771.
This gallery offers weavings, ceramics, baskets, jewelry, and other Native American artifacts, as well as some contemporary paintings. Appropriately, it's across the street from the Denver Art Museum. Open Monday through Friday from 10am to 6pm and on Saturday from 11am to 4pm.

PIRATE: A CONTEMPORARY ART OASIS, 3659 Navajo St. Tel. 458-6058.
Across the South Platte in northwest Denver, Pirate treads the cutting edge in work of all types. Open on Friday from 7 to 10pm and on Saturday and Sunday from noon to 5pm.

JOAN ROBEY GALLERY, 939 Broadway. Tel. 892-9600.
Part of a four-gallery downtown complex known as Broadway Central Galleries,

the Robey Gallery specializes in three-dimensional sculpture and wall art. Open Monday through Friday from 10am to 6pm and on Saturday from 10am to 4pm.

CARL SIPLE GALLERY, 1401 17th St., at Market. Tel. 292-1401.

Established national and emerging regional artists are represented at this beautiful gallery in lower downtown. Open Monday through Friday from 11am to 5pm and Saturday from noon to 4pm.

THE SQUASH BLOSSOM, 1428 Larimer St. Tel. 572-7979.

Southwestern-style paintings, Hispanic folk art and furniture, and jewelry, pottery, and weavings by Pueblo and Navajo peoples are presented at Larimer Square.

TURNER GALLERY, 301 University Blvd. Tel. 355-1828.

Colorado's oldest gallery specializes in traditional art forms, including oils and Colorado landscapes by contemporary and deceased American and European painters. Its collection also includes etchings, engravings, and antique botanicals. Open on Monday from 10am to 4pm and Tuesday through Saturday from 9am to 5:30pm.

BOOKS

TATTERED COVER BOOKSTORE, 2955 E. First Ave., opposite Cherry Creek Shopping Center. Tel. 322-7727 or toll free 800/833-9327.

This bookstore is so big it provides maps to help you find your way through its maze of shelves, which contain just about every book anybody could possibly want. There are comfortable chairs placed strategically throughout the building for those who want to check out the first chapter before buying or to rest up after a hike to the fourth floor. The store also has an extensive selection of newspapers and magazines, a bargain book section, free gift wrapping, disabled access to all four floors via elevator, mail order, and out-of-print search services. Storytelling takes place in the children's section each Tuesday at 11am and Saturday at 10:30am. Open Monday through Saturday from 9:30am to 9pm and Sunday from 10am to 6pm.

DEPARTMENT STORES

FOLEY'S, at Cherry Creek Shopping Center. Tel. 333-8555.

The Rocky Mountain region's largest retailer sells everything from clothing to kitchenware to sporting goods to children's toys. There are several stores in the Denver area, mainly in shopping malls.

JOSLIN'S, 16th Street Mall, at Curtis St. Tel. 534-0441.

Denver's oldest department store specializes in brand-name merchandise at value prices.

DISCOUNT SHOPPING

CASTLE ROCK FACTORY SHOPS, I-25, Exit 1184, about 20 minutes south of Denver. Tel. 688-2800.

This outlet mall between Denver and Colorado Springs has more than 50 manufacturer's stores, including Corning/Revere, Levi's, Van Heusen, Bass, Boston Traders, Guess, Farberware, Woolrich, and Toy Liquidators, plus a food court. Although many prices are no better than you'll find during a sale at your local mall or discount store, there's a good selection and a few real bargains, especially on end-of-season items and irregulars. Open Monday through Saturday from 9am to 9pm and Sunday from 11am to 6pm.

FASHIONS

BANANA REPUBLIC, 535 16th Street Mall. Tel. 595-8877.

This travel and safari merchandiser has developed a name for functional but attractive men's and women's wear.

FASHION BAR, 16th Street Mall, at Tremont Place. Tel. 620-9811.

Women's and men's clothing in a wide range of styles and prices are the specialty of Fashion Bars, found throughout Colorado.

LAWRENCE COVELL, The Shops at Tabor Center. Tel. 595-8300.
This upscale shop offers contemporary men's and women's fashions, including designer clothing by Giorgio Armani, Hugo Boss, Valentino, and Byblos.

MILLER STOCKMAN WESTERN WEAR, 1600 California St., at 16th Street Mall. Tel. 825-5339.
In business since 1918, this purveyor of western wear stocks more than 400 pairs of cowboy boots.

SHEPLERS, 8500 E. Orchard Rd., Tech Center. Tel. 773-3311.
The world's largest western store and catalog merchant sells every piece of clothing you'll need. Also at 10300 Bannock St., west off I-25, Northglenn (tel. 450-9999).

FOOD

ALFALFA'S, 201 University Blvd. Tel. 320-0700.
Already an institution in the Denver area, this huge natural-foods store—50,000 square feet in area—helps perpetuate Coloradans' healthy life-styles. No food sold here contains any artificial flavoring or preservative, nor was any grown using pesticides, chemicals, or other additives. There's a juice and health-food bar as well. This Cherry Creek–area store opened in 1990; others are in Boulder and Littleton.

STEPHANY'S CHOCOLATES, 4969 Colorado Blvd., north of I-70. Tel. 355-1522.
Denver's largest manufacturer and wholesaler of gourmet confections is best known for the Denver Mint and Colorado Almond Toffee. In business for more than three decades, it offers tours by appointment. There are several retail outlets around the city.

GIFTS & SOUVENIRS

COLORADO HISTORY MUSEUM STORE, 1300 Broadway. Tel. 866-4993.
This museum shop carries unique made-in-Colorado gifts and souvenirs, including Native American jewelry and sand paintings, plus an excellent selection of western books.

EARTH WORKS, LTD., 1421-B Larimer Square. Tel. 825-3390.
Handcrafted work by Colorado artisans is sold here, including pottery, jewelry, sculptures, photos, and clothing. Open seven days a week.

LOKSTOK 'N BAREL, 1421 Larimer St. Tel. 825-3436.
This Larimer Square outlet sells a variety of western and wildlife bronze sculptures, aspen vases, jewelry, antique toy reproductions, and more.

JEWELRY

JOHN ATENCIO, Writer Square, 1512 Larimer St. Tel. 534-4277.
An award-winning designer, Atencio sells one-of-a-kind, handcrafted gold jewelry. Many pieces are set with precious or semiprecious stones. Open Monday through Thursday from 10am to 5:30pm and on Friday and Saturday from 10am to 5pm.

SHALAKO EAST, 3023 E. Second Ave. Tel. 320-5482.
Native American jewelry is the specialty of this store, which also carries a variety

of arts-and-crafts products. Open Monday through Saturday from 10am to 9pm and on Sunday from noon to 6pm.

MALLS & SHOPPING CENTERS

CHERRY CREEK SHOPPING CENTER, 3000 E. First Ave., between University Blvd. and Steele St. Tel. 388-3900.
Saks Fifth Avenue, Neiman Marcus, Foley's, and Lord & Taylor anchor this deluxe million-square-foot mall, with more than 130 shops, restaurants, and services, including an eight-screen movie theater. Across the street is Cherry Creek North, an upscale neighborhood retail area. Open Monday through Friday from 10am to 9pm, Saturday from 10am to 7pm, and Sunday from noon to 6pm.

LARIMER SQUARE, 1400 block of Larimer St. Tel. 534-2367.
This restored quarter of old Denver (see "The Top Attractions" in "Attractions," above) includes numerous art galleries, boutiques, restaurants, and nightclubs. The Market is an excellent place to have breakfast or lunch or sip on an espresso. Most shops are open Monday through Friday from 10am to 7pm, Saturday from 10am to 6pm, and on Sunday from noon to 5pm. Restaurants and nightclubs vary.

THE SHOPS AT TABOR CENTER, 16th Street Mall, between Larimer and Arapahoe Sts. Tel. 534-2141.
Some 70 specialty shops are in this 2-block, glass-enclosed galleria. The Bridge Market offers a changing showcase of gifts and collectibles, while the PicNic Court has over a dozen dining opportunities. Open Monday through Saturday from 10am to 9pm and on Sunday from noon to 5pm.

TIVOLI DENVER, 901 Larimer St., at Auraria Pkwy. Tel. 629-8712.
Transformed from a 19th-century brewery (see "Architectural Highlights" in "Attractions," above), this exciting theme mall combines shops, restaurants, and nightclubs into one cohesive whole. Shops are open Monday through Saturday from 10am to 9pm and on Sunday from noon to 5pm. A free shuttle trolley runs throughout the day between Civic Center Park, Larimer Square, and Tivoli Denver.

MARKETS

MILE HIGH FLEA MARKET, 7007 E. 88th Ave., at I-76, Henderson. Tel. 289-4656.
Though it's some 15 miles northeast of downtown Denver, this huge market attracts over a million shoppers a year to its 80 paved acres. Besides closeouts, garage sales, and seasonal merchandise, it has more than a dozen places to eat and snack. Open year-round, on Wednesday, Saturday, and Sunday from 6am to 5pm. Admission is $2 Saturday to Sunday, $1 Wednesday, free for children under 12.

4. EVENING ENTERTAINMENT

Denver's performing arts and nightlife scene, an important part of life in this sophisticated western city, is anchored by the 4-square-block, $80-million Denver Performing Arts Complex, located downtown just a few blocks from major hotels. The complex contains nine theaters, a concert hall, and the nation's first symphony hall in the round; it is home to the Colorado Symphony, Colorado Ballet, Opera Colorado, and the Denver Center for the Performing Arts, the latter an umbrella organization for resident and touring theater companies.

In all, Denver has 30 theaters, more than 100 cinemas, and dozens of concert halls, nightclubs, discos, and bars. Numerous clubs offer country-and-western music; jazz, rock, and comedy acts are also popular.

Current entertainment listings can be found in special Friday-morning sections of the two daily newspapers, the *Denver Post* and the *Rocky Mountain News*. *Westword*, a weekly newspaper distributed free throughout the city every Wednesday, has perhaps the best listings of all; it focuses on arts, entertainment, and local politics.

Tickets for nearly all major entertainment and sporting events can be obtained from **TicketMaster** (tel. 290-TIXS for information). Credit-card orders can be placed on American Express, Discover, MasterCard, or VISA. There are cash-only TicketMaster outlets at selected Gart Brothers sporting goods stores (including 10th Street and Broadway) and Sound Warehouses. The agency adds a $3 charge to every ticket, in addition to the 10% city seat tax.

The **Ticket Bus,** an English double-decker on the 16th Street Mall at Curtis Street, sells tickets on a cash-only basis for many live theater performances as well as all events sold through TicketMaster. Half-price tickets may be available on the day of the performance. The Ticket Bus is open Monday through Friday from 10am to 6pm and on Saturday from 11am to 3pm.

Discount tickets are often available for midweek and matinee performances.

THE PERFORMING ARTS

MAJOR PERFORMING ARTS COMPANIES

Classical Music & Opera

COLORADO SYMPHONY ORCHESTRA, Denver Performing Arts Complex, 1031 13th St. Tel. 98 MUSIC.

Home for this international-caliber orchestra is Boettcher Concert Hall—the nation's first symphony hall in the round. Huge discs suspended from the ceiling help create perfect acoustics. The orchestra's classical concerts are interspersed with pops concerts featuring top touring celebrities.

Concerts are scheduled Thursday through Saturday evenings and Sunday afternoon. During the summer season, the orchestra makes outdoor appearances at the Fiddler's Green Amphitheatre and other outdoor and indoor venues.

DENVER CHAMBER ORCHESTRA, 1616 Glenarm Place, Suite 1360. Tel. 825-4911.

Celebrating its 25th anniversary in 1994, this 38-member chamber orchestra, under conductor Paul Lustig, performs at Trinity Methodist Church, 18th Avenue and Broadway, and the Arvada Center for the Arts and Humanities.

OPERA COLORADO, 695 S. Colorado Blvd., Suite 20. Tel. 778-6464.

Internationally renowned singers take the lead roles each spring and fall. Three operas (twelve performances) are performed, with English subtitles, at the Boettcher Concert Hall in the Denver Performing Arts Complex in spring and Temple Hoyne Buell Theatre in fall. The schedule typically is three nights—a Tuesday, Friday, and Saturday—at 8pm, followed by a 2pm Sunday matinee.

Prices: Tickets, $15–$70.

Theater Companies

DENVER CENTER FOR THE PERFORMING ARTS, Denver Performing Arts Complex, 1245 Champa St. Tel. 893-4000 or 893-DCPA for recorded information.

An umbrella organization for resident and touring theater, youth outreach, and conservatory training, the DCPA includes the following:

Denver Center Theatre Company, the largest professional resident theater company in the Rockies region. With 40 artists on its payroll, the troupe performs 8 to 12 plays in repertory from late fall to early spring in all four theaters of the Helen Bonfils Theatre Complex (tel. 893-4100). The company produces classical and contemporary dramas, innovative revivals of musicals, and premieres of new plays.

Associated with the company is the National Theatre Conservatory, chartered by Congress in 1984, an institute of advanced theatrical education.

Denver Center Productions includes the Robert Garner/Center Attractions, which brings touring Best of Broadway shows like *Phantom of the Opera* and *Miss Saigon* and many Broadway-bound musicals, to the Auditorium Theatre and Temple Hoyne Buell Theatre.

The Denver Center Recording and Research Center does pioneering research on the voice, including environmental, physiological, and psychological effects.

Prices: Denver Center Theatre Company prices vary according to performance, $15–$25; Robert Garner/Center Attractions, $15–$60.

Dance Companies

COLORADO BALLET, 999 18th St., Suite 1645. Tel. 298-0677.

The city's premier professional resident ballet company performs in the Auditorium Theatre at the Denver Performing Arts Complex. The classical program always includes *The Nutcracker* during the Christmas season.

CLEO PARKER ROBINSON DANCE ENSEMBLE, 119 23rd St. Tel. 295-1759.

A highly acclaimed multicultural modern dance ensemble, the Cleo Parker Robinson group performs in its own Shorter Church Building in the Five Points neighborhood north of downtown. It offers a varied selection of performances each year, many on tour.

MAJOR CONCERT HALLS & ALL-PURPOSE AUDITORIUMS

ARVADA CENTER FOR THE ARTS AND HUMANITIES, 6901 Wadsworth Blvd., Arvada. Tel. 431-3080.

This multidisciplinary arts center is in use almost every day of the year for performances by its resident theater company; concert music and dance; historical museum and art-gallery exhibitions; and community education programs. The main auditorium seats 800.

The center is open Monday through Friday from 9am to 10pm, on Saturday from 9am to 5pm, and on Sunday from 1 to 5pm. Call for information on specific programs.

DENVER PERFORMING ARTS COMPLEX, 14th and Curtis Sts. Tel. 640-2862 or 893-4100 for box office.

Covering four square blocks in downtown Denver from Cherry Creek to 14th Street and Champa Street to Arapahoe Street, the Performing Arts Complex is impressive even to those not attending a performance. Free guided tours of the complex are offered by appointment.

Components include the Helen G. Bonfils Theatre Complex (tel. 893-4000), with four theaters seating 157 to 547; the state-of-the-art Temple Hoyne Buell Theatre (tel. 640-2862), seating 2,830; the Auditorium Theatre (tel. 640-2862), seating 2,060; and the Galleria Theatre (tel. 893-4000), seating 240. It also contains the impressive Boettcher Concert Hall (tel. 640-2862), seating 2,634 for music-in-the-round performances of symphony and opera, as well as a restaurant and shopping promenade.

FIDDLER'S GREEN AMPHITHEATRE, 6350 Greenwood Plaza Blvd., Englewood. Tel. 741-5000.

Outdoor summer concerts at the Museum of Outdoor Arts feature national and international stars in rock, jazz, classical, and country music. There's also a pops subscription series presented by the Colorado Symphony Orchestra. The amphitheater has 7,500 reserved seats and room for another 10,500 on its spacious lawn. It's open May to September.

MCNICHOLS ARENA, 1635 Bryant St. Tel. 640-7300.

Though this arena beside Mile High Stadium is home to the National Basketball Association's Denver Nuggets much of the year, it's also a perfect locale for concerts and other shows—many of which are moved here from outdoor amphitheaters when weather intervenes. There's seating for 18,500.

PARAMOUNT THEATRE, 1631 Glenarm Place. Tel. 534-8336.

A historic-preservation group bought this impressive early 20th-century downtown theater in 1978 and returned its gilded columns and emblazoned walls to their former glory. Now the 2,054-seat theater is a wonderful place to enjoy an eclectic series of jazz concerts, pop and folk performances, high-brow lectures, and films like the annual Warren Miller ski movies.

RED ROCKS AMPHITHEATRE, Hogback Rd., Morrison. Tel. 640-7300.
Denver's favorite venue for top-name outdoor summer concerts is set in the Rocky Mountain foothills, 12 miles from Denver via I-70 west. The amphitheater is flanked by 400-foot-high red sandstone rocks, and at night, with the lights of Denver spread across the horizon, the atmosphere is magical.

The Beatles performed here, as have top symphony orchestras from around the world plus Paul Simon, Sting, Lyle Lovett, and Merle Haggard.

The amphitheater seats 9,000; only 2,173 of which are reserved.

THEATERS

AVENUE THEATER, 2119 E. 17th Ave. Tel. 321-5925.
Off-Broadway plays and musicals are presented in an intimate 100-seat theater. The company is best known locally for *Chicken Lips,* an improvisational comedy.

EL CENTRO SU TEATRO, 4725 High St. Tel. 296-0219.
A Hispanic theater and cultural center, El Centro presents bilingual productions on a regular basis.

EULIPIONS CULTURAL CENTER, 2715 Welton St. Tel. 295-6814.
This multicultural theater in the Five Points neighborhood specializes in works by African American playwrights. It seats 300.

GERMINAL STATE, 44th and Alcott Sts. Tel. 455-7108.
In this 100-seat theater, plays by modern playwrights, such as Brecht, Albee, and Pinter, are presented.

DINNER THEATERS

THE COUNTRY DINNER PLAYHOUSE, 6875 S. Clinton St., Englewood. Tel. 799-1410.
A preshow buffet dinner is followed by live Broadway musicals and other productions, like *Steel Magnolias* and *It's a Wonderful Life.* The playhouse seats 481. Shows are Tuesday through Sunday nights, with matinees on Saturday and Sunday.

THE CLUB & MUSIC SCENE
COMEDY CLUBS

COMEDY WORKS, 1226 15th St. Tel. 595-3637.
This Larimer Square Club, going strong since 1981, is packed Tuesday through Sunday evenings, with various touring big-name acts, many whom have appeared on HBO, Showtime, and other television specials. Roseanne Arnold performed here early in her career, as did Jay Leno, Jerry Seinfeld, and Judy Tenuta. Call for reservations.
Admission: $5–$10.

THE COMEDY CLUB, 10015 E. Hampden Ave., at Havana St. Tel. 368-8900.
National headliners often make their way to this club, located just within Denver's southwestern city limits. The club is open Wednesday through Sunday evenings. Reservations are suggested.
Admission: $5–$8.

COUNTRY MUSIC

THE GRIZZLY ROSE, 5450 N. Valley Hwy. Tel. 295-1330.
Consistently rated as the top country-and-western dance club in the area, this huge dance hall is located at Exit 215 of I-25. There's a 5,000-square-foot dance floor beneath a 1-acre roof, and it draws national acts like Garth Brooks, Willie Nelson,

and Tanya Tucker. Bands perform every night of the week. Sunday is family night and is reserved for local entertainers. The café serves a full-service menu.
Admission: $3–$15.

ROCK

HERMAN'S HIDEAWAY, 1578 S. Broadway, near Iowa Ave. Tel. 777-5840.
Readers of the *Rocky Mountain News* named Herman's the best place to hear original music by bands on their way up. Open daily, there's live music Wednesday through Saturday nights, featuring contemporary rock groups such as the Subdudes and reggae from the likes of the Healers.
Admission: $2–$15, depending on band.

I-BEAM, 1427 Larimer St. Tel. 534-2326.
A downtown rock emporium on Larimer Square, the I-Beam features live rock bands, occasional jazz, and deejays playing Top-40 dance tunes nightly. There are also billiard tables.
Admission: Free, or about $5, depending on band.

JIMMY'S GRILLE, 320 S. Birch St., at Leetsdale. Tel. 322-5334.
If you're looking for live reggae, this is the place to go, at least on Thursday, Friday, and Saturday nights. Other nights you might catch blues, jazz, or whoever might be in town, but it's always live. Jimmy's also has drink and Tex-Mex food specials galore and special events such as the annual pig roast in May. Denverites consider this the best place in town to party.
Admission: Free to $5, depending on band.

JAZZ, BLUES & FOLK MUSIC

EL CHAPULTEPEC, 1962 Market St. Tel. 295-9126.
By 10pm on a weekend night, it's almost impossible to get through the door here. There's no room to dance, and you can hardly hear the music over the buzz of the crowd, but jazz at El Chapultepec, on the edge of lower downtown, has become a sort of late-night institution in Denver. Open seven nights a week.
Admission: Free.

FALCONE'S, 1096 S. Gaylord St., at 11th Ave. Tel. 777-0707.
This lively little club in the Washington Park neighborhood presents live jazz Wednesday through Saturday nights. Open daily except Monday from 5:30pm to 2am.
Admission: Two-drink minimum per person.

THE MERCURY CAFE, 2199 California St., at 22nd St. Tel. 294-9281.
It's hard to classify the Mercury in any one genre of music. There's always live something Wednesday through Sunday, but the offerings range from avant-garde jazz to classical violin and harp to down-home blues to South American folk to progressive rock. Admission varies with performer.

DANCE CLUBS & DISCOS

ALFIE'S, 9700 E. Iliff Ave., near S. Parker Rd. Tel. 752-4990.
Deejays play alternative music nightly for dancing. A big draw here is the domestic bottled beer special: just $1, nightly from 5 to 11pm. Alfie's opens daily at 5pm.
Admission: $1 Fri–Sat.

THE BAR SCENE

The first permanent structure ever built on the site of modern Denver was a saloon, and the city hasn't lost a step in the century and a quarter since. Today there are sports bars, brew pubs, outdoor café bars, English pubs, Old West saloons, city-overlook bars, art deco bars, even bars that don't serve alcohol.

Glendale, an enclave completely surrounded by southeastern Denver where

Colorado Boulevard crosses Cherry Creek, has long been recognized as headquarters for Denver's singles scene. An unusual zoning situation has resulted in over a dozen drinking establishments built into a small, concentrated area. Other "strips" can be found along East Hampden Boulevard, South Monaco Parkway, and along East and West Colfax Avenue.

Following are some popular bars and pubs:

BULL & BUSH, 4700 S. Cherry Creek Dr., Glendale. Tel. 759-0333.

This re-creation of a famous London pub offers good imported beer always, and Sunday Dixieland jazz by regional groups like the Boom Town Stompers.

CRUISE ROOM BAR, in the Oxford Alexis Hotel, 1600 17th St., at Wynkoop St. Tel. 628-5400.

Modeled after a bar aboard the *Queen Mary* in the 1930s, this charming hotel lounge, recently restored to its art deco best, has all the atmosphere of an oceangoing cruise ship.

JACKSON'S HOLE SALOON, 990 S. Oneida St., at E. Leetsdale Dr. Tel. 388-2883.

This huge sports bar boasts more than 100 television sets for every satellite game that any viewer could possibly want. "We cover the world in sports" is its motto. Couch potatoes also rave about its hamburgers. Other Jackson's Holes are on Kipling Street at Sixth Avenue in Lakewood (tel. 238-3000), west of downtown, and in Thornton Town Center at 1001 Grant St., Thornton (tel. 457-2100), north of Denver.

MILE HIGH SALOON, 4451 E. Virginia Ave., Glendale. Tel. 399-5606.

Sensitively termed "a gentlemen's cabaret," this is in fact Denver's most sophisticated strip bar. Besides the beautiful women who work here, it offers a full dinner menu and plenty of TVs for men who'd rather watch football.

ROCK BOTTOM BREWERY, 1001 16th St. Tel. 534-7676.

Brewing beer is fun, but sampling it is more fun. Rock Bottom Brewery should definitely be included in your "pub crawl." There's a great view of the brewing equipment, and if you're there Saturday between 11am and 2pm there are tours and tastings. Rock Bottom offers a standard brew pub menu, starting at $6, that includes a half-pound burger, buffalo fajitas, and chicken potpie, plus dinner entrées like grilled fresh salmon and filet mignon.

WYNKOOP BREWING CO., 1634 18th St., at Wynkoop St. Tel. 297-2700.

This very popular microbrewery, located in a renovated 1899 mercantile building, was Denver's first microbrewery. Tours are given Saturdays from 1 to 5pm, and half-gallon and gallon containers of beer are available to go. There's a billiards hall and cabaret, plus a good restaurant (see "Dining," in Chapter 4). For nonbeer drinkers, the Wynkoop has some of the best lemonade you'll find in Denver.

5. EASY EXCURSIONS FROM DENVER

Golden, Georgetown, Idaho Springs, and Central City make up the fabled Gold Circle. The first big strikes came almost simultaneously near Central City and Idaho Springs in 1859. The Gold Circle towns boomed and died first with gold, then with silver . . . and now they're experiencing a third boom with tourism.

GOLDEN

Golden, 12 miles west of downtown Denver via U.S. 6 or Colo. 58 off I-70, is better known for its Coors Brewery (founded in 1873) and the Colorado School of Mines (established in 1874) than for its years as territorial capital. About 15,000 people now live in the small city at the foot of the Rockies.

Major annual events are Buffalo Bill Days, the third weekend of July, Oktoberfest in September, and the Jefferson County Fair in October. For tourist information, contact the **Greater Golden Area Chamber of Commerce,** 611 14th St. (P.O. Box 1035), Golden, CO 80402 (tel. 303/279-3113).

WHAT TO SEE & DO

Historic downtown Golden focuses around the Territorial Capitol in the Loveland Building at 12th Street and Washington Avenue. Built in 1861, it housed the first state legislature from 1863 to 1867, when the capital was moved to Denver. Today it contains the Silverheels Restaurant. The Armory, 13th Street and Arapahoe Street, is the largest cobblestone structure in the United States; 3,300 wagonloads of stone and quartz were used in its construction. The Rock Flour Mill Warehouse, Eighth Street and Cheyenne Street, dates from 1863; it was built with red granite from nearby Golden Gate Canyon and has original cedar beams and wooden floors.

The **Golden DAR Pioneer Museum,** 911 10th St. in the Golden Municipal Building (tel. 278-7151), has an impressive collection of furniture, household articles, photographs, and other items, including a re-created 19th-century parlor and boudoir. It's open Memorial Day to Labor Day, Monday through Saturday from 11am to 4pm; the rest of the year, Monday through Saturday from noon to 4pm. Admission is free.

The **Astor House Hotel,** 822 12th St. (tel. 278-3557), charges $1 for hourly guided tours of the oldest native stone structure in Colorado, built in 1867. It's open in summer, Monday through Saturday from 10am to 4pm; in winter, Monday through Saturday from 10am to 3pm. While there, obtain a walking-tour guide for the 12th Street Historic District.

The **Rocky Mountain Quilt Museum,** 1111 Washington Ave. (tel. 277-0377), has a changing collection of more than 100 antique and contemporary quilts, and offers tours and classes. It's open Tuesday through Saturday from 10am to 4pm; admission is $1 for nonmembers. Local crafters work is for sale in the gift shop.

BOETTCHER MANSION, 900 Colorow Rd., on Lookout Mountain. Tel. 526-0855.

This Jefferson County estate was built by Charles Boettcher in 1917 as a summer home and hunting lodge. The historic home, now open to visitors, with changing art and history exhibits, also hosts conferences, weddings, and community events. A 1¼-mile nature trail winds through the 110-acre property, among ponderosa pines and mountain meadows. A nature center (tel. 526-0594) is also located on the property.

Admission: Free.

Open: Mansion, Mon–Sat 8am–5pm or by appointment; trails, 8am–dark; nature center, Tues–Sun 10am–4pm.

BUFFALO BILL MEMORIAL MUSEUM, 987½ Lookout Mountain Rd. Tel. 526-0747.

William Frederick Cody, the most famous of all western scouts, is buried atop Lookout Mountain south of Golden. The adjacent musuem has memorabilia from the life and legend of "Buffalo Bill," who rode for the Pony Express, organized buffalo hunts for foreign royalty, and toured the world with his Wild West Show. The museum, which is reached via Exit 256 from I-70, is in 66-acre Lookout Mountain Park, a Denver municipal park popular for picnicking.

Admission: $2 adults, $1.50 seniors, $1 children 6–15, free for children under 6.

Open: May–Oct, daily 9am–5pm; Nov–Apr, Tues–Sun 9am–4pm. **Closed:** Christmas.

COLORADO RAILROAD MUSEUM, 17155 W. 44th Ave. Tel. 279-4591 or toll free 800/365-6263.

Occupying a replica of an 1880 railroad depot, this museum is a must-stop for every railroad buff visiting the Denver area. On display are more than four dozen narrow- and standard-gauge locomotives and cars, plus other historic equipment and artifacts, historic photos and documents, and model trains. In fact, the exhibits cover 12 acres, including the two-story depot. You can climb up into many of the old locomotives and wander through the parlor cars. The museum also has an excellent gift and souvenir shop, selling hundreds of railroad-related items from coffee mugs to posters to T-shirts. The museum is located two miles east of Golden. Follow the signs from I-70, Exit 265.

Admission: $3 adults, $1.50 children under 16, $6.50 families.

Open: June–Aug, daily 9am–6pm; Sept–May, daily 9am–5pm. **Closed:** New Year's morning, Thanksgiving, Christmas.

COLORADO SCHOOL OF MINES GEOLOGY MUSEUM, 16th and Maple Sts. Tel. 273-3815.

Exhibits here include a replica of a gold mine, minerals from around the world, gemstones and precious metals, a replica of Clear Creek Cave, and other displays depicting Colorado's rich mining history. The Colorado School of Mines, founded in 1869, has an enrollment of 2,800.

Admission: Free.

Open: School year, Mon–Sat 9am–4pm, Sun 1–4pm, but closed for school holidays; summer, Mon–Sat 9am–4pm.

COORS BREWING COMPANY, 13th and Ford Sts. Tel. 277-BEER.

The world's single largest brewery, producing 1.5 million gallons of beer each day, Coors conducts free public tours of its brewery, followed by free samples of beer. Tours leave a central parking lot at 13th and Ford streets, where visitors pile onto a bus for a short drive through historic Golden before arriving at the brewery. There, a 30-minute walking tour covers the history of the Coors family and company, the barley-malting process, the 13,640-gallon gleaming copper kettles, and the entire process all the way to bottling. Children are welcome, and arrangements can be made for disabled or foreign-speaking visitors. There's also a gift shop.

Admission: Free.

Open: Mon–Sat 10am–4pm. **Closed:** Sundays and holidays.

FOOTHILLS ART CENTER, 809 15th St. Tel. 279-3922.

Housed in an 1872 Presbyterian church of Gothic architecture, which is on the National Historic Register, this exhibition center developed out of the annual Golden Sidewalk Art Show. The center features national and regional exhibits that change every four to six weeks. The Roundel Gallery gift shop is stocked with crafts from local artisans.

Admission: Free.

Open: Mon–Sat 9am–4pm, Sun 1–4pm.

GOLDEN GATE CANYON STATE PARK, Golden Gate Canyon Rd., Colo. 46. Tel. 592-1502.

Hiking, fishing, and nature study are the main pursuits at this state park, about 15 miles northwest of Golden. The Panorama Point Overlook, reached by car, gives a view of 100 miles of the Continental Divide. The park visitor center, open year-round, has an ecological and historical display and schedules various summer nature programs.

Admission: $3 per vehicle; campsites cost another $7 per vehicle per night.

Open: Daily year-round.

HAKUSHIKA SAKE USA, 4414 Table Mountain Dr. Tel. 279-7253.

The Hakushika company, founded in 1662 and today one of Japan's foremost saké makers, has opened a brewery in Golden that produces saké for distribution throughout the United States and Europe. Saké, considered the national drink of Japan, is made from fermented steamed rice, has an alcohol content of 16%, and is traditionally, but not exclusively, drunk with meals.

Guided tours, by reservation only, follow a glass-enclosed mezzanine that provides an excellent view of the entire brewing and bottling process. Visitors also see displays of traditional saké brewing techniques, and a fantastic exhibit of Japanese art from the

19th and early 20th centuries. There is also a tasting room and gift shop, and children are welcome. The Hakushika Saké brewery is located in an industrial park, surrounded by Coors Brewing Company warehouses and offices. Follow West 44th Avenue east from Golden to McIntyre Street, turn left, go 0.2 mile, turn left onto Service Drive, and then left onto Table Mountain Drive, where Hakushika is located.
Admission: Free.
Open: Mon–Sat 10am–4pm by reservation.

HERITAGE SQUARE, U.S. 40. Tel. 279-2789.

A shopping, dining, and entertainment village with a Wild West theme, Heritage Square features Victorian specialty shops, a small museum, several fine restaurants, and a dinner theater. Warm weather rides include go-carts, bumper boats, a water slide, a bungee tower, and a 2,350-foot alpine slide with bobsled-style carts. The Lazy H Chuckwagon serves dinner and presents a western-style show, and there's an ice-cream parlor and beer garden. It's located three-quarters of a mile south of the U.S. 6 and U.S. 40 interchange.
Admission: Free, but activities have their own charges.
Open: Memorial Day–Labor Day, daily 10am–9pm; the rest of the year, Mon–Sat 10am–6pm, Sun noon–6pm.

MOTHER CABRINI SHRINE, I-70, Exit 259, Lookout Mountain. Tel. 526-0758.

A 22-foot statue of Christ stands at the top of a 373-step stairway, adorned by carvings representing the stations of the cross and mysteries of the rosary. Terra-cotta benches provide respites along the way. The shrine is dedicated to America's first citizen saint, St. Frances Xavier Cabrini, who founded the Order of the Missionary Sisters of the Sacred Heart. They have a convent here with a gift shop.
Admission: By donation.
Open: Summer, daily 7am–7pm; winter, daily 7am–5pm; gift shop, daily 9am–5pm.

NATIONAL EARTHQUAKE INFORMATION CENTER, 1711 Illinois St. Tel. 273-8500.

The U.S. Geological Survey operates this facility to collect rapid earthquake information, transmit warnings via the Earthquake Early Alerting Service, and publish and disseminate earthquake data. Tours of 30 to 45 minutes can be scheduled.
Admission: Free.
Open: By appointment only, Mon–Fri 9–11am and 1–3pm.

RED ROCKS PARK AND AMPHITHEATRE, Hogback Rd., Morrison. Tel. 575-2638.

The road winds between spectacular 400-foot-high red sandstone spires and ledges at this area south of Golden. In their midst is the 9,000-seat Red Rocks Amphitheatre, famed for its wide-ranging summer concert series (see "Evening Entertainment," above). It is reached from the Morrison/Red Rocks exit off I-70.
Admission: Free except for scheduled concerts.
Open: Daily year-round.

WHERE TO STAY

HOLIDAY INN–DENVER WEST, 14707 W. Colfax Ave., Golden, CO 80401. Tel. 303/279-7611 or toll free 800/729-2830. 225 rms (all with bath). A/C TV TEL

$ Rates: $65–$77 single; $75–$87 double. Special wedding rates available. AE, CB, DC, DISC, MC, V.

The highlight of this property is its Holidome Indoor Recreation Center—complete with indoor lap pool, miniature golf course, exercise room, whirlpool, video arcade, and games room. The Dining Deck Restaurant serves three meals daily, and the Brass

Rail Lounge offers live music. There's also a coin-operated guest laundry and coffee machines in the rooms. Guest rooms are extremely spacious, with all standard furnishings as well as a desk for business travelers. Fax and copy machine available. The hotel is just off I-70 at Exit 262.

TABLE MOUNTAIN INN, 1310 Washington Ave., Golden, CO 80401. Tel. 303/277-9898 or toll free 800/762-9898. Fax 303/271-0298. 29 rooms, 3 suites (all with bath). A/C TV TEL

$ Rates: $85–$95 single or double; $115–$135 suite. AE, DC, DISC, JCB, MC, V.
This beautiful new property, which opened in downtown Golden in July 1992, has Southwest charm and beautiful views of the surrounding mesas. You'll find Santa Fe-style furnishings and ceiling fans in all rooms, and most rooms have wet bars and either balconies or patios. There is a full-service restaurant serving excellent southwestern cuisine, plus bar. Guests have use of a nearby health club, and rooms for the disabled and nonsmokers are available. Local calls are free, and fax and photocopy services are available. There are also meeting and banquet facilities. Pets are not accepted.

WHERE TO DINE

BRIARWOOD INN, 1630 Eighth St., Golden. Tel. 279-3121.
   Cuisine: AMERICAN/CONTINENTAL. **Reservations:** Recommended.
$ Prices: Main courses $20–$30; lunch $9–$15. AE, CB, DC, MC, V.
   Open: Lunch Mon–Fri 11am–2:30pm; dinner nightly 5:30–10pm; brunch Sun 10:30am–2:30pm.
One of the most celebrated restaurants in the greater Denver area, the Briarwood is noted for its gourmet food and attentive service. The decor is understated elegance—white linen and candlelight in an informal western atmosphere. Those who don't dine enjoy the cocktail lounge. The inn is at the junction of U.S. 6 and Colo. 58 west of downtown Golden.

CENTRAL CITY/BLACK HAWK

The area once called "the richest square mile on earth" is trying to relive its glory days with a return to gambling. Central City and its neighbor Black Hawk, plus Cripple Creek, west of Colorado Springs, began legalized limited-stakes **casino gambling** in October 1991. Now, in addition to exploring the historic charm of these Victorian towns, visitors can ante up, with $5-maximum bets on poker and blackjack and rows of shiny electronic slot machines.

Located 35 miles west of Denver via I-70 or U.S. 6 and Colo. 119, Central City is at the head of Gregory Gulch, where John Gregory made Colorado's first major gold strike in 1859. By the 1870s the town had grown to become the most important trade and cultural center of the central Rockies. After a decline at the turn of the 20th century, an Opera Festival, started in the 1930s, revitalized the town.

Today Central City is a National Historic District with one of the finest collections of Victorian buildings in the West. Its main street has been used in many western films, including the television miniseries *Centennial*.

The route to Central City from Denver goes through Clear Creek Canyon to Black Hawk, established in 1867 as the milling and smelting center for Central City ore. A mile farther, through Gregory Gulch, lies Central City. For information on attractions and travel services contact the Central City Public Information Office, P.O. Box 249, Central City, CO 80427 (tel. 303/582-1889 or toll free 800/542-2999); or Gilpin County Chamber of Commerce, P.O. Box 343, Black Hawk, CO 80422 (tel. 303/582-5077).

WHAT TO SEE & DO

With the advent of gambling, Black Hawk and Central City have changed considerably; the casinos are fast becoming the focal point. Because of this, some of the old tourist attractions have disappeared or cut back their hours, so it's best to call first if there are specific sites you want to visit.

Among casinos, a must-see is the **Teller House,** 120 Eureka St. (tel. 279-3200), with its famous "Face on the Barroom Floor," painted in 1936, and the inspiration for a cabaret opera which is still performed by the Central City Opera. The Teller House also contains a museum that shows off its Victorian charms, with tours offered daily from 9am to 4:30pm.

The Toll Gate Saloon and Gambling Hall, 108 Main St. (tel. toll free 800/800-LUCK), has a video arcade for children and live entertainment. Other **major casinos** include Bullwhackers, with casinos in both Central City and Black Hawk; the Glory Hole in Central City; and Gilpin Hotel Casino in Black Hawk. Most casinos have at least one restaurant and bar and use food and drink specials to lure gamblers through their doors.

Those looking for something to see outside the gambling halls can begin a **walking tour** on lower Lawrence Street at the Gilpin County Historical Museum (tel. 582-5283). Formerly a high school, it now houses antiques and artifacts from the mining era. Admission is $3 for adults, free for children under 12. It's open late May through early September, daily from 10am to 4pm; September to November, Saturday and Sunday from 9am to 5pm. The museum also operates the sporadically operational Black Hawk & Central City Narrow Gauge Railroad.

As you walk through town, you'll notice the solidity of the buildings. A great fire razed the town in 1874, after which stone and brick construction were exclusively used. An example of Cornish stone masonry is St. Paul's Episcopal Church. The granite Raynold's Building withstood the fire when the proprietor hung wet blankets over the windows and doors, thus preventing blasting powder kept in the cellar from blowing up the town. West on Eureka Street is the Register-Call Building, the oldest commercial building in the town still in use, housing the oldest newspaper in the state, a weekly. Interesting murals are on the walls of the Masonic Temple on the third floor of this building. Nearby, the oldest city hall in Colorado was originally built of logs in 1862 by the county sheriff, and over the years it has been used as a jail and courthouse. Farther west on Eureka Street is the Gilpin County Courthouse.

Beyond this are the Thomas Home and the Lost Gold Mine, both offering visitor tours. On the south side of Eureka Street are the famous Opera House and Teller House.

LOST GOLD MINE, 231 Eureka St., Central City. Tel. 642-7533.

Visitors walk down the main shaft of an old mine, viewing actual veins of gold and seeing the original 19th-century tools used here. An airshaft lets light in from 125 feet above the mine. At the tour's conclusion, visitors can buy gold-nugget jewelry and other souvenirs from a gift shop.

Admission: $4 adults, $3 seniors, $2 children 5–11, free for children under 5.

Open: Summer, daily 8am–8pm; call for winter hours.

OPERA HOUSE, 120 Eureka St., Central City. Tel. 297-8306.

Built in 1878 by public subscription, the Opera House has walls of native granite four feet thick. Inside are three-dimensional murals lighted by a great crystal chandelier. Hickory chairs are inscribed with the names of historic Colorado characters and actors from all over the world who appeared on the Opera House stage. But the Opera House went into a gradual decline with the end of mining and was used for minstrel shows, wrestling matches, high school graduations, and silent movies before being shuttered for a time.

Descendants of pioneer Coloradans reopened it for the first annual opera festival in 1932. The festival continues every year from mid-June through mid-August. Operas presented in recent years have included Puccini's *Tosca,* Strauss's *Die Fledermaus,* and Gounod's *Romeo and Juliet.* Tickets run $20 to $45, depending on seating and performance dates. For tickets or information, call 292-6700.

Admission: $3 adults, $2.50 seniors and children.

Open: Summer, daily 10am–2pm; the rest of the year, Thurs–Mon 10am–2pm.

THOMAS HOME, 209 Eureka St., Central City. Tel. 582-5093 or 582-5011 evenings.

A handsome 1874 home in the American Renaissance style, this house was boarded up in 1917 with all the family furnishings inside, and was only reopened in 1986! Everything remains intact: quilts on the beds, clothes in the closets, family photos, 13 different styles of clocks, calendars dating from the 1870s. The architecture features Doric columns, pedimented windows, and a secluded patio terraced with a mortarless rock wall.

Admission: $3 adults, free for children.

Open: June–Aug, daily 10am–5:30pm; Sept–Nov and Feb–May, Sat–Thurs 11am–4pm; Dec–Jan, Sat–Sun 11am–4pm.

IDAHO SPRINGS

The "Oh My God" dirt road winds dangerously from Central City through Virginia Canyon to Idaho Springs. Most visitors prefer to take I-70 directly to this community, 35 miles west of Denver. Site of a major gold strike in 1859, Idaho Springs today beckons visitors to try their luck at panning for any gold that may still remain. The **Argo Gold Mill and Museum,** 2350 Riverside Dr. (tel. 567-2421), offers tours daily, year-round, from 10am to 7pm. Visitors tour the Double Eagle Gold Mine, relatively unchanged since the early miners first worked it over 100 years ago, and the mill, where ore was processed into gold. Also at the mine and mill, you can ride the **Argo Express,** a one-half scale replica of a turn-of-the-century steam locomotive.

Still being worked is **Phoenix mine** on Trail Creek Road (tel. 567-0422), where you can don a hard hat, follow a working miner through narrow tunnels, and dig out your own ore sample. Open daily from 10am to 6pm, the tours are informal and entertaining, and after the tour participants receive their membership cards in the Independent Mining Association. Take your camera and flash—mines are dark!

Lesser metals now provide miners their work in these hills: uranium, tungsten, zinc, molybdenum, and lead are worked, and there is a 5-mile-long tunnel linking some of these mines a third of a mile below ground.

The Colorado School of Mines in Golden uses the **Edgar Experimental Mine,** less than a mile north of Idaho Springs on Eighth Avenue (tel. 567-2911), as a research area and teaching facility for high-tech mining practices. Underground walking tours of 60 to 90 minutes are offered to the public throughout the year: mid-June through August, Tuesday through Saturday from 8am to 4:30pm; other times by appointment. Tour rates: $4 adults, $2 ages 6 to 16, under 6 free, $3 over 60.

Just outside of town at 302 Soda Creek Rd. is the **Indian Springs Resort** (tel. 567-2191), a great place for a soak in the hot springs after a long day of skiing or hiking. There's a covered swimming pool and indoor and outdoor private baths. Lodging, meals, and weekend entertainment are also offered here.

Idaho Springs is the starting point for a 28-mile drive to the summit of 14,260-foot **Mount Evans.** Colorado 103 winds through Arapahoe National Forest, along Chicago Creek, to **Echo Lake Park,** another of the Denver mountain parks with fireplaces, hiking trails, fishing, and a shelter house. From here, Colo. 5–the highest paved auto road in North America—climbs to Mount Evans's summit. It is generally open from Memorial Day to Labor Day and is free.

Another way to see the country is by **horseback.** A&A Historical Trails Stables, 2380 Riverside Dr. (tel. 567-4808), offers a variety of trail rides, including breakfast and moonlight rides, plus pony rides for children.

For additional **information** on Idaho Springs, contact the Idaho Springs Chamber of Commerce, P.O. Box 97, Idaho Springs, CO 80452 (tel. 303/567-4382 or toll free 800/685-7785). Information on Idaho Springs, Empire, Georgetown, and Silver Plume can be obtained from the Clear Creek County Tourism Board, Box 100, Idaho Springs, CO 80452 (tel. 303/567-4660 or toll free 800/88-BLAST).

WHERE TO STAY

H&H MOTOR LODGE, 2445 Colorado Blvd. (P.O. Box 1359) Idaho Springs, CO 80452. Tel. 303/567-2838 or toll free 800/445-2893. 19 rooms (all with bath). TV TEL

$ **Rates:** $35–$60 single or double; kitchenettes $10 extra. AE, CB, DC, DISC, MC, V.

Clean, comfortable rooms at reasonable prices are what you'll find at this mom-and-pop motel on the east side of Idaho Springs. Rooms are well lit, bright and cheery, with either two doubles or a queen-size bed. The motel offers cable TV with HBO and a hot tub and sauna. Several larger family units are also available. Pets are welcome. Some rooms have air conditioning.

GEORGETOWN

A pretty village of Victorian-era houses and stores, Georgetown, 45 miles west of Denver on I-70 at an elevation of 8,500 feet, is named for an 1860 gold camp. But the town boomed more in the 1870s with silver. This is the best preserved of the foothills mining towns: It didn't suffer a major fire in its formative years. Perhaps to acknowledge their prayers, townspeople built eye-catching steeples on top of their firehouses, not their churches.

For **information** on attractions and travel services, contact the Georgetown Chamber of Commerce, P.O. Box 444, Georgetown, CO 80444 (tel. 303/569-2888), or Historic Georgetown, Inc., P.O. Box 667, Georgetown, CO 80444 (tel. 303/569-2840). A visitor information center, open in summer, is at Sixth Street across from the post office in Georgetown.

WHAT TO SEE & DO

The Georgetown–Silver Plume Mining Area, including this community and the adjacent hamlet of Silver Plume, was declared a National Historic Landmark District in 1966. More than 200 of its buildings have been saved and restored through the efforts of the Georgetown Society, a nonprofit organization dedicated to preserving historic structures. The Hamill House and Hotel de Paris are open to public tours.

A convenient place to begin a **walking tour** of downtown Georgetown is the Old County Courthouse at Sixth Street and Argentine Street. Now the Community Center and tourist information office, it was built in 1867. Across Argentine Street is the Old Stone Jail (1868); three blocks south, at Third and Argentine, is the Hamill House (see below).

Sixth Street is Georgetown's main commercial strip. Walk east from the Old Courthouse to see, on your left, the Masonic Hall (1891), the Fish Block (1886), the Monti and Guanella Building (1868), and the Cushman Block (1874); and on your right, the Hamill Block (1881) and the Kneisel & Anderson Building (1893). The Hotel de Paris is at the corner of Sixth and Taos. Nearly opposite, at Sixth and Griffith, is the Star Hook & Ladder Building (1886), along with the town hall and marshall's office.

If you turn south on Taos Street, you'll find Grace Episcopal Church (1869) at Fifth Street and the Maxwell House (1890) a couple of steps east on Fourth. Glance west on Fifth to see Alpine Hose Company No. 2 (1874) and the Courier Building (1875). North on Taos Street from the Hotel de Paris are the Old Georgetown School (1874), at Eighth Street; First Presbyterian Church (1874), at Ninth; Our Lady of Lourdes Catholic Church (1918), at Ninth; and the Old Missouri Firehouse (1870), at 10th and Taos.

If you turn west on Ninth at the Catholic church, you'll find two more historic structures: the Bowman-White House (1892), at Rose and Ninth, and the Tucker-Rutherford House (circa 1860), a miner's log cabin with four small rooms on Ninth Street at Clear Creek, with a trapper's cabin in back.

Special events during the year in Georgetown include a Fasching winter carnival in February; an antique fair and Swedish festival (Midsummer's Day) in June; an auction in Hamill House in July and August; an aspen festival in September; and a Christmas market with seasonal foods, folk dancing, a Santa Lucia procession, and caroling in early December.

GEORGETOWN LOOP RAILROAD, Loop Dr., near Sixth St., Georgetown. **Tel. 569-2403** or 670-1686 in Denver.

An 1884 railroad bridge serves this restored narrow-gauge line, which runs daily trips in summer between Georgetown and Silver Plume. The steel bridge is 300 feet long and 95 feet high and was considered an engineering miracle a century ago. Though the direct distance between the terminals is 2.1 miles, the track covers 4.5 miles, climbing 638 feet in 14 sharp curves and switchbacks, crossing Clear Creek four times, and culminating with a 360° spiraling knot. Passengers may make round-trips from either end: The whole trip takes about 2½ hours, including an optional walking tour of the Lebanon Mine and Mill, which can be reached only by train. They also offer Trails and Rails Mountain Bike Tours and Rentals and have a Depot Express Café, open 8am to 6pm daily.

Admission: $14 adults, $7.75 children 4–15, for train and mine tour; $10.50 adults, $6 children, for train ride only; no charge for children under 4 not occupying a seat.

Open: Memorial Day–Labor Day, daily 9am–4:30pm; Labor Day to early Oct, Sat–Sun only noon–3pm. Departures from Georgetown and from Silver Plume. There's no mine tour on the final run.

HAMILL HOUSE, Third and Argentine Sts. Tel. 569-2840.

Built in country Gothic revival style, it dates to 1867, when it was owned by a silver speculator, William Hamill, and was the town's most ambitious residence. A carriage house and office occupy two stone structures behind the main house, and a delicately carved outhouse had two parts, one for the family with walnut seats, and the other for servants with pine seats. When acquired by Historic Georgetown, Inc., in 1971, the house had the original woodwork, fireplaces, and wallpaper. Restoration work on the upper stories is continuing.

Admission: $2.50 adults, $1.50 seniors, and 50¢ children 12–16, under 12 free.

Open: Memorial Day–Sept 30, daily 10am–5pm; Oct–May, Sat–Sun noon–4pm.

HOTEL DE PARIS, Sixth and Taos Sts. Tel. 569-2311.

The builder of the hotel, Louis Dupuy, once wrote an explanation of his desire to build a French inn so far away from his homeland: "I love these mountains and I love America, but you will pardon me if I bring into this community a remembrance of my youth and my country." The hotel opened in 1875 and soon became famous for its French provincial luxuriousness.

Today the hotel is a historic museum run by the National Society of Colonial Dames of America. The hotel is embellished with many of its original furnishings: Haviland china, diamond-dust mirrors, a big pendulum clock, paintings and etchings of the past century, carved walnut furniture, lace curtains and draperies of tapestry, as well as Dupuy's considerable library. An antique stove and other cooking equipment occupy the kitchen; the wine cellar has some early wine barrels, with their labels still in place.

Admission: $3 adults, $1.50 seniors, $1 children, under 12 free.

Open: Memorial Day–Sept 30, daily 10am–5pm; Oct–May, Thurs–Sun noon–4pm.

WHERE TO STAY

GEORGETOWN BAEHLER RESORT SERVICE, P.O. Box 247, Georgetown, CO 80444. Tel. 303/569-2665.

$ Rates: Average $150 double, plus damage deposit. Weekly rates begin at $800 for 6 nights. MC, V.

This central booking agency will place you in a historic home for the length of your stay in Georgetown. Facilities vary widely with properties.

THE PECK HOUSE HOTEL AND RESTAURANT, 83 Sunny Ave., P.O. Box 428, Empire, CO 80438 (on U.S. 40 off I-70, Exit 232). Tel. 569-9870. 11 rooms (9 with private bath).

$ Rates: $45–$95 double. AE, CB, DC, JCB, MC, V.

Colorado's oldest continually operated hotel is in the tiny community of Empire, 5 minutes from Georgetown and about 45 minutes from downtown Denver. Established in 1862, it was originally a stagecoach stop, serving travelers and immigrants from the East Coast seeking adventure and fortune in the

Old West. Today, the Victorian elegance of the Peck House brings to mind a time when well-to-do ladies in plumed hats and full skirts would alight from a carriage for a visit. Rooms are decorated with rich-wood antiques and many have claw-footed tubs. There's a wide veranda, offering a fine view of the Empire Valley, and an antique-filled parlor that contains reading matter and historic photos of the Peck family and the Empire area. The hotel also has a spa with Jacuzzi that accommodates 12, and a restaurant and lounge (see "Where to Dine," below).

WHERE TO DINE

HAPPY COOKER, 412 Sixth St., Georgetown. Tel. 569-3166.
   Cuisine: INTERNATIONAL.
$ Prices: $3–$8. MC, V.
   Open: Summer, Mon–Fri 8am–4pm, Sat–Sun 8am–7pm; winter, Mon–Fri 8am–4pm, Sat–Sun 8am–6pm.

Unusual soups, homemade breads, crêpes, and quiches are the specialties in this converted home in Georgetown's historic business district, but you'll also find more stick-to-your-ribs type selections such as lasagne, barbecued beef, and a variety of healthy sandwiches. Also offered are spiced teas, hot spiced cider, wine, and beer. There's an outside patio for warm-weather dining.

THE PECK HOUSE HOTEL AND RESTAURANT, 83 Sunny Ave., Empire (on U.S. 40 off I-70, Exit 232). Tel. 569-9870.
   Cuisine: INTERNATIONAL. **Reservations:** Recommended.
$ Prices: Appetizers $5–$8; lunch $3–$9; dinner $14–$20. Sunday brunch $12.
   Open: Lunch Mon–Sat 11am–4pm, summer only; year-round, dinner Sun–Thurs 4–9pm, Fri–Sat 4–10pm; year-round, brunch Sun 10am–2pm. Check on Sunday holiday schedules.

The historic Peck House (see "Where to Stay," above) offers fine dining, a historic atmosphere, and magnificent views. The restaurant features nightly specials, such as alder-smoked trout, seafood strudel, or beef Wellington. Regular offerings include New York steak, trout amandine, raspberry duck, and beef and oyster pie. But save some room for dessert—the Peck House is famous for its hot-fudge cake and raspberry Romanoff. The Sunday brunch, a local tradition, features entrées such as eggs Benedict, smoked trout with eggs, and steak with eggs, plus fresh fruit and homemade breads. Lunches, served only in summer, include half-pound cheeseburgers, a sausage-and-cheese platter, barbecued chicken, and a variety of sandwiches.

THE PLACE, 715 Seventh St., Georgetown. Tel. 569-2552.
   Cuisine: AMERICAN.
$ Prices: Breakfast $3.25–$7.45; lunch $5.25–$7.95; dinner $10.95–$15.95. AE, MC, V.
   Open: Mon–Fri 11am–8pm, Sat–Sun 8am–8pm.

A family restaurant serving made-from-scratch meals, this is a favorite of Georgetown residents looking for good food at reasonable prices. Burgers and sandwiches are featured at lunch, and the dinner menu has the standard favorites of steak, fish, chicken, pork, and pasta. The weekend breakfasts include bacon and eggs and the other usual offerings.

COLORADO SPRINGS

Nearly two centuries ago, in 1806, army lieutenant Zebulon Pike led a company of soldiers on a trek of exploration around the base of an enormous mountain toward which they had been marching for over 100 miles. He called it "Grand Peak," declared it unconquerable, and moved on.

Today, the 14,110-foot mountain we now know as Pikes Peak has been conquered so often that an auto highway and a cog railway ascend it. And where previously there was naught but sagebrush-speckled prairie, today a thriving city sprawls.

Neither mineral wealth nor ranching was the cornerstone of the city; instead, 19th-century tourism was responsible. In fact, when founded in 1871, Colorado Springs was the first genuine resort community west of Chicago.

General William J. Palmer, builder of the Denver & Rio Grande Railroad, established the resort on his rail line at 6,035 feet elevation, at the confluence of two creeks. The state's growing reputation as a health center, with its high mountains and mineral springs, convinced him to build at the foot of Pikes Peak. It would lure affluent easterners, he said—so he named the resort Colorado Springs, because most of the fashionable resorts back east were "springs." The mineral waters at Manitou were only five miles distant, and soon Palmer exploited them—installing as resident physician one Dr. Samuel Solly, who exuberantly trumpeted the benefits of Manitou's springs in print and in person.

The gold strikes of the 1890s at Cripple Creek, on the southwestern slope of Pikes Peak, added a new dimension to Colorado Springs life. Among those who cashed in on the boom was Spencer Penrose, a middle-aged Philadelphian and Harvard graduate who came to the Springs in 1892, made some astute investments, and became very rich. Penrose, like Palmer, a man ahead of his time, believed that the automobile would revolutionize life in the United States. He promoted the creation of new highways, and to show the effectiveness of motor cars in the mountains, built (in 1913–15) the Pikes Peak road with more than $250,000 of his own money. During World War I, at a cost of over $2 million, he built the Broadmoor, Colorado's most luxurious hotel, at the foot of Cheyenne Mountain.

World War II brought the defense industry. Camp Carson and Ent Air Force Base were built in 1942. On the north side of Colorado Springs, the $200-million U.S. Air Force Academy opened to cadets in 1958. With this military presence, it's no surprise that numerous high-technology corporations have chosen to locate in Colorado Springs as well.

Modern Colorado Springs is a growing city of 281,000 that retains the feel and mood of a small western town. Visitors come to see the Air Force Academy, marvel at

WHAT'S SPECIAL ABOUT COLORADO SPRINGS

Natural Spectacles
- [ ] Pikes Peak summit, reached by cog railway, road, or trail, for its unparalleled view.
- [ ] Garden of the Gods, a tract of red sandstone pinnacles 300 million years old, home to a remarkable variety of fauna and flora.
- [ ] Cave of the Winds, a geological wonderland 10 minutes from downtown.

Architectural Highlights
- [ ] The Broadmoor (1918), built in the style of grand foreign hotels by Warren and Wetmore, architects of New York's Grand Central Terminal.
- [ ] Colorado Springs Fine Art Center (1936), a community arts center of monolithic concrete design, built by John Gaw Meem of Santa Fe.
- [ ] Cadet Chapel (1958) with its 17 soaring spires on the Air Force Academy campus.

Museums
- [ ] Western Museum of Mining and Industry, where the history and practice of mining come to life.
- [ ] The Pro Rodeo Hall of Fame and American Cowboy Museum, immortalizing the most "western" of sports.
- [ ] The May Natural History Museum, featuring a world-famous collection of 7,000 tropical insects and other invertebrates.

- [ ] Colorado Springs Pioneers Museum, which tells the story of Colorado Springs, and is housed in a magnificent historic building.

American Heritage
- [ ] The U.S. Air Force Academy (4,000 cadets), with a museum and other public areas.
- [ ] The U.S. Olympic Training Center.

Events/Festivals
- [ ] Pikes Peak Auto Hill Climb, an international July 4 "race to the clouds" since 1916.
- [ ] Pikes Peak or Bust Rodeo in August, now in its sixth decade.
- [ ] Territory Days (May) and Springspree (June), street festivals with food and live entertainment.

For the Kids
- [ ] Cheyenne Mountain Zoo, with 600 animals on the side of Cheyenne Mountain.
- [ ] Ghost Town, where youngsters can relive the rough-and-tumble days of the Old West.
- [ ] North Pole, where Santa Claus shares the magic of Christmas even in the heat of summer.

the scenery of Garden of the Gods and Pikes Peak, and explore the history of the American West.

1. ORIENTATION

ARRIVING

BY PLANE The **Colorado Springs Airport,** 5750 E. Fountain Blvd. (tel. 719/596-0188), is not a commuter satellite of Denver. But over 100 direct, major-carrier flights arrive at and depart from the Springs daily from Chicago, St. Louis, Dallas/Fort Worth, Phoenix, Las Vegas, Salt Lake City, and Albuquerque. And the airport is just a short drive from major hotels, in the southeastern part of the city.

Major airlines serving Colorado Springs include American (tel. toll free 800/433-7300), America West (tel. 630-0737 or 800/228-7862), Continental (tel. 473-7580 or toll free 800/525-0280), Delta (tel. toll free 800/221-1212), Trans World (tel. 599-4400 or toll free 800/221-2000), and United (tel. toll free 800/241-6522).

Regional and commuter airlines connect Colorado Springs with Denver, Albuquerque, and other cities; they include Mesa (tel. 591-6211 or toll free 800/637-2247).

Getting to & from Airport   The Airport Shuttle Service (tel. 719/578-5232) operates direct ground service from the Colorado Springs airport to local hotels and the Denver airport. The cost is $25 airport-to-airport, with a three passenger minimum.

City bus fare from the airport to downtown is 75¢. Taxi service to hotels runs $7 to $9.

BY BUS   TNM&O Coaches, 120 S. Weber St. (tel. 719/635-1505), has regular daily arrivals and departures to towns, cities, and resort communities throughout the state. Call for route, fare, and schedule information.

BY CAR   The principal artery to and from the north (Denver: 70 miles) and south (Pueblo: 42 miles), Interstate 25 bisects Colorado Springs. U.S. 24 is the principal east-west route through the city.

Visitors traveling via I-70 from the east can take Exit 359 at Limon and follow U.S. 24 into the Springs. Traveling via I-70 from the west, the most direct route is Exit 201 at Frisco, then Colo. 9 (via Breckenridge) 53 miles to Hartsel Junction, and then U.S. 24 east 66 miles to the Springs.

TOURIST INFORMATION

Offices of the **Colorado Springs Convention and Visitors Bureau** are at 104 S. Cascade Ave., Colorado Springs, CO 80903 (tel. 719/635-7506, or toll free 800/DO-VISIT; fax 719/635-4968). Ask for the "Official Visitors Guide to Colorado Springs and the Pikes Peak Region," a 64-page compendium with a comprehensive listing of accommodations, restaurants, and all other visitor services in the area.

The **Visitor Information Center,** located in the same Sun Plaza Building at the corner of Cascade Avenue and Colorado Avenue, is open in summer, daily from 8:30am to 5pm; in winter, Monday through Friday from 8:30am to 5pm. From I-25, take the Bijou St. exit, head east, and turn right at the second stoplight onto Cascade. Just past the Antler's Hotel turn right onto Colorado Avenue, and almost immediately left into the parking lot for the Visitor's Center. The center also operates a weekly events line with a 24-hour recording (tel. 635-1723).

Additional information on regional attractions can be obtained from the Manitou Springs Chamber of Commerce, 354 Manitou Ave., Manitou Springs, CO 80829 (tel. 719/685-5089 or toll free 800/642-2567), or Pikes Peak Country Attractions Association, at the same address (tel. 719/685-5894 or toll free 800/525-2250).

CITY LAYOUT

It's easy to get around central Colorado Springs, laid out as it is on a classic grid pattern.

If the I-25/U.S. 24 interchange is the center of the city, downtown Colorado Springs lies in the northeast quadrant—bounded on the west by I-25 and on the south by U.S. 24 (Cimarron Street). Boulder Street to the north and Wahsatch Avenue to the east complete the downtown frame. Nevada Avenue (U.S. 85) parallels the freeway for 15 miles through the city, intersecting it twice; Tejon Street and Cascade Avenue also run north-south through downtown between Nevada and the freeway. **Colorado Avenue** and **Platte Avenue** are the busiest east-west downtown cross streets.

West of downtown, Colorado Avenue extends through the historic **Old Colorado City** district and the quaint foothill community of **Manitou Springs,** rejoining U.S. 24—itself a busy but less interesting artery—as it enters Pike National Forest.

South of downtown, Nevada Avenue intersects Lake Avenue, the principal boulevard into the Broadmoor, and proceeds south as Colo. 115 past Fort Carson. North and east of downtown, Academy Boulevard (Colo. 83) is the street name to remember. From the south gate of the Air Force Academy north of the Springs, it winds through residential hills, crosses Austin Bluff Parkway, then runs without a curve 8 miles due south, finally curving west to intersect I-25 and Colo. 115 at Fort Carson. U.S. 24, which exits downtown as Platte Avenue, and Fountain Boulevard, which leads to the airport, are among its cross streets. Austin Bluff Parkway extends west of I-25 as **Garden of the Gods Road,** affording access to that natural wonder.

City street addresses are divided by Pikes Peak Avenue into "north" and "south"; by Nevada Avenue into "east" and "west."

A basic but efficient Colorado Springs map can be found in the center of the city's "Official Visitors Guide." Inquire at the visitor information center or local bookstores for more detailed maps (an excellent one I recommend is the Pierson Graphics Corp. Colorado Springs & Monument Valley Street Map).

2. GETTING AROUND

BY BUS   The city bus service is provided by **Colorado Springs Transit** (tel. 475-9733). Buses operate 6am to 6pm Monday through Saturday, with some routes having limited service until 10pm. Fares on in-city routes are 75¢ for adults; 35¢ for children 6 to 11, senior citizens, and the disabled; and free for children under 6. Fares for routes outside city limits are 25¢ higher. Bus schedules can be obtained at terminals, city libraries, and the Colorado Springs Convention and Visitors Bureau.

In Manitou Springs the **Town Trolley** operates daily from Memorial Day to Labor Day and on a limited schedule in the weeks preceding Christmas and weekends during April, May, September, and October, weather permitting. The open-sided trolleys provide 1-hour guided tours through Manitou Springs and a portion of Garden of the Gods. A $2 1-day pass allows riders to stop to see the sights and then continue the tour later. Children under 12, with parents, ride free. During the summer, trolleys run every half hour from 9am until 8pm.

BY TAXI   Call **Yellow Cab** (tel. 634-5000). Fares are $3 for the first mile, $1.35 for each additional mile, plus 50¢ per adult passenger. Taxis are not normally hailed on the streets. A few stands are at the major hotels.

BY CAR   For regulations and advice on driving in Colorado, see "Getting Around" in Chapter 2. The **American Automobile Association (AAA)** maintains an office in Colorado Springs at 3525 N. Carefree Circle (tel. 719/591-2222), open Monday through Friday from 8:30am to 5:30pm and on Saturday from 9am to 1pm.

Parking   Most downtown streets have parking meters, with rates of 25¢ an hour—have your change ready. Look for city-run parking lots, which charge 25¢ per hour and also offer day rates. Outside of downtown, free parking is generally available on side streets.

Car Rentals   Car-rental agencies in Colorado Springs—some of which have offices in or near downtown as well as at the municipal airport—include: **Avis** (tel. 596-2751 or toll free 800/831-2847); **Budget,** 303 W. Bijou St. (tel. 574-7400 or toll free 800/527-0700); **Dollar** (tel. 591-6464 or toll free 800/800-4000); **Enterprise,** 803 W. Colorado Ave. (tel. 636-3900); **Hertz,** 5750 E. Fountain Blvd. (tel. 596-1863 or toll free 800/654-3131); **National** (tel. 596-1519 or toll free 800/227-7368); **Payless,** 1645 Newport Rd. (tel. 597-4444 or toll free 800/PAYLESS); or **Thrifty,** 4180 Center Park Dr. (tel. 574-2472 or toll free 800/367-2277).

ON FOOT   Each of the main sections of town can be easily explored without a vehicle. It's fun, for instance, to wander the winding streets through Manitou Springs or explore the Old Colorado City "strip." Between neighborhoods, however, distances are considerable. Unless you're particularly fit, it's wise to take a bus or a taxi.

FAST COLORADO SPRINGS

American Express To report a lost card, call toll free 800/528-4800; to report lost traveler's checks, call toll free 800/221-7282.

Area Code The area code for Colorado Springs is 719.

Babysitters Front desks or concierges at major hotels often can make arrangements on your behalf. Otherwise, try ABC Baby Sitting Agency (tel. 635-4229).

Banks Leading banks, all with downtown branches, include Bank One Colorado Springs (tel. 471-5000) and Norwest Bank (tel. 636-1361). Most banks are open Monday through Thursday from 9am to 4pm and on Friday from 9am to 6pm.

Plus System (tel. toll free 800/THE-PLUS) cash machines can be found at strategic locations throughout the city.

Dentist For 24-hour referrals, call the Colorado Springs Dental Society Emergency and Referral Service (tel. 473-3168).

Doctor For referrals, call Memorial Hospital Physician Referral (tel. 444-CARE) or the Colorado Springs Doctors Exchange (tel. 632-1512). Minor illnesses and injuries are treated outpatient, and emergencies are tended 24 hours, at the Colorado Springs Medical Center, 5209 S. Nevada Ave. (tel. 475-7700) and four other locations.

Drugstores Reliable prescription services are available at Walgreen's Drug Stores, whose 24-hour store is located at 2727 Palmer Park Blvd. (prescription information tel. 473-9090; general information tel. 473-9092).

Emergencies For police, fire, or medical emergencies, call 911. To reach Poison Control, dial 630-5333. For the 24-hour Rape Hot line, call toll free 800/551-0008.

Eyeglasses You can get 1-hour replacement of lost or broken glasses at Pearle Vision in Chapel Hills and Citadel malls. Another choice is Lenscrafters, at the corner of Vickers and North Academy Boulevard (tel. 548-8650); and for unique frames as well as other optical services, stop at Charlotte's, 2501 W. Colorado Ave. (tel. 473-8066), in Old Colorado City.

Hairdressers & Barbers Those looking for a quick trim or the full treatment have plenty of choices. Locals swear by Old Colorado Stylist, 2616 W. Colorado Ave., suite 12 (tel. 632-0066), where walk-ins are welcome. You might also try Middleton Salon, 5747 N. Academy Blvd., at Vickers Street (tel. 548-1543). Cost Cutters Family Hair Care has seven shops in the city, including Citadel and Chapel Hills malls.

Hospitals Full medical services, including 24-hour emergency treatment, are offered by Memorial Hospital, 1400 E. Boulder St. (tel. 475-5000 or 475-5221 for emergency); and St. Francis Hospital, 825 E. Pikes Peak Ave. (tel. 636-8800; or 636-8850 for emergencies). Both are just east of downtown. Penrose Hospital, 2215 N. Cascade Ave. (tel. 630-5000; or for emergency 630-5333), and Penrose Community Hospital, 3205 N. Academy Blvd. (tel. 591-3000; or for emergency 591-3216), are on the north side.

Information See "Orientation," at the beginning of this chapter.

Laundry/Dry Cleaning Nearly every major hotel offers valet drop-off and pick-up service, but the charge can be steep. Few have guest laundries. Your hotel can direct you to the nearest coin laundrette. For dry cleaning, One Hour Cleaners has two locations in the city, including 1859 S. Nevada Ave. (tel. 473-1597).

Libraries The main library in Colorado Springs, the Penrose Public Library, is located at 20 N. Cascade Ave. (tel. 531-6333), in the heart of downtown. There are branches throughout the metropolitan area. A local library card is required to check out material. Open Monday through Thursday from 10am to 9pm, Friday and Saturday from 10am to 6pm. The East Library and Information Center, 5550 N. Union Blvd. (tel. 531-6333), is also open Sundays from 1 to 5pm.

Liquor Laws   See "Fast Facts: Colorado" in Chapter 2.

Lost Property   Consult the city police (tel. 632-6611).

Newspapers/Magazines   The *Gazette Telegraph* is published daily in Colorado Springs and is by far the city's most widely read newspaper. Both Denver dailies—the *Denver Post* and *Rocky Mountain News*—are also sold at newsstands throughout the city. *Springs* magazine and *Steppin' Out* are free monthly arts-and-entertainment tabloids. *USA Today* and the *Wall Street Journal* can be purchased on the streets and at major hotels.

Photographic Needs   Try 50-Minute Photo at 6902 N. Academy Blvd. (tel. 598-6412). For camera and video supplies and repairs, go to Robert Waxman Camera and Video, 1850 N. Academy Blvd. (tel. 597-1575), or Shewmaker's Camera Shop, downtown at 30 N. Tejon St. (tel. 636-1696).

Police   In an emergency, dial 911. For standard business, call 632-6611.

Post Office   The Main Post Office is downtown at 201 E. Pikes Peak Ave. (tel. 570-5339), open Monday through Friday from 7:30am to 5pm. There are many other branches. For late-night pick up, you'll have to visit the General Mail Facility, 3655 E. Fountain Blvd. (tel. 570-5377).

Radio/TV   More than a dozen AM and FM radio stations in the Colorado Springs area cater to all musical, news, sports, and entertainment tastes. Among them are KCME (88.7 FM) for classical, KILO (93.9 FM) for album-oriented rock, KKFM (96.5 FM) for classic rock, KGFT (100.7 FM) and KCBR (1040 AM) for contemporary Christian, KCMN (1530 AM) for big band and hit parade, KKCS (101.9 FM) and KRDO (1240 AM) for new country, KKLI (106.3 FM) for light adult contemporary, and KVOR (1300 AM) for all news. Major television stations include Channel 5 (NBC), 8 (PBS), 11 (CBS), 13 (ABC), and 21 (FOX). Cable or satellite service is available at most hotels.

Religious Services   Most major religious denominations, and many minor ones, are represented in Colorado Springs. Check the *Yellow Pages* for a complete listing of houses of worship.

Safety   Colorado Springs is a very safe city, but use common sense when you visit. Stay alert. Be aware of your immediate surroundings, and keep a close eye on your possessions. Be especially careful with cameras, purses, and wallets, all favorite targets of thieves and pickpockets.

Shoe Repairs   Shoes and boots are quickly repaired, sometimes while you wait, at Andy's Shoe Repair, 2234 East Pikes Peak Ave. (tel. 632-9990).

Taxes   Colorado state sales tax is 3%. Each county, city, and town tacks on additional local taxes, including bed taxes for lodging. In Colorado Springs the sales tax is 6.4% and the lodging tax is 8.6%. Rates in Manitou Springs are 7.5% for general sales tax and 9.52% for lodging.

Telephone/Fax   Local calls are normally 25¢. Facsimiles can be transmitted by most major hotels at a nominal cost to guests.

For directory assistance, dial 1-411 for Colorado Springs and southeast Colorado. Dial 1-555-1212 for Denver and the rest of the state.

Useful Telephone Numbers   Road conditions (635-7623); ski conditions statewide (tel. 831-SNOW); time (tel. 630-1111); and weather (tel. 475-7599).

3. ACCOMMODATIONS

The rates listed here are the officially quoted off-the-street prices, or "rack rates," and don't take into account any individual or group discounts.

In these listings, the price ranges, based on summer rates for double rooms, are: "Very Expensive," more than $200; "Expensive," $110 to $200; "Moderate," $65 to

$110; "Budget," less than $65. An additional 8.7% city bed tax (8.6% in Colorado Springs, 9.52% in Manitou Springs) is added to all bills.

VERY EXPENSIVE

THE BROADMOOR, Lake Circle, at Lake Ave. (P.O. Box 1439), Colorado Springs, CO 80901. Tel. 719/634-7711 or toll free 800/634-7711. Fax 719/577-5779. 532 rms, 18 suites. A/C TV TEL

$ Rates: Summer, $215–$280 single or double; $350–$1,740 suite. Winter, $135–$175 single or double; $220–$1,170 suite. Winter packages may cost as little as $52.50 per person per night. CB, DC, MC, V. **Parking:** Free.

A Colorado Springs institution and a tourist attraction in its own right, the Broadmoor is a sprawling resort complex of pink Mediterranean-style buildings and modern additions at the foot of Cheyenne Mountain. It began in 1885 as the dream of a German count, who envisioned a sort of American Monte Carlo. James de Pourtales constructed a Georgian casino on a small lake and laid trolley lines from downtown Colorado Springs, 5 miles away. But the casino burned in 1897 and a planned grand hotel was never built. It was up to Spencer Penrose, two decades later, to take up where Count de Pourtales had left off. Built in the Italian Renaissance style, the Broadmoor opened in 1918. Its marble staircase, brass chandeliers, della Robbia tile, hand-painted beams and ceilings, and carved marble fountain remain spectacles today, along with a priceless art collection featuring original work by Toulouse-Lautrec and Ming dynasty ceramicists. The first names entered on the guest register were those of John D. Rockefeller, Jr., and his party.

Today there are guest rooms in three separate buildings—Broadmoor Main, adjacent Broadmoor South, and Broadmoor West, on the site of the original casino across Broadmoor Lake—on the 3,000-acre grounds. Guest rooms are spacious and luxurious, as might be expected. Recently refurbished, all contain early 20th-century antiques and original works of art. Rooms typically have two queen-size or one king-size bed, desks and tables, plush seating, secluded luggage areas, and excellent lighting. Service is impeccable: The hotel staffs two employees for every room.

Dining/Entertainment: Charles Court (see "Dining," below) is the Broadmoor's finest restaurant. The Tavern (see "Dining," below) focuses on steak and seafood and offers an option of dining in a tropical Garden Room or with live background music. The Lake Terrace Dining Room is especially popular for Sunday brunch ($18.50, children ages 4 to 12 $10, under 4 free). The elegant Penrose Room, on the ninth floor of Broadmoor South, serves wild game, new American cuisine, and to-die-for desserts; open for dinner only, its main dishes run $18 to $32. More casual are the Broadmoor Golf Club (members and hotel guests only), with continental breakfast ($6.25), luncheon soups, salads, and sandwiches ($5.50 to $12.75), and light dinner dishes ($18.50 to $25); the Golden Bee (see "Evening Entertainment," below) pub fare ($6.75 to $10); and Julie's, a sidewalk café and ice-cream shop. There are four lounges, one in each building. Across Lake Circle is the Broadmoor International Theatre.

Services: 24-hour room service, full concierge service, valet laundry, no-smoking rooms, facilities for the disabled, shuttle bus between buildings.

Facilities: Sports facilities include 3 golf courses, 3 swimming pools, 16 tennis courts (4 indoor), squash court, trap and skeet-shooting grounds, bicycle rental, exercise room, aerobics classes, saunas, Jacuzzi, Broadmoor World Arena (ice skating and hockey), and Spencer Penrose Stadium (rodeo and equestrian). There are 19 shops (boutiques, galleries, jeweler, florist, druggist, hair salon, travel agent, and gift shop), a cinema, a car-rental agency, a post office, and a service station. Up to 1,600 at a sitting can be accommodated for meetings; there are 30 meeting rooms and a conference center. The hotel owns El Pomar Carriage House Museum, the Broadmoor International Theatre, Cheyenne Mountain Zoo, and Will Rogers Shrine of the Sun.

CHEYENNE MOUNTAIN CONFERENCE RESORT, 3225 Broadmoor Valley Rd., Colorado Springs, CO 80906. Tel. 719/576-4600 or toll free 800/428-8886. Fax 719/576-4711. A/C TV TEL

$ Rates: Summer, $200–$275 single, $310–$400 double; winter, $150–$200 single, $230–$310 double. 30-day advance booking requested. AE, CB, DC, DISC, MC, V. **Parking:** Free.

Designed specifically to attract conferences, this fine resort in southern Colorado Springs hosts independent travelers as space permits. Rates listed above are conference rates. Eight satellite lodges surround a large main lodge, all of them built of rough-hewn cedar with massive beams and native moss rock. A skylit cathedral ceiling gives the central lobby a majestic feel.

Every guest room has a private deck or balcony, most of them with an impressive view toward the southern Rockies. Because of the business orientation, all have comfortable work areas with computer outlets and modern capability. Most rooms have two double beds, dressers and easy chairs, a vanity and separate dressing table, and built-in hair dryers. The "executive king" also features a large private Jacuzzi. Local phone calls are 50¢.

Dining/Entertainment: Remington's (see "Dining," below) has been voted Colorado Springs's "most romantic" restaurant. The Mountain View Dining Room wins raves for its buffet: all-you-can-eat breakfast ($8.95) and lunch ($12.95) spreads. A limited but changing choice of dinner dishes ($15 to $23) always includes beef, seafood, poultry, and another meat in new American preparations. The Will Rogers Lounge features a piano bar and bands playing light contemporary music during the summer season.

Services: Room service most hours, concierge, valet laundry, no-smoking rooms, facilities for the disabled.

Facilities: A 35-acre lake with a swimming beach, boat and sailboard rentals, and trout fishing; 18 hole golf course, 18 tennis courts (6 indoors), four swimming pools (one indoor), fitness center with weight equipment and racquet courts, bicycle path and rentals, adult games room (billiards, cards, other table games); state-of-the-art conference facilities include 32 meeting rooms that handle up to 420 for banquets.

EXPENSIVE

THE ANTLERS DOUBLETREE HOTEL, 4 S. Cascade Ave., Colorado Springs, CO 80903. Tel. 719/473-5600 or toll free 800/222-TREE. Fax 719/444-0417. 284 rms, 6 suites (all with bath). A/C TV TEL

$ Rates: Summer, $125 single or double. Winter, $105 single or double. Year-round, $200–$750 suite. AE, CB, DC, DISC, ER, JCB, MC, V. **Parking:** $4 per day.

The Antlers has been a Colorado Springs landmark for more than a century—although there have been three different Antlers on the same site. The first two were built by city founder Gen. William Palmer. A turreted Victorian showcase built in 1883, it was named for the general's collection of deer and elk trophies. After it was destroyed by fire in 1898, Palmer built an extravagant Italian Renaissance–style building that survived until 1964, when it was leveled to make room for the new Antlers Plaza. That in turn was closed for over a year after it was purchased by Doubletree Hotels—and reopened only in October 1990 after a dramatic face-lift.

Antique black-walnut nightstands from the old Antlers provide a touch of historic continuity in every guest room. The rooms, appointed in brown and beige shades, feature king-size, queen-size, or double beds, armoires with televisions, clock radios, two telephones (50¢ for local calls), and ample closet space. Corner rooms are larger, with desks. The 13th-floor concierge level has a hospitality room and additional amenities.

The hotel offers a full range of services, including a fitness center, indoor pool, and whirlpool. It has two restaurants, including Colorado Springs first microbrewery, Judge Baldwin's (see "Dining," below).

COLORADO SPRINGS MARRIOTT, 5580 Tech Center Dr., Colorado Springs, CO 80919. Tel. 719/260-1800 or toll free 800/228-9290. Fax 719/260-1492. 302 rms, 8 suites (all with bath). A/C TV TEL

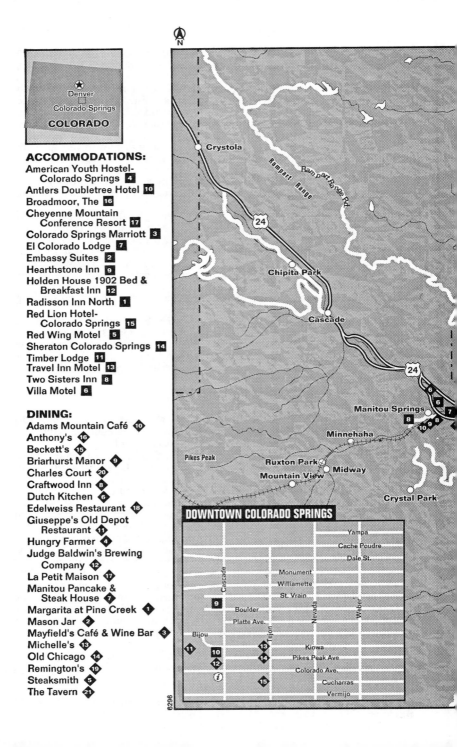

COLORADO

★ Denver
□ Colorado Springs

ACCOMMODATIONS:
American Youth Hostel-
   Colorado Springs **4**
Antlers Doubletree Hotel **10**
Broadmoor, The **16**
Cheyenne Mountain
   Conference Resort **17**
Colorado Springs Marriott **3**
El Colorado Lodge **7**
Embassy Suites **2**
Hearthstone Inn **9**
Holden House 1902 Bed &
   Breakfast Inn **12**
Radisson Inn North **1**
Red Lion Hotel-
   Colorado Springs **15**
Red Wing Motel **5**
Sheraton Colorado Springs **14**
Timber Lodge **11**
Travel Inn Motel **13**
Two Sisters Inn **8**
Villa Motel **6**

DINING:
Adams Mountain Café **10**
Anthony's **16**
Beckett's **15**
Briarhurst Manor **9**
Charles Court **20**
Craftwood Inn **8**
Dutch Kitchen **6**
Edelweiss Restaurant **18**
Giuseppe's Old Depot
   Restaurant **11**
Hungry Farmer **4**
Judge Baldwin's Brewing
   Company **12**
La Petit Maison **17**
Manitou Pancake &
   Steak House **7**
Margarita at Pine Creek **1**
Mason Jar **2**
Mayfield's Café & Wine Bar **3**
Michelle's **13**
Old Chicago **14**
Remington's **19**
Steaksmith **5**
The Tavern **21**

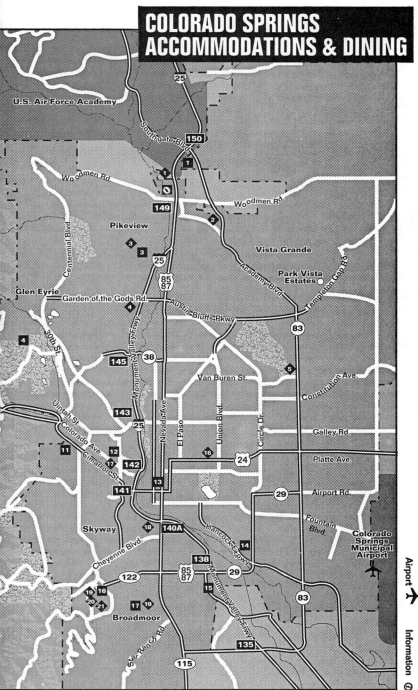

COLORADO SPRINGS
ACCOMMODATIONS & DINING

U.S. Air Force Academy

Pikeview

Glen Eyrie

Vista Grande

Park Vista Estates

Skyway

Broadmoor

Colorado Springs Municipal Airport

$ Rates: Year-round, $120 single, $130 double, $180 suites. AE, CB, DC, DISC, MC, V. **Parking:** Free.

Set atop a low hill overlooking the businesses of the Colorado Springs Technological Center, the red-brick Marriott dominates the surrounding scenery. The interior was designed to incorporate the red sandstone colors of the natural landscape. In the lobby, a large fireplace set against tall picture windows gives warmth to cool nights.

Guest rooms have mauve or lime color schemes and handsome wood furnishings. All have a king-size or two double beds, a large desk with telephone (75¢ local calls) and computer modem jack, easy chair with ottoman, full-length mirrors, vanities, in-room movies, and AM/FM radio alarm clocks. "Executive kings," some of them reserved for women travelers, have a sitting room separate from the bedroom. The concierge level offers complimentary breakfasts, an honor bar, and upgraded amenities.

The hotel offers a full range of services, including indoor and outdoor pools, an exercise room, and sauna.

EMBASSY SUITES, 7290 Commerce Center Dr., Colorado Springs, CO 80919. Tel. 719/599-9100 or toll free 800/EMBASSY. Fax 719/599-4644. 207 suites (all with bath). A/C TV TEL

$ Rates (including full breakfast): $109 single; $119 double. AE, CB, DC, DISC, MC, V. **Parking:** Free.

Entering this hotel, with its central atrium, is like walking into a South American garden. Waterfalls feed a recycling stream that runs through jungle vegetation, in the midst of the red tile and decorative ironwork of a Spanish colonial hacienda.

Standard suites have a living area and a separate bedroom. Cooking facilities include a microwave, refrigerator, wet bar, and coffee maker. There's a table with seating for four and a sleeper sofa in the living area. The bedroom has a king-size bed, or oversized double, private deck or balcony, wardrobe closet, armoire with remote-control cable TV, clock radio, and telephone (50¢ local calls).

The hotel offers a full range of services and dining and other facilities.

RED LION HOTEL–COLORADO SPRINGS, 1775 E. Cheyenne Mountain Blvd. (I-25 at Circle Dr.), Colorado Springs, CO 80906. Tel. 719/576-8900 or toll free 800/547-8010. Fax 719/576-4450. 293 rms, 6 suites (all with bath). A/C TV TEL

$ Rates: $89–$129 single; $99–$139 double; $295–$425 suite. AE, CB, DC, DISC, ER, MC, V. **Parking:** Free.

The most impressive features of this hotel are its two courtyards. One, sporting a fountain and sun deck, provides a pleasant view for inward-looking rooms in this five-story property. The second offers a sunny recess for coffee-shop diners.

The spacious guest rooms have two queen-size beds (no doubles) or a king size, a desk/dresser, table and chairs, and two vanities. All but 50 of the rooms have a private balcony. The appointments are dark desert rose or cypress green. Business travelers appreciate the two-line phones (local calls 50¢), modem hookups, and separate sitting area in the "king" rooms.

The hotel offers a full range of services and dining and other facilities.

SHERATON COLORADO SPRINGS HOTEL, 2886 S. Circle Dr. (I-25, Exit 138), Colorado Springs, CO 80906. Tel. 719/576-5900 or toll free 800/325-3535 worldwide, toll free 800/635-3304 direct. Fax 719/576-7695, ext. 1717. 486 rms, 16 suites (all with bath). A/C TV TEL

$ Rates: $65–$115 single; $80–$130 double; inquire for suites. AE, CB, DC, DISC, MC, V. **Parking:** Free.

Eleven acres of landscaped grounds and a beautiful skylit indoor garden set this Sheraton apart from others. The grounds feature trees, waterfalls, and three plaza-style courtyards. The indoor garden offers a pool, Jacuzzi, and patio dining among palms and other tropical plants.

The rooms are equally inviting. Double rooms have private balconies, views of the indoor or outdoor pool, and desks, along with standard features such as clock radios, full-size mirrors, and vanities. North wing rooms lack the private deck, but offer refrigerators and built-in hair dryers. A half-dozen bilevel suites have a king-size bed in a loft and a sleeper sofa downstairs.

The hotel offers a full range of services and dining and other facilities.

MODERATE

HEARTHSTONE INN, 506 N. Cascade Ave., Colorado Springs, CO 80903. Tel. 719/473-4413 or toll free 800/521-1885. 23 rms (all with bath). A/C

$ Rates (including full breakfast): $80–$140 double, single $10 less per night. AE, MC, V. **Parking:** Free.

This elegant small downtown hotel is actually two historic homes (one built in 1885, the other in 1900) connected by a carriage house. Listed on the National Register of Historic Places, and the winner of numerous preservation awards, the inn is decorated with fascinating old photographs and antiques, as well as reproduction king- and queen-size brass beds.

Each room has a personality of its own. The Study, for instance, is a parlor-style room with built-in bookcases and a fireplace. The Solarium has an open-air latticed porch. The Sewing Room has an antique treadle sewing machine that functions as a nightstand. The third-floor Loft has three dormer windows, a queen-size brass bed, and a tiny child's bed with a child-size rocking chair.

Breakfasts are fantastic—imaginative variations of the standard eggs, cheese, and meat, plus home-baked breads and fruit dishes. There are no televisions or telephones in the rooms, but the innkeeper will take messages. There is a common parlor with games, a piano, and fresh coffee. Pets and smoking are not permitted.

HOLDEN HOUSE 1902 BED & BREAKFAST INN, 1102 W. Pikes Peak Ave., Colorado Springs, CO 80904. Tel. 719/471-3980. 5 rms (all with bath). A/C

$ Rates (including full breakfast): $65–$95 single or double. AE, CB, DC, DISC, MC, V. **Parking:** Free.

Innkeepers Sallie and Welling Clark restored this storybook colonial revival–style Victorian, and its adjacent 1906 carriage house, and filled the rooms with antiques and family heirlooms. Located near Old Colorado City, it has a living room with a tile fireplace, a front parlor with a television, and verandas where gourmet breakfast is served on warm summer mornings.

The guest rooms are named after Colorado mining areas, and each contains some memorabilia of that district. All have queen-size beds and three have fireplaces. Largest is the turreted Aspen Suite, with a romantic "tub for two." The Cripple Creek and Leadville rooms, although smaller, are comfortably individualistic. In the

---

(F) FROMMER'S COOL FOR KIDS:
HOTELS

Hearthstone Inn *(see p. 113)* Well-behaved children who respect antique furnishings will be delighted by the toddler-size bed and rocking chair in the Loft.

Radisson Inn North *(see p. 114)* Kids like the 24-hour pool and video games, and for teens looking to "hang out," Chapel Hills Mall is right across the street.

Sheraton Colorado Springs Hotel *(see p. 112)* Two swimming pools, a separate children's pool, shuffleboard, and a putting green will keep the kids happy.

Carriage House, the gabled Goldfield Suite features a skylight above the bed and a cozy "tub for two"; the Silverton Suite has a four-poster bed and claw-foot tub.

Smoking, children, and pets are not permitted. (The two resident cats, Ming Toy & Muffin, claim prior tenancy.) Those with allergies should request the cat-free Carriage House.

RADISSON INN NORTH, 8110 N. Academy Blvd. (I-25, Exit 150A), Colorado Springs, CO 80920. Tel. 719/598-5770 or toll free 800/333-3333. Fax 719/598-3434. 193 rms, 7 suites (all with bath). A/C TV TEL
$ Rates: Mid-May to Sept, $70–$90. Oct to mid-May, $60–$80. Year-round, $145–$225 suite. AE, CB, DC, DISC, ER, MC, V. **Parking:** Free.

The nearest full-service hotel to the Air Force Academy has a large and beautiful atrium, with fountains spurting beneath a skylight. Guest rooms have king-size or double beds, light-wood furnishings, dressing tables, and remote-control TV with in-house movies. There are also three large Jacuzzi suites.

Boondoggle's Eating and Drinking Establishment serves three meals daily beneath the atrium skylight. The hotel has a 24-hour indoor pool, hot tub, sauna, guest laundry, gift shop, video games, complimentary airport shuttle, and is located within easy walking distance of Chapel Hills Mall.

TWO SISTERS INN, 10 Otoe Place, Manitou Springs, CO 80829. Tel. 719/685-9684. 4 rms (2 with bath), 1 cottage with bath.
$ Rates (including full breakfast): $59 with shared bath, $70 with bath; $90 cottage. DISC, MC, V. **Parking:** Free.

Built by two sisters in 1919 as a boardinghouse, this bed and breakfast, not far from the Pikes Peak Cog Railway, is still owned and operated by two women—sisters in spirit if not actually in blood. Wendy Goldstein and Sharon Smith have furnished the four bedrooms and separate honeymoon cottage with family heirlooms and photographs, in a style best described as "informal elegance."

Rooms in the main house feature Victorian frills and furnishings, such as quilts and claw-foot bathtubs. The cottage, with a separate bedroom and living room, has a feather bed, gas log fireplace, refrigerator, and shower with skylight.

There are fresh flowers in each room, and homemade chocolates and baked goods are served in the evenings. Well behaved children over 10 are permitted, but smoking and pets are not.

VILLA MOTEL, 481 Manitou Ave., Manitou Springs, CO 80829. Tel. 719/685-5492 or toll free 800/341-8000. 47 rms (all with bath, 7 with kitchen). A/C TV TEL
$ Rates: Memorial Day–Labor Day, $66–$74 single or double. Early Oct to early May, $29 single; $35–$43 double. Shoulder periods, $46–$52 single or double. Kitchenettes, $78–$84. AE, CB, DC, DISC, MC, V.

A two-story chalet-style motel opposite a streamside city park, the Villa has numerous facilities that make it a popular place for families. All rooms have ceramic tile baths, cable TV, radios, free local phone calls, and courtesy coffee and tea service. The motel has a heated pool and whirlpool, as well as a coin-op laundry. Seven units have kitchenettes. Kids are welcome; pets are not.

BUDGET

AMERICAN YOUTH HOSTEL–COLORADO SPRINGS, 3704 W. Colorado Ave., Colorado Springs, CO 80904. Tel. 719/475-9450. 48 dormitory beds.
$ Rates: $10 for AYH members. No credit cards. **Closed:** Mid-Sept to mid-May.

Located in the Garden of the Gods Campground, this hostel—comprised of a series of streamside cabins—is blessed with a remarkably beautiful location. As with all hostels, toilets and showers are shared, and there's a laundry and telephone. This hostel also has a huge swimming pool and hot tub. Located on a city bus line, it's open mid-May to mid-September only, and only to AYH and IYH members.

EL COLORADO LODGE, 23 Manitou Ave., Manitou Springs, CO 80829.

Tel. 719/685-5485 or toll free 800/782-2246. Fax 719/685-4645. 27 cabins (8 with kitchen, all with bath). A/C TV TEL
$ Rates: Summer, $40–$85. Winter rates up to 30% less. AE, DC, DISC, MC, V.
Most of the cabins in this southwestern-style lodge have fireplaces and beamed ceilings. Each cabin has from one to three clean, well-appointed rooms and can accommodate from two to six people. Kitchenettes are fully equipped with cooking utensils and dishes. The lodge boasts the largest outdoor swimming pool in Manitou Springs. Pets are not allowed.

RED WING MOTEL, 56 El Paso Blvd., at Beckers Lane, Manitou Springs, CO 80829. Tel. 719/685-9547 or toll free 800/RED-9547. 27 rms (10 with kitchen, all with bath). A/C TV TEL
$ Rates: Mid-May to mid-Sept, $47–$54. Mid-Sept to mid-May, $32–$40. Kitchenettes, $5 additional. AE, CB, DC, DISC, MC, V.
Set back a block off busy Manitou Avenue, this motel faces a fenced-in heated swimming pool with a kids' slide and sun deck. Nearby is a covered patio for picnicking. The spacious rooms have basic furnishings, ceramic tile bath, in-room coffee, and hot-water heating. Ten have kitchenettes.

TIMBER LODGE, 3627 W. Colorado Ave., Colorado Springs, CO 80904. Tel. 719/636-3941 or toll free 800/448-6762. 25 rms. A/C TV TEL
$ Rates: $44–$98 per cabin, which sleeps two to six people; slightly less in winter. AE, DC, DISC, MC, V.
Rustic outside but modern inside is the best way to describe these comfortable separate and duplex cabins along a creek on the west side of Colorado Springs. Half of the rooms offer kitchen facilities, and all have knotty pine interiors and cable TV. No pets.

TRAVEL INN, 512 S. Nevada, Colorado Springs, CO 80903. Tel. 719/636-3986. 36 rms. A/C TV TEL
$ Rates: Mid-May to mid-Sept, $37–$45. Mid-Sept to mid-May, $31–$39. AE, CB, DC, DISC, MC, V.
Clean, comfortable, and centrally located, this older well-maintained motel has no pool, but it offers in-room coffee and cable TV at very good rates.

CAMPING

GARDEN OF THE GODS CAMPGROUND, 3704 W. Colorado Ave., Colorado Springs, CO 80904. Tel. 719/475-9450 or toll free 800/345-8197.
$ Rates: $17–$22 for two people. Extra person $2. AE, MC, V. **Closed:** Mid-Oct to mid-Apr.
Near the park, this large tree-shaded campground offers 250 full R.V. hookups, an adults-only section, and additional tent sites. It has tables, a barbecue pit, bathhouses, a grocery, laundry, heated swimming pool, Jacuzzi, playground, and games room.

MUELLER STATE PARK, P.O. Box 49, Divide, CO 80814. Tel. 719/687-2366. Reservations, toll free 800/678-2267. 90 sites.
$ Rates: $3 per vehicle park entrance fee, plus camping fee of $7 for walk-in sites, $10 for drive-in sites with electricity. MC, V for reservations, cash only at the park.
Located on the west slope of Pikes Peak, this park is ideal for campers who want to get away from it all, but still have a hot shower and modern restroom at the end of the day. To reach the park entrance take Highway 24 west from Colorado Springs to Divide (25 miles), then go 3½ miles south on Highway 67.

4. DINING

The categories below define a "Very Expensive" restaurant as one in which most dinner main courses are priced above $20; "Expensive," $15 to $20 for main courses; "Moderate," $10 to $15; "Inexpensive," $6 to $10; and "Budget," less than $6.

VERY EXPENSIVE

CHARLES COURT, Broadmoor West, in the Broadmoor, Lake Circle. Tel. 634-7711.
Cuisine: CONTEMPORARY AMERICAN. **Reservations:** Recommended.
$ Prices: Breakfast $7.75–$15.50, appetizers $5.50–$12, main dinner courses $17–$35. CB, DC, MC, V.
Open: Breakfast daily 7–10am; dinner daily 6:30–9:30pm.
The English country-manor atmosphere of this outstanding restaurant, with picture windows looking across Broadmoor Lake to the renowned Broadmoor Hotel, lends itself to a fine dining experience complete with attentive service.

The creative menu changes seasonally, but you'll usually find such delicacies as Colorado lamb chops, medallions of beef Madeira, salmon filet, and a wild-game selection such as free-range black-buck antelope with hot blueberry sauce and corn-nugget yam chips. And there's always a fantasy of dessert selections.

REMINGTON'S, in the Cheyenne Mountain Conference Resort, 3225 Broadmoor Valley Rd. Tel. 719/576-4600.
Cuisine: CONTINENTAL. **Reservations:** Recommended.
$ Prices: Appetizers $3.75–$7.25; main courses $18.50–$25. A 15% service charge is added to all bills. AE, CB, DC, DISC, MC, V.
Open: Dinner seatings from 6–9pm.
Named one of the country's top 25 restaurants by the American Culinary Institute, this is also Colorado Springs' "most romantic" restaurant, according to readers of the daily *Gazette Times*. An intimate 18-table gem in a spacious resort lodge, the walls are adorned with contemporary art, but the magnificent view outside attracts more attention.

Diners can begin with oyster Padua (in beluga caviar) or a crab-and-asparagus terrine. Classic Caesar and wilted-spinach salads are prepared table side. Main dishes range from Remington's trio (beef, lamb, and veal with charcutière sauce), and duckling Aberdeen (in a cider sauce), to lobster tail saffron beurre blanc. A creative fixed-price menu ($30.95) changes every two months.

EXPENSIVE

BRIARHURST MANOR, 404 Manitou Ave., Manitou Springs. Tel. 685-1864.
Cuisine: CONTINENTAL/AMERICAN. **Reservations:** Suggested.
$ Prices: Appetizers $3.95–$15; main courses $10.50–$29.50. Seniors' and children's portions and prices. AE, CB, DC, MC, V.
Open: Dinner Mon–Sat 6–10:30pm; Sunday brunch 11am–3pm.
The original 1876 stone home of Manitou Springs founder Dr. William Bell, this magnificent Tudor mansion has all the style of an English country house. Its pink sandstone walls are accented by the emerald green of surrounding grounds. Designated for demolition in 1975, the restaurant was purchased by chef Sigi Krauss, an East German who came to Colorado Springs after 10 years in Vail. Krauss restored its rich wood interior, including a Gothic oak staircase, and turned it into a world-renowned restaurant.

The Briarhurst features meticulously prepared selections ranging from Rocky Mountain rainbow trout to Colorado lamb chops to a vegetarian platter. There are also homemade pastas, chicken and seafood, and a variety of exquisite beef dishes. Not to be missed is the Wednesday night all-you-can-eat candlelight buffet, with a marvelous array of delicacies from around the world, from appetizers to dessert.

CRAFTWOOD INN, 404 El Paso Blvd., Manitou Springs. Tel. 685-9000.
Cuisine: ROCKY MOUNTAIN. **Reservations:** Recommended.
$ Prices: Appetizers $3.50–$7; main courses $9.50–$23.50. MC, V.
Open: Dinner daily 5–10pm.

An English country Tudor building with beamed ceilings, stained-glass windows, and a copper-hooded fireplace, the Craftwood Inn was built in 1912 as a coppersmith shop. Today this excellent restaurant specializes in game and other regional cuisine—dishes such as juniper venison, grilled piñon trout, and roast pheasant with zinfandel sauce. You can also have roast duck, beef tenderloin, or a vegetarian platter. Save room for dessert, though. You won't believe the bittersweet chocolate pâte, jalapeño white-chocolate mousse with raspberry sauce, or prickly pear sorbet. The restaurant also boasts an excellent wine list.

To reach the Craftwood Inn, turn off Manitou Avenue at the Buffalo Bill Wax Museum; go uphill one block, and turn left onto El Paso Boulevard.

LA PETITE MAISON, 1015 W. Colorado Ave. Tel. 632-4887.
   Cuisine: CONTEMPORARY. **Reservations:** Recommended.
$ **Prices:** Appetizers $2.95–$5.25; main courses $12.95–$18.75; early evening (5–6:30pm) lighter fare $6.95–$11.95.
   Open: Tues–Sat 5–10pm.

This delightful 1894 Victorian cottage is home to a gem of a restaurant, providing a blend of classic French and modern southwestern cuisine, served in a friendly, intimate setting to the strains of recorded chamber music. The service is impeccable, and the food top rate.

Chef Holly Mervis is a fanatic about using only the freshest and finest ingredients and has gained local fame for her imaginative variations on classic recipes. Recommendations include lamb chops dijonnaise and sautéed beef tenderloin with Danish bleu-cheese sauce. And you'll also enjoy the southwestern chicken with black beans and avocado compote, sautéed duck breast, Spanish ragoût of pork, or fresh fish.

There's an excellent wine cellar with about 150 choices, and be sure to try the white-chocolate cheesecake with strawberry sauce for dessert. This is where locals go to celebrate special occasions.

THE MARGARITA AT PINE CREEK, 7350 Pine Creek Rd. Tel. 598-8667.
   Cuisine: INTERNATIONAL. **Reservations:** Recommended.
$ **Prices:** Fixed-price meal $6.75 at lunch, $17 at dinner Tues–Fri, $23 Sat, $9–$15 Sunday brunch. AE, CB, DC, MC, V.
   Open: Lunch Tues–Fri 11:30am–2pm; dinner Tues–Sat 6–9pm; brunch Sunday 10:30am–2pm.

Local newspaper readers say this restaurant has the "best ambience" in Colorado Springs. Located at the north end of the city, near the Woodmen Road exit from I-25, the Margarita occupies a modified southwestern structure with tile floors and stuccoed walls. A tree-shaded outdoor patio is open in summer.

Lunches feature a choice of soup (usually a beef barley and a seafood or mushroom bisque), salad, and homemade bread. There is also a southwestern special. Six-course dinners Tuesday through Friday include a Mexican selection and two continental choices. Saturday night there's a special baroque dinner featuring continental cuisine accompanied by live chamber music, and the Sunday brunch features a classic brunch menu. Those who are vegetarians or have other dietary restrictions are invited to call ahead for special arrangements.

STEAKSMITH, 3802 Maizeland Rd., at Academy. Tel. 596-9300.
   Cuisine: STEAK/SEAFOOD. **Reservations:** Recommended.
$ **Prices:** Appetizers $2.95–$5.50, main courses $10.50–$23.95. AE, DC, MC, V.
   Open: Mon–Sat 5:30–10pm, Sun 4–9pm. Open for cocktails from 4pm daily.

Voted by local newspaper readers as having the best steaks, seafood, and service in Colorado Springs, as well as being their all time favorite restaurant, the Steaksmith works hard to maintain its reputation. In addition to a wide choice of top-quality beef, the restaurant offers excellent seafood, including Alaskan king crab, Australian lobster tails, and large Gulf shrimp.

A sign of its success, diners are warned that the prime rib and fresh seafood specials often sell out early in the evening. The menu also features baby-back pork ribs and several chicken entrées, a variety of appetizers and homemade soups, and dessert specials such as homemade caramel piñon nut ice cream. A children's menu is also available.

THE TAVERN, Broadmoor Main, at the Broadmoor, Lake Circle. Tel. 634-7711.
    Cuisine: STEAK/SEAFOOD. **Reservations:** Recommended.
$ **Prices:** Appetizers $5–$9.50; main courses $7.50–$17 at lunch, $10–$27.50 at dinner. Children's menu $3.25–$4.25. CB, DC, MC, V.
    Open: Lunch daily 11am–2pm; dinner daily 5–10pm.
Original Toulouse-Lautrec lithographs on the walls mark the Tavern as a place with unusual class . . . and a few unexpected surprises. The main restaurant features live background music, both at noon and at night. Adjoining is the Garden Room, richly planted with tropical foliage. In either room, service is impeccable—and this is the Broadmoor's informal dining spot!

    Lunch specials include a London broil *au jus,* seafood crêpes Louise, Welsh rarebit, or a variety of sandwiches and salads. Dinners are more elaborate: Choose from prime rib, filet mignon, chateaubriand for two, blackened or broiled salmon or swordfish, or half a roast duck or chicken.

MODERATE

ANTHONY'S, 1919 E. Boulder St. Tel. 471-3654.
    Cuisine: ITALIAN. **Reservations:** Recommended for groups of 5 or more.
$ **Prices:** Appetizers $3.50–$5.95; lunch $4.15–$8.95; dinner $6.95–$14.95. AE, DISC, MC, V.
    Open: Lunch Mon–Fri 11am–2pm; dinner Tues–Thurs and Sun 5–9pm, Fri–Sat 5–10pm.
Located in a quiet eastside neighborhood, Anthony's is a tranquil escape from a hectic day. In summer, it has an outdoor patio for dining; in winter, a blazing fire keeps you warm. All pastas, from manicotti to fettuccine, are homemade. Chicken parmigiana and saltimbocca alla romana are favorite dishes of regulars. All dinners come with soup, salad, and garlic bread, and a plate of linguine accompanies meat dishes.

BECKETT'S, 128 S. Tejon St. Tel. 633-3230.
    Cuisine: AMERICAN.
$ **Prices:** Lunch $4.65–$8.95; dinner $7.45–$14.95. AE, MC, V.
    Open: Lunch Mon–Sat 11am–2pm; dinner daily 5–10pm.
Located downtown in the 1890s Alamo Building, Beckett's has a classic brew-house atmosphere of stone and dark wood. Five handcrafted beers from Boulder Brewery are poured here—my favorite is Red Dog, a medium-bodied ale—along with a wide selection of bottled beer. The lounge menu includes steak burgers, Bratwurst, Buffalo wings, and armadillo eggs (fried jalapeños stuffed with cream cheese). There's a patio beer garden in warmer weather, and the restaurant features rotisserie chicken, alder-smoked salmon, baby-back ribs, pasta, and steak. There's live entertainment in the lounge Thursday, Friday, and Saturday evenings.

EDELWEISS RESTAURANT, 34 E. Ramona Ave. Tel. 633-2220.
    Cuisine: GERMAN. **Reservations:** Recommended.
$ **Prices:** Appetizers $4.25–$5.75, lunch $3.45–$6.75; dinner $10.95–$15.50. AE, CB, DC, DISC, MC, V.
    Open: Lunch Mon–Fri 11:30am–2pm; dinner Sun–Thurs 5–9pm, Fri–Sat 5–9:30pm.
A lovely stone building with a big inside fireplace and outside patio, the Edelweiss underscores its Bavarian atmosphere with strolling folk musicians on weekend nights. Located south of I-25 near the intersection of South Tejon Street and Cheyenne Boulevard, just west of Nevada Avenue, it offers a hearty menu of Jägerschnitzel,

Wiener Schnitzel, Sauerbraten, Bratwurst, and other old-country specials—as well as New York strip steak and fresh fish and chicken dishes. Don't miss the fruit strudels for dessert!

THE HUNGRY FARMER, 575 Garden of the Gods Rd. Tel. 598-7622.

Cuisine: CONTINENTAL. **Reservations:** Accepted.
$ **Prices:** Lunch $4–$6.50; dinner $9.95–$15.50. AE, CB, DC, DISC, MC, V.
Open: Lunch Mon–Fri 11:30am–2:30pm; dinner Mon–Sat 5–10pm, Sun noon–9pm.

Famous for its generous portions and prime rib, this restaurant has a farm atmosphere, complete with bales of hay, that makes it a favorite among kids. There's a large selection of steak, chicken, seafood, ribs, and veal, and all dinners include the bottomless bucket of soup, corn on the cob, salad, potato, homemade oatmeal muffins, and cinnamon rolls. Children have their own menu, and if you order a cup of coffee you get a little show—high-pouring, they call it. There's also a full-service bar.

MAYFIELD'S CAFE AND WINE BAR, 802 Village Center Dr. Tel. 528-8400.

Cuisine: NEW AMERICAN. **Reservations:** Recommended.
$ **Prices:** Breakfast $1.95–$5.95; appetizers $3.75–$4.25; main courses $4.75–$5.95 at lunch, $11.95–$14.50 at dinner. AE, DISC, MC, V.
Open: Breakfast Mon–Fri 6–9am; lunch Mon–Fri 11am–2:30pm; dinner Tues–Sat 5–9pm.

Floral wreaths and garlands of peach and mauve haphazardly adorn this contemporary restaurant, located in the Rockrimmon neighborhood in the northwestern part of Colorado Springs. Recipes tend to be invented here more frequently than at other restaurants—but they rarely if ever fail. Tried and true are a variety of salads and pastas for lunch. Feeling adventurous? Come for dinner. The dinner menu changes daily, and you can be assured that whatever is offered during your visit won't be boring. Be prepared for creations such as red-chili steak tartare, fresh grilled mahimahi with papaya salsa, curried roast game hen, and chocolate-hazelnut cheesecake for dessert.

INEXPENSIVE

GIUSEPPE'S OLD DEPOT RESTAURANT, 10 S. Sierra Madre St. Tel. 635-3111.

Cuisine: ITALIAN/AMERICAN.
$ **Prices:** Lunch $3.95–$9.75; dinner $5.75–$14.95. AE, CB, DC, DISC, MC, V.
Open: Daily 11am–11pm.

Old Engine 168 occupies a place of honor in front of this restaurant, lodged in a restored Denver & Rio Grande train station downtown. Spaghetti, lasagne, and stone-baked pizza are house specialties. On the American side of the ledger, you can get a full slab of baby-back ribs, an engineer's cut of prime rib, a pepper steak flamed with cognac, fried chicken, or Louisiana shrimp crèole.

JUDGE BALDWIN'S BREWING COMPANY, the Antlers Doubletree Hotel, 4 S. Cascade Ave. Tel. 473-5600.

Cuisine: AMERICAN.
$ **Prices:** $3.95–$8.95. AE, CB, DC, DISC, MC, V.
Open: Sun–Thurs 11am–11pm; Fri–Sat 11am–midnight.

 Judge Baldwin's, like many good brew pubs, takes just as much pride in its food as it does in its handcrafted beer. The great tasting burgers are made from one-half pound of fresh ground beef, charbroiled to order. For the more health conscious, you can get the same thing made with ground turkey. There's also a pasta of the day, black-bean chili, a huge club sandwich, beer-batter shrimp, a turkey sandwich, pizza, and the highly recommended killer quesadillas, which are flour tortillas filled with Jack and Cheddar cheese and jalapeño peppers. The menu also lists a variety of soups and salads, and strangely enough, everything here goes well with Judge Baldwin's excellent beers (see "The Bar Scene," below).

THE MASON JAR, 5050 N. Academy Blvd. Tel. 598-1101.
    Cuisine: AMERICAN.
$ Prices: Lunch or dinner $4.60–$12. Children's meals $2.40. DISC, MC, V.
    Open: Daily 11am–10pm.
The Mason Jar caters to every member of the family. Children, for instance, get crayons and coloring pages, as well as a more manageable menu selection. This is basic American country cuisine: fried chicken, pork chops, prime rib, seafood, sandwiches, and fresh-baked desserts. There's a second Mason Jar in Old Colorado City at 2925 W. Colorado Ave. (tel. 632-4820).

OLD CHICAGO, 118 N. Tejon St. Tel. 634-8812.
    Cuisine: PASTA/PIZZA.
$ Prices: Lunch $4.50–$8.95; dinner $5.50–$11. AE, MC, V.
    Open: Lunch Mon–Sat 11am–4pm; dinner Sun–Thurs 4–10pm, Fri–Sat 4–11pm.
The door handles are made of Chicago Cubs bats. Etched-glass dividers in the restaurant depict the Chicago skyline as seen from Lake Michigan. This is Colorado, not Illinois, but everybody loves the Cubs. A special feature is the pasta bar—6 sauces daily (from a list of 18) to cloak your spaghetti, linguine, or fettuccine. Old Chicago boasts 25 draft and 85 bottled beers; drink them all and you'll be a "Hall of Foam" member.
    There are Old Chicagos throughout the Front Range, including another restaurant on the north side at 7115 Commerce Center Dr. (tel. 593-7678).

BUDGET

ADAMS MOUNTAIN CAFE, 733 Manitou Ave., Manitou Springs. Tel. 685-1430.
    Cuisine: INTERNATIONAL/NATURAL FOODS.
$ Prices: Breakfast $1.85–$5.25; lunch $2.50–$5.95; dinner $5.95–$12. No credit cards.
    Open: Breakfast/lunch daily 7:30am–3pm; dinner Mon–Sat 5–9pm.
The Victorian dining room offers live acoustic guitar Tuesdays and Thursdays, along with a healthy, varied menu. About half the delicious meals are vegetarian; the rest are chicken, turkey, or shrimp. Try whole-grain fruit pancakes for breakfast, an Indonesian tempeh sandwich for lunch, and spinach lasagne or a chicken burrito for dinner.

DUTCH KITCHEN, 1025 Manitou Ave., Manitou Springs. Tel. 685-9962.

 FROMMER'S COOL FOR KIDS:
RESTAURANTS

Edelweiss Restaurant (see p. 118) Kids will enjoy the strolling musicians playing German folk music on weekends, and they'll love the apple and cherry strudels.

Giuseppe's Old Depot Restaurant (see p. 119) An original locomotive stands outside this old Denver & Rio Grande Railroad station. Spaghetti and pizza are always great kids' food.

The Mason Jar (see p. 120) The friendly staff gives children crayons and coloring pages to keep them busy as they wait for their meal, ordered off a kids' menu.

Cuisine: AMERICAN.
$ Prices: Lunch $3.25–$4.95; dinner $5.25–$6.75.
Open: Sat–Thurs 11:30am–3:30pm and 4:30–8pm. Closed mid-Dec to mid-March.

Good, homemade food served in a casual, friendly atmosphere is what you'll find at this relatively small restaurant that has been owned and operated by the Flynn family since 1959. The corned beef is always good, and if you're there in summer be sure to try the fresh rhubarb pie. Other house specialties include buttermilk pie and homemade soups. Fourteen brands of bottled beer are available, served in frosted mugs.

MANITOU PANCAKE AND STEAK HOUSE, 26 Manitou Ave., Manitou Springs. Tel. 685-9225.
Cuisine: AMERICAN.
$ Prices: Breakfast $2–$6.85; breakfast buffet $4.90 adults, $2.90 children 7–12, $1.90 children under 7; lunch and dinner $1.70–$7.95. MC, V.
Open: Memorial Day–Labor Day 6am–8pm, Labor Day–Memorial Day, 6am–2pm.

Perhaps the best bargain in town, this popular restaurant serves a 10-ounce New York strip steak with two vegetables and bread for just $6.20. There are a variety of home-cooked plate specials for lunch and dinner, including pot roast, grilled ham, and chicken and dumplings. The breakfast menu features a variety of omelets, and a fantastic all-you-can-eat breakfast buffet is served from 7 to 11am daily during the summer, and Saturdays and Sundays at other times.

MICHELLE'S, 122 N. Tejon St. Tel. 633-5089.
Cuisine: AMERICAN/GREEK/SOUTHWEST.
$ Prices: Breakfast $2.50–$4.75; lunch and dinner $3.50–$5.95; snacks and salads $1.25–$5.50.
Open: Mon–Thurs 9am–11pm, Fri–Sat 9am–midnight, Sun 10am–11pm.

Talk about an eclectic menu, it's amazing how many different things Michelle's does well, and at very reasonable prices. Since opening in 1952 this restaurant has been known for its excellent handmade chocolates, fresh churned ice cream, and Greek specialties like gyros and spanakopita. But it also has great burgers, croissant sandwiches, a half-dozen different salads, numerous omelets, and a delicious breakfast burrito. A three page ice-cream menu includes everything from a single scoop of vanilla to the "Believe It or Not Sundae," featured in *Life Magazine* in November 1959, weighing 42 pounds and including every flavor of ice cream Michelle's makes.

There is also a Michelle's in the Citadel Shopping Center, at East Platte Avenue and North Academy Boulevard (tel. 597-9932).

---

5. ATTRACTIONS

The attractions of the Pikes Peak region can be placed in two general categories: "natural," such as Pikes Peak, Garden of the Gods, and Cave of the Winds, and "historic and educational," including the Air Force Academy, Olympic Training Center, museums, historic homes, and art galleries. And there are also the gambling houses of Cripple Creek. Those who recently arrived in Colorado from sea-level areas might want to leave mountain excursions, such as the cog railway to the top of Pikes Peak, for close to the end of their stay, to allow their bodies to adapt to the lack of oxygen at higher elevations. See "Health & Insurance" in Chapter 2 of this book.

SUGGESTED ITINERARIES

IF YOU HAVE ONE DAY Start early at the **Garden of the Gods,** a unique geological site featuring red sandstone pillars, and **Cave of the Winds,** an underground cavern. Then head downtown to the **Pioneers Museum** for an

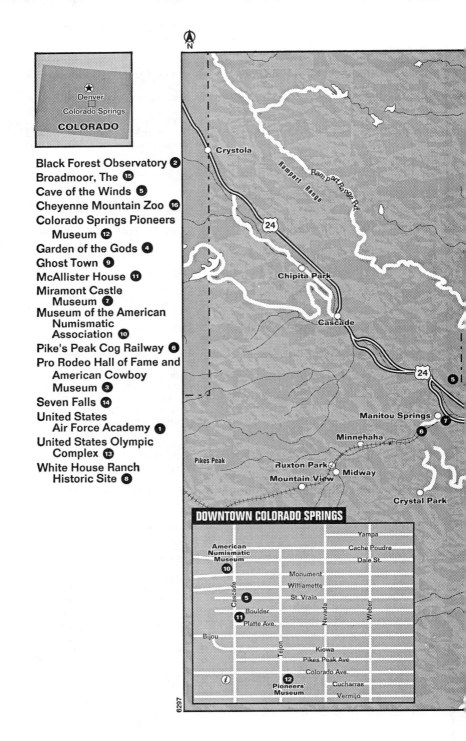

★ Denver
☐ Colorado Springs
COLORADO

Crystola

Rampart Range Rd

Rampart Range

24

Chipita Park

Cascade

24

❺

Manitou Springs ❼

Minnehaha ❻

Pikes Peak

Ruxton Park

Mountain View   Midway

Crystal Park

DOWNTOWN COLORADO SPRINGS

American
Numismatic
Museum ❿

Yampa

Cache Poudre

Dale St.

Monument

Williamette

St. Vrain

Cascade

❺

Boulder

⓫ Platte Ave.

Bijou

Nevada

Weber

Tejon

Kiowa

Pikes Peak Ave

Colorado Ave.

ⓘ

⓬ Pioneers'
Museum

Cucharras

Vermijo

6297

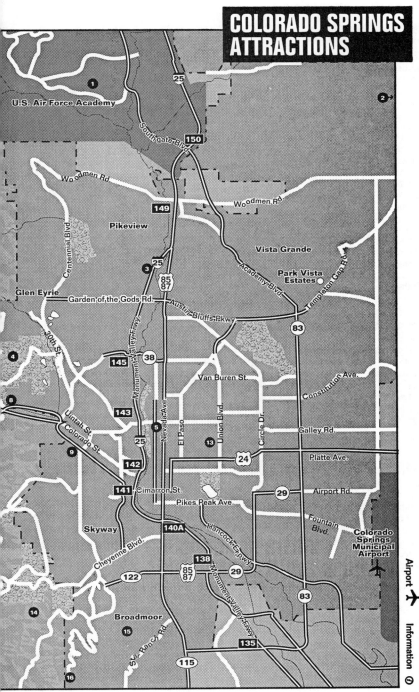

COLORADO SPRINGS ATTRACTIONS

U.S. Air Force Academy

Pikeview

Vista Grande

Park Vista Estates

Glen Eyrie

Garden of the Gods Rd.

Austin Bluffs Pkwy.

Academy Blvd.

Templeton Gap Rd.

Van Buren St.

Constitution Ave.

Galley Rd.

Platte Ave.

Cimarron St.

Pikes Peak Ave.

Airport Rd.

Skyway

Hancock Expwy.

Fountain Blvd.

Colorado Springs Municipal Airport

Cheyenne Blvd.

Broadmoor

Monument Valley Frwy.

Woodmen Rd.

Southgate Blvd.

Centennial Blvd.

30th St.

Uintah St.

Colorado St.

Nevada Ave.

El Paso

Union Blvd.

Circle Dr.

Airport ✈

Information ⓘ

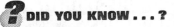

- Katherine Lee Bates wrote the words to "America the Beautiful" after seeing the view from the top of Pikes Peak in 1893.
- The Pikes Peak Auto Hillclimb is the second-oldest car race in America, after the Indianapolis 500.
- The U.S. Air Force Academy is one of Colorado's foremost tourist attractions, drawing over one million visitors per year.
- The North American Air Defense Command (NORAD) in Colorado Springs is the continent's first warning system of a nuclear-missile strike.
- Nikola Tesla, inventor of the first alternating-current electrical system, created artificial lightning above his Colorado Springs home at the turn of the 20th century.

overview of the history of the region. After lunch tour the **Air Force Academy,** and if time remains, visit the **Pro Rodeo Hall of Fame.**

IF YOU HAVE TWO DAYS Spend your first day as suggested above.

Begin day 2 with a 1-hour tour of the **Olympic Training Center,** followed by stops at **Ghost Town** and **Van Briggle Art Pottery.** After lunch visit **Old Colorado City, McAllister House,** the **Fine Arts Center,** and the **Museum of the American Numismatic Association.**

IF YOU HAVE THREE DAYS Spend your first two days as suggested above.

Head to **Manitou Springs** for the free 1-hour guided mineral springs historical **walking tour.** Then visit **Miramont Castle** and the **Manitou Cliff Dwellings.** Check out the Manitou Springs shops and galleries, have lunch, and then hop on the **cog railway** for a trip to the top of Pikes Peak. If time remains, stop at the **Pike's Peak Auto Hill Climb Museum.**

IF YOU HAVE FIVE OR MORE DAYS Spend your first three days as suggested above.

On day 4, catch up on some of the Colorado Springs sights you might have missed, such as the **May Natural History Museum of the Tropics,** the **Western Museum of Mining and Technology,** the **World Figure Skating Hall of Fame,** and the **Nikola Tesla Museum of Science and Industry.**

For your fifth day consider visits to the **Black Forest Observatory,** the **Cheyenne Mountain Zoo,** the **North Pole, Seven Falls,** and day trips to **Cripple Creek, Florissant Fossil Beds National Monument,** and the **Royal Gorge.**

THE TOP ATTRACTIONS

UNITED STATES AIR FORCE ACADEMY, off I-25, Exit 156B. Tel. 472-2555.

Colorado Springs's pride and joy got its start in 1954, when Congress authorized the establishment of a U.S. Air Force Academy and selected this 18,000-acre site—on a broad mesa buffered on the west by the Rockies, 12 miles north of downtown—from among 400 other locations. The first class of cadets enrolled in 1958. Each year since, about 4,000 cadets have begun the four years of rigorous training required to become air force officers.

Approach the academy through the North Gate, off I-25, Exit 156B. Soon after entering the grounds, at the intersection of North Gate Boulevard and Stadium Boulevard, you'll see an impressive outdoor B-52 display. Where North Gate Boulevard becomes Academy Drive, another mile or so farther, look to your left to see the Cadet Field House, where basketball and ice hockey games are played (see "Sports & Recreation," below), and the Parade Ground, where cadets can be spotted marching some Saturday mornings and on special occasions.

Academy Drive soon curves to the left. Six miles from the North Gate, signs mark the turnoff to the Barry Goldwater Air Force Visitor Center. Open daily year-round, it has a variety of exhibits and films on academy history and cadet life, extensive literature and self-guided tour maps, and the latest information and schedules on academy activities. There's also a large gift shop, coffee shop, public telephones, and restrooms.

A short trail from the visitor center leads to the Cadet Chapel. Its 17 gleaming aluminum spires soar 150 feet skyward, and within are separate chapels for the major Western faiths. The public can visit Monday through Saturday from 9am to 5pm and on Sunday from 1 to 5pm. The chapel is closed for five days around graduation and during special events.

Also within easy walking distance of the visitor center are the Academy Planetarium (tel. 472-2778), a classroom for astronomy, physics, and navigation classes that offers periodic free public programs; Arnold Hall (tel. 472-4499), the social center (open daily from 9am to 5pm), which offers historical exhibits, a cafeteria, and a theater featuring a variety of public shows and lectures throughout the year; and Harmon Hall (tel. 472-2520), the administration building, where potential cadets can obtain admission information.

After leaving the visitor center, continue south, then east, on Academy Boulevard to Stadium Boulevard, where you can't miss Falcon Stadium on your left. If you're in town in the fall, try to attend a football game.

Turn right on Stadium Boulevard and follow it out to South Gate Boulevard, which leaves the academy grounds at I-25, Exit 150B. En route, you'll pass the Thunderbird Airmanship Overlook, where you might be lucky enough to watch cadets parachuting, soaring, and practicing their takeoffs and landings in U.S. Air Force Thunderbirds.

For specific information about the academy, write Visitor Services Division, Directorate of Public Affairs, U.S. Air Force Academy, Colorado Springs, CO 80840.

Admission: Free.

Open: Daily 9am–5pm; additional hours for special events.

PIKES PEAK COG RAILWAY, 515 Ruxton Ave., Manitou Springs. Tel. 685-5401.

A century old in 1991, the train to the summit of the Front Range's most imposing mountain is more popular than ever. The first passenger train climbed 14,110-foot Pikes Peak on June 30, 1891. Steam power was slowly replaced by diesel between 1939 and 1957. Four custom-built Swiss twin-unit rail cars, each seating 216 passengers, were put into service in 1989. It takes 75 minutes to ascend and to descend the 9-mile line, with grades up to 25°; including a stay of 40 minutes on top of the mountain, a round-trip requires 3¼ hours.

The journey is exciting from the start, but passengers begin to "ooh" and "ah" when the track leaves the aspen and pine forests and creeps above the timberline at about 11,500 feet. The view from the summit takes in Denver, 75 miles north; New Mexico's Sangre de Cristo range, 100 miles south; the Cripple Creek mining district, on the mountain's western flank, and wave after wave of Rocky Mountain subranges to the west; and the seemingly endless sea of Great Plains to the east. The Summit House at the top of Pikes Peak has a restaurant and gift shop.

Take a jacket or sweater, because it can be very cold and/or windy at the top. If you've got cardiac or respiratory restrictions, give this trip a miss.

Admission: $21 adults, $9.50 children under 12 (but those under 5 held on lap are free).

Open: June–Aug, eight departures daily; in May and Sept–Oct, two to six departures daily. Definite May–Oct departures from Manitou Springs at 9:20am and 1:20pm. Reservations recommended.

COLORADO SPRINGS PIONEERS MUSEUM, 215 S. Tejon St. Tel. 578-6650.

Housed in the former El Paso County Courthouse, built in 1903 and listed on the National Register of Historic Places, this museum is an excellent place to begin your visit to Colorado Springs. Exhibits show the community's history including its beginning as a fashionable resort, the railroad and mining eras, and its growth and change into the 20th century.

IMPRESSIONS

The air is so refined that you can live without much lungs.
—SHANE LESLIE, *AMERICAN WONDERLAND*, 1936

You can ride an over 80-year-old Otis bird-cage elevator to the original courtroom, where several Perry Mason episodes were filmed. Recent renovation has uncovered gold and silver images of goddesses, painted on the courtroom walls as a political statement when the country was changing from a gold to silver monetary standard.

The museum also contains the Victorian home and furnishings of writer Helen Hunt Jackson, several art galleries, a section on the history of blacks in the region, plus Native American artifacts, turn-of-the-century toys, quilts, and clothing.

Admission: Free.

Open: Tues–Sat 10am–5pm, Sun 1–5pm.

GARDEN OF THE GODS, Ridge Rd., I-25, Exit 146. Tel. 578-6933.

One of the West's most unique geological sites, the Garden of the Gods was a wintering place of Ute tribespeople until a century ago. The Native Americans were no doubt impressed by the spectacular red sandstone pillars, sculpted by rain and wind, freezing and thawing, over 300 million years. The 1,300-acre park was deeded to the city in 1909.

Located where several life zones and ecosystems converge—Great Plains grass-lands, Southwest piñon and juniper, Rocky Mountain pine forests—the park harbors a variety of plant and animal communities. Oldest survivors in the park are the ancient, twisted junipers, some 1,000 years old. The strangest animals are honey ants, which gorge themselves with honey in the summer and fall to become living honey pots to feed their colonies during winter hibernation.

Hiking maps are available at the **visitor center,** which also offers displays on the history, geology, plants, and wildlife of the park. Twice a day in summer, park naturalists host 45-minute walks through the park and afternoon interpretive programs. You may spot technical rock climbers on some of the park spires (they must first register at the visitor center).

In the center of the park is the pueblo-style Hidden Inn, built in 1917 and decorated with Navajo sand paintings. A wide selection of southwestern arts and crafts and other souvenirs are sold, and light refreshments are available at the Patio Café.

Also in the park is the **White House Ranch Historic Site** (see "More Attractions," below).

Admission: Free.

Open: Park, May–Oct, daily 5am–11pm; Nov–Apr, daily 5am–9pm. Visitor center, early June to Labor Day, daily 9am–5pm; Labor Day to early June, daily 10am–4pm. **Directions:** Take Garden of the Gods Road west off I-25 (Exit 146) and turn south on 30th Street, or follow Ridge Road north off U.S. 24 or Colorado Avenue.

UNITED STATES OLYMPIC COMPLEX, 1 Olympic Plaza, corner of Boulder St. and Union Blvd. Take I-25, Exit 143. Tel. 578-4618.

When NORAD and the Air Defense Command moved their operations into Cheyenne Mountain in 1978, this 36-acre site in the middle of Colorado Springs became home to the U.S. Olympic Committee. Today the complex provides a sophisticated training center for more than half of the 41 U.S. Olympic sports, including swimming, basketball, and gymnastics. From 14,000 to 17,000 athletes of all ages train or attend developmental programs each year.

Visitors should stop first at the visitor center for a free guided tour, starting every 30 minutes in summer and every hour during the winter. Tours begin with a film on the U.S. Olympic effort, and then take in the Sports Center, with five gymnasiums and a weight-training room; the Indoor Shooting Center with two 50-meter ranges; a new training gymnasium, and a swimming complex with a huge 50-meter 10-lane pool.

A gift shop next to the visitor center sells Olympic-logo merchandise, with proceeds going to support training programs. One mile south of the Olympic Complex, in Memorial Park off Union Boulevard, is the 7-Eleven Velodrome, with a banked track for bicycle and roller speed skating.

Admission: Free.

Open: Summer, Mon–Sat 9am–5pm, Sun 10am–4pm; winter, Mon–Sat 9am–4pm, Sun noon–4pm.

MORE ATTRACTIONS
ARCHITECTURAL HIGHLIGHTS

THE BROADMOOR, Lake Circle, at Lake Ave. Tel. 634-7711.
This famous Italian Renaissance–style resort hotel has been a Colorado Springs landmark since it was built by Spencer Penrose in 1918. (See "Accommodations," above.)
Admission: Free.
Open: Daily year-round.

MIRAMONT CASTLE MUSEUM, 9 Capitol Hill Ave., Manitou Springs. Tel. 685-1011.
Built into a hillside by a wealthy French priest as a private home in 1895, and converted by the Sisters of Mercy into a sanitorium in 1907, this unique Victorian mansion has always inspired curiosity. At least nine identifiable architectural styles are incorporated into the structure, among them Gothic, Romanesque, Tudor, and Byzantine. The "castle" has four stories, 28 rooms, 14,000 square feet of floor space, and 2-foot-thick stone walls. One room is a miniature museum, another a model railroad museum. Light meals and tea are served from 11am to 4pm in the Queen's Parlour during the summer. The mansion is just off Ruxton Avenue, en route from Manitou Avenue to the Pikes Peak Cog Railway.
Admission: $3 adults, $1 children 6–12, free for children under 6.
Open: June–Aug, daily 10am–5pm; Sept–May, daily 12–3pm; Victorian Christmas, three weekends beginning Thanksgiving weekend, Fri–Sun noon–4pm.

HISTORIC BUILDINGS

MCALLISTER HOUSE, 423 N. Cascade Ave., at St. Vrain St. Tel. 635-7925.
This Gothic cottage, listed in the National Register of Historic Places, was built of brick in 1873 when the builder, an army major named Henry McAllister, learned that the local wind was of such force as to have blown a train off the tracks nearby! It contains many original furnishings, including three marble fireplaces. The house is now owned by the Colonial Dames of America, whose very knowledgeable volunteers lead guided tours.
Admission: $2 adults, $1 seniors and students, 75¢ children 6–16, free for children under 6.
Open: Summer, Wed–Sat 10am–4pm, Sun noon–4pm; winter, Thurs–Sat 10am–4pm.

WHITE HOUSE RANCH HISTORIC SITE, Gateway Rd., Garden of the Gods. Tel. 578-6777.
The history of three different pioneer eras comes to life at this working ranch at the east entrance to Garden of the Gods park. Visitors can see how Coloradans lived during the homestead era (1868), the ranch era (1895), and the estate period (1907). Guides in period clothing compare the life-styles of the three eras, and there is a working blacksmith shop and demonstrations of historical agricultural techniques. Besides the original homestead, general store, and ranch, there's a nature trail for the blind.
Admission: $3 adults, $2 seniors, $1 children 6–12, free for children under 6.
Open: Early June to August, Wed–Sun 10am–4pm; Sept and Thanksgiving through Christmas, Sat 10am–4pm, Sun noon–4pm; Jan–May, open only selected weekends for special events.

MUSEUMS & GALLERIES

COLORADO SPRINGS FINE ARTS CENTER, 30 W. Dale St., west of N. Cascade Ave., I-25, Exit 143. Tel. 634-5581.
Georgia O'Keeffe, John James Audubon, John Singer Sargent, Charles Russell,

Albert Bierstadt, Nicolai Fechin, and other famed painters and sculptors are represented in the permanent collection of the Fine Arts Museum here, one of several facilities that call the center home. Opened in 1936, the center now also houses a 450-seat performing arts theater, 27,000 volume art research library, the Bemis Art School offering visual arts and drama classes, the Taylor Museum displaying the cultural history of the Southwest, a tactile gallery for the visually impaired, and a delightful sculpture garden. Changing exhibits in the North and East Galleries showcase local collections, as well as touring international exhibits. Designed by renowned Santa Fe–architect John Gaw Meem, the art-deco style building reflects southwestern mission and pueblo influences.

Admission: Galleries and museum, $3 adults, $1.50 seniors and students, free for children under 6. Free for everyone Sat 10am–noon. Separate admission for performing-arts events.

Open: Galleries and museum, Tues–Fri 9am–5pm, Sat 10am–5pm, Sun 1–5pm. Closed federal holidays.

GHOST TOWN, 400 S. 21st St., Old Colorado City. Tel. 634-0696.

Comprised of authentic 19th-century buildings relocated from other parts of Colorado, this "town" is out of the elements and under cover in Old Colorado City. There's a sheriff's office, jail, saloon, general store, livery stable, blacksmith shop, rooming house, assayer's office, and more. Animated frontier characters tell stories of the Old West, while a shooting gallery, antique arcade machines, and nickelodeons provide additional entertainment.

Admission: $3.75 adults, $2 children 6–16, under 6 free.

Open: Summer, Mon–Sat 9am–7pm, Sun noon–6pm; call for winter hours.

HALL OF PRESIDENTS LIVING WAX STUDIO, 1050 S. 21st St., Old Colorado City. Tel. 635-3553.

More than 100 life-size wax figures, all crafted at Madame Tussaud's London studios, are assembled in 26 room-size chapters of American history.

Admission: $4 adults, $2 children 6–11, free for children under 6.

Open: Memorial Day–Labor Day, daily 9am–9pm; Labor Day–Memorial Day, daily 10am–5pm.

MANITOU CLIFF DWELLINGS MUSEUM, U.S. 24, Manitou Springs. Tel. 685-5242.

Before Mesa Verde and other archeological treasure troves were protected by the National Park Service, zealous scientists horded many of the finest artifacts. Some of those artifacts have been reacquired and are displayed in this excellent relocated 12th-century cliff village, built by archeologists in Phantom Cliff Canyon around 1900. Native American dancers perform during the high tourist season.

Admission: $4 adults, $2 children 7–11, free for children under 7.

Open: June–Aug, daily 9am–8pm; Apr and May, Sept, Oct, daily 9am–6pm. **Closed:** Nov–Mar.

MAY NATURAL HISTORY MUSEUM OF THE TROPICS, 710 Rock Creek Canyon Rd. Tel. 576-0450.

One of the world's outstanding collections of giant insects and other tropical invertebrates is presented at this museum. James F. May (1884–1956) spent more than half a century exploring the world's jungles while compiling this illustrious collection of about 7,000 arthropods. The new Museum of Space Exploration is also located in the John May Museum Center, adjacent to the Golden Eagle Ranch R.V. park and campground, four miles south of the Colorado Springs city limits, a mile west of Colo. 115 opposite Fort Carson.

Admission: $4.50 adults, $2.50 children.

Open: May–Sept, daily 9am–6pm. **Closed:** Oct–Apr.

MUSEUM OF THE AMERICAN NUMISMATIC ASSOCIATION, 818 N. Cascade Ave. Tel. 632-2646.

The largest collection of its kind west of the Smithsonian Institute consists of eight galleries of coins, tokens, medals, and paper money from around the world. There's also a collectors' library, a gallery for the visually impaired, and an authentication department.

Admission: Free, but donations are welcome.

Open: Memorial Day–Labor Day, Mon–Sat 8:30am–4pm. Labor Day– Memorial Day, Mon–Fri 8:30am–4pm.

NIKOLA TESLA MUSEUM OF SCIENCE AND TECHNOLOGY, 2220 E. Bijou St. Tel. 475-0918.

Science buffs will love this small but fascinating collection of early electronics and related gadgets. The museum's primary purpose is to display and demonstrate some of the many inventions of Nikola Tesla (1856–1943), who was awarded over 100 U.S. patents, and is credited with accidentally throwing all of Colorado Springs into darkness during one of his many experiments. Tesla, a contemporary of Thomas Edison's, perfected alternating current and invented the Tesla coil, a transformer used to produce high-frequency power. Guided hands-on tours are usually given daily at 2pm, and possibly at other times. The museum also includes an extensive science and technology bookstore.

Admission: $4 adults, $2 children under 14 and seniors.

Open: Mon–Fri 10am–4pm, Sat 9am–4pm. **Closed:** Holidays.

PETERSON AIR AND SPACE MUSEUM, Peterson Air Force Base main gate, off Hwy. 24. Tel. 556-4915.

Through its exhibits this museum traces the history of Peterson Air Force Base, NORAD, the Air Defense Command, and Air Force Space Command. Of special interest are 17 historic aircraft, including P-47 Thunderbolt and P-40 Warhawk fighters from World War II, plus jets from the Korean War to the present. There's also a small gift shop with air- and space-related posters, videos, and souvenirs.

Admission: Free.

Open: Tues–Fri 8:30am–4:30pm, Sat 9:30am–4:30pm. **Closed:** Sundays, Mondays, and holidays.

PIKES PEAK AUTO HILL CLIMB EDUCATIONAL MUSEUM, 135 Manitou Ave., Manitou Springs. Tel. 685-4400.

Commemorating the nation's second-oldest auto race, after the Indianapolis 500, this museum displays nearly a century of memorabilia and historic photos, and close to two dozen race cars dating from the 1920s to today. Racing legends including Mario Andretti, Parnelli Jones, and Al and Bobby Unser have competed in the annual July Fourth race—156 turns on a gravel highway, ending 14,110 feet above sea level.

Admission: $3 adults, $2 seniors, free for children under 12.

Open: May–Oct 1, daily 9am–5pm. **Closed:** Oct 2–Apr.

PRO RODEO HALL OF FAME AND AMERICAN COWBOY MUSEUM, 101 Pro Rodeo Dr., off Rockrimmon Blvd. W I-25, Exit 147. Tel. 528-4764.

A multimedia theatrical presentation sketches the history of cowboys and rodeos in the West. Displays on the development of ropes, saddles, chaps, and boots are seen in Heritage Hall. A special video technique gives viewers a realistic, jouncing ride atop a wild Brahma bull in a Theater II film sequence. Showcases of photos, trophies, belt buckles, and memorabilia honor rodeo greats in the Hall of Champions.

Admission: $5 adults, $2 children 5–12, free for children under 5.

Open: Daily 9am–5pm. **Closed:** New Year's Eve and Day, Easter, Thanksgiving, and Christmas.

WESTERN MUSEUM OF MINING AND INDUSTRY, Gleneagle Drive, at I-25, Exit 156A. Tel. 488-0880.

Historic hard-rock mining machinery and other equipment from Cripple Creek and other turn-of-the-century Colorado gold camps form the basis of this museum's 3,000-plus item collection. There's an operating Corliss steam engine with a 17-ton flywheel, a life-size underground mine reconstruction, an actual 1890s mill, and a new exhibit on mining-town life that shows how early western miners and their families lived. Visitors can also pan for gold and view an 18-minute multiprojector slide presentation on life in the early mining camps.

The museum's 27-acre exhibit site is located just east of the north gate of the U.S. Air Force Academy.

Admission: $5 adults, $4 seniors 60 and older and students 13–17, $2 children 5–12, and free for children under 5.

Open: Mon–Sat 9am–4pm, Sun noon–4pm; call for hours Dec–Feb.

WORLD FIGURE SKATING MUSEUM AND HALL OF FAME, 20 First St. Tel. 635-5200.

The only museum of its kind in the world, this is where you can see 1,200 years of ice skates, from early skates of bone to highly decorated cast-iron examples to the skates of today. There are skating costumes, medals, and other memorabilia, changing exhibits, films, a library, and gift shop. A gallery exhibits skating-related paintings, including works by 17th century Dutch artist Pieter Brueghel and Americans Winslow Homer and Andy Warhol.

Admission: Free.

Open: June–Aug, Mon–Sat 10am–4pm; Sept–May, Mon–Fri 10am–4pm.

NATURAL ATTRACTIONS

BLACK FOREST OBSERVATORY, 12815 Porcupine Lane. Tel. 495-3828.

The observatory may not be "natural," but the heavens it studies are as pure as exist! The only public observatory in Colorado offers public viewing by reservation. It's located off Colo. 83 east of the Air Force Academy and north of Research Parkway. Take Exit 151 off I-25.

Admission: $8 per person.

Open: By reservation only.

CAVE OF THE WINDS, U.S. 24, Manitou Springs. Tel. 685-5444.

Discovered by two boys on a church outing in 1881, this impressive underground cavern has offered public tours for well over a century. The 40-minute Discovery Tour takes visitors along a well-lit 3-quarter-mile trail through 20 subterranean chambers, complete with classic stalagmites, stalactites, crystal flowers, and limestone canopies. In the Adventure Room, modern lighting techniques return visitors to an era when spelunking was done by candle and lantern. There's also a physically demanding, 2½-hour Wild Tour that's guaranteed to get participants dirty: Armed only with flashlights and helmets, adventurers slither and scramble through remote tunnels of the Manitou Grand Caverns system.

Admission: $8 adults, $4 children 6–15, free for children under 6.

Open: Memorial Day–Labor Day, daily 9am–9pm; Labor Day–Memorial Day, daily 10am–5pm. Adventure Tours depart every 15 minutes. Wild Tours are conducted three times daily in summer, other times by reservation.

SEVEN FALLS, South Cheyenne Canyon, west on Cheyenne Blvd. Tel. 632-0765.

A spectacular 1-mile drive through a box canyon, including a transit of the Pillars of Hercules where the canyon narrows to just 42 feet, climaxes at these cascading falls. Seven separate waterfalls dance down a granite cliff, illuminated during the summer months by colored lights. A new elevator takes visitors to the Eagle Nest viewing platform. A mile-long trail atop the plateau passes the grave of 19th-century author Helen Hunt Jackson (*Ramona*) and ends at a panoramic view of Colorado Springs.

Admission: $5.75 adults, $3 children 6–12, free for children under 6.

Open: Memorial Day–Labor Day, daily 8am–11pm; other months, reduced hours.

NEIGHBORHOODS

MANITOU SPRINGS, Manitou Ave. off U.S. 24 West.

Actually a separate town with its own government, Manitou Springs is one of the country's largest National Historic Districts. Legend has it that Ute Indians named the springs Manitou, their word for "Great Spirit," because they believed that the Great Spirit had breathed into the waters to create the natural effervescence of the springs. Called the Saratoga of the West a century ago, when trips to "take the waters" were in fashion, even President Ulysses S. Grant visited.

Today, the community offers the breathtaking sight of Pikes Peak, plus a step back in history to magnificent Victorian buildings, many housing fascinating shops, galleries, and restaurants. An effort is underway to reestablish the lure of the mineral springs, with restoration and preservation of spring houses and many of the original 28 mineral springs.

OLD COLORADO CITY, Colorado Ave., between 21st and 31st Sts.

Founded in 1859, before Colorado Springs itself, Colorado City boomed in the 1880s after General Palmer's railroad came through. Tunnels led from the respectable side of town to the saloon and red-light district so that city fathers could carouse without being seen going or coming back—or so the legend goes. Today this historic district has an interesting assortment of shops, galleries, and restaurants.

PANORAMAS

PIKES PEAK HIGHWAY, off U.S. 24 at Cascade. Tel. 684-9383.

There is perhaps no view in Colorado to equal the 360° panorama from the 14,110-foot summit of Pikes Peak. Whether by cog railway (see "The Top Attractions," above) or private vehicle, the ascent—though not for the faint of heart—is one that no able-bodied visitor should miss. This 19-mile toll highway (paved for 7 miles, all-weather gravel thereafter) starts at 7,400 feet, some 4 miles west of Manitou Springs. There are numerous photo stops en route up the mountain, and restaurant/gift shops at 11 miles and at the summit. Deer, mountain sheep, and other animals can often be seen on the slopes, especially above the timberline (around 11,500 feet).

This 156-curve toll road is the site of the annual July 4 Pikes Peak Auto Hill Climb, the Pikes Peak Marathon footrace in August, and the New Year's Eve climb and fireworks show.

Admission: $5 adults, $2 children 6–11, free for children under 6.

Open: June 10–Labor Day, daily 7am–6:30pm; Apr–June 9 and Labor Day to the first major snowfall (late Oct), 9am–3pm. **Closed:** Late Oct to Mar.

PARKS & GARDENS

CHEYENNE MOUNTAIN ZOO, Zoo Rd. off Mirada Rd. Tel. 475-9555.

Located south of the Broadmoor hotel on the cool lower slopes of Cheyenne Mountain, 6,800 feet above sea level, this menagerie claims to be America's only mountain zoo. Not large by big-city standards, it nevertheless boasts some 600 animals from the familiar to the exotic—tigers, lions, elephants, hippopotamuses, monkeys, giraffes, and many more. New exhibits include rocky cliffs for mountain goats, a pebbled beach for penguins, and an animal-contact area where children can pet certain creatures. There's even an antique carousel!

Admission to the zoo includes road access to the Will Rogers Shrine of the Sun, a tall granite structure built without nails in 1937 as a memorial to the beloved humorist. Inside is a pictorial biography of Rogers; outside, an impressive view of the surrounding countryside.

Admission: $5.75 adults, $4.75 seniors, $3 children 3–11, free for children under 3.

Open: Summer, daily 9am–6pm; winter, daily 9am–5pm.

MONUMENT VALLEY PARK, Monument Creek from Bijou St. north to Fontanero St. Tel. 578-6640.

This long, slender park follows Monument Creek through downtown Colorado Springs beside the I-25 freeway. At its south end are formal zinnia, begonia, and rose gardens. In the middle are demonstration gardens of the Horticultural Art Society.

There are softball/baseball fields, a swimming pool, volleyball and tennis courts, children's playgrounds, picnic shelters, and two trails—the 4¼-mile Monument Creek Trail for walkers, runners, and cyclists, and the 1-mile Monument Valley Fitness Trail at the north end of the park, beside Bodington Field.

Admission: Free.

Open: Daily year-round.

MUELLER STATE PARK, P.O. Box 49, Divide, CO 80814. Tel. 719/687-2366.

Among Colorado's newest state parks, Mueller has 12,000 acres of prime scenic beauty along the west slope of Pikes Peak. There are 90 miles of trails, designated for hikers, horseback riders, and mountain bikers, with opportunities to observe elk, bighorn sheep, and the park's other wildlife. The best times to spot wildlife are spring and fall, just after sunrise and just before sunset. There are ranger-led hikes and campfire programs in an 80-seat amphitheater. To reach the park entrance take Highway 24 west from Colorado Springs to Divide (25 miles), then go 3½ miles south on Highway 67. (See "Camping" section.)

Admission: $3 per vehicle for day use.

Open: Daily 6am–10pm.

NORTH CHEYENNE CAÑON PARK, Cheyenne Blvd. west of 21st St. Tel. 634-9320 or 578-6146.

This small piece of the Rocky Mountains is entirely within the Colorado Springs city limits. North Cheyenne Creek races across pinkish-red Pikes Peak granite formations, dropping 1,800 feet in five miles in a series of cascades and waterfalls. The elevation range supports a variety of native grasses and wildflowers, including numerous rare orchids, as well as a White Fir Botanical Preserve. There are six picnic areas in the park and several hiking trails, the longest of which is the 3-mile Columbine Springs Trail. Exhibits on history, geology, flora, and fauna can be found at the visitor center at the foot of Helen Hunt Falls; nature walks and interpretive programs leave from here daily in summer.

The Starsmore Discovery Center, at the entrance to the park, has maps, information, and interactive exhibits for all members of the family, including audio-visual programs and a climbing wall where you can learn about rock climbing.

Admission: Free.

Open: Park, May–Oct, daily 5am–11pm; Nov–Apr, daily 5am–9pm. Starsmore Discovery Center, early June to Labor Day, daily 9am–5pm; Labor Day to early June, Wed–Sun 10am–4pm. Helen Hunt Falls Visitor Center, early June to Labor Day, daily 9am–5pm; Sept–Oct, Sat–Sun 10am–4pm, closed Sept to early June.

PALMER PARK, Maizeland Rd. off Academy Blvd. Tel. 578-6640.

Deeded to the city in 1899 by its founder, Gen. William Jackson Palmer, this 722-acre preserve features hiking, biking, and equestrian activities spread across a low mesa in central Colorado Springs. It boasts a variety of minerals (including quartz, topaz, jasper, and tourmaline), a rich vegetation (including a yucca preservation area), and considerable wildlife. The **Edna Mae Bennet Nature Trail** is a self-guided excursion; there are numerous other trails, including those shared with riders from the adjoining **Mark Reyner Stables.** The park also includes 12 separate picnic areas, softball/baseball fields, and volleyball courts.

Admission: Free.

Open: Daily year-round.

COOL FOR KIDS

In addition to the listings below, children will also enjoy the following attractions described in "More Attractions" above: Hall of Presidents Living Wax Studio, May Natural History Museum of the Tropics, Miramont Castle Museum, Cheyenne Mountain Zoo, and Ghost Town.

ARCADE AMUSEMENTS, INC., 930 Block Manitou Ave., Manitou Springs. Tel. 685-9815.

Among the West's oldest and largest amusement arcades, this game complex just might be considered a hands-on arcade museum, as well as a fun arcade for kids of all ages. There are some 250 machines, from original working penny pinball machines to modern video games, skee-ball, and 12-player horse racing.

Admission: Free, with arcade games ranging from 1¢ to 75¢.

Open: First weekend in May through Labor Day, daily 10am–midnight.

BOARDWALK USA, Pioneer Plaza Mall at Circle Dr. and Galley Rd., Tel. 637-PLAY.

This entertainment center has plenty to do for kids of all ages, including bumper cars, an 18-hole miniature golf course, large video game room, virtual reality, and an indoor theme park just for younger children (under four feet tall).

Admission: $5 for 1 hour plus $1 more for each additional hour, $10 for all day.

Open: School days 11am–10pm; school holidays, weekends, and summer, 9am–midnight.

BUFFALO BILL WAX MUSEUM, 404 W. Manitou Ave., Manitou Springs. Tel. 685-5900.

The legends of the Old West—Kit Carson and Davy Crockett, Jesse James and his gang, Wyatt Earp's gunfight at the OK Corral—are depicted by over 100 life-size wax figures in 32 realistic displays.

Admission: $3.50 adults, $1.50 children 6–16, free for children under 6.

Open: Apr 15–30, daily 10am–4pm; May–Aug, daily 9am–9pm; Sept and Oct, daily 10–5pm. **Closed:** Nov–Apr 14.

MANITOU WATER SLIDE, 324 Manitou Ave., Manitou Springs. Tel. 685-5867.

This water park has more than the thrilling slides. It includes a miniature golf course and the Miracle House, where gravity isn't what you thought it was.

Admission: $7 for 2 hours, $9 for all day; slide, $4.50 for 10 rides; miniature golf, $3; Miracle House, $1.

Open: Memorial Day weekend to Labor Day, daily 10am–8pm (golf until 11pm).

NORTH POLE, foot of Pikes Peak Hwy. off U.S. 24, 5 miles west of Manitou Springs. Tel. 684-9432.

Santa's workshop is busy from mid-May right up until Christmas Eve. Not only can kids visit shops where elves have some early Christmas gifts for sale, but they can also see Santa himself and whisper their requests into his ear. This 25-acre storybook village features numerous rides, including a miniature train and the *Enterprise* space shuttle, as well as magic shows and musical entertainment, snack shops, and an ice-cream parlor.

Admission: $7.50 ages 2–59, $3 seniors 60 and over, free for children under 24 months.

Open: May 15–31, Fri–Wed 9:30am–6pm, June–Aug, daily 9:30am–6pm, Sept–Dec 24, Fri–Tues 10am–5pm. **Closed:** Christmas–May 14.

ORGANIZED TOURS

Half- and full-day bus tours of Colorado Springs, Pikes Peak, the Air Force Academy, and other nearby attractions are offered by Gray Line Tours, doing business as **Pikes Peak Tours,** 3704 W. Colorado Ave. (tel. 719/633-1181 or toll free 800/345-8197). A variety of tours are offered May through October, including an excursion to Royal Gorge and white-water rafting trips. Prices range from $15 to $50 per person.

Historic walking tours, and other customized individual and group tours are available from **Talk of the Town,** 1313 Sunset Rd. (tel. 633-2724), which also publishes a book of walking tours, *Trips on Twos,* and a book of driving tours, *Trips on Wheels,* available at local bookstores.

A free Downtown Walking Tour brochure, with a map and descriptions of more than 30 historic buildings, can be obtained at the Visitors and Convention Bureau and local businesses.

Another free brochure, titled "Old Colorado City," not only shows the location of more than a dozen historic buildings, but also lists shops, galleries, and other businesses.

The **Town Trolley** provides tours and transportation through Manitou Springs and into part of Garden of the Gods during summer. See the "Getting Around" section at the beginning of this chapter for details.

Highly recommended is the ✪ **Mineral Springs Historical Walking Tour,** with members of the Mineral Springs Foundation leading free 1-hour walks through the community, discussing its history and stopping for samples of water from the different mineral springs. You'll hear about the discovery and founding of the springs, as well as the personalities and fortunes made and lost.

Contact the Manitou Springs Chamber of Commerce (tel. 685-5089 or toll free 800/642-2567) for reservations.

6. SPORTS & RECREATION

SPECTATOR SPORTS

AUTO RACING   The annual Pikes Peak Auto Hill Climb (tel. 685-4400), known as "the Race to the Clouds," is held annually on July 4. An international field of drivers negotiate the winding, hairpin turns of the final 12.4 miles of the Pikes Peak Highway, to the top of the 14,110-foot mountain.

BASEBALL   The Colorado Springs Sky Sox of the Pacific Coast League, a Colorado Rockies AAA farm team, play a full 144-game season, with 72 home games at Sky Sox Stadium, 4385 Tutt Ave. (tel. 597-3000). The season begins the second week of April and runs through Labor Day. Games are played afternoons and evenings. Tickets are $5.50 for reserved seating, $3.50 for general admission. Call the stadium or check the newspaper sports pages for schedule information.

The Air Force Academy plays a spring schedule (February to May) against major college competition.

BASKETBALL   The Air Force Academy plays a full major-college schedule against NCAA Division 1 competition, primarily against Western Athletic Conference foes. The 30-game season begins in late November and continues until about early March. Home contests are played in Cadet Field House (tel. 472-1895).

FOOTBALL   Those same Air Force Academy Falcons, winners of the 1990 Liberty Bowl and members of the Western Athletic Conference, play an 11-game season from September to November. Falcon Stadium (tel. 472-1895 for ticket information) seats 52,153 fans. Call for schedules and ticket information.

GREYHOUND RACING   The Rocky Mountain Greyhound Park, 3701 N. Nevada Ave., I-25, Exit 148A (tel. 719/632-1391) has pari-mutuel dog races from April to September, Wednesday through Saturday at 7:30pm and Sunday, Monday, Wednesday, and Saturday at 1pm. Admission is $1; reserved clubhouse seats are $2. Children are welcome.

There is simulcast greyhound wagering October to March.

ICE HOCKEY   There are not one, but two outstanding college ice-hockey teams in Colorado Springs. The Air Force Academy, of course, plays its home games during the winter season at the Cadet Field House (tel. 472-1895). Colorado College, a small but highly acclaimed 4-year institution in downtown Colorado Springs, plays its home hockey matches at the Broadmoor World Arena, 125 El Pomar Rd. (tel. 577-5795). Call for schedules and ticket information.

RODEO   The Pikes Peak or Bust Rodeo, held annually (since 1941) in early August, is a major stop on the Professional Rodeo Cowboys Association circuit. Its purse of over $150,000 makes it the second-largest rodeo in Colorado (after Denver's National Western Stock Show), 15th in North America. Events are held at 1:30pm and 7:30pm at 10,000-seat Penrose Stadium, 1045 W. Rio Grande Ave. off Eighth Street (tel. 635-3547). Various events around the city, including a parade, observe rodeo week.

SOCCER   Not only does the Air Force Academy have one of the nation's premier collegiate soccer teams, but it also hosts the annual Pikes Peak Invitational Soccer Tournament (tel. 590-9977). Youth teams from 22 states compete in June on the academy athletic fields.

RECREATION

Most of the state and federal agencies that deal with aspects of outdoor recreation are headquartered in Denver. There are branch offices in Colorado Springs for the Colorado Division of Parks and Outdoor Recreation, 2128 N. Weber St. (tel. 471-0900); the Colorado Division of Wildlife, at 2126 N. Weber St. (tel. 473-2945); and the U.S. Forest Service, Pike National Forest Ranger District, 601 S. Weber St. (tel. 636-1602).

Leading sporting-goods dealers in the city include Grand West Outfitters, 3250 N. Academy Blvd. (tel. 596-3031), and Mountain Chalet, 226 N. Tejon St. (tel. 633-0732).

AERIAL SPORTS   Novices can get lessons in hang-gliding from the Eagle's Nest School of Hang Gliding, P.O. Box 25985, Colorado Springs, CO 80936 (tel. 719/594-0498). Classes are conducted year-round by reservation, at a site 15 miles south of the city.

The Black Forest Soaring Society, 24566 David Johnson Loop, Elbert, CO 80106 (tel. 303/648-3623), some 30 miles northeast of the Springs, offers glider rides, rentals, and instruction.

Those wanting to rise above it all in a hot-air balloon can contact several commercial ballooning companies for tours, champagne flights, and weddings, including High But Dry Balloons, P.O. Box 49006, Colorado Springs, CO 80949 (tel. 719/260-0011). On Labor Day weekend, the Colorado Springs Balloon Classic sees more than 100 hot-air balloons launched from the city's Memorial Park. Admission is free. (Tel. 473-2120).

BICYCLING   Aside from the 4-mile loop trail around Monument Valley Park (see "Parks & Gardens" in "Attractions," above), there are numerous other urban trails for bikers. Inquire at the city's Visitor Information Center, 104 S. Cascade Ave. (tel. 635-1632), for the Colorado Springs Area Bicycle Access Map.

Off-road mountain biking has become "the thing to do" in Colorado in recent years. Challenge Unlimited, 204 S. 24th St. (tel. 633-6399 or toll free 800/798-5954), hosts fully equipped, guided rides for every level of experience, including a 19-mile ride down the Pikes Peak Highway.

FISHING   Most Colorado Springs anglers drive south 40 miles to the Arkansas River, or west to the Rocky Mountain streams and lakes, like Eleven Mile Canyon Reservoir and Spinney Mountain Reservoir on the South Platte River west of Florissant. Bass, catfish, walleye pike, and panfish are found in the streams of eastern Colorado; trout is the preferred sport fish of the mountain regions.

IMPRESSIONS

Could one live in constant view of these grand mountains without being elevated by them into a lofty plane of thought and purpose?
—GEN. WILLIAM J. PALMER, Founder of Colorado Springs, 1871

Angler's Covey, 917 W. Colorado Ave. (tel. 471-2984), is a specialty fly-fishing shop and a good source of general fishing information for southern Colorado. It offers guided half- and full-day trips, as well as licenses, rentals, flies, tackle, and so forth.

Just one-half hour from Colorado Springs, Rainbow Falls Park, P.O. Box 9062, Woodland Park, CO 80866 (tel. 687-9074), offers a relaxing family fishing vacation, with no state licenses required. There are also horseback trail rides, hay-wagon rides, tent and R.V. camping, and cabins.

GOLF Among public courses: Cimarron Hills Golf Club, 1850 Tuskegee Place (tel. 597-2637); Patty Jewett Golf Course, 900 E. Española Street (tel. 578-6827); Pine Creek Golf Club; 9850 Divot Trail (tel. 594-9999); and Valley Hi Municipal Golf Course, 610 S. Chelton Rd. (tel. 578-6351). Call for current greens fees and to reserve tee times.

The Springs's finest golf clubs are private. Guests can enjoy the 54-hole Broadmoor Golf Club (tel. 577-5790) at the Broadmoor hotel. It has courses designed by Robert Trent Jones and Arnold Palmer, two driving ranges, and two pro shops. Ditto the Cheyenne Mountain Conference Resort, 3225 Broadmoor Valley Rd. (tel. 576-4600).

HIKING Opportunities abound in municipal parks (see "Parks & Gardens" in "Attractions," above) and Pike National Forest, which bounds Colorado Springs to the west. The U.S. Forest Service district office can provide maps and general information.

Especially popular are the 7.5-mile Waldo Canyon Trail, with its trailhead just east of Cascade off U.S. 24; the 10-mile Mount Manitou Trail, starting in Ruxton Canyon above the hydroelectric plant; and the 12-mile Barr Trail to the summit of Pikes Peak. Mueller State Park (tel. 687-2366), 3½ miles south of Divide en route to Cripple Creek, has 90 miles of hiking and backpacking paths.

HORSEBACK RIDING The Mark Reyner Stables, 3524 Paseo Rd., at Palmer Park (tel. 634-4173), and the Academy Riding Stables, 4 El Paso Blvd., near the Garden of the Gods (tel. 633-5667), offer guided trail rides for children and adults by reservation.

HUNTING Opportunities for hunters abound in the plains east of Colorado Springs (especially for waterfowl) and in the Rockies west of the city (for deer, bear, even cougars). For information and license requirements, consult the Colorado Division of Wildlife or the U.S. Forest Service, Pike National Forest.

ICE SKATING The Plaza Ice Chalet, 111 S. Tejon St. (tel. 633-2423), is open for public ice skating daily, with year-round instruction and rentals. Broadmoor World Arena, 125 El Pomar Rd. (tel. 577-5795), offers instruction and skate rental at times not already reserved for technical figure skaters or hockey teams. The arena has hosted four world figure-skating championships and it's the site of the Broadmoor Ice Revue the first week in July and the "Christmas Pops and Ice Show" each December. Call for prices and schedules.

RIVER RAFTING Colorado Springs is only 40 miles from the Arkansas River near Cañon City. Among the licensed white-water outfitters who tackle the Royal Gorge is Echo Canyon River Expeditions, P.O. Box 1002, Colorado Springs, CO 80901 (tel. 719/275-3154 or toll free 800/748-2953 April to September). Half-day to 3-day trips on "mild to wild" stretches of river are offered. The company uses state-of-the-art equipment, including self-bailing rafts, and has excitement for all ages. Costs range from $28 to $295.

SKIING The nearest major ski areas are Breckenridge, 105 miles northwest, and Monarch, 120 miles west near Garfield.

SWIMMING If your accommodation doesn't have a pool of its own, visit Municipool, 270 Union Blvd. (tel. 578-6634). There are also two water slides and an 18-hole miniature golf course at Manitou Water Park, 327 Manitou Ave., Manitou Springs (tel. 685-5867).

TENNIS   Many city parks have tennis courts, including Memorial Park, at the corner of Hancock and Pikes Peak avenues. Call for information (tel. 578-6676).

7. SAVVY SHOPPING

Five principal areas attract shoppers in Colorado Springs. The Manitou Springs and Old Colorado City neighborhoods are best for souvenir hunting and arts-and-crafts galleries. The Citadel and Chapel Hills malls combine major department stores with a variety of fashionable boutiques. Downtown Colorado Springs, of course, also has numerous fine shops.

Shopping hours vary from store to store and from shopping center to shopping center. In general, it's safe to say that shops will be open Monday through Friday from 10am to 9pm, on Saturday from 10am to 6pm, and on Sunday from noon to 5pm. Stores that cater to tourists have longer hours in summer, shorter hours in winter. Some may close their doors entirely between October and April.

SHOPPING A TO Z

ANTIQUES

THE ANTIQUE EMPORIUM AT MANITOU SPRINGS, 719 Manitou Ave., Manitou Springs. Tel. 685-9195.
The shop's 4,000 square feet of floor space amply displays furniture, china, glassware, books, collectibles, and primitives.

THE VILLAGERS, 2426 W. Colorado Ave., Old Colorado City. Tel. 632-1400.
A diverse array of quality antiques and collectibles are sold. All proceeds go to Cheyenne Village, a community of adults with developmental disabilities.

ART

BUSINESS OF ART CENTER, 513 Manitou Ave., Manitou Springs. Tel. 685-1861.
This renovated historic building is home to numerous artists' studios and a resource library, as well as a contemporary gallery and retail shop. Fine paintings and limited-edition prints, ceramics, textiles, sculpture, jewelry, and other works are displayed and sold. There's also an art-activities area for children. Open Monday through Saturday from 10am to 6pm; Sunday from noon to 6pm.

COLORADO SPRINGS ART GUILD/GALLERY, 2501 W. Colorado Ave., #206. Tel. 389-0303.
A showcase for local artists, the guild has promoted fine arts in the Colorado Springs area since the 1940s. It sponsors quarterly and annual juried shows and classes. Open Monday through Saturday from 10am to 5pm.

COMMONWHEEL ARTISTS CO-OP, 102 Cañon Ave., Manitou Springs. Tel. 685-1008.
Local artists and craftspeople share responsibilities for this cooperative gallery, which features changing exhibits each month.

EL DORADO FINE ARTS GALLERY, 2504 W. Colorado Ave., Old Colorado City. Tel. 634-4075.
Paintings in all media, sculpture, pottery, prints, and art cards are exhibited.

THE FLUTE PLAYER GALLERY, 2501 W. Colorado Ave., Old Colorado City. Tel. 632-7702.

This gallery offers contemporary and traditional Indian jewelry, Pueblo pottery, Navajo weavings, and Hopi kachina dolls.

MICHAEL GARMAN GALLERIES, 2418 W. Colorado Ave., Old Colorado City. Tel. 471-9391.

Garman's lifelike sculpted miniatures delight everyone. His Old West dioramas are noteworthy, but slices of urban life and traditional Americana are equally wonderful.

BOOKS

THE CHINOOK BOOKSHOP, 210 N. Tejon St. Tel. 635-1195 or toll free 800/999-1195.

This is a gem of a bookstore, with 75,000 titles, including an extensive western Americana collection. There's an entire room devoted to maps and globes.

CRAFTS

THE CANDLE SHOPPE, 2421½ W. Colorado Ave., Old Colorado City, Tel. 633-4856.

Candles in all shapes, scents, and sizes are offered in this unique shop, or you can dip your own. Among the 25,000 candles are a 20-pound wax grizzly bear and religious and historic figures that are much too beautiful to burn.

VAN BRIGGLE ART POTTERY, 600 S. 21st St., Old Colorado City. Tel. 633-7729.

Founded in 1900 by Artus Van Briggle, who applied Chinese matte glaze to Rocky Mountain clays and imaginative art nouveau shapes, this is one of the oldest active art potteries in the United States. Today artisans demonstrate their craft, from "throwing on the wheel" to glazing and firing. Finished works are sold in a showroom. Free tours are available, 8:30am to 4:30pm, Monday through Saturday. Finished works are sold in the showroom, starting at $8.

DISCOUNT SHOPPING

CURRENT FACTORY OUTLET, 3106 N. Stone Ave. Tel. 630-7446.

Not just a factory-owned store, but a real outlet, with cardboard boxes piled with closeouts, seconds, and shopworn items, including gift wrap, greeting cards, crafts, and other selections from the Current Catalogue. Open 9am to 6pm weekdays, 9am to 5pm Saturdays, and noon to 5pm Sundays. And they'll ship your purchases.

FASHIONS

LORIG'S, 31 S. Tejon St. Tel. 633-4695.

This downtown store has been serving Colorado's real cowboys for 60 years, with authentic western wear from all major manufacturers.

M.J. CREATIONS, 130 N. Tejon St. Tel. 632-4133.

Classic and innovative women's fashions for moderate prices, with an emphasis on active wear.

MOUNTAIN MOPPETS, 3532 W. Colorado Ave., Old Colorado City. Tel. 633-3473.

This shop offers a wide assortment of children's wear for infants through preteen.

WESTERN WAREHOUSE, 5506 N. Academy Blvd. Tel. 590-9711.

This full-service western-wear outlet boasts more than 5,000 pairs of boots in stock, as well as a Native American jewelry counter.

FOOD

PATSY'S CANDIES, 1540 S. 21st St. Tel. 633-7215.
A popular chocolate and confection manufacturer, Patsy's offers factory tours for groups, by appointment. There's also a retail outlet here.

GIFTS & SOUVENIRS

KRIS KRINGLE LTD., 2619 W. Colorado Ave., Old Colorado City. Tel. 633-1210.
It's Christmas all year-round in this overstuffed shop, especially for fans of model trains, dollhouses, and miniatures.

MUSHROOM MONDAY T-SHIRTS, 941 Manitou Ave., Manitou Springs. Tel. 685-1142.
This large, well-established souvenir shirt shop has more than 100 shirt styles and colors, in all sizes. Thousands of designs can be applied with custom screen printing.

SIMPICH CHARACTER DOLLS, 2413 W. Colorado Ave., Old Colorado City. Tel. 636-3272.
Exquisite handmade dolls are the creation of this specialty shop. Take a free self-guided tour of the assembly plant, where workers explain the process of making, and when necessary repairing, the intricately detailed collectors' dolls. The shop is open Monday through Saturday from 10am to 5pm.

SWISS MISS SHOP, 8455 U.S. 24 West, Cascade. Tel. 684-9679.
Seemingly transplanted from the Alps, this gallery sells European-style gifts such as music boxes, cuckoo clocks, beer steins, Hummel figurines, and Tom Clark gnomes. One mile west of the Pikes Peak turnoff; open Monday through Saturday from 10am to 5pm.

JEWELRY

ALL THAT GLITTERS, 2518 W. Colorado Ave., Old Colorado City. Tel. 475-7160.
This well-established Colorado Springs jeweler is known for beautiful custom gold work and one-of-a-kind designer jewelry.

MANITOU JACK'S TRADING CO., 742 Manitou Ave., Manitou Springs. Tel. 685-5004.
Black Hills gold, 10- and 14-karat, is the specialty here. There's also an extensive collection of Native American jewelry, pottery, sand paintings, and other art. The shop will create custom jewelry and perform repairs.

MEGEL & GRAFF JEWELERS LTD., 12 E. Pikes Peak Ave. Tel. 632-2552.
A downtown institution since 1949, this well-respected shop offers full-service jewelry repair, often while you wait, plus a large selection of diamonds and gems.

MALLS & SHOPPING CENTERS

CHAPEL HILLS MALL, 1710 Briargate Blvd. (N. Academy Blvd., at I-25, Exit 150A). Tel. 594-0111.
Joslins, Sears, Mervyn's, and K-Mart are among the 130-plus shops here. There's also a Gart Bros. sporting goods, a Fashion Bar, a cinema complex, and a dozen food outlets from Greek to Chinese. Open Monday through Saturday from 10am to 9pm and on Sunday from 11am to 6pm.

THE CITADEL, 750 Citadel Dr. E. (N. Academy Blvd., at E. Platte Ave.). Tel. 591-2900.
Southern Colorado's largest mall has 175 shops, including Foley's Department Store, J. C. Penney's, Office Depot, Miller Stockman, Eddie Bauer, and the Disney Store. There's a four-screen movie theater, and Picnic-on-the-Terrace has 17 food outlets. Open Monday through Friday from 10am to 9pm, Saturday from 10am to 7pm, and Sunday from noon to 7pm.

WINE

PIKES PEAK VINEYARDS, 3901 Janitell Rd. (I-25, Exit 138). Tel. 576-0075.

This small award-winning winery produces 8 to 10 moderately priced red, white, and blush wines, including a popular "Coyote White." Tours and tastings are offered in summer daily from 11am to 5pm; in winter, most Saturdays from 10am to 4pm or by appointment.

8. EVENING ENTERTAINMENT

The Colorado Springs entertainment scene is spread throughout the metropolitan area. Pikes Peak Center, the Colorado Springs Fine Arts Center, City Auditorium, Colorado College, and the various facilities at the U.S. Air Force Academy are all outstanding venues for the performing arts. The city also supports dozens of cinemas, nightclubs, bars, and other after-dark attractions.

Current weekly entertainment schedules can be found in the Friday *Gazette Telegraph*. Consult also the listings in *Springs* magazine and *Steppin' Out,* free monthly tabloids.

Tickets for nearly all major entertainment and sporting events can be obtained from TicketMaster (tel. 520-9090), although visitors may find it more convenient to stop at a TicketMaster outlet, including Sound Warehouse at 1877 S. Nevada Ave. (tel. 475-7171) or Disc Jockey Records in Chapel Hills Mall (tel. 260-1995).

THE PERFORMING ARTS

MAJOR PERFORMING ARTS COMPANIES

Classical Music & Opera

COLORADO OPERA FESTIVAL, 27 S. Tejon St. Tel. 473-0073.

Three performances of a classical opera are presented every year in late July at the Pikes Peak Center. Recently, Mozart's *The Magic Flute* drew capacity crowds. English-language productions feature nationally known opera singers.

Admission: Tickets, $12–$50.

COLORADO SPRINGS SYMPHONY ORCHESTRA, 619 N. Cascade Ave. Tel. 633-4611.

This fine professional orchestra annually performs two dozen classical concerts, as well as youth and pops concerts, chamber concerts, a summer series, and two Christmastime institutions—*The Nutcracker* ballet and "Christmas Pops on Ice" at the Broadmoor World Arena. Most performances are at the Pikes Peak Center.

Admission: Tickets, $5–$27.

Theater Companies

BLUEBARDS, Arnold Hall Theater, U.S. Air Force Academy. Tel. 472-4499.

The Air Force Academy's cadet theater group performs to appreciative townspeople as well as fellow cadets.

STAR BAR PLAYERS, Lon Chaney Theatre, City Auditorium, 221 E. Kiowa St. Tel. 578-6855.

This resident theater company presents four full-length plays a year, two studio productions, and a children's Christmas show.

Dance Companies

COLORADO SPRINGS DANCE THEATRE. 7 E. Bijou St., Suite 213, Colorado Springs, CO 80903. Tel. 630-7434.

This nonprofit organization presents dance companies from around the world at

Pikes Peak Center and other venues. Recent productions have included Mikhail Baryshnikov's Company, Joffrey Ballet, New Zealand Ballet, Ballet Folklorico of Mexico, and other traditional, modern, ethnic, and jazz dance programs. Call or write for a brochure.

Admission: $13–$30, with discounts for students and seniors.

ROCKY MOUNTAIN CLOGGERS, P.O. Box 16706, Colorado Springs, CO 80935. Tel. 392-4791.

The 14 members of this national exhibition clog-dance team perform some three dozen shows in the Colorado Springs area each year. Call or write for a current schedule.

MAJOR CONCERT HALLS & ALL-PURPOSE AUDITORIUMS

ARNOLD HALL THEATER, Cadet Social Center, U.S. Air Force Academy. Tel. 472-4499.

Everything from stage plays to lectures to concerts by top-name national and international performers takes place at this campus auditorium. Call for a current schedule.

CITY AUDITORIUM, 221 E. Kiowa St. Tel. 578-6652.

Conventions, trade shows, and concerts are regularly scheduled in the main hall. The Lon Chaney Theatre, with its resident Star Bar Players, is active with stage productions. There's also a small restaurant, the Curtain Call Café.

COLORADO SPRINGS FINE ARTS CENTER, 30 W. Dale St. Tel. 634-5581.

The performing-arts schedule at this civic facility (see "Museums & Galleries" in "Attractions," above) includes the "Just for Kids" Theater, a repertory theater company, dance programs and concerts, and several film series.

PIKES PEAK CENTER, 190 S. Cascade Ave. Tel. 520-7469.

The primary performing-arts facility in Colorado Springs, this 2,000-seat concert hall in the heart of downtown has been acclaimed for its outstanding acoustics. The city's symphony orchestra and dance theater call it home. Top-flight touring entertainers, Broadway musicals, and symphony orchestras make appearances here as well.

DINNER THEATER

ABOUT TOWN DINNER THEATRE, 530 Blackhawk Ct., Colorado Springs, CO 80919. Tel. 593-7303.

Entertaining comedies are the specialty of this theater troupe, whose recent performances have included Neil Simon's *Last of the Red Hot Lovers* and *The Odd Couple,* and *Murder at the Howard Johnson's,* by Ron Clark and Sam Bobrick. Call for times and locations.

Admission: $18–$27 for dinner buffet or cocktail show.

FLYING W RANCH, 3330 Chuckwagon Rd. Tel. 598-4000 or toll free 800/232-FLYW.

This working cattle and horse ranch just north of the Garden of the Gods treats visitors to a western village of a dozen restored buildings and a mine train. The western stage show features bunkhouse comedy, cowboy balladry, and foot-stompin' fiddle, banjo, and guitar music. From mid-May through September the town opens each afternoon at 4:30pm, with a chuck-wagon dinner served ranch style at 7:15pm and the show at 8:30pm. The winter steak house is open October to December and March to May on Friday and Saturday evenings, with seatings at 5 and 8pm.

Admission: Chuck-wagon dinners $12.50 adults, $6 for children 8 and younger; winter steak house $17 adults, $7 for children 8 and younger.

IRON SPRINGS CHATEAU, 444 Ruxton Ave., Manitou Springs. Tel. 685-5104 or 685-5572.

Located near the foot of the Pikes Peak Cog Railway, this popular comedy/drama dinner theater urges patrons to boo the villain and cheer the hero. Past productions have included *Farther North to Laughter or Buck of the Yukon, Part Two,* and *When the Halibut Start Running or Don't Slam the Door on Davy Jones Locker.* A family-style dinner, served Tuesday through Sunday from 6 to 7:15pm, offers all you can eat of oven-baked chicken and barbecued ribs. You'll need reservations. Show time is 8:30pm, followed by a sing-along intermission and a vaudeville-style olio show. The theater is closed the last two weeks of January and first two weeks of February.

Admission: Tickets, dinner and show, $18 adults, $17 seniors, $10 children; show only, $10 adults, $9 seniors, $6.50 children.

THE CLUB & MUSIC SCENE

COMEDY CLUBS

JEFF VALDEZ' COMEDY CORNER, 1305 N. Academy Blvd. Tel. 591-8200.

Rated one of the top-10 comedy clubs in the United States, the Comedy Corner features local and touring stand-up comedians Wednesday through Sunday. Doors open at 7pm; shows are at 8:30pm Wednesday, Thursday and Sunday, and at 8pm and 10:30pm Friday and Saturday.

Admission: $4–$15, depending on performer.

COUNTRY & ROCK MUSIC

COWBOYS, 3910 Palmer Park Blvd. Tel. 596-1212.

Two-steppers and country-and-western music lovers flock to this east-side club, open daily from 4pm to 2am.

Admission: Sun–Tues $1; Wed $3 women, $4 men; Thurs free for women, $2 men; Fri–Sat $2 women, $3 men.

THE CLUB HOUSE RESTAURANT AND UNDERGROUND PUB, 130 E. Kiowa St. Tel. 633-0590.

This popular hangout for college students and other young people offers progressive rock on its basement stage. Open daily from 11am to 2am.

Admission: Free Mon–Wed, $2–$4 Thurs–Sun.

JAZZ, BLUES & FOLK MUSIC

POOR RICHARD'S RESTAURANT, 324 N. Tejon St. Tel. 632-7721.

An eclectic variety of performers appear here several nights each week, presenting everything from acoustic folk to Celtic melodies, jazz to bluegrass. Open daily till 10pm.

Admission: Usually free.

DANCE CLUBS & DISCOS

MAXI'S LOUNGE, in the Red Lion Hotel, 1775 E. Cheyenne Mountain Blvd., at I-25. Tel. 576-8900.

A disc jockey plays rock classics of the 1960s through the 1980s for dancing most nights. Open daily at 4:30pm.

Admission: Free.

THE BAR SCENE

BECKETT'S RESTAURANT AND BREWPUB, 128 S. Tejon St. Tel. 635-3535.

Five different handcrafted ales and stouts, including Harvest Wheat, Red Dog Ale, and Grizzly Brown, highlight the drink menu at this casually elegant spot. Steak, seafood, and pasta dishes dominate the meal menu.

THE GOLDEN BEE, lower level entrance of the Broadmoor International Center, Lake Circle. Tel. 634-7111.

An opulent English pub was disassembled, shipped from Great Britain, and reassembled piece by piece to create this delightful drinking establishment. You can drink imported Bass Ale by the yard if you choose, while enjoying a beef-and-kidney pie or other English specialties.

JUDGE BALDWIN'S BREWING COMPANY, in the Antlers Doubletree Hotel, 4 S. Cascade Ave. Tel. 473-5600.

Although Judge Baldwin's offers more than a dozen designer beers from around the United States, look around this cheery bar and you'll see that practically everyone is drinking the Judge's own. And with good reason, it's good. The most popular is amber ale, served with a pretzel, but those preferring a richer brew might try the nut brown ale. Or order a sampler and try all four.

THE RITZ GRILL, 15 S. Tejon St. Tel. 635-8484.

Especially popular with young professionals after work and the chic clique later in the evening, this restaurant-lounge, with a large central bar, brings an art deco feel to downtown Colorado Springs.

LASER LIGHT SHOW

LASER CANYON, Cave of the Winds, U.S. 24, Manitou Springs. Tel. 685-5446.

Laser light-show enthusiasts won't want to miss this one. Effects 15 stories high and half a mile long are projected within a canyon adjacent to Cave of the Winds, enhanced by a concert sound system. There's one show nightly at 9pm, May 1 through Labor Day.

Admission: Tickets, $5 adults, $3 children 6–15, free for children under 6.

9. EASY EXCURSIONS FROM COLORADO SPRINGS

CRIPPLE CREEK

This famous old mining town on Pikes Peak's southwestern flank was known as the world's greatest gold camp after the precious mineral was first discovered here in 1890. By the time mining ceased in 1961, over $800 million worth of ore had been taken from the surrounding hills. Today, with limited-stakes casino gambling, residents of this picturesque mountain village—45 miles west of Colorado Springs via U.S. 24 west and Colo. 67 south—await a different kind of gold rush.

During its heyday at the turn of the century, Cripple Creek (elevation 9,494 ft.) had a stock exchange, two opera houses, five daily newspapers, 16 churches, 19 schools, and 73 saloons, plus an elaborate streetcar system and a railroad depot that saw 18 arrivals and departures a day. In the year 1900, $10 million in gold was found. It was said that the nearby community of Victor (elevation 9,693 ft.), six miles south, had streets that were literally paved with gold—poorer grades of ore not fit for the mills.

The Cripple Creek area has known some famous folk over the years. Lowell Thomas was a newspaper reporter in Victor, where Jack Dempsey fought his first professional fight in the Gold Coin Club. Bernard Baruch was a telegrapher at the Midland terminal depot. Texas Guinan, the New York burlesque queen, started in show biz as a church organist in Anaconda. Groucho Marx, stranded without money for a cigar, drove a grocery wagon in Cripple Creek for a time.

Today Cripple Creek has several dozen casinos, most lining Bennett Avenue, cashing in not only on the lure of gambling, but on the nostalgia and excitement of the turn-of-the-century style gambling houses that were once prominent throughout the Old West. Although gamblers must be at least 21 years old, some casinos offer special children's areas, and there are plenty of other activities for families to do together.

Among casinos, stop at Johnny Nolon's Saloon and Gambling Emporium, in a historic building at 301 E. Bennett Ave. (tel. 689-2080), with over 100 slot machines, blackjack and poker, and live jazz and ragtime music. Nearby, the Imperial Hotel and Casino at the corner of Third and Bennett (tel. 689-2922) presents classic melodrama during the summer in its Gold Bar Room (see "Where to Stay," below). At Old Chicago Casino at 419 E. Bennett Ave. (tel. 689-7880), you can play poker, blackjack, and feed the one-armed bandits, while sampling some of the casino's 110 national and international beers (see "Where to Dine," below).

Some casinos use food-and-drink specials to lure customers in the doors, so it is often worth checking out the competition as you walk down Bennett Avenue.

One of the town's unique attractions is a herd of wild donkeys—descendants of the miners' runaways—that roam freely through the hills and into the streets during the summer months. The year's biggest celebration, Donkey Derby Days in late June, is climaxed by a donkey race from Victor to Cripple Creek.

For travel information on the area, contact the Cripple Creek Chamber of Commerce, P.O. Box 650, Cripple Creek, CO 80813 (tel. 719/689-2169 or toll free 800/526-8777); or the Victor Chamber of Commerce, P.O. Box 83, Victor, CO 80860 (tel. 719/689-3211).

WHAT TO SEE & DO

CRIPPLE CREEK DISTRICT MUSEUM, east end of Bennett Ave. Tel. 689-2634.

Located in the old Midland Terminal Depot, this outstanding small museum is packed with turn-of-the-century relics. There is a floor of Victorian rooms, a floor of transportation and mining artifacts, an adjacent assay office where fire-testing of local ores persists, a new gold ore exhibit, and a heritage gallery with a natural-history display, old photographs, and paintings. Of special interest are multilevel glass models of district mines.

Admission: $2.25 adults, 50¢ children 7 to 12, free for children under 7.
Open: Summer, 9am–5pm daily; rest of year, noon–4pm Sat–Sun.

CRIPPLE CREEK & VICTOR NARROW GAUGE RAILROAD CO., Midland Terminal Depot, east end of Bennett Ave. Tel. 689-2640.

Before or after a museum tour, many visitors board this old train for a 4-mile narrated, historic tour past abandoned mines to the ghost town of Anaconda. A 15-ton "iron horse" steam locomotive pulls the train out of the station approximately every 45 minutes beginning at 10am, Memorial Day weekend through the first weekend of October.

Admission: $6.50 adults, $3.25 children 12 and under.
Open: Memorial Day weekend to first weekend of Oct; first run 10am, last run 4pm.

MOLLIE KATHLEEN GOLD MINE, Colo. 67 North. Tel. 689-2465.

Rated by the National Geographic Society as the single most outstanding tour in Colorado, this is a rare chance to spend time inside an actual gold mine. Experienced hard-rock miners join visitors on a 1,000-foot underground descent to explain and demonstrate the mining process. Gold production ceased at the Mollie Kathleen in 1961 because of the high costs of hard-rock mining, but the equipment remains in place. Guides point out gold veins and give visitors a free ore specimen.

Admission: $7 adults, $3.50 children 5 to 12, children under 5 free.
Open: Memorial Day–Oct, 9am–5pm daily.

OLD HOMESTEAD PARLOUR HOUSE, 353 E. Myers Ave. Tel. 689-3090.

The last and most elegant of Cripple Creek's infamous brothels stands alone on an otherwise deserted street, one block south of Bennett Avenue. Now a museum, the house has such original fixtures as velvet drapes, Persian carpets, and a 17th-century

liquor cabinet. The tour includes music and entertainment rooms, a dining area, and the five second-floor bedrooms.
Admission: $3.
Open: Summer, daily 10am–5pm.

VICTOR/LOWELL THOMAS MUSEUM, City Hall, Third and Victor Sts., Victor. Tel. 689-2766.

Memorabilia from the days when Victor was known as "the city of mines," and a family collection memorializing hometown boy Lowell Thomas, are the focuses of this small museum.
Admission: $1 adults, free for children under 12.
Open: May 1–Oct 15, daily 9am–5pm.

Scenic Drives

Three separate drives of particular beauty offer alternatives to Colo. 67 out of Cripple Creek and Victor. None is paved, all are narrow and winding, but all are passable to everyday vehicles under normal road and weather conditions. All are roughly 30 miles in length, but require some 90 minutes to negotiate.

The **Gold Camp Road** leads east from Victor to Colorado Springs via the North Cheyenne Cañon. Teddy Roosevelt said that this trip up the old Short Line Railroad bed had "scenery that bankrupts the English language."

The **Phantom Canyon Road** leads south from Victor to Florence, following another old narrow-gauge railroad bed known as the Gold Belt Line. Ghost towns and fossil areas mark this route.

The **Shelf Road** leads south from Cripple Creek to Cañon City on an old toll stage route blasted out of the sidewall of Fourmile Canyon. This route is not recommended to anyone afraid of heights, and should definitely be avoided when the road is wet, unless you have a four-wheel-drive vehicle.

WHERE TO STAY

CRIPPLE CREEK HOSPITALITY HOUSE AND TRAVEL PARK, 600 N. "B" St., Cripple Creek, CO 80813. Tel. 719/689-2513. 18 rms (9 with bath). 40 campsites. TV
$ Rates: $45–$75 hotel, $15 campsite. DISC, MC, V.

This Victorian hotel one-half mile from town was once the local hospital, but now, with period furnishings, it offers a quiet alternative to the casinos on Bennett Avenue. Situated on 20 acres, there is a playground, recreation room with pool table, and cable TV in all rooms.

IMPERIAL HOTEL, Third St. and Bennett Ave., Cripple Creek, CO 80813. Tel. 719/689-7777 or toll free 800/235-2922. 26 rms, 2 suites (11 with bath). A/C TV
$ Rates: $65–$85 single or double. DISC, MC, V.

Built in 1896 following a disastrous fire that razed most of the city, the fully renovated Imperial is the only original Cripple Creek hotel still standing. Except for a few years during World War II, it has been in continuous operation. Every room is a little different, and many share baths, but all are furnished with Victorian antiques.

The hotel has a restaurant and five bars, the best known of which is the Red Rooster—so called because of its international collection of roosters. The Imperial Players, the longest-running melodrama company in the United States, perform in the Gold Bar Room Theatre in summer. Tickets are $8 to $10.

VICTOR HOTEL, Fourth St. and Victor Ave, Victor, CO 80860. Tel. 719/689-3553 or toll free 800/748-0870. 30 rms (all with bath). TV TEL
$ Rates: $75–$90 single; $80–$95 double. AE, DISC, MC, V.

Offering a panoramic view of the mountains, this four-story Victorian hotel was extensively renovated in 1992 and offers queen-size beds, cable television, and lots of Victorian charm. Historic touches include the original 1899 Otis bird-cage elevator. A continental breakfast is included, and the hotel has a full-service restaurant featuring American and continental cuisine.

WHERE TO DINE

OLD CHICAGO CASINO, 419 E. Bennett Ave. Tel. 689-7880.
Cuisine: ITALIAN/AMERICAN.
$ Prices: $2.50–$8.95 entrées. AE, MC, V.
Open: Sun–Thurs 11am–9pm, Fri–Sat 11am–11pm.
Old Chicago has restaurants throughout Colorado's Front Range that feature top-quality pastas, pizza, and sandwiches, along with 110 different beers from around the world. The Cripple Creek casino and restaurant has a pasta bar, pizzas, a good selection of sandwiches, and excellent burgers.

FLORISSANT

A small village 35 miles west of Colorado Springs on U.S. 24, Florissant was given the French name for "flowering" because its hillsides are ablaze with wildflowers in spring.

There's superb **fishing** at lakes and streams in this area, particularly for German browns and cutthroats at Spinney Mountain Reservoir west of here. And the 7,000-acre **Dome Rock State Wildlife Area** to the east attracts nature-loving hikers with its elk, bighorn sheep, eagles, and other creatures. Half a mile south on Teller County Road No. 1 is the Florissant Fossil Beds National Monument.

FLORISSANT FOSSIL BEDS NATIONAL MONUMENT, P.O. Box 185, Florissant, CO 80816. Tel. 748-3253.
The fossils in this 6,000-acre National Park Service property are preserved in rocks of ancient Lake Florissant, which existed 26 to 38 million years ago. Volcanic eruptions over half a million years trapped plants and animals under layers of ash and dust; the creatures were fossilized as the sediment settled and became shale.

The detailed impressions, first discovered in 1874, offer the most extensive record of this kind in the world today. Some 80,000 specimens have been removed by scientists, including 1,100 separate species of insects! Dragonflies, beetles, ants; every known species of fossil butterfly in the New World; plus spiders, fish, some mammals and birds—all are perfectly preserved from as long ago as 35 million years. Leaves from birches, willows, maples, beeches, and hickories, and needles from fir trees and sequoias, are plentiful. Palm trees show how the climate has changed.

Mudflows also buried forests during this long period of time, petrifying the trees where they stood. Nature trails pass petrified sequoia stumps, one 10 feet in diameter and 11 feet high. All told, the national monument has some 14 miles of hiking trails.

There's a display of carbonized fossils at the visitor center, which also offers interpretive programs.

An added attraction within the national monument is the homestead of Adeline Hornbek, who pioneered the land here with her children in 1878.

A 16-mile paved road connects Florissant directly with Cripple Creek.
Admission: $2, maximum $4 per family.
Open: June–Sept, daily 8am–7pm; the rest of the year, daily 8am–4:30pm.
Closed: New Year's Day, Thanksgiving, and Christmas.

BOULDER

Known primarily as a young people's town, Boulder (pop. 100,000) is a sophisticated university community, a center for high-technology industries, and one of America's outdoor-sports capitals. The University of Colorado has been here since 1877, but it is only in the decades since World War II that the city has blossomed.

Set at the foot of the Flatirons of the Rocky Mountains, just 30 miles northwest of downtown Denver and only 74 feet higher than the "Mile High City," Boulder was settled by hopeful miners in 1858 and named for the large rocks in the area. Welcomed by Chief Niwot and the resident southern Arapahoe tribespeople, the miners struck gold in the nearby hills the following year. By the 1870s Boulder had become a regional rail and trade center for mining and farming. The university, founded later that decade, became the economic mainstay after the bottom fell out of mining around the turn of the century.

Since the 1950s Boulder has grown as a center for scientific and environmental research. The National Center for Atmospheric Research, the National Bureau of Standards, the Solar Forecast Center, and other modern governmental institutions located here. IBM, Storage Tek, Ball Aerospace, and other forward-looking private firms followed. (To some folks, Boulder is "Silicon Mountain.")

1. ORIENTATION

ARRIVING

BY AIR   Boulder doesn't have its own commercial airport. Air travelers must fly into Denver's Stapleton International Airport, then make ground connections to Boulder.

Getting Into Town   The Boulder Airporter limo van (tel. 303/321-3222) leaves Denver hourly from 8am to 10:15pm, and Boulder hourly from 6am to 8pm; weekends and holidays have a more restricted schedule. Pick ups in Boulder are scheduled from certain hotels, on call from others, and from the University of Colorado campus. One-way fare is $9.50 per person for the 40-minute drive from the airport, or $12 for door-to-door pick-up service.

International Boulder Limousine Airport Express (tel. 449-5466) charges $45 plus 20% gratuity to take two people from Boulder to Denver Airport in a formal limousine; $55 plus 20% gratuity for up to six people in a stretch limousine.

By Boulder Yellow Cab (tel. 442-2277), the airport fare is $40 one way, for one to five passengers.

Regional Transportation District (RTD) buses (tel. 299-6000) make one-way airport runs for $2.50 (exact change required). Trips start from or end at the main terminal at 14th Street and Walnut Street hourly, daily from 6am to 11pm.

BY CAR   The Boulder Turnpike (U.S. 36) departs I-25 north of Denver and passes

WHAT'S SPECIAL ABOUT BOULDER

People-Watching
- [ ] The Pearl Street Mall, once the haunt of "Mork and Mindy," still frequented by a fascinating cross section of people.
- [ ] The University of Colorado, the leading institute of higher learning in the Rockies.

Natural Attractions
- [ ] The Flatirons, a dramatic geologic uplift that creates a jagged wall behind Boulder.
- [ ] Boulder Creek Path, a 9-mile path and park through the middle of the city.

Industrial Tours
- [ ] The National Center for Atmospheric Research, which studies global warming, acid rain, and other world problems.
- [ ] Celestial Seasonings, the company that made herbal teas fashionable, imports 100 ingredients from 35 countries.
- [ ] Rockies Brewing Co., the nation's first microbrewery (in 1979).

The Arts
- [ ] The Colorado Music Festival, with top classical artists from all over the world.

- [ ] Leanin' Tree Museum of Western Art, one of the largest private collections of western art.
- [ ] The Colorado Shakespeare Festival, rated one of the top three in the U.S.

Events/Festivals
- [ ] The Kinetic Conveyance Challenge, with the most creative and bizarre human-powered land vehicles and sea vessels imaginable.
- [ ] The Boulder Creek Festival, with a parade, art show, and lots of food and fun activities.
- [ ] The Boulder Bach Festival.

Sports
- [ ] The University of Colorado football team, national collegiate champion in 1990, attracting tens of thousands of fans to home games.
- [ ] The Number One sports town in America according to *Outside* magazine.
- [ ] The Jose Cuervo Volleyball Tournament.

---

through the suburbs of Westminster, Broomfield, and Louisville before reaching Boulder some 25 minutes later.

If you're coming in from the north, take the Longmont exit from I-25 and follow Colo. 119 all the way. Longmont is 7 miles due west of the freeway; Boulder is another 15 miles southwest via the Longmont Diagonal Highway.

Other routes leading into and out of Boulder are U.S. 36 north to Lyons and Rocky Mountain National Park; Colo. 119 west to Nederland and Central City; Colo. 93 south to Golden; and Colo. 7 east to Brighton.

TOURIST INFORMATION

The **Boulder Convention and Visitors Bureau,** 2440 Pearl St. (at Folsom Street), Boulder, CO 80302 (tel. 303/442-2911, or toll free 800/444-0447), is open Monday through Friday from 9am to 5pm with excellent maps, brochures, and general information on the city.

From Memorial Day to Labor Day, there is a visitor **information** center at the Davidson Mesa overlook, a couple of miles southeast of Boulder on U.S. 36 from Denver.

CITY LAYOUT

From the mountains on Boulder's west, numbered north-south streets run east, beginning with Third Street. (The eastern city limits are at 61st Street, although the numbers run all the way to the Boulder County line at 124th Street in Broomfield.) U.S. 36, where it does a 45° turn to the north upon entering Boulder, becomes 28th Street, a major commercial artery. The Longmont Diagonal Highway (Colo. 119 east), coming in from the northeast, intersects 28th at the north end of the city.

To reach downtown Boulder from the highway, turn west on Canyon Boulevard (Colo. 119 west) and north on Broadway, which would be 12th Street if it had a number. It's two blocks to the Pearl Street Mall, a 4-block pedestrians-only strip from 11th Street to 15th Street that constitutes the historic downtown district. Boulder's few one-way streets circle the Mall: 15th Street is one way north, 11th and 14th one way south, Walnut Street (a block south of the Mall) one way east, and Spruce Street (a block north) one way west.

Broadway continues across the Mall, eventually joining U.S. 36 north of the city. South of Arapahoe Avenue, Broadway turns to the southeast, skirting the University of Colorado campus and becoming Colo. 93 (the Foothills Highway to Golden) after crossing Baseline Road. Baseline follows a straight line from east Boulder, across U.S. 36 and Broadway, past Chautauqua Park and up the mountain slopes. To its south, Table Mesa Drive pursues a similar course.

The Foothills Parkway (not to be confused with the Foothills Highway) is the principal north-south route on the east side of Boulder, extending from U.S. 36 at Table Mesa Drive to the Longmont Diagonal; Arapahoe Avenue, a block south of Canyon Boulevard, continues across 28th Street as Colo. 7, the main east-west route.

2. GETTING AROUND

BY BUS The Regional Transportation District (RTD), 14th Street and Walnut Street (tel. 299-6000), operates Monday through Friday from 5am to midnight and on Saturday and Sunday from 6am to midnight. Fares within the city are 60¢, (15¢ for seniors). A 10-ride book costs $4.75. There are schedules at the depot, the Chamber of Commerce, and other locations around the city.

BY TAXI Boulder Yellow Cab (tel. 442-2277) offers 24-hour service. Rates are $1.20 at flag fall and $1.20 per mile, prorated. It's almost always necessary to call for a taxi.

BY CAR For regulations and advice on driving in Colorado, see "Getting Around" in Chapter 2. There's a local office of the American Automobile Association (AAA) at 1933 28th St. (tel. 442-0383). Open Monday to Friday 8:30am to 5:30pm, Saturday 9am to 1pm.

Parking Most downtown streets have parking meters, with rates of about 25¢ per half hour. Downtown parking lots get about 35¢ for 3 hours before 5pm. Parking is hard to find around the Pearl Street Mall. Outside downtown, free parking is generally available on side streets.

Car Rentals Car-rental agencies in Boulder include: **Avis,** 4700 Baseline Rd. (tel. 499-1136, or 800/331-1212); **Budget,** 1345 28th St. (tel. 444-9054 or toll free 800/527-0700); **Hertz,** 1760 14th St. (tel. 443-3520 or toll free 800/654-3131); and **National,** 2960 Center Green Court (tel. 442-5110 or toll free 800/227-7368).

BY BICYCLE Boulder is a wonderful place for bicycling, with bike paths throughout the city and an extensive trail system leading for miles beyond (see "Sports & Recreation," below).

Among several places that rent mountain and touring bikes are Doc's Ski and

Sports, 629 S. Broadway (tel. 499-0963), and Full Cycle, 1211 13th St., near campus (tel. 440-7771). Rates are typically $12 for 3 hours or less, and about $20 a day.

If the shop is out of the "Boulder Bicycling Map" ($3), check with the Boulder Chamber of Commerce, 2440 Pearl St. (tel. 442-1044), or GoBoulder (tel. 441-4260).

ON FOOT   Many of Boulder's attractions can best be seen by pure foot power, especially around the Pearl Street Mall and University of Colorado campus.

FAST FACTS   BOULDER

Area Code   The telephone area code for the Boulder region is 303.

Babysitters   Front desks at major hotels often can make arrangements on your behalf. The city Child Care Referral Service (tel. 441-3180), open Monday through Friday from 1 to 5pm, can also help.

Banks   Most banks are open Monday through Thursday from 9am to 5pm, on Friday from 9am to 6pm, and Sat 9am to noon. Major banks include 1stBank, 6500 Lookout Rd. (tel. 530-1000); Bank One, 2500 Arapahoe Ave. (tel. 443-4933); and Colorado National Bank, Crossroads Mall, 28th Street and Arapahoe Avenue (tel. 444-1234). Plus System (tel. toll free 800/THE-PLUS) cash machines can be found at strategic locations throughout the city.

Drugstores   Reliable prescription services are available at the Medical Center Pharmacy in the Boulder Medical Center, 2750 N. Broadway (tel. 440-3111), and Jones Drug and Camera Center, 1370 College Ave. (tel. 443-4420). If it's 3 in the morning and you can't get your prescription, call a hospital.

Emergencies   For police, fire, or medical emergencies, call 911. For Colorado State Patrol emergencies, call 303/239-4501.

Eyeglasses   You can get fast repairs or replacement of lost or broken glasses at Boulder Optical, 1928 14th St. (tel. 442-4521), just off the Pearl Street Mall.

Hairdressers/Barbers   A couple of good bets on the Mall are Barbara the Barber, 1035 Pearl St. (tel. 449-3061), and Pompadours, 1320 Pearl St., Suite 200 (tel. 938-8015). For budget cuts, try Supercuts, Crossroads Shopping Mall (tel. 449-6901).

Hospitals   Full medical services, including 24-hour emergency treatment, are available at Boulder Community Hospital, 1100 Balsam Ave., at North Broadway (tel. 440-2037).

Information   See "Orientation," above.

Laundry/Dry Cleaning   Most major hotels offer valet drop-off and pick-up service. Some motels may have guest laundries. A popular student laundromat is Duds 'n Suds, in the Crossroad Commons, 2317 30th St. (tel. 440-WASH), so named because the washing machines share turf with a tavern! For dry cleaning, try Dependable Cleaners, Village Shopping Center, Folsom Avenue south of Canyon Boulevard (tel. 443-0290).

Libraries   The main branch of the Boulder Public Library is at 10th Street and Arapahoe (tel. 441-3100). It's open Monday through Thursday from 9am to 9pm, on Friday and Saturday from 9am to 6pm, and on Sunday from noon to 6pm. A local library card is required to check out material. Visitors are also welcome to use the University of Colorado's Norlin Library.

Liquor Laws   See "Fast Facts: Colorado" in Chapter 2.

Lost Property   Consult the Boulder Police (tel. 441-4444).

Newspapers/Magazines   Boulder's *Daily Camera* is an award-winning daily newspaper. Many townspeople also read the campus paper, the *Colorado Daily,* available all over town. Both Denver dailies—the *Denver Post* and *Rocky Mountain News*—are also sold at newsstands throughout the city, as are the *New York Times, Wall Street Journal,* and *Christian Science Monitor.* The free *Boulder* magazine, published three times a year, lists seasonal events and other information on restaurants and the arts.

Photographic Needs   For standard processing requirements (including

2-hour slide processing) as well as custom lab work, see Photo Craft Laboratories, at 3550 Arapahoe Ave. (tel. 442-6410). For equipment, supplies, and repairs, see Mike's Camera, 1637 Pearl St. (tel. 443-1715).

Police   In an emergency, dial 911. For standard business, call 441-4444.

Post Office   The Main Post Office is downtown at 15th Street and Walnut Street (tel. 938-1100), open Monday through Friday from 7:30am to 5:30pm, Saturday from 10am to 2pm.

Radio/TV   Boulder radio stations include KBCO (1190 AM and 97.3 FM) for alternative rock; KBOL (1490 AM) for news, sports, and contemporary rock; and KGNU (88.5 FM), public radio. Boulder also is within reception range of most Denver stations. The local cable TV channel is 28. For other stations, see "Fast Facts: Denver" in Chapter 4.

Religious Services   Not only are most major religious denominations represented in Boulder, but the city is a major center for followers of New Age and Eastern belief systems. Check the *Yellow Pages* for a complete listing.

Safety   Although Boulder is generally a very safe city, it is not crime free, and visitors should stay alert and use common sense, especially when exploring unfamiliar sections of the city after dark. Cameras and other valuables should be locked out-of-sight in car trunks or other safe places when not in use.

Shoe Repairs   Shoes and boots are quickly repaired, often while you wait, at Action Shoe Repair, 2709 Arapahoe Ave. (tel. 440-3737).

Taxes   Colorado state sales tax is 3%, Boulder area taxes are 3.66%—a total of 6.66%.

Telephone/Fax   Local calls are normally 25¢. Facsimiles can be transmitted by most major hotels at a nominal cost to guests, or 24 hours a day from Kinko's, 1717 Walnut St. (tel. 449-7100). For directory assistance, dial 1-411.

Useful Telephone Numbers   The poison control center (tel. 629-1123), rape crisis hot line (tel. 443-7300), road conditions (tel. 639-1111 for a recording or 639-1234 statewide), ski reports (tel. 831-7669 for a recording), weather (tel. 398-3964).

3. ACCOMMODATIONS

These categories define price ranges: "Expensive," more than $100 per night double; "Moderate," $70 to $100; "Inexpensive," $40 to $70; "Budget," less than $40 per night double. An additional 9.5% sales tax is levied onto all bills, and is not included in the rates.

EXPENSIVE

CLARION HARVEST HOUSE, 1345 28th St., Boulder, CO 80302. Tel. 303/443-3850 or toll free 800/545-6285. Fax 303/443-1480. 264 rms, 5 suites. A/C TV TEL

$ Rates: Nov–May 15, $89–$112 single; $113–$133 double. May 16–Aug, $99–$122 single; $119–$142 double. Sept–Oct, $95–$115 single; $115–$135 double. Year-round suites, $150–$395. AE, CB, DC, DISC, JCB, MC, V. **Parking:** Free.

Few downtown hotels anywhere could have grounds as spacious and lovely as the Harvest House, dubbed the Clarion chain's "hotel of the year" for 1990. Located on the mountain side of U.S. 36 as it enters Boulder from Denver, the Harvest House looks like almost any other four-story hotel from the front. But the hotel's backyard

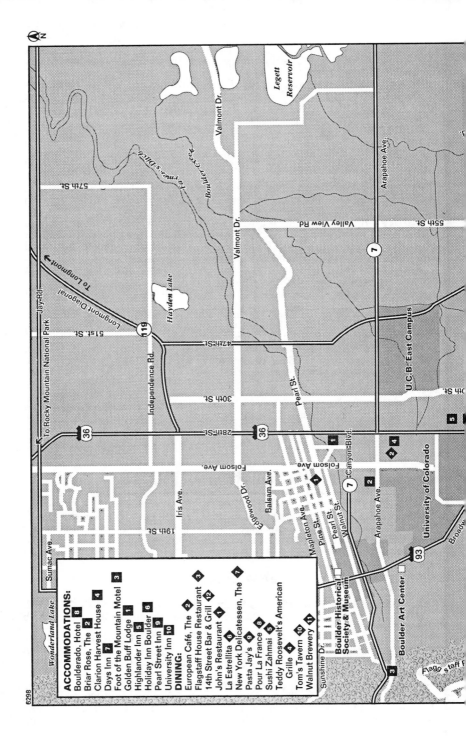

ACCOMMODATIONS:
Boulderado, Hotel **8**
Briar Rose, The **2**
Clarion Harvest House **4**
Days Inn **7**
Foot of the Mountain Motel **3**
Golden Buff Lodge **1**
Highlander Inn **5**
Holiday Inn Boulder **6**
Pearl Street Inn **9**
University Inn **10**

DINING:
European Café, The **2**
Flagstaff House Restaurant **3**
14th Street Bar & Grill **12**
John's Restaurant **1**
La Estrellita **6**
New York Delicatessen, The **7**
Pasta Jay's **9**
Pour La France **8**
Sushi Zahmai **5**
Teddy Roosevelt's American
Grille **4**
Tom's Tavern **10**
Walnut Brewery **11**

6298

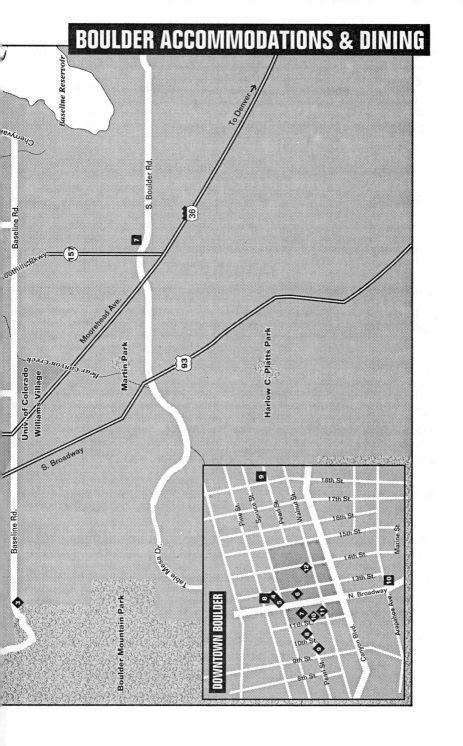

BOULDER ACCOMMODATIONS & DINING

melds into a park surrounding the east end of the 9-mile Boulder Creek Path, a worthy object of city pride (see "Attractions," below). Guests can swim, ride bicycles, play tennis or volleyball, and pretend they're at a country resort.

No guest room has less than a "deluxe" designation. All rooms have one king-size or two double beds, a lounge chair and ottoman, remote-control TV, and direct-dial phone (50¢ local calls). Spacious VIP Tower accommodations have upgraded amenities such as hair dryers and bathrobes, daily newspapers, and an extra phone jack for a computer modem; they also include a continental breakfast and cocktail hour in the wing's Club Room.

Dining/Entertainment: The hotel's new restaurant, Bel Gusto d'Italia, specializes in home-style northern Italian cuisine, with lunches from $7.50 to $12.50, and dinners ranging from $7.50 to $20.00. The restaurant is open daily from 6:30am to 10pm. Champ's, a popular sports bar with a big fireplace, is also open daily.

Services: Room service, valet laundry, no-smoking rooms, facilities for the disabled.

Facilities: 15 tennis courts (5 indoors), indoor lap pool and hot tub, outdoor swimming pool and hot tub, baby pool, exercise room, bicycle rentals at Boulder Creek Path, playground, volleyball and basketball courts; meeting space for up to 700.

MODERATE

THE BRIAR ROSE, 2151 Arapahoe Ave., Boulder, CO 80302. Tel. 303/442-3007. 9 rms (all with bath). A/C TEL
$ Rates (including continental breakfast): May–Oct, $74–$99 single; $89–$109 double. Nov–Apr, $69–$95 single; $84–$105 double. AE, DC, MC, V.

A country-style brick home set amid a lovely garden, this midcity bed and breakfast might remind you of Grandma's. Every room is furnished with period antiques, from the bedrooms to the parlor to the back sun porch. Each guest room has handmade feather comforters and fresh fruit and flowers; tea and coffee are always on in the dining room. You even get a chocolate at bedtime.

Five rooms are in the main house, four in a separate "cottage." Of the first five, two deluxe rooms have their own fireplaces and big queen-size featherbeds. One room with twin beds is available. All four cottage rooms, all recently redecorated, have either patios (downstairs) or balconies (upstairs). Breakfast may be continental, but it's gourmet: croissants, granola, fresh nut breads, yogurt with fruit, and much more.

DAYS INN BOULDER, 5397 S. Boulder Rd., Boulder, CO 80303. Tel. 303/499-4422 or toll free 800/325-2525. Fax 303/494-0269. 72 rms, 2 suites (all with bath). A/C TV TEL
$ Rates (including continental breakfast): Summer, $69 single; $74 double. Winter, $49 single or double. Suites $20 additional year-round. AE, CB, DC, DISC, MC, V.
Parking: Free.

One of the best values you'll find, this four-story hotel, with a great view of the mountains, looks and feels like it should cost much more. Perhaps that's because, unlike many franchise hotels, the owner is also the manager, and the pride of ownership shows.

Rooms are large, with mahogany-finish solid-wood furniture, including night tables on each side of the beds. The continental breakfast is excellent, and each room has cable television and a radio. All rooms have desks, computer modem phone hookups are available in-room, and fax and photocopy services are available at the front desk. There's a seasonal outdoor heated pool and an attached sports bar and lounge where you can get pizza, sandwiches, and similar fare. The hotel accepts small pets.

HOTEL BOULDERADO, 2115 13th St., at Spruce St., Boulder, CO 80302. Tel. 303/442-4344 or toll free 800/433-4344. Fax 303/442-4378. 133 rms, 27 suites (all with bath). A/C TV TEL
$ Rates: $109–$129 single; $121–$141 double; $149–$161 suite. Extra person $12. AE, CB, DC, DISC, JCB, MC, V. **Parking:** Free.

Opened on January 1, 1909, this elegant and historic hotel still has the same Otis elevator that wowed visiting dignitaries on opening day. The colorful leaded-glass ceiling and cantilevered cherry-wood staircase are other reminders of days past, along with the rich woodwork of the balusters around the mezzanine and the handsome armchairs and settees in the main-floor lobby.

The original five-story hotel, just a block off the Pearl Street Mall, has 42 bright and cozy guest rooms, every one a little bit different. All have been recently renovated down to the wiring and plumbing, but they retain a Victorian flavor with their antique furnishings (including desks), floral wallpaper, and other touches. The construction a few years ago of a spacious North Wing almost quadrupled the number of rooms, while perpetuating the turn-of-the-century feel in the wallpaper and reproduction antiques. Every room has a clock radio and hair dryer; deluxe units also have vanities and refrigerators.

The Hotel Boulderado's Christmas tree, a 24-footer with 1,000 white lights, is a Boulder tradition.

The hotel offers a full range of services and dining and other facilities.

HOLIDAY INN BOULDER, 800 28th St., Boulder, CO 80303. Tel. 303/443-3322 or toll free 800/465-4329. Fax 303/443-0397. 165 rms (all with bath). A/C TV TEL

$ Rates: May 15–Aug, $69–$89 single; $79–$99 double. Sept–May 14, $61–$79 single; $69–$89 double. AE, CB, DC, DISC, JCB, MC, V. **Parking:** Free.

Located at the south end of Boulder on the U.S. 36 Frontage Road near the Baseline Road exit, this hotel has one of the nicer "Holidomes" around. The central garden atrium features an indoor swimming pool fed by a fountain, a large adjacent whirlpool, and comfortable café seating.

Standard rooms have a king-size or two double beds, southwestern-theme decor, watercolors of the city, and all the usual furnishings. Executive rooms are a little larger, with desks and clock radios. Local phone calls are 50¢. Most rooms face the atrium, though some have outside entrances.

The hotel offers a full range of services and dining and other facilities.

PEARL STREET INN, 1820 Pearl St., Boulder, CO 80302. Tel. 303/444-5584 or toll free 800/232-5949. 6 rms, 1 suite (all with bath). A/C TV TEL

$ Rates (including continental breakfast): Apr–Sept, $78–$108 single; $88–$118 double. Oct–Mar, $68–$88 single; $78–$98 double. AE, MC, V. **Parking:** Free.

This wonderful guest house, three blocks east of the Pearl Street Mall, is a restored turn-of-the-century Victorian with a contemporary wing added in 1985. It offers the best of both worlds: bed-and-breakfast intimacy with private entrances, along with some of the luxury touches of a large hotel.

Rooms, all of which face a central courtyard, feature a crisp, bright decor with antique furnishings—a sort of meeting of the old and the new. Every room has a private bath and fireplace. Breakfast and afternoon tea or wine and cheese are served in the courtyard or a quiet dining room. Fax and photocopy service is available.

INEXPENSIVE

BEST WESTERN GOLDEN BUFF LODGE, 1725 28th St., Boulder, CO 80301. Tel. 303/442-7450 or toll free 800/999-BUFF. Fax 303/442-8788. 104 rms, 8 suites (all with bath). A/C TV TEL

$ Rates: May–Sept, $62–$70 single; $72–$80 double; $70–$90 suite. Oct–Apr, $52–$60 single; $57–$65 double; $60–$80 suite. 20%–25% less for stays of 2 weeks or longer. AE, CB, DC, DISC, MC, V. **Parking:** Free.

This one- and two-story motel takes up a full city block. Rooms are spacious, with queen-size beds, small working desks with phones (free local calls), refrigerators, clock radios, and hair dryers. A few kitchen units are available. Over half of the rooms are no-smoking, and air-filtration units are available on request.

The Golden Buff Restaurant, open Monday through Thursday from 6:30am to 9pm, Friday and Saturday from 6:30am to 10pm, and Sunday 7 to 9pm, is a popular family restaurant. Beef, chicken, vegetarian, and Mexican dishes run $3.95 to $8.95. The motel offers room service. Other facilities include an outdoor swimming pool (seasonal), whirlpool, saunas, exercise room, mountain-bike rentals, and a guest laundry. Up to 50 people can be accommodated for meetings.

HIGHLANDER INN, 970 28th St., Boulder, CO 80303. Tel. 303/443-7800 or toll free 800/525-2149. Fax 303/443-7800, ext. 155. 48 rms, 24 suites (all with bath). A/C TV TEL

$ Rates: May 15–Oct 15, $60–$66 single; $67–$72 double; $67–$79 suite. Oct 16–May 14, $45–$48 single; $46–$52 double; $50–$62 suite. AE, CB, DC, DISC, MC, V. **Parking:** Free.

The comfortable lobby of this motel features a volume of menus of Boulder restaurants, a nice touch for visitors. Standard guest rooms are in the rear of the motel, shielded from traffic noise by solid brick walls. Units have queen-size or double beds, HBO, coffee and tea, and direct-dial phones (35¢ local calls). The motel also has 12 two-bedroom suites (one room with a king-size bed and a refrigerator, the second room with two double beds) and 12 apartments for long-term rentals, with fully equipped kitchenettes and microwaves. No-smoking rooms are available.

Free coffee, tea, and hot chocolate are always on in the lobby. There's a 24-hour desk (with sundry sales), fax and copy machine available, a guest laundry, outdoor swimming pool, and meeting rooms. Pets are welcome.

UNIVERSITY INN, 1632 Broadway, near Arapahoe Ave., Boulder, CO 80302. Tel. 303/442-3830 or toll free 800/258-7917. 39 rms (all with bath). A/C TV TEL

$ Rates: $45–$80 single; $50–$90 double. AE, DC, DISC, MC, V. **Parking:** Free.

Conveniently located between campus and the Pearl Street Mall, and within walking distance of both, this two-story motel has distinctive sky-blue trim on white brick. The simple, cozy rooms have king-size, queen-size, or double beds, light-wood furnishings, refrigerators, cable TV with a movie channel, and direct-dial phones (25¢ local calls). Most have showers only; if you need a room with a bathtub, ask. Family rooms and no-smoking rooms are available. There's a guest laundry and outdoor heated swimming pool. No pets.

BUDGET

FOOT OF THE MOUNTAIN MOTEL, 200 Arapahoe Ave., Boulder, CO 80302. Tel. 303/442-5688. 18 rms (all with bath). TV TEL

$ Rates: $45–$60 double. AE, DISC, MC, V.

A series of rustic log cabins (with bright-red trim) near the east gate of Boulder Canyon, this motel dates to 1930, but has been fully modernized. Across the street is Eben Fine Park, at the top end of the Boulder Creek Path. Behind the cabins is an acre of park and picnic land. Despite their age, the cabins are very nice, with pine walls, queen-size or double beds, cable TV with HBO, refrigerators, and private hot-water heaters. There's complimentary coffee in the office every morning. Pets are welcome.

BOULDER INTERNATIONAL YOUTH HOSTEL, 1127 12th St. (P.O. Box 1705), Boulder, CO 80306-1705. Tel. 303/442-0522.

$ Rates: $11 for dorm beds; private rooms $25 single, $30 double. No credit cards.

As at most youth hostels, guests come here expecting to share—and they do. Toilets, showers, kitchen, laundry, and TV room are communal. Individual phones can be arranged for private rooms (with deposit), but others share a phone. Just two blocks from the University of Colorado campus, the hostel is open for registration daily from 7:30 to 10am and from 5pm to 1am. During summer, additional facilities are available at 1107 12th St. Traveler's checks are accepted.

4. DINING

Dining in this university town tends to be more casual than in Denver (with a few notable exceptions), at least as wide ranging in terms of ethnic variety, but no less expensive. In this listing, I consider a "Very Expensive" restaurant to be one in which most dinner main courses are priced above $20; "Expensive," $15 to $20; "Moderate," $10 to $15; "Inexpensive," $7 to $10; and "Budget," less than $7. Several restaurants offer discounted meals before 6:30pm.

There are over 300 restaurants in this city of 100,000-plus, fully one-third of them in a 12-square-block chunk of downtown—between Ninth Street and 15th Street on the Pearl Street Mall or its flanking streets, Walnut and Spruce. Nevertheless, especially in summer and on weekends, dinner reservations are advised. A few restaurants may expect gentlemen to wear a coat and tie. It's appropriate to tip 15% to 20% of your tab.

VERY EXPENSIVE

FLAGSTAFF HOUSE RESTAURANT, 1138 Flagstaff Rd., west up Baseline Rd. Tel. 442-4640.
    Cuisine: NEW AMERICAN/REGIONAL. **Reservations:** Required.
$ Prices: Appetizers $8–$18; main courses $21–$39. AE, DC, MC, V.
    Open: Dinner only, Sun–Fri 6–10pm, Sat 5–10pm.

Folks drive all the way from Denver to dine at the Flagstaff House for its spectacular nighttime view of the lights of Boulder, spread out 1,000 feet below. A local institution since 1951, the restaurant has an elegant, candlelit dining room and glass walls that make the most of its location. But while the scenery is magnificent, it's the food and attentive service that bring patrons back again and again.

The menu, which changes daily, is eclectic, with an excellent selection of seafood and Rocky Mountain game, all prepared with a creative touch. Typical appetizers include smoked rabbit or duck, oysters, wild mushrooms, and cheeses. Entrées, many of which are seasonal, might include Colorado buffalo, Australian lobster tail, quail, elk filet, Canadian halibut, and soft-shell crabs. There are dessert soufflés, an award-winning wine cellar with over 1,000 varieties, and an impressive selection of after-dinner drinks.

EXPENSIVE

JOHN'S RESTAURANT, 2328 Pearl St. Tel. 444-5232.
    Cuisine: CREATIVE CONTINENTAL. **Reservations:** Highly recommended.
$ Prices: Appetizers $5–$7.50, main courses $13–$20. AE, DISC, MC, V.
    Open: Daily 6–10pm.

This unimposing beige house on the south side of Pearl Street occupies the former premises of an antique store. Chef John Bizzarro—yes, that's his name—opened his restaurant in 1974, drawing raves from all who have eaten here. Meals are served by candlelight in several interconnected rooms; the walls are decorated with work by local artists and photographers.

The menu is an olio of classic French, Spanish, and Italian dishes, tossed with some Cajun and Southwest creations and liberally seasoned with Bizzarro's own deft touch. You can start with duck-liver pâté with pistachios, oysters in brandy and cream, or a Hopi squash with green chiles and cilantro, then move to the main dishes: mariscos Catalan, chicken Agrigento, filet mignon au poivre, or sweetbreads Madeira, for example. Finish up with John's Chocolate Intensity (a trademarked dessert) or a mocha soufflé glaze.

MODERATE

THE EUROPEAN CAFE, in the Arapahoe Village Shopping Center, 2460 Arapahoe Ave. Tel. 938-8250.
    Cuisine: CONTINENTAL. **Reservations:** Recommended.
$ Prices: Appetizers $5.95–$6.95; main courses $5.95–$7.95 at lunch, $11.95–$16.95 at dinner. AE, MC, V.
    Open: Lunch Mon–Fri 11am–2pm; dinner Mon–Sat 5:30–10pm, Sun 5:30–9:30pm.

Simple and elegant, this entirely nonsmoking restaurant belies its location in a shopping center with fine presentation and cuisine. The decor features glass-top tables, large mirrors, strong flower arrangements, and a soft burgundy color scheme.

The luncheon menu features salads (such as the asparagus salad with avocados and enoki mushrooms), pastas, and light dishes. Dinners typically start with an appetizer such as pâté, escargots, or smoked salmon with caviar; and continue with a continental delight of seafood, poultry, beef, or lamb. One favorite is mesquite-grilled Cajun-spiced tuna. The wine list is superb, the dessert menu scrumptious.

14TH STREET BAR & GRILL, 1400 Pearl St. Tel. 444-5854.
Cuisine: AMERICAN GRILL. **Reservations:** Not required.
$ Prices: Appetizers and salads $2.50–$6.95; main courses $4.95–$15.95. MC, V.
Open: Mon–Thurs 11:30am–10pm, Fri–Sat 11:30am–midnight, Sun 5–10pm.

An open, airy restaurant, entirely nonsmoking, with big windows facing the corner of 14th and Pearl, this is as good a place for people-watching as it is for dining—and it's great for dining! The open wood grill and pizza oven, abstract modern art on the walls, and long (and crowded) bar let you know that this is a place where creative people like to have fun.

The lunch menu offers spinach, pasta, and southwestern chicken salads; grilled sandwiches; pastas; and unusual homemade pizzas, such as one with chorizo sausage, garlic, and roasted green chiles, another with shrimp, spinach, olives, and feta cheese. The dinner specials (4pm on Monday to Thursday, 7pm on weekends) change nightly, but could feature cioppino served with a side of angel-hair pasta, roasted chicken in a prosciutto-mushroom sauce, or beef tenderloin stuffed with cheese and cilantro.

SUSHI ZANMAI, 1221 Spruce St. Tel. 440-0773.
Cuisine: JAPANESE. **Reservations:** Requested for groups of 4 or more.
$ Prices: Lunch $5–$7; dinner $8–$14. AE, MC, V.
Open: Lunch Mon–Fri 11:30am–2pm; dinner daily 5–10pm.

This place has been rated the best Japanese restaurant for years by local newspaper readers. All food is prepared in Japanese cookware in traditional ways while you watch at the hibachi steak table, the sushi bar, or table side. There are lunch specials and sushi happy hour specials during lunch and dinner. Karaoke sing-along takes place every Saturday from 10pm to midnight.

TEDDY ROOSEVELT'S AMERICAN GRILLE, in the Hotel Boulderado, 2115 13th St. 442-4560.
Cuisine: AMERICAN. **Reservations:** Accepted.
$ Prices: Main courses $2–$8 at breakfast, $2–$10 at lunch, $4–$15 at dinner. AE, CB, DC, DISC, MC, V.
Open: Breakfast Mon–Fri 6:30–10:30am; lunch daily 11am–2:30pm; limited lunch menu daily 2:30–5pm; dinner daily 5–10pm; breakfast Sat–Sun 7am–11am.

Housed in the Hotel Boulderado's original 1909 dining room, this restaurant offers a wide variety of made-from-scratch creations in an open, rustic atmosphere. There's a huge moose head looking down from a rock wall, antler light fixtures, and photos of T.R. keeping an eye on things.

Breakfasts include standard fare such as ham and eggs, plus skillet dishes, great warm sticky buns, and Rocky Mountain trout. For lunch there's a good selection of sandwiches, burgers, and salads. A favorite at lunch or dinner is roasted chicken with woodland mushroom pasta. At dinner you can have the Rough Rider steak, a charbroiled 10-ounce sirloin served with wild Colorado mushrooms; spit roasted chicken or prime rib; or pork tenderloin with chili pomegranate sauce. Attached to the restaurant is a coffee shop serving espressos, pastries, and malts.

INEXPENSIVE

LA ESTRELLITA, 2037 13th St. Tel. 939-8822.
Cuisine: MEXICAN.
$ Prices: Appetizers $2.25–$5; meals $5–$10.50. AE, MC, V.
Open: Mon–Thurs 11am–10pm, Fri–Sat 11am–11pm (bar open Fri–Sat until 2am), Sun 4–10pm.

Drawing on recipes developed by his parents at the original La Estrellita in Fort

Lupton in the 1950s and 1960s, John Montoya established this restaurant in 1986—and it's still growing in popularity. You'll get all the standard tacos, tostadas, enchiladas, tamales, and chile relleños here, in generous portions, as well as a few surprises: costillas adobadas (Mexican-style ribs), Indian tacos, stuffed sopaipillas, and more. Fajitas are a big seller. Selected as one of the 50 Best Mexican Restaurants in the U.S. by *Hispanic Magazine.*

PASTA JAY'S, 925 Pearl St. Tel. 444-5800.
   Cuisine: ITALIAN. **Reservations:** Not accepted.
$ **Prices:** Appetizers $2.25–$4.75; meals $5.95–$11.50. MC, V.
   Open: Mon–Sat 11am–10:30pm.

Expect a long line when you arrive at this Mediterranean bistro, with its red-checked tablecloths indoors and its huge outdoor patio facing Pearl Street. Pasta Jay's is on a first-name basis with many of its customers, and they keep coming back—prepared to wait an hour or two, unless they come before 6pm. Good food, generous portions, and low prices are the attractions here: manicotti, gnocchi, tortellini, rigatoni, eggplant or chicken parmigiana, and other Italian classics. Jay's also has great pizza, and sandwiches before 5pm. Try one of the incredible ice-cream pies for dessert. No smoking is permitted; beer and wine are served.

WALNUT BREWERY, 1123 Walnut St., near Broadway. Tel. 447-1345.
   Cuisine: AMERICAN.
$ **Prices:** Appetizers $3.45–$5.95; lunch $4.95–$8.50; dinner $7.50–$14.95. MC, V.
   Open: Lunch daily 11am–4pm; dinner Mon–Thurs 5–11pm, Fri–Sat 5pm–midnight, Sun 5–10pm.
This looks as a brewery should. Brick walls, prominent brew tanks, warehouselike decor, big beer-label signs against one wall. Order an appetizing taster of the brewery's six handcrafted beers, but don't ignore the food. Lunches feature the brew burger and the brewer's club, as well as enchiladas and superb, beer-battered fish-and-chips. The Mexican treats remain on the dinner menu, along with a varied selection that includes lasagne and other pastas, brown ale chicken, alder-smoked salmon, tenderloin of beef with roasted garlic, and Danish baby-back ribs.

BUDGET

THE NEW YORK DELICATESSEN, 1117 Pearl St. Tel. 449-5161.
   Cuisine: DELI.
$ **Prices:** $2–$8.95. AE, MC, V.
   Open: Summer, daily 8am–9pm; winter, daily 8am–8pm.
Remember television's "Mork and Mindy"? Back in the 1970s, Robin Williams and Pam Dawber made their home-away-from-home at this authentic New York–style deli on the Pearl Street Mall. Enjoy Dagwood-style sandwiches, Coney Island hot dogs, or Reuben sandwiches. Soups, salads, and pastries are prepared fresh daily. The extensive menu also includes pizza and 15 different burgers. There's booth seating or a great outside deck for dining in, and take-out service is welcomed.

POUR LA FRANCE, 1001 Pearl St. Tel. 449-3929.
   Cuisine: FRENCH BISTRO.
$ **Prices:** Breakfast $1.10–$5.95; lunch $3.95–$6.95; dinner $4.25–$10.95. MC, V.
   Open: Mon–Sat 7am–midnight, Sun 8am–10pm.
A café and bistro on the mall, Pour La France is like a Paris brasserie—a casual sidewalk café with an awning shading outdoor diners and big windows giving the same view to those eating inside. You can start your day with a double espresso and Grand Marnier french toast or eggs Benedict, and a few hours later return for a gourmet salad or a pissaladière (a French bread pizza). Dinners feature a variety of pasta dishes plus daily specials, and the desserts are a chocolate lover's dream.

TOM'S TAVERN, 11th and Pearl Sts. Tel. 443-3893.
   Cuisine: AMERICAN.

$ Prices: $4.50–$6.95. CB, DC, DISC, MC, V.
Open: Daily 11:30am–12:30am.

Boulder's most popular place for a good hamburger, Tom's has been a neighborhood institution for three decades. Located in a turn-of-the-century building that once housed an undertaker, the tavern offers vinyl-upholstered booths indoors, a row of patio seating outdoors. Besides the one-third-pound burgers and other sandwiches, Tom's serves dinner anytime: a 10-ounce steak, fried chicken, or a vegetarian casserole, all in the $6 range.

5. ATTRACTIONS

Boulder is more a place to explore for its "feel," its atmosphere, than for any one or two particular attractions. The University of Colorado, the Pearl Street Mall, and the Boulder Creek Path are most typically "Boulder." But there's plenty more.

THE TOP ATTRACTIONS

BOULDER CREEK PATH, 55th St. and Pearl Pkwy. to Arapahoe Ave. and Canyon Blvd. Tel. 441-3400.

This nature corridor cuts a 9-mile swath through Boulder, from east to west along the rushing waters of Boulder Creek, but it doesn't even require so much as a street crossing. The peaceful, wooded path deals with traffic by a series of bridges and underpasses, linking several of the city's parks with the University of Colorado campus, government buildings, and other points of interest. It's a special favorite of walkers, runners, and bicyclists.

The eastern access to the path is from 55th Street at Pearl Parkway, just south of Valmont Road. Look for prairie-dog colonies and wetlands, where up to 150 species of birds have been identified. At 30th Street south of Arapahoe Road, it cuts through Scott Carpenter Park (named for Colorado's native-son astronaut), popular for swimming in summer and sledding in winter. Between 28th Street and Folsom Road, it skirts the grounds of the Clarion Harvest House (see "Accommodations," above), with its extensive recreational facilities (including bicycle rentals) and its underground fish observatory. The university's Folsom Stadium is just a few steps up the hill to the south.

A historic train and bandstand mark Central Park at Broadway and Canyon Boulevard. Here, the trail is just 2½ blocks south of the Pearl Street Mall. In short order, you'll pass the Boulder Municipal Building, the City of Boulder Sculpture Park, fishing ponds where kids under 12 can angle for free and keep their catch, and the Boulder Justice Center, a merging of courts and jail facilities. Near Third and Canyon, look for the Xeriscape Garden, where drought-tolerant plants are used to test reduced water usage.

At the west end of the Boulder Creek Path is Eben G. Fine Park, named for the discoverer of Arapahoe Glacier, a major source of municipal water. There are plans underway extending the path up Boulder Canyon to connect with other byways, thus creating a regional bicycle-pedestrian trail system.

PEARL STREET MALL, Pearl St. from 11th to 15th Sts.

This four-block-long tree-lined pedestrian mall marks at once Boulder's downtown core and its center for dining, shopping, strolling, and (especially) people-watching. Musicians, mimes, jugglers, and other buskers hold forth on the landscaped mall day and night, winter and summer; and you'll find everyone from starched-shirted lawyers to dreadlocked Rastafarians watching the shows. Buy your lunch from one of the many vendors and sprawl on the grass in front of the courthouse to rest and eat. Locally owned businesses and galleries share the mall with trendy boutiques, sidewalk cafés, and major chains including Esprit, Peppercor, Banana Republic, and Pendleton. There's a wonderful play area for youngsters—

climbable boulders set in gravel—the kids love it. Don't miss the bronze bust of Chief Niwot, king of the southern Arapahoe, in front of the Boulder County Courthouse between 13th and 14th. Niwot, who welcomed the first Boulder settlers, was killed in southeastern Colorado in the Sand Creek Massacre of 1864.

UNIVERSITY OF COLORADO, east side of Broadway between Arapahoe Ave. and Baseline Rd. Tel. 492-1411.

The largest university in the state, with 25,000 students (including 4,000 graduate students) and 1,600 acres, the University of Colorado dominates all else in Boulder. Its student population, its cultural and sports events, and its intellectual atmosphere have shaped Boulder into the city it is today. It's one of 12 universities in the U.S. that has a NASA program.

Old Main, on the Norlin Quadrangle, was the first building erected after the university was established in 1876. At first it housed the entire school. Later, pink sandstone buildings of Italian Renaissance style came to predominate on campus. Of special interest are the C.U. Heritage Center, on the third floor of Old Main; the University of Colorado Museum (see "More Attractions," below), a natural-history museum in the Henderson Building on Broadway; the Mary Rippon Outdoor Theatre, behind the Henderson Museum, site of the annual Colorado Shakespeare Festival; the Fiske Planetarium and Science Center, between Kittredge Loop Drive and Regent Drive on the south side of campus; and the Norlin Library, on the Norlin Quadrangle, the largest research library in the state, with extensive holdings of American and English literature. Prospective students and their parents can arrange campus tours through the admissions office (tel. 492-6301).

NATIONAL CENTER FOR ATMOSPHERIC RESEARCH, 1850 Table Mesa Dr. Tel. 497-1173.

I. M. Pei designed this striking pink sandstone building overlooking Boulder from high atop Table Mesa in the southwestern foothills. Scientists here study such phenomena as the greenhouse effect, wind shear, sunspots, and tides to gain a better understanding of the earth's atmosphere. Satellites, weather balloons, interactive computer monitors, robots, and supercomputers that can simulate the world's climate are among the technological tools on display. The center also hosts a changing art exhibit.

Admission: Free.

Open: Self-guided tours, Mon–Fri 8am–5pm, Sat–Sun and holidays 9am–3pm; guided tours, June–Sept, Mon–Sat at noon and by appointment.

MORE ATTRACTIONS

INDUSTRIAL TOURS

CELESTIAL SEASONINGS, 4600 Sleepytime Dr., off Spine Rd. and Longmont Diagonal. Tel. 530-5300.

The nation's leading manufacturer of herbal teas moved into a modern new building in northeastern Boulder in late 1990. The tour is an experience for the senses. The company, which began in a Boulder garage in the 1970s, now produces more than 40 varieties of teas from over 100 different herbs and spices, which it imports from 35 foreign countries. Here at the plant, you'll observe everything from the importation bays to the blending process to packaging, from the production of tea bags to boxing for shipment. The tour lasts about one hour. The visitor center includes a retail outlet.

Admission: Free.

Open: Daily for tours; call ahead for schedule. Reservations are highly recommended for groups.

ROCKIES BREWING COMPANY, 2880 Wilderness Place, near Valmont Rd. Tel. 444-8448.

From the grinding of the grain to the bottling of the beer, the 25-minute tour of this microbrewery—America's original, trendsetting "designer" brewery—ends as all brewery tours should: in the pub. Tours lead past glistening copper vats that turn out 200 kegs of beer a day. (The mammoth Coors brewery in Golden produces 300,000

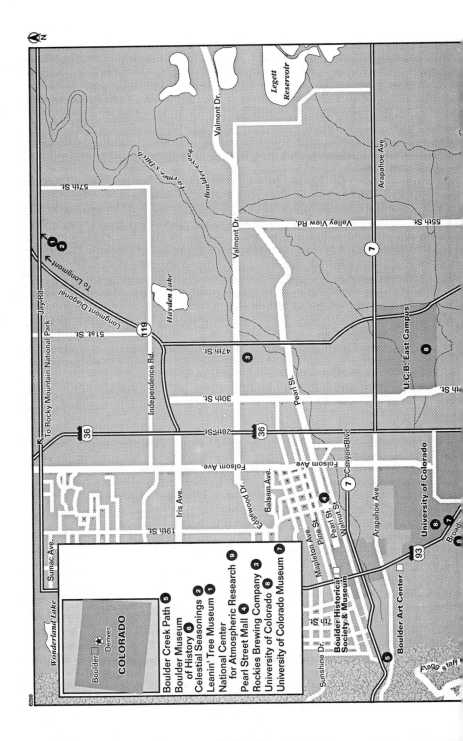

COLORADO

Boulder ☐ ★ Denver

Boulder Creek Path ❺
Boulder Museum
  of History ❻
Celestial Seasonings ❷
Leanin' Tree Museum ❶
National Center
  for Atmospheric Research ❾
Pearl Street Mall ❹
Rockies Brewing Company ❸
University of Colorado ❽
University of Colorado Museum ❼

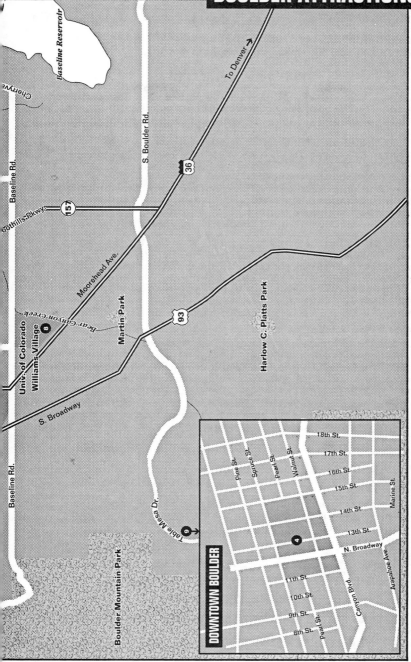

To Denver

Baseline Reservoir

Cherryv...

Baseline Rd.

S. Boulder Rd.

Foothills Pkwy.

Baseline Rd.

157

36

Moorehead Ave.

Bear Canyon Creek

93

Martin Park

Harlow C. Platts Park

Univ. of Colorado

Williams Village

8

S. Broadway

Baseline Rd.

Table Mesa Dr.

9

Boulder Mountain Park

DOWNTOWN BOULDER

18th St.

17th St.

16th St.

15th St.

14th St.

13th St.

Pine St.

Spruce St.

Pearl St.

Walnut St.

Marine St.

N. Broadway

4

11th St.

10th St.

9th St.

8th St.

Pearl St.

Canyon Blvd.

Arapahoe Ave.

kegs an hour!) The pub is actually a restaurant that overlooks the bottling area. The menu features such choices as soup, fresh salads, and sandwiches. Lunches run $5 to $7.

Admission: Free.
Open: Mon–Sat 11am–midnight; tours, Mon–Sat 2pm.

MUSEUMS & GALLERIES

BOULDER MUSEUM OF HISTORY, 1206 Euclid Ave. Tel. 449-3464.

Ensconced on University Hill in the 1899 Harbeck House, a French château-style sandstone mansion with a Dutch-style front door and Italian tile fireplaces, this museum has an impressive collection of over 25,000 artifacts, 111,000 photographs, and 486,000 documents. Built by a New York merchant who maintained a direct line to Wall Street, it features a Tiffany window on the stairway landing, a built-in buffet with leaded-glass doors, and hand-carved mantels throughout. Mannequins are busy cooking in the authentic old-fashioned kitchen. The wardrobes in the upstairs bedrooms contain an extensive collection of Victorian and Edwardian clothing, and there are exquisite quilts on the beds.

Admission: $1 suggested donation.
Open: Tues–Fri 10am–4pm, Sat noon–4pm; in summer only, also Sun 1–4pm.

COLLAGE CHILDREN'S MUSEUM, 2065 30th St. Tel. 440-9894.

This is a museum where children from preschool through elementary grades are encouraged to touch, dress up, and get involved. The museum has 4,700 square feet of custom-designed interactive exhibits, created to stimulate the imagination. Children under 12 must be accompanied by adults, but adults can play, too.

Admission: $2 per person, $7 per family.
Open: Wed 2–5pm, Thurs–Sat 10am–5pm, Sun 1–5pm.

LEANIN' TREE MUSEUM OF WESTERN ART, 6055 Longbow Dr., off Spine Rd. and Longmont Diagonal. Tel. 530-1442.

You may know Leanin' Tree as the world's largest publisher of western-art greeting cards. What's not so well known is that here, upstairs in the corporate headquarters, is an outstanding collection of 200 original paintings and 80 bronze sculptures by contemporary artists—all depicting scenes from the Old or New West. Represented are award-winning pieces from the National Academy of Western Art and Cowboy Artists of America. Many of the works have been reproduced on the company's greeting cards, for sale in the downstairs shop.

Admission: Free.
Open: Mon–Fri 8am–4:30pm, Sat 10am–4pm.

UNIVERSITY OF COLORADO MUSEUM, University of Colorado, Henderson Bldg., Broadway between 15th and 16th Sts. Tel. 492-6892 or 492-6165.

The natural history and anthropology of the Rocky Mountains and Southwest are the focus of this campus museum, founded in 1902. Anasazi pottery, dinosaurs, and antique Pueblo, Navajo, and Spanish colonial textiles are featured exhibits, along with collections in geology, paleontology, botany, entomology, zoology, and the arts. The main gallery has special displays that change throughout the year.

Admission: Free.
Open: Mon–Fri 9am–5pm, Sat 9am–4pm, Sun 10am–4pm.

PARKS & GARDENS

CHAUTAUQUA PARK, Ninth St. and Baseline Rd. Tel. 442-3282 or 440-3776 (restaurant).

During the late 19th and early 20th centuries, more than 400 Chautauquas—adult education and cultural entertainment centers—sprang up around the United States. This 26-acre city park, on a hillside above downtown, is one of the few remaining Chautauqua parks in the country. In summer, it still hosts a wide-ranging program of music, dance, theater, and film, including the Colorado Music Festival (see "The Performing Arts" section). There are playgrounds, picnic grounds, tennis courts, and hiking trailheads. The historic Chautauqua Dining Hall, which first opened on July 4, 1898, serves three meals daily at moderate prices, Memorial Day through Labor Day, and since they don't take reservations, expect a long wait—maybe an hour. There is some lodging available in cottages of varying sizes.

ELDORADO CANYON STATE PARK, Colo. 170, Eldorado Springs. Tel. 494-3943.
Eight miles southwest of Boulder, this 845-acre park is known around the world for the technical rock climbing offered by the sheer sandstone walls of Eldorado Canyon, reaching heights of 850 feet. If you're not a climber yourself, it's equally exciting to watch others scale the walls. There is also picnicking, hiking, and fishing, but no camping.
Admission: $3 per vehicle.

COOL FOR KIDS

City parks, Collage Museum, and the University of Colorado's Fiske Planetarium offer the best diversions for children.

On the Boulder Creek Path (see "The Top Attractions," above), youngsters are charmed by the **underwater fish observatory** behind the Clarion Harvest House. They can feed the huge trout (25¢ machines cough up handfuls of fish food) swimming behind a special glass barrier on the creek. Farther up the path, on the south bank around Sixth Street, **Kids' Fishing Ponds** stocked by the Boulder Fish and Game Club are open to children under the age of 12. There's no charge for either activity.

In summer, the Boulder Parks and Recreation Department (tel. 441-3400) schedules a variety of music, dance, and theater performances for children in some of its 56 parks. Three year-round sports centers have **public pools;** South Boulder Recreation Center, 1360 Gillaspie Dr. (tel. 441-3448), East Boulder Community Center, 5660 Sioux Dr. (tel. 441-4400), and North Boulder Recreation Center, 3170 Broadway (tel. 441-3444). Call for schedules and times.

The **Collage Children's Museum** has hands-on exhibits. The **Fiske Planetarium** (tel. 492-5002) has an after-school and summer Science Discovery Program and Saturday "Stories Under the Stars." Friday nights they sometimes offer a light show followed by looking through the telescope at the stars.

6. SPORTS & RECREATION

SPECTATOR SPORTS

The major attraction is University of Colorado college baseball, basketball, and football. For tickets write or phone the Ticket Office, Campus Box 372, Boulder, CO 80309 (tel. 303/49-BUFFS).

VOLLEYBALL It may seem out of place here in the mountains, but each June sees the Jose Cuervo Doubles Volleyball Tournament, a professional beach-volleyball tournament that attracts the best two-person teams in the nation. It takes place at the Boulder Reservoir, 5100 N. 51st St. (tel. 441-3468). There's a separate division for amateurs in this tournament, played at the South Boulder Recreation Center, 1360 Gillaspie Dr. (tel. 441-3410).

RECREATION

Boulder is without doubt one of the leading outdoor-sports towns in North America. The city itself owns 6,000 acres of park lands, including more than 200 miles of hiking trails and long stretches of bicycle paths. Several canyons lead down from the Rockies directly into Boulder, attracting mountaineers and rock climbers. Families enjoy picnicking and camping in the beautiful surroundings. It seems that everywhere you look, men and women of all ages are running, walking, biking, skiing, or otherwise active.

Well-established sporting-goods stores in the city include Chivers Sports, 2000 30th St. (tel. 442-2493), which focuses on skiing, tennis, swimming, and soccer; and Doc's Ski and Sport, 629 S. Broadway (tel. 499-0963), which sells, rents, and repairs skis, mountain bikes, and rollerblades.

BICYCLING Some days, you may see more bikes than cars in Boulder. Paths run along many of the city's major arteries, and local racing and touring events are scheduled year-round. For current information on biking events, the best places to ride, and equipment sales and repairs, check with University Bicycles, 839 Pearl St. (tel. 444-4196). The shop also provides rentals of bikes and in-line skates at its outlet a block away, at Pearl and Eighth (tel. 449-2562). Rentals for mountain and road bikes start at $14 for a half day, and rentals for three-speeds and cruisers begin at $10 for a half day. In-line skate rentals start at $8 for two hours.

For maps of the city's 40 miles of bike paths, stop at either of the University Bicycles stores, or the city's alternative transportation program, Go Boulder, P.O. Box 791, Boulder, CO 80306 (tel. 303/441-4260). Each July, the city, county, and university cosponsor Boulder Bike week, which includes races, a kids' bike rodeo, safety forum, and maintenance clinics.

CLIMBING If you're interested in tackling the nearby mountains and cliffs with ropes and pitons, contact the Boulder Mountaineer, 1335 Broadway (tel. 442-8355), or the International Alpine Climbing School (tel. 494-4904).

The Flatiron Range, easily visible from downtown Boulder, and nearby Eldorado Canyon are two favorites among expert rock scalers.

FISHING Favored fishing areas near Boulder include Boulder Reservoir, North 51st Street, 1½ miles north of Jay Road, northeast of the city off the Longmont Diagonal; Lagerman Reservoir, west of North 73rd Street off Pike Road, about 15 miles northeast of the city, where nonmotorized boats can be used; Barker Reservoir, just east of Nederland on the Boulder Canyon Drive (Colo. 119), for bank fishing; and Walden Ponds Wildlife Habitat, about 6 miles east of downtown on North 75th Street. Don't forget to get a license and check local laws (see "Sports & Recreation" in Chapter 1 for details).

GOLF Local courses include the Coal Creek Golf Course, 585 W. Dillon Rd., Louisville (tel. 666-PUTT); the Flatiron Golf Course, 5706 Arapahoe Ave. (tel. 442-7851); and the Lake Valley Golf Course, Neva Road off U.S. 36 north (tel. 444-2114).

HEALTH CLUBS Among private clubs with wide-ranging facilities are the Boulder Athletic Club, 1715 15th St. (tel. 442-9790); the Flatiron Athletic Club, 505 Thunderbird Dr. (tel. 499-6590); and the Rallysport Health and Fitness Club, 2727 29th St. (tel. 449-4800).

The city operates the North Boulder Recreation Center, 3170 Broadway (tel. 441-3444), the East Boulder Community Center, 5660 Sioux Dr. (tel. 441-4400), and the South Boulder Recreation Center, 1360 Gillaspie Dr. (tel. 441-3448).

HIKING & BACKPACKING From Chautauqua Park, Ninth Street and Baseline Road (tel. 441-3408), rangers lead hikes and offer advice on trips into Boulder Mountain Parks. These include 4,625 acres bordering the Boulder city limits to the west and south, including the Flatirons and Flagstaff Mountain. You can pick up a "Boulder Mountain Park Trail Map" from the city Chamber of Commerce, 2440 Pearl St. (tel. 442-1044). A very popular hike is the Enchanted Mesa Trail, which leaves from Chautauqua Park, joins the longer Mesa Trail, and follows the ridge of the Flatirons about 6 miles to Eldorado Springs.

Boulder County Parks offer nice day hikes into the Betasso Preserve, 6 miles west of Boulder off Sugarloaf Road; Boulder Falls, 8 miles west of the city on Boulder Canyon Drive; and Walker Ranch, 8½ miles southwest via Flagstaff Road.

Numerous Roosevelt National Forest trailheads leave the Peak to Peak Highway (Colo. 72) west of Boulder. Check with the U.S. Forest Service, Boulder Ranger District, 2995 Baseline Rd. (tel. 444-6600). West of Boulder, on the Continental Divide, is the Indian Peaks Wilderness Area (tel. 444-6003). More than half of the area is fragile alpine tundra; permits are required from June 1 to September 15. North of Boulder, via Estes Park, is Rocky Mountain National Park (tel. 586-2371), covered in Chapter 9.

HORSEBACK RIDING Several area ranches offer day rides and pack trips, including Bar A Stables, 6000 W. Coal Creek Dr., Louisville (tel. 499-4464); and Lazy Ranch Riding Stables, Eldorado Springs (tel. 499-4940).

RUNNING The best place to get information about running or walking is the Runners Roost, 1129 Pearl St. (tel. 443-9868), which sells shoes and apparel and acts as headquarters for the many race events the city hosts. Most of these are "fun runs," varying in distance from 5km to a half marathon (13 miles), which occur throughout the year.

The Bolder Boulder (tel. 444-RACE), held every Memorial Day, attracts 20,000 runners who circle the 10km course.

SKIING Friendly Eldora Mountain Resort (tel. 440-8700) is just 21 miles (about a 40-minute drive) west of downtown Boulder via Highway 119 through Nederland. RTD buses leave Boulder for Eldora daily at 8:10am during ski season. Recently, the resort added a large new ski-school building and expanded the area's snowmaking capacity for a longer season.

For downhill skiers and snowboarders, Eldora has 34 trails geared primarily to the novice and intermediate, but with some expert terrain among its 210 acres. Fifteen runs are lighted for night skiing Thursday through Saturday. The area has five double-chair lifts, two surface lifts, and a vertical rise of 1,400 feet. Adult tickets are $29 for a full day, $21 for a half day, $15 at night. Seniors 65 to 69 pay $13; those 70 and over ski free. Children 6 to 12 pay $13 or $11 for a half day or at night; those 6 and under ski free. The season extends from mid-November to early April, snow permitting.

For cross-country skiers, Eldora has 50km (31 miles) of trails, about half groomed, and an overnight hut available by reservation. About 15% of the trails are rated easy, 50% intermediate, and 35% difficult. Rates are $9 for a full day of track skiing, $6 for a half day.

You can get equipment rentals at Crystal Ski Shop, 3216 Arapahoe Ave. (tel. 449-7669). Mountain Sports, 821 Pearl St. (tel. 443-6770), specializes in equipment for backcountry trips: cross-country, telemark, and touring skis, plus snowshoes.

HANG-GLIDING The atmospheric conditions generated by the peaks of the Front Range are ideal for year-round hang-gliding. The Cloud Base, 5534 Independence Rd. (tel. 530-2208), offers rides and lessons from the Boulder Municipal Airport, 2 miles northeast of downtown.

SWIMMING There are five public pools within the city. Indoor pools, all open daily year-round, are at the North Boulder Recreation Center, 3170 Broadway (tel. 441-3444), the East Boulder Community Center, 5660 Sioux Dr. (tel. 441-4400), and the South Boulder Recreation Center, 1360 Gillaspie Dr. (tel. 441-3448). Outdoor pools, both open daily from Memorial Day to Labor Day, are Scott Carpenter Pool, 30th Street and Arapahoe Avenue (tel. 441-3447), and Spruce Pool, 21st Street and Spruce Street (tel. 441-3446).

TENNIS There are more than 30 public courts in the city. The North and South Boulder Recreation Centers (see "Swimming," above) each have four lighted courts and accept reservations. Others are at Arapahoe Ridge Park, Eisenhower Drive south of Arapahoe Street; Chautauqua Park, Ninth Street and Baseline Road; Columbine Park, 20th Street and Glenwood Street; and Martin Park, 36th Street and Eastman Street.

WATER SPORTS For boat or canoe rentals, sailboard instruction, or swimming (and tanning) at a sandy beach, head for Boulder Reservoir (tel. 441-3456), on North 51st Street off the Longmont Diagonal northeast of the city.

7. SAVVY SHOPPING

SHOPPING A TO Z
ANTIQUES

ART SOURCE INTERNATIONAL, 1237 Pearl St. Tel. 444-4080.
Natural-history prints, maps, and rare books on western Americana—all from the 18th and 19th centuries—are the specialty here, along with a collection of one-of-a-kind, turn-of-the-century Colorado photographs. Open Monday through Saturday from 10am to 6pm and on summer Sundays from noon to 5pm.

ARTS & CRAFTS

ART MART, 1222 Pearl St. Tel. 443-8248.
More than 300 local artisans are represented in this gallery, which presents their watercolors, pastels, ceramics, hand-blown glass, and Native American jewelry and textile art. Open Monday to Thursday 10am to 10pm, Friday to Saturday 10am to 11pm, and Sunday 11am to 9pm, with shorter hours in winter.

BOULDER ART CENTER, 1750 13th St., between Arapahoe Ave. and Canyon Blvd. Tel. 443-2122.
Two exhibition galleries display the works of local, state, and contemporary national artists at this nonprofit art center. There are also frequent live performances of music, dance, and poetry readings in the center. Open Tuesday through Saturday from 11am to 5pm and on Sunday from noon to 4pm.

BOULDER ARTS AND CRAFTS COOPERATIVE, 1421 Pearl St. Tel. 443-3683.
Almost 100 Colorado artists and craftsworkers sell their work, all handcrafted originals, through this shop. Prices range from $2 to thousands, with most items less than $50. Open Monday through Saturday from 10am to 6pm and on Sunday from 11am to 6pm.

COYOTE GALLERY, 1401 Pearl St. Tel. 444-3323.
Leading contemporary southwestern artists display their paintings, pottery, wood carvings, jewelry, textiles, and other crafts. Open Monday through Wednesday from 9:30am to 6:30pm and Thursday through Saturday from 9:30am to 9pm (in summer also on Sunday from noon to 5pm).

HANDMADE IN COLORADO, 1426 Pearl St. Tel. 938-8394.
A small cooperative of local artists make everything right here—including weavings, quilts, stained glass, jewelry, and ceramics. Open Monday through Saturday from 10am to 6pm and on Sunday from 11am to 5pm (until 9pm in summer and on holidays).

MACLAREN/MARKOWITZ GALLERY, 1011 Pearl St. Tel. 449-6807.
Works by nationally known artists in a variety of mediums and styles are presented here, including metal sculpture, Southwest jewelry, and ceramics. Open Monday through Friday from 10am to 9pm, Saturday from 10am to 5:30pm, and on Sunday from noon to 5pm.

FASHIONS

ALPACA CONNECTION, 1326 Pearl St. Tel. 447-2047.
Natural fiber clothing from around the world, including alpaca-and-wool sweaters from South America, are featured at this shop, which is open seven days a week.

ZIPPETY DOO-DA, 2425 Canyon Blvd. Tel. 449-2522.
It's all for the kids here—children's clothing and accessories, including such lines as Flapdoodles, Mousefeathers, and Monkeywear, from newborn to size 14. There's a play area for kids while parents shop. Open Monday through Friday from 10am to 6pm, on Saturday from 10am to 5:30pm, and on Sunday from noon to 5pm.

FOOD

ALFALFA'S, 1651 Broadway. Tel. 442-0997.
The original Alfalfa's—a natural-foods supermarket that has since expanded to three locations in greater Denver and one in Fort Collins—is here in Boulder. Even if you're not cooking for yourself, stop for a sandwich, salad, or a drink at the juice bar. Open Mon–Sat 8am–10pm, Sun 8am–9pm.

GIFTS & SOUVENIRS

ANGELS FOR ALL SEASONS, 3100 S. Sheridan Blvd. Tel. 935-7033.
If you believe in angels, this is the place to come. Angels are the specialty here—wood, porcelain, pottery, paper—plus cards, prints, and even angel music.

ECOLOGY HOUSE, 1441 Pearl St. Tel. 444-7023.
Every gift in the shop, from T-shirts to jewelry, sculpture to stained glass, has an environmental theme. Part of the proceeds from every sale go to environmental causes. Open daily from 10am to 8pm.

TRADERS OF THE LOST ART, 1429 Pearl St. Tel. 440-9664.
This import shop carries incense candles, cards, jewelry, and colorful clothing and accessories from Asia, Africa, South America, and other locations around the world.

JEWELRY

FLORENCE BEAR JEWELRY & ANTIQUES, 2014 Broadway. Tel. 443-6311.
Native American jewelry, including many hard-to-find pieces, highlight this shop, in business for two decades. Gold and silver work is also presented. Open Monday through Saturday from 10:30am to 5:30pm and on Sunday from 1 to 5pm, with extended hours in summer.

MALLS & SHOPPING CENTERS

ARAPAHOE VILLAGE SHOPPING CENTER, 2640 Arapahoe Ave., at Folsom Ave.
This is one of several mid-size shopping centers near the junction of Arapahoe and 28th Street.

CROSSROADS MALL, 28th St. between Pearl St. and Arapahoe Ave.
This 160-store shopping center is anchored by Sears, J. C. Penney's, Foley's, and Mervyn's. There are also a wide variety of clothiers, jewelers, and stationers, at least half a dozen restaurants, and various other shops. A marked "Walkers Track" attracts locals on rainy days.

PEARL STREET MALL, Pearl St. from 11th to 15th Sts.
The core of downtown Boulder, the mall contains a wide choice of shops, galleries, and restaurants. See "The Top Attractions" in "Attractions," above.

8. EVENING ENTERTAINMENT

Boulder is a highly cultured community, especially noted for its summer music, dance, and Shakespeare festivals. But major entertainment events take place here year-round, both downtown and on the University of Colorado campus.

There's also a wide choice of nightclubs and bars—but it hasn't always been so here. Boulder was dry for 60 years, from 1907 (13 years before national Prohibition) until 1967! The first new bar in the city, the Catacombs in the Hotel Boulderado, finally opened in 1969.

Current entertainment schedules can be found in the *Daily Camera*'s weekly *Friday Magazine;* in either of the Denver dailies, the *Denver Post* or the *Rocky Mountain News;* or in *Westword,* the Denver weekly. Tickets for nearly all major entertainment and sporting events can be obtained from **TicketMaster** (tel. 290-TIXS) or its outlets, including Gart Bros. Sporting Goods (tel. 449-9021). Credit-card orders can be placed on American Express, MasterCard, or VISA. The agency adds a $3 charge to every ticket.

THE PERFORMING ARTS

MAJOR PERFORMING ARTS COMPANIES & EVENTS

Classical Music & Opera

ARTIST SERIES, Macky Auditorium Concert Hall, University of Colorado. Tel. 492-8423, or for tickets, 492-8008.

Such famed and varied international artists as Isaac Stern, Dave Brubeck, Dance Brasil, and the Royal Philharmonic Orchestra of London have appeared in Boulder through this annual subscription series. Emerging and regional artists also perform on and off campus.

BOULDER BACH FESTIVAL, 2010 14th St. Tel. 494-3159.

First presented in 1981, this celebration of the music of Johann Sebastian Bach includes performances and lectures during April and May.

BOULDER INTERNATIONAL CHAMBER PLAYERS. Tel. 447-8364.

Artists present an eclectic mix of music, from Beethoven sonatas to the classical sarod and tabla of North India. Performances are scheduled at various locales around the city.

BOULDER PHILHARMONIC ORCHESTRA. Tel. 449-1343.

This acclaimed community orchestra performs an annual fall-to-spring season at Macky Auditorium, bringing in world-famous artists who have included violinist Nadia Salerno Sonnenberg, singer Marilyn Horn, guitarist Carlos Montoya, and pianist Pinchus Zuckerman plus regional artists. Conductor Oswald Lehnert also presents *The Nutcracker* ballet with the Boulder Ballet Ensemble, Thanksgiving weekend. Tickets are $8 to $25.

Dance Companies

BOULDER BALLET ENSEMBLE. Tel. 442-6944.

This community group, established in 1984, is best known for its production of *The Nutcracker* with the Boulder Philharmonic on Thanksgiving weekend.

FESTIVALS

COLORADO DANCE FESTIVAL, P.O. Box 356, Boulder, CO 80306-0356. Tel. 303/442-7666.

Dancers from all over the world flock to Boulder for this 4-week event each July. Diverse performances are interspersed with classes, workshops, lectures, film and video screenings, and panel discussions.

COLORADO MUSIC FESTIVAL, 1035 Pearl St., Suite 302, Boulder, CO 80302. Tel. 303/449-1397.

The single biggest arts event of every year in Boulder lasts seven weeks, from mid-June to early August. Principal musicians from the world's leading orchestras comprise the Colorado Festival Orchestra, under the direction of Giora Bernstein, and present four performances a week at the acoustically revered Chautauqua Auditorium. Visiting artists and conductors add to the high standard of classical and contemporary performances. The festival has been held since 1976. There's a children's concert in late June and a special holiday concert on the Fourth of July.

COLORADO SHAKESPEARE FESTIVAL, Campus Box 261, University of Colorado, Boulder, CO 80309. Tel. 303/492-1527 or 492-0554.

Considered one of the top three Shakespearean festivals in the United States, this 7½-week event annually attracts more than 55,000 theatergoers between late June and mid-August. Held since 1958 in the University of Colorado's Mary Rippon Outdoor Theatre, and indoors at University Theatre, it offers 14 performances of each of four of the great bard's plays. Actors, directors, designers, and everyone associated with the productions are fully schooled Shakespearean professionals.

Performances are Tuesday through Sunday at 8:30pm (8pm for the indoor play), with 2pm matinees about twice a week. Tickets run $12 to $30 for a single performance, $42 to $90 for a four-play package.

During the festival, company members conduct 45-minute backstage tours at 6pm before each show. The tour reveals actors and technicians preparing for that evening's performance, and includes a visit to the company's costume exhibit. Adults pay $3; children 5 to 11, $2.

MAJOR CONCERT HALLS, THEATERS & ALL-PURPOSE AUDITORIUMS

CHAUTAUQUA AUDITORIUM, 900 Baseline Rd. Tel. 422-3282.

First opened on July 4, 1898, this National Historic Landmark in Chautauqua Park is an all-wood building notable for the clarity of its acoustics. Home of the Chautauqua Summer Festival, the auditorium hosts popular concerts, lectures, and dance and theater performances throughout the summer. Also in the historic park are the Community House, which features a more intimate program; and the Dining Hall, open from late May through Labor Day.

THE GUILD THEATRE, 4840 Sterling Dr. Tel. 442-1415.

The Upstart Crow community theater group offers a four-play season of classical plays at the Guild Theatre in the early autumn, late autumn, winter, and spring. The Boulder Acting Conservatory Theatre, for children 5 to 18, also makes its home here, as does Actors Ensemble, which presents contemporary plays.

MACKY AUDITORIUM CONCERT HALL, University of Colorado, University Ave. and Macky Dr. Tel. 492-8423 or 492-8008 for tickets.

The campus concert hall is home to the Boulder Philharmonic Orchestra and to major touring concert acts throughout the year.

MARY RIPPON OUTDOOR THEATRE, University of Colorado, Hellems Bldg., Broadway between 15th and 16th Sts. Tel. 492-0554.

Home of summer Shakespeare since 1944, and the official birthplace of the Colorado Shakespeare Festival in 1958, this beautiful garden theater was built by the Works Progress Administration in 1936 and named for the university's first woman professor. Nestled in the courtyard between the Hellems and Henderson buildings, it seats 1,004.

THE NOMAD PLAYHOUSE, 1410 Quince St. Tel. 443-7510.

The Nomad Players stage five productions a year, September to June, including musicals, comedies, dramas, and children's programs.

SPACE FOR DANCE, 3404 Walnut St. Tel. 444-1357.

A variety of local dance troupes use this space for productions and workshops, frequently two or more weekends a month.

DINNER THEATER

BOULDER DINNER THEATER, 5501 Arapahoe Ave. Tel. 449-6000.

Servers pull double duty here: First they bring you dinner in this cabaret-style theater; then they perform popular Broadway musicals without missing a beat. Dinner is served Tuesday through Sunday at 6:15pm, with show time at 8pm. There's also a 12:15pm Sunday matinee (show time 2pm).

Admission: $24–$34 for dinner and show with discounts for children and seniors on weeknights.

THE CLUB & MUSIC SCENE
COUNTRY & ROCK MUSIC

BOULDER CITY LIMITS, 47th St. and Longmont Diagonal. Tel. 444-6666.
Boulder's only country-and-western nightclub offers live swing and two-step music Wednesday through Saturday nights. Open daily with drink specials and theme nights.
Admission: Free or $2–$5, depending on night.

FOX THEATRE, 1135 13th St. Tel. 447-0095.
A variety of live music is presented here seven nights a week, from psychedelic rock to blues, featuring a mix of local, regional, and national talent. The converted movie theater has three bars, plus a café, open from 9am each day.
Admission: From free to $20, depending on performer.

J. J. McCABE'S SEAFOOD SHANTY, 945 Walnut St. Tel. 449-4130.
There's live rock, blues, and reggae music at this casual downtown café-bar. Also a lot of big-screen sports TVs.
Admission: $1–$4.

TULAGI, 1129 13th St. Tel. 442-1369.
An informal college bar on the Hill off campus, Tulagi features live rock music most nights.

JAZZ, BLUES & FOLK MUSIC

BRILLIG CAFE AND BAKERY, 1322 College Ave. Tel. 443-7461.
This college hangout brings back the image of the Greenwich Village coffeehouses of the 1960s, except with better food. There's acoustic music every Thursday evening, with an extensive selection of coffees, teas, and homemade baked goods. The Brillig also serves vegetarian lunches and dinners.
Admission: Free.

MEZZANINE LOUNGE, in the Hotel Boulderado, 13th and Spruce Sts. Tel. 442-4344.
Light jazz combos or soloists perform in Victorian surroundings, a great place to have a conversation with friends without being overwhelmed by loud music.
Admission: Free.

DANCE CLUBS & DISCOS

BENTLEY'S, in the Broker Inn, 30th St. and Baseline Rd. Tel. 449-1752.
There's live and recorded dance music at this flashy singles bar that tends to attract young professionals rather than a college crowd. There are happy-hour specials Monday through Friday from 4 to 7pm and Tuesday night is comedy night.
Admission: $3 cover on comedy night.

POTTER'S, 1207 Pearl St. Tel. 444-3100.
The Pearl Street Mall's most popular dance club features recorded music, nightly "special events," big-screen TV for major sports, and two pool tables. Open daily.
Admission: Free.

THE BAR SCENE
PUBS & WINE BARS

THE JAMES PUB, 1922 13th St. Tel. 449-1922.

Every important city has an Irish pub, and this is Boulder's. You'll find Harp Lager among the dozen beers on tap, Irish coffee, and such pub grub as corned beef and cabbage. Irish musicians even perform on occasion. Come for lunch (11am to 11pm) or dinner (5 to 11pm) or for happy hour after 10pm. There's a Sunday brunch at 11am.

WALNUT BREWERY, 1123 Walnut St., near Broadway. Tel. 447-1345.

The second-largest microbrewery in the United States (in terms of beer production) has its restaurant/bar/brewery in a historic brick warehouse a block off the Pearl Street Mall. Six beers are regularly brewed on the premises—Big Horn Bitter, Swiss Trail Wheat Ale, Buffalo Gold Premium Ale, Old Elk Brown Ale, the James Irish Red Ale, and Devil's Thumb Stout—plus seasonal specials like Spiranthes Ale, made from a white orchid grown locally. You can get half-gallon jugs to go.

THE CORNER BAR, in the Hotel Boulderado, 13th and Spruce Sts. Tel. 442-4344.

Probably the best bar in Boulder for people-watching, this Hotel Boulderado institution features sandwiches, soups, a fresh-oyster bar and an extensive list of wines by the glass. It's a local lunch spot.

OLD CHICAGO, 1102 Pearl St. Tel. 443-5031.

A pizza-and-pasta chain found throughout the Front Range, Old Chicago has two trademarks: its list of 110 beers from around the world (ask for a passport) and its sports-bar focus on Chicago teams (Cubs, White Sox, Bears, Bulls, Black Hawks).

THE SINK, 1165 13th St. Tel. 444-SINK.

The spacey wall murals are straight out of the 1960s, but this off-campus establishment has actually been open since 1949. There's a full bar and live music. Talk to students in the "Ratroom," or dine on burgers or "ugly crust" pizza. Open daily from 11am to 2am.

THE WALRUS, 11th and Walnut Sts. Tel. 443-9902.

This is where local university students come to play games—6 pool tables, plus foosball, shuffleboard, video games, and more—or to down happy-hour deals on beer while circulating from table to table to see friends.

WEST END TAVERN, 926 Pearl St. between 9th and 10th Sts. Tel. 444-3535.

The West End seems to have a lock on the annual "best neighborhood bar" balloting conducted by the *Daily Camera*. Sunny afternoons find dozens of Boulderites perched on the tavern's roof garden, and evenings see them tuned in to a wide-ranging selection of jazz, blues, or other live music in the trendy bar. Fare includes hot chili, pizza, and charbroiled sandwiches.

CHAPTER 8

NORTHEASTERN COLORADO

1. FORT COLLINS
- **WHAT'S SPECIAL ABOUT NORTHEASTERN COLORADO**

2. LOVELAND

3. GREELEY

4. FORT MORGAN

It would be hard to describe northeastern Colorado more perfectly or succinctly than with the now-famous words of "America the Beautiful" penned by Katherine Lee Bates after her ascent of Pikes Peak in 1893.

Here indeed are the spacious skies, stretching without obstacle or interruption hundreds of miles eastward from the foot of the Rocky Mountains.

Here are the golden, rolling, irrigated fields of wheat and corn, spreading along the valleys of the South Platte and Republican rivers and their tributaries, such as the Cache la Poudre and Big Thompson.

The western edge of this magnificent country is defined by the regal Rockies themselves. Impressive geological features mark the foothills, where the mountains meet the Great Plains at Fort Collins and Loveland.

A different Colorado exists on the sparsely populated plains, one that inspired James Michener's novel *Centennial*. Alive are memories of the Comanche buffalo hunters who first inhabited the region; trailblazers and railroad crews who opened up the area to white settlement; hardy pioneer farmers who endured drought, economic ruin, and so many other hardships; and ranchers like John W. Iliff, who carved a feudal empire built on longhorn cattle. Pioneer museums, frontier forts, old battlefields, and preserved downtown districts won't let history die. Vast open stretches—wetlands swollen with migrating waterfowl, the starkly beautiful Pawnee National Grassland—remain to remind us that Colorado wilderness is not the sole domain of the Rockies.

1. FORT COLLINS

65 miles N of Denver, 34 miles S of Cheyenne, Wyo.

GETTING THERE **By Plane** Most visitors to Fort Collins fly into Denver International Airport (see Chapter 4). The Airport Express (tel. 482-0505) provides shuttle services from the airport to Fort Collins.

The small Fort Collins–Loveland Municipal Airport (tel. 669-7182), off I-25 Exit 259, 10 miles south of Fort Collins, is served by Continental Express from Denver (toll free 800/525-0280) and also handles charters. Private planes land at the Fort Collins Valley Airpark, County Road 9E off Mulberry Street (tel. 484-4186).

WHAT'S SPECIAL ABOUT NORTHEASTERN COLORADO

Natural Attractions

☐ Poudre Canyon, containing the Cache la Poudre River, the first Colorado river designated a National Wild and Scenic River.

☐ Pawnee National Grassland, where the federal government and ranchers work to enhance wildlife habitat and reduce soil erosion.

The Arts

☐ Benson Park Sculpture Garden in Loveland, site every August of the largest outdoor sculpture show and sale in the U.S.

Museums

☐ Fort Morgan Museum, tracing Native American history back 13,000 years to Clovis points.

☐ Meeker Home Museum in Greeley, the original home of Union Colony founder Nathan Cook Meeker.

Industrial Tour

☐ Anheuser-Busch Brewery in Fort Collins, home of the company's famous Clydesdales.

Special Events

☐ Valentine's Day in Loveland, with its annual remailing of cards and love letters with a Cupid cachet and postmark.

☐ The Brush Rodeo, held over the Fourth of July weekend, the world's largest amateur rodeo.

Historic Villages

☐ Greeley's Centennial Village, with 22 buildings recalling life from the 1860 agricultural colony era to the 1920s.

By Bus   Greyhound/Trailways, 501 at Riverside Avenue (tel. 221-1327), provides intercity service, with major connections from Denver and Cheyenne.

By Car   Coming from south or north, take I-25, Exit 269 (Mulberry Street, for downtown Fort Collins), Exit 268 (Prospect Road, for Colorado State University), or Exit 265 (Harmony Road, for south Fort Collins). From Rocky Mountain National Park, follow U.S. 34 to Loveland, then turn north on U.S. 287. The drive takes about 1¼ hours from Denver or Estes Park, about 40 minutes from Cheyenne.

SPECIAL EVENTS   The first weekend in May, Cinco de Mayo is celebrated in Old Town and Lee Martinez Park; the third weekend in August, New West Fest takes place in Old Town and Library Park; the third week in September is Balloon Fest, on Mulberry Street near I-25; and in mid-October, go to Old Town for Oktoberfest.

A trading post was established here in 1862 on the Cache la Poudre River, named for a powder cache left by French fur trappers. A stage station and army camp, commanded by Lt. Col. William O. Collins, followed. The fort was abandoned in 1867, but the settlement prospered, first as a quarrying and farming center, and by 1910 in sugar-beet processing.

Today Fort Collins is regarded as one of the fastest-growing cities in the United States, with an average annual growth rate of 3.5%. Population leaped from 43,000 in 1970 to 65,000 in 1980 to 87,800 in the 1990 census, not including the many Colorado State University students. CSU was established in 1879; today it is nationally known for its forestry and veterinary medicine schools, and its research advances in space engineering and bone cancer. Major employers in the city are the Anheuser-Busch Brewery and Hewlett-Packard computer systems. The National Institute of

Standards and Technology, which coordinates the precise universal time and frequency, transmitting it to radios all over the world, is also located here.

ORIENTATION

INFORMATION

The Fort Collins Convention & Visitors Bureau has a visitor information center at 420 S. Howes St., Suite 101 (P.O. Box 1998), Fort Collins, CO 80522 (tel. 303/482-5821 or toll free 800/274-FORT). That's two blocks west of the intersection of College Avenue and Mulberry Street.

CITY LAYOUT

Fort Collins is located at the foot of the Rockies on the Cache la Poudre River, a major tributary of the South Platte. Downtown "Fort" is four miles due west of I-25. College Avenue (U.S. 287) is the main north-south artery and the city's primary commercial strip; Mulberry Street (Colo. 14), which crosses I-25 at Exit 269, the major Fort Collins interchange, is the main east-west thoroughfare.

Downtown Fort Collins extends north of Mulberry on College to Jefferson Street; Old Town is contained in a triangle bounded by College, Jefferson, and Mountain Avenue, which parallels Mulberry four blocks to its north. The main Colorado State University campus is in the mile-square sector bounded by Mulberry Street on the north, Prospect Road on the south, College Avenue on the east, and Shields Street on the west. Drake Road, Horsetooth Road, and Harmony Road cross College Avenue at 1-mile intervals south of Prospect. Taft Hill Road and Overland Trail parallel College at 1-mile intervals west of Shields; Lemay Avenue and Timberline Road are at 1-mile intervals east.

GETTING AROUND

BY BUS   The city bus system, known as Transfort (tel. 221-6620), operates nine routes throughout Fort Collins Monday through Saturday from 6:30am to 6:30pm, except major holidays. Most buses are accessible to the disabled; call for information. Fares are 75¢ for adults, 35¢ for seniors, the disabled, and youths 6 to 17, children under 6 ride free; exact change is required. A 10-ride ticket is $5.

BY TAXI   Taxi service is provided 24 hours a day by Shamrock Yellow Cab (tel. 224-2222).

BY BICYCLE   There are more than 75 miles of designated bikeways in Fort Collins, including the 5-mile Spring Creek Trail and the 6-mile Poudre River Trail. Rent bikes from Lee's Cyclery, 202 W. Laurel St. (tel. 482-6006), and ask for the free "Tour de Fort" bicycle route map from Lee's, the visitor information center, or city offices. Bicycles are not allowed on College Avenue.

FAST FACTS

The **area code** is 303. In case of **emergency,** call 911; for standard business, call police at 221-6540 or the Larimer County sheriff at 498-5100. The **Poudre Valley Hospital** is at 1024 Lemay Ave. (tel. 495-7000), between Prospect Road and Riverside Avenue just east of downtown. *The Coloradoan,* a Gannett **newspaper,** is published daily. The main **post office** is located at 301 E. Boardwalk Dr. (tel. 225-4100). State and county **tax** adds 8.95% to hotel bills.

WHAT TO SEE & DO

OLD TOWN, between College and Mountain Aves. and Jefferson St.
    A red-brick pedestrian walkway, flanked by street lamps and surrounding a

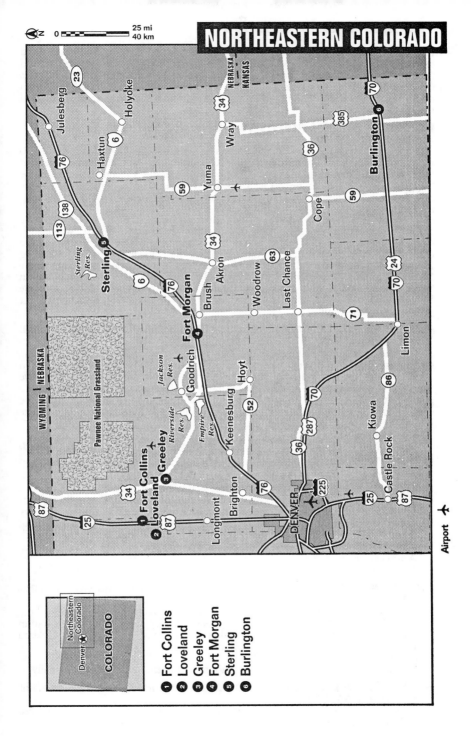

NORTHEASTERN COLORADO

0 25 mi / 40 km

COLORADO
Northeastern Colorado
Denver

1 Fort Collins
2 Loveland
3 Greeley
4 Fort Morgan
5 Sterling
6 Burlington

Airport ✈

bubbling fountain, is the focus of this restored historic district. The main plaza extends diagonally northeastward from the intersection of College Avenue and Mountain Avenue; on either side are shops and galleries, restaurants and nightspots. Outdoor concerts and a string of special events keep the plaza lively, especially from midspring to midfall. Walking-tour maps are usually available from individual merchants and city offices.

COLORADO STATE UNIVERSITY, University and College Aves. Tel. 491-1101.

Fort Collins revolves around the university, with its 20,000 students and 4,500 more faculty and staff. Founded in 1879 as Colorado State Agricultural College, and later renamed Colorado A&M, its athletic teams are still affectionately called the "Aggies," though they've been the Rams for decades. The A constructed on the hillside behind Hughes Stadium by students and faculty in December 1923 helps keep the name alive.

Campus visits usually start at the Administration Building, on the Oval where the school began, or Lory Student Center, University Avenue and Center Avenue (tel. 491-6444), which houses a cafeteria, bar, bookstore, activities center, ballroom, and other facilities. Appointments can be made to visit the renowned Veterinary Teaching Hospital, 300 W. Drake Rd. (tel. 221-4535), and the Equine Teaching Center at the Foothills Campus, Overland Trail (tel. 491-8373). The CSU Art Department, on Pitkin Street (tel. 491-6774), has five different galleries with revolving exhibits; and the University Theatre in Johnson Hall, on East Drive (tel. 491-5116), presents student productions year-round.

ANHEUSER-BUSCH BREWERY, 2351 Busch Dr. (I-25, Exit 271). Tel. 490-4691.

Opened in mid-1988, the brewery has become one of Fort Collins's leading employers—and its top tourist attraction. Six million gallons of beer are produced here each year, and distributed to 10 western states. Tours of the brewing facility leave from the visitors center, which includes exhibits on the Anheuser-Busch company, a gift shop and tasting room. Tours take about 1¼ hr. You needn't join a tour to visit the elegant barn that's home to the giant Clydesdale draft horses, used to promote Budweiser and other Busch beers since 1933.

Admission: Free.

Open: May–Oct, daily 9:30am–5pm; Nov–Apr, Wed–Sun 10am–4pm. **Closed:** Some major holidays.

AVERY HOUSE, 328 W. Mountain Ave. Tel. 221-0533.

Custom-built in 1879 for banker-surveyor Franklin Avery and his wife, Sara, this Victorian home at the corner of Mountain Avenue and Meldrum Street was constructed of red-and-buff sandstone from the quarries west of Fort Collins. The city purchased the house in 1974, and is continuing to restore it to its original Victorian splendor—from furniture to wallpaper to wall-papered ceilings. The grounds, with their gazebo, carriage house, and fountain, are popular for weddings and receptions.

Admission: By donation.

Open: Sun and Wed 1–3pm except Easter, Christmas, and New Year's Day.

THE FARM AT LEE MARTINEZ PARK, 600 N. Sherwood St. Tel. 221-6665.

City slickers can visit the country while in the city. Oats are available to feed the animals. Early 20th-century farm machinery is on display; country crafts are sold in the Silo Store. Special programs are scheduled year-round, and there are weekend pony rides for the kids in spring and summer.

Admission: Free; pony rides $2.

Open: Wed–Sat 10am–5:30pm, Sun noon–5:30pm; hours change seasonally.

FORT COLLINS MUNICIPAL RAILWAY, west end of Mountain Ave., at City Park. Tel. 224-5372.

This is one of the few remaining original trolley systems in the nation, a restored 1919 Birney streetcar running on its original track along Mountain Avenue for 1½ miles from City Park to Sherwood Street. It's certainly more for fun than practical urban transport.

Admission: $1 adults, 75¢ seniors, 50¢ children 12 and under.

Open: May–Sept, weekends and holidays only noon–5pm.

FORT COLLINS MUSEUM, 200 Mathews St. Tel. 221-6738.

Located in the 1904 Carnegie Library Building just a block south of Old Town, this museum boasts the largest collection of Folsom points of any western museum, plus military artifacts from Fort Collins, and pioneer and Victorian objects. There is an 1850s cabin, the 1864 log officers' mess known locally as "Auntie Stone's cabin," and a log one-room schoolhouse built in 1905.

Events include Rendezvous, a reenactment of the fur-trading era, in June; and Skookum Day, a living history day with an ice-cream social and children's activities, the third Saturday in July. The museum has a gift shop.

Admission: Free, with a suggested donation of $2.50.

Open: Tues–Sat 10am–5pm, Sun noon–5pm. **Closed:** Mondays and major holidays.

SWETSVILLE ZOO, 4801 E. Harmony Rd. Tel. 484-9509.

Don't come to Bill Swets's zoo expecting to find animals—not live ones, that is. The Sculpture Park is a menagerie of over 120 dinosaurs and other real and imaginary animals, flowers, and windmills—all constructed from car parts, farm machinery, and other scrap metal. Inside a small building is the Bungled Jungle—a wondrous series of imaginative creatures that boggle the mind and tickle the funnybone. There's also a miniature 3-quarter-mile steam train visitors can ride summer weekends and holidays, and an outdoor exhibit of old farm equipment and a 10-seat bicycle. The zoo is southeast of Fort Collins, on the east side of I-25 at Exit 265. Take your camera!

Admission: By donation.

Open: Daily dawn–dusk, year-round.

WHERE TO STAY

MODERATE

FORT COLLINS MARRIOTT, 350 E. Horsetooth Rd., Fort Collins, CO 80525. Tel. 303/226-5200 or toll free 800/548-2635. Fax 303/226-5200, request fax. 215 rms (all with bath), 13 suites. A/C TV TEL

$ Rates: $79–$109 single Mon–Fri, $69–$89 Sat–Sun; $89–$119 double Mon–Fri, $79–$99 Sat–Sun; $96–$400 suite. AE, CB, DC, DISC, ER, MC, V. **Parking:** Free.

Located in south Fort Collins, the Marriott boasts a direct walkway to the city's largest shopping center, Foothills Fashion Mall, as well as other shops and banks. The spacious lobby, which makes nice use of pink marble, is built around a central gas fireplace.

Most rooms have light-pastel decor, a king-size or two double beds, and standard hotel furnishings. Vanities are outside the bathroom. TVs offer in-room movies; local phone calls are 75¢.

The hotel offers a full range of services and dining and other facilities.

HOLIDAY INN UNIVERSITY PARK, 425 W. Prospect Rd., Fort Collins, CO 80524. Tel. 303/482-2626 or toll free 800/HOLIDAY. Fax 303/493-6265. 208 rms (all with bath), 51 mini-suites. A/C TV TEL

$ Rates: $83–$90 single; $94–$100 double; $94–$106 mini-suite. AE, CB, DC, DISC, JCB, MC, V. **Parking:** Free.

Conveniently located across the street from the Colorado State University main campus and adjacent to the Spring Creek trail for bikers and runners, this is the city's largest hotel. It's built around a beautiful central atrium with a three-story waterfall, trees, and standing plants.

Standard rooms have one king-size or two oversize double beds, and all standard hotel furnishings, including a credenza with remote-control television, direct-dial phone (local calls 75¢), and attractive serigraphs on the walls. Appointments are light blue and beige.

The hotel offers a full range of concierge services and dining and other facilities.

INEXPENSIVE

ELIZABETH STREET GUEST HOUSE, 202 E. Elizabeth St., Fort Collins, CO 80524. Tel. 303/493-BEDS. 3 rms (1 with bath).

$ Rates (including full breakfast): $43–$56 single or double without bath, $58–$71 single or double with bath. There's a 10% discount after the 4th night. AE, MC, V.

This 1905 American Foursquare brick home, just a block from CSU, at Elizabeth Street and Remington Street, is a little like grandma's house. There's a three-story dollhouse at the entrance and various dolls and other miniatures on shelves throughout, as well as impressive leaded windows and oak woodwork. Guest rooms are individually decorated with antiques and country crafts. The Alaska Room has a private bath; other rooms share 1½ baths. No smoking is permitted in the rooms. Guests have access to a TV, phone, and refrigerator. Coffee and tea are always available.

HELMSHIRE INN BED & BREAKFAST, 1204 S. College Ave., Fort Collins, CO 80524. Tel. 303/493-4683. Request fax. 26 rms (all with bath). A/C TV TEL

$ Rates (including breakfast): $59 single; $69 double. Discounts for stays over 5 days. AE, DC, MC, V.

A three-story custom-built inn across College Avenue from the CSU campus at Edwards Street, the Helmshire has a lobby like a living room and a lovely adjoining dining room, where buffet breakfasts and catered dinners are served. Each guest room is a little different, but every one has a private bath and kitchenette (with refrigerator, microwave oven, wet bar, and utensils), and is furnished with antiques and re-creations. Ask for a back room—they're quieter. Local phone calls are 30¢. Infants are welcome. The building has an elevator and facilities for the disabled. About three rooms are nonsmoking.

BUDGET

MULBERRY INN, 4333 E. Mulberry St., Fort Collins, CO 80524. Tel. 303/493-9000 or toll free 800/234-5548. Fax 303/224-9636. 116 rms (all with bath), 4 suites. A/C TV TEL

$ Rates: $35–$50 single; $40–$55 double. Suites $85–$95; Jacuzzi units $60–$75. AE, CB, DC, DISC, MC, V.

Most rooms in this recently upgraded motel have queen-size beds, a desk with a phone (local calls free), a television with in-room movies, and other standard furnishings. There are double Jacuzzis in 32 rooms; some suites have Jacuzzis, wet bars, and large private decks. There's a restaurant, lounge, heated, seasonal outdoor swimming pool, no-smoking rooms, and facilities for the disabled.

BUDGET HOST INN, 1513 N. College Ave., Fort Collins, CO 80524. Tel. 303/484-0870 or toll free 800/825-4678. 29 rms (all with bath), 1 suite. A/C TV TEL

$ Rates: Mid-May to Sept, $36–$52 single or double; Oct to mid-May, $28–$38 single or double. AE, CB, DC, DISC, ER, MC, V.

A property at the north end of town, on U.S. 287 near Willox Lane, this pleasant motel has been owned and operated by Tom and Karen Weitkunat since 1975. Kids enjoy its playground equipment, while adults like the outdoor hot tub. Ten units have full kitchens; all have coffee makers. Half of the rooms have a shower, so if you need a tub, request it. Rooms have direct-dial phones (free local calls) and remote-control televisions. Fax and copy machine available.

WHERE TO DINE

EXPENSIVE

NICO'S CATACOMBS, 115 S. College Ave. Tel. 482-6426.

Cuisine: CONTINENTAL. **Reservations:** Recommended.
$ Prices: Appetizers $4.25–$7.50; main courses $11.95–$25. AE, CB, DC, MC, V.
Open: Dinner only, Mon–Sat 5–10pm.

If Frank Sinatra hung out in northern Colorado, you'd probably find him at Nico's. A classic, dimly lit cellar restaurant, with a richly decorated lounge separated from the main dining room by a stained-glass partition, Nico's features table-side service and daily specials (including fresh seafood) announced on blackboards.

You can start with a shellfish dish such as mussels Marseille, or perhaps the pâté maison, then move on to rack of lamb paloise, steak Diane flambé, or chateaubriand bouquetière for two. The lounge also serves a pre- and posttheater menu that features a "macho platter" of fried alligator, juliennes of rattlesnake, and Rocky Mountain oysters. The Catacombs also has an award-winning wine cellar, considered the best in northern Colorado.

THE WINE CELLAR, 3400 S. College Ave. Tel. 226-4413.

Cuisine: CONTINENTAL. **Reservations:** Highly recommended.
$ Prices: Appetizers $4.95–$9.95; main courses $4.95–$11.95 at lunch, $14–$32.95 at dinner. AE, DC, DISC, MC, V.
Open: Lunch Mon–Fri 11am–2pm; Sun brunch 10am–2pm; dinner Sun–Thurs 5–9pm, Fri–Sat 5–10pm.

Perhaps the city's most elegant restaurant, the Wine Cellar is not a cellar at all. It maintains an Old World look, with small wine casks atop room dividers, lush plants and dimly lit lamps suspended from the ceilings, and a double-sided fireplace separating the dining area from the spacious lounge. An outdoor deck is especially popular on summer weekends, and there's live jazz in the lounge nightly.

Lunches feature a good selection of salads and sandwiches, including a Cajun grilled chicken-breast sandwich. Customized omelets, shrimp, and crab are featured during the Sunday brunch, and favorite dinner entrées include beef Wellington, veal Florentine, fresh seafood, and pasta primavera. Try the raspberry bash for dessert. The Wine Cellar has an excellent wine cellar, with many varieties available by the glass.

MODERATE

JAY'S AMERICAN BISTRO, 151 S. College Ave. Tel. 482-1876.

Cuisine: CREATIVE AMERICAN. **Reservations:** Accepted.
$ Prices: Appetizers $4.50–$6.95; main courses $2.50–$7 at lunch, $6.95–$15.95 at dinner. AE, DISC, MC, V.
Open: Mon–Sat 11am–10pm.

An eclectic menu, the work of local artists on the walls, and a friendly atmosphere are what you'll find at Jay's, located near the CSU campus. Appetizers include crab cakes and peanut shrimp in red chile sauce, and there's also a decidedly Southwest influence in many of the main entrées, such as seafood enchilada, or chipolte pasta, a smoked jalapeño pasta with tequila lime sauce. Other choices include northern Italian style–pastas, a variety of fresh seafood, steak, veal, and California-style pizza.

CUISINE! CUISINE!, 130 S. Mason St. Tel. 221-0399.

Cuisine: CONTINENTAL. **Reservations:** Recommended.
$ Prices: Appetizers $5–$7; main courses $4–$7 at lunch, $9–$18 at dinner. AE, DC, DISC, MC, V.
Open: Lunch Mon–Sat, 11am–2pm; dinner Mon–Thurs 5–9pm, Fri–Sat 5–9:30pm.

Creativity emanates from every corner of Cuisine! Cuisine!, abstract paintings and prints cover the walls of three small rooms, and modern jazz and semiclassical music wafts from the sound system. Fresh flowers and oil candles help contribute to the serene atmosphere. The cuisine is most creative of all. The theme menu changes monthly, often with international influences. A meal might include an appetizer of Cajun prawns in shiitake mushroom sauce, followed by a *queso flameado*—a baked white Cheddar flamed with brandy and a side of homemade raspberry peach chutney.

Other choices are the "turf and surf" dish of lamb chops and scallops, seared tuna steak with a roasted red-pepper crab sauce, and pork tenderloin pressed in macadamia-nut flour and sautéed. There's always something on the menu for vegetarians.

INEXPENSIVE

BISETTI'S, 120 S. College Ave. Tel. 493-0086.
   Cuisine: ITALIAN. **Reservations:** Not accepted.
$ Prices: Appetizers $3.95–$6.95; main courses $4.25–$6.95 at lunch, $6.50–$13.95 at dinner. AE, CB, DC, DISC, MC, V.
   Open: Lunch Mon–Fri 11am–2pm; dinner Mon–Thurs 5–9pm, Fri–Sun 5–9pm.
The first thing you'll notice upon entering this long-standing family business is the ceiling: From one end to the other dangle empty Chianti bottles signed by over a decade of consumers. This is a dark, candlelit room; two adjoining rooms are brighter and more modern. The menu features a variety of homemade pastas, from spaghetti and lasagne to rigatoni and manicotti. Full main courses include veal saltimbocca, basil fettuccine with chicken, and smoked salmon Alfredo. Come before 6:30pm Monday through Saturday for early-bird dinner specials as low as $5.25.

NATE'S STEAK & SEAFOOD PLACE, Cottonwood Corners, S. College Ave. at Horsetooth Rd. Tel. 223-9200.
   Cuisine: STEAK/SEAFOOD. **Reservations:** Accepted.
$ Prices: Appetizers $2.95–$5.25; main courses $3.95–$5.95 at lunch, $6.95–$13.95 at dinner. AE, CB, DC, DISC, MC, V.
   Open: Sun–Thurs 11am–10pm, Fri–Sat 11am–11pm.
There's a vaguely Cape Cod feel to this casual south-end establishment, with seascapes and yachting pictures. A daily list of fresh seafood catches—prepared as you like them—highlights the menu; the other house specialty is prime rib. There's also a variety of steaks, ribs, and barbecued chicken at dinnertime; soups, salads, and sandwiches for lunch. An outdoor patio draws crowds on summer afternoons.

BUDGET

AVOGADRO'S NUMBER, 605 S. Mason St. Tel. 493-5555.
   Cuisine: AMERICAN and NATURAL.
$ Prices: Breakfast $1.50–$4.25; lunch or dinner $2.95–$4.45. MC, V.
   Open: Mon–Thurs 7am–11pm, Fri 7am–midnight, Sat 8am–midnight, Sun 8am–11pm.
A college hangout just north of campus, Avogadro's is a throwback to the 1960s with its macramé room dividers and jungle-theme wall mural. The menu runs the gamut from steaks and hamburgers to tempeh burgers, omelets to granola, with a wide selection of coffees, bagel sandwiches, subs, and home-baked desserts. There's live bluegrass music Friday and Saturday nights.

COOPER SMITH'S PUB & BREWING, 5 Old Town Sq. Tel. 498-0483.
   Cuisine: ENGLISH/AMERICAN. **Reservations:** Accepted for parties of eight or more.
$ Prices: $4.95–$8.95. AE, MC, V.
   Open: Wed–Sat 11am–2am, Sun–Tues 11am–midnight.
This modern brew pub isn't just a place for beer drinking. Within its brick walls is an open kitchen that prepares such traditional pub specialties as fish-and-chips, bangers and mash, and Highland cottage pie. You can also get local treats like catfish Delacroix as well as hamburgers, other sandwiches, salads, and soups. A late-night menu is served Monday through Saturday until 1am and on Sunday until 11pm. There's also a children's menu.

EL BURRITO, 404 Linden St. Tel. 484-1102.
   Cuisine: MEXICAN.
$ Prices: $2.95–$8.95. AE, CB, DC, MC, V.
   Open: Sun–Thurs 11am–9pm, Fri–Sat 11am–10pm.
Mama Godiñez has been concocting her authentic Mexican specialties at this tiny

north-of-downtown restaurant. Year-in, year-out, Fort Collins residents have voted it the spot with the best burritos in town. It's also got great tacos, enchiladas, and chiles rellenos.

SILVER GRILL CAFE, 218 Walnut St., Old Town. Tel. 484-4656.
  Cuisine: AMERICAN.
$ Prices: Breakfast or lunch $2–$5.75. MC, V.
  Open: Mon–Sat 6am–2pm, Sun 7am–1pm.

Continually operated since 1933, this working man's café attracts blue- *and* white-collar types, as well as seniors, students, and families. When there's a line outside, as there often is on weekends, coffee is served to those waiting! Come for the giant cinnamon rolls, or standard American fare: eggs and pancakes, biscuits 'n' gravy for breakfast; burgers and other sandwiches for lunch; "noontime dinners" like chicken-fried steak and roast beef. Everything's prepared fresh daily. Grilling and frying is done in salt-free and cholesterol-free vegetable oil.

SPORTS & RECREATION
SPECTATOR SPORTS

The Colorado State University Rams, which play in the Western Athletic Conference, provide the main attraction for fans of spectator sports. Football games are at CSU Hughes Stadium, Overland Trail near County Road 42C; basketball is played at Moby Arena, North Drive near Shields Street on the main campus; and the baseball field is on South Drive near Shields. For tickets, call 491-7267.

RECREATION

HORSETOOTH RESERVOIR   The city's most popular area for outdoor recreation is Horsetooth Reservoir, only about 15 minutes west of downtown, just over the first ridge of the Rocky Mountain foothills. The 7-mile-long, man-made lake—on the site of the 19th-century Stout Quarry and community—is named for the distinctive tooth-shaped rock that has long been an area landmark. It's reached via County Road 44E or 42C, both off Overland Trail, or County Road 38E off Taft Hill Road (tel. 226-4517).

There are boat rentals for waterskiing and fishing at the North Inlet Bay Marina, 4314 Shoreline Rd., and a campground and swimming beach in the South Bay area. Sailboarding and even scuba diving are also popular. The Foothills Trail for hikers and mountain bikers runs along the east side of the reservoir from Dixon Dam north to Michaud Lane. Horsetooth Mountain Park, on the reservoir's southwestern shore, has 25 miles of hiking and cross-country skiing trails. Near the north end of the lake is a Sports Cycle Park for motorcycles and all-terrain vehicles, as well as snowmobiles in winter.

On the northwestern shore of the lake is Lory State Park (tel. 493-1623), reached through Laporte. It has hiking and horse trails, and plenty of opportunities for rock climbing. The top of Arthur's Rock—a hike of 2 miles—offers a marvelous view across Fort Collins and the northeastern Colorado plains. In the park is the Double Diamond Stable (tel. 224-4200), where horse rentals, guided rides, and chuck-wagon dinners are arranged.

OTHER PARKS   Major Fort Collins parks include: City Park, 1500 W. Mulberry St. (tel. 484-6686), with boat rentals, miniature train rides, a nine-hole golf course, and an outdoor swimming pool; Edora Park, 1420 E. Stuart St. (tel. 221-6679), whose Edora Pool and Ice Center (EPIC) (tel. 221-6683) is considered one of the finest indoor swimming pools and ice rinks in the United States; Lee Martiñez Park, 600 N. Sherwood St. (tel. 221-6665), notable not only for its farm (see "What to See & Do" above) but for its fishing and horseback riding opportunities; and Rolland Moore Park, 2201 S. Shields St. (tel. 221-6667), which features a complex for racquetball and handball players. You'll find picnic grounds, tennis courts, and softball fields at all four parks.

PARTICIPATORY SPORTS Fort Collins offers a number of possibilities. (See also "Other Parks" above).

Biking Bicyclists (see "Getting Around," above), hikers, and joggers use two asphalted trails through the city: Poudre River Trail, southeast from North Taft Hill Road to East Prospect Road; Spring Creek Trail, west from East Prospect Road to West Drake Road; and an earthen trail: Foothills Trail, parallel to Horsetooth Reservoir from Dixon Reservoir north to Campeau Open Space and Michaud Lane.

Fishing & Hunting Fishing-and-hunting opportunities abound in the nearby Roosevelt National Forest. For further information, contact the U.S. Forest Service, Estes-Poudre Ranger District, 148 Remington St. (tel. 482-3822), or Redfeather Ranger District, 1311 S. College Ave., third floor (tel. 498-1375); and the Colorado Division of Wildlife, 317 W. Prospect Rd. (tel. 484-2836).

Golf For golfers, Fort Collins has four public courses, including Collindale Golf Course, 1441 E. Horsetooth Rd. (tel. 221-6651), and Southridge Greens, 5750 S. Lemay Ave. (tel. 226-2828); plus a private country club.

River Rafting River-rafting enthusiasts can get half-day trips on the Cache la Poudre and full-day rides down the North Platte with Rocky Mountain Adventures, P.O. Box 1989, Fort Collins (tel. 493-4005 or toll free 800/858-6808), or A Wanderlust Adventure, 3500 Bingham Hill Rd. (tel. 484-1219 or toll free 800/745-7238).

Skiing Cross-country skiers can stay overnight in a backcountry yurt system owned by Never Summer Nordic (tel. 482-9411). The yurts are located near Cameron Pass, west of Fort Collins off Colo. 14 in Roosevelt National Forest.

Swimming The recently refurbished indoor Mulberry pool, 424 W. Mulberry St. (tel. 221-6659), has lap lanes, a diving area, and "Elrog the Frog," a poolside slide. The pool is open all afternoons and most evenings. The City Park Center and Outdoor Pool, 1599 City Park Ave. (tel. 484-6686), is open afternoons during warm weather. There is also a wading pool. Edora Pool and Ice Center (EPIC), at 1801 Riverside Dr. in Edora Park, (tel. 221-6683), has swimming and water exercise programs and diving. It is open afternoons and evenings.

SHOPPING

Visitors enjoy shopping in **Old Town Square,** at Mountain Avenue and College Avenue. Shops of note here include the **Walnut Street Gallery,** Building 21, Old Town Square (tel. 221-2383), which displays the work of nationally and regionally known artists; and **Trimble Court Artisans,** 118 Trimble Court (tel. 221-0051), an arts-and-crafts co-op just off the main plaza.

Also downtown is the **One West Art Center,** 201 S. College Ave. at Oak Plaza (tel. 482-ARTS), housed in a 1911 Italian Renaissance–style building that for six decades was the Fort Collins post office. The visual-arts complex now has three galleries, an art school, library, and a gift shop. It's open Wednesday through Saturday from 10am to 5pm.

Northern Colorado's largest enclosed shopping mall is the **Foothills Fashion Mall,** 215 E. Foothills Pkwy., at College Avenue and Horsetooth Road (tel. 226-5555). Anchored by four department stores—Foley's, J. C. Penney's, Sears, and Mervyn's—it has more than 110 specialty stores and a food court, and is open Monday through Friday from 10am to 9pm, on Saturday from 10am to 6pm, and on Sunday from noon to 5pm (closed major holidays).

EVENING ENTERTAINMENT

THE PERFORMING ARTS Fort Collins's principal venue for the performing arts is **Lincoln Center,** 417 W. Magnolia St., at Meldrum Street (tel. 221-6730). Built in 1978, the center includes the 1,180-seat Performance Hall and the 220-seat Mini-Theatre, as well as an art gallery and an outdoor sculpture garden. It is home to the Fort Collins Symphony, the Canyon Concert Ballet, the Larimer Chorale, the

OpenStage Theater, and the Children's Theater. Annual concert, dance, children's, and travel film series are presented.

The **Fort Collins Symphony** (tel. 482-4823), established in 1948, performs both classical and pops music plus special events—such as *The Nutcracker* (with the Canyon Concert Ballet) during the Christmas season, and a collaboration with the Larimer Chorale in the spring. On summer nights, the orchestra plays frequent outdoor concerts at various locations.

The **OpenStage Theatre Company** (tel. 484-5237) is the leading professional stage group. It offers five contemporary adult productions annually, as well as various popular, classical, operatic, and musical pieces through the season.

Notable **summer concert series** are the Lincoln Center Brown-Bag Lunches (tel. 221-6730), the Old Town Evening Concerts (tel. 484-6500), and the CSU–Lory Student Center Lagoon Concert Series (tel. 491-5402), all offering a range of jazz, contemporary, and classical music. Also on the CSU campus, the **Theatre Under the Stars** (tel. 482-4823) features three plays on alternating nights late June through July.

NIGHTCLUBS   The college crowd does its drinking and mingling at **Fort Ram,** a large dance club near the railroad tracks at 450 N. Linden St. (tel. 482-5026). There's live music a few blocks away in Old Town at **Linden's Bourbon Street,** 214 Linden St. (tel. 484-1780), the spot for blues and reggae, and the **Old Town Ale House,** 25 Old Town Sq. (tel. 493-2213), for all types of live music. Or try the **Wine Cellar,** 3400 S. College Ave. (tel. 226-4413), for jazz Thursday through Saturday. A regular is Mark Sloniker, a Fort Collins resident who's developing a national following. Country-and-western dancers head for the **Sundance,** 2716 E. Mulberry St. (tel. 484-1600).

Many Fort Collins folk head 24 miles up the Poudre River to the **Mishawaka Inn,** 13714 Poudre Canyon, Colo. 14 (tel. 482-4420), where top regional bands—and occasional national acts—perform. Keep an ear open for the Subdudes, a Fort Collins rock band with a growing national following.

THE BAR SCENE   Cooper Smith's Pub & Brewing, 5 Old Town Sq. (tel. 498-0483), attracts everyone from students to business executives with its pub menu and custom beers, including Poudre Pale Ale and Horsetooth Stout. Nearby, **Old Chicago,** 147 S. College Ave. (tel. 482-8599), features an international list of 125 beers. There's a dance floor downstairs at **Washington's,** 132 Laporte Ave. (tel. 493-1603), a lively bar with eclectic decor. The **County Cork Pub,** 313 W. Drake Rd. (tel. 226-1212), is a popular Irish-style bar.

MOVIES   There are well over a dozen cinemas, including the **University Mall Triplex Theaters 123,** 2273 S. College Ave. (tel. 221-4375), and the off-campus favorite, the **Aggie Theatre,** 204 S. College Ave. (tel. 224-3772).

EASY EXCURSIONS FROM FORT COLLINS

Both the Poudre Canyon and Red Feather Lakes are in Roosevelt National Forest. For further **information,** contact the Fort Collins offices of the U.S. Forest Service: Estes-Poudre Ranger District, 148 Remington St. (tel. 482-3822), or Redfeather Ranger District, 1311 S. College Ave., third floor (tel. 498-1375).

POUDRE CANYON   Running about 70 miles up Colo. 114 west of Fort Collins, this beautiful canyon follows the Cache la Poudre River to its source near the Continental Divide at 10,276-foot Cameron Pass. The first Colorado river with a national Wild and Scenic River designation, the Cache la Poudre offers outstanding trout fishing and white-water rafting, as well as picnicking, camping, hiking, and wildlife watching (deer and bighorn sheep) near its banks.

The upper canyon was the site for the first episode of the TV miniseries *Centennial.* Near the top of the canyon, the Rawah Wilderness encompasses the alpine lakes of the Medicine Bow Mountains, much loved by backpackers and horse packers. The Cameron Pass area is used by snowmobilers and cross-country skiers in winter.

The scenic drive begins 10 miles northwest of Fort Collins, where Colo. 14 turns west off U.S. 287.

RED FEATHER LAKES Located about 45 miles northwest of Fort Collins, this cluster of small lakes attracts fishermen as well as campers, hikers, and cross-country skiers. The high-plateau village, which offers lodging and basic amenities, is reached by turning left at Livermore, about 21 miles north of Fort Collins on U.S. 287.

A short distance from the Livermore turnoff, on the North Fork of the Cache la Poudre, is a historic 1880s guest ranch, the Cherokee Park Ranch, P.O. Box 97, Livermore, CO 80536 (toll free 800/628-0949). Open mid-May to early October, it offers an all-inclusive 1-week package—including lodging, meals, and a variety of outdoor sports—at a price of $925 for adults, $500 to $650 for children. Daily rates available during May and September.

---

2. LOVELAND

52 miles N of Denver, 13 miles S of Fort Collins

GETTING THERE By Plane Visitors who fly into Denver International Airport can reach Loveland aboard the Airport Express (tel. 482-0505) airport shuttle service.

The small Fort Collins–Loveland Municipal Airport, 4824 Earhart Dr., Loveland (tel. 669-7182), off I-25, Exit 259, seven miles northeast of downtown Loveland, is served by United Express (tel. 663-4614) and Continental Express from Denver (tel. 663-0962 or toll free 800/525-0280) and also handles charters.

By Bus Greyhound, 1630 N. Lincoln Ave. (tel. 669-8579), provides intercity service.

By Car Loveland is at the junction of U.S. 287 and U.S. 34. Coming from south or north, take I-25, Exit 257. From the west (Rocky Mountain National Park) or east (Greeley), follow U.S. 34 directly to Loveland. The drive takes about one hour from Denver or Estes Park.

ESSENTIALS Orientation Loveland is on the banks of the Big Thompson River, at the foot of the Rockies. The city is notable for more than a dozen lakes within or just outside the city limits—including Lake Loveland, just west of city center. U.S. 34, known as Eisenhower Boulevard, the main east-west thoroughfare, does a slight jog around the lake. Lincoln Avenue (one way northbound) and Cleveland Avenue (one way southbound) comprise U.S. 287 through the city. The main downtown district is along Lincoln and Cleveland south of Seventh Street, seven blocks south of Eisenhower.

Information Contact the Loveland Chamber of Commerce, 114 E. Fifth St. (at Cleveland Avenue), Loveland, CO 80537 (tel. 303/667-6311).

Getting Around Taxi service is provided 24 hours a day by Shamrock Yellow Cab (tel. 667-6767).

Fast Facts The **area code** is 303. In case of **emergency,** call 911: for standard business, call the police at 667-2157. The **hospital** is McKee Medical Center, 2000 N. Boise Ave. (tel. 669-4640) in the northeastern part of the city. The *Reporter-Herald* **newspaper** is published daily. The main **post office** is at 446 E. 29th St. (tel. 667-0344), just off Lincoln. State and county **tax** adds 8.95% to hotel bills.

SPECIAL EVENTS Loveland features the Annual Rotary Sweetheart Sculpture Show and Sale in February, the Ethnic Food Fest in June, the Corn Roast Festival, and the Larimer County Fair and Rodeo in August, and a Pumpkin Festival in October.

To get your Valentine's Day cards remailed from Loveland before February 14, you must address and stamp them, leaving room on the lower left of the envelopes for the special Loveland cachet, and mail them in a large envelope to Postmaster, Attn.: Valentines, Loveland, CO 80538. Mark SPECIAL HANDLING on the outer envelope.

The earliest settlements in the Big Thompson Valley were a trading post in the late 1850s and a community that grew around a flour mill in the late 1860s. Loveland was platted in 1877 on a wheat field near the tracks of the Colorado Central Railroad and was named for railroad president W. A. H. Loveland. That "lovestruck" monicker later proved fortuitous, for today Loveland has gained fame as the "Sweetheart City": Some 300,000 Valentine's Day cards are remailed from here every February with a Loveland postmark and cachet. At other times of the year the city is an agricultural center, especially for sugar-beet production. The population is around 37,000.

WHAT TO SEE & DO
ATTRACTIONS
In-Town Attractions

BENSON PARK SCULPTURE GARDEN, 29th St. between Aspen and Beech Sts. Tel. 663-2940.

A large number of sculptures are permanently displayed among the trees and plants at this city park. More significantly, this is the site of "Sculpture in the Park," the largest outdoor sculpture show and sale in the United States. Held annually in August, it features work by more than 160 sculptors. There are numerous studios and two casting foundries near the park, which is located opposite the northwest shore of Lake Loveland.

BOYD LAKE STATE RECREATION AREA, 3720 N. County Rd., Box 11C. Tel. 669-1739.

One of the largest lakes in the northern Front Range is located just a mile east of downtown Loveland via Madison Avenue and County Road 24E. The park here is geared to water sports, including water skiing, sailing, and windsurfing. There are white sand beaches for swimming, modern campsites, and excellent fishing (especially for walleyes).

LOVELAND CIVIC CENTER, Third and Adams Sts. Tel. 667-6130.

City offices, the Loveland Public Library, a senior citizens' center, the Chilson Recreation Center (see "Sports & Recreation" section below), and the Foote Lagoon and Performance Center are located here. The complex includes 17 landscaped acres and a 35-foot water fountain incorporated into a 400-seat outdoor amphitheater.

LOVELAND MUSEUM AND GALLERY, 503 N. Lincoln Ave. at E. Fifth St. Tel. 962-2410.

Exhibits of local historical artifacts and the work of regional and national artists fill this fine small museum. A "Life on Main Street" display depicts Loveland at the turn of the 20th century. Art exhibits change monthly. The museum also sponsors programs on art and history, workshops, concerts, and field trips.

Admission: Free.

Open: Tues–Wed and Fri 10am–5pm, Thurs 10am–9pm, Sat 10am–4pm, Sun noon–4pm.

Nearby Attractions

U.S. 34 west of Loveland follows the Big Thompson River through Big Thompson Canyon for 30 miles to Estes Park, the gateway to Rocky Mountain National Park. After passing **Devil's Backbone,** an unusual geological formation, this marvelously scenic route enters the canyon about 9 miles from Loveland. You can stop at **Viestenz-Smith Mountain Park,** 4 miles farther, with hiking trailheads, picnicking, and playground areas. The one small community along this route, Drake, another 4 miles past the mountain park, has cabins, food, and other facilities. A side route from Drake follows the North Fork of the Big Thompson through tiny Glen Haven, beside the Comanche Peak Wilderness, to Estes Park.

SPORTS & RECREATION

Loveland has over 900 acres in 24 parks. **North Lake Park,** at 29th and Taft streets, has a swim beach, tennis-and-racquetball courts, a playground, and a miniature narrow-gauge train, the Buckhorn Northern. Golfers enjoy two 18-hole municipal **golf courses:** Loveland and Marianna Butte and the Par 3 Cattail Golf Course. For full information on these and other recreation sites, contact **Loveland Parks and Recreation,** 700 E. Fourth St. (tel. 962-2727).

For year-round indoor fitness and recreation, the **Chilson Recreation Center,** located in the Loveland Civic Center, Third and Adams streets (tel. 962-2FUN), provides an eight-lane lap pool, water slide, whirlpools, an aerobic studio, and three gyms.

Greyhounds run from March through May at **Cloverleaf Kennel Club,** 2527 W. Frontage Rd. (tel. 667-6211). Satellite events are presented all year at the track, just off U.S. 34 at I-25.

Loveland's proximity to Rocky Mountain National Park offers many hardier challenges. One outfit taking advantage is the **Buckhorn Llama Co.** (tel. 667-7411), based in Masonville, a small community about 10 miles northwest of Loveland via County Road 27. A day hike and lunch with a llama runs $35 to $50 per person; wilderness pack trips of three to five days are also arranged. Or do it yourself and rent a llama for $25 per day.

EVENING ENTERTAINMENT

The Performing Arts **Outdoor concerts** and presentations are staged all summer long at Foote Lagoon, in Civic Center Park, and at Peters Park, next to the Loveland Museum and Gallery. The museum is the city's year-round cultural center, for performing as well as fine arts. Call 962-2410 for the current schedule of events.

WHERE TO STAY

BEST WESTERN COACH HOUSE RESORT, 5542 E. U.S. 34, Loveland, CO 80537. Tel. 303/667-7810 or toll free 800/528-1234. 88 units (all with bath). A/C TV TEL

$ Rates: Apr, $31–$44 single; $36–$50 double. May–June 18 and Sept (after Labor Day to Oct), $36–$50 single; $41–$55 double. June 19–Labor Day, $41–$55 single; $46–$60 double. AE, CB, DC, DISC, MC, V.

Nestled beside U.S. 34 as it enters Loveland from the east, this expansive, modern motel features indoor-and-outdoor swimming pools, a tennis court, whirlpool bath, barbecue area, moderately priced restaurant (serving three meals daily), and lounge. Rooms have king-size or queen-size beds, TV with in-room movies, and direct-dial phones. Pets are accepted.

BUDGET HOST EXIT 254 INN, 2716 S. E. Frontage Rd., I-25, Loveland, CO 80537. Tel. 303/667-5202 or toll free 800/825-4254. 30 units (all with bath). A/C TV TEL

$ Rates: $28–$34 single; $36–$40 double, hot-tub room $58. AE, CB, DC, DISC, MC, V.

An inexpensive alternative beside the freeway, this motel has individually heated rooms with king-size or queen-size beds, satellite TV, and direct-dial phones (free local calls). One room has a hot tub. There's a coin-operated laundry, a playground for the kids, and a restaurant nearby. Small pets are permitted with deposit. The motel is accessible to the disabled.

LOVELANDER BED AND BREAKFAST INN, 217 W. Fourth St., Loveland, CO 80537. Tel. 303/669-0798. 11 rms (all with bath).

$ Rates (including full breakfast): $69–$105 single; $79–$115 double. AE, DISC, MC, V.

Bob and Marilyn Wiltgen's rambling 1902 Victorian, just west of downtown, is undoubtedly Loveland's most charming accommodation. Every room has period antiques, including vintage iron or hardwood beds, writing tables, and claw-foot bathtubs. All rooms have private baths, one has a steam shower for two, and two have whirlpools. Breakfast is served in the dining room or on the terrace, and complimentary fruit, homemade cookies, and beverages are offered. Outside, guests can enjoy rose-and-herb gardens. Neither pets nor smoking are permitted; children over 10 are welcome. Fax service is available.

SYLVAN DALE GUEST RANCH, 2939 N. County Rd. 31D, Loveland, CO 80538. Tel. 303/667-3915. 28 units (all with bath).

$ Rates: Mid-June to Aug, $687 per person for 6 night package; Sept to mid-June, $55–$95 double for "bunk and breakfast." No credit cards (personal and traveler's checks accepted).

A working cattle-and-horse ranch on the banks of the Big Thompson River 7½ miles west of Loveland, the Jessup family urges guests to join in with daily ranch chores and roundups. There's horseback riding, an outdoor pool, tennis-and-volleyball courts, lakes stocked with rainbow trout, an indoor recreation room, and a kids' play area. The ranch has 14 rooms in its Wagon Wheel Lodge, four duplex cabins, and two large individual cabins. Summer guests must schedule 3- or 6-day full-board stays; the rest of the year, overnight guests are welcomed. The ranch offers complimentary van service from Loveland for packages.

WHERE TO DINE

THE PEAKS CAFE, 425 E. Fourth St. Tel. 669-6158.
  Cuisine: NATURAL FOODS.
$ Prices: Breakfast $1.25–$2.95; lunch $1.50–$4.75.
  Open: Mon–Fri 7am–4pm, Sat 8am–3pm.

Come in the morning for breakfast burritos, porridge, yogurt parfait, or the weekly Wednesday "pancake fest." Lunch offers salads, soups, a healthy spinach lasagne, "build-your-own" deli sandwiches, and other health-conscious foods. The café also serves home-baked goods, ice cream, and espressos.

THE SUMMIT, 3208 W. Eisenhower Blvd. (U.S. 34). Tel. 669-6648.
  Cuisine: STEAK/SEAFOOD. **Reservations:** Recommended.
$ Prices: Appetizers $3.50–$6.95; main courses $5.50–$7.50 at lunch, $7.45–$18.95 at dinner. AE, DC, V.
  Open: Lunch Mon–Fri 11:30am–2pm; dinner Sun–Thurs 5–9:30pm, Fri–Sat 5–10:30pm; brunch Sun 10am–2pm.

Arguably Loveland's finest restaurant, the Summit offers magnificent views of the Rockies from its location off U.S. 34, as it heads west toward Estes Park. The menu features three cuts of prime rib, New York and sirloin steaks, tenderloin of elk, chicken piccata or chipeta, fresh fish, shrimp Diane, Alaskan snow crab, and much more. There are wines by the glass, espresso drinks, and homemade pies.

---

3. GREELEY

54 miles N of Denver, 30 miles SE of Fort Collins

GETTING THERE By Plane Visitors who fly into Denver International Airport can travel on to Greeley with the Rocky Mount Shuttle (tel. 356-3366) and Airport Express (tel. 352-0505).

The Greeley–Weld County Airport, 600 Crosier Ave. (tel. 356-9141), east of the city, serves private planes and charters.

By Bus Greyhound, 902 Seventh Ave. (tel. 353-5050), provides intercity service.

By Car Greeley is located at the intersection of U.S. 34 (east-west) and U.S. 85 (north-south). The city is exactly midway between Denver and Cheyenne, Wyo.—both of which are more directly reached by U.S. 85 than by I-25. U.S. 34 heads west 17 miles to I-25, beyond which are Loveland and Rocky Mountain National Park. To the east, U.S. 34 ties Greeley to Fort Morgan via I-76, 37 miles away.

ESSENTIALS **Orientation** Greeley is located on the Cache la Poudre River just west of the point where it joins the South Platte. Laid out on a standard grid, it's an easy city in which to find your way around—provided you don't get confused by the numbered streets (which run east-west) and numbered avenues (which run north-south). It helps to know which is which when you're standing at the corner of 10th Street and 10th Avenue. Eighth Avenue (U.S. 85 north) and 11th Avenue (U.S. 85 south) are the main north-south streets through downtown. Ninth Street is U.S. 34 Business, jogging into 10th Street west of 23rd Avenue. The U.S. 34 Bypass joins U.S. 85 in a cloverleaf just south of town.

Information Contact the Greeley Convention & Visitors Bureau, 1407 Eighth Ave., Greeley, CO 80631 (tel. 303/352-3566).

Getting Around The city bus system, with the highly imaginative name of the **Bus,** provides in-town transportation. Its main terminal is at 1200 A St. (tel. 353-2812). Taxi service is provided 24 hours a day by **Shamrock Yellow Cab** (tel. 352-3000). There's also a service for the elderly and disabled called **Medicab** (tel. 686-1111).

Fast Facts The **area code** is 303. In case of **emergency,** call 911: for standard business, call the police (tel. 350-9600) or the Weld County Sheriff (tel. 356-4015). The **hospital,** North Colorado Medical Center, is at 1801 16th St. (tel. 352-4121), just west of downtown. The *Greeley Tribune* **newspaper**—named, of course, for the *New York Tribune* that contributed to the city's founding—is published daily. The main **post office** is at 925 11th Ave. (tel. 353-0398). State and county **tax** adds 6.7% to hotel bills.

SPECIAL EVENTS The UNC Jazz Festival is held on the last weekend of April at the University of Northern Colorado (tel. 351-2200). The last week of June and the first week of July the Independence Stampede is held in Island Grove Park, 14th Avenue and A Street (tel. 356-2855 or 356-7787). The Weld County Fair, in August, is also at Island Grove Park (tel. 356-4000).

Greeley is one of the few cities in the world that owes its existence to a newspaper. It was founded in 1870 as a sort of prairie Utopia by Nathan C. Meeker, farm columnist for the *New York Tribune*. Meeker named the settlement—first known as Union Colony—in honor of his patron, *Tribune* publisher Horace Greeley. Through his widely read column, Meeker recruited more than 100 pioneers from all walks of life and purchased a tract on the Cache la Poudre from the Denver Pacific Railroad.

City lots were laid out surrounded by farms, and each colonist contributed a membership fee, giving them the right to a farm parcel and an option on a town lot. Lots had to be improved within one year for the claim to continue valid. Proceeds from the sale of town lots went for projects for "the common good." Within a year, the colony's population was at 1,000. Greeley himself, an unsuccessful 1872 presidential candidate, visited the city in late 1870.

The population has been growing steadily ever since: At the 1990 census, it was nearly 60,000. Greeley's economy is supported almost exclusively by agriculture, with more than 96% of Weld County's 2.5 million acres devoted to either farming or raising livestock. A combination of irrigated and dry-land farms produce grains (including oats, corn, and wheat) and root vegetables (especially sugar beets, onions, potatoes, and carrots).

WHAT TO SEE & DO

ATTRACTIONS

In-Town Attractions

CENTENNIAL VILLAGE, Island Grove Park, 1475 A St., at N. 14th Ave. Tel. 350-9224.
This collection of buildings, depicting life in Greeley between 1860 and 1920, was

established as a 1976 Bicentennial project. Visitors enter the 5½-acre site through an old railroad depot; inside are 16 historic buildings and six reproductions, among them homestead houses, a one-room school, newspaper office, log-cabin courthouse, and rural church. Selma's Store sells crafts and regional history books.

Admission: $2.50 adults, $2 seniors, and $1 children 6–16, children under 6 are free.

Open: Memorial Day–Labor Day, Tues–Sat 10am–5pm, Sun 1–5pm; mid-Apr to Memorial Day and Labor Day to mid-Oct, Tues–Sat 10am–3pm. Guided tours are available.

MEEKER HOME MUSEUM, 1324 Ninth Ave. Tel. 353-9221.

This two-story adobe brick residence, built in 1870 for Greeley founder Nathan Cook Meeker, is on the National Register of Historic Places. The Union Colony era (1870–85) is interpreted through guided tours of the home, which is furnished with Meeker family belongings and 19th-century antiques.

Admission: $2.50 adults, $2 seniors, $1 children 6–16, children under 6 are free.

Open: Memorial Day–Labor Day, Tues–Sat 10am–5pm, Sun 1–5pm; Labor Day to mid-Oct and mid-April to Memorial Day, Tues–Sat 10am–3pm.

GREELEY MUNICIPAL MUSEUM, 919 Seventh St. Tel. 350-9220.

Housed in the east wing of the Civic Center, the museum contains an archives with the original Union Colony records, a Colorado Collection with many rare and out-of-print books about the state, and a gallery of changing exhibits pertaining to Greeley and Weld County history.

Admission: Free.

Open: Tues–Sat 9am–5pm.

Nearby Attractions

NORTH OF GREELEY The **Pawnee National Grasslands** (tel. 353-5004) begins about 25 miles northeast of Greeley and extends for about 60 miles east, to the boundary of Weld County. Nomadic Native American tribes lived in this desertlike area until the late 19th century; farmers subsequently had little success in cultivating the grasslands. Today the region is administered by the U.S. Forest Service, which works with ranchers to enhance the wildlife habitat, reduce soil erosion, and provide clean water. Activities on public land include hiking, horseback riding, hunting, camping, and picnicking. Antelope, coyotes, and prairie dogs are among the prolific wildlife.

There are many ways to the grasslands; one is to follow U.S. 85 north 11 miles to Ault, then east on Colo. 14 toward Briggsdale, 23 miles away.

On the south side of the grasslands, west of Briggsdale, are the two **Pawnee Buttes,** part of a steep, curving escarpment that cuts down from Wyoming. These sedimentary rock formations, once native lookout posts, stand half a mile apart and rise 350 feet above the plains.

SOUTH OF GREELEY South from Greeley, U.S. 85 travels south-southeast to Denver. There are interesting stops en route in **Platteville,** 16 miles from Greeley; **Fort Lupton,** 25 miles; and **Brighton,** 32 miles.

Just south of Platteville is **Fort Vasquez,** 13412 U.S. 85 (tel. 785-2832). A historical adobe reconstruction of a fur trader's fort of the 1830s, it has exhibits on trapping and trading, on the indigenous Plains tribe, and displays of artifacts excavated at the fort. It's open Memorial Day weekend to Labor Day, Monday through Saturday from 10am to 5pm and on Sunday from 1 to 5pm, with limited hours through September. Admission is free.

The **Fort Lupton Museum,** at 453 First St. (Hwy. 52), Fort Lupton (tel. 857-1634), is a small potpourri museum featuring south Weld County artifacts; it's open Monday through Friday, 9am to 4pm year-round, plus Sun 1am to 4pm June to August.

Brighton's **Front Wheel Drive Auto Museum,** 250 N. Main St. (tel. 659-6536 evenings), is open by appointment only. The technical-and-historical exhibits show designs used in front-wheel-drive automobiles from the 1890s to 1980s.

The **Adams County Museum And Cultural Center,** 9601 Henderson Rd., Brighton (tel. 659-7103), presents exhibits depicting the history of the area. Among displays are a blacksmith shop with a working forge and a 1920s parlor. The museum is open Monday through Saturday from 10am to 4:30pm.

SPORTS & RECREATION

FOOTBALL The Denver Broncos of the National Football League hold their preseason training camp at the University of Northern Colorado for six weeks during July and August. For practice and scrimmage information, call 351-2007.

RODEO The Greeley Independence Stampede comes to town for two weeks, starting in late June. Hundreds of professional cowboys compete for over $150,000 in prize money at Greeley's Island Grove Park. Festivities include concerts by top country-western music stars, a carnival, a children's rodeo, fireworks, and a parade. For information and tickets, call 303/356-7787 or toll free 800/982-BULL.

EVENING ENTERTAINMENT

THE PERFORMING ARTS Greeley's cultural focus is the **Union Colony Civic Center,** 10th Avenue at Seventh Street (tel. 356-5555 or 356-5000 for the box office). Opened in late 1988, the center hosts national touring artists and companies in the 1,700-seat Monfort Concert Hall or the 220-seat Hensel Phelps Theatre. The Greeley Civic Theater stages four to six plays a year, and the Greeley Philharmonic Orchestra, the oldest orchestra west of the Mississippi River, has an October-to-May season with about 10 performances.

The Little Theatre of the Rockies offers five summer-stock productions with a company of professionals and drama students. The University Garden Theater is the scene of Concerts Under the Stars in July and August, presented by the Colorado Philharmonic, the Greeley Summer Symphonic Band and Festival Choir, and others. For information or tickets to any of these events, call the University of Northern Colorado box office at 351-2200.

A 3-day **jazz festival** (tel. 351-2200) is held on the UNC campus in late April or early May. Cultural programs scheduled by the university are also open to the public (tel. 351-2265).

The annual **Arts Picnic** (tel. 350-9451), held the last full weekend in July in Lincoln Park, Ninth Street and Tenth Avenue, offers live entertainment, hands-on activities for children, over 200 arts-and-crafts booths, and 30 food booths.

Among Greeley's more popular **nightspots** are Potato Brumbaugh's Restaurant & Saloon, 2400 17th St. (tel. 356-6340), and the Smiling Moose Bar & Grill, 2501 11th Ave. (tel. 356-7010).

WHERE TO STAY

BEST WESTERN RAMKOTA INN & CONFERENCE CENTER, 701 Eighth St., Greeley, CO 80631. Tel. 303/353-8444 or toll free 800/528-1234. Fax 303/353-4269. 148 rms (all with bath), 4 suites. A/C TV TEL
$ Rates: $50–$55 single; $58–$63 double. AE, CB, DC, DISC, MC, V.
This former Radisson property is located downtown on Business Route 85. It offers a heated indoor swimming pool, in-room movies, a restaurant and a lounge. The hotel has no-smoking rooms, facilities for the disabled, and fax service.

HOLIDAY INN OF GREELEY, 609 Eighth Ave., Greeley, CO 80631. Tel. 303/356-3000 or toll free 800/HOLIDAY. 100 rms (all with bath). A/C TV TEL
$ Rates: Mar–Aug, $55 single, $62 double; Sept–Feb, $45 single, $52 double. AE, CB, DC, DISC, MC, V.
A newly renovated downtown hotel, this Holiday Inn offers guests an outdoor heated swimming pool, in-room movies, free local phone calls, and a coin-operated laundry. Camfield's restaurant serves three moderately priced meals daily, and the lounge is a popular evening oasis. Pets are accepted.

WINTERSET INN, 800 31st St., Evans, CO 80620. Tel. 303/339-2492
or toll free 800/777-5088. 47 rms (all with bath), 2 suites. A/C TV TEL
$ Rates: June to early Sept, $32 single, $32–$37 double. Early Sept to May, $26 single; $29–$33 double. Suites $46. AE, CB, DC, DISC, MC, V.

A lower-cost alternative to the downtown hotels, the Winterset is located two blocks south of the U.S. 34 bypass in the neighboring community of Evans. All rooms have satellite TV with in-room movies and access to the heated swimming pool. Pets are accepted with payment of a $10 deposit. There are nonsmoking rooms and complimentary morning coffee.

WHERE TO DINE

THE ARMADILLO, 111 S. First St., La Salle. Tel. 284-6560.
Cuisine: MEXICAN.
$ Prices: $4.95–$8.95. AE, MC, V.
Open: Sun–Thurs 11am–9pm, Fri–Sat 11am–10pm.

Occupying a large brick building beside the Union Pacific tracks in La Salle, five miles south of Greeley, this Mexican establishment offers an extensive-and-varied menu. You'll get all the usual meals here—enchiladas, tamales, and the like—and excellent fajitas. Every meal comes with rice, salad, and beans.

CABLE'S END, 3780 W. 10th St. Tel. 356-4847.
Cuisine: ITALIAN.
$ Prices: Dinner $6.95–$13.95. AE, DC, DISC, MC, V.
Open: Mon–Sat 11am–1am, Sun 11am–11pm.

Locally famous for its homemade pastas, including spaghetti and ravioli, Cable's End also offers fresh seafood, prime rib, steaks, chicken . . . and pizza. There's a seafood-and-pasta special on Friday night, a prime-rib-and-pasta special on Saturday. Kids eat for $1 from the children's menu on Sunday, there are $3.95 pasta specials Monday through Friday from 11am to 2pm, and on Monday night, it's all the spaghetti you can eat for $2.95. Don't miss the homemade cheesecake. Soup, salads, and sandwiches are the lunch fare.

POTATO BRUMBAUGH'S RESTAURANT & SALOON, 2400 17th St. Tel. 356-6340.
Cuisine: AMERICAN. **Reservations:** Suggested.
$ Prices: Lunch $4.95–$7.95; dinner $9.95–$17.95. AE, CB, DC, MC, V.
Open: Lunch Mon–Fri 11:15am–2pm; dinner Mon–Sat 5–10pm. **Closed:** New Year's and Christmas days.

Named for a character in James Michener's *Centennial,* this casually elegant restaurant in the Cottonwood Square shopping center follows the novel's theme in its western decor. The menu features steaks, prime rib, poultry, fresh seafood, and a variety of light dishes.

---

4. FORT MORGAN

81 miles NE of Denver, 45 miles SW of Sterling

GETTING THERE By Plane Denver International Airport is less than 90 minutes away. There are small municipal airfields for private planes and charters in Fort Morgan and Brush, 10 miles east.

By Train Amtrak trains make daily stops on the Denver to Chicago route at the Fort Morgan depot, located on Ensign Street south of Railroad Avenue (toll free 800/872-7245).

By Bus Greyhound provides intercity service. The bus station is on West Platte Avenue between Euclid Street and West Street (tel. 876-8072).

By Car Fort Morgan is located on U.S. 34 at I-76, the main east-west route between Denver and Omaha, Nebr. U.S. 34 proceeds west to Greeley and Estes Park, east to Wray and southern Nebraska. Colorado 52 is the principal north-south route through Fort Morgan.

ESSENTIALS Orientation Situated in the South Platte River valley is Fort Morgan's appropriately named principal east-west thoroughfare, Platte Avenue. The north-south artery, Main Street, divides it and other streets into east and west designations. I-76 exits onto Main Street north of downtown.

Information Contact the Fort Morgan Area Chamber of Commerce, 300 Main St. (P.O. Box 971), Fort Morgan, CO 80701 (tel. 303/867-6702).

Fast Facts The **area code** is 303. In case of **emergency,** call 911. The Colorado Plains Medical Center is located at 1000 Lincoln Ave., Fort Morgan (tel. 303/867-3391). The main **post office** is at 300 State St. between Kiowa Avenue and Beaver Avenue, a block east of Main. State and county **tax** adds 6.7% to hotel bills.

SPECIAL EVENTS The Fort Morgan area offers the following: the Brush Spring Festival, in May or early June in Brush; Huck Finn & Becky Thatcher Days, in June in Fort Morgan; the Tin Man Triathlon, in June in Fort Morgan; the Morgan County Fair, in August in Brush; and the Spanish Fiesta, in September in Fort Morgan.

Established as a military outpost in 1864, the original Fort Morgan housed about 200 troops who protected stagecoaches and pioneers traveling the Overland Trail from marauding Cheyenne and Arapahoe warriors. The threat had passed by 1870 and the fort was dismantled. But the name stuck when the city was founded in 1884 by an irrigation engineer from Greeley.

The town grew in the 20th century with the establishment of the Great Western Sugar Company for sugar-beet processing and with a pair of oil discoveries in the 1920s and 1950s. Cattle ranching has always been important. Today Fort Morgan has a population of about 8,500.

The city's most famous citizen was big-band leader Glenn Miller, who graduated from Fort Morgan High School in 1921 and formed his first band, the Mick-Miller Five, in the city.

WHAT TO SEE & DO
ATTRACTIONS

FORT MORGAN MUSEUM, City Park, 414 Main St. Tel. 867-6331.

An impressive collection of northeastern Colorado Indian artifacts, beginning with Clovis points 13,000 years old, is the highlight of this museum—the smallest one in Colorado to be accredited by the American Association of Museums. Other permanent exhibits focus on farming, ranching, and the railroad history of Morgan County, including old Fort Morgan, and a display on the life of native son Glenn Miller. The 1920s Hillrose Drugstore soda fountain, a town social center, has been fully restored.

Admission: Free.

Open: Mon and Fri 10am–5pm, Tues–Thurs 10am–5pm and 6–8pm, and Sat 11am–5pm.

FORT MORGAN HISTORICAL DRIVING TOUR. Tel. 867-6331.

Obtain a brochure from the museum or chamber of commerce for a self-guided tour to 13 sites around Morgan County. Included are a monument marking the site of Old Fort Morgan on Riverview Avenue at Lake Street, three blocks east of Main off I-76; Rainbow Bridge, a 1923 engineering marvel and National Historic Site on Colo. 52 at Riverside Park; remains of the Overland Trail, which parallels I-76 on its north side for 4 miles west from the Fort Morgan exit; and Orchard, a community 22 miles west of Fort Morgan on Colo. 144, where part of the TV miniseries *Centennial* was filmed. Many sets are still standing, including the Railroad Arms Hotel.

OASIS ON THE PLAINS MUSEUM, 6877 County Rd. 14. Tel. 432-5200.

This working ranch museum displays artifacts, antiques, collectibles, and other items of interest in the northeastern Colorado plains.

Admission: Free (donations appreciated).
Open: Sun noon–4pm, or by appointment.

SHERMAN STREET NATIONAL HISTORIC DISTRICT, 400 and 500 blocks of Sherman St. Tel. 867-6331.

Four Victorian mansions built between 1886 and 1926 are of special interest. Located on either side of East Platte Avenue, six blocks east of Main Street, they include the Warner House, an 1886 Queen Anne home; the Curry House, an 1898 Queen Anne Victorian home with decorative spindlework porches, a barn, carriage house, and water tower; the Graham House, a 1914 American Foursquare home; and the Bloedorn House, a 1926 brick Georgian revival–style house. Each is associated with a prominent city pioneer and are still private homes, not open to the public.

The Fort Morgan Museum publishes a walking-tour brochure both for Sherman Street and for the 9-block downtown district, the latter noting 44 buildings that made up the early town. These are available at the Chamber of Commerce at 300 Main St.

SPORTS & RECREATION

Impressive **Riverside Park,** off Main Street between I-76 and the South Platte River, offers facilities for swimming and tennis, an archery range, a nature trail, a handful of campsites, and ice skating in winter. Best of all, it's free.

Some 25 miles northwest of Fort Morgan is **Jackson Lake State Recreation Area,** 26363 Morgan County Rd. 3 (tel. 645-2551), off Colo. 144, 2½ miles north of Goodrich. The park offers a variety of water sports on a 2,700-acre reservoir. There are more than 200 campsites, sandy beaches for swimming, boating, and waterskiing. Anglers fish year-round for walleye, bass, catfish, and panfish. Hunters pursue waterfowl, game birds, and rabbits in a tightly controlled Labor Day-to-Memorial Day season. Bikers and hikers are always welcome. Watch for bald eagles, deer, beaver, and turkeys—especially in the mornings. Skaters and cross-country skiers enjoy the lake in winter. There's a fee for overnight use.

The **Brush Rodeo,** the world's largest amateur rodeo, is held in the town of Brush, 10 miles east, over the Fourth of July weekend.

WHERE TO STAY

BEST WESTERN PARK TERRACE MOTOR HOTEL, 725 Main St., Fort Morgan, CO 80701. Tel. 303/867-8256 or toll free 800/528-1234. 24 rms (all with bath). A/C TV TEL

$ Rates: $40 single; $44–$60 double. AE, CB, DC, DISC, MC, V.
A pleasant property four blocks south of I-76, the Park Terrace has rooms with queen-size beds, individual heating, full baths, direct-dial phones, and cable TV with HBO. There's a swimming pool and restaurant, serving three meals daily. Pets are accepted.

BUDGET HOST EMPIRE MOTEL, 1408 Edison St., Brush, CO 80723. Tel. 303/842-2876 or toll free 800/BUD-HOST. 19 rms (all with bath). A/C TV TEL

$ Rates: Summer, $28–$32 single; $32–$40 double. Winter, $25–$27 single; $30–$38 double. AE, CB, DC, DISC, MC, V.
A comfortable, clean, small roadside motel in Brush, about 10 miles from Fort Morgan, this mom-and-pop operation provides a good night's sleep at a bargain rate. All rooms are on one floor, with at-door parking, and the motel has cable TV. Nonsmoking rooms are available. Pets are not accepted.

CENTRAL MOTEL, 201 W. Platte Ave., Fort Morgan, CO 80701. Tel. 303/867-2401. 11 rms (all with bath), 6 suites. A/C TV TEL

$ Rates: May–Oct, $32 single; $37–$42 double. Nov to Apr, $30 single; $35–$39 double. AE, CB, DC, DISC, MC, V.
If you're staying more than a day or two, consider the Central: Refrigerators and

microwaves are available at no extra charge, and there are six two-bedroom suites. Rooms have king- or queen-size beds, individual hot-water heating, remote-control cable TV with HBO, and direct-dial phones. There are no-smoking rooms and facilities for the disabled; pets require advance approval. VCR rental and fax are available.

WHERE TO DINE

COUNTRY STEAK OUT, 19592 E. 88th Ave., Fort Morgan. Tel. 867-7887.
   Cuisine: STEAK. **Reservations:** Accepted.
$ **Prices:** $4.95–$15.95. AE, MC, V.
   Open: Tues–Sat 11am–9pm, Sun 11am–2pm.
This is the place for steak. This open-and-airy restaurant, with high ceilings and lots of wood and brick, is a favorite of locals. In addition to the great steaks, there are excellent homemade soups, daily luncheon specials, and an extensive salad bar at lunch and dinner.

EASY EXCURSIONS FROM FORT MORGAN

BRUSH Brush, 10 miles east of Fort Morgan on I-76 and U.S. 34, is an attractive town in its own right. With a population of 4,200, it is the second-largest community in Morgan County. The Brush Area Chamber of Commerce, 301 Edison St., Brush, CO 80723 (tel. 303/842-2666), has **information.**

The **All Saints Church of Eben Ezer,** 122 Hospital Rd. (tel. 842-2861), is on the National Register of Historic Places. Founded as a tuberculosis sanitorium in 1903, it was dedicated as a church in 1918. Its pointed Gothic arches, pitched beamwork ceiling, and art-glass windows are reminiscent of a 12th- or 13th-century Danish structure; in fact, the crown prince and princess of Denmark visited in 1918, and there's a Danish Pioneer Museum on site. Open Monday through Friday from 8am to 5pm; free admission.

WRAY Wray (pop. 2,300), about 10 miles from the Nebraska state line, is the Yuma County seat. The **Wray Museum,** 205 E. Third St. (tel. 332-5063), open Tuesday through Saturday from 10am to 5pm and on Sunday by appointment (free admission), displays native artifacts, pioneer memorabilia and photographs, a Battle of Beecher Island diorama, and replicas from Smithsonian-sponsored digs in the area. **Flirtation Point,** the oddly named first Masonic Temple in eastern Colorado, was built with stones from all 48 contiguous states. Just east of town, the human-made **Lions Amphitheater** on Fourth Street provides a stage for concerts, sunrise services, and graduation ceremonies in a beautiful sandstone canyon. Also, just off U.S. Hwy. 34, is the Wray Fish Hatchery, Colorado's largest warm-water **hatchery.** Free tours are available Monday through Wednesday.

Beecher Island Battleground, a National Historic Site 17 miles south off U.S. 385, commemorates one of the last skirmishes between white pioneers and Native Americans in Colorado, in September 1868. Today the site offers camping, picnicking, and hiking. There's hiking, fishing, and hunting as well as excellent opportunities for wildlife photography in the **Sandsage and Stalker Lake State Wildlife Areas,** both west of Wray off U.S. 34 (tel. 332-5382).

You can learn more about the Wray area from the Wray Tourism Center at the Wray Museum (see above), or the Yuma County Tourism Information Center, 330 E. Third St., Wray, CO 80758 (tel. 303/332-4828). For information about all of eastern Colorado, consult Colorado Plains, Inc., P.O. Box 324, Wray, CO 80758 (tel. 303/332-4364).

THE NORTHERN ROCKIES

The northern half of the Colorado Rockies is truly the climax of U.S. mountain wilderness, the crown on the head of the great range that dominates the American West.

This is rugged beauty at its best, extending on either side of the meandering Continental Divide down sawtooth ridgelines, through precipitous river canyons, and across broad alpine plains. Here, snowfall is measured in feet, not inches; when spring's golden sun finally melts away the frost, amazing arrays of alpine wildflowers greet the new beginning.

These Rockies are known as America's winter playground, and that's as it should be. Names of the region's resorts roll off the tongues of skiing households throughout the world, and are a part of the lore and legend of the sport: Aspen, Vail, Steamboat Springs, Breckenridge.

But this is also wonderful summer recreation territory. No one knows that better than Coloradans themselves, who flock here in every season to feel a oneness with the wilderness. Although out-of-state tourists predominate in July and August, locals opt for May and September as their favorite months: The temperature is only slightly lower, and there's more room to spread their wings.

One resort town that thrives on summer business is Estes Park, the gateway to Rocky Mountain National Park. To the northwest is Steamboat Springs, first and foremost a ranching town. Real cowboys—not urban imitations—share the streets with skiers and other vacationers.

Winter Park—remarkably, a mountain park owned by the City of Denver—may not get as much publicity as other Rockies resorts, but it soon may. Though it's now a relatively laid-back community, somewhat off the beaten track, it's miles closer to the Front Range than other leading resorts.

Summit County, perhaps, has more major ski areas within a half-hour's drive of one another than anywhere else in the country. Breckenridge, Copper Mountain, Keystone, Arapahoe Basin, and (just across the Continental Divide) Loveland Basin make this a winter sportsman's dream. Dillon Reservoir at Frisco is a major summer destination for boaters.

Year after year, Vail is voted America's single favorite ski resort. Why? For one, accessibility: The community is right on I-70. The mountain offers seemingly endless terrain for all abilities of skier. The town, only three decades old, has evolved into a high-class European-style enclave where traffic is restricted but the "beautiful people" are not. It's a charmer, though not a cheap one.

Aspen, too, is synonymous with Colorado and the Rocky Mountains. The town has kept its Victorian mining-town atmosphere while becoming, since the 1940s, the quintessential ski-resort community. It's as popular with the mink-stole set as with the blue-jeans-and-flannel-shirt generation. But, like Vail, prices in Aspen are very high.

☑

WHAT'S SPECIAL ABOUT THE NORTHERN ROCKIES

Natural Spectacles

- ☐ Rocky Mountain National Park in Estes Park, with some of the most spectacular mountain scenery you'll find anywhere in the American West.
- ☐ Maroon Bells, west of Aspen, among the most photographed mountains in the Rockies.
- ☐ Betty Ford Alpine Gardens in Vail, billed as the highest public gardens in the world.

Museums

- ☐ MacGregor Ranch Museum in Estes Park, a working ranch where you can see what life was like in the late 1800s.
- ☐ Estes Park Area Historical Museum, with a furnished pioneer cabin, hands-on activities for kids, and more.
- ☐ Tread of Pioneers Museum in Steamboat Springs, a beautifully restored Victorian home with exhibits on local ranch life and the history of skiing in Steamboat Springs.

- ☐ Frisco Historic Park, with turn-of-the-century buildings including a one-room schoolhouse, a trapper's cabin, and a jail.
- ☐ Colorado Ski Museum in Vail, everything there is to know about the history of skiing in Colorado.
- ☐ National Mining Hall of Fame and Museum, in Leadville, where you'll see minerals, crystals, mining equipment, and a walk-through, life-size model of a hard rock mine.

Activities

- ☐ Skiing at the world famous resorts of Vail, Aspen, and Steamboat Springs, with night skiing at Copper Mountain.
- ☐ Hiking in Routt National Forest and Rocky Mountain National Park.
- ☐ River rafting on the Arkansas River.

1. ESTES PARK

71 miles NW of Denver, 42 miles SW of Fort Collins

GETTING THERE By Plane Visitors fly into Denver International Airport, and continue to Estes Park with Charles Tour and Travel Services (see below).

By Bus Charles Tour and Travel Services (tel. 303/586-5151 or toll free 800/950-DASH) connects the town with Boulder and Denver.

By Car The most direct route is U.S. 36 from Denver and Boulder. At Estes Park, that highway joins U.S. 34, which runs up the Big Thompson River Valley from I-25 and Loveland, and continues through Rocky Mountain National Park to Granby. An alternative scenic route to Estes Park is Colo. 7, the "Peak-to-Peak Scenic Byway" that transits Central City (Colo. 119), Nederland (Colo. 72), and Allenspark (Colo. 7) under different designations.

SPECIAL EVENTS Area events include: the Stanley Steamer Tour, in May in Estes Park; the Rooftop Fair and Rodeo, in the third week of July in Estes Park; Western Days, in the third week of July in Grand Lake; the Estes Park Music Festival, during July and August in Estes Park; the Grand Lake Yacht Club Regatta, the second week of August in Grand Lake; the Americade of the Rockies Motorcycle Rally, during Labor Day week in Estes Park; the Scottish-Irish Highland Festival, in the second weekend of September in Estes Park; and the Elk Festival, in late September in Estes Park.

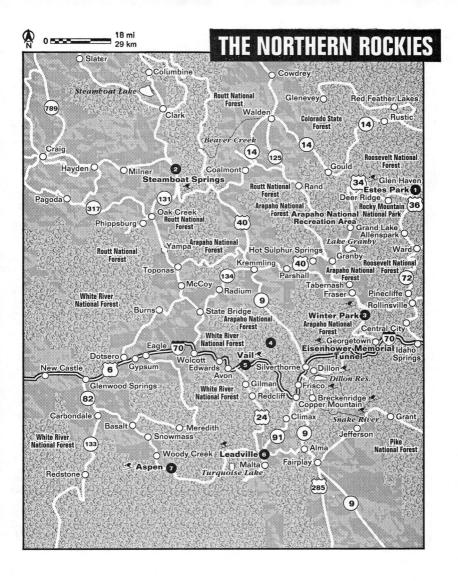

THE NORTHERN ROCKIES

The Northern Rockies

Denver

COLORADO

❶ Estes Park
❷ Steamboat Springs
❸ Winter Park
❹ Summit County
❺ Vail
❻ Leadville
❼ Aspen

Unlike other Colorado mountain communities, most of which got their starts in mining, Estes Park has always been a resort town. Long known by Utes and Arapahoes, the mountain park (7,522 ft.) was discovered in 1859 by rancher Joel Estes. He soon sold his homestead to Griff Evans, who built it into a dude ranch. One of Evans's guests, the British earl of Dunraven, was so taken by the region, he purchased most of the valley and operated it as his private game reserve until thwarted by such settlers as W. E. James, who built Elkhorn Lodge as a "fish ranch" to supply Denver restaurants.

But the growth of Estes Park is inextricably linked with two individuals: Freelan Stanley and Enos Mills. Stanley, a Bostonian who with his brother Francis had invented the kerosene-powered Stanley Steamer automobile in 1899, settled in Estes Park in 1907, launched a Stanley Steamer shuttle service to and from Denver, and in 1909 built the landmark Stanley Hotel. Mills, an innkeeper-turned-conservationist author and lecturer, was the prime advocate for the creation of Rocky Mountain National Park. President Woodrow Wilson signed the bill creating the 400-square-mile park in 1915; today it attracts over 2.8 million visitors annually.

ORIENTATION

INFORMATION The Estes Park Area Chamber of Commerce, P.O. Box 3050, Estes Park, CO 80517 (tel. 303/586-4431 or toll free 800/44-ESTES), has a visitor center on U.S. 34, just east of its junction with U.S. 36. For information on the national park, write or phone Park Headquarters, Rocky Mountain National Park, Estes Park, CO 80517 (tel. 303/586-2371).

CITY LAYOUT U.S. 34 and U.S. 36 enter Estes Park from the east, on either side of Lake Estes. The highways proceed together through downtown Estes Park as Elkhorn Avenue; U.S. 34 Bypass branches to the north and west as Wonderview Avenue, rejoining Elkhorn on the west side of town as Fall River Road and paralleling Fall River as it climbs into Rocky Mountain National Park. U.S. 36, now known as Moraine Avenue, turns south and west off Elkhorn at a town-center intersection; it follows Glacier Creek to the junction of Bear Creek Road, then ascends to the national park headquarters and visitor center.

GETTING AROUND

During the summer, the **Estes Park Trolley** (tel. 586-8866) operates on five routes daily from 10:30am to 10pm. Cost of a full-day pass is $4, which is good on all routes. Single round-trip tickets cost $2, and a one-way ticket is $1. The trolleys serve many motels, hotels, campgrounds, shopping, dining, and sightseeing areas.

Also in summer, a free national-park **shuttle bus** runs from the Glacier Basin parking area to Bear Lake. Departures are every 12 to 30 minutes between 8am and 5:30pm daily, from Memorial Day to mid-August, weekends only from mid-August to mid-September.

There's year-round taxi service with **Estes Park Tour and Taxi** (tel. 586-8440). Road tours into Rocky Mountain National Park and other area points of interest are conducted throughout the summer season by **Charles Tour and Travel Services** (tel. 303/586-5151 or toll free 800/950-DASH). Rates start as low as $10 and go up to $45 for full-day tours. Four-wheel-drive backcountry tours are conducted by **American Wilderness Tours,** 481 W. Elkhorn Ave. (tel. 586-4237), with rates starting at $15.

FAST FACTS

In case of **emergency,** call 911; for regular business, contact the Estes Park Police or the Larimer County Sheriff, both located at 170 MacGregor Ave. (tel. 586-4465). In the national park, call 586-2371 for emergencies. The **hospital,** Estes Park Medical Center is at 555 Prospect Ave. (tel. 586-2317). The **post office** is at 215 W. Riverside

Dr. (tel. 586-8177). For **road information,** call 586-4000. State and local **tax** add 8.2% to hotel bills.

WHAT TO SEE & DO
ATTRACTIONS

ROCKY MOUNTAIN NATIONAL PARK, Estes Park, CO 80517-8397. Tel. 303/586-2371.

⭐ Snow-covered peaks stand over lush valleys and shimmering alpine lakes. Certainly, this sort of beauty is not unusual in the Colorado Rockies—but the variety in ecological zones, which change with elevation, is. At lower elevations, about 7,500 to 9,000 feet, ponderosa pine and juniper cloak the sunny southern slopes, with Douglas fir on the cooler northern slopes. Blue spruce and lodgepole pine cling to streamsides, with occasional groves of aspen. Elk and mule deer thrive here. On higher slopes, forests of Englemann spruce and subalpine fir take over, interspersed with wide meadows alive with wildflowers in the spring and summer. This is also bighorn sheep country. Above about 10,500 feet the trees become increasingly gnarled and stunted, until they finally disappear and alpine tundra takes over. Fully one-third of the park is in this bleak world, many of its plants identical to those found in the Arctic.

Within the 415 square miles (265,726 acres) protected by the national park are 17 mountains above 13,000 feet. Longs Peak, at 14,255 feet, is the highest.

✪ **Trail Ridge Road,** which cuts west through the middle of the park from Estes Park, then south down its western boundary to Grand Lake, is one of America's great alpine highways. Climbing to 12,183 feet near Fall River Pass, it's the highest continuous paved highway in the United States. Depending on snowfall, the road is open from Memorial Day to mid-October. The 48-mile scenic drive from Estes Park to Grand Lake takes about three hours, allowing for stops at numerous scenic outlooks. Exhibits at the **Alpine Visitor Center** (open in summer daily from 9am to 5pm) at Fall River Pass, 11,796 feet above sea level, explain life on the alpine tundra.

Fall River Road, the original park road, leads to the pass from Estes Park via Horseshoe Park Junction. West of the Endovalley picnic area, the road is one-way uphill. As you negotiate its gravelly switchbacks, you get a clear idea of what early auto travel was like in the West. This road, too, is closed in winter.

One of the few paved roads in the Rockies that leads into a high mountain basin is Bear Lake Road. As a result, it's one of the most crowded. Numerous trails converge at Bear Lake, southwest of park headquarters via Moraine Park.

Wise visitors to the national park avoid crowds by putting on a backpack or climbing onto a horse. Rocky Mountain has 355 miles of trails leading into all corners of the park (see "Sports & Recreation," below). Backcountry permits are required for overnight hikes; they're obtained free at park headquarters and ranger stations. Backcountry camping is limited to one week from June to September. The park also offers fishing and mountaineering, plus cross-country and downhill skiing in winter.

Entering the park from Estes Park, it's wise to make your first stop at **Park Headquarters,** U.S. 36 west of Colo. 66 (tel. 586-2371). There's a good interpretive exhibit here, a wide choice of books and maps for sale, and general park information. It's open in summer, daily from 8am to 9pm; in winter, daily from 8am to 5pm. The **Kawuneeche Visitor Center** (open in summer daily from 7am to 7pm; winter, daily from 8am to 4:30pm) is located at the Grand Lake end of the Trail Ridge Road (tel. 303/887-3331 or 627-3471). Besides the Alpine Visitor Center, the **Moraine Park Museum** (open mid-June to mid-September, from 9am to 5pm), on Bear Lake Road (tel. 586-3777), also has full visitor facilities, in addition to its excellent natural-history exhibits. The new **Lily Lake Visitor Center,** eight miles south of Estes Park on Highway 7, also offers nature walks and information on Roosevelt National Forest. Campfire talks and interpretive ranger programs are offered at each visitor center between June and September. Consult the biweekly "High Country Headlines" newsletter for scheduled activities, which vary from photo walks to fly fishing and orienteering.

The park has five **campgrounds** with a total of 589 sites. Nearly half (247) are at Moraine Park; another 150 are at Glacier Basin. Moraine Park, Timber Creek (100 sites), and Longs Peak (26 tent sites) are open year round; Glacier Basin and Aspenglen (54 sites) are seasonal. Camping is limited to three days at Longs Peak and seven days at the other sites. Arrive early in summer if you hope to snare one of these first-come/first-served campsites. Moraine Park and Glacier Basin require reservations Memorial Day through early September. Contact Mistix, P.O. Box 85705, San Diego, CA 92186-5705, or call toll free 800/365-2267, up to eight weeks in advance.

Admission: $5 per week per vehicle; camping, summer $9 per campsite, off-season $7 per campsite.

Open: Park, daily year-round; high country, summer only, as snow conditions permit.

ENOS MILLS CABIN, Colo. 7 opposite Longs Peak Inn. Tel. 586-4706.

The cabin and 200-acre homestead of the late 19th-century conservationist is open to the public as a museum. Visitors are asked to honk their car horns when they arrive at the parking area, and Enda Mills Kiley will guide them down a nature trail to the cabin while discussing her father's life and work. Memorabilia in the homestead cabin include copies of Mills's 15 books, and the cameras that took thousands of photographs. Enos Mills encouraged the appreciation of the Rocky Mountains, and was a driving force behind the establishment of Rocky Mountain National Park.

Admission: Free.

Open: Memorial Day–Labor Day, daily 10am–5pm. By appointment in other seasons.

ESTES PARK AREA HISTORICAL MUSEUM, 200 Fourth St. at State Hwy. 36. Tel. 586-6256.

The lives of early homesteaders in Estes Park are depicted in this excellent, small museum, which includes a completely furnished turn-of-the-century log cabin, old ranch wagons, and an original Stanley Steam Car. The museum also has a discovery room for kids, with hands-on activities, and the story behind the book *A Lady's Life in the Rocky Mountains,* written in the late 1800s by Englishwoman Isabella Bird. The museum distributes a historical walking-tour brochure for downtown Estes Park and also sponsors a variety of lectures and other programs.

Admission: $2 adults, $1 children 12 and under, $5 families.

Open: May–Sept, Mon–Sat 10am–5pm, Sun 1–5pm; March, April, Oct, Dec, Sat 10–5, Sun 1–5; call for hours at other times.

MACGREGOR RANCH MUSEUM, Devil's Gulch Rd. Tel. 586-3749.

This 1873 ranch, located north of Estes Park off the U.S. 34 Bypass, not only shows what ranching was like in the last century but also offers spectacular views of the Rocky Mountains. Still a working ranch with about 125 head of black angus cattle, visitors are invited to tour the MacGregor family's large ranch house, with turn-of-the-century fashions and antiques. The ranch also features a smokehouse, root cellar, milk house, and a blacksmith shop.

Admission: Free.

Open: Memorial Day–Labor Day, Tues–Sat 11am–5pm.

PROSPECT MOUNTAIN AERIAL TRAMWAY, 420 E. Riverside Dr. Tel. 586-3675.

Panoramic views of Longs Peak and the Continental Divide, plus Estes Park village itself, are afforded by this lift. Its lower terminal is one block south of the post office. Its upper terminal has a gift shop and snack bar. Numerous trails converge atop the mountain.

Admission: $6 adults, $3 children under 12.

Open: Mid-May to Mid-Sept, daily 9am–6:30pm.

SPORTS & RECREATION

Estes Park is a major center for outdoor recreation. Aside from the Rocky Mountain National Park (see "Attractions," above), many activities take place in the 1,240-

square-mile Roosevelt National Forest. Obtain **information** on hiking, horseback riding, fishing, and other sports from the Estes-Poudre Ranger District Office, 148 Remington St. (P.O. Box 2747), Estes Park, CO 80517 (tel. 303/856-3440).

Within the city, the Estes Valley Recreation & Park District, 690 Big Thompson Hwy. (tel. 586-8191 or 800/345-2361 in Colorado), is in charge of a marina, two golf courses, a swimming pool, tennis courts, and other facilities.

BICYCLING Bicyclists pay a $3 weekly fee to enter Rocky Mountain National Park. A free park brochure provides information on safety, accommodations, regulations, and describes various suggested routes. Rentals and repairs are available at Colorado Bicycling, 184 E. Elkhorn Ave. (tel. 586-4241).

BOATING The Lake Estes Marina, 1770 Big Thompson Hwy. (tel. 586-2011), offers rentals of motorboats, sailboats, paddleboats, canoes, and sailboards. Windsurfing lessons are available by appointment. The marina is open Memorial Day to mid-September.

FISHING Four species of trout are fished in national park and national forest streams and lakes: brown, rainbow, brook, and cutthroat. A state fishing license is required ($18.25 for a 5-day nonresident license, if you're 15 or older); live bait is not permitted. Bear Lake is closed to fishing, as are some lakes and streams at the east side of the park. Get a license and regulations at area sporting-goods stores.

Another alternative is Trout Haven Trout Farm, 8100 Moraine Ave., west of town on U.S. 36 (tel. 586-5525), where you don't need a fishing license. Not only is all equipment provided, but they'll even clean and cook your fish for you! Rainbows run 10 to 28 inches, and you pay by the inch for what you catch. Open seven days a week, May to September, 8am to sunset.

GOLF There are two courses: Estes Park Golf Course (18 holes), 1080 S. St. Vrain St. (tel. 586-8146); and Lake Estes Executive Golf Course (9 holes), 690 Big Thompson Hwy. (tel. 586-8176). Working on your putting? Try Tiny Town Miniature Golf (19 holes), 840 Moraine Ave. (tel. 586-6333).

HIKING & BACKPACKING The national park visitor center has U.S. Geological Survey topographic maps and guidebooks for sale, and rangers will be happy to suggest trails that are lightly used. One trail that is decidedly *not* lightly used is the Deer Ridge Trail, with a trailhead in downtown Estes Park!

Easy to moderate trails include the Alberta Falls Trail from the Glacier Gorge Parking Area (0.6 mile) and the Bierstadt Lake Trail from the Bear Lake Parking Area (1.6 miles). Moderately difficult trails include the Emerald Lake Trail from the Bear Lake Parking Area (1.8 miles), the Fern Lake Trail from Moraine Park (3.8 miles), the Finch Lake Trail from the Wild Basin Ranger Station (4.5 miles), and the Lulu City Trail from the Colorado River Trailhead (3.1 miles). Strenuous trails include the Lawn Lake Trail from Horseshoe Park (6.2 miles) and the Timber Lake Trail from near Never Summer Ranch (4.8 miles).

Remember that overnight camping in backcountry areas requires a park permit.

HORSEBACK RIDING Stables where horses can be hired for a variety of guided rides are found at several locations in and outside the national park. Sombrero Ranch Stables is opposite the Lake Estes dam on the Big Thompson Highway (U.S. 34) (tel. 586-4577). The National Park Village Stables are at National Park Village North on U.S. 34 west, Fall River Road (tel. 586-5269); the Cowpoke Corner Corral is at Glacier Lodge on the YMCA road (tel. 586-5890). You can also try Wild Basin Livery at the southernmost entrance to the park, 14 miles south of Estes Park off Highway 7 (tel. 747-2454). Hi Country Stables is inside the park—call for reservations (Glacier Creek Stables; tel. 586-3244, and Moraine Park Stables, tel. 586-2327).

Day hikes with llamas are offered by Walkabout Llama Hikes (tel. 586-5940) and Keno's Llama & Guest Ranch (tel. 586-2827).

MOUNTAINEERING The Colorado Mountain School, P.O. Box 2062, Estes Park, CO 80517 (tel. 303/586-5758), is a national park sanctioned technical climbing school that caters to all ages and a summer-winter guide service. The most popular climb is Longs Peak (the highest mountain in the park). It can be ascended by those without experience via the "Keyhole," but its north and east faces are for experts only. Longs Peak information is available from the ranger station at the trailhead (tel. 586-4975).

RIVER RAFTING   For trips down the Colorado River contact Rapid Transit Rafting, P.O. Box 4095, Estes Park, CO 80517 (tel. 303/586-8852 or toll free 800/367-8523).

SKIING   If you're headed into the backcountry for Nordic skiing, stop by the national park headquarters for a permit and a brochure titled "Ski Touring in Rocky Mountain National Park." Some backcountry areas are closed because of avalanche danger.

SNOWMOBILING   Snowmobiling is permitted on the west side of the park only. Register at the Kawuneeche Visitor Center, at the Grand Lake end of Trail Ridge Road (tel. 303/887-3331).

SWIMMING   The Estes Park Aquatic Center, 660 Community Dr. (tel. 586-2340), is open for public and lap swims, lessons, water aerobics, and aquanistics. Call for current schedules. Admission is $2 for adults, $1.50 for children and seniors, $5 family rate.

SHOPPING

The Galleries of Estes Park Association, P.O. Box 987, Estes Park, CO 80517, publishes a directory of nearly two dozen village art galleries. Of special note is the **Art Center of Estes Park** in the Stanley Village Shopping Center, Wonderview Avenue at U.S. 34 (tel. 586-5882). One of its galleries represents local artists; the other offers changing exhibits of a wide range of media. Classes, programs, and tours are offered. Open Memorial Day to September, daily from 11am to 5pm; October to December, Thursday through Saturday from 11am to 4pm.

Interesting collections of galleries and gift shops include the **Old Church Shops,** 157 W. Elkhorn Ave., and **Sundance Center for the Arts,** 150 E. Riverside Dr. Also look for **Garth's Glassworks Studio & Gallery,** 323 W. Elkhorn Ave. (tel. 586-8619), with sales and demonstrations of hand-blown glass; and **Serendipity Trading Company,** 117 E. Elkhorn Ave., traders in Native American arts and crafts.

Ten miles south of Estes Park via Colo. 7 is the **Charles Eagle Plume Indian Store & Museum** (tel. 586-4710). A University of Colorado graduate now deceased, Eagle Plume was one-fourth Native American (Blackfoot) and a true entertainer and entrepreneur. His fascinating collection of museum-quality artifacts is not for sale, but the trading post has much more that is: crafts, pottery, jewelry, baskets, rugs, and more. It's open mid-May to mid-September, daily from 9am to 5pm.

EVENING ENTERTAINMENT

The **Stanley Hotel** (see "Where to Stay," below), 333 Wonderview Ave. (tel. 303/586-3371 or toll free 800/ROCKIES), is the focus for the performing arts in Estes Park. Summer and fall theater seasons are offered in Stanley Hall Thursday through Sunday nights, with optional dinner reservations preceding the show; and a **Fine Arts Concert Series** offers symphony-and-chamber music in the Music Room at 2pm every Sunday throughout the year. In summer, the **Estes Park Music Festival** also presents classical concerts at 8pm on Monday nights in July. The Fine Arts Guild of the Rockies (tel. 586-5035) sponsors a variety of visual-and-performing arts shows throughout the year.

Nine miles south of Estes Park off Colo. 7, the **Rocky Ridge Music Center,** 465 Longs Peak Rd. (tel. 586-4031), offers a series of 20 concerts over six weeks beginning in late June.

The **Lazy B Ranch,** 1915 Dry Gulch Rd. (tel. 586-5371 or toll free 800/228-2116), offers a chuck-wagon supper and western show. There's also a program on the history of western music. To reach Lazy B, take U.S. 34 east from Estes Park about 1½ miles, turn left at Sombrero Stables, and follow the signs. Open early June into

September. The **Barleen Family Country Music Dinner Theatre,** Woodstock Drive at Colo. 7 (tel. 586-5749), offers dinner followed by a stage show of country western, gospel, popular music, and comedy. Open June through September.

For live music and dancing, check out **Lonigan's Saloon,** 110 W. Elkhorn Ave. (tel. 586-4346).

WHERE TO STAY

For help finding accommodations, call the Estes Park Area Chamber of Commerce Lodging Referral Service (tel. 303/586-4431 or 800/44-ESTES).

EXPENSIVE

BOULDER BROOK, 1900 Fall River Rd. (P.O. Box 2255), Estes Park, CO 80517. Tel. 303/586-0910 or toll free 800/238-0910. 16 suites. TV TEL
$ Rates: $89–$125 double; spa suites $139–$169. AE, DISC, MC, V.

It would be hard to find a more beautiful setting for a lodging establishment. Surrounded by tall pines, all suites face the Fall River and have private riverfront decks. There's also a year-round outdoor hot tub. Inside, there are one bedroom suites or spa suites, with either full kitchens or wet bars. The spa suites, of course, contain two-person spas, plus a fireplace, sitting rooms with cathedral ceilings, king-size beds, and cable TV with VCR. The one-bedroom suites offer king-size beds, plus window seats, two televisions, and baths with whirlpool tub and shower combinations. Fax and photocopy service is available.

RIVERSONG, Lower Broadview Dr. off Mary's Lake Rd. (P.O. Box 1910), Estes Park, CO 80517. Tel. 303/586-4666. 9 rms (all with bath).
$ Rates (including breakfast): $75–$150 single; $85–$160 double. MC, V.
A 1920 Craftsman mansion on the Big Thompson River, this elegant bed-and-breakfast has 27 forested acres with hiking trails and a trout pond, as well as prolific wildlife. It's at the end of a country lane, the first right off Mary's Lake Road after it branches off U.S. 36 south.

The cozy bedrooms, all named after wildflowers, are decorated with a blend of antique and modern country furniture. Various rooms have ornate brass beds, claw-foot tubs, and all but one have fireplaces. All have private bathrooms, four with jetted tubs for two; but none have phones or TVs—it's designed that way. Smoking is not permitted.

Hosts Sue and Gary Mansfield will prepare gourmet candlelight dinners by advance arrangement, but you must supply your own alcoholic beverage.

STANLEY HOTEL, 333 Wonderview Ave. (P.O. Box 1767), Estes Park, CO 80517. Tel. 303/586-3371 or toll free 800/ROCKIES. 92 rms (all with bath), 8 condo suites. TV TEL
$ Rates: May 15–Oct 15, $75–$115 single; $80–$120 double; $150 condo suites. Discounts offered Oct 16–May 14. AE, DISC, JCB, MC, V.
F. O. Stanley, inventor of the Stanley Steamer automobile, built this elegant, white-pillared hotel in 1909. The equal of European resorts of the time, it was built into solid rock at a 7,800-foot elevation on the eastern slope of the Colorado Rockies. Today the hotel is a registered National Historic District. Of course, a Stanley Steamer is on display in the lobby. As is often the case in historic hotels, every room is different in size and shape. Rooms have assorted views of Long's Peak, Lake Estes, and surrounding hillsides.

Dining/Entertainment: A classic American menu is served year-round in the hotel's restaurant, open for breakfast, lunch, and dinner. There are dinner/big-band shows and dinner/theater productions, and every Sunday year-round the Stanley presents its award-winning, free concert series and champagne buffet brunch. Pianists perform nightly in the Dunraven Grille.

Services: Room service.

Facilities: Heated outdoor swimming pool, Jacuzzi, exercise room, Polo/Ralph Lauren shop, gift shop, and a gallery with one of the largest collections of antiquities for sale in the western United States.

STREAMSIDE CABINS, 1260 Fall River Rd., Moraine Rte. (P.O. Box 2930), Estes Park, CO 80517. Tel. 303/586-6464. 19 suites (all with bath). TV

$ Rates: June–Sept, $105–$170 single or double; Oct–May, $50–$165 single or double. AE, DISC, MC, V.

These 16 acres on the Fall River, less than a mile west of Estes Park via U.S. 34, are surrounded by woods and meadows rife with wildflowers. They are a lure to wildlife. Deer, as well as some of the elk and occasional bighorn sheep, are such regular visitors that they've been given names.

Everything is top drawer in these solid-wood cabins. In fact, the semiweekly *Trail-Gazette* newspaper has rated them the "Best Lodging in Estes" for several years. Most have beamed cathedral ceilings, skylights, and southwestern country decor. Furnished like condominiums, they have wall-to-wall carpeting, king- and queen-size beds, Jacuzzi tubs or steam baths, full fireplaces, cable television, decks or patios with gas grills, and (with only two exceptions) full electric kitchens equipped for gourmet chefs. Romantic suites pamper couples through an "Affairs of the Heart" package.

WIND RIVER RANCH, Colo. 7 (P.O. Box 3410), Estes Park, CO 80517. Tel. 303/586-4212, or toll free 800/523-4212. 15 rms, 10 cabins (all with bath).

$ Rates (including full board): $155 single; $250–$284 double. Discounts for children, weekly rates available. DISC, MC, V. **Closed:** Mid-Sept to early June.

Owned and operated by the Irvin family since 1973, this 120-year-old guest ranch is located 7¼ miles south of Estes Park on the Peak-to-Peak Highway, at the 9,000-foot level in the Tahosa Valley. Guests stay in one- or two-bedroom cabins. All guests share the ranch house's big living room, dining room, huge fireplace, library, and games area.

Dining/Entertainment: Prices include all meals, but you must supply your own alcoholic beverages. A varied entertainment program (six nights a week, in season) may have a musician one night, a naturalist's lecture the second, a bingo game the third, and a movie the fourth.

Facilities: Heated swimming pool, hot tub, trout-stocked fish pond. Day-camp program for children 4 to 12, Monday through Friday. The stables have 40 horses for riding: 1-hour lessons are $15, all-day rides are $45, and 1-week use of a horse is $150.

MODERATE

BALDPATE INN, 4900 S. Colo. 7 (P.O. Box 4445), Estes Park, CO 80517. Tel. 303/586-6151. 13 rms (4 with bath), 2 cabins.

$ Rates (including full breakfast): $65 single or double without bath, $78 single or double with bath; $100–$125 cabin. DISC, MC, V. **Closed:** Nov–Apr.

★ Built in 1917, the Baldpate was named for the novel *Seven Keys to Baldpate,* a murder mystery in which seven visitors believe he or she possesses the only key to the hotel. Guests today can watch several movie versions of the story, read the book, and add their keys to the hotel's collection of more than 20,000 keys.

Seven miles south of Estes Park, adjacent to Rocky Mountain National Park at an elevation of 9,000 feet, the inn's lobby has a stone fireplace where homemade cookies are served each evening. The early 20th-century style rooms are each unique, with handmade quilts on the beds. Pets are not allowed.

BEST WESTERN LAKE ESTES RESORT, 1650 Big Thompson Hwy. (U.S. 34) (P.O. Box 1466), Estes Park, CO 80517. Tel. 303/586-3386 or toll free 800/292-8439. 56 rooms (all with bath), 8 suites. TV TEL

$ Rates: June–Sept, $65–$105 single or double; $80–$140 suites. Oct–May, $52–$59 single or double; $70–$120 suites. AE, CB, DC, DISC, JCB, MC, V.

Perhaps the distinguishing feature of this motel is the 5,000-gallon Jacuzzi tub (it seats 30) that's housed inside a solarium-greenhouse, adjacent to the outdoor swimming pool. There's also a sports court, children's playground, sauna, and guest laundry.

Rooms, in two buildings, have fine cherry-wood furnishings and other special touches, like hair dryers and phones in every bathroom. A dozen rooms with king-size beds have views across Lake Estes. Fireplace suites have desks, two TVs, and three phones. Family units sleep six to eight, and the new Chalet Suites have fireplaces, jacuzzis, and kitchenettes. No-smoking rooms are available. Pets are not permitted.

CASTLE MOUNTAIN LODGE, 1520 Fall River Rd., Moraine Rte., Estes Park, CO 80517. Tel. 303/586-3664. 28 cabins. TV
$ Rates: Mid-June to August, $65–$125 single or double; $139–$230 two- and three-bedroom cabins. $5 per person extra for three or more in cabin. Discounts of about 15% for stays of 3 nights; special weekly rates. Fall-and-spring rates 27–37% less; winter rates, 37–50% less. AE, DISC, MC, V.

These modern rustic cabins on Fall River, in a wooded tract facing Castle Mountain, offer guests a wide choice of options. No two cabins are alike, ranging in size from studio cottages to three-bedroom units. All except a pair of studios have full kitchens with refrigerators. Most cabins have fireplaces, hideabed sofas, barbecues, and outdoor furniture.

There is a playground for children, and a "peripatetic pet policy" allows critters for $5 a day by advance arrangement.

ESTES PARK CENTER/YMCA OF THE ROCKIES, 2515 Tunnel Rd., Estes Park, CO 80511-2800. Tel. 303/586-3341 or from Denver direct 623-9215. 565 rms, 201 cabins.
$ Rates: Summer, lodge $41–$78 per room; cabins $49–$199. Winter, lodge $30–$57; cabins $100–$204. R.V. campsites $12–$16. Weekly rates. No credit cards.

Extremely popular, this family resort is an ideal place to get away from it all or use as home base while exploring the Estes Park area. Lodge units are basic, with three-quarters or full bath. The spacious mountain cabins have two to four bedrooms that sleep up to 10, and complete kitchens. Some cabins have fireplaces and telephones. YMCA membership is required, and is sold at a nominal additional charge. The center occupies 860 wooded acres, and offers hiking, horseback riding, miniature golf, swimming, fishing, bicycling, tennis, and cross-country skiing. Pets are permitted in some cabins, but not in lodge rooms. R.V.'ers will find all the usual amenities, including full hookups, hot showers, and a heated pool. Ground tents are not allowed.

GLACIER LODGE, Hwy. 66 (P.O. Box 2656), Estes Park, CO 80517. Tel. 303/586-4401. 3 rms (all with bath), 23 cottages. TV
$ Rates: Early June to mid-Sept, $48–$82 rooms; $84–$120 cottages. Late May to early June and mid- to end of Sept, $38–$72 rooms; $74–$110 cottages. Oct to late May, $32–$38 rooms; $60–$87 cottages. MC, V.

Deer and elk frequently visit these lovely cottages, spread across 15 acres of woodland by the Big Thompson River. You've even got to cross a rustic bridge to get to them. Poolside chalets are 1½-bedroom cabins with a loft, full kitchen, and fireplace. Cozy, homey river duplexes have outside decks overlooking the stream. River triplexes are similar, ranging from earthy to country quaint in decor. The lodge has a swimming pool, sports court, playground, fishing, lending library, and its own stables. Every Tuesday evening in summer there's a western steak fry at Campfire Corral; on Friday nights, a "buckaroo roundup" for kids 4 to 10 (there's an additional fee for this).

HOLIDAY INN OF ESTES PARK, U.S. 36 and Colo. 7 (P.O. Box 1468), Estes Park, CO 80517. Tel. 303/586-2332 or toll free 800/HOLIDAY. Fax 303/586-2332, ext. 299. 150 rms (all with bath). A/C TV TEL
$ Rates: Summer, $79–$95 single or double; $139–$155 suite. Winter, $49–$65 single or double; $89–$109 suite. Children under 18 eat and stay free in same room with adult. AE, CB, DC, DISC, JCB, MC, V.

The modern lodge at first appearance leads you to believe that this may not be a typical Holiday Inn—but the cavernous HoliDome, with its indoor swimming pool, reaffirms your faith in the chain. Most rooms have two double beds; a handful have balconies overlooking the indoor pool. All have standard furnishings, HBO, and direct-dial phones (free local calls).

The restaurant lounge serves three meals daily, including Sunday champagne brunch; no smoking is permitted in the restaurant. The motel offers no-smoking rooms, room service, valet or guest laundry, a fitness room, and games room. Facilities for the disabled are available. A conference center handles 1,000, theater style.

INEXPENSIVE

ALL BUDGET INN, 945 Moraine Ave., Estes Park, CO 80517. Tel. 303/586-3485 or toll free 800/628-3438. 15 rms (all with bath). TV
$ Rates: June 16–Oct 14, $52–$90 single or double; Oct 15–June 15, $35–$50 single or double. MC, V. **Parking:** Free.
Top-quality budget lodging is what you'll find here. Rooms have cable TV with HBO, and there is free coffee and at-door parking. The rooms, extensively remodeled in recent years, are individually decorated. Some have minikitchens and several units have fireplaces. Located adjacent to the entrance to Rocky Mountain National Park, don't be surprised to see a deer or elk peering in your motel-room window, especially in spring. Pets are not accepted; most rooms are nonsmoking.

ALLENSPARK LODGE, Colo. 7 Business Loop (P.O. Box 247), Allenspark, CO 80510. Tel. 303/747-2552. 14 rms (5 with bath).
$ Rates (including continental breakfast): Mid-May to October, $31–$70 single or double; Nov to mid-May, $31–$70 single or double. DISC, MC, V.
There's a historic ambience to this three-story lodge, built in 1933 of native stone and hand-hewn ponderosa alpine logs. Located 16 miles south of Estes Park, in a tiny village at the southeast corner of the national park, the lodge has four bedrooms with private baths and six others which share. Every room has mountain views and original handmade 1930s pine furniture. At the top end is the Hideaway Room, with a brass bed, bear-claw tub, and fine linens; the lowest-priced room is the Bear Cub Room, with a single twin bed. Guests share the stone fireplace in the Great Room, Ping-Pong and pool in the Game Room, books in the Library, and breakfast, afternoon wine, and hors d'oeuvres in the Wilderquest Room.

COLORADO COTTAGES, 1241 High Dr., Moraine Rte., Estes Park, CO 80517. Tel. 303/586-4637 or toll free 800/468-1236. 10 rms, 1 suite (all with bath). TV
$ Rates: Mid-June to Labor Day, $61–$74 single or double; $96 suite. Labor Day to Oct and Apr to mid-June, $47–$59 single or double; $79 suite. Closed Nov–Mar. AE, DISC, MC, V.
These tiny blue-slate, shingled cabins have fully equipped kitchenettes with refrigerators, a fireplace (with wood provided), heater, queen-size or double beds, tiny three-quarter baths, barbecues, and picnic tables. Furnishings are basic. Three units are modernized, with a microwave in place of a stove, and a full bath. Some rooms sleep as many as eight. There's a playground for kids.

BUDGET

H-BAR-G RANCH HOSTEL, 3500 H-Bar-G Rd., off Dry Gulch Rd. (P.O. Box 1260), Estes Park, CO 80517. Tel. 303/586-3688. 100 beds.
$ Rates: $8 per bed. Hostelling International memberships required and available; annual membership fees: $25 for adults (18–54), $15 for seniors (55+), $10 for youth (under 18), $35 for families.
Bring your own bedding (sleeping bag or sheet sack) to throw on your dormitory bunk, and be prepared to pitch in with daily chores. That's the hosteler's way. There are separate accommodations for men and women, and family cabins, each with private bath, by advance reservation, and everyone shares the kitchen and games room. Hiking trails lead into the national forest from the hostel; you'll also find tennis-and-volleyball courts, barbecues, and fireplace. Check in between 5:15 and 9pm, or wait for daily pick ups at 5pm at the Estes Park Tourist Information Center. The hostel is 5½ miles northeast of Lake Estes, in the national forest at an elevation of 8,200 feet, and has easy access to the national park. Open Memorial Day to Labor Day.

CAMPGROUNDS

Aside from the Rocky Mountain National Park campgrounds, discussed above, these are among the commercial sites in the Estes Park area.

MARY'S LAKE CAMPGROUND, 2120 Mary's Lake Rd. (P.O. Box 2514), Estes Park, CO 80517. Tel. 303/586-4411 or toll free 800/445-6279. 150 sites.
$ Rates: $15.50–$19.50 per campsite for two people. Extra person $2.
Forty of the campsites are reserved for tenters; the remainder are for recreational vehicles. Most R.V. spaces have sewer hookups, as well as water and electricity. The campground has bathhouses, a laundry, playground, basketball court, small store, heated swimming pool, and games room; firewood is available, and pets are allowed. Fishing licenses and bait and tackle are available for shore fishing at the lake and stream fishing in the national park.

NATIONAL PARK RESORT, 3501 Fall River Rd., Moraine Route, Estes Park, CO 80517. Tel. 303/586-4563. 100 sites.
$ Rates: $16.50–$18.50 per campsite for two people. Extra person $1.50. DISC, MC, V.
This wooded campground can accommodate both tents and R.V.s. Full hookups include electric, water, sewer, and cable TV. Facilities include bathhouses and a laundry; firewood is available and pets are permitted. Open May through September; cabins available year-round.

SPRUCE LAKE R.V. PARK, Rte. 36 and Mary's Lake Rd. (P.O. Box 2497), Estes Park, CO 80517. Tel. 303/586-2889. 110 sites.
$ Rates: $15–$23 with hookups. MC, V.
Considered among the top R.V. parks in Colorado, Spruce Lake has a heated pool, free miniature golf, a large playground, stocked private fishing lake, large sites, and spotless rest-room/shower facilities. There are Sunday pancake breakfasts and weekly ice-cream socials, and like almost everywhere in Estes Park, the scenery is spectacular. Ground tents are not permitted, and pets are allowed, but must be walked within your campsite or carried or driven from the R.V. park. Open from March 15 to December 15. Reservations are strongly recommended, especially in summer.

WHERE TO DINE

EXPENSIVE

THE FAWN BROOK INN, Colo. 7 Business Loop, Allenspark. Tel. 747-2556.
   Cuisine: CONTINENTAL. **Reservations:** Required.
$ Prices: Appetizers $9.85–$13.85; main courses $21.50–$34.
   Open: May 1–Oct 15, dinner Tues–Sat 5–9pm, Sun 4–8:30pm.
Very "olde countrye" in appearance, this establishment, 16 miles south of Estes Park, belies its rustic atmosphere by serving up what many consider the finest gourmet cuisine and intimate service in the Rocky Mountain National Park area. The menu focuses on continental dishes with a German flair.
   Start with a wild-game pâté, langoustine rémoulade, or Caesar salad prepared table side. Then move on to a wide choice of main dishes, such as sweetbreads Monte Carlo, chateaubriand, sole meunière, or a fresh seafood selection. Leave room for the superb desserts.

LA CHAUMIERE, U.S. 36, Pinewood Springs. Tel. 823-6521.
   Cuisine: FRENCH/CONTINENTAL. **Reservations:** Suggested.
$ Prices: Appetizers $2.50–$5.75; main courses $11.50–$17.50. AE, MC, V.
   Open: Dinner only, Tues–Sat 5:30–8:30pm, Sun 1–8pm.
A romantic atmosphere, good food, and homemade ice cream are three good reasons to visit this small restaurant, 12 miles southeast of Estes Park en route to Lyons. The menu changes frequently, but usually includes specialties such as filet mignon, sautéed

sweetbreads with wild rice, poached breast of chicken, spinach pasta, roast duckling, and a vegetarian platter.

MODERATE

THE DUNRAVEN INN, 2470 Hwy. 66. Tel. 586-6409.
   Cuisine: ITALIAN. **Reservations:** Highly recommended.
$ **Prices:** Appetizers $3.95–$5.95; main courses $7.95–$15.50. DC, MC, V.
   Open: Summer, dinner only, Mon–Sat 5–11pm, Sun 5–10pm; winter, dinner only, Mon–Sat 5–10pm, Sun 5–9pm.

The *Mona Lisa* is everywhere in this self-proclaimed "Rome of the Rockies." Every possible design of the *Mona,* from a mustachioed lady to opera posters, has found its way onto the walls—as well as autographed dollar bills, posted by their former owners. The provincial charm extends to the cuisine. House specialties are scampi, veal parmigiana, chicken cacciatore, and Dunraven italiano: a charbroiled sirloin steak in a sauce of green peppers, black olives, mushrooms, and tomatoes. There's a wide choice of pastas, seafoods, vegetarian plates, and coffee and dessert specials. There's also a children's menu.

GAZEBO RESTAURANT ON THE PARK, 225 Park Lane. Tel. 586-9564.
   Cuisine: INTERNATIONAL. **Reservations:** Recommended.
$ **Prices:** Appetizers $2.50–$6.50; lunch $4.25–$10.95; Sun brunch $5.50–$10.50; dinner $8.50–$15.95. 20% discount for seniors. AE, MC, V.
   Open: Daily 11:30am–9pm.

Now in a beautiful new building across from City Hall, flanking downtown Bond Park in the heart of Estes Park. There's outdoor seating and the views are spectacular. You can get standard beef, veal, poultry, seafood, and vegetarian dishes here, but for something different try spuntini, a hollowed-out *boule* of homemade bread, filled with chili, beef stew, or a seafood or chicken casserole, and served with a salad. For dinner, try Khyber chicken or cubed beef, marinated overnight in yogurt and spices, broiled, and served with a chutney relish.

THE OTHER SIDE, 900 Moraine Ave. Tel. 586-2171.
   Cuisine: AMERICAN/INTERNATIONAL. **Reservations:** Recommended.
$ **Prices:** Breakfast $3.25–$6.75; lunch entrées $4.95–$7.50; dinner entrées $6.75–$15.25. AE, DISC, MC, V.
   Open: Summer, daily 7:30am–2pm, 5–9:30pm. Winter, Mon–Fri 11am–2pm, 5–9:30pm; Sat–Sun 7:30am–2pm, 5–9:30pm.

This comfortable, attractive, modern restaurant lets you view ducks and muskrats in a nearby pond or gaze at a cozy fire in the fireplace. But the real reason to come here is the food. Specialties include prime rib, rainbow trout, smoked barbecued ribs, veal picatta, and chicken scampi. Lunches include burgers, salads, and hot-and-cold sandwiches; at breakfast you'll find all the usual entrées, including eight different kinds of three-egg omelets.

INEXPENSIVE

ED'S CANTINA & GRILL, 362 E. Elkhorn Ave., at the junction of U.S. 34 and U.S. 36. Tel. 586-2919.
   Cuisine: MEXICAN/AMERICAN. **Reservations:** Accepted.
$ **Prices:** Breakfast $2.75–$5.75; lunch and dinner $4.25–$9.75. AE, MC, V.
   Open: Daily 7am–11pm.

Although primarily a Mexican restaurant, there's pretty much something for everyone here: burgers, a Philly steak sandwich, roasted chicken, and barbecued beef, as well as Mexican combination plates, fajitas, burritos, tacos, and enchiladas.

LA CASA, 222 E. Elkhorn Ave. Tel. 586-2807.
   Cuisine: MEXICAN/CAJUN. **Reservations:** Recommended.
$ **Prices:** $6.95–$14.95. AE, DC, DISC, MC, V.
   Open: Daily 11am–10pm.

One thing that the Mexican and Cajun cuisines have in common, besides the Gulf of

Mexico, is a high level of spiciness. You'll get that at the Estorito family's fun restaurant on Estes Park's main street. In summer, there's seating in a lovely outdoor garden. Try blackened shrimp, voodoo chicken, or a spicy beef burrito.

MOUNTAINEER RESTAURANT, 540 S. St. Vrain St., Hwy. 7. Tel. 586-9001.
   Cuisine: AMERICAN. **Reservations:** Not necessary.
$ Prices: Breakfast $1.95–$5.95; lunch $2.45–$5.75; dinner $5.95–$7.50. MC, V.
   Open: Daily 6am–8:30pm.

Candy Edward's bargain eatery is a family favorite, just outside downtown. Have an omelet or steak and eggs for breakfast, a chili dog or a shrimp basket for lunch, southern fried chicken or liver and onions for dinner.

AN EASY EXCURSION FROM ESTES PARK
GRAND LAKE

The west gateway to Rocky Mountain National Park is at ♦ **Grand Lake,** a village with board sidewalks and a few horses still being ridden along the main drag. There's an information center on U.S. 34 at the turnoff into town. Located in the shadow of Shadow Mountain at the park's southwestern corner, the community—at 8,370-feet elevation—is actually within Arapahoe National Recreation Area, which encompasses Grand Lake and two other larger bodies of water: Shadow Mountain Reservoir and Lake Granby.

   In summer, it's easy to get to Grand Lake, 48 miles from Estes Park via the Trail Ridge Road (U.S. 34). In winter, when Grand Lake is a ski-touring and snowmobiling mecca, it's a bit trickier. From Denver, it's 101 miles: Travel west on I-70 42 miles to the Empire exit; follow U.S. 40 through Winter Park, 47 miles to Granby; then turn north on U.S. 34 another 14 miles to Grand Lake. The drive is beautiful and well worth the time.

WHAT TO SEE & DO   The Grand Lake Yacht Club, the world's highest-altitude yacht club, hosts the **Grand Lake Regatta** and the **Lipton Cup Races** in August. The club was organized in 1902, when sails were added to rowboats; it began the regatta 10 years later. Sailboats from around the world compete to win the prestigious Lipton Cup, given to the club by Thomas Lipton in 1912. Grand Lake, which reaches a depth of 400 feet, is the largest natural lake in the state; it is linked by channels to the other two large lakes, both of them dammed portions of the Colorado River. Water from the three is pumped under the mountains via the Alva Adams Tunnel to the Big Thompson River and Lake Estes, where it is channeled to the plains for irrigation. The national recreation area that encompasses the lakes offers boating, fishing, hiking, horseback riding, cross-country skiing, snowmobiling, picnicking, and camping. There's also an 18-hole championship golf course, altitude 8,420 feet, in Grand Lake, and marinas on each of the lakes.

   Tours are offered at the Granby Pumping Plant. The **Kaufman House,** on Pitkin Avenue, an early log structure, serves as the museum of the Grand Lake Historical Society, and is open to the public. A summer repertory company stages **theater productions.** For **information** on these and other attractions and activities, contact the Grand Lake Chamber of Commerce, P.O. Box 57, Grand Lake, CO 80447 (tel. 303/627-3402).

WHERE TO STAY   There are about three dozen motels, guest ranches, and lodges with cabins in the Grand Lake area. Two are **Grand Lake Lodge,** 15500 Hwy. 34 (Box 569), Grand Lake, CO 80447 (tel. 303/627-3967 or 303/759-5848 in winter), overlooking the lake, with cabins at $40 to $60; and the **Bighorn Lodge,** 613 Grand Ave. (P.O. Box 1260), Grand Lake, CO 80447 (tel. 303/627-8101 or toll free 800/621-5923), a main-street hotel with 20 rooms at $45 to $75 double.

WHERE TO DINE   The **Corner Cupboard Inn,** 1028 Grand Ave. (tel. 627-3813), offers aged prime meats and family dining in a building dating to 1881. Other likely dining establishments are the **Mountain Inn,** 612 Grand Ave. (tel. 627-3385), and (for breakfast and lunch only) the **Chuck Hole Café,** 1119 Grand Avenue (tel.

627-3509). **Grand Lake Lodge** (see "Where to Stay" above) has an excellent restaurant.

---

2. STEAMBOAT SPRINGS

158 miles NW of Denver, 335 miles E of Salt Lake City, Utah

GETTING THERE By Plane The Steamboat Springs Airport (known as the "STOLPort"), four miles west of town on Elk River Road (tel. 879-9042), is served by Continental Express (tel. 303/879-2648 or toll free 800/525-0280), with connections to and from Denver International Airport several times daily, year-round.

From mid-December through March, the Yampa Valley Regional Airport, 22 miles west of Steamboat Springs near Hayden (tel. 276-3669), greets Boeing 727s, 737s, and 767s. American Airlines (toll free 800/443-7300) offers daily nonstop service from Chicago, Dallas/Fort Worth, and Los Angeles, and Saturday nonstops from Newark and San Jose; Continental Airlines (toll free 800/525-0280) has daily nonstops from Denver and Saturday nonstops from Cleveland and Houston; and Northwest Airlines (toll free 800/225-2525) has daily nonstops to and from Minneapolis/St. Paul.

For transportation between Steamboat and the airports, call Alpine Taxi and Limo (tel. 879-3294 or toll free 800/343-7433).

By Bus Greyhound 30060 W. U.S. Hwy. 40 (tel. 879-0866), offers daily intercity service. Steamboat Express, 1401 Lincoln Ave. (tel. 303/879-3400 or toll free 800/825-8383), a service of Panorama Coaches, travels daily in ski season between Denver International Airport and Steamboat Springs.

By Car The most direct route to Steamboat Springs from Denver is to take I-70 west 68 miles to Silverthorne, Colo. 9 north 38 miles to Kremmling, and U.S. 40 west 52 miles to Steamboat. (*Note:* Rabbit Ears Pass, 25 miles east of Steamboat, can be treacherous in winter.) If you're traveling east on I-70, exit at Rifle, proceed 90 miles north on Colo. 13 to Craig, then take U.S. 40 east 42 miles to Steamboat. From Fort Collins, take Colo. 14 west 147 miles via Walden. From Salt Lake City or the Pacific Northwest, you have two choices: Either follow U.S. 40 east through Vernal; or take I-80 east through Rock Springs, Wyo., exit at Creston (82 miles east of Rock Springs), take Wyo. 789/Colo. 13 south 91 miles to Craig, then turn east on U.S. 40.

Car Rentals Car rentals are available at the airports. At Steamboat Springs Airport, try Advantage (tel. 879-5737), Avis (tel. 879-3785), Budget (tel. 879-3103), Hertz (tel. 870-0880), or National (tel. 879-0800). At Yampa Valley Airport, look for Budget (tel. 276-3612), Dollar (tel. 276-3702), and Hertz (tel. 276-3304).

SPECIAL EVENTS Area events include the Cowboy Downhill, the second week of January; the Winter Carnival, the first full week of February; the Cardboard Classic and Ski Area Closure, over the second weekend of April; the Yampa River Festival, over the first weekend of June; Cowboy Roundup Days, over the Fourth of July weekend; Rainbow Weekend, on the third weekend of July; the Vintage Auto Race and Aircraft Fly-in, over the Labor Day weekend; the Ski Area Opening, on Thanksgiving weekend; and the Torchlight Parade, on New Year's Eve.

N umerous mineral springs and abundant wild game made this a summer playground for Ute tribespeople for centuries before the arrival of the white man. Mid-19th-century trappers swore they heard the chugging sound of "a steamboat comin' 'round the bend" until investigation revealed a bubbling mineral spring. Prospectors never thrived here, as they did elsewhere in the Rockies, though coal mining has proven profitable. Ranching and farming—cattle and sheep, hay, wheat, oats, and barley—were the economic mainstays until tourism became paramount, and agriculture remains of key importance to the community.

Skiing has been synonymous with Steamboat ever since Carl Howelsen, a

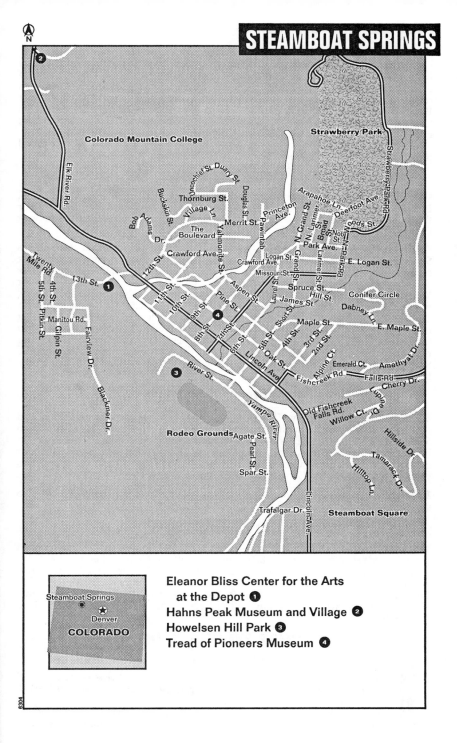

STEAMBOAT SPRINGS

Eleanor Bliss Center for the Arts
   at the Depot ❶
Hahns Peak Museum and Village ❷
Howelsen Hill Park ❸
Tread of Pioneers Museum ❹

Norwegian ski-jumping and cross-country champion, moved to the town in 1914. He lived in Steamboat for seven years, during which time he built the ski area that bears his name (Howelsen Hill) and organized the first Winter Carnival. Development of Storm Mountain began in 1958; the mountain officially opened in 1963, and was renamed Mount Werner after the 1964 avalanche death in Europe of Olympic skier Buddy Werner, a Steamboat native and prime backer of the resort. The Steamboat Ski Company, established in 1970, has put tens of millions of dollars into resort improvements in the past two decades. Continuing expansion is planned.

Today Steamboat Springs, at an elevation of 6,700 feet, has a year-round population of about 6,700, and beds for 16,000 visitors.

ORIENTATION

INFORMATION The Steamboat Springs Chamber Resort Association, 1255 S. Lincoln Ave. (P.O. Box 774408), Steamboat Springs, CO 80477 (tel. 303/879-0740 or 879-0880), provides visitor information. There's a second office on the third floor of Gondola Square (tel. 879-0882).

CITY LAYOUT There are really two Steamboats. The ski resort, known here as Steamboat Village, is about two miles southeast of the town itself, a division that seems to work well for everyone. If you're coming in from Denver, U.S. 40 approaches Steamboat from the south and parallels the Yampa River through town. Mount Werner Road, which turns east off U.S. 40, leads directly to the resort community, centered around Mount Werner Circle and Ski Time Square. U.S. 40 is known as Lincoln Avenue through the town of Steamboat, where it is crossed by Third Street through 13th Street. You'll cross the Yampa to Howelsen Hill and River Street if you turn left on Fifth Street; wind uphill to the Strawberry Park Hot Springs if you turn right on Seventh Street, and find your way to the Steamboat Springs Airport and Steamboat Lake if you turn right on Elk River Road (County Road 129), half a mile beyond 13th.

GETTING AROUND

BY BUS Steamboat Springs Transit (tel. 879-3717) serves the downtown area and the resort and its condominium community. During ski season, buses run from 5:30am to 2:30am, with buses every 15 minutes during peak hours. After skiers go home, buses run less frequently, from 7am to 10pm, about once every half hour during peak travel times. Cost is 50¢ per person, but those 60 and older or 5 and younger ride free.

BY TAXI Steamboat Taxi (tel. 879-3335) and Alpine Taxi-Limo (tel. 879-8294) also serve the community.

FAST FACTS

The **area code** is 303. In case of **emergency,** call 911: for regular business, contact the police at 840 Yampa Ave. (tel. 879-1144) or the Routt County Sheriff at 30007 W. U.S. 40 (tel. 879-1090). **Routt Memorial Hospital,** 80 Park Ave., off Seventh Street (tel. 879-1322), provides 24-hour medical service. A **pharmacy** is City Market, 1825 Central Park Plaza (tel. 879-7317). The **post office** is at 200 Lincoln Ave. (tel. 879-0363). For **road information,** call 879-1260. State and local **tax** add 9.2% to hotel bills.

WHAT TO SEE & DO
ATTRACTIONS

STEAMBOAT SKI AREA, Steamboat Ski & Resort Corporation, 2305 Mt. Werner Circle, Steamboat Springs, CO 80487. Tel. 303/879-6111, toll free 800/922-2722, or 879-7300 for daily ski reports.

When devoted skiers think of Steamboat, the first things that come to mind are "champagne powder" and aspen glades. Because of a unique localized weather system, an average of 27 feet (325 inches) of light, dry snow is dumped on the mountain each winter.

Four peaks comprise Mount Werner. **Christie Peak,** the lower mountain area, is ideal for beginners. **Thunderhead Peak,** served by the "Silver Bullet" gondola, is mainly intermediate. Three separate restaurants, not counting the ski-school cafeteria, are located at the gondola terminal, and Billy Kidd, the 1970 world ski champion and director of skiing at Steamboat for two decades, makes a ski run from here with anyone who cares to join him, Monday through Saturday at 1pm, whenever he's in town—which is most of the winter.

Storm Peak accesses the extreme "Chutes" area, advanced mogul runs and powder bowls, as well as "Buddy's Run," one of the Rockies' great intermediate cruisers. The most famous tree runs—"Shadows" and "Twilight"—are on **Sunshine Peak,** along with more bump runs and cruising slopes. In Rendezvous Saddle, midmountain at the foot of "High Noon," are two more restaurants, including Ragnar's gourmet Scandinavian café.

The vertical here is the second highest in Colorado: 3,665 feet, from base (6,900 feet) to summit (10,565 feet). Skiable terrain of 2,500 acres (61% groomable) includes 107 named runs, served by 20 lifts—the eight-passenger gondola, two express quad chairs, one quad chair, six triple chairs, seven double chairs, a ski-school chair, and two surface lifts. That gives Steamboat an hourly uphill capacity of over 29,941 skiers.

Admission: Tickets, $41 per day adults, $39 per day if a multiday ticket is purchased; $24 per day youth. Full-rental packages average $16; 2-hour lessons are $32. Kids under 12 ski free with parents who purchase a 5-or-more-day lift ticket and stay in a Chamber Resort Association member accommodation.

Open: Thanksgiving–Easter, daily 8:30am–4pm.

ELEANOR BLISS CENTER FOR THE ARTS AT THE DEPOT, 13th St. between the Yampa River and the railroad tracks. Tel. 879-4434 or 879-9008.

The historic Steamboat Springs train depot is now the home of the Steamboat Arts Council, which coordinates music, dance, theater, and visual-arts activities in the upper Yampa Valley. The Depot Gallery here has changing exhibits and shows year-round of local-and-regional artists.

Admission: Free.

Open: Mon–Fri 9am–5pm and some weekends.

FISH CREEK FALLS, Fish Creek Falls Rd. Tel. 879-1870.

A footpath leads to a historic bridge at the base of this breathtaking 283-foot waterfall. There's also a special overlook with a short one-eighth mile trail and ramp designed for the disabled, as well as a picnic area and hiking trails. The falls are just four miles from downtown Steamboat in Routt National Forest. Turn right off Lincoln Avenue onto Third Street, go one block, and turn right again onto Fish Creek Falls Road.

HAHNS PEAK MUSEUM AND VILLAGE, Routt County Rd. 129. Tel. 879-6781.

This historic gold-mining town, while not exactly thriving, still clings to life 24 miles north of Steamboat Springs, near Steamboat Lake. Established in 1860, it was the scene in 1898 of a famous jailbreak by members of the Butch Cassidy gang, and its 1911 schoolhouse is listed in the National Register. The small museum contains interesting memorabilia. While in town, stop at the **Things and Stuff** shop, next door to the museum, which sells scenic photos of the area and a variety of souvenirs. Pyramid-shaped Hahns Peak, elevation 10,389 feet, may be ascended by Jeep trail. En route to Hahns Peak, stop at the **Clark Store,** 54175 Routt County Rd. 129 (tel. 879-3849), an old-fashioned country store with a post office, library, fishing equipment, ski rentals, and ice-cream cones.

HOWELSEN HILL PARK, River St. Tel. 879-4300.

The community's pride and joy is this beautiful park and recreation complex on the south side of the Yampa River, opposite downtown via Fifth Street. Howelsen Hill (see "Sports & Recreation," below) was Steamboat's original ski area, and is still nationally important as a Nordic site. The Lodge at Howelsen Hill offers an exhibit on the history of local skiing. The park also is the location of the **Romick Rodeo Arena,** where the Professional Rodeo Cowboy Association holds a weekly series from mid-June to Labor Day, as well as facilities for tennis, softball, soccer, volleyball, skateboarding, horseback riding, winter ice skating, summer roller skating, and hiking. There are picnic areas and playgrounds.

Admission: Free (fee for rodeo).
Open: Daily 8am–10pm.

JEAN PAUL LUC WINTER DRIVING SCHOOL, Mount Werner Rd. (P.O. Box 774167), Steamboat Springs, CO 80477. Tel. 879-6104.

America's first school of ice driving is a terrific way to learn safe winter driving, the hands-on way. Director Jean-Paul Luc, a former world-class rally driver from France, instructs courses on a 1-mile circuit—packed with frozen water and snow, and guarded by high snow banks—at the foot of Mount Werner. Classes combine personal-and-videotape instruction with on-track practice.

Price: $80 for a 3-hour course, up to $290 for a 2-day course.
Open: Mid-Dec to mid-Mar, daily 9am–5pm. Course admission by appointment only. **Closed:** Mid-Mar to mid-Dec.

TREAD OF PIONEERS MUSEUM, 800 Oak St., at Eighth St. Tel. 879-2214.

⭐ This beautifully restored Victorian home features exhibits on pioneer ranch life, Colorado's Ute Indians, and the history of skiing in Steamboat Springs, as well as changing exhibits on various subjects. The museum also shows how a well-to-do family in Steamboat Springs would have lived about 1910.

The museum offers video programs on local history, guided tours Tuesdays from noon to 1pm during the winter and summer, and an excellent museum shop. Ask for a copy of the Steamboat Springs self-guided historical walking-tour brochure, which includes 10 easy-to-reach sites.

Admission: $2.50 adults, $1 children 6–12, $5 families.
Open: Daily 11am–5pm, except Mon–Fri 11am–5pm during May, Oct, and Nov.

BUD WERNER MEMORIAL LIBRARY, 1289 Lincoln Ave. Tel. 879-0240.

A collection of skiing memorabilia, focusing on Steamboat's Werner family, long considered the "first family" of ski racing in the Colorado Rockies, is the highlight of a visit. The library is a full-service facility with books and current periodicals.

Admission: Free.
Open: Mon–Thurs 9am–8pm, Fri 9am–6pm, Sat 9am–5pm, Sun noon–5pm.

SPORTS & RECREATION

Most outdoor recreation pursuits are enjoyed in 1.1-million-acre **Routt National Forest,** which virtually surrounds Steamboat Springs. With elevations ranging from 6,750 to 13,553 feet, the national forest offers opportunities for camping, hiking, backpacking, mountain biking, horseback riding, fishing, hunting, snowmobiling, snowshoeing, cross-country skiing, and more. Less than 25 miles east of Steamboat is the 9,426-foot **Rabbit Ears Pass** area, which takes its name from a unique summit rock formation said to resemble rabbit ears. For Routt National Forest information, check with the Hahns Peak District office, 57 10th St. (tel. 879-1870).

Two wilderness areas in the forest are easily reached from Steamboat. Immediately north of town is the **Mount Zirkel Wilderness Area,** a region of rugged peaks approached through 10,800-foot Buffalo Pass, on Forest Road 60 off Strawberry Park Road via Seventh Street. Southwest of Stillwater Reservoir, some 40 miles south of Steamboat via Colo. 131 through Yampa, is the **Flat Tops Wilderness Area,** notable for its alpine meadows and sheer volcanic cliffs. No motorized vehicles or mountain bikes are allowed in wilderness areas.

Some 27 miles north of Steamboat Springs on Routt County Road 129 is the **Steamboat Lake State Recreation Area** (tel. 879-3922), encompassing 1,053-acre Steamboat Lake and 190-acre Pearl Lake. Activities at the two lakes include summer camping (there are 183 campsites), picnicking, fishing, hunting, boating (with rentals), waterskiing (on Steamboat Lake only), swimming, canoeing, horseback riding, and nature walks. In winter, there's ice fishing, cross-country skiing, snowmobiling, and snowshoeing. Day use fee is $3 per vehicle.

Information on most activities can be obtained from the Steamboat Springs Parks and Recreation Department (tel. 879-4300). Agencies that will arrange activities for visitors, both summer and winter, include the Steamboat Activity Center, 720 Lincoln Ave. or Gondola Square, Steamboat Village (tel. 303/879-2062) and Windwalker Tours (tel. 879-8065).

BALLOONING   Get a bird's-eye view of Steamboat and the Yampa River Valley, summer or winter, while floating quietly aloft in a colorful hot-air balloon. Operators include Aero Sports (tel. 879-7433), Balloons Over Steamboat (tel. 879-3298), Eagle Balloon Tours (tel. 879-8687), and Pegasus Balloon Tours (tel. 879-9191 or toll free 800/748-2487). A 30-minute ride runs about $75; a full hour, about $130.

BICYCLING   The new 5-mile, dual-surface Yampa River Trail connects downtown Steamboat Springs with Steamboat Village, and links area parks and national forest trails. The Mount Werner Trail links the river to the ski area, which itself has numerous slopes open to mountain bikers in summer. Spring Creek Trail climbs from Yampa River Park into the Routt National Forest. Touring enthusiasts can try the 110-mile loop over Rabbit Ears and Gore passes, rated one of the 10 most scenic rides in America by *Bicycling* magazine.

You can rent bikes from Sore Saddle Cyclery, Central Park Plaza and three other locations (tel. 879-1675); Steamboat Trading Company, 1850 Ski Time Square Dr. (tel. 879-0083); and Ski Haus International, 1450 S. Lincoln Ave. (tel. 879-0385 or toll free 800/932-3019). Typical rates are $10 for a half day, $16 for a full day.

Free tours of Moots Cycles Bicycle Factory, 1136 Yampa St. (tel. 879-1675), a custom bicycle frame builder, are offered by appointment.

BOATING   At Steamboat Lake (tel. 879-4404 for the marina) and at Stagecoach Reservoir, 17 miles southeast of Steamboat Springs off County Road 14 (tel. 736-8342), there are ample opportunities for water lovers. Canoes, paddleboats, and sailboards can be rented for $10 1 hour, $15 2½ hours, $20 4 hours, or $30 8 hours; Hobie Cats and Laser sailboats run $39 one hour, $59 2½ hours, or $79 8 hours; motorboats for fishing start at $35 for 4 hours.

DOG SLEDDING   Dog sledding is offered by the Steamboat Sled Dog Express (tel. 879-4662).

FISHING   There are nearly 150 lakes and reservoirs, and almost 600 miles of streams, in Routt County. Trout—rainbow, brown, brook, and cutthroat—are prolific. Buggywhip's Fish & Float Service (tel. 303/879-8033 or toll free 800/759-0343) leads half- and full-day stream-wading and float-fishing trips on the Yampa, Elk, North Platte, and Green rivers for rates starting at $90. Creative Sports, 431 Pine St. (tel. 879-1568), offers fly-fishing and fly-tying classes, as well as guided fishing trips, year-round.

You can get equipment, licenses, and information from Bear Paw Sporting Goods, 1106 Lincoln Ave. (tel. 879-8154), or Steamboat Springs Sporting Goods, 908 Lincoln Ave. (tel. 879-7774). Visitors are welcome at the Finger Rock Fish Rearing Unit of the Colorado Department of Wildlife, 5 miles south of Yampa on Colo. 131 (tel. 638-4490).

GOLF   The Sheraton Steamboat Resort and Conference Center, Clubhouse Drive (tel. 879-2220), designed by Robert Trent Jones, Jr., in 1972, is considered one of the Rockies' finest courses. The 18-hole, 6,906-yard course offers spectacular scenery and challenging fairways. Greens fees from mid-May through September are $48 for Sheraton guests, $73 for the public; from April to mid-May and October until the snow falls, it's $33 for Sheraton guests, $48 for the public. There are discounts for late-afternoon tee times. Call for information on lessons, clinics, and packages.

Steamboat Golf Club, U.S. 40 west of town (tel. 879-4295), is a 9-hole course; greens fees are $17 for 9 holes, $25 for 18 holes. The course is open to members only on Saturday and Sunday mornings, but open to the public most other times. Inner Links, 1855 Ski Time Square Dr. in the Torian Plum Plaza (tel. 879-2916), is an ideal winter remedy for the snowbound golfer. A life-size video simulation that puts you on some of the world's finest courses, it's almost like an indoor driving range!

HIKING & BACKPACKING   Visit the Routt National Forest district office, 57 10th St. (tel. 879-1870), for detailed area maps and trail information. There are many, many opportunities in the Mount Zirkel Wilderness Area, immediately north of Steamboat, and the Flat Tops Wilderness Area, 48 miles southwest. An especially fascinating 4-hour day hike in the Flat Tops area takes you from Stillwater Reservoir to the Devil's Causeway, with unforgettable views. Backpacking-and-camping rentals are offered by Ski Haus International, 1450 S. Lincoln Ave. at Pine Grove Road (tel. 879-0385).

HORSEBACK RIDING   Several area ranches offer trail rides by the hour, the half day, or overnight. They include Del's Triangle 3 Ranch, 55675 County Rd. 62 in Clark (tel. 879-3495); Elk River Guest Ranch, 29840 County Rd. 64 in Clark (tel. 879-6220); Glen Eden Stables, 61276 County Rd. 129 (tel. 879-3864 or 879-5736); Steamboat Lake Outfitters, Steamboat Lake (tel. 879-4404); and Sunset Ranch, 42850 County Rd. 129 (tel. 879-0954). Typical adult rates are $15 for a 1-hour ride, $50 for a half day, $75 for a full day, including lunch.

There's also a summer equestrian program at the Steamboat Resort (tel. 879-6111), with guided rides leaving half hourly, 10:30am to 2:30pm, from the Thunderhead gondola terminal.

HOT SPRINGS   More than 150 mineral springs are located in and around the Steamboat Springs area. Black, Heart, Iron, Lithia, Soda, Sulphur, and Steamboat—the springs for which the town was named—are located in parks of Steamboat Springs. Their healing and restorative qualities were recognized for centuries by Utes. James Crawford, the first white settler in this town, in 1875, regularly bathed in Heart Spring and helped build the first log bathhouse over it in 1884.

Today Heart Spring is part of the Steamboat Springs Health & Recreation complex, 136 Lincoln Ave. (tel. 879-1828), in downtown Steamboat Springs. Besides the human-made pools into which the spring's waters flow, there's a lap pool, a water slide, a weight room, tennis courts, fitness classes, and massage therapy. Suits and towels can be rented for $1.50; pool admission is $5 for adults, $3.50 for youths 13 to 17, and $2 for children under 13 and seniors. It's open daily from 7am to 10pm. The slide is open noon to 6pm in summer, and 4 to 8pm in winter.

The Hot Springs at Strawberry Park (tel. 879-0342) are 7 miles north of downtown. It's a wonderful experience to spend a moonlit evening in a sandy-bottomed, rock-lined soaking pool, kept between 102° and 104°; with snow piled high around you. Follow Strawberry Park Road, off Park Avenue via Seventh Street. Open daily from 10am to midnight; admission is $5. Massages are available, and cabins can be rented year-round.

A free city parks department brochure, "The Springs of Steamboat: A Walking Tour," will acquaint you with other mineral springs in the town area.

HUNTING   There's big-game hunting in Routt National Forest for deer, elk, antelope, moose, black bear, and mountain lion, and in adjacent areas for waterfowl, ground birds, and small mammals. The Steamboat Springs Chamber Resort Association (tel. 879-0880) has Division of Wildlife hunting information and regulations, and a list of guides and outfitters.

ICE SKATING   The Howelsen Ice Skating Rink, 243 River Rd. (tel. 879-0341), rents skates, offers lessons, and organizes ice-hockey and broomball competitions. Admission is $3.50 for adults, $2 for children 13 and under; skate rentals are $3 for adults, $2 for children. The rink has roller and in-line skating in the summer.

KAYAKING   There are kayak gates on the Yampa River, with major competitions the second weekend of June every year during the Yampa River Festival. If you have an interest in this exciting water sport, talk to the Mountain Sports Kayak School, 1835 Central Park Dr. (tel. 879-8794).

MOUNTAINEERING   Mountain climbing in the summer becomes ice climbing in the winter, and there's plenty of both in the Steamboat area. Consult Backdoor Sport of Steamboat, 811 Yampa St. (tel. 879-6249), or Rocky Mountain Ventures, 208 Ninth St. (tel. 879-4857).

RIVER RAFTING   White-water trips on numerous Colorado rivers are offered by Buggywhip's Fish & Float Service (tel. 303/879-8033 or toll free 800/759-0343), and Adventures Wild Rafting (tel. 303/879-8747 or toll free 800/825-3989). The Yampa, Cross Mountain Fork, North Platte, Eagle, Roaring Fork, Green, Colorado, and Arkansas rivers are tackled by these companies, which charge from $25 for a half day on the Yampa through town to $95 for a full day or $300 plus for an extended trip on expert (Class IV and V) rapids.

RODEO   The Romick Rodeo Arena at Howelsen Hill Park (tel. 879-0880) is the site each year, from mid-June to Labor Day, of the 13-week Summer of ProRodeo Series of the Professional Rodeo Cowboy Association. Some of the world's best compete in Brahma bull riding, bareback and saddle bronc riding, steer wrestling, calf roping, team roping, and barrel racing. In the Wrangler Ram Scramble, children are invited to try to pluck a ribbon from the tail of a ram for a special prize. Rodeo tickets are $7.50 for adults, $2 for children.

SKIING   Besides the Steamboat Ski Area (see "Attractions," above), there's Howelsen Hill (tel. 879-8499), which opened in 1915 and has remained open every winter since. The first accredited public-school ski classes in North America were taught on this slope. The hill, which offers day-and-night skiing, has 30 acres of terrain served by a double-chair and a poma lift. Vertical rise is 440 feet, to a 7,136-foot summit elevation. Tickets are $8 for adults, $4 for children (11am to 10pm Monday through Friday, Saturday and Sunday 9am to 10pm). The bobsled run costs $7 per trip.

   Howelsen Hill has bred more North American skiers for international competition than any other—primarily because of its ski-jumping complex. The U.S. ski-jumping team trains each year on the 20-, 30-, 50-, 70-, and 90-meter jumps.

   Cross-country skiers usually make their first stop at the Steamboat Ski Touring Center at the Sheraton Steamboat Resort and Conference Center, Clubhouse Road (tel. 879-8180 or toll free 800/848-8878). Some 25km (15 miles) of groomed cross-country trails are set across the fairways beside Fish Creek, near the foot of the mountain. The daily trail fee is $8.50; rental packages run $10. There are also lessons, equipment rentals, and citizens' races.

   There are many other touring areas throughout Routt National Forest. Obtain trail maps and information from the national forest district office, 57 10th St. (tel. 879-1870). Popular areas include Rabbit Ears Pass, 25 miles east of Steamboat on U.S. 40, and Dunkley Pass, 25 miles south on Colo. 131. Guided backcountry ski tours are offered by Rocky Mountain Ventures, 208 Ninth St. (tel. 879-4857).

   The cross-country trails and rustic resort atmosphere of the Home Ranch, 54880 County Rd. 129 (tel. 879-1780), in the Elk River Valley 18 miles north of Steamboat, have been widely praised.

   Ski-and-snowboard rental, sales, and repairs are offered by a variety of Steamboat-area shops, among them Inside Edge Sports (tel. 879-1250), Powder Pursuits (tel. 879-9086), Ski Haus International (tel. 879-0385), Sport Stalker at the Gondola (tel. 879-0371), and Ski Time Square (tel. 879-2445), and Terry Sports (tel. 879-8414 or toll free 800/233-SKIS).

SLEIGH RIDES   Take a sleigh ride to dinner with Double Runner Sleigh Rides (tel. 879-8877), Franni's Sleigh and Dinner Rides (tel. 879-1312). Several local guest ranches also offer horse-drawn sleigh trips, including Sunset Ranch (tel. 879-0954).

SNOWMOBILING   Snowmobilers consider the Continental Divide Trail, running over 50 miles from Buffalo Pass, north of Steamboat, to Gore Pass, west of Kremmling, to be one of the finest maintained trails in the Rockies. For information, check with Routt National Forest or with the Routt Powder Riders snowmobile club, P.O. Box 43, Steamboat Springs, CO 80477 (tel. 303/879-3731). Many guest ranches and other agencies offer winter tours, including Emerald Mountain Snowmobile Tours (tel. 879-8065), High Mountain Snowmobile Tours (tel. 879-9073), Steamboat Outfitters (tel. 879-4404 or toll free 800/342-1889), and Steamboat Snowmobile Tours (tel. 879-6500).

SWIMMING   Many hotel-and-condominium properties have their own swimming pools. You'll also find pools at the Glen Eden Resort, 54737 County Rd. 29, Clark (tel. 879-3907); the Steamboat Athletic Club, 33250 Storm Meadows Dr. (tel. 879-1036); and the Steamboat Springs Health & Recreation, 136 Lincoln Ave. (tel. 879-1828).

SHOPPING

Lincoln Avenue, between 5th and 9th streets, is where most of the more interesting shops and galleries are located. You won't find many bargains here, but there are a number of shops with unique merchandise. Stop at **Artisans' market** (tel. 879-7512), 626 Lincoln Ave., a nonprofit cooperative of local artists; and **Steamboat Art Company** (tel. 879-3383), 903 Lincoln Ave., which sells a huge selection of jewelry, plus pottery, stained glass, limited edition prints, and regional items.

The Silver Spur (tel. 879-3880), 842 Lincoln Ave., specializes in one-of-a-kind custom jewelry from precious metals and gems. The shop also does jewelry repairs. **The Front Page** (tel. 879-2180), corner of 5th and Lincoln, has a wide selection of gifts, including brass pots, hand-loomed place mats, pottery, and jewelry. If you forgot to pack your cowboy hat, there's a tremendous selection of Stetson and other fine brands, plus just about everything else a westerner wears, at **F. M. Light & Sons,** 826 Lincoln Ave. (tel. 879-1822). And while hardware stores might not be on everyone's list of tourist sites, take a few minutes to stop at **Bogg's Hardware,** 730 Lincoln Ave. (tel. 879-6250), where you'll find snowshoes, art and antiques, and just about every kitchen gizmo ever made.

Lyon's Corner Drug & Soda Fountain, at the corner of Ninth and Lincoln, is not only a drugstore and card shop; it also has a great old Wurlitzer jukebox spinning golden oldies, and an old-time soda fountain where you can get real malts, ice-cream sodas, and sundaes.

EVENING ENTERTAINMENT

THE PERFORMING ARTS   Summer is a busy time for the performing arts in Steamboat. The **Strings in the Mountains Chamber Music Festival,** P.O. Box 774627, Steamboat Springs, CO 80477 (tel. 303/879-5056), offers six performances a week, Tuesday through Sunday, for five weeks, mid-July to mid-August, featuring members of major national symphony orchestras. Tickets are $4 to $10 on Tuesday and Wednesday, free for Thursday student performances, $10 for Friday celebrity recitals, $12 for Saturday-night concerts, and varied prices for Sunday evening jazz, bluegrass, country western, or theater performances.

"Strings" overlaps with the **Perry-Mansfield Performing Arts Camp,** at 40755 County Rd. 36 (tel. 879-7125), whose alumni include actors Dustin Hoffman and Lee Remick and dancer José Limon. The camp has operated continually since 1913. Youth 10 and older are taught theater, music, dance, and riding from the third week of June to the first week of August. One dance and three theater productions are staged to sell-out audiences in the camp's Julie Harris Theater.

The **Steamboat Community Players** produce several stage plays over the course of the year, including a couple in the summer. The troupe performs at the Seventh Street Playhouse, Seventh Street and Aspen Street (tel. 879-3254).

THE CLUB & BAR SCENE   The nightlife scene, while never dull, comes especially alive in winter as *après-ski.* At Steamboat Village, the **Inferno,** Gondola Square (tel. 879-5111), is a hot dance club for the 20s set, with live music; the rustic **Tugboat Saloon & Eatery,** Ski Time Square (tel. 879-7070), attracts more of a local crowd for rock music and dancing with live music from 9pm; and **Buddy's Run,** in the Sheraton Steamboat Resort (tel. 879-2220), does a quick change from a foot-of-the-slopes bar to an early evening comedy club. Other lively bars include

Mather's Bar, 420 Yampa Ave., Craig (tel. 824-9946), with live music weekends, pool, and shuffleboard; and **Dos Amigos,** at 1910 Mount Werner Rd. (tel. 879-4270), a friendly neighborhood Mexican restaurant and bar.

In downtown Steamboat, the **Old Town Pub & Restaurant,** Sixth Street and Lincoln Avenue (tel. 879-2101), has big-screen ski movies; and **Buffalo Wild Wings and Weck** ("BW-3"), 729 Lincoln Ave. (tel. 879-2431), has live music weekends ($1 to $3 cover charge). Sundance Plaza, midway between the resort and downtown, offers the **Steamboat Saloon** (tel. 879-7797), a country-and-western nightclub.

WHERE TO STAY

Rates are highest during the Christmas holiday season: mid-December through New Year's Day. Next highest is the "regular" February to March season. "Value" season is usually January, and "low" seasons run from the beginning of ski season (Thanksgiving) to mid-December and April until the area closes. Rates are normally much lower during the summer season, Memorial Day to mid-October. Because vacancy rates are so high during shoulder seasons—April to May and October to November—many accommodations close at these times.

Steamboat Reservation Services (toll free 800/922-2722) can make all lodging bookings and any other travel arrangements for visitors to Steamboat Springs.

VERY EXPENSIVE

CHATEAU CHAMONIX, 2340 Apres Ski Way, Steamboat Springs, CO 80487. Tel. 303/879-7511 or toll free 800/833-9877. Fax 303/879-9321. 27 units (all with bath). A/C TV TEL
$ Rates: Two-bedrooms, $115–$130 summer (Easter–Thanksgiving), $225–$240 low-season, $365–$440 regular-and-value seasons, $550–$600 Christmas season; three-bedrooms, $175–$200 summer, $275 low-season, $455–$545 regular-and-value seasons, $700–$750 Christmas season. MC, V. **Parking:** Free covered lot.

Located a few steps from the base of the Silver Bullet gondola, this is one of the most convenient accommodations at Steamboat Village. Two buildings have condominium units with private decks facing the slopes. All have fireplaces and fully equipped kitchens with refrigerators, washers and dryers, wet bars, VCRs, and furnishings of pine, walnut, or oak. Most of the units are two-bedroom suites, with twin beds in one room, a king-size bed in the master bedroom, and a Jacuzzi tub in the adjoining private bathroom. Local calls are free.

Facilities: Swimming pool, outdoor hot tub, sauna, ski lockers, conference room.

THE HOME RANCH, 54880 Routt County Rd. 129 (P.O. Box 822), Clark, CO 80428. Tel. 303/879-1780 or toll free 800/223-7094. Fax 303/879-1795. 13 units (all with bath). TV TEL
$ Rates (including full board): Summer, $350–$415 lodge room; $400–$475 cabin; $800 two-bedroom cabin; children $115–$150 extra. Winter, $320–$390 lodge room; $380–$465 cabin; $775 two-bedroom cabin; children $100–$145 extra. AE, MC, V.

Acclaimed by *Travel & Leisure* magazine and the *Los Angeles Times*, Ken and Cile Jones's Home Ranch injects a large dose of luxury into the Elk River Valley, 19 miles north of Steamboat. By summer a guest ranch that draws horse lovers and fly fishers, it becomes in winter a refuge for cross-country skiers. The Main House has a particularly welcoming ambience with its leather couches, huge stone fireplace, grand piano, paintings and crafts by local artisans, and library.

Lodge rooms, with king-size beds, are furnished with antiques and reproductions. Two rooms have charming children's lofts. Special touches include humidifiers, hair dryers, bathrobes, and coffee makers. Each of the "modern rustic" guest cabins, 5 to 10 minutes' walk from the lodge, has a Jacuzzi tub on its porch; they also boast antique furnishings, native crafts, original artwork, hair dryers, coffee makers . . . and bootjacks, to avoid tracking the stable mud into the house. On your bed at night, you'll get a "Far Side" cartoon instead of a chocolate: "It's better for your teeth," the Joneses explain.

Dining/Entertainment: Three gourmet meals a day are served family style in the Main House. There are no menu choices, so the staff must be advised in advance of special dietary requirements.

Services: Airport transfers, weekly laundry, children's counselor, masseuse on call; 1:1 staff-to-guest ratio.

Facilities: Heated swimming pool, sauna, Jacuzzis; stable with horseback riding and lessons; fly-fishing lessons and 2 miles of private river; guided hiking trips into the Mount Zirkel Wilderness; cross-country skiing equipment, lessons, and 40km (25 miles) of set tracks.

TORIAN PLUM AT STEAMBOAT, 1855 Ski Time Square Dr., Steamboat Springs, CO 80487. Tel. 303/879-8811 or toll free 800/228-2458. Fax 303/879-8485. 47 units (all with bath). TV TEL

$ Rates: One-bedroom, $109 summer, $160 early/late season, $395 preholiday season, $455 holiday season, $295 and $235 value season, $375 and $340 regular ski season; two-bedroom, $125 summer, $195 early/late season, $535 preholiday season, $625 holiday season, $395 and $295 value season, $545 and $495 regular ski season; three-bedroom, $145 summer, $235 early/late season, $695 preholiday season, $795 holiday season, $525 and $395 value season, $665 and $595 regular ski season. AE, MC, V. **Parking:** Free underground lot.

This slope-side ski-in/ski-out condominium development has one-, two-, and three-bedroom units with handsome light-wood furnishings. Each unit has a fully equipped and tiled kitchen (with microwave and dishwasher), washer/dryer, whirlpool tub, gas fireplace, private balcony, cable TV with HBO and VCR, and ski locker.

The manager is Steamboat Premier Properties, Ltd., which also operates the neighboring Bronze Tree and Trappeur's Crossing condominium developments. All have equivalent facilities and summer rates; regular ski-season rates for a two-bedroom condo start at $385 at the Bronze Tree, $295 at Trappeur's.

Services: Concierge during ski season, daily housekeeping, shuttle van, bell staff, 24-hour front desk.

Facilities: Outdoor heated swimming pool, outdoor-and-indoor hot tubs, sauna, four summer tennis courts.

EXPENSIVE

THE RANCH AT STEAMBOAT, 1 Ranch Rd. (off Clubhouse Dr.), Steamboat Springs, CO 80487. Tel. 303/879-3000 or toll free 800/525-2002. Fax 303/879-5409. 88 units (all with bath). TV TEL

$ Rates: $110–$135 one- and two-bedrooms in summer, $275–$350 during the regular ski season, $400 during the Christmas season; three- and four-bedroom units are higher. AE, MC, V. **Parking:** Free private garages.

Spread across a 36-acre hillside on Burgess Creek, not far from Ski Time Square, these one- to four-bedroom condominiums offer a peaceful, quiet location. They're especially popular for company getaways.

The two-story condo units are furnished in deluxe style, with full kitchens (including microwaves), large fireplaces, private barbecue decks, and washer/dryer facilities. There's a direct entrance from the private garage into the kitchen. The price of local phone calls is 50¢.

Services: Full front-desk services, shuttle vans.

Facilities: Swimming pool, hot tubs, saunas, recreation center, weight room, tennis courts; meeting facilities for 200.

SHERATON STEAMBOAT RESORT, Base Village (P.O. Box 774808), Steamboat Springs, CO 80477. Tel. 303/879-2220 or toll free 800/848-8878. Fax 303/879-7686. 270 rms (all with bath), 29 suites and condos. A/C TV TEL

$ Rates: Late May to mid-Oct, $69–$109; winter, low-season $99–$129, value season $169–$199, Christmas and regular season $189–$249. Children under 17

stay free in parents' room in summer. AE, CB, DC, MC, V. **Parking:** Free underground lot. **Closed:** 1 month in spring and 1 month in fall.

Steamboat Springs's premier hotel property is located in the heart of Ski Time Square, at the foot of the "Silver Bullet" gondola. The Sheraton opens directly onto the ski slopes, and every room has a view of the mountain, valley, or slopes. In summer, sports lovers enjoy its golf club, one of the finest in the Rockies.

Opened in the mid-1970s, the hotel was fully renovated in 1993. A typical room has two queen-size beds, a private balcony, in-room movies, and a large closet with full mirror doors.

Dining/Entertainment: Remington's fine dining establishment has a view straight up the Headwall chair lift. Breakfast (6:30 to 11am), Sunday brunch, and dinner (5:30 to 10pm) are served daily. The restaurant has Steamboat's largest soup-and-salad bar; steak, seafood, and poultry dishes run $11.75 to $18.95. Buddy's Run, open winters only, serves skiers' breakfasts and lunches from 7am to 5pm; in the early evening, it's a comedy club. The hotel also has H. B. Longbaugh's sports bar and Cinnamon's pastry shop.

Services: Room service (7am to 10pm), concierge (8am to 6pm), valet and guest laundry, children's summer day-camp program, no-smoking rooms, facilities for the disabled.

Facilities: Golf club and cross-country ski course (see "What to See & Do," above), year-round heated swimming pool, hot tubs, saunas, massage, games room, gift-and-sundry shop, ski storage and rental; meeting facilities for 800.

MODERATE

THE HARBOR HOTEL, 703 Lincoln Ave. (P.O. Box 774109), Steamboat Springs, CO 80477. Tel. 303/879-1522 or toll free 800/543-8888, 800/334-1012 in Colorado. Fax 303/879-1737. 62 units (all with bath). TV TEL

$ Rates (including continental breakfast): $50–$90 single or double in summer (Easter–Thanksgiving), $57–$98 in low ski season, $91–$161 in value-and-regular season, $149–$196 season; $85–$109 condos in summer and low-season, $138–$201 in value-and-regular seasons, $253–$322 at Christmas. AE, CB, DC, DISC, JCB, MC, V. **Parking:** Free, off street.

A European-style hotel that dates to 1940, the Harbor has expanded in recent years with an adjoining motel and condominium complex. Guests still enter the hotel through polished bronze doors from a turn-of-the-century London bank, and register in a small, antique-filled lobby. This isn't a Victorian showcase, but the decor is simple and homey.

Each of the 15 hotel guest rooms has a different design. All offer period furnishings. Motel units (23), are good, basic, economical rooms. Downtown Steamboat's only condos (24) have well-equipped kitchens with stoves, microwaves, and refrigerators. Local phone calls cost 50¢, long-distance access to AT&T operator is free.

Services and facilities include free bus pass, hot beverages, Wednesday après-ski party, ski storage, Jacuzzis, sauna, steam room, gift shop, and boutique.

SKY VALLEY LODGE, 31490 E. U.S. 40 (P.O. Box 3132), Steamboat Springs, CO 80477. Tel. 303/879-7749 or toll free 800/538-7519. Fax 303/879-6044. 24 rms (all with bath or shower). TV TEL

$ Rates (including continental breakfast): May–Thanksgiving, $58–$78 single or double. Winter, $75–$105 single or double in low-season, $155–$195 in Christmas season, $90–$130 in value season, $125–$155 in regular season. Extra person $10. AE, CB, DC, DISC, MC, V. **Parking:** Free. **Closed:** Mid-Apr to late May.

Located below Rabbit Ears Pass with a spectacular view of the upper Yampa River Valley, this lodge—actually two rustic lodges, 8½ miles east of Steamboat Springs—offers country-manor charm in a woodsy setting. Guests get to know each other while sitting around a big fireplace in the main living-room area.

Each cozy room is a bit different, but all have an alpine pension atmosphere. Only four units have full baths; others have showers only, and sinks are in the bedroom. There are king-size and queen-size brass beds and wood beds, and several daybeds; floral decor predominates. Local calls cost 50¢.

Gourmet family-style dinners are served Wednesday through Sunday in winter, with a choice of three main courses each night. A full bar opens at 3pm daily. Services and facilities include a shuttle to the Ptarmigan Inn at the foot of the ski slopes, where equipment can be stored; outdoor hot tub, coed saunas, games room.

INEXPENSIVE

THE INN AT STEAMBOAT BED & BREAKFAST, 3070 Columbine Dr. (P.O. Box 775084), Steamboat Springs, CO 80477. Tel. 303/879-2600 or toll free 800/872-2601. Fax 303/879-9270. 31 rms, 1 suite (all with bath). TV TEL

$ Rates: May–Thanksgiving, $45 single; $56 double; additional person $6. Thanksgiving–April, $61 single; $149 double; additional person $10. AE, DISC, MC, V. **Parking:** Free.

A large ranch-style bed-and-breakfast, the inn is one of the least expensive accommodations in the Steamboat Village area, surrounded by upscale condominiums. Etched-pine decor and a large stone fireplace add flair. The inn has an outdoor swimming pool, sauna, service bar, and game room, and offers ski-tuning services and a private ski shuttle to the mountain.

Rooms are spacious units with queen-size and double beds. Sliding glass doors lead to private decks. The TV rests on a long credenza. Local phone calls are free. Rates include an extensive continental breakfast in spring, summer, and fall, and a full breakfast in the winter, served in the quaint dining room. The entire inn is nonsmoking.

RABBIT EARS MOTEL, 201 Lincoln Ave. (P.O. Box 770573), Steamboat Springs, CO 80477. Tel. 303/879-1150 or toll free 800/828-7702. Fax 303/870-0483. 65 rooms (all with bath). A/C TV TEL

$ Rates: Summer, $50–$70 single; $56–$76 double. Winter, $70–$90 single; $76–$96 double. AE, CB, DC, DISC, MC, V. **Parking:** Free.

Built in 1952, this property was extensively remodeled recently and offers a very attractive alternative to the higher-priced condos and lodges in town. All rooms have coffee makers, clock radios, and color cable remote TV, and some of the larger units have private balconies and hideabed couches. Some also come with refrigerators. Discount passes to the hot springs (across the street) are provided to guests, who can also easily walk to the local bus, downtown shopping and dining, and Howelsen Park. Nonsmoking rooms are available, and pets are welcome.

STEAMBOAT BED & BREAKFAST, 442 Pine St. (P.O. Box 772058), Steamboat Springs, CO 80477. Tel. 303/879-5724. 6 rms (all with bath).

$ Rates (including full breakfast): Mid-Apr to mid-Nov, $65 single; $75 double. Mid-Nov to mid-Apr $85 single; $85–$125 double. DISC, MC, V. **Parking:** Off street.

Steamboat Springs's first house of worship, an 1891 Congregational Church that lost its steeple and top floor to a lightning strike, is now a fine bed-and-breakfast with many stained glass windows. Today there are beautiful antiques in every room, reproduction antique beds, and hardwood floors. Guests share a huge living/dining room with a stone fireplace and complimentary fresh fruit and baked goods, an upstairs library, a hot tub, and a music conservatory with a piano . . . and a television. Smoking and pets are not allowed.

STEAMBOAT VALLEY GUEST HOUSE, 1245 Crawford Ave. (P.O. Box 773815), Steamboat Springs, CO 80477. Tel. 303/870-9017 or toll free 800/530-3866. 4 rooms (all with bath).

$ Rates (including full breakfast): Spring and fall, $55–$90. Summer and ski season, $70–$120. Higher during holidays. MC, V. **Parking:** Free.

This western-style log house has spectacular views of the ski area and town. The four guest rooms are all decorated with antiques and family treasures. Three of the rooms have queen-size beds, and the honeymoon suite has a king bed and ceramic fireplace. Breakfasts are different each day, and might include Swedish pancakes or a green chili cheese soufflé. A common room has a fireplace, grand piano, and TV, and guests have access to a cordless phone. Smoking and pets are not permitted. Children are accepted on a limited basis.

WHERE TO DINE
EXPENSIVE

HAZIE'S, Thunderhead Terminal, Silver Bullet Gondola. Tel. 879-6111, ext. 465.

    Cuisine: CREATIVE CONTINENTAL. **Reservations:** Recommended for lunch, required for dinner.

$ **Prices:** Lunch appetizers $3.75–$6.25, main courses $6.95–$10.95; four-course fixed-price dinner $45, including round-trip gondola ride. AE, MC, V.

    Open: Lunch daily 11:30am–2:30pm; dinner Tues–Sat 6:30–10:30pm.

Steamboat's most exciting dining experience can be found at the top of the gondola, midway up Mount Werner. The views of the upper Yampa River valley are spectacular by day, romantic by night, as the lights of Steamboat Springs spread out at the foot of the mountain. Lunch features a chicken Durango salad, Hazie's buffalo burger, veal Yorkshire, and fettuccine Alfredo. But it's at dinner that Hazie's really struts its stuff. This is a package deal: round-trip gondola transportation and four courses—an appetizer, soup or salad, main course, and dessert—for $45. You can start with smoked Norwegian salmon or escargots bourguignonne à la fromage, then select from a choice of eight main dishes, such as shrimp cilantro, pheasant aux pêches, and beef Wellington. Desserts are made fresh daily. Service is impeccable, and there's an extensive wine selection. Don't feel that you must wear a coat and tie. A neat ski sweater and slacks will do just fine. Evening child care is available.

RAGNAR'S, Rendezvous Saddle, Sunshine Peak. Tel. 879-6111, ext. 465.

    Cuisine: SCANDINAVIAN/CONTINENTAL. **Reservations:** Recommended for lunch, required for dinner.

$ **Prices:** Lunch appetizers $4.50–$6.95, main courses $6.75–$11.95; fixed-price four-course dinner $59 (children 12 and under $42), including gondola-and-sleigh rides. AE, DISC, MC, V.

    Open: Ski season only, lunch daily 11:30am–2:15pm; dinner Thurs–Sat at 6pm.

    Closed: Off-season.

Travel by moonlight, across the midmountain slopes, to a Scandinavian-style dinner at this charming restaurant. Named for Norwegian ski jumper Ragnar Omtvedt, Ragnar's has skis, snowshoes, and various bric-a-brac on its walls, and lacy window curtains facing the High Noon slopes.

    Main-course choices include oven-baked salmon with puff pastry and white asparagus, roast chicken stuffed with juniper berries and garnished with a chestnut sauce, or mesquite-broiled filet mignon; and delectable homemade desserts. For midday lunch, consider *fyldt pandekager* (seafood crêpes), *stekt lammekølle* (leg of lamb), or a *smørrebrød* platter (an assortment of open-face sandwiches).

MODERATE

DOS AMIGOS, 1910 Mount Werner Rd., Ski Time Sq. Tel. 879-4270.

    Cuisine: MEXICAN. **Reservations:** Accepted.

$ **Prices:** Appetizers $1–$6.25; main courses $5.95–$15.95. AE, DC, MC, V.

    Open: Winter, bar menu 2:30pm–midnight; dinner 5–10pm daily. Summer, daily 3:30pm–midnight; dinner Tues–Sun 5:30–10pm.

The mountain's oldest Mexican café, established in 1975, is a casual place dominated by its large and popular bar. Pictures cover the stuccoed walls, and green plants add a homey ambience. Start with a margarita or two, then try some of the authentic cuisine—such as Yucatán sopa de lima (a savory chicken, lime, and tortilla soup).

Main courses range from Mexican blackened snapper to chimichangas, tacos, and enchiladas.

LA MONTAÑA, Village Center Shopping Plaza, 2500 Village Dr. at Apres Ski Way. Tel. 879-5800.

    Cuisine: MEXICAN/SOUTHWESTERN. **Reservations:** Recommended.

$ **Prices:** Appetizers $3.75–$8.95; main courses $8.95–$17.95. DISC, MC, V.

    Open: Dinner only, daily 5–10pm (bar daily 3:30pm–midnight in winter, 4:30pm–midnight in summer). Closed Sun–Tues spring and fall.

This isn't your everyday Mexican restaurant: It's a gourmet experience. The festive decor sets the mood, with greenhouse dining and handsome photos by owner Tom Garrett decorating the stuccoed walls elsewhere.

Start with the restaurant's award-winning grilled braided sausage, a mesquite-grilled combination of elk, lamb, and chorizo sausage. Then choose between sizzling fajitas (with chicken, pork, shrimp, beef, or elk); traditional southwestern dishes such as red-chile pasta; or such Tex-Mex favorites as enchiladas and chiles rellenos. Perhaps the epicure's choice would be the elk tenderloin.

ORE HOUSE AT THE PINE GROVE, 1465 Pine Grove Rd. at U.S. 40. Tel. 879-1190.

    Cuisine: GAME/STEAK/SEAFOOD. **Reservations:** Recommended.

$ **Prices:** Appetizers $3.75–$7.95; main courses $7.95–$29.50. AE, DISC, MC, V.

    Open: Dinner only, daily 5–10pm (bar open to 2am, to midnight Sun).

The century-old barn of the late, lamented Pine Grove Ranch was converted into this restaurant in 1971. Steamboat residents and visitors alike appreciate the rustic atmosphere. Artifacts such as wagon wheels and a sleigh decorate the walls. Many folks come here for the ranch-raised game, including buffalo-and-elk steaks. It's also known for its steak and prime rib and Rocky Mountain rainbow trout and fresh seafood. There's a kids' menu too.

INEXPENSIVE

BUFFALO WILD WINGS AND WECK [BW-3], 729 Lincoln Ave. Tel. 879-2431.

    Cuisine: AMERICAN. **Reservations:** Not necessary.

$ **Prices:** $1.90–$12. AE, MC, V.

    Open: Mon–Sat 11am–2am, Sun 11am–2am.

Locals love "BW-3," downtown Steamboat's only late-night dining establishment. "Weck" is a German-style Kimmelweck roll, on which buffalo-and-beef burgers, char-grilled steaks, and barbecues are served. As the name implies, spicy chicken wings are another house specialty. There's dancing here, too, to a compact-disc jukebox or live bands, and the bar stocks 18 draft beers and 24 bottled beers.

CUGINO'S PIZZERIA, INC. 825 Oak St. Tel. 879-5805.

    Cuisine: ITALIAN. **Reservations:** Not accepted.

$ **Prices:** Appetizers $2–$4.50; entrées $3.50–$12.50. No credit cards.

    Open: Daily 11am–10pm.

Local families pack this restaurant in downtown Steamboat Springs, and with good reason—generous portions and low prices. The decor is simple, with posters from Italian operas. The extensive menu includes pizza, of course, plus hoagies and steak sandwiches, pasta, seafood, and calzones. Those with healthy appetites might want to try a stromboli—fresh-baked pizza dough stuffed with mushrooms, onions, peppers, mozzarella and provolone cheeses, ham, Genoa salami, and capacola. A vegetarian version is also served.

THE TUGBOAT SALOON & EATERY, Ski Time Sq. Tel. 879-7070.

    Cuisine: AMERICAN. **Reservations:** Not accepted.

$ **Prices:** Breakfast/lunch $2.95–$7.95; dinner $4.95–$7.95. AE, DC, DISC, MC, V.

    Open: Winter, daily 7:30am–10pm; summer, daily 11am–10pm (bar open Mon–Sat to 2am, Sun to midnight). **Closed:** April 15–June 10.

Oak floors and rough barn-wood walls cloaked with game-and-fishing trophies, sports memorabilia, and celebrity photographs are the trademark of this foot-of-the-slopes establishment. The hand-carved cherry-wood bar, circa 1850, came from the Log Cabin Saloon in Baggs, Wyo., a Butch Cassidy hangout; look for the bullet hole in one of the columns. Budget fare includes omelets and *huevos* (Mexican egg dishes) for breakfast, a variety of burgers, burritos, and deli sandwiches for lunch, and dinner. Many folks sup on nachos, teriyaki wings, and other generous appetizer plates. Live music starts nightly at 9:30pm.

EASY EXCURSIONS FROM STEAMBOAT SPRINGS

U.S. 40 west from Steamboat Springs leads 25 miles to **Hayden,** a ranching center of about 2,000 people that has preserved a strong Old West flavor. Points of interest include the **Hayden Heritage Center,** 300 W. Pearl St. (tel. 276-4380), open Friday through Sunday from 11am to 5pm, located in the 1918 railroad depot; and the **Old Hayden Trading Company,** 108 Walnut St. (tel. 276-4247), an authentic trading post with a jewelry and leather workshop.

South and east from Steamboat, U.S. 40 passes through Rabbit Ears Pass and Muddy Pass en route to **Kremmling** (pop. 1,300), 52 miles away. As the road passes through rolling hills, watch for cowboys at work on local ranches—this is the real thing, not Hollywood. Kremmling, at an elevation of 7,364 feet, is a center for **hunting, fishing,** and **rafting.** Check with Whitewater Rafting Monarch Guides, in Eagle (tel. 524-7444 or toll free 800/882-3445). The **Kremmling Museum,** in the old jail on Town Square, offers displays of area history. Stop at the Kremmling Chamber of Commerce, next door at 213 Park Center Ave. (tel. 724-3472), if the museum is closed.

Colorado 131 follows the Yampa River south from Steamboat, branching off U.S. 40 just south of Steamboat Village. It's 74 winding miles from Steamboat to I-70 at Wolcott, through the villages of **Oak Creek, Phippsburg, Yampa,** and **Toponas,** old ranching and coal-mining towns. Locals in Oak Creek, 22 miles from Steamboat, swear by the Chinese food at Chelsea's on Main Street (tel. 736-8538), open nightly except Mondays, from 5 to 11pm, and usually closed the months of May and November. Landmark buttes, glaciated valleys, and fossil deposits add to the scenic beauty of this route. **State Bridge,** 15 miles from I-70, is where the highway crosses the Colorado River and rail line; it's a rafting center.

Just past Rabbit Ears Pass, Colo. 14 turns east off U.S. 40 for a 122-mile passage to Fort Collins. The highlight of this drive is the **North Park** area, a broad, high basin surrounded by various Rocky Mountain ranges, and a paradise for ranchers—as well as hunters and anglers. The population center is Walden (pop. 950); get outdoor recreation **information** here from the North Park District office of Routt National Forest, 612 Fifth St. (tel. 723-4707). Worth a visit is the **North Park Pioneer Museum,** 460 McKinley St. (tel. 723-4711), open in summer, Tuesday through Sunday from noon to 6pm, or by appointment.

3. WINTER PARK

67 miles W of Denver

GETTING THERE By Plane Visitors fly into Denver International Airport, and may continue to Winter Park aboard Home James vans (tel. 303/726-5060 or toll free 800/451-4844) which leave Denver 10 times daily during ski season, less frequently in summer.

By Train Winter Park Resort claims to be the only ski area in the United States to have rail service directly to the slopes. The dramatically scenic ✪ Rio Grande Ski Train between Denver and Winter Park has been making regular runs over the same route since 1940, stopping just 50 yards from the foot of the lifts. On its 2-hour run, the train climbs almost 4,000 feet and passes through 29 tunnels (including the 6.2-mile Moffat Tunnel). The train, which operates weekends from December 18 to April (but not Christmas), leaves Denver promptly at 7:15am and Winter Park at 4:15pm. Same-day round-trip fare is $30 coach or $45 for first class which includes a continental breakfast and snacks on the return trip. For ticket information, call 303/296-I-SKI (303/296-4754).

The Amtrak *California Zephyr* stops daily in Fraser, 2 miles north of Winter Park, on its Chicago–Denver–San Francisco–Los Angeles route. The rail line's "Snowball Express" package brings thousands of skiers to Winter Park each year. Call toll free 800/USA-RAIL for schedules and fares from your city.

By Bus   Greyhound/Trailways, U.S. 40 at Vasquez Road (tel. 292-6111), offers regular service on the main route between Denver and Steamboat Springs.

By Car   From Denver or any other points east and west, take I-70, Exit 232, at Empire and climb 24 miles over Berthoud Pass on U.S. 40 to Winter Park. U.S. 40 links Winter Park directly to Steamboat Springs, 101 miles northwest, and, via U.S. 34 (at Granby) and Rocky Mountain National Park, to Estes Park, 84 miles north.

SPECIAL EVENTS   Winter Park area events include the First Interstate Bank Cup ski races, in early February; the Subaru U.S. Alpine Championships, in late March; the Spring Splash (Ski Area Closing Day), in mid-April; High Country Stampede Rodeo, every Saturday night from early July through August; the Alpine ArtAffair, late July; Rocky Mountain Wine and Food Festival, in early August; King of the Rockies Mountain Bike Festival, in late August; and the Torchlight Parade, on Christmas Eve.

Originally a Ute and Arapahoe hunting ground, the Fraser Valley was first settled by whites in the 1850s. The laying of a rail track over Rollins Pass in 1905, and the completion of the 6.2-mile Moffat Tunnel in 1928, opened the forests of Grand County to logging, which long supported the local economy while providing Denver with raw materials for its growth.

The opening of the Winter Park ski area in January 1940, at the west portal of the Moffat Tunnel, helped induce the Colorado ski boom. Owned by the city of Denver and operated by a private corporation, it is today the fourth-largest ski resort in the state (after Aspen, Vail, and Steamboat). The long-term master plan for the resort includes construction of a 4.1-mile highway tunnel for more rapid road access from Denver and Boulder, and development of a major base village.

Winter Park's elevation is 9,110 feet. The year-round population is 548 in Winter Park and 538 more in neighboring Fraser, plus there are beds for over 13,000 overnight guests in peak summer or winter seasons.

ORIENTATION

INFORMATION   Main sources of visitor information are the Winter Park/Fraser Valley Chamber of Commerce, P.O. Box 3236, Winter Park, CO 80482 (tel. 303/726-4118, for general information, or for lodging call toll free 800/722-4118), and the Winter Park Resort, P.O. Box 36, Winter Park, CO 80482 (tel. 303/726-5514). The chamber of commerce Visitor Center, off U.S. 40 on Vasquez Road, is open daily from 8am to 6pm year-round.

CITY LAYOUT   U.S. 40, or Winter Park Drive runs almost directly north-south through the community. Coming from Denver, you first cross Berthoud Pass, and 15 miles later see the Winter Park Resort on your left. About 1 mile farther is downtown Winter Park; Vasquez Road, one of the few side roads with accommodations, is the first major left turn as you arrive. Two miles farther on U.S. 40 is **Fraser,** site of the Amtrak terminal and several condominium developments.

GETTING AROUND

The **Ski Lift** (tel. 390-LIFT), a free local shuttle service, runs to/from most accommodations and the Winter Park Resort base area in winter. **Home James**

Taxi Service (tel. 726-5060) does the yeoman's share of taxi work. "Skierized" **car rentals** are available from Hertz (tel. 303/726-8993 or toll free 800/654-3131).

FAST FACTS

The **area code** is 303. In case of **emergency,** call 911; for regular business, contact the Grand County Sheriff (tel. 726-5666). The **hospital,** Winter Park Medical Center, U.S. 40 in downtown Winter Park (tel. 726-9616), and 7 Mile Medical Clinic, at the Winter Park Ski Area (tel. 726-8066), can handle most medical emergencies. The **post office** is in the heart of Winter Park on U.S. 40. For **road information,** call 639-1111. State, county, and city **taxes** add 9.2% to hotel bills.

WHAT TO SEE & DO
ATTRACTIONS

WINTER PARK RESORT, Winter Park Recreational Association, P.O. Box 36, Winter Park, CO 80482. Tel. 303/726-5514 or 303/892-0961 in Denver or toll free 800/453-2525 for lodging or 900/950-5550 ($1.25 for the first minute, 95¢ for each additional minute) for daily ski reports.

Winter Park is one of those rare resorts that seem to have something for everyone. Experts drool over the chutes and steep mogul runs on Mary Jane mountain, but intermediates and beginners are well served on other slopes. Moreover, Winter Park is noted for wide-ranging programs for children and the disabled.

The resort includes three interconnected mountain areas totaling 113 trails on 1,311 acres of skiable terrain. Twenty lifts include 5 high-speed express quads, 5 triples, and 10 double chair lifts, providing an uphill capacity of 32,450 skiers per hour.

Winter Park Mountain has 12 lifts and 44 trails, with mostly beginner and intermediate terrain. A new $2-million **Learn to Ski Park** encompasses 20 acres of prime beginner terrain served by 3 lifts.

Mary Jane Mountain has 6 chair lifts and 49 trails on intermediate and expert terrain. **Vasquez Ridge,** the resort's third mountain area, offers primarily intermediate terrain on its 13 trails. All are served by 1 quad lift. Fans of tree-line skiing will like **Parsenn Bowl,** more than 200 acres of open-bowl and gladed-tree skiing that fan out from the summit at North Cone and merge with Mary Jane's Backside.

Annual snowfall at Winter Park averages 30 feet—more than any other major destination resort in Colorado. The vertical drop is 3,060 feet, from the 9,000-foot base to the 12,060-foot summit off North Cone. There are nine restaurants and three bars, including the Lodge at Sunspot, a mountaintop restaurant.

Winter Park's 32,000-square-foot **Children's Center,** first of its kind at a ski resort, includes a play area, a rental shop, restrooms, and a children's instruction hill. The **National Sports Center for the Disabled,** founded in 1970, is the largest program of its kind in the world. Each year, more than 2,500 children and adults take over 23,000 lessons, at a cost of $70 (including full-day lift ticket, private lesson, and adaptive equipment). The half-day rate is $35.

Admission: Tickets, $38 per day adults, $25 half day, $33 per day for multiday tickets; $17 per day children 6–13 and seniors 62–69; free for those under 6 and over 69. Special beginner's lift rates. Full-rental packages are available; lessons run $15–$40. Snowboard lessons also available.

Open: Third week of Nov to third week of Apr, Mon–Fri 9am–4pm, Sat–Sun and holidays 8:30am–4pm. **Closed:** Late Apr to late Nov.

COZENS RANCH HOUSE RESTORATION MUSEUM, U.S. 40 between Winter Park and Fraser. Tel. 726-5488.

A series of 1870s ranch buildings, including a family residence, a small hotel, a stage stop, and the original Fraser Valley post office, have been restored by the Grand County Historical Association. They give a glimpse of life in Colorado's pioneer era.

Admission: $2 adults, $1 children.

Open: Dec 15–Apr 11, Tues–Sun, 11am–4:30pm; June 15–Sept 15, daily 11am–4:30pm.

RIO GRANDE CABOOSE MUSEUM, Ski Train Terminal, Winter Park Resort. Tel. 726-5514.

A vintage 1945 caboose has been converted to a ski museum, with a display of ski memorabilia and historical photos showing the half-century development of the Winter Park ski area. It doubles as a visitor information center. Around the base of the mountain are exhibits on ski patrol, ski lifts, and snowmaking technology.

Admission: Free.

Open: Summer, daily 9am–5pm; call for winter hours.

SPORTS & RECREATION

A majority of recreational pursuits in the Fraser Valley area are undertaken in **Arapahoe National Forest** (tel. 887-3331).

ALPINE SLIDE   Colorado's longest alpine slide, at 1½ miles, thrills summer visitors to Winter Park Resort (tel. 726-5514).

BICYCLING   As a mountain-biking center, Winter Park has won national recognition for its expansive trail system and established race program. Many of the off-road bike trails connect to 600 miles of backcountry roads and trails in the adjacent national forest. The King of the Rockies Off-Road Stage Race, held each year in August, is one of the top professional mountain-bike races in America; part of it is run on the 30-mile Tipperary Creek Trail, generally considered Colorado's best mountain-bike trail.

Bike rentals and repairs are available at numerous locations, including Winter Park Sports Shop, Kings Crossing Shopping Center, Winter Park Drive at Kings Crossing Road and Winter Park Ski Shop, Ltd., at the foot of the ski slopes (tel. 303/726-5554 or toll free 800/222-7547), and Europa Sports, Gasthaus Eichler, Winter Park Drive at Vasquez Creek (tel. 303/726-5133 or toll free 800/543-3899). For specific information on trails and races, call the Winter Park/Fraser Valley Chamber of Commerce (tel. 726-4118, ext. 4).

BOATING   The Arapahoe National Recreation Area, 30 miles north via U.S. 34, has marinas on three large lakes—Lake Granby, Shadow Mountain Reservoir, and Grand Lake. See "An Easy Excursion from Estes Park," above, for details.

FISHING   Fraser Valley and surrounding Grand County are renowned among anglers. Head to Williams Fork Reservoir and the Three Lakes District for kokanee salmon, lake trout, brookies, and browns. Fishing ponds stocked with various species are in Fraser, across from the Fraser Valley Center on U.S. Highway 40. The upper pond is reserved for children and people in wheelchairs; the lower pond is open to everyone. Ponds are opened and stocked by mid-May.

GOLF   Pole Creek Golf Course, 11 miles northwest of Winter Park on U.S. Highway 40 (tel. 726-8847), considered among the finest mountain courses in the state, continues to be highly rated by *Golf Digest* magazine. Mountain views on the Ron Kirby/Gary Player–designed course are terrific. There's also a full-service pro shop, driving range, lessons, club rentals, and a restaurant.

HIKING & BACKPACKING   Check with Arapahoe National Forest (tel. 887-3331) for trail maps and other information. Beautiful Rocky Mountain National Park (see "Estes Park," above) is less than an hour's drive north.

HORSEBACK RIDING   Several stables offer rides into Arapahoe National Forest (tel. 887-3331). Check with the Horses at Beavers (tel. 726-9247) or Broken Spur Stables (tel. 887-2152).

ICE SKATING   There's ice skating on outdoor rinks at Meadowridge Resort (tel. 726-4253) and Fraser Valley Elementary School (tel. 726-4708), both in Fraser. Rentals are available; call for hours. Another rink is open to the public at Snow Mountain Ranch–YMCA of the Rockies, Tabernash (tel. 887-2152).

RIVER RAFTING   Half-day, full-day, and multiday trips on the Colorado,

Arkansas, Eagle, North Platte, and other rivers are offered by numerous local outfitters, including Colorado River Runs (tel. toll free 800/826-1081), Mad Adventures (tel. 303/726-5290 or toll free 800/451-4844), Raven Adventure Trips (toll free 800/332-3381). Adult rates start around $55 for a full day.

RODEO Every Saturday night for eight weeks, beginning the Fourth of July weekend, the High Country Stampede Rodeos hold forth at Fraser's John Work Arena (tel. 726-4118, ext. 4). Professional and top amateur cowboys compete in bronco riding, calf roping, and other events. A barbecue precedes the rodeo.

ROLLER SKATING There's public roller skating at the Snow Mountain Ranch–YMCA of the Rockies (tel. 887-2152).

SKIING [ALPINE] The Winter Park Resort (see "Attractions," above) isn't the only mecca for winter-sports enthusiasts. Alpine skiers, for instance, have a nearby small resort to explore.

Silver Creek Ski Area, U.S. 40, Granby (tel. 303/887-3384 or toll free 800/448-9458), is a small family-oriented area mainly known for its beginner's area and intermediate slopes. With a 1,000-foot vertical drop to a base elevation of 8,200 feet, it is served by three double chairs and a triple chair. Full-day tickets are $26 for adults, $12 for juniors (6 to 12) and seniors (60 to 69). Under 6 and over 69 ski free. Equipment rentals start at $12 for adults, $8 for children. Special beginner lesson/lift/rental packages run $36.

See "Skiing (Nordic)," below for additional sources of equipment rentals.

SKIING [NORDIC] The outstanding cross-country skiing in the Fraser Valley area is highlighted by what the *Denver Post* calls "the best touring center in Colorado." The Devil's Thumb–Idlewild Cross-Country Centers have more than 90km (56 miles) of groomed trails linking Ski Idlewild, in the town of Winter Park (tel. 726-5564), with the Devil's Thumb Ranch, on Grand County Road 83, 6½ miles north of Fraser (tel. 726-8231). Full rentals and instruction are available at both centers, along with guided 6-hour backcountry tours and a telemark hill at Devil's Thumb.

Trail fees for adults are $8 for a full day; children 6 to 12 and seniors, $5 for a full day; under 6, free. Full-day rentals, including trail pass, are $15 for adults, $12 for children and seniors, $7 for children under 6. Group lessons are $15 for adults, $12 for children and seniors, including the trail fee.

Snow Mountain Ranch–YMCA Nordic Center, on U.S. 40 between Tabernash and Granby (tel. 887-2152), features 65km (40 miles) of groomed trails for all abilities, including 3km (2 miles) of lighted track for night skiing. The trail fee is $6 for adults ($4 for Y members), $2 for children 6 to 12. Rentals are $10 for adults, $5 for children.

For other Nordic opportunities, talk to local ski shops or Arapahoe National Forest (tel. 887-3331).

Rental equipment for downhill or cross-country skiing can be obtained from more than a dozen outlets in the Winter Park area, including Flanagan's Ski Rentals, U.S. 40, Winter Park (tel. 726-4412 or toll free 800/544-1523); and Sport Stalker, U.S. 40 at Cooper Creek Square (tel. 726-8873 or toll free 800/525-5520).

SLEIGH RIDES Opportunities abound for horse-drawn sleigh rides. Jim's Sleigh Rides (tel. 726-5527) takes you through woods and meadows along the Fraser River on a 1¼-hour trip, at a cost of $12 for adults and $9 for children 12 and under. Sleigh rides are also provided by Ray's Sleighs, at Devil's Thumb Ranch (tel. 887-3114); and Broken Spur Ranch and Stables (tel. 887-2152, ext. 4146).

For sleigh rides that end up at elaborate dinners, call Dashing Through the Snow Sleigh Rides (tel. 726-5376); or Dinner at the Barn (tel. 726-4923).

Dog Sled Rides of Winter Park (tel. 725-3508) offers unique sled rides, pulled by teams of Siberian huskies, through the beautiful Arapaho National Forest. Cost is $80, based on two people per sled.

SNOWMOBILING Snowmobile rentals and guided tours are offered by Trailblazer Snowmobile Tours, Fraser Valley Tubing Hill (tel. 303/726-8452 or toll free 800/669-0134). Boots and helmets are provided. Rates are about $35 an hour.

SWIMMING   There are public pools at the Snowblaze Athletic Club, Winter Park (tel. 726-9342 or 726-5701), with a $5 daily walk-in fee, which includes full club usage; and the Snow Mountain Ranch–YMCA of the Rockies, Tabernash (tel. 887-2152), which charges $3 for a non-YMCA-member day pass.

TENNIS   Public tennis courts can be found at the Fraser Community Center, Fraser (tel. 726-4708).

TUBING [SNOW]   The Fraser Valley Tubing Hill, Fraser (tel. 726-5954), offers a return to childhood for many adults. For $8 an hour by day, $9 an hour by night (for additional hours, subtract $1 from first hour's rate), you can slide down a steep hill in a big inner tube. Open Monday through Friday from 4 to 10pm and on Saturday, Sunday, and holidays from 10am to 10pm.

MISCELLANEOUS   Children and adults alike enjoy getting lost and found at the A'Maze Labyrinth 'n' Grill's human maze, Safeway Center, U.S. 40, Winter Park (tel. 726-9555). There are also miniature golf, video games, and food.

EVENING ENTERTAINMENT

Several outstanding music events are hosted in summer at Winter Park Resort. The **American Music Festival** (the third weekend of July), and the **Winter Park Jazz Festival** (the third weekend of July) all draw nationally known performing artists, including Bonnie Raitt, Lyle Lovett, Wynton Marsalis, David Sanborn, and Harry Connick, Jr.

There's live music and dancing at the **Slope,** on U.S. 40 half a mile from the ski resort (tel. 726-5727); rock disco with occasional country-and-western bands at the **Stampede,** Cooper Creek Square (tel. 726-9433); and live rock music Wednesday through Saturday nights at the **Crooked Creek Saloon** in downtown Fraser (tel. 726-9250).

First-run movies are presented nightly at the **Silver Screen Cinema** (tel. 726-5390). Tickets cost $5 for adults, $3 for children under 13 and senior citizens.

WHERE TO STAY

There are more than 100 accommodation properties in the Fraser Valley, including hotels, condominiums, family-style mountain inns (serving breakfast and dinner daily), European Plan lodges, and motels. Bookings can be made by **Winter Park Central Reservations,** P.O. Box 36, Winter Park, CO 80482 (tel. 303/726-5587, 303/447-0588 in Denver, or toll free 800/453-2525). The agency can also book air-and-rail tickets, rental cars, airport transfers, lift tickets, ski-school lessons, ski rentals, and many other activities.

Ski-season rates vary according to skier traffic. Although there are slight differences in seasonal definitions among accommodations, most have their highest rates during the 2-week Christmas–New Year's period (referred to here as "Christmas"). Next busiest is "peak" season (February and March), followed by "value" season (most of January) and "low" season (mid-November to mid-December and early to mid-April, when the area closes). "Summer" season runs from mid-April to mid-November, though many accommodations close their doors during the April to May "mud season" and again mid-October to mid-November. There's some gray area from lodge to lodge about where one "season" ends and another "begins," so confirm rates before booking.

EXPENSIVE

C LAZY U RANCH, Colo. 125 (P.O. Box 378), Granby, CO 80446. Tel. 303/887-3344. 18 rms, 21 cottages (all with bath).
$ Rates (including full board): Early June to late Sept (weekly), $1,325–$1,600 single, $2,125–$2,385 double. Christmas (6–7 night minimum), $1,200–$2,300 single; $1,075–$1,500 double. Jan–Mar (2 night minimum), $163–$225 single; $106–$174 double. **Closed:** Late Sept to Dec 21 and Apr 1–May 30.
Regarded by some as the finest guest ranch in the United States, the C Lazy U offers a

little of everything for summer-and-winter visitors. Located 7½ miles northwest of Granby on Willow Creek, a rich trout-fishing stream, it's a great place for riding enthusiasts: You get your own horse for a week! Included in the rates are riding instruction and trail rides with a real western wrangler.

Ranch accommodations include 18 lodge rooms, 20 two-bedroom cottages or duplexes, and a three-bedroom cottage. All have full or three-quarter baths; some have fireplaces. No pets are permitted.

Dining/Entertainment: Full gourmet meals are served in the dining room to guests only, and there's a cocktail lounge. Country-and-western bands, square dancing, staff shows, and cookouts are occasional features.

Services: Children's and teenagers' program; nature program.

Facilities: Heated swimming pool, Jacuzzi, sauna, tennis and racquetball courts, skeet-shooting range, ice skating, cross-country ski trails, children's playground; guest laundry.

MODERATE

THE INN AT SILVER CREEK, U.S. 40 (P.O. Box 4222), Silver Creek, CO 80446. Tel. 303/887-2131 or toll free 800/926-4386. 223 rms, 119 suites (all with bath). A/C TV TEL
$ Rates: Summer and peak season, $49 single or double; $128 suite. Christmas, $129 single or double; $218 suite. Low-and-value seasons, $37 single or double; $98 suite. AE, CB, DC, DISC, MC, V.

This outstanding year-round resort is located 15 miles north of Winter Park and 2 miles southeast of Granby. It's becoming a popular conference location with its meeting area, fine restaurants, all-seasons athletic facilities, and a full range of services.

Every room is luxurious, with a whirlpool and steam cabinet in the bath. Each unit has a full deck or balcony and cable TV with in-room movies. Third-floor rooms and suites have vaulted ceilings, skylights, and lofts. Suites and efficiencies have a fireplace, wet bar (with refrigerator and microwave), and dining-and-living areas.

IRON HORSE RESORT RETREAT, 257 Winter Park Dr. (P.O. Box 1286), Winter Park, CO 80482. Tel. 303/726-8851 or toll free 800/621-8190. 76 rms, 44 suites (all with bath). A/C TV TEL
$ Rates (single or double): Peak season, $110 lodge room; $145 studio; $225–$320 one-bedroom; $295–$390 two-bedroom. Christmas, $150 lodge room; $205 studio; $320–$415 one-bedroom; $395–$510 two-bedroom. Value season, $100 lodge room; $115 studio; $170–$265 one-bedroom; $245–$315 two-bedroom. Low-season, $75 lodge room; $85 studio; $125–$195 one-bedroom; $185–$230 two-bedroom. Summer, $60–$65 lodge room; $75–$80 studio; $95–$130 one-bedroom; $125–$160 two-bedroom. AE, CB, DC, DISC, MC, V.
Parking: Free, underground.

Billing itself as Winter Park's only ski-in/ski-out lodging, the Iron Horse—so named for its proximity to the Rio Grande Railroad that serves the resort—can be reached via a bridge off the ski (or summer bike) trail from Mary Jane Mountain to the Winter Park base. Most folks, however, make their first visit to this fine hotel by road.

Every unit has a kitchen with microwave, a private deck or balcony, a fireplace (with wood provided daily), and cable color television. The light southwestern decor and handsome wood furnishings feel right at home in the pine forests. There are one- and two-bedroom suites, as well as 16 Premium Suites with wet bars, washer/dryers, jetted tubs, skylights, and a 10-person dining area.

The resort offers a full range of services as well as dining, athletic, and meeting-room facilities.

SNOWBLAZE, U.S. 40 (P.O. Box 66), Winter Park, CO 80482. Tel. 303/726-5701 or toll free 800/525-2466. 73 units.
$ Rates (single or double): Low-season, $77 studio; $155 two-bedroom; $180 three-bedroom. Value season, $98 studio; $198 two-bedroom; $265 three-bedroom. Pre-Christmas, $124 studio; $237 two-bedroom; $316 three-bedroom. Christmas, $196 studio; $383 two-bedroom; $506 three-bedroom. Summer, $70

studio; $99 two-bedroom; $130 three-bedroom (additional summer discounts certain months). AE, CB, DC, MC, V.

One of Winter Park's more prestigious condominium developments, Snowblaze features the Fraser Valley's leading athletic club on site. The units are in downtown Winter Park, 1½ miles from the ski area by shuttle. All rooms have full baths (one per bedroom), fully equipped kitchens, electric stoves and/or microwaves, and color TVs. Two- and three-bedroom units also have fireplaces (with wood provided) and private dry saunas. All have simple but handsome decor, with big picture windows and rich wood furnishings. Winter Park Adventures, the property management firm for Snowblaze, has 14 other area properties and a variety of packages.

THE VINTAGE, 100 Winter Park Dr. (P.O. Box 1369), Winter Park, CO 80482. Tel. 303/726-8801 or toll free 800/472-7017. Fax 303/726-9230. 101 rms, 20 suites (all with bath). A/C TV TEL

$ Rates: Summer, $75–$85 studio; $85–$160 suite. Winter, $110–$120 studio; $145–$475 suite. AE, DC, DISC, MC, V.

Châteaulike, the Vintage rises five stories above the foot of Winter Park's ski slopes, not far from the Mary Jane base facilities. A full-service resort hotel, it offers convenient access, excellent dining and atmosphere, and luxury accommodations. Every room in the hotel has a view of either the Winter Park slopes or the Continental Divide. Even the studio efficiencies have fireplaces and kitchens, as well as cable television. Birch furnishings accent light-pastel appointments to yield a modern mountain atmosphere.

The hotel offers a full range of services as well as athletic-and-meeting facilities.

INEXPENSIVE

DEVIL'S THUMB RANCH RESORT, Grand County Rd. 83 (P.O. Box 21, Winter Park, CO 80482), Tabernash, CO 80478. Tel. 303/726-5632 or toll free 800/933-4339. 21 rms (all with bath), 2 cabins, 2 dormitories.

$ Rates: Winter, $65–$130 single; $84–$130 double; $140–$170 cabin single or double; $28 dorm bed. Summer, $45–$105 single; $50–$105 double; $105–$130 cabin single or double; $20 dorm bed. JCB, MC, V.

This is the sort of place that attracts outdoor sports lovers by droves. Established in 1937, the ranch—eight miles north of Winter Park—is as famous today for its cross-country skiing in winter (see "Sports & Recreation" in "What to See & Do," above) as for its horseback riding and mountain biking in summer. Accommodations are available for all pocketbooks, from a honeymoon cabin with a four-poster lodgepole pine bed to eight-bed dormitory rooms in the Bunkhouse. Most guests stay in the elegant log Elk Lodge, where they have cozy rooms with private baths, and access to a spa, sauna, TV, and billiards room. The Ranch House Restaurant and Saloon lure Winter Park residents for regional cuisine at moderate prices.

ENGELMANN PINES, 1035 Cranmer Ave. (P.O. Box 1305), Winter Park, CO 80482. Tel. 303/726-4632, or toll free 800/992-9512. 6 rms (2 with bath).

$ Rates (including full breakfast): Winter, $75–$85 shared bath; $95 private bath. Summer, $65–$75 shared bath; $85 private bath. AE, MC, V.

Antique furnishings add a country touch to this contemporary home outside Winter Park. Heinz and Margaret Engel serve Swiss confections and other treats around their large fireplace in winter, and invite guests to catch the free shuttle to the ski resort or from the Amtrak station. In summer, mountain bikers and hikers appreciate the same trailhead across the street that cross-country skiers use in winter. Guests have full use of the kitchen. Some rooms have Jacuzzis and balconies. No smoking or pets are allowed, and children are welcome.

GÄSTHAUS EICHLER, 78786 U.S. 40 at Vasquez Creek (P.O. Box 430), Winter Park, CO 80482. Tel. 303/726-5133 or toll free 800/543-3899. 15 rms (all with bath). TV TEL

$ Rates: Summer, $25–$35 per person per unit, double occupancy. Winter,

$55–$75 per person per unit, double occupancy. AE, DC, MC, V. **Closed:** Mid-Apr to May.

When Hans and Hannelore Eichler moved to Colorado from their hometown of Duisburg, Germany, they brought with them their concept of what an alpine *Gästhaus* ought to be like. The charm of this small inn is exactly what you'd expect to find at a European resort. Lace curtains and down comforters grace each room, and private whirlpool baths are available. The Eichlers' daughter Anke and her husband, Kurt, manage Europa Sports on the premises, and the Gästhaus Eichler Restaurant is an unforgettable experience.

SNOW MOUNTAIN RANCH—YMCA OF THE ROCKIES, U.S. 40 near Tabernash (P.O. Box 169), Winter Park, CO 80482. Tel. 303/887-2152 or 303/443-4743 in Denver. 178 lodge rms, 40 cabins, 53 campsites.
$ Rates: $30–$57 lodge room; $100–$204 cabin (sleeping 5–12). Camping $12–$16. Weekly rates. No credit cards.

This YMCA ranch, and a sister property outside Estes Park, are enormously popular among Denverites and other Rocky Mountain–area residents. The ranch offers both bunk beds in lodge rooms—some with full baths, others with central showers—and housekeeping cabins of two to five bedrooms with fireplaces. YMCA membership is required, and will be sold by the ranch for a nominal additional charge. Facilities here include two restaurants, a gift shop, coin-op laundry, indoor swimming pool, tennis court, ice-skating rink, cross-country skiing/mountain bike trails, horse stables, hay/sleigh rides, and a playground.

SOMETHING SPECIAL, A Country Home Bed & Breakfast, 1848 Grand County Rd. 83 (P.O. Box 800), Winter Park, CO 80482. Tel. 303/726-5360. 3 rms (1 with bath).
$ Rates (including breakfast): Summer, $60–$70; winter, $70–$85. AE.

Located on 14 wooded acres near Devil's Thumb Ranch, 8 miles north of Winter Park, this quaint bed-and-breakfast is the home of Noel Wilson, widow of former Winter Park Ski School director Bill Wilson. Noel has three cozy rooms, one with a private bath, available year-round; she offers spectacular views, plus down comforters, an outdoor cookout area, and complimentary evening refreshments. Guests may use the kitchen, but no smoking is permitted.

WOODSPUR, Van Anderson Dr. (P.O. Box 249), Winter Park, CO 80482. Tel. 303/726-8417 or toll free 800/626-6562. 32 rms (all with bath).
$ Rates: Nov–Apr (including breakfast and dinner), $77 single; $134 double; $37 children 5–11 in room with parents. May–Oct (including continental breakfast), $39 single; $56 double; $22 children 5–11 in room with parents. Special rates for three or more in room. MC, V.

A rustic mountain lodge off Vasquez Road, the Woodspur has all the earmarks of a classic ski lodge. Most rooms have queen-size or double beds and either two or four single bunks, encouraging sharing by groups of young people. They've all got private baths, but only a dozen rooms (those without bunk beds) have tubs; most have showers only. Winter rates include home-cooked dinners as well as breakfasts. Guests share a gigantic stone fireplace, library, recreation room, outdoor Jacuzzi, sauna, and frontier-style bar.

BUDGET

HOSTELLING INTERNATIONAL—WINTER PARK AYH, opposite Cooper Creek Square, U.S. 40 (P.O. Box 3323), Winter Park, CO 80482. Tel. 726-5356. 6 rms (none with bath).
$ Rates: Winter, $11 for Youth Hostel Association members, $14 for nonmembers; summer, $8 for members, $10 for nonmembers. MC, V.

Six large mobile homes contain rooms with two to six bunk beds each, as well as three rooms with double beds for couples. Everyone shares the living room, four kitchens, and baths. There's no curfew or age restrictions, but you'll have to reserve ahead in winter, July, and August.

WHERE TO DINE

EXPENSIVE

GÄSTHAUS EICHLER, U.S. 40 at Vasquez Creek. Tel. 726-5133.

Cuisine: GERMAN. **Reservations:** Recommended.

$ **Prices:** Dinner, appetizers $5.95–$9.50; main courses $12.95–$30. AE, DC, MC, V.

Open: Breakfast daily 7:30–10am; lunch daily 11:30am–2pm; dinner daily 5–9pm. **Closed:** Mid-Apr through May.

A delightful Teutonic atmosphere dominates this outstanding restaurant, located on the bottom floor of a European-style pension. Start your gourmet dinner with baked Camembert or traditional potato pancakes. Then contemplate which of the house specialties you'll try: Rindsrouladen (stuffed rolled beef with red cabbage); Jägerschnitzel (pork in a mushroom-and-onion sauce), or Huhner ragoût (chicken simmered in chardonnay). Be sure to leave room for a strudel!

RESTAURANT ON THE RIDGE, Meadow Ridge Resort Clubhouse, Fraser. Tel. 726-4000.

Cuisine: STEAK/SEAFOOD. **Reservations:** Recommended.

$ **Prices:** Appetizers $5–$7.50; main courses $5–$10 at lunch, $8–$25 at dinner. AE, MC, V.

Open: Mon–Sat 11am–10pm, Sun 9:30am–1pm and 5–10pm.

Spacious but intimate, casual but elegant, this restaurant occupies the glass-enclosed dining room and outdoor deck of a condominium-complex clubhouse in Fraser. The cuisine is an interesting blend of continental (chicken Oscar, fettuccine carbonara), steaks (sirloin, New York strip), and seafood (Alaskan king crab, fresh fish). There are terrific views of the mountains.

SOUFFLES, Park Place Shopping Center, U.S. 40. Tel. 726-9404.

Cuisine: CREATIVE CONTINENTAL. **Reservations:** Recommended.

$ **Prices:** Appetizers $6.75–$7.50; main courses $9.50–$24.50. AE, MC, V.

Open: Nov 15–Apr 15, dinner only, daily 4–10pm. **Closed:** Apr 16–Nov 14.

It's a shame this restaurant is open only five months a year, because nonskiers never get a chance to experience it. Oil candles cast their glow through intimate dining rooms, and impressionist paintings of ski slopes adorn the walls. Light jazz is piped through the dining area, while 1960s music livens the adjacent lounge. Dessert? Order a hot soufflé, of course.

MODERATE

THE LAST WALTZ, King's Cross Shopping Center, U.S. 40. Tel. 726-4877.

Cuisine: AMERICAN/MEXICAN.

$ **Prices:** Breakfast $2.95–$6.95; lunch $2.75–$6.95; dinner appetizers $3.25–$6.75, main courses $5.95–$14.95. AE, CB, DC, DISC, MC, V.

Open: Daily 7am–9pm.

A favorite place for locals who enjoy good home-cooking, this café treads the line between cultures at every meal: flapjacks, lox and bagels, or migas (a south-of-the-border egg scramble) for breakfast; Cajun-blackened ham, Rocky Mountain Reuben, or quesadilla (Mexican cheese) sandwiches for lunch. In the evening, you'll have to decide between crabmeat enchiladas and the like, or swear your allegiance to a honey-and-pecan fried chicken, pork chops, fish-and-chips, or a 12-ounce rib-eye steak. Children's and senior's portions available.

DENO'S SWISS HOUSE, U.S. 40, downtown Winter Park. Tel. 726-5332.

Cuisine: BISTRO.

$ **Prices:** Appetizers $2.95–$9.95; main courses $5.25–$19.95. AE, MC, V.

Open: Daily 11am–11pm.

Locals frequent and visitors always seem to find this self-proclaimed "mountain bistro" on Winter Park's main drag. With its casual atmosphere and impressive bar scroll—75 national-and-international beers, over 300 varietal wines—it might be written off as a pub. But the cuisine is indeed gourmet: pasta dishes such as angel hair with wild mushrooms, a New York steak with Gorgonzola-brandy sauce, fresh fish, and chicken or veal marsala. There's a good choice of sandwiches, pizzas, and salads, 3 to 5pm and late night.

DOUGALS RESTAURANT, in the Silverado II Hotel, 380 Alpine Vista. Tel. 726-8732.

Cuisine: AMERICAN. **Reservations:** Recommended.

$ Prices: Breakfast buffet $5.50; dinner appetizers $5.50–$7.95; dinner main courses $4.95–$15.95. AE, MC, V.

Open: Winter, breakfast daily 7:30–10:30am; dinner daily 5–10pm. Summer, dinner Tues–Sun 5:30–9:30pm.

Family-style dining with real mashed potatoes, country gravy and hot biscuits are the trademark of this popular restaurant. You can get a complete dinner, such as fried chicken, veal parmesan, trout amandine, or prime rib, complete with every extra you can think of, including dessert. Or, from the à la carte menu, you can order chicken potpie, stew, or a hamburger. There are nightly specials and children's portions.

INEXPENSIVE

BEV'S BUNNERY, Park Place Center. U.S. 40. Tel. 726-5774.

Cuisine: BAKERY/DELI.

$ Prices: Breakfast $1.75–$4.95; lunch $1.25–$4.95. MC, V.

Open: Daily 7am–8pm.

You can't come to Bev's without trying the home-baked breads—such as Bavarian farmers rye, six grain, or wheat-and-honey Müsli. Enjoy large omelettes, french toast, hot homemade soup, or a thick deli-style sandwich. And leave room for one of Bev's scrumptious desserts.

CROOKED CREEK SALOON & EATERY, U.S. 40, Fraser. Tel. 726-9250.

Cuisine: AMERICAN/MEXICAN.

$ Prices: Breakfast $1.95–$5.95; lunch $2.95–$7.95; dinner appetizers $1.50–$5.95, main courses $3.95–$14.95. MC, V.

Open: Daily 7am–10pm (bar, Mon–Sat 7am–2am, Sun 7am–midnight).

The Fraser Valley's favorite drinking spot, the Crooked Creek is opening eyes with biscuits and gravy, an egg burrito, and steak and eggs, while its late-night crowd is still in dreamland. You can get an Awesome Fatboy Burger (10 oz. of ground beef) and a variety of chicken sandwiches most anytime, or St. Louis style ribs, panfried trout, or London broil after 5pm.

---

4. SUMMIT COUNTY

67 miles W of Denver, 114 miles NW of Colorado Springs, 23 miles E of Vail

GETTING THERE **By Plane** Visitors fly into Denver International Airport, and continue to Frisco, Breckenridge, Keystone, and/or Copper Mountain via shuttle. Resort Express (tel. 303/468-7600 or toll free 800/334-7433), and Vans to Breckenridge (tel. 303/668-5466 or toll free 800/222-2112) offer shuttles; People's Choice Transportation (tel. 303/659-7780 or toll free outside Colorado 800/777-2388) offers luxury transport to Summit County resorts.

By Bus Greyhound (tel. 303/468-1938) makes stops in Frisco, Copper Mountain, and Keystone.

By Car I-70 runs through the middle of Summit County. For Keystone, exit on U.S. 6 at Dillon; the resort is 6 miles east of the interchange. For Breckenridge, exit on Colo. 9 at the county seat of Frisco; the resort town is 10 miles south. Copper Mountain is right on I-70 at the Colo. 91 interchange.

SPECIAL EVENTS Summit County offers the following events: the Ullr Fest, on the third week of January, in Breckenridge; the Ski Fiesta, on the fourth Saturday of February, in Keystone; the John Elway Celebrity Ski Race and Eenie Weenie Bikini Contest, over the first weekend of April, in Copper Mountain; the Beachin' at the Basin Spring Skiing Blowout, over the Memorial Day weekend, in Arapahoe Basin; the Keystone Music Festival, from late June to mid-August, in Keystone; the National Festival of Music at Breckenridge from late June through late August; Michael Martin Murphey's West Fest, over Labor Day weekend, in Copper Mountain; the Breckenridge Festival of Film, in the third week of September, in Breckenridge; Frisco Founders Day, on the third weekend of September, in Frisco; and the American International Snow Sculpture Championships, during the third week of January, in Breckenridge.

Summit County boomed during the late 19th-century silver and gold rushes. The single largest gold nugget ever found in Colorado—13 pounds, 7 ounces—was uncovered in 1887 by Breckenridge miner Tom Groves. Copper Mountain gained a reputation for the copper ore it produced around the same time, and Frisco was home to 3,500 miners, 19 dance halls, and 20 saloons. Dillon, relocated from its original townsite (flooded by the construction of Dillon Reservoir), once boasted the world's longest and highest ski jump. Historical sites throughout the county are readily shown by the Summit County and Frisco historical societies.

The economy of modern Summit County is tied to the growth in recreational sports—skiing in the winter; fishing, hiking, and biking in the summer—and to the real-estate boom that has accompanied it. Though skiers began coming to Arapahoe Basin in 1945 and to Loveland, just outside the county, in 1955, the winter-sports boom truly began with the opening of Breckenridge resort in 1961. Keystone opened in 1969 and Copper Mountain in 1972, putting five ski resorts within a 10-mile radius of Dillon Reservoir. Resort expansion and community growth continues today.

ORIENTATION

Summit County's elevation at Dillon Reservoir is 9,015 feet; Keystone is at 9,300 feet, Breckenridge at 9,600 feet, and Copper Mountain Village at 9,700 feet. Full-time population of the county is about 5,000, some 25% of whom live in the county seat of Frisco.

INFORMATION The main source of visitor information for the entire region is the Summit County Chamber of Commerce, P.O. Box 214, Frisco, CO 80443 (tel. 303/668-0376 or 668-5800). The chamber has an information center at the junction of Colo. 9 and U.S. 6 (Summit Boulevard at Main Street), en route from I-70 to Breckenridge.

For additional information on the resort communities, contact the Breckenridge Resort Chamber, 309 N. Main St. (P.O. Box 1909), Breckenridge, CO 80424 (tel. 303/453-6018; for central reservations toll free 800/800-BREC or 800/221-1091); for information and reservations for activities in Breckenridge, contact the Activity Center (tel. 303/453-5579); the Copper Mountain Resort Chamber, P.O. Box 3003, Copper Mountain, CO 80443 (tel. 303/968-6477); Keystone Resort, P.O. Box 38, Keystone, CO 80435 (tel. 303/468-2316; or toll free outside Colorado 800/525-1309, within Colorado 800/222-0188); or the Lake Dillon Resort Association, P.O. Box 446, Dillon, CO 80435 (tel. 303/468-6222 or toll free 800/365-6365).

COUNTY LAYOUT The heart of Summit County is Dillon Reservoir, its arms reaching like an octopus to the southwest, where the county seat, Frisco, is located; to the south, pointing directly up the Blue River toward Breckenridge; to the north, site of the town of Dillon; and to the east, up U.S. 6, the artery to Keystone, Arapahoe Basin, and Loveland Pass. I-70 follows the western shore of the lake, separating Dillon from Silverthorne at the top end and swinging past Copper Mountain (six miles south of Frisco) before climbing over Vail Pass.

GETTING AROUND

Summit Stage (tel. 453-1241 or 453-1339) provides *free* year-round service between Frisco, Dillon, Silverthorne, Keystone, Breckenridge, and Copper Mountain, daily from 6:30am to 11:30pm mid-June to mid-September; shorter hours the rest of the year. Expresses serve all destinations but Silverthorne during peak travel hours.

Taxi service is provided by **Around Town Taxi** (tel. 453-TAXI) in Breckenridge. You can get around Breckenridge on the free **Town Trolley** (tel. 453-2251), and there's also free shuttle service within the Keystone Resort (tel. 453-5241).

FAST FACTS

The **area code** for all of Summit County is 303. In case of **emergency,** call 911; for regular business, call the Summit County Sheriff (tel. 453-2232). **Hospitals** include the Provenant Medical Center at Summit, 0038 County Rd. 1030, Frisco (tel. 668-3300), and the Breckenridge Medical Center, Village at Breckenridge Resort, 555 S. Park St., Plaza II, Breckenridge (tel. 453-9000). **Post offices** are at 65 W. Main St., Frisco (tel. 668-5505), and 300 S. Ridge St., Breckenridge (tel. 453-2310). State and county **taxes** add 9.45% to hotel bills. For **weather** and **road conditions,** call 453-1090.

WHAT TO SEE & DO

ATTRACTIONS

BRECKENRIDGE SKI AREA, Breckenridge Ski Corporation, P.O. Box 1058, Breckenridge, CO 80424. Tel. 303/453-5000 or 303/453-6118 for 24-hour ski conditions.

Spread across four large mountains on the west side of the town of Breckenridge, this area ranks third in size among Colorado's ski resorts. Once known for its wealth of open, groomed beginner-and-intermediate slopes, Breckenridge in recent years has expanded its acreage for expert skiers as well.

Peak 8, the original ski mountain, is highest of the three at 12,998 feet and has the greatest variety. **Peak 9,** heavily geared to novices and intermediates, rises above the principal base area. **Peak 10,** served by a single quad chair, is predominantly expert territory. The vast back bowls of Peak 8, and the North Face of Peak 9, are likewise advanced terrain. There are restaurants high on Peaks 8 and 9, and three cafeterias at the base of the slopes. A fourth ski mountain, Peak 7, is scheduled to open in 1994.

All told, the resort has 1,900 skiable acres, with 126 trails served by 16 lifts—four high-speed quad superchairs, one triple chair, eight double chairs, and three surface lifts for beginners—for an uphill capacity of 24,430 skiers per hour. Available vertical is 3,398 feet; average annual snowfall is 255 inches (over 21 feet).

Among Breckenridge's more interesting programs are its **Women's Ski Seminars,** taught exclusively by women for women skiers of all abilities. Four such seminars are offered during the year, over 3-day weekends in December, January, February, and March. "Women only" ski-school classes are available throughout the ski year.

Admission: Full-day lift ticket, $39 a day adults, to as low as $30 a day for multiday tickets; $18 a day children 6–12 and seniors 60–69; free for children under 6 and seniors over 69. Full-day class lessons, $39.

Open: Third Sat of Nov to the third Sun of Apr, daily 8:30am–3:45pm. **Closed** (for skiing): Last week of Apr to third week of Nov.

COPPER MOUNTAIN RESORT, P.O. Box 3001, Copper Mountain, CO 80443. Tel. 303/968-2318 or toll free 800/458-8386; or 303/968-2100 or toll free 800/457-5429 for snow report.

From Copper Mountain village, the avalanche chutes on the west face of Ten Mile Mountain seem to spell out the word SKI. Though this is a natural coincidence, Arapaho National Forest officials like to say that Copper has "terrain created for skiing."

What makes Copper special is its topography, naturally dividing the mountain into beginner, intermediate, and expert areas. The "American Flyer" lift serves the gentle novice runs on the lower slopes of 12,313-foot **Union Peak,** up to the right of the main day lodge, while the "American Eagle" climbs to the intermediate trails on the western flank of 12,360-foot **Copper Peak.** The eastern flank of Copper Peak drops off more sharply, and it is here, and in the high-altitude Spaulding and Resolution bowls, that most of the expert terrain lies.

The area has a vertical drop of 2,760 feet and 1,330 patrolled acres of skiing, with an additional 350 acres open to guided "extreme" skiing. The 96 trails are served by 20 lifts—two high-speed quad superchairs, six triple chairs, eight double chairs, and four beginners' surface lifts—for an uphill capacity of 28,250 skiers per hour. The average annual snowfall is 255 inches (21 feet, 3 inches).

There are two restaurants on the mountain, and several more in the base village. Also at the base are 25km (15 miles) of cross-country track, an ice-skating pond, a full-service racquet and athletic club, and other amenities of a totally self-contained resort village.

Admission: Tickets, $37 a day adults, to as low as $30 a day for multiday tickets; $16 a day children 12 and under, $23 a day seniors 60–69; free for seniors over 70 and children 3 and under. Equipment rentals average $19 a day; full-day class lessons start at $37. AE, DC, DISC, MC, V.

Open: Mid-Nov to late Apr, Mon–Fri 9am–4pm, Sat–Sun 8:30am–4pm. **Closed:** Late Apr to mid-Nov.

KEYSTONE RESORT, P.O. Box 38, Keystone, CO 80435. Tel. 303/468-2316 or toll free 800/222-0188; or 303/468-4111 for snow report.

Keystone is not only a superb mountain for intermediate skiers, it's also the single largest night-skiing mountain in America. It's possible to take the gondola to dinner in the Summit House atop 11,640-foot Keystone Mountain, then spend several hours working off your meal on 13 cruising trails, some as long as 3 miles.

The resort here (see "Where to Stay," below) was built from the ground up, and ski-area development has proceeded in much the same fashion. Spacious **Keystone Mountain** offers 599 acres of intermediate terrain and ample beginner slopes. Over its back side are **North Peak** and the **Outback** region, both with advanced intermediate and expert runs. A second gondola now connects the Summit House with the Outpost, a new restaurant atop 11,660-foot North Peak. Keystone also manages **Arapahoe Basin** (see "Sports & Recreation," below), 5 miles distant.

Keystone's vertical drop is 2,340 feet; the North Peak/Outback complex has 1,920 of its own. Together, they offer 1,737 acres of skiing, 89 trails, and 19 lifts—including two connecting high-speed gondolas, four quad chairs, three triple chairs, six double chairs, and four surface lifts. Total uphill capacity is over 26,000 skiers per hour. Average annual snowfall is 230 inches (about 19 feet).

Admission: Lift tickets, $39 a day adults, to as low as $30 a day for multiday tickets; $21 seniors 60–69; over 70 ski free; $17 a day children 12 and under, or $15 a day for multiday tickets. Ticket prices include Arapahoe Basin and Breckenridge Ski Resort. Equipment rentals average $17 a day; 2½-hour class lessons start at $30. MC, V.

Open: Late Oct to early June, daily 9am–9pm. **Closed:** Early June to late Oct.

AMAZE 'N BRECKENRIDGE, 710 S. Main St., Breckenridge. Tel. 453-7262.

Colorado's largest human maze, this two-level labyrinth of twists and turns offers prizes to participants who can "beat the clock." There's also a grill-style restaurant, an indoor miniature golf course, and a video arcade.

Admission: $4 adults, $3 children 5–12, free for children under 5. Additional maze runs $2.

Open: Dec 21–Jan 15 11am–7pm. Call for summer hours. **Closed:** Fall to mid-Dec.

BRECKENRIDGE NATIONAL HISTORIC DISTRICT, Breckenridge. Tel. 453-9022.

The entire Victorian core of this 19th-century mining town has been carefully preserved. Colorfully painted shops and restaurants occupy the old businesses and homes, most of them dating from the 1880s and 1890s. The Summit Historical Society conducts guided 2-hour walking tours beginning from the Breckenridge Activity Center, 201 S. Main St. The main historic district focuses on Main Street, and extends east for two blocks on either side of Lincoln Avenue, for four blocks to High Street. Among the 254 buildings in the district are the 1909 **Summit County Courthouse,** 200 E. Lincoln Ave.; and the **1896 William Harrison Briggle House,** 104 N. Harris St., which houses the historical society's decorative-arts museum. The society also leads tours to the outskirts of town to visit the underground shaft of the hard-rock **Washington Gold Mine** and the gold-panning operation at **Lomax Placer Gulch.**

Admission: Tours, $3–$5 adults, $2 ages 4–12.

Open: June–Aug, Mon–Sat 10am–4pm by appointment.

FRISCO HISTORIC PARK, 120 Main St. (at Second St.), Frisco. Tel. 668-3428.

✪ Eight historic buildings, including the town's original 1881 jail, one-room schoolhouse, log chapel, and homes dating to the 1880s, comprise this beautifully maintained historic park. The schoolhouse contains displays and artifacts on Frisco's early days, and a trapper's cabin contains a hands-on exhibit of animal pelts. Artisans sell their wares in several of the buildings, and special programs are scheduled during the summer. A self-guided walking tour of historic Frisco can be obtained at the park.

Admission: Free.

Open: Summer, Tues–Sun 11am–4pm; winter, Tues–Sat 11am–4pm.

SUMMITT HISTORICAL MUSEUM, 403 LaBonte St., Dillon. Tel. 468-6079.

A one-room country school—filled with such artifacts of early Colorado education as desks with inkwells, McGuffey readers, and scientific teaching apparatus—is the highlight of Dillon's "historic park." Also on the site are the 1885 Lula Myers ranch house and the depression-era Honeymoon Cabin. All buildings were moved from Old Dillon (now beneath the waters of the reservoir) or Keystone. Tours are conducted to the 1884 Montezuma Schoolhouse, located at 10,200 feet elevation in the 1860s mining camp of Montezuma.

Admission: By donation.

Open: Dillon Museum, Memorial Day–Labor Day, Wed–Sun 11am–4pm; or by appointment. Montezuma Schoolhouse, July 4 to mid-Aug, Sat only.

SPORTS & RECREATION

Two national forests—**Arapaho National Forest** and **White River National Forest**—overlap the boundaries of Summit County. These recreational playgrounds offer opportunities not only for downhill and cross-country skiing, but also for hiking and backpacking, horseback riding, boating, fishing, hunting, and bicycling in summer, and for snowmobiling and other cold-weather pursuits in winter. White River National Forest encompasses the **Eagles Nest Wilderness Area** and Arapaho National Forest includes **Green Mountain Reservoir,** both in the northern part of the county.

The U.S. Forest Service's Dillon Ranger District (tel. 468-5400) has maps and guides to hiking trails, bike paths, campsites, and two- and four-wheel-drive tours. The USFS's "Recreation Opportunity Guide" is available at visitors centers.

ALPINE SLIDE Peak 8 at Breckenridge has a dual-track alpine slide during the summer months. Call 453-5000 for schedules and ticket information.

BICYCLING Whether you're a touring bicyclist or a mountain biker, Summit County can accommodate you. There are more than 40 miles of paved bicycle paths in the county, including a 35-mile path from Breckenridge (with a spur from Keystone) to Frisco and Copper Mountain, continuing across Vail Pass to Vail. This spectacularly beautiful two-lane path is off-limits to motorized vehicles of any kind.

More energetic cyclists can try the Devil's Triangle, a difficult 80-mile loop that begins and ends in Frisco after climbing four mountain passes (including 11,318-foot Fremont Pass) and visiting five towns.

Numerous trails beckon mountain bikers into the wilderness. Some of them retrace 19th-century mining roads and burro trails, often ending in ghost towns.

Summit County's premier race event for mountain bikers is the annual Fall Classic, a 2-day, three-stage race organized by the Breckenridge Fat Tire Society (tel. 453-1872). Several Summit Mountain Challenges are organized as recreational races for beginners as well as experts.

Rentals and general information can be obtained from the Knorr House, 303 S. Main St., Breckenridge (tel. 453-2631); Kodi Rafting & Bikes, Bell Tower Mall, Breckenridge (tel. 453-2194); and Wilderness Sports, 171 Blue River Pkwy., Silverthorne (tel. 468-8519). For repairs try Cycopath Skis & Bikes, 303½ N. Main St., Breckenridge (tel. 453-4614).

BOATING Summit County is graced by two beautiful mountain lakes for watersports enthusiasts: Dillon Reservoir, often called Lake Dillon, on I-70 between Dillon and Frisco; and Green Mountain Reservoir, about 25 miles northwest of Silverthorne on Colo. 9.

At 9,000 feet elevation, Dillon Reservoir claims to be the home of America's highest yacht club. Colorful regattas are scheduled most weekends throughout the summer. The Dillon Marina, 300 Marine Dr., Dillon (tel. 468-5100), offers hourly rentals of powerboats, sailboats, fishing boats, and pontoon boats in summer daily between 8am and 7pm. Lake tours and canoe rentals are available from Osprey Adventures, 810 Main St., Frisco (tel. 668-5573).

The marina at Green Mountain Reservoir in Heeney (tel. 369-4632) also rents boats. Sailing, waterskiing, and board sailing are popular activities.

DOG SLEDDING You can get pulled behind a team of nine huskies with Snow Cap's Dog Sled Rides, Breckenridge (tel. 453-0276). Five different trips leave daily in winter between 9:30am and 1:30pm.

FISHING There are great trout streams throughout the county. Popular for brook, brown, cutthroat, lake, and rainbow trout, as well as kokanee salmon, are the Blue River, Ten Mile River, Snake River, and Straight Creek. For lake fishing, try Dillon Reservoir, Green Mountain Reservoir, and Pass Lake. The Blue River, from Lake Dillon Dam to its confluence with the Colorado River at Kremmling, is rated a Gold Medal–category fishing stream.

Mountain Angler, 311 S. Main St., Breckenridge (tel. 453-4665), offers year-round guide service, fly-fishing instruction, and tackle-and-license sales.

GOLF The county has four golf courses. The Breckenridge Golf Club, 200 Clubhouse Dr., Breckenridge (tel. 453-9104), is a public course designed by Jack Nicklaus. The Copper Creek Golf Club, 104 Wheeler Place, Copper Mountain Resort (tel. 968-2339), at 9,650 feet is the highest 18-hole course in North America. The Keystone Ranch Golf Course, Keystone Ranch Road, Keystone (tel. 468-4250), designed by Robert Trent Jones, Jr., is rated by *Golf Digest* as the leading resort course in Colorado, and one of the top 50 in the United States. The Eagles Nest Golf Club, Colo. 9, three miles north of Silverthorne (tel. 468-0681), is another 18-hole course.

HIKING & BACKPACKING The Colorado Trail cuts a swath through Summit County. It enters from the east across Kenosha Pass, follows the Swan River to its confluence with the Blue River, then climbs over Ten Mile Mountain to Copper Mountain. The trail then turns southerly toward the Tennessee Pass, north of Leadville.

There are myriad hiking opportunities in the national forests and the Eagles Nest Wilderness Area. Consult the U.S. Forest Service office, the Breckenridge Activity Center (453-5579), or a visitor information center for maps and details.

HORSEBACK RIDING One of the most popular rides in Summit County is the 7am breakfast ride offered by Breckenridge Stables, just above the Alpine Super Slide parking area, 1700 Ski Hill Rd., Breckenridge (tel. 453-4438). Call for reservations for this and other rides. The Eagles Nest Equestrian Center, Colo. 9, three miles north of Silverthorne (tel. 468-0677), offers trail rides in summer, sleigh rides in winter.

ICE SKATING All three major resort communities boast groomed ponds for ice skating. Rentals and lessons are available at all. Keystone Lake is the largest outdoor rink in the United States; it's open in winter, daily from 10am to 5pm and 6 to 10pm. Maggie Pond, at the base of Peak 9 at Breckenridge, is open daily from 9am to 9pm. Copper Mountain's West Lake offers free skating for resort guests daily from noon to 10pm.

RIVER RAFTING Trips through the white water of the Blue River—which runs through Breckenridge to Frisco—as well as longer journeys on the Colorado and Arkansas rivers are offered by various companies. They include the Adventure Company, 101 Ski Hill Rd., Breckenridge (tel. 453-0747); Kodi Rafting & Bikes, Bell Tower Mall, Breckenridge (tel. 303/453-2194 or toll free 800/525-9624); and Performance Tours, 110 Ski Hill Rd., Breckenridge (tel. 303/453-0661 or toll free 800/328-RAFT).

SKIING [ALPINE] One of the highlights of skiing in Summit County is the Ski the Summit Pass (tel. 468-6607), an interchangeable multiday ticket that allows purchasers to ski at Breckenridge, Copper Mountain, Keystone, and Arapahoe Basin for one price. It can be bought at any of the resorts; the cost is $145 for adults, $68 for children 12 and younger, for 4 days of skiing in a 5-day period. Other packages, including full season passes, are also available.

The three larger resorts are discussed in "Attractions" above. The fourth, Arapahoe Basin, on U.S. 6, between Keystone and Loveland Pass, is one of Colorado's oldest, having opened in 1945. It is now operated by Keystone Resort, P.O. Box 38, Keystone, CO 80435 (tel. 303/468-2316 or toll free 800/222-0188). Several features make Arapahoe exceptional. Most of its acreage is intermediate-and-expert terrain, much of it above timberline, and it is traditionally the last Colorado ski area to close for the season—often not until early June. Arapahoe offers a 1,670-foot vertical, from its summit at 12,450 feet to its base at 10,780 feet. It is served by one triple and four double chairs. Full-day tickets are $35 for adults, $17 for seniors 60 to 69 and children 6 to 12; children under 6 and seniors over 69 ski free.

Just across the county line, on the east side of I-70's Eisenhower Memorial Tunnel through the Continental Divide, is the Loveland ski area, P.O. Box 899, Georgetown, CO 80444 (tel. 303/569-3203). Comprised of Loveland Basin and Loveland Valley, it was created in the late 1930s by a Denver ski club because of its heavy annual snowfall (375 inches, or more than 31 feet). You can still see the original rope-tow cabins from 1942, when all-day tickets cost $2. (Tickets are now $32 for adults, $16 for seniors 60 to 69, $13 for children 6 to 12; children under 6 ski free.) There's good beginner-intermediate terrain here, with a vertical of 1,680 feet and a base elevation of 10,600 feet. Lifts include one quad chair, two triples, and five doubles. The resort is Colorado's first to open, in mid-October, and it generally remains open until mid-May.

Skiers who want a backcountry experience on untracked wilderness peaks can call Colorado Heli Ski in Frisco (tel. 303/668-5600 or toll free 800/TRY-HELI-SKI). Helicopters serve 150 square miles of the White River National Forest, at a cost of $80 to $425 for scenic charters and guided runs.

There are literally dozens of shops throughout Summit County from which to rent or buy ski equipment and clothing. They include Blue River Sports, 600 S. Park St., Breckenridge (tel. 303/453-1110 or toll free 800/525-9823), across the street from the Peak 9 Quicksilver lift; Mountain View Sports, Mountain View Plaza, U.S. 6, Keystone (tel. 468-0396); Rebel Sports, 315 Main St., Breckenridge (tel. 453-2565) and 100 Ski Hill Rd., Breckenridge (tel. 453-4224); and Virgin Islands Ski Rental, Summit Place Shopping Center, U.S. 6 off I-70, Exit 205, Silverthorne (tel. 303/468-6655 or toll free 800/525-9186).

SKIING [NORDIC] The Frisco Nordic Center, on Colo. 9 east of Frisco (tel. 668-0866), sits on the shore of Dillon Reservoir. Its trail network includes 35km (21 miles) of set tracks and access to backcountry trails. The lodge has a snack bar and a shop with rentals and retail sales; cross-country instruction is also offered. The masterplan for the Nordic Center was developed by Olympic silver medalist Bill Koch, probably America's greatest Nordic skier of the last 50 years. Open November to April, daily from 9am to 4pm, it charges $8 a day for adult tickets.

Peak's Trail connects the Frisco Nordic Center to the Breckenridge Nordic Ski Center, on Willow Lane near the foot of Peak 8 (tel. 453-6855), and the Whatley Ranch, two miles north of Breckenridge (tel. 453-2600). Trail tickets are interchangeable among the three centers. Copper Mountain has its own Trak Cross-Country Center at Union Creek (tel. 968-2318, ext. 6342), at the west end of the resort village. See "Skiing (Alpine)" for more equipment rental information.

SLEIGH RIDES Sleigh rides are offered by Alpine Adventures, Breckenridge (tel. 453-0111); Eagles Nest Sleigh Rides, Colo. 9, Silverthorne (tel. 468-0677); Nordic Sleigh Rides, Ski Hill Road, Breckenridge (tel. 453-2005); and Two Below Zero Sleighrides, Frisco Nordic Center (tel. 453-1520).

SNOWBOARDING Snowboard enthusiasts can get equipment and lessons from First Tracks Snowboarding Ltd., 311 S. Main St., Breckenridge (tel. 453-4049).

SNOWMOBILING Snowmobilers can join guided tours or rent machines from Eagles Nest Snowmobile Center, Colo. 9, three miles north of Silverthorne (tel. 468-0677); Swan River Adventure Center, 216 S. Main St., Breckenridge (tel. 303/453-7604 or toll free 800/477-0144); or Tiger Run Tours, 128 S. Main St., Breckenridge (tel. 453-2231). The latter company leads tours to old ghost towns and mining camps, including an excursion to the Dry Gulch gold camp for dinner.

WINTER ADVENTURE PARK At Summit Adventure Park, 16197 Colo. 9 at Swan Mountain Road, east of Frisco (tel. 303/453-0353 or toll free 800/253-0723), you can take a guided snowmobile trip, ride an inner tube down a 45° slope, race around the Yamaha Snoscoot track, or enjoy a sleigh ride. There are fees for each activity. Open in winter, daily from 8am to 10pm.

SHOPPING

IN BRECKENRIDGE A variety of shops and galleries occupy the historic buildings along Breckenridge's Main Street.

Of particular interest in the realm of art are the work of R. C. Gorman, Star York, and other New Mexico artisans in the **Meerdink Village Galleries,** Plaza Building 1 in the Village at Breckenridge Resort, 655 S. Park St. (tel. 453-9688); Bev Doolittle's striking camouflage oils at the **Silver Shadows Gallery** in the Four Seasons Mall, 411 S. Main St. (tel. 453-4938); and the unique handcrafted jewelry in the **Skilled Hands Gallery,** 110 S. Main St. (tel. 453-7818).

The **Silverthorne Factory Stores** has 53 outlet shops—from fashion-and-athletic wear to home accessories. Take I-70, Exit 205. Open Monday to Saturday 9am to 9pm, Sunday 10am to 6pm.

EVENING ENTERTAINMENT

SPECIAL EVENTS The **National Festival of Music at Breckenridge** is held each summer in the new $2.7-million Riverwalk Center. Presented by the Breckenridge Music Institute's Chamber and National Repertory Orchestras, the festival offers more than 50 concerts, plus workshops and special programs for children and senior citizens. Concerts take place from late June through late August, and tickets cost from $10 to $15, with $2 discounts for seniors and students under 18. There is also a free Fourth of July concert, and a free children's program in early July. Contact the Breckenridge Music Institute, P.O. Box 1254, Breckenridge, CO 80424 (tel. 303/453-2120).

Genuine Jazz in July, the second weekend of the month, showcases Colorado jazz ensembles with styles ranging from Dixieland to bebop to New Age.

Breckenridge bars and nightclubs host Friday- and Saturday-night performances; a weekend pass to all participating clubs costs $25, or $15 for 1 night. Free Saturday- and Sunday-afternoon concerts are outdoors at Maggie Pond, at the base of Peak 9. Call 303/453-6018 for more information.

The **Breckenridge Festival of Film,** held the third full weekend of September, attracts Hollywood directors and actors to town to discuss over 20 films in all genres. The casual interaction between stars and attendees makes this festival unique. Past guests have included Alan Arkin, Angie Dickinson, Elliot Gould, James Earl Jones, Malcolm McDowell, Mary Steenburgen, Rod Steiger, Donald Sutherland, and Jon Voight. Contact the Breckenridge Festival of Film office for information (tel. 453-6200).

Every Labor Day weekend, Copper Mountain is the scene for country singer **Michael Martin Murphey's West Fest.** The 3-day event focuses on the art, culture, and music of the American West with a full slate of guest appearances. For information, contact Copper Mountain Resort (tel. 968-2882).

BARS & CLUBS   Breckenridge is the nightlife capital of Summit County, but every community has its watering holes and dance spots.

Popular bars in Breckenridge include the **Breckenridge Brewery & Pub,** 600 S. Main St. (tel. 453-1550), whose microbrews include Avalanche, a full-bodied amber ale called "the one you can't get away from"; and **JohSha's,** 500 S. Park St. (tel. 453-4146), currently the most popular live-music dance club in town.

In Frisco, **Moose Jaw Food & Spirits,** 208 Old Main St. (tel. 668-3931), is a burgers, pool, and darts hangout; **Frisco's Bar and Grill,** located upstairs at the Boardwalk Building, 720 Granite, has lunch-and-dinner specials, and serves cocktails til 2am. Silverthorne's **Old Dillon Inn,** 321 Blue River Pkwy. (tel. 468-2791), serves terrific margaritas across an 1875 Old West bar. Copper Mountain offers live music for dancing at **O'Shea's Copper Bar** in the Copper Junction Building (tel. 968-2318, ext. 6504). In Dillon, the **Snake River Saloon,** 23074 U.S. 6 (tel. 468-2788), has live rock music nightly all winter, weekends in summer, and has been called one of America's great ski bars by *Playboy.*

THEATER   The **Backstage Theatre,** Bell Tower Mall, in the Village at Breckenridge, 605 S. Park St. (tel. 453-0199), has presented fine theater for 20 years. Open winter and summer.

WHERE TO STAY

Thousands of rooms are available at the various Summit County resorts at any given time. Even so, during peak seasons, finding accommodation may be difficult. **Summit County Central Reservations** (toll free 800/365-6365) can assist, as can **Copper Mountain Central Reservations** (toll free 800/525-3891), and **Breckenridge Central Reservations** (tel. 303/453-2918 or toll free 800/800-BREC or 800/221-1091).

Seasons vary somewhat from hotel to hotel, condo to condo, but some generalizations can be made. Rates will be highest during the holiday season—mid-December through the New Year's holidays—and next highest during the peak ski season, January through March. (Some establishments discount January and even early February, focusing higher rates on school vacation periods.) Early ski season (until mid-December) and late season (the first few weeks of April) are almost as low-priced as summer. The spring "mud season" (the end of ski season until the end of public school in June), and fall (usually mid-September to mid-November), are the least expensive times.

BRECKENRIDGE

Expensive

BEAVER RUN RESORT AND CONFERENCE CENTER, 620 Village Rd. (P.O. Box 2115), Breckenridge, CO 80424. Tel. 303/453-6000 or toll free 800/288-1282. Fax 303/453-4284. 224 rms, 326 suites. TV TEL

$ Rates: Mid-Apr to mid-Nov, $80–$85 single or double; $95–$100 studio; $100–$130 one-bedroom; $140–$190 two-bedroom. Mid-Nov to mid-Dec, $147 single or double; $165 studio; $200–$235 one-bedroom; $315–$400 two-bedroom. Holiday periods, $220 single or double; $265 studio; $310–$370 one-bedroom; $525–$610 two-bedroom. Jan to mid-April, $110–$165 single or double; $140–$205 studio; $165–$265 one-bedroom; $260–$450 two-bedroom. AE, CB, DC, DISC, JCB, MC, V. **Parking:** Free underground lot.

Over 800 staff serve guests at this spacious conference hotel, which consists of four separate buildings connected by covered walkways. Located at the foot of the Peak 9 slopes, with superb year-round athletic facilities, this is a favorite of corporate visitors.

Room styles vary from standard hotel rooms to four-bedroom premium suites. Hotel rooms are simple but nice, with southwestern motifs; they have two queen-size beds and the usual furnishings. Deluxe studios have intimate double spa tubs, efficiency kitchenettes, and soft contemporary pastel decor. One-bedroom units all have fireplaces and balconies, plus full kitchens with refrigerators. Two-bedroom town homes have two queen-size beds in one room, one in the other, and two bathrooms; including the hideaway sofa, they can sleep eight.

Dining/Entertainment: Spencer's Steak and Spirits is one of Breckenridge's outstanding restaurants, serving three meals daily in a casual contemporary setting. Steak-and-seafood choices dominate the dinner menu, priced $15.95 to $24.95. Meals are also served in the Copper Top Bar and Restaurant (winter only) and G. B. Watson's Mercantile deli/pizzeria. Tiffany's Night Club dominates the evening lounge action all year; three other bars include one poolside, open in winter.

Services: Concierge, valet laundry, free shuttle, ski storage, day-care program (winter), no-smoking rooms, facilities for the disabled.

Facilities: Outdoor and indoor/outdoor swimming pools, eight hot tubs, saunas, massage therapy, weight-and-exercise room, a tennis court, miniature golf, games room, four guest laundries, ski shops, gift shops, meeting space for 650.

THE LODGE AT BRECKENRIDGE SPA, 112 Overlook Dr. (P.O. Box 391), Breckenridge, CO 80424. Tel. 303/453-9300 or toll free 800/736-1607. Fax 303/453-0625. 45 suites. TV TEL

$ Rates: Mid-Nov to mid-Apr (except holidays), $125 single; $135–$195 double; $200 suite. Christmas and spring vacation (Feb) weeks, $135 single; $155–$215 double; $230 suite. Mid-Apr to mid-June and late Sept to mid-Nov, $85 single; $95–$130 double; $155 suite. Mid-June to late Sept, $105 single; $115–$150 double; $175 suite. **Closed:** May. AE, DISC, MC, V.

From below, this refurbished log building—a European-style spa with a Rocky Mountain atmosphere—looks like a mountaintop Tibetan monastery. Once you've entered through the landscaped garden, you'll find a superb view. Stone fireplaces and deer-antler chandeliers add a regional touch.

Each room has a different theme, but all feature country elegance in a rustic setting. They typically have hardwood floors, Southwest decor and artwork, balconies (or views), and two queen-size beds. The Longs Peak Room has colorful floral prints in a rustic setting, pedestal sinks, and other antique touches. The Mount Lincoln Room has a Native American theme; the Crestone Peak Room, quilts. Suites have sitting areas and kitchens with refrigerators and microwaves.

Dining/Entertainment: Dinners ($13.95 to $19.95) feature international dishes, steaks, and seafood. Summer buffets are presented on an outdoor deck. Breakfast runs $6.95 to $9.95.

Services: Room service, concierge, complimentary shuttle for skiers and dinner guests.

Facilities: Full spa services (massage, wraps, skin treatments, fitness consultations), three-story athletic club (with weight/exercise facilities and racquetball courts), outdoor swimming pool, hot tub, sauna; meeting space for 100.

RIVER MOUNTAIN LODGE, 100 S. Park St. (P.O. Box 7188), Breckenridge, CO 80424. Tel. 303/453-4711 or toll free 800/325-2342, 800/553-4456 in Colorado. Fax 303/453-1763, ext. 7012. 55 suites. TV TEL

$ Rates (including breakfast): Winter, $95–$175 studio; $135–$220 one-bedroom. Summer, $70–$110 studio; $80–$120 one-bedroom. Studio lofts and penthouses (both sleep four) also available. AE, DISC, MC, V. **Parking:** Free underground lot. Cross a covered bridge over the Blue River to reach this pleasant accommodation at the foot of Peak 9. Very popular with vacationing British skiers, it has an English-pub-style Fireside Lounge at the entry. You can ski in from the slopes on the Four o'Clock Run, but you must hop a shuttle to the lifts.

One of the truly nice features is that every guest room has a private washer/dryer! Studios have a queen-size Murphy bed and sofa sleeper, a full kitchen, and a balcony or walkout patio. The one-bedroom units have queen-size beds, fireplaces, and walk-through baths. Studio lofts have an additional queen with a sky-lit three-quarter bath at the top of a circular staircase.

Dining/Entertainment: A lounge is open daily in winter, weekends the rest of the year.

Services: Facilities for the disabled.

Facilities: Small health club with weights, steam room, sauna, aerobics studio, tanning; ski shop; three hot tubs (two outdoors); meeting space for 100.

THE VILLAGE AT BRECKENRIDGE, 655 S. Park St. (P.O. Box 8329), Breckenridge, CO 80424. Tel. 303/453-2000 or toll free 800/800-7829. Fax 303/453-3116. 60 rms, 395 suites. TV TEL

$ Rates: Mid-Apr to mid-Dec, $85 single or double; $90–$105 studio; $125 one-bedroom; $175–$235 two-bedroom; $225–$335 three-bedroom. Holiday, $155 single or double; $175–$190 studio; $280 one-bedroom; $365–$625 two-bedroom; $565–$850 three-bedroom. Regular season, $130–$145 single or double; $142–$175 studio; $200–$230 one-bedroom; $270–$475 two-bedroom; $400–$775 three-bedroom. AE, DISC, MC, V. **Parking:** Free underground lot. As the name implies, this really is a village. Eleven buildings, spread across 18½ acres of grounds, include guest rooms, restaurants, lounges, ski-and-sports shops, clothing stores, recreation centers, and everything else a visitor might need. The lower terminal of Peak 9's Quicksilver Chair is within the Village, so you could enjoy a Breckenridge ski vacation without seeing anything else of Breckenridge!

Accommodations run the gamut from hotel rooms and studios with kitchenettes to three-bedroom condominium suites. Standard hotel rooms are in the Village Hotel, studio suites in the Liftside Inn, deluxe hotel suites in the Hotel Breckenridge, condominium units in Plaza Condominiums, and deluxe condo units in the Châteaux. All are tastefully appointed; hotel rooms, though lacking the cooking facilities of other units, still feature coffee makers for early morning get-up-and-go.

Dining/Entertainment: Ten restaurants and lounges are part of the complex. Serving steak, pasta, Mexican, Chinese, and other foods, they include the Breckenridge Cattle Co. in Plaza I, the Café Breck in Plaza III, Jake T. Pounder's in the Village Hotel, the Village Pasta Company, and Bamboo Gardens in the Bell Tower Mall. The Gold Strike Saloon at the base of Peak 9 is a town watering hole.

Services: Ski storage, concierge, babysitting, valet laundry, no-smoking rooms, facilities for the disabled.

Facilities: Two health clubs, with 12 indoor/outdoor hot tubs, steam room, saunas, two swimming pools, racquetball, weight-and-exercise equipment, massage therapy, chiropractor, and paddleboats in summer; meeting space for 600; 26 guest laundries, hair salon, video arcade.

Moderate/Inexpensive

BRECKENRIDGE RESORT CONDOMINIUMS, 105 S. Park St. (P.O. Box 2009), Breckenridge, CO 80424. Tel. 303/453-2222 or toll free 800/525-2258. 81 suites (all with bath).

$ Rates: Summer, $70–$135 one-bedroom; $84–$150 two-bedroom; $100–$165 two-bedroom plus loft; $200–$450 three-bedroom. Winter, $105–$195 one-bedroom; $125–$295 two-bedroom; $185–$350 two-bedroom plus loft; $275–$650 three-bedroom. Weekly and monthly rates in summer. AE, DISC, MC, V. **Parking:** Free underground lot.

Actually two condominium complexes (Sawmill Creek and Sundowner II), these comfortable accommodations are close to both downtown and the ski area. Most units have mountain views, or are nestled among tall pines, and provide ski lockers.

Inside, it's just like home, assuming your home has a fireplace, cable television, phone, completely furnished kitchen with microwave, spacious living room, and from one to three bedrooms. Some of the two-bedroom condos at Sawmill Creek also have lofts and can accommodate up to 10 people. Most units also have washers and dryers. Sawmill Creek has a centrally located indoor Jacuzzi, and at Sundowner II there's an outdoor hot tub and heated year-round swimming pool.

RIDGE STREET INN BED & BREAKFAST, 212 Ridge St. (P.O. Box 2854), Breckenridge, CO 80424. Tel. 303/453-4680. 6 rms (4 with bath).

$ Rates (including full breakfast): Summer, $65–$70 with private bath; $60 with shared bath. Regular season, $90–$95 with private bath; $80 with shared bath. Early and late season, $75–$80 with private bath; $65 with shared bath. Holiday, $95–$100 with private bath; $85 with shared bath. All rates are for single or double occupancy. MC, V.

This 1890 Victorian style inn, located in the heart of the Breckenridge Historic District, is close to restaurants, shops, the town trolley, and shuttle services. The star of the inn is the Parlor Suite, furnished with butter-print antiques. It has bay windows, a queen size bed, a large private bath, a TV, and private entrance. Rooms with private baths also have TVs; the two rooms that share a bath also share a TV lounge. Home-cooked breakfasts might include waffles, fresh strawberry crêpes, or omelets. Children over five are welcome. Smoking is not permitted, and pets are not accepted.

SWISS INN BED AND BREAKFAST, 205 S. French St. (P.O. Box 556), Breckenridge, CO 80424. Tel. 303/453-6489. Fax 303/453-4915. 4 rms (all with bath), 2 dorms (shared bath).

$ Rates (including full breakfast): Winter, $85–$100 single or double; $30–$40 dorm bed. Summer, $35–$60 single or double; $15–$30 dorm bed. MC, V.

This is an elegantly restored 1910, three-level Victorian, ideally located on the shuttle-bus line two blocks off Main Street. They serve delicious full breakfasts and provide afternoon snacks. There are dormitory bunks for frugal travelers. All guests converge on two cozy lounges with Franklin-style fireplaces—one with cable TV, the other a reading room—or the hot tub, especially popular in winter.

WILLIAMS HOUSE 1885 BED & BREAKFAST, 303 N. Main St. (P.O. Box 2454), Breckenridge, CO 80424. Tel. 303/453-2975 or toll free 800/795-2975 outside Colorado. 4 rms (all with bath).

$ Rates (including full breakfast): Winter, $96–$140 single or double. Holiday periods, $135–$160 single or double. Summer, $69–$96 single or double. AE

Late 19th-century antiques grace every room of this charming historic home, originally the home of Emma Asminta Williams. Diane Jaynes and Fred Kinat now own the bed-and-breakfast, which has two parlors with fireplaces. The front parlor is a quiet haven for reading, while the back parlor has a television, VCR, and stereo. New in 1994 will be the Honeymoon Cottage with a Jacuzzi for two. Baked egg dishes are the breakfast favorite. Smoking, children, and pets are all taboo.

COPPER MOUNTAIN

CLUB MED–COPPER MOUNTAIN, 50 Beeler Place, Copper Mountain, CO 80443. Tel. 303/968-2161 or toll free 800/CLUB-MED. Fax 303/968-2166.

$ Rates (per person, double occupancy; minimum stay 1 week): Weekly, $940–$1,240; Christmas week, $1,450. **Closed:** Late Apr to early Nov. AE, MC, V.

One of only two American entries in this famed international chain of "jet-set" resorts (the other is in Florida), Club Med occupies a modern seven-story lodge near the west end of Copper Mountain village. The main doors open to a central cocktail lounge beside a cozy fireplace, creating an immediate atmosphere of leisure.

Guest rooms are simple but adequate. All have twin beds or king on request, full bathrooms, and attractive appointments. Many have mountain views.

One of the main draws is the 40-instructor Club Med ski school, the only one in the United States that uses the French method of training. Adult and children's lessons, as well as snowboarding instruction, are offered.

Dining/Entertainment: The main dining room serves three buffet-style meals daily. On the lower level are a more intimate restaurant for private dining, and a nightclub featuring live entertainment and dancing.

Services: Transportation from Denver airport (fee).

Facilities: Outdoor Jacuzzi, sauna, exercise-and-aerobics classes, big-screen TV, theater, boutique, ski-rental shop, guest laundry.

COPPER MOUNTAIN RESORT, I-70, Exit 195 (P.O. Box 3001), Copper Mountain, CO 80443. Tel. 303/968-2882 or toll free 800/458-8386. Fax 303/968-2308. 600 units (all with bath). TV TEL

$ Rates: Early and late season, $80–$120 single or double; $135–$170 one bedroom; $215–$265 two-bedroom. Regular season, $160–$170 single or double; $210–$240 one-bedroom; $335–$405 two-bedroom. Holiday season, $145–$199 single or double; $200–$280 one-bedroom; $285–$399 two-bedroom. Summer, $90 single or double; $125 one-bedroom; $200 two-bedroom. Higher rates for three- and four-bedroom suites and penthouse suites. AE, CB, DC, DISC, JCB, MC, V.

The vast majority of rooms in Copper Mountain village are condominium units, managed by the resort's Copper Mountain Lodging Services division or five other private management firms. The Copper Mountain Resort Association provides central reservation services for all. Ranging from simple hotel rooms and efficiency studios to luxurious town homes of one to four bedrooms along the golf course, they are all within walking distance of ski lifts.

All guests register at the Village Square, at the end of Ten Mile Circle; rooms here have kitchens, fireplaces, and a sort of whitewashed Santa Fe appearance. The five-story Telemark Inn, on Beeler Place, features one-bedroom lofts and Murphy-bed studios with full kitchens and fireplaces. At the other end of the spectrum, the Woods and the Greens at Copper Creek are elegant homes away from home.

Dining/Entertainment: Resort restaurants include the Clubhouse (tel. 968-2882, ext. 6514), serving breakfast and lunch year-round, winter fondues, and summer barbecues Wednesday through Sunday evenings. Farley's Tavern and Steakhouse, in the Snowflake Building (tel. 968-2577), features steaks and seafood. Others are O'Shea's Copper Bar, in the Copper Junction Building (see "Where to Dine," below); Pesce Fresco, on the first floor of the Mountain Plaza Building (ext. 6505), with seafood-and-pasta specialties and a seasonal jazz piano bar; and Rackets Restaurant, in the athletic club (see "Where to Dine," below). There are several other restaurants in the village, and four more on the mountain. The Copper Commons lounge in the day lodge also offers après-ski entertainment.

Services: Concierge, shuttle service, valet laundry, ski storage, no-smoking rooms, facilities for the disabled.

Facilities: Guests have free use of the $3-million Copper Mountain Racquet and Athletic Club, which has a swimming pool, hot tubs, saunas, steam rooms, weight-and-exercise room, tanning beds, racquetball and indoor tennis courts, a nursery, and a pro shop. Individual properties may also have a pool, sauna, and/or Jacuzzi. Most have guest laundries. Other resort facilities include a medical center, fire station, travel agency, post office, service station, chapel, grocery and many other shops. There's meeting space for 700.

DILLON/SILVERTHORNE

ALPEN HUTTE, 471 Rainbow Dr. (P.O. Box 919), Silverthorne, CO 80498. Tel. 303/468-6336. 66 dormitory beds (shared bath).

$ Rates: Winter, $18–$25 dorm bed; summer, $12–$15 dorm bed. DISC, MC, V.

Summit County's response to European skiers' hostels, the Alpen Hutte has much in common with its youth-hostel cousins: midday closure (9:30am to 3:30pm), a midnight curfew, and a handful of in-house regulations. But it remains one of the best deals around for hard-core skiers. There are two to eight bunks per room, and two large bathrooms per floor. One bedroom is disabled-equipped. Amenities include game rooms, fireplace, lounges, reading rooms, picnic areas, and a free shuttle bus year-round to the ski areas and towns.

FRISCO

HOLIDAY INN–SUMMIT COUNTY, I-70, Exit 203 (P.O. Box 10), Frisco, CO 80443. Tel. 303/668-5000 or toll free 800/782-7669. Fax 303/668-0718. 213 rms, 5 suites (all with bath). A/C TV TEL

$ Rates: Nov–Apr, $119–$125 single; $119–$135 double. Spring and Fall, $49–$59 single; $49–$69 double. Summer, $55–$81 single; $55–$91 double. Children 19 and under stay free in parents' room. AE, DC, DISC, MC, V.

Located beside the shoreline wetlands of Dillon Reservoir, this Holiday Inn— centrally located to all of Summit County's ski resorts—maintains the feel of a ski lodge with its warm fireplace seating. During the winter season this is a milieu for ski-movie parties with hot-chocolate and spiced-wine parties.

Many second-floor rooms have balconies with views across the lake. All have standard hotel furnishings; most feature two double beds or a queen-size bed and sleeper sofa. Decor is light pastel with rich blue carpeting. Local phone calls are 50¢.

The restaurant specializes in salads and sandwiches for lunch, steaks and seafood for dinner. The hotel lounge offers free hors d'oeuvres during its 4 to 6pm happy hour.

Services and facilities include room service, valet laundry, no-smoking rooms, facilities for the disabled; HoliDome with indoor swimming pool, Jacuzzi, steam room, tanning booth, tennis courts, exercise-and-weight room, games area with pool tables, and a video arcade; ski rentals and repairs; guest laundry; gift shop; meeting space for 250. Pets are allowed.

TWILIGHT INN, 308 Main St. (P.O. Box 397), Frisco, CO 80443. Tel. 303/668-5009 or toll free 800/262-1002. 12 rms (8 with bath).

$ Rates (including continental breakfast): Winter, $70–$80 double without bath, $95–$120 double with bath; summer, $40–$50 double without bath, $47–$73 double with bath. AE, DISC, MC, V. **Parking:** Private off street.

Most rooms in this modern country bed-and-breakfast inn, located in downtown Frisco, have private decks or balconies and antique furnishings. Guests can relax around the fireplace in the large living room or in front of the television in the cozy library. Amenities include a hot tub, exercycle, steam room, laundry room, kitchen use, and locked storage area. Children are catered to with cribs and high chairs, and some pets may be accepted. There are disabled-accessible rooms.

KEYSTONE

KEYSTONE RESORT, U.S. 6 (P.O. Box 38), Keystone, CO 80435. Tel. 303/468-2316 or toll free 800/222-0188. Fax 303/468-4105. 1,127 units (all with bath). TV TEL

$ Rates (single or double): Studio or one bedroom: early and late ski season $115–$125; high-season $185–$210; summer $55–$185. Higher rates for deluxe units and two- to four-bedroom condos. Children under 18 stay free in parents' room. AE, CB, DC, DISC, MC, V.

Spacious Keystone Resort has two main centers of activity. One is Keystone Lake, and the second is Keystone Mountain House Village, a mile east at the foot of the ski lifts. River Run Plaza, by the gondola terminal east of the Mountain House Village, and Old Keystone Village, west of the lodge en route to Keystone Ranch, are other areas of development.

All 152 rooms in the Keystone Lodge, a member of the Preferred Hotels Worldwide group, are oriented for mountain views. The pleasant rooms, spacious and without frills, all have cable TV with in-room movies, radios, phones, and refrigerators. The Keystone Mountain Inn, with 103 ski-in, ski-out rooms, is mainly efficiency studios with kitchens, along with a few one-bedroom suites (some with private spas).

Keystone Condominiums comprise 850 condo units and private homes, ranging in size from one to four bedrooms. There's access to Jacuzzis, saunas, and swimming pools at all of them, along with daily housekeeping, kitchens, and fireplaces.

Dining/Entertainment: All told, there are 26 places to eat in Keystone. There's fine dining at the Keystone Ranch (see "Where to Dine," below); the Garden Room for continental cuisine and the Bighorn Room for steaks, both in the Keystone Lodge; RazzBerry's in the Keystone Mountain Inn; and the SkiTip Lodge (see below). Families can find three meals a day at the Edgewater Café (in the Lodge), enjoy seafood meals at the Commodore Restaurant, relax with burgers and Mexican food in the mining decor of Ida Belle's Bar and Grille, put away pizza at the Last Chance Saloon, grab a sandwich at the Tip Top Deli, or attend a Thursday-night barbecue and barn dance at Keystone Stables (summer only). Atop Keystone Mountain, reached via gondola, is the Outpost, whose elegant centerpiece—the Alpenglow Stube—serves elegant wild game and other regional dishes, at a price to match the view.

Services: Room service, concierge, valet parking, valet laundry, free shuttle-bus system (operates three times hourly between the Lodge, Mountain Village, and other developments).

Facilities: 11 swimming pools, saunas, Jacuzzis, fitness center with weight room, indoor/outdoor tennis center (14 courts), golf, bicycle paths, stables, boating, llama trekking, ice skating; children's center, science school, day-camp program, petting farm, "Family Fun Park" (with volleyball, horseshoes, playground, and a tepee); guest laundries, boutiques, ski shops, many other stores; the $10-million Keystone Conference Center with meeting space for 1,800.

SKI TIP LODGE, 764 Montezuma Rd. (P.O. Box 38), Keystone, CO 80435. Tel. 303/468-4202 or toll free 800/222-0188. 11 rms (9 with bath). **$ Rates** (including continental breakfast in summer, full breakfast in winter): Summer, $45–$55 single; $70–$90 double. Winter, low-season, $51–$121 single; $75–$145 double; high-season, $66–$136 single; $60–$160 double. AE, CB, DC, MC, V.

In stark contrast to Keystone's modern core, the historic SkiTip offers a serene, rustic setting. Nestled in a pine forest by the Snake River, about two miles east of Keystone Resort and a brisk walk from the River Run Plaza gondola terminal, the lodge dates back to the 1880s, when it was a stagecoach stop on the way to the Montezuma gold mines. Arapahoe Basin developer Max Dercum bought it in the 1940s and turned it into the first skiers' guest lodge in Colorado. He sold the property to Keystone Resort in 1983, but its rough-hewn log construction has been maintained.

Eleven rooms are appointed with antiques, quilts, and lace curtains. Two rooms share baths. There's no TV or phone, so guests are encouraged to fraternize with other visitors around the fireplace or in the Rathskeller bar.

Dining/Entertainment: Four-course dinners are served nightly in a country-inn atmosphere (see "Where to Dine," below).

Facilities: Two tennis courts, nature trails; all Keystone Resort facilities are available to SkiTip Lodge guests.

CAMPGROUNDS

Many of the **Arapaho National Forest** campgrounds (tel. 303/468-5400) in Summit County are found around the shores of Dillon Reservoir. **Heaton Bay** (72 sites), **Peak One** (79 sites), **Pine Cove** (50 sites), and **Prospector** (107 sites)—all on Dam Road north of Frisco or on Colo. 9 south toward Breckenridge—have water and other facilities.

Reservations (toll free 800-283-2267) are accepted for Heaton Bay and Peak One, and are highly recommended. Campers are also advised to get to other campgrounds early in the day to claim sites, especially on weekends.

Numerous other campgrounds are around Green Mountain Reservoir, 25 miles north of Silverthorne on Colo. 9. They include **Cataract Creek** (4 primitive sites), **Elliot Creek** (dispersed camping with space for 60 vehicles), **McDonald Flats** (13 sites), and **Prairie Point** (33 sites).

All campgrounds charge a $6 to $8 overnight fee per vehicle, except Cataract Creek, which is free.

WHERE TO DINE

BRECKENRIDGE

Expensive

BRIAR ROSE RESTAURANT, 109 E. Lincoln St. Tel. 453-9948.
   Cuisine: REGIONAL/STEAK/SEAFOOD. **Reservations:** Recommended.
$ Prices: Appetizers $6; main courses $10–$26. AE, DISC, MC, V.
   Open: Dinner only, daily 5–10pm.

Located uphill from the Main Street traffic light, the Briar Rose is arguably the town's most elegant restaurant. Classical paintings, fine music, and white-linen service underscore the sophistication. The adjoining trophy lounge has big-game heads, a few paintings and a hundred-year-old bar.

You can start with escargots, crab-stuffed mushrooms or homemade soup. Dinners feature game when available—usually elk, moose, buffalo, and caribou. Other popular choices include slow-cooked prime rib, veal, steaks, duck, and seafood. Vegetarian meals are also available, plus a children's menu, and an extensive wine list.

Moderate

ADAMS STREET GRILL, Main and Adams Sts. Tel. 453-4700.
   Cuisine: INTERNATIONAL. **Reservations:** Recommended.
$ Prices: Appetizers $5.50–$6.95; main courses $4.95–$6.95 at lunch, $8.95–$16.95 at dinner. MC, V.
   Open: Summer, Mon–Thurs 11am–10pm, Fri 11am–11pm, Sat 10am–11pm, Sun 10am–10pm; winter, 11am–10pm. Earlier closing in spring and fall.

There are five different seating levels at this popular restaurant, which has two outdoor decks—one overlooking Main Street, a second facing Ten Mile Mountain. The interior offers understated Southwest decor, with a tile floor and a rose-and-dark-aquamarine color scheme. The menu has a little of everything, starting with a pasta bar. You can also get international cuisine with a southwestern accent, or opt for something homespun such as shrimp Adams Street—sautéed with green peppers, tomatoes, and mushrooms and served on linguine with a cream sauce. There are regional game specials; American standards such as barbecued pork spareribs, steak teriyaki, and honey-almond chicken; and vegetarian dishes.

BRECKENRIDGE CATTLE CO., Plaza I Bldg., The Village at Breckenridge Resort, 655 S. Park St. Tel. 453-3111.
   Cuisine: STEAKS/SEAFOOD. **Reservations:** Recommended.
$ Prices: Appetizers $4–$10.75; main courses $10.95–$21.95. AE, MC, V.
   Open: Dinner only, daily 5–10pm.

The large windows of this classic western steak house overlook Maggie Pond, site of year-round activity. The specialty is prime rib, but the menu also includes pasta stir-fries, a 16-ounce T-bone miner's stew, pork chops, and chicken. Early diners (5 to 6pm) save 20% on their tabs. There's also a children's menu.

HEARTHSTONE CASUAL DINING, 130 S. Ridge St. Tel. 453-1148.
   Cuisine: NEW AMERICAN/STEAKS. **Reservations:** Recommended.
$ Prices: Appetizers $2.95–$6.95; main courses $3.95–$7.95 at lunch, $9.95–$18.95 at dinner. AE, MC, V.
   Open: Lunch Mon–Sat 11am–3pm; dinner Sun–Thurs 4:30–9:30pm, Fri–Sat 4:30–10:30pm; brunch Sun 10am–3pm.

This wonderful restaurant in the 1886 Kaiser House is among Breckenridge's favorites. Blue on the outside, with white trim and wrought iron, it has a rustic yet elegant interior decor. There are fine views across the Ten Mile Range from the upstairs lounge. You can get great lunches here—jalapeño-wrapped shrimp, turkey-and-avocado sandwiches, half-pound burgers—but dinner is the meal "to die for." Start with baked Brie or steamed mussels. Then mull over your main dish: fresh seafood, such as Hearthstone shrimp (with garlic and ginger) or yellowfin tuna; Hearthstone chicken; a variety of steaks and slow-roasted prime rib. Vegetarian choices are also offered. An early diners' menu, offered from 4:30 to 5:30pm, cuts a couple of dollars off dinner prices.

POIRRIER'S CAJUN CAFE, 224 S. Main St. Tel. 453-1877.
   Cuisine: CAJUN/CREOLE. **Reservations:** Recommended.
$ **Prices:** Appetizers $4.95–$8.95; main courses $5.95–$9.95 at lunch, $8.95–$19.95 at dinner. AE, DISC, MC, V.
   Open: Lunch daily 11:30am–2pm; dinner daily 5:30–10pm.
This Reliance Place brownstone is straight out of New Orleans, with sidewalk café seating behind a wrought-iron railing. Two rooms inside display harlequin masks and photos of Louisiana. Indeed, owners Bobby and Connie Poirrier are native Cajuns from Louisiana. For lunch, order yourself a "po-boy," New Orleans–style red beans and rice, or seafood gumbo. At dinnertime, there's poisson Hymel (a catfish filet surrounded with crayfish étoufée, served with steamed rice and gumbo), blackened catch of the day, chicken à la Poirrier (with a mushroom sauce), and rib-eye steak. Finish your meal with Lafayette bread pudding. A children's menu is available, and they have early diner's prices.

TILLIE'S, 215 S. Ridge St. Tel. 453-0669.
   Cuisine: AMERICAN. **Reservations:** Recommended at dinner.
$ **Prices:** Appetizers $2.75–$4.95; main courses $5.75–$6.50 at lunch, $10.95–$16.95 at dinner. MC, V.
   Open: Summer, daily 11am–10pm. Winter, daily 11am–11pm. Sun open 9am for breakfast.
A chainsaw-carved eagle doing duty as a flagstaff greets visitors to this backstreet Victorian bar and grill. Once inside, the tin ceiling, leaded-glass windows, and marble-top bar lend a late 19th-century ambience. Gourmet hamburgers—8 ounces of grilled beef on a French roll—and homemade soups are the rage at lunchtime. Dinner features barbecued country-style pork ribs, New York strip steak, and teriyaki kebabs. They've added a low-cal, low-fat menu. Don't miss the "morning after" breakfast special on Sunday: 50¢ for eggs, sausage, home fries, and toast when you buy a bloody Mary or any other cocktail.

Inexpensive

THE BLUE MOOSE, 540 S. Main St. Tel. 453-4859.
   Cuisine: INTERNATIONAL. **Reservations:** Not necessary.
$ **Prices:** Breakfast $2.95–$4.50; lunch/dinner $4.25–$14.95. MC, V.
   Open: Daily 7am–2pm; dinner Thurs–Mon 3–9pm. **Closed:** Dinner in spring and fall.
This small café has a huge local following, perhaps because it caters to vegetarians as much as to meat eaters. For every beef burger there's a felafel burger, for every drunken chicken (marinated in tequila and lime) there's a stir-fry wok dish, and for every steak au poivre there's a pasta Alfredo. Fresh seafood is available nightly. There's a deck for warm-weather dining—with a great view of the Ten Mile Range.

BRECKENRIDGE BREWERY AND PUB, 600 S. Main St. Tel. 453-1550.
   Cuisine: AMERICAN/SOUTHWEST. **Reservations:** Not accepted.
$ **Prices:** Appetizers $1–$5; lunch $3.75–$7.50; dinner $5.95–$9.95. DISC, MC, V.
   Open: Daily 11am–midnight.
★ This brew pub was designed around its brewery, giving diners a first-hand view of the brewing process. Try the India Pale Ale, or the Avalanche—a local favorite. Lunch choices include fish-and-chips, half-pound burgers, charbroiled chicken sandwiches, and chicken or vegetable burritos. The menu also includes, for the dinner crowd, grilled salmon, roasted chicken, and rib-eye steak with fried green tomatoes. Desserts are homemade, and this brew pub also caters to abstainers—they brew their own root beer.

HORSESHOE II RESTAURANT, 115 S. Main St. Tel. 453-7463.

Cuisine: AMERICAN. **Reservations:** Not accepted.
$ Prices: Breakfast $2.75–$5.95; lunch $3.95–$6.50; dinner $8.95–$15.95. AE, MC, V.
Open: Daily 7:30am–10pm.

A classy family-style restaurant in a historic 19th-century building, the Horseshoe II (yes, there was once a I) is set in the heart of downtown Breckenridge. It has two outdoor patios, ornate walls and ceilings, lace curtains, and mounted horseshoes (of course). The bar is equally popular for espressos and alcoholic beverages, with an extensive selection of draft beer, including microbrewing choices.

You can get three meals a day here, starting with breakfasts, including the Breck-Mex Express and the HAB (high-altitude breakfast) consisting of two eggs, two pancakes, breakfast meat, and juice. Lunch offers salads, burgers, and sandwiches. Dinners are more elaborate, and feature the likes of pecan-and-chicken stir-fry, chicken-fried steak, fresh grilled Colorado trout, prime rib, and fresh salmon.

MI CASA, 600 Park Ave. Tel. 453-2071.
Cuisine: MEXICAN. **Reservations:** Not accepted.
$ Prices: Appetizers $3.95–$5.95; main courses $4.25–$9.95. AE, MC, V.
Open: Dinner only, daily 5–10pm (bar open at 3pm).

A large room with stuccoed walls, tile floor, wooden furniture, and baskets of silk flowers hanging from a beamed ceiling, Mi Casa is arguably Breckenridge's best Mexican restaurant. Its adjoining cantina is among the most popular, with margaritas by the liter and tequila (pronounced "ta-*kill*-ya") shooters. House specialties include snapper al ajillo (with garlic), and Acapulco scallops, Standard burritos, tostadas, and enchiladas are also on the menu. There's a children's menu, as well as a few non-Mexican steaks and burgers.

PASTA JAY'S, 326 S. Main St. Tel. 453-5800.
Cuisine: ITALIAN. **Reservations:** Not accepted.
$ Prices: Appetizers $2.25–$4.25; meals $4.50–$9.95. MC, V.
Open: Mon–Sat 11am–10:30pm.

This casual Mediterranean-style bistro occupies a modern log cabin in the Centennial Square plaza on Jefferson Avenue. Like its namesake in Boulder, it has a crowded outdoor deck, low prices, and generous portions of good food. Pastas, eggplant or chicken parmigiana, and pizza are especially good. Sandwiches are available before 5pm. Smoking isn't allowed.

COPPER MOUNTAIN

O'SHEA'S COPPER BAR, Copper Junction Bldg. opposite Mountain Plaza. Tel. 968-2882, ext. 6504.
Cuisine: AMERICAN/MEXICAN. **Reservations:** Not necessary.
$ Prices: Breakfast $2.95–$4.95; appetizers $1.95–$4.95; main courses $5.95–$12.95. AE, CB, DC, DISC, JCB, MC, V.
Open: Winter, daily 7am–10pm; summer, daily 11am–9pm.

There are two floors to this restaurant—a casual, mountain-style café on the top level, and a sports bar in the basement. There are buffets for all meals, including Mexican dishes at lunch and prime rib at dinner. Or order off the menu: huevos rancheros in the morning, a bad-boy salad or motherlode burger at midday, mesquite chicken or buffalo shrimp at night. There's a kids' menu, but here's good news: Kids' items are free with an adult dinner main dish!

RACKETS, in the Copper Mountain Racquet and Athletic Club, Copper Road at Ten Mile Circle. Tel. 968-2882, ext. 6386.
Cuisine: SOUTHWESTERN. **Reservations:** Recommended.
$ Prices: Appetizers $3.95–$5.95; main courses $3.95–$8.95 lunch, $11.95–$24.95 dinner. AE, CB, DC, DISC, MC, V.
Open: Summer, lunch Tues–Sun 11am–2pm; dinner 5–10pm. Winter, dinner only, daily 4–10pm. Closed: After Labor Day through mid-December, and after Easter through mid-June.

The second floor of an athletic club may seem an unlikely location for a fine restaurant, but it works. Guests enter through a fireside seating area. Handsome wood decor is an earmark of the main restaurant, and there's outdoor patio seating as well. Rackets features a southwestern grill menu with seafood, chicken, and rib eye, plus an extensive soup-and-salad bar and homemade breads.

DILLON/SILVERTHORNE

THE HISTORIC MINT, 341 Blue River Pkwy., Silverthorne. Tel. 468-5247.
   Cuisine: STEAK/SEAFOOD. **Reservations:** Recommended.
$ **Prices:** Appetizers $3.95–$6.95; main courses $7.95–$15.95. AE, MC, V.
   Open: Dinner only, daily 5–10pm (bar opens at 4pm).
Cook your own dinner on a charcoal grill amid rough-hewn plank walls in a historic 1862 building. Steaks, chicken, and fresh seafood—including tuna, mahimahi, snapper, salmon, and swordfish, depending on availability—are available. There are awesome appetizers and delicious desserts. All dinners include the fabulous salad bar.

PUG RYAN'S, 101 Village Place, Dillon. Tel. 468-2145.
   Cuisine: STEAK/SEAFOOD. **Reservations:** Recommended.
$ **Prices:** Appetizers $4.95–$7.95; main courses $10.95–$18.95. AE, MC, V.
   Open: Dinner only, daily 5–10pm.
From the deck of Dillon's oldest steak house you can gaze across Marina Park to the waters of Dillon Reservoir. Diners enjoy fresh oysters on the half shell while watching the sun set, then cut into slow-roasted prime rib or the daily seafood special. Children are welcome everywhere but the Fireside Lounge.

FRISCO

CHARITY'S, 307 Main St., Frisco. Tel. 668-3644.
   Cuisine: INTERNATIONAL. **Reservations:** Recommended.
$ **Prices:** Appetizers $2.95–$5.95; main courses $4.95–$8.95 at lunch, $5.95–$15.95 at dinner. AE, MC, V.
   Open: Lunch daily 11:30am–3pm; dinner daily 5–10pm.
Charity's offers a wide selection of pastas, Mexican foods, and grill items. South-of-the-border items include chimichangas, enchiladas, chile rellenos, chile verde, and Navajo tacos. There's plenty of fresh seafood: grilled salmon, trout Grand Marnier, and shrimp scampi, for instance. Southwestern lime chicken, charcoal-broiled steaks, pasta, burgers, and miner's stew fill out the varied menu.

GOLDEN ANNIE'S, 603 Main St., Frisco. Tel. 668-0345.
   Cuisine: STEAK/SEAFOOD. **Reservations:** Recommended.
$ **Prices:** Appetizers $2.95–$6.95; main courses $4.95–$9.95 at lunch, $5–$19.95 at dinner. AE, MC, V.
   Open: May–Oct, lunch daily 11:30am–3pm; year-round, dinner daily 5–10pm.
Golden Annie's was a late 19th-century claim at the mining camp of Masontown, overlooking Frisco from Mountain Royal. Local legend says that the mine, along with Masontown, was destroyed by an avalanche on New Year's Eve 1912. But fortuitously, no one was home: They were all celebrating in Frisco. Today this mesquite grill and bar serves steaks (New York, rib eye, T-bone, filet mignon), seafood (snapper, swordfish, salmon, shrimp, fresh catch), fajitas, barbecues, and "finger food."

KEYSTONE

KEYSTONE RANCH, Keystone Ranch Rd. Tel. 468-4161.
   Cuisine: CREATIVE REGIONAL. **Reservations:** Required.
$ **Prices:** Six-course dinner begins at $47. AE, DISC, MC, V.
   Open: Daily 6pm–midnight. Also June–Sept Golfer's Lunch 11:30am–2pm.
A working cattle ranch for over three decades until 1972, the Keystone Ranch now boasts riding stables, a fine golf course, and this outstanding gourmet restaurant built of pine logs from the forest that surrounds it. Utes and Arapahoes made their summer

camps in the 19th century where the golf course now lies, at the foot of Keystone Mountain; it doesn't take much imagination here to visualize the smoke of their campfires in the twilight.

The food here is as delicious as the setting. The six-course menu offers a choice of appetizer, followed by a soup, a salad, and a fruit sorbet to cleanse the palate. Main dishes, which vary seasonally, might include Silver City beef, straw potato and mushroom cakes, or Willow Creek Muscovy duck. Local game and fresh seafood dishes are prepared with whim and inspiration, depending on what's available. Desserts include Gorgonzola apple tart, chocolate piñon torte, and hazelnut logs with dried cherries.

There's no smoking in the restaurant. You won't need a tie, gentlemen, but wear slacks and your best ski sweater.

SKI TIP LODGE, 764 Montezuma Rd. Tel. 468-4202.
   Cuisine: REGIONAL. **Reservations:** Required.
$ Prices: Four-course dinner $42. AE, CB, DC, MC, V.
   Open: Winter, lunch daily 11:30am–2pm; dinner daily 5:45–9pm. Summer, dinner Thurs–Tues 5:45–9pm.

Some say the food at this casual country inn, an 1880s stagecoach stop, is the best in Summit County. A nightly choice of meat, poultry, and seafood dishes is offered, which might include roast loin of pork, trout sautéed with pecans and lemon butter, or apple-smoked Cornish hens with wild rice. Soup, salad, home-baked bread, and delectable desserts are included. Lunches offer all the soup and bread you can eat. There's a full lounge. Smoking is not permitted.

5. VAIL

109 miles W of Denver, 150 miles E of Grand Junction

GETTING THERE   By Plane   From mid-December to early April, visitors can fly directly into Vail/Beaver Creek Jet Center, 35 miles west of Vail near the town of Eagle, at I-70, Exit 140 or 147 (tel. 303/524-7700 or 949-5480).

Most visitors fly into Denver International Airport and continue to Vail aboard any of four shuttle services: Airport Transportation Service (tel. 303/476-7576 or toll free 800/247-7074); Colorado Mountain Express (tel. 303/949-4227 or toll free 800/525-6363); Vail Valley Transportation (tel. 303/476-8008 or toll free 800/882-8872); or Vans to Vail (tel. 303/476-4467 or toll free 800/222-2112).

By Bus   Coaches of Greyhound (tel. 303/476-5137) stop in Vail at the Vail Transportation Center, South Frontage Road at East Meadow Drive. For Beaver Creek, they stop in the village of Avon.

By Car   Vail is right on the I-70 corridor, so it's exceedingly easy to find your way there. Just take Exit 176, whether you're coming from the east (Denver) or the west (Grand Junction). A more direct route from the south may be U.S. 24 through Leadville; this Tennessee Pass road joins I-70 five miles west of Vail.

SPECIAL EVENTS   The Vail area holds the following annual events: the Mountain Man Winter Triathlon, on the first weekend of February, in Beaver Creek; Taste of Vail, over the first weekend of April, in Vail; Kick-off to Summer, over Memorial Day weekend, in Vail/Lionshead; the Salute to the USA, on July 4, in Avon; the Bravo! Colorado Music Festival, from early July to early August, in Vail and Beaver Creek; the Vail Arts Festival, from early July to early August, in Vail/Lionshead; the Eagle County Fair and Rodeo, on the second weekend of August, in Eagle; the Beaver Creek Arts Festival, over the third weekend of August, in Beaver Creek; and VailFest, in mid-September, in Lionshead.

Native American Ute tribespeople didn't take kindly to the first incursions into this valley by white gold seekers in the 1850s and 1860s. They set the forests alight in "spite fires"—burnings that created the wide-open ridges and back bowls that have made Vail Mountain famous as a ski resort today.

But no substantial amount of gold was found in the Gore Valley, as it was then known, and until U.S. 6 was built through Vail Pass (named for a highway engineer) in 1939, the only inhabitants were a handful of sheep ranchers. Veterans of the 10th Mountain Division, who trained during World War II at Camp Hale, 23 miles south of the valley, returned in the 1950s to ski the Rockies. One of them, Peter Seibert, urged development of this mountain land in the White River National Forest. His investment company began construction in 1962, and the entire ski resort—immediately among the three largest ski areas in the United States—was completed and ready to open in December 1963. Additional ski-lift capacity made Vail America's largest ski resort by 1964.

A Tyrolean-style pedestrian village grew around the base, attracting many rich and famous citizens—among them former President Gerald Ford. Readers of *Ski* and *Snow Country* magazines annually vote the resort the country's most popular.

ORIENTATION

The town of Vail is located at an elevation of 8,150 feet. The year-round population is around 4,000.

INFORMATION　For information or reservations in the Vail Valley, contact the Vail Valley Tourism and Convention Bureau, 100 E. Meadow Dr., Vail, CO 81657 (tel. 303/476-1000 or toll free 800/525-3875); Vail Associates, Inc., P.O. Box 7, Vail, CO 81658 (tel. 303/476-5601 or toll free 800/525-2257); or the Eagle Valley Chamber of Commerce, P.O. Box 964, Eagle, CO 81631 (tel. 303/328-5220).

The TCB's information centers are located at the parking structures in Vail and Lionshead on South Frontage Road, open daily.

CITY LAYOUT　There's no getting around the fact that narrow Vail Valley, hemmed in on the south and north by steep mountains, is in a long strip along Gore Creek. In fact, as you come in from the east across Vail Pass, you'll find a whole strip of separate communities: East Vail (Exit 180), Vail (Exit 176), West Vail (Exit 173), Minturn and Eagle-Vail (Exit 171), Avon and Beaver Creek (Exit 167), and Edwards (Exit 163).

The town of Vail is mostly on the south side of the interstate, which you exit on Vail Road. The two main skiing areas are Vail Village, slightly to the east, and Lionshead, to the west. Because much of Vail is open to pedestrians only, it's wise to park in one of the major garages off South Frontage Road, then get hold of one of several available tourist maps to find your way through the network of lanes.

GETTING AROUND

The Town of Vail runs a **free shuttle-bus service** between 7am and 1am daily. Shuttles in the Vail Village–Lionshead area run every three to five minutes, and there are regularly scheduled trips to West Vail and East Vail. There's also free transportation between Beaver Creek Resort and the village of Avon (tel. 949-1938). Buses between Vail and Beaver Creek, an 11-mile trip, run daily from 5:30am to midnight, for a nominal fee.

Vail Valley Taxi (tel. 476-TAXI) operates throughout the area, around-the-clock.

For **auto rentals,** try Hertz (tel. 303/524-7177 or toll free 800/654-3131), at the Vail/Beaver Creek Jet Center in Eagle, or Thrifty (tel. 303/949-7787 or toll free 800/367-2277).

FAST FACTS

The **area code** is 303. In case of an **emergency,** call 911; for regular business, contact the Vail Police (tel. 479-2200). The **hospital,** Vail Valley Medical Center, is on West Meadow Drive between Vail Road and East Lionshead Circle (tel. 476-2451). The **post office** is on North Frontage Road West, opposite Donovan Park (tel.

476-5217). For **road information,** call 479-2226. State, county, and city **taxes** add 8.2% to hotel bills in Vail, 9.4% in Beaver Creek.

WHAT TO SEE & DO
ATTRACTIONS

VAIL MOUNTAIN, Vail Associates, Inc., P.O. Box 7, Vail, CO 81658. Tel. 303/476-5601 or toll free 800/525-2257; or 303/476-4888 for daily snow reports. Fax 303/949-2315.

In his *Skiing America* guide, author Charles Leocha writes, "Vail comes closest of any resort in America to epitomizing what many skiers would call perfection." I agree. You can arrive at the base village, unload and park your car once, and never have to drive again until it's time to go. You'll find all the shops, restaurants, and nightlife you could ever want within a short walk from your hotel or condominium. And the skiing is unparalleled.

The area boundaries stretch 7 miles from east to west along the ridge top, from Outer Mongolia to Game Creek Bowl, and the skiable terrain is measured at 3,834 acres. Virtually every lift on the front (north-facing) side of the mountain has runs for every level of skier, with a predominance of novice-and-intermediate terrain. (The longest run, 4½-mile **Riva Ridge,** is mainly intermediate.) The world-famous **Back Bowls** are decidedly *not* for beginners, and there are few options for intermediates. The seven bowls—from west to east, Sun Down, Sun Up, Tea Cup, China, Siberia, Inner Mongolia, and Outer Mongolia—are strictly for advanced and experts; snow-and-weather conditions determine just *how* expert you ought to be. They are served by only three lifts, one of them a short surface lift to access the Mongolias. One trip down the Slot or Rasputin's Revenge will give you a fair idea of just how good you are.

From Mongolia Summit, at 11,450 feet, Vail has a vertical drop on the front side of 3,250 feet; on the back side, 1,850 feet. Average annual snowfall is 334 inches (nearly 28 feet). All told, there are 120 named trails served by 20 lifts—a gondola, nine quad chairs, two triple chairs, six double chairs, and two surface lifts—with a skier capacity of 35,820 per hour. Meet the Mountain tours begin at Wildwood Shelter, atop Lift 3 (Hunky Dory), Sunday through Tuesday at 1pm; and former U.S. Olympic medalist Cindy Nelson, the director of skiing here, invites advanced-and-intermediate skiers to join her on a run on Friday at 1pm.

Ten **mountain restaurants** include two that ask for reservations: the Cook Shack (tel. 479-2030), with creative American cuisine at the Summit, and the Wine Stube (tel. 479-2034) at Eagle's Nest, with international cuisine atop the Lionshead Gondola. The Native American–themed Two Elk Restaurant on the Far East summit has southwestern cuisine and pasta, baked potato, and salad bars. Wok 'n' Roll, in China Bowl, is a ski-by pagoda with Asian fast food; the Dog Haus offers ski-by hot dogs at the foot of the Avanti Express; Wildwood Shelter specializes in smoked or barbecued foods; Eagle's Nest has salad, potato, and pasta bars. And Mid-Vail has two levels of cafeterias: Golden Peak and Trail's End serve breakfast, lunch, and après-ski drinks.

Vail has an outstanding children's program. The **Golden Peak Children's Skiing Center** (tel. 479-2040) and the **Lionshead Children's Skiing Center** (tel. 479-2042) are under the aegis of the Ski School. Call 479-2048 for recorded information on a wide range of day and night family activities. There are daily NASTAR races on Race Track run.

Admission: Tickets, $42 per day adults, $39 per day for multiday tickets, $37 for a half day; $29 per day children 12 and under, $24 for a half day; $32 per day seniors 65–69; free for seniors 70 and older. Multiday tickets are interchangeable between Vail and Beaver Creek. For rental packages call 303/479-2050.

Open: Thanksgiving to the third week of Apr, daily 8:30am–3:30pm.

BEAVER CREEK RESORT, Vail Associates, Inc., P.O. Box 7, Vail, CO 81658. Tel. 303/949-5750 or toll free 800/525-2257; or 303/476-4889 for daily snow report. Fax 303/949-2315.

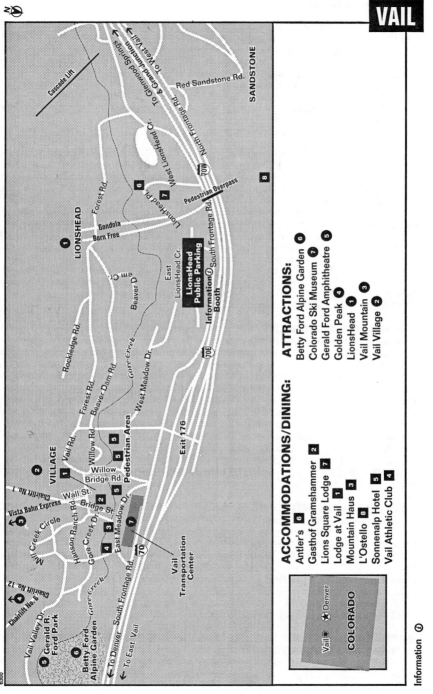

VAIL

ACCOMMODATIONS/DINING:

Antler's **6**
Gasthof Gramshammer **2**
Lions Square Lodge **7**
Lodge at Vail **1**
Mountain Haus **3**
L'Ostello **8**
Sonnenalp Hotel **5**
Vail Athletic Club **4**

ATTRACTIONS:

Betty Ford Alpine Garden **6**
Colorado Ski Museum **7**
Gerald Ford Amphitheatre **5**
Golden Peak **4**
LionsHead **1**
Vail Mountain **3**
Vail Village **2**

COLORADO
Vail ●   ★ Denver

Information ⓘ

Vail's "other" mountain is an outstanding resort in its own right, one with a more secluded atmosphere than its better-known neighbor. Located up a valley 1½ miles off the I-70 corridor, Beaver Creek combines European château–style elegance in its base village with expansive slopes for novice-and-intermediate skiers. The Grouse Mountain lift reaches previously inaccessible expert terrain.

From the village, the Centennial Express lift to **Spruce Saddle** reaches wide-open northwest-facing midmountain slopes and the **Stump Park** beginners' area. Opposite, the Strawberry Park lift accesses **Larkspur Bowl** and the **McCoy Park** cross-country area at 9,840 feet. Three other lifts—Larkspur, Grouse Mountain, and Westfall (serving the expert Birds of Prey area)—leave from **Red-Tail Camp** at midmountain.

Beaver Creek's vertical is 3,340 feet, from the 8,100-foot base to the 11,400-foot summit. There are 1,125 developed acres, though Vail Associates are licensed to develop up to 5,600: plans are on the drawing board. Currently, 10 lifts (two quad chairs, four triples, and four doubles) serve 59 trails with a capacity of 17,228 skiers per hour. Average annual snowfall is 330 inches.

There are five **mountain restaurants,** including the widely praised Beano's Cabin. Others include Rafters, at Spruce Saddle (tel. 949-6050 for reservations), the Spruce Saddle Cafeteria, the Red-Tail Camp fast-food stop, and McCoy's, offering breakfast, lunch, and après-ski entertainment at the base.

Admission: Tickets, $43 per day adults, $40 per day for multiday tickets, $38 for a half day; $28 per day children 12 and under, $23 for a half day; $30 per day seniors 65–69; free for seniors 70 and older. Multiday tickets are interchangeable between Beaver Creek and Vail. Full-rental packages average $16.

Open: Daily 8:30am–3:30pm.

COLORADO SKI MUSEUM, Vail Transportation Center, on Level 3, just below the information center, Vail. Tel. 476-1876.

The history of more than a century of Colorado skiing—from the boards that mountain miners first strapped on their feet, to the post–World War II resort boom, to Coloradans' success in international racing—is depicted in this popular showcase. Also included are the evolution of ski equipment and fashions, and the role of the U.S. Forest Service. There's one room devoted to the 10th Mountain Division, the only division of the military trained in winter warfare. A theater presents historical and current ski videos. The museum incorporates the Colorado Ski Hall of Fame, with plaques and photographs honoring Vail founder Peter Seibert, filmmaker Lowell Thomas, Olympic skier Buddy Werner, and others.

Admission: $1 adults, 50¢ children 12–18, free for children under 12.

Open: Tues–Sun 10am–5pm. **Closed:** May and Oct, except by appointment.

EAGLE COUNTY HISTORICAL SOCIETY MUSEUM, Chambers Park, Fairgrounds Rd., Eagle. Tel. 328-6464.

Located in a large early 20th-century barn on the Eagle River, this museum presents exhibits that document the history of the valley from prehistoric Native Americans to modern day. Displays in a nearby caboose describe the importance of rail traffic. The society also operates the **Gore Creek Schoolhouse Museum** at Ford Park in Vail and the **Red Cliff Museum** in the 19th-century town hall at Red Cliff, 12 miles south of I-70 off U.S. 24.

Admission: Free.

Open: Summer, daily 9am–4pm.

BETTY FORD ALPINE GARDENS, Ford Park, S. Frontage Rd. east of Vail Village, Vail. Tel. 476-7471.

Billed as "the highest public gardens in the world," this peaceful tract features more than 1,500 hardy perennials from around the world, along with an experimental rock garden and a meditation garden, employing elements of Chinese Zen and Japanese moss gardens. The gardens are disabled accessible.

Admission: Free.
Open: Snowmelt to snowfall, daily dawn–dusk.

SPORTS & RECREATION

BALLOONING   Camelot Balloons (tel. 476-4743) and AeroVail (tel. 476-7622) fly year-round, including champagne-breakfast flights.

BICYCLING   Casual summer visitors can take the Lionshead Gondola to Eagle's Nest on Vail Mountain, rent mountain bikes (and helmets) there, and cruise downhill on what *had* been ski runs to return their bikes at the base of the gondola.

But there are many other choices for avid bikers, both on backcountry trails and road tours. The 13½-mile Vail Pass Bikeway connects the mountain village to Copper Mountain, from which additional bike paths lead to Breckenridge and Keystone. Another popular trip is the 15-mile Red Sandstone Road to Piney Lake, beginning from North Frontage Road West a mile west of the Vail exit from I-70.

Curtain Hill Sports, next to the village ticket office, at 254 Bridge St. (tel. 476-5337), is among many sporting-goods companies that rent mountain-and-touring bicycles.

BOBSLEDDING   The ✪ Vail Bobsled runs a 3,200-foot course beginning just below Mid-Vail near the Short Cut run. The ride lasts about one minute and costs $15 per ride per person. Helmets are provided.

FISHING   The streams and mountain lakes surrounding Vail are rich with rainbow, brook, brown, and cutthroat trout, and mountain whitefish. Gore Creek through the town of Vail is one popular anglers' venue, especially toward evening from its banks in the Vail Golf Course. Also good are the Eagle River, joined by Gore Creek 5 miles downstream near Minturn; the Black Lakes near the summit of Vail Pass; and 60-acre Piney Lake (see directions under "Bicycling," above). At the latter site, the Piney River Ranch, c/o Vail Associates, P.O. Box 7, Vail, CO 81658 (tel. 303/476-3941), will rent canoes and small boats for fishing, and also will supply fly rods and waders.

For a fishing trip call Nova Guides, P.O. Box 2018, Vail, CO 81658 (tel. 303/949-4232).

For your fishing supplies stop at American Angler, 225 Wall St. (tel. 476-1477).

GOLF   There are four 18-hole public courses and one private club in the Vail valley. Play dates depend on snow conditions, but usually are mid-May to mid-October.

Generally considered the outstanding area course is the Beaver Creek Resort Golf Club, 75 Offerson Road, Beaver Creek (tel. 949-7123), designed by Robert Trent Jones, Jr. The Vail Golf Club, 1778 Vail Valley Dr., Vail (tel. 479-2260), and the private, Jack Nicklaus–designed Country Club of the Rockies at Arrowhead resort, 2 miles west of Beaver Creek on U.S. 6 (tel. 926-3080), co-host the annual Gerald R. Ford Invitational Golf Tournament in August.

Other courses include the Eagle-Vail Golf Course, 0431 Eagle Dr., Avon (tel. 949-5267), a challenging course with the lowest greens fees and rentals in the valley; and the private Singletree Golf Course, 1265 Berrycreek Rd., Edwards (tel. 926-3533), 7 miles west of Beaver Creek off I-70, Exit 163, which opens earlier than the other courses (April 1) because of its lower elevation.

HIKING & BACKPACKING   The surrounding White River National Forest has a plethora of trails leading to pristine lakes and spectacular panoramic views. The Holy Cross Wilderness Area to the southwest of Vail, encompassing 14,005-foot Mount of the Holy Cross, has more than 100 miles of trails; so awesome is this region that it was nearly awarded national monument status in the 1950s, rejected only because of its relative inaccessibility and short recreational season. Nearly as impressive is the Eagle's Nest Wilderness Area to the north. For information on these and other hiking areas, consult the Holy Cross Ranger District Office, 24747 U.S. Hwy. 24 (P.O. Box 190), Minturn, CO 81645 (tel. 303/827-5715).

Among the less strenuous walks in the immediate Vail area is the 11-mile Two Elk Trail, a National Scenic Trail. It starts in East Vail, just south of the Gore Circle Campground on old U.S. 6, and ends in Minturn.

For supplies and more information, visit Vail Mountaineering, 500 Lionshead Mall, Vail (tel. 476-4223).

HORSEBACK RIDING The Spraddle Creek Ranch, 100 N. Frontage Rd. E., Vail (tel. 476-6941), is geared for family day outings. Located across I-70 from the Vail interchange, it features a pony ring for children.

For more serious pack trips, visit Beaver Creek Stables at the Beaver Creek Resort (tel. 845-7770) or Piney River Ranch, 15 miles north of Vail via Red Sandstone Road (tel. 476-3941).

ICE SKATING There's year-round public skating at the John A. Dobson Ice Arena, East Lionshead Circle (tel. 479-2270); admission is $4 for adults, $3 for children 17 and under. Skate rentals cost $2. Nottingham Lake in Avon (tel. 949-4280) has afternoon-and-evening skating, as well as a hockey rink and speed-skating lane. The Vail Golf Club, 1778 Vail Valley Dr. (tel. 476-8366), has a small outdoor rink.

RIVER RAFTING The Eagle River, just a few miles west of Vail, offers excellent white water during the summer, especially during the May-June thaw. Families can enjoy the relatively gentle (Class II to IV) lower Eagle, west of Minturn; the upper Eagle, above Minturn, is significantly rougher (Class IV to V rapids). The Colorado and Arkansas rivers are also readily accessible—the former at State Bridge, 35 miles northwest via Colo. 131, and the latter at Buena Vista, 73 miles south via U.S. 24.

Rafting companies include Nova Guides, P.O. Box 2018, Vail, CO 81658 (tel. 303/949-4232), and Colorado River Runs, running the rivers for 20 years, Star Route, Box 32, Bond, CO 80423 (tel. 303/653-4292 or toll free 800/826-1081). Rates typically run $40 to $75 for a full-day journey, including lunch; $25 to $50 for a half-day trip.

SKIING [ALPINE] There's another ski resort in Eagle County: Arrowhead at Vail, P.O. Box 3418, Vail, CO 81658 (tel. 303/926-3029 or toll free 800/332-3029). Located 2 miles west of Beaver Creek on U.S. 6, it's a small family-oriented area, with one high-speed quad-chair lift and a beginners' surface lift serving 11 runs, nearly all of them for intermediates or novices. The mountain has a 1,700-foot vertical, from a base elevation of 7,400 feet to the summit of 9,100. With annual snowfall of just 115 inches (not quite 10 feet), it doesn't open until Christmas week, but then stays open until early April, daily from 9am to 3:30pm. Full-day tickets are $28 for adults, $19 for children 16 and under and seniors 65 to 69; family rates are available.

Adventurous downhillers who want to get away from the crowded slopes can try helicopter skiing with Colorado Heli-Ski USA (tel. 303/668-5600 or toll free 800/HELI-SKI); or snow-cat tours with Nova Guides (tel. 949-4232), Piney River Ranch (tel. 476-3941), or Resolution Snotours (tel. 476-2556).

For rentals or sales of ski equipment, there are many, many options. Try American Ski Exchange, 225 Wall St., Vail (tel. 476-1477); Christy Sports, 182 Avon Rd., Avon (tel. 949-0241); or Kenny's Double Diamond Ski Shop, 520 Lionshead Mall, Vail (tel. 476-5500). You can outfit the children, meanwhile, at KidSport, 122 E. Meadow Dr., Vail (tel. 303/476-1666 or toll free 800/833-1729).

SKIING [NORDIC] Cross-country skiers needn't feel left out by the emphasis on downhill skiing here. Each of the resorts has ample Nordic terrain set aside, and there's a tremendous system of winter trails through the surrounding mountains.

Vail's Golden Peak Cross-Country Skiing Center (tel. 845-5313), located at the bases of Chairs 6 and 12 at Vail Village, has 20km (12 miles) of trails, part of them on the Vail Golf Course. In addition, an 8-mile (13km) track extends to the Vail Nordic Center, 75 S. Frontage Rd. E. (tel. 479-4391); in summer, this is the Vail Nature Center.

Beaver Creek Resort has a Nordic skiing center on its golf course, and a 30km (18-mile) mountaintop track system in 9,840-foot McCoy Park (tel. 949-5750, ext. 4313), atop the Strawberry Park Chair (Lift 12). Most of the high-altitude terrain here is intermediate, though there's some for both beginners and advanced cross-country skiers; telemarking lessons are available.

All these areas are open for lessons and touring daily from 10am to 4pm, with rentals of cross-country equipment, snowshoes, and sleds.

For general information on the wonderful network of backcountry trails in the Vail area, consult the Holy Cross Ranger District Office, White River National Forest, P.O. Box 190, Minturn, CO 81645 (tel. 303/827-5715). Of particular note is the system of trails known as the Tenth Mountain Division Hut System. Generally following the World War II training network of the Camp Hale militia, the trails cover 273 miles and link Vail with Leadville and Aspen with Arrowhead; the two sections now connect. There are 14 overnight cabins, and more are being built. Hikers and mountain bikers also use this trail. For reservations and other information, contact the association at 1280 Ute Ave., Aspen, CO 81611 (tel. 303/925-5775).

For more information on equipment rentals, see "Skiing (Alpine)," above.

SLEIGH RIDES   Steve Jones' Sleigh Rides (tel. 845-7770) offers afternoon rides and dinner packages.

SNOWMOBILING   Three tours daily—lunch, afternoon, and dinner—are conducted at the Piney River Ranch, Red Sandstone Road (tel. 476-3941). You can also go snowmobiling with Nova Guides (tel. 949-4232) or Timberline Tours (tel. 476-1414).

SWIMMING   Call for free-swim hours at the public Eagle-Vail Swim Club, 0099 Eagle Drive, Avon (tel. 949-4257). Numerous private clubs in Vail offer swimming for a fee; they include the Vail Athletic Club, 352 E. Meadow Dr. (tel. 476-0700), and the Vail Run Resort, 1000 Lionsridge Loop (tel. 476-1500).

TENNIS   There are many public courts in the Vail valley, including nine at Golden Peak, at the foot of Lift 6, and six at Ford Park, on South Frontage Road east of Vail Village. Lofty guest and court fees are charged by resort condominiums with indoor/outdoor courts, including the Vail Racquet Club, 4690 Racquet Club Dr. (tel. 476-4840).

SHOPPING

Vail is noted for its fine-art galleries. Among the many of note are **Knox Galleries,** 100 E. Meadow Dr. (tel. 476-5171), with life-size sculpture gardens and impressionist paintings, with galleries also in Beaver Creek and Denver; **Gotthelf's Gallery,** 122 E. Meadow Dr. (tel. 476-1777), featuring fine art glass and innovative jewelry; and **Vail Fine Art Gallery,** 141 E. Meadow Dr. (tel. 476-2900), specializing in American and international masters. For a full gallery listing and information on their evening art walks, contact the **Vail Valley Arts Council,** P.O. Box 1153, Vail, CO 81658 (tel. 949-1626).

Vail and Beaver Creek also have a large number of fine clothiers and jewelers, along with every other kind of shop.

EVENING ENTERTAINMENT

THE PERFORMING ARTS   The summer season's big cultural event is the **Bravo! Colorado Music Festival,** from July 4 through the first week of August. Established in 1988, the festival features everything from classical orchestral and chamber music to vocal and pops, from baroque to modern jazz, foreign ethnic performances to youth concerts. Performance days and times vary, but there are typically chamber-music concerts on Tuesday at 6pm at the Chapel at Beaver Creek (tickets: $17.50), major concerts on Saturday and Sunday at 6pm at the Gerald Ford Amphitheatre in Ford Park, Vail (tickets: $12.50), and more intimate presentations in Vail Interfaith Chapel (tickets: $17.50). For tickets or more information, contact the festival office at 953 S. Frontage Rd., Suite 104, Vail, CO 81657 (tel. 303/476-0206).

The **Bolshoi Ballet Academy at Vail,** a satellite school to the famous Bolshoi of Moscow, teaches the Russian style of artistic expression to about 50 young dancers from the United States, Canada, and Mexico. The parent Bolshoi Ballet Academy of Moscow performs with the Vail Academy during its annual residency in August. Also in August they host the Paul Mitchell International Evening of Dance, featuring couples from around the world. For information, contact the Vail Valley Foundation, P.O. Box 309, Vail, CO 81658 (tel. 303/476-9500).

Vail's Ford Amphitheatre hosts **Hot Summer Nights** concerts of contemporary rock or jazz every Friday evening of July and August. Beaver Creek Resort's **Jazz on the Green,** which runs late June through Labor Day weekend, features regional jazz sounds from across America on Sunday at noon on the resort's south lawn.

DANCE CLUBS Vail's greatest concentration of nightclubs can be found in a 1½-block stretch of Bridge Street from Hanson Ranch Road north to the covered bridge over Gore Creek. From mountainside to creek, they include the **Club** (tel. 479-0556), the **Red Lion** (tel. 476-7676), and **Vendetta's** (tel. 476-5070). All have music for dancing: either live rock, rhythm-and-blues, or disco.

Just off Bridge Drive on Gore Creek Drive is **Sheika's,** a lively disco at Gasthof Gramshammer (tel. 476-1515). There is a dance club in the Evergreen Lodge (the **Altitude Club**), 250 S. Frontage Rd. W. (tel. 476-7810).

Country music enthusiasts find swing and two-step on the dance floor at the **Sundance Saloon,** Sunbird Lodge, Lionshead Gondola (tel. 476-3453); or the **Jackalope,** West Vail Mall (tel. 476-4314).

BARS & PUBS Piano bars draw quieter types to **Babau's Café** at L'Ostello, 705 W. Lionshead Circle (tel. 476-2050); **Mickey's** featuring Vail's original Piano Man, in the Lodge at Vail, 174 E. Gore Creek Dr. (tel. 476-5011); and **Ludwig's** in the Sonnenalp Hotel, 20 Vail Rd. (tel. 476-5656). Acoustic guitarists soothe nerves at the **Hong Kong Café,** Wall Street (tel. 476-1818), and **C. J. Capers,** 2211 N. Frontage Rd. W. (tel. 476-5306).

In Beaver Creek, the place to go is the **Beaver Trap Tavern,** St. James Place (tel. 845-8930).

One of Vail's newest establishments is the **Hubcap Brewery and Kitchen,** at the Crossroads Shopping Center, West Meadow Drive at Willow Bridge Road (tel. 476-5757). Vail's first brew pub, the Hubcap invites beer connoisseurs to relax on its large deck and sip such homemade delights as White River Wheat Ale and Rainbow Trout Stout.

WHERE TO STAY

In general, winter season is mid-November to mid-April; summer is the opposite, mid-April to mid-November. Prices are lowest in summer, highest during the Christmas holiday period, and they remain relatively high through the prime January-to-March ski season. Early and late winter seasons (mid-November to mid-December and April until area closing) are moderately priced.

VAIL

Expensive

THE LODGE AT VAIL, 174 E. Gore Creek Dr., Vail, CO 81657. Tel. 303/476-5011 or toll free 800/231-0136. Fax 303/476-7425. 138 rms, 84 suites. TV TEL

$ Rates: Winter, $290–$425 single or double; $445–$1,475 suite. Summer, $120–$160 single or double; $185–$450 suite. 2-week minimum stay over Christmas holidays. AE, DC, MC, V. **Parking:** Free.

Vail's original deluxe hotel—owned by Venice Simplon Orient Express—sits at the base of the Vista Bahn Express in the heart of Vail Village. (Follow Vail Road south from the main Vail interchange, through two lights and around a curve to the left, to the end of the road.) As with most Vail properties, once you've parked, you needn't use your car again until you return home. Everything you need is within a few steps: winter-and-summer recreation, restaurants, lounges, boutiques, galleries—and stunning views.

The lodge offers deluxe hotel rooms and one-, two-, and three-bedroom suites. All have private balconies, mahogany furnishings and paneling, minirefrigerators, full-view mirrors, and floral-pattern appointments. The bathrooms, finished with marble, feature hair dryers, phones, and heated towel racks. Suites, each with a fireplace and full kitchen, are individually owned and decorated by their personal owners, with touches that vary from French provincial to Colorado western.

Dining/Entertainment: The five-star Wildflower Inn (see "Where to Dine," below) serves creative American cuisine in a garden atmosphere. The Café Arlberg offers a deluxe breakfast buffet, lunch, and country Italian cuisine on winter evenings. Mickey's piano bar has featured Mickey Poage at the ivories for over 17 years.

Services: 24-hour room service, concierge, valet laundry, international currency exchange, business center, babysitting, ski storage, no-smoking rooms.

Facilities: Heated swimming pool, Jacuzzis, sauna, exercise room, six tennis courts, gift shop, meeting space for 175.

L'OSTELLO, 705 W. Lionshead Circle, Vail, CO 81657. Tel. 303/476-2050, or toll free 800/283-VAIL. Fax 303/476-9265. 50 rms. TV TEL

$ Rates: Winter, early/mid/late season, $170–$245 double; holiday-and-peak season (Feb–Mar), $240–$295 double. Summer, $60–$100 double. AE, MC, V.
Parking: Free.

A European-style mountain inn just 100 yards from the Lionshead Gondola terminal, L'Ostello lives up to its claim of being "long on sophistication but short on formality." "The Refuge," as its Italian name translates, has a big central fireplace completely surrounded by sunken seating, and one of the Vail Valley's outstanding restaurants.

Guest rooms are fairly simple. Older rooms have a double Murphy bed, a double sofa sleeper, light-wood furnishings, and a wet bar. Renovated rooms have a rich contemporary appearance and feature individual home-entertainment centers. A compact-disc and video-cassette library is complimentary to guests.

Dining/Entertainment: L'Ostello restaurant has won national acclaim for its northern Italian cuisine (see "Where to Dine," below). Babau's Café offers light meals daily from 4:30pm, and major jazz piano entertainment Tuesday through Sunday nights. Breakfast is served daily from 7 to 10am in the L'Ostello dining room.

Services: Room service, concierge, valet laundry, complimentary *USA Today* (delivered to your room each morning).

Facilities: Heated outdoor swimming pool, fitness center, massage room, meeting space for 100.

SONNENALP RESORT, 20 Vail Rd., Vail, CO 81657. Tel. 303/476-5656 or 800/654-8312. Fax 303/476-1639. 80 rms, 100 suites. TV TEL

$ Rates (including full breakfast): Winter, $175–$295 single or double; $250–$800 suite. Summer, $105–$135 single or double; $150–$445 suite. DC, MC, V.
Parking: Free.

This is one of Vail's more unusual hotels, encompassing three separate buildings that extend—interrupted by other properties—for two blocks along the south side of Gore Creek, from the covered bridge across Willow Bridge Road to the Vail Interfaith Chapel. Each building has the warmth and ambience of a small inn in Bavaria, the original home of owners Rosana and Johannes Fässler. Yet the hotel is able to offer the amenities of a large resort complex complete with golfing at the Singletree Golf Course (see "Sports & Recreation" in "What to See & Do," above), 13 miles east near Edwards. There's an extensive hotel activities program both winter and summer.

Creek-side, garden-level, and Village View hotel rooms, and a wide variety of suites, are furnished with loving detail. From carved pine armoires to down comforters and pillows, all furniture and appointments are imported from the German Alps—right down to staff uniforms.

Dining/Entertainment: Ludwig's (see "Where to Dine," below) is an intimate creek-side dining room serving continental and new American cuisines. The casual Bully Pub features soup-and-salad bar, pastas, pizzas, and sandwiches. The Swiss Chalet offers traditional Swiss foods: raclette and cheese and beef fondues.

Services: Room service, concierge, valet laundry.

Facilities: Full European health spa and cosmetic boutique, two heated outdoor swimming pools, hot tubs, four tennis courts, golf course (with Swing Dynamics Institute); kindergarten program for children; meeting space for 150.

VAIL ATHLETIC CLUB, 352 E. Meadow Dr. (at Vail Valley Dr.), Vail, CO 81657. Tel. 303/476-0700 or toll free 800/822-4754. Fax 303/476-6451. 31 rms, 7 suites. TV TEL

$ Rates (including continental breakfast): Winter, $175–$355 single or double; $335–$240 suite. Summer, $115 single or double; $235 suite. AE, DISC, MC, V. **Parking:** Free.

Located in the heart of Vail Village on the banks of Gore Creek, Vail Athletic Club is within walking distance of the ski lifts, shops, dining, restaurants, and nightlife, and is also the only hotel in the village with its own spa and fitness club. The hotel's restaurant, Terra Bistro, serves dinner.

Rooms have either two queen-size beds or one king, plus small refrigerators and humidifiers. Each suite has a kitchen, a living room with fireplace and deck, one bedroom, and two full baths.

Services: Room service, concierge, valet laundry, babysitting, ski storage, facilities for the disabled.

Facilities: Athletic club and spa (with a swimming pool, racquetball-and-squash courts, four Jacuzzis, steam, sauna, extensive cardiovascular area, and other facilities), gift shop, guest laundry, beauty salon; meeting space for 100.

Moderate

ANTLERS AT VAIL, 680 W. Lionshead Place, Vail, CO 81657. Tel. 303/476-2471 or toll free 800/843-VAIL. Fax 303/476-4146. 69 suites (all with bath). TV TEL

$ Rates: Winter, $185–$675; summer, $85–$190. AE, DC, DISC, MC, V. **Parking:** Free.

These luxurious condominium units near the foot of the Lionshead Gondola have a long reputation for friendly service and unobstructed views up Vail Mountain. Units range in size from studios to three-bedroom suites; each has a full-size, fully equipped kitchen, a fireplace, a private view balcony, and satellite TV (with HBO and free VCR). Facilities include a heated outdoor swimming pool, Jacuzzi, sun deck, two saunas, guest laundry, and ski storage. There's meeting space for 150.

GASTHOF GRAMSHAMMER, 231 E. Gore Creek Dr., Vail, CO 81657. Tel. 303/476-5626. 24 rms, 4 suites (all with bath). Fax 303/476-8816. TV TEL

$ Rates: Winter, $195–$250 single or double; $240–$555 suite. Summer, $75–$80 single; $85–$118 double; $125–$375 suite. AE, DC, MC, V. **Parking:** Free.

Austria natives Pepi and Sheika Gramshammer built this Tyrolean lodge three decades ago and watched Vail Village grow up around it. The Gramshammers still greet guests personally at their lodge, which maintains a deluxe European-style ambience all the way to the goose-down comforters. There's a wide choice of room types: standard (two double beds), deluxe (two queen size or one king size), deluxe with kitchenette, studio apartment, studio suites with connecting bedroom, one-bedroom apartment, two-bedroom suite, and family suite.

Pepi's Restaurant serves continental cuisine for lunch and dinner; the Antlers Room specializes in wild game and veal. Pepi's Bar frequently has live music, and Sheika's Night Club is popular for disco dancing. The lodge also has a sports equipment and fashion shop.

LION SQUARE LODGE, 660 W. Lionshead Place, Vail, CO 81657. Tel. 303/476-2281 or toll free 800/525-5788. Fax 303/476-7423. 28 rms, 75 suites (all with bath). TV TEL

$ Rates: Winter, $130–$290 lodge; $180–$465 one-bedroom; $305–$725 two-bedroom. Summer, $90 lodge; $110 one-bedroom; $180 two-bedroom. AE, CB, DC, DISC, JCB, MC, V. **Parking:** Free.

A ski-in, ski-out property on Gore Creek at the base of the Lionshead Gondola, the Lion Square offers deluxe lodge rooms or one-, two-, and three-bedroom condominiums. All condo units have mountain views, spacious living rooms with balconies and fireplaces, and fully equipped kitchens.

There are complimentary coffee, cookies, and newspapers in the lobby each morning, and the K.B. Ranch Co. serves steak-and-seafood dinners. The lodge offers concierge, valet laundry, and a free local shuttle van. Facilities include a heated outdoor swimming pool, hot tubs, sauna, ski-and-bicycle storage, and meeting space for 400.

MOUNTAIN HAUS AT VAIL, 292 E. Meadow Dr. (P.O. Box 1748), Vail, CO 81657. Tel. 303/476-2434 or toll free 800/237-0922. Fax 303/476-3007. 10 rms, 64 suites (all with bath). TV TEL
$ Rates: Winter, $120–$390 single or double; $215–$830 suite. Summer, $90–$165 single; $90–$350 double; $215–$830 suite. AE, DISC, MC, V.

Located in Vail Village on East Meadow Drive at Bridge Street, at the covered bridge across Gore Creek, these privately owned condominiums have been individually decorated by their owners. Guests can choose between handsome hotel rooms and spacious one- to four-bedroom condo units. All have fireplaces (wood is provided), private balconies, and fully equipped kitchens. Two-bedroom units sleep six: There's a sleeper sofa in the living room, two bathrooms, and a ski room at the entrance.

The Mountain Haus has a heated outdoor swimming pool, indoor-and-outdoor Jacuzzis, men's and women's steam rooms and saunas, a guest laundry, and valet laundry service. The desk is staffed 24 hours.

Inexpensive

**PARK MEADOWS LODGE, 1472 Matterhorn Circle, Vail, CO 81657. Tel. 303/476-5598. Fax 303/476-3056. 27 units (all with bath). TV TEL
$ Rates:** Winter, $54–$125; summer, $38–$68. Weekly rates available; children 12 and under stay free in parents' room. MC, V.

Located in West Vail, adjacent to the bicycle path and only an 8-minute walk from the Cascade Village Lift and the terminus of the free Vail shuttle, the Park Meadows is one of the few family-style economy lodges left in the Vail valley. All rooms— efficiency studios, one-bedroom and two-bedroom suites—have kitchenettes with microwaves and hideaway sofas. There's a central sitting area with a large fireplace and board games, a recreation room with a pool table, a hot tub in an outdoor courtyard, and a coin laundry.

THE ROOST LODGE, 1783 N. Frontage Rd. W., Vail, CO 81657. Tel. 303/476-5451 or toll free 800/873-3065. 72 rms (all with bath). TV TEL
$ Rates (including continental breakfast): Winter, $58–$114; summer, $39–$59. MC, V.

Personal attention in a country-inn atmosphere is the boast of the Roost, a family-run ski lodge on the north side of I-70 in West Vail. Rooms are cozy, with pleasing appointments. The lodge has an enclosed outdoor swimming pool, Jacuzzi, and sauna, and is accessible to the disabled. In the summer guests enjoy white-water rafting and mountain biking. A free lodge shuttle runs to Vail Village on the hour, daily from 8am to 10pm.

WEST OF VAIL
Expensive

BEAVER CREEK LODGE, 26 Avondale Lane (P.O. Box 2578), Beaver Creek, CO 81620. Tel. 303/845-9800 or toll free 800/732-6777. Fax 303/845-8242. 71 suites. A/C TV TEL
$ Rates: $90–$430 suites. AE, CB, DC, MC, V. **Parking:** Free underground valet parking.

The phrase "casually elegant" can be overworked, but it fits this all-suite property. Located in the heart of Beaver Creek at the foot of the Centennial Express Lift, it's built around an interior atrium, but it avoids the institutional appearance of many other atrium hotels.

The hotel's 71 efficiency suites have handsome oak furnishings and paneling throughout. All have queen or king-size beds and sleeper sofas, fully equipped kitchenettes with microwave ovens and wet bars, gaslight fireplaces, humidifiers, two TVs (one with a VCR), and two phones.

Dining/Entertainment: The Black Diamond Bar and Grill serves a breakfast buffet, lunch, and dinners of gourmet continental and new American cuisine. Dining indoors is bistro style; outside, there's a viewing deck. Many folks gravitate to the Atrium Lobby Bar for après-ski.

Services: Room service, 24-hour concierge, ski valet, individual ski lockers.

Facilities: Indoor/outdoor swimming pool, Jacuzzi, steam room, sauna, exercise equipment, ski-rental shop, retail shops and boutiques; meeting space for 200.

HYATT REGENCY BEAVER CREEK, P.O. Box 1595, Avon, CO 81620. Tel. 303/949-1234 or toll free 800/233-1234. Fax 303/949-4164. 295 rms. MINIBAR TV TEL

$ Rates: Winter, $365–$500; $855–$2,280 suite. Spring, $100–$300; $315–$925 suite. Summer, $185–$350; $415–$970 suite. Fall, $175–$295; $315–$1,040 suite. All rates single or double. Children 18 or under stay free in parents' room. AE, CB, DC, DISC, JCB, MC, V. **Parking:** $10 valet.

An architecturally unique hotel at the foot of the Beaver Creek lifts, this ski-in/ski-out Hyatt blends features of medieval European alpine monasteries with Rocky Mountain styles and materials. The exterior is native stone, offset with stucco and rough timbers; a domed cupola, peaked roofs, and copper flashing are singular touches. The interior is of rough-hewn pine and sandstone; wall-size fireplaces enhance numerous cozy alcoves furnished with overstuffed chairs and sofas. Elk-antler chandeliers and works by contemporary artisans lend a western ambience.

Guest rooms have a European country elegance, knotty-pine furnishings, and a stenciled border to the ceiling and walls. The raised beds have dust ruffles, pillow shams, and quilted comforters. The TV and minibar are in an armoire. Most rooms have private balconies. The bathroom features a marble-top vanity, hair dryer, heated towel rack, and coffee maker.

Dining/Entertainment: The Patina Ristorante, open for three meals daily, has an open fireplace for cold days and an outdoor terrace for warm ones. The menu offers everything from gourmet northern Italian and continental cuisine to light snacks. The Crooked Hearth serves prime rib, fish, and other selections around another large fireplace, and offers live entertainment most nights. The Double Diamond Deli has all manner of snacks and even prepares picnic baskets for mountain hikes and rides. The Lobby Lounge Tavern, open only to hotel guests in winter, has entertainment during evening cocktails, and McCoy's Café offers quick meals and a daily après-ski party. The Hyatt has a cozy library with books and chessboards.

Services: Room service, concierge, complimentary ski valet, Camp Hyatt children's day program.

Facilities: Full-service health spa (with indoor/outdoor swimming pool, six open-air Jacuzzis, saunas, weight-and-exercise room, aerobics and water aerobics classes, facials, massages, and herbal wraps), six tennis courts; retail boutiques, jewelry, and sportswear; meeting space for 750.

THE LODGE AT CORDILLERA, 2205 Cordillera Way (P.O. Box 1110), Edwards, CO 81632. Tel. 303/926-2200 or toll free 800/548-2721. 28 rms and suites. A/C TV TEL

$ Rates (including breakfast): Winter, $155–$430; summer, $130–$325. AE, CB, DC, JCB, MC, V. **Parking:** Free valet parking.

Like a mountain château in the Pyrenees of southwestern France, this luxurious hideaway nestles in 3,200 acres of private forest 13 miles west of Vail, and about 3 miles from Beaver Creek. Chinese slate roofs crown the sophisticated edifice of native woods, stone, and stucco.

The same Rocky Mountain timber and stone, along with elegant wrought iron, are used in the handsome, residential-style guest rooms. Handworked Spanish and French furnishings lend an Old World touch. More than half the rooms feature wood-burning fireplaces; all have king- or queen-size beds with down comforters, remote-control cable television, and most have private balconies or decks with views of the New York Range of the Rockies.

Dining/Entertainment: The Restaurant Picasso is one of the Vail Valley's finest dining establishments (see "Where to Dine," below). A European buffet breakfast, included with the room bill, is also served here. The Lobby Lounge presents piano music Wednesday through Sunday in season.

Services: Room service, concierge, valet laundry.

Facilities: European spa and salon (outdoor swimming pool and 25m/82-ft. indoor lap pool, indoor-and-outdoor Jacuzzis, steam room and sauna in men's and women's locker rooms, weight-and-exercise room, aerobics, massage, hydrotherapy, body treatments), a new 18-hole Hale Irwin signature golf course, 15 miles of mountain-biking or cross-country skiing trails, two tennis courts; meeting space for 125.

THE PINES LODGE, Scott Hill Rd. (P.O. Box 36), Beaver Creek, CO 81620. Tel. 303/845-7900 or toll free 800/859-8242. Fax 303/845-7809. 60 rms. TV TEL

$ Rates (including continental breakfast): Winter, $195–$425 single or double; $575–$1,400 suite. Summer, $79–$125 single or double; $270–$405 suite. MC, V. **Parking:** Covered valet parking.

Pine-and-aspen groves camouflage this handsome lodge, situated on a hillside overlooking Beaver Creek Resort from the west. Skiers can easily come and go from the Strawberry Park Lift to the hotel, which has a stately, almost Tudor-style elegance.

Rooms are furnished in Bavarian charm, with a southwestern ambience. They've got adobe walls and natural-pine furniture, as well as a panoramic view of the resort village. Each room has a king-size or two double beds with goose-down comforters. Amenities include terry-cloth robes, and every room has a video-cassette recorder with its television; the hotel maintains a free video library for guests.

Dining/Entertainment: Gourmet continental dinners are served nightly in the Pines Room.

Services: Ski valet, business center.

Facilities: Heated outdoor swimming pool, Jacuzzi, steam rooms, fitness center, games room, recreation programs; meeting space for 150.

Moderate

EAGLE RIVER INN, 145 N. Main St. (P.O. Box 100), Minturn, CO 81645. Tel. 303/827-5761 or toll free 800/344-1750. 12 rms (all with three-quarter bath). TV

$ Rates (including breakfast): Winter, single or double, $98–$108 early and late season, $160–$170 regular season, $182–$192 holiday periods; summer, $89 single or double. MC, V.

Built in 1894 when the Denver & Rio Grande Railroad first made the village of Minturn a stop on its route, the picturesque Eagle River Inn has had many incarnations. Its latest make-over, in 1986, turned it into a fine bed-and-breakfast. It feels like Santa Fe throughout, from the *sala*-style lobby (complete with *kiva* fireplace, *bancos,* and other southwestern-style furnishings) to the bright and breezy second- and third-story guest rooms. The rooms feature tiled three-quarter baths and down comforters.

Breakfast is "gourmet continental," including homemade granola, fresh fruit, and baked goods. The hot tub on a deck overlooking the Eagle River is always available. Smoking and pets are not permitted.

Inexpensive

COMFORT INN, 0161 W. Beaver Creek Blvd. (P.O. Box 5510), Avon, CO 81620. Tel. 303/949-5511 or toll free 800/423-4374. Fax 303/949-7762. 143 rms, 4 suites (all with bath). A/C TV TEL

$ Rates (including continental breakfast in winter): Winter, $79–$195 single or double. Summer, $69–$79 single or double; $59–$84 suite. AE, DC, DISC, ER, JCB, MC, V. **Parking:** Free.

A four-story hotel just off the I-70 Avon/Beaver Creek interchange, this comfortable franchise establishment has a big fireplace in its lobby lounge and modified southwestern decor. Most of the spacious rooms have two queen-size beds; a few boast king-size beds. All rooms have remote-control cable television. No-smoking rooms are available. There's indoor ski storage and a free shuttle to Beaver Creek Resort, a heated outdoor pool, a Jacuzzi, and a guest laundry.

CAMPING

SYLVAN LAKE STATE PARK, Brush Creek Rd., 16 miles south of Eagle. Tel. 303/625-1607. 50 sites.

$ Rates: $6 per site, plus $3 state parks pass. No credit cards.

Two separate campgrounds on this beautiful 40-acre trout-fishing lake in the White River National Forest accommodate tents and recreational vehicles. There are bathhouses, fire pits, water, and other facilities.

WHERE TO DINE

VERY EXPENSIVE

BEANO'S CABIN, foot of Larkspur Lift, Beaver Creek Resort. Tel. 949-9090.

Cuisine: REGIONAL. **Reservations:** Required.

$ Prices: Fixed-price, $69 adults, $46 children under 12. MC, V.

Open: Dinner daily 5:30-9:30pm (departures from Rendezvous Cabin).

One splurge that every Beaver Creek visitor should make is the sleigh-ride dinner trip (or in summer, the horse-drawn wagon ride) to Beano's. This isn't the log homestead that Chicago lettuce farmer Frank "Beano" Bienkowski built on Beaver Creek Mountain in 1919—it's far more elegant. Diners board the 42-passenger, snow-cat-driven sleighs at the base of the Centennial Lift, arriving 15 minutes later for a candlelit dinner around a crackling fire with musical entertainment.

Diners choose from eight entrées, which always include beef, lamb, seafood, chicken, and pasta. Vegetarian meals may be requested. Desserts are included; a favorite is the warm pecan square with whisky sauce. Ask about the availability of the Sunday brunch.

L'OSTELLO, 705 W. Lionshead Circle. Tel. 476-2050.

Cuisine: NORTHERN ITALIAN. **Reservations:** Recommended.

$ Prices: Appetizers $7-$15, main courses $22-$33. AE, MC.

Open: Dinner only, daily 6-10pm.

Under the same ownership as New York's *nuova cuccina* Andiamo, L'Ostello ("The Refuge") is an ultracontemporary dining room in a small European-style hotel. Tiny hanging halogen light fixtures, unusual metal chairs with embroidered cushions, and a tile floor provide the atmosphere.

You can start with such appetizers as tuna carpaccio or roasted-eggplant soup. The fine choice of dishes changes on a regular basis, but may include crabmeat ravioli with ginger-carrot broth, roast rack of lamb with potato gnocchi, or roasted chicken with sweet roasted garlic. Vegetables are grilled and served with three different accompaniments: tapenade, pesto, and a sun-dried-tomato pesto.

RESTAURANT PICASSO, in the Lodge at Cordillera, 2205 Cordillera Way, Edwards. Tel. 926-2200.

Cuisine: MODERN FRENCH. **Reservations:** Recommended.

$ Prices: Appetizers $5-$10; lunch $6-$15; dinner $22-$30. AE, MC, V.

Open: Daily lunch noon-2pm; dinner 6:30-10pm.

Original works by Pablo Picasso actually hang on the walls of this sophisticated restaurant, which combines European elegance with Rocky Mountain splendor. Chef Fabrice Beaudoin creates memorable meals, using only the freshest ingredients each evening to prepare a variety of gourmet delicacies.

EXPENSIVE

THE BRISTOL AT ARROWHEAD, Country Club of the Rockies, 0676 Sawatche Dr., Edwards. Tel. 926-2111.

Cuisine: CREATIVE AMERICAN. **Reservations:** Recommended.

$ Prices: Appetizers $6.25-$8.95; main courses $16.50-$25.50. AE, MC, V.

Open: Lunch daily 11:30am–3pm; dinner daily 6–10pm.

You can enjoy a sleigh ride for dinner, but unlike Beano's, that's a fringe benefit here, not the means to the end. The dining room at this popular golf-and-ski resort center, 2½ miles west of Beaver Creek off I-70, Exit 163, is decidedly not far off the beaten path.

The menu is inspired by imagination and international culinary knowledge. Appetizers include lobster quesadilla, four cheeses baked in filo, and artichoke half-moon pasta. There are fresh cooked seafood specials daily, as well as grilled quail, roasted chicken, and filet mignon grilled to perfection.

CHANTICLER, 710 W. Lionshead Circle. Tel. 476-1441.
   Cuisine: CONTINENTAL. **Reservations:** Recommended.
$ Prices: Appetizers $7.50–$9.95; main courses $16.75–$27.25. AE, DC, DISC, MC, V.
   Open: Dinner only, daily 6–10pm.

Victorian surroundings greet you in this intimate French-country restaurant in the Vail Spa. Pewter antiques and fine artwork grace the shelves and walls, and beautiful brass chandeliers hang over the candlelit tables. Service is attentive but not intrusive.

Wild game, fresh fish, fowl, and steaks grace the menu. Only the freshest ingredients are used, and the pastries are all homemade. There's also an extensive wine list.

THE GOLDEN EAGLE INN, Village Hall, Beaver Creek Mall. Tel. 949-1940.
   Cuisine: CREATIVE AMERICAN.
$ Prices: Appetizers $4.50–$8.50; main courses dinner $13.95–$23.95, lunch $8.50–$12.95. AE, MC, V.
   Open: Daily 11:30am–midnight.

Sidewalk tables on the Beaver Creek promenade are the outstanding feature of this restaurant, owned by Austrian Pepi Langeggar of Vail's Tyrolean Inn. Appetizers include a baked almond-coated Brie and venison in phyllo with mushroom cream. Main courses feature loin of elk, rack of lamb, grilled pheasant breast with a red-currant and amaretto sauce, pastas, and fresh seafood.

IMPERIAL FEZ, 1000 Lions Ridge Loop. Tel. 476-1948.
   Cuisine: MOROCCAN. **Reservations:** Recommended.
$ Prices: Fixed-price dinner $28 for five courses, $33 for six courses. MC, V.
   Open: Dinner only, daily 5–10pm.

Here you find yourself in a giant Moroccan tent when you walk through the door. Owner Rafih Benjelloun will seat you on cushions at a low, round table, then spread white towels across your laps to keep you from being too messy while you eat with your fingers. (Finger bowls are provided.) Belly dancers and sword dancers add to the entrancing atmosphere.

Main courses cover a wide range of foods and preparations, like apricot lamb, fish in paprika sauce, Moroccan baked beef tajine, or spicy quail M'shui. There are also poultry, prawns, and vegetarian offerings. For dessert, have a cup of mint tea and a chocolate b'stella.

SWEET BASIL, 193 E. Gore Creek Dr. Tel. 476-0125.
   Cuisine: CREATIVE AMERICAN. **Reservations:** Recommended.
$ Prices: Appetizers $6–$11.50; main courses $4–$8.95 at lunch, $19–$25 at dinner. AE, MC, V.
   Open: Lunch daily 11:30am–2:30pm; dinner daily 5:30–10pm.

Simple modern decor, with contemporary art on the peach-colored walls and tasteful use of mirrors and large windows, is the earmark of this pleasant restaurant. A deck looks out on the Lodge Promenade in the center of Vail Village. Diners can sit at private tables or be served at the wine bar.

Fish and seafood predominate on this creative-and-delicious menu. Specialties include saffron and angel-hair pasta with lobster, scallops and shrimp, and grilled ginger-cured salmon. But there's also rack of lamb, grilled pork chop, and roast filet mignon.

TYROLEAN INN, 400 E. Meadow Dr. Tel. 476-2204.

Cuisine: REGIONAL/CONTINENTAL. **Reservations:** Recommended.
$ Prices: Appetizers $5.75–$8.95; main courses $14.95–$29.95. AE, DC, MC, V.
Open: Dinner only, daily 5:30–10pm.

The Langeggar family are proud of their Old World roots. Pepi established this Vail landmark more than two decades ago, and the ambience today remains decidedly alpine, with gracious, friendly service and authentic Tyrolean decor. In the summer, there's dining on an outdoor patio beside gurgling Gore Creek.

Wild game, when available, is the house specialty: venison sauerbraten, pheasant Kroatzbeere—or for the total experience, the wild-game medley of wild boar Budapest, elk forestière, and caribou Midnight Sun. You'll always find such items as pepper steak Madagascar, wienerschnitzel, and Muscovy duck.

WILDFLOWER INN, in the Lodge at Vail, 174 E. Gore Creek Dr. Tel. 476-8111.

Cuisine: CREATIVE AMERICAN. **Reservations:** Recommended.
$ Prices: Appetizers $6–$21; main courses $19–$32. AE, DC, MC, V.
Open: Dinner only, Wed–Mon 6–10pm.

Fine china, silver, and crystal grace the lodge's upscale dining room, a garden affair on the second floor, with a broad outdoor deck facing Vail Mountain. Foie-gras terrine and salt-cod ravioli are among the appetizers. Then come the delightful main dishes: grilled duck breast on spinach pancakes with a red-pepper sauce, sautéed anglerfish with fried shallots, braised Sephardic short ribs, and roast veal breast with matzoh stuffing.

MODERATE

BLU'S, 193 E. Gore Creek Dr. Tel. 476-3113.

Cuisine: INTERNATIONAL. **Reservations:** Recommended at dinner.
$ Prices: Appetizers $6.25–$9.25; main courses $6.50–$17.95; breakfast/lunch $4.50–$7.95. MC, V.
Open: Daily 9am–11pm.

This eatery, located down the stairs from the Children's Fountain by Gore Creek, off Willow Bridge Road, is a local favorite—in no small part because it offers breakfasts daily until 5pm for late risers.

There's a wide selection of breakfast/lunch items including green eggs and ham, omelettes, vegetarian specialties, pasta dishes, salads, sandwiches, and burgers. The emphasis is Continental during dinner, with fresh seafood, pasta, mustard pepper steak, Gypsy schnitzel and an extensive wine list.

HUBCAP BREWERY AND KITCHEN, Crossroads Shopping Center, W. Meadow Dr. at Willow Bridge Rd. Tel. 476-5757.

Cuisine: AMERICAN. **Reservations:** Not accepted.
$ Prices: Appetizers $2.25–$7.25; main courses $4.75–$6.95 lunch, $6.95–$14.95 dinner. AE, MC, V.
Open: Daily 11:30am–1am.

A state-of-the-art brew pub, with a glass-enclosed brew house, this establishment serves real, unfiltered, unpasteurized beer. Sandwich offerings include grilled chicken, BLT, steak, and tuna. There are also burgers, salads, and soups. Dinner selections, which come with homemade beer bread, include grilled quail, barbecued chicken and ribs, fresh seafood, New York strip steak, a vegetarian platter, and fish-and-chips. There's Mom's apple pie for dessert.

LUDWIG'S, in the Sonnenalp Hotel, 20 Vail Rd. Tel. 476-5656.

Cuisine: CREATIVE CONTINENTAL. **Reservations:** Recommended.
$ Prices: Appetizers $5.25–$7.50; main courses $12.25–$19.50; breakfast buffet $12; Sun brunch $11.50–$22. MC, V.
Open: Breakfast Mon–Sat 7–11am; dinner only, Thurs–Tues 5:30–10:30pm; Sun brunch 7am–noon, winter only.

Chef Mark Spitzer is the only "master chef" designated by Les Chaînes des Rôtissieures in the state of Colorado, and that's reason enough to visit this classical European dining room. Named after Bavaria's King Ludwig, it has an intimate creek-side location and frequent "opera dinners," featuring resident musician Cindy Saunders at the piano. Your meal might start with a gravlax of smoked salmon, a lobster bisque, or a wilted-spinach salad. For a main course, consider grilled venison sausage with polenta cakes, sautéed Gulf shrimp in a citrus beurre blanc, or tenderloin of beef.

MONTAUK SEAFOOD GRILL, 549 Lionshead Mall. Tel. 476-2601.
Cuisine: SEAFOOD. **Reservations:** Recommended.
$ Prices: Appetizers $5.95–$7.95; main courses $15.95–$21.95. AE, MC, V.
Open: Daily 5–10pm.
Gary Boris, the managing partner of this seafood grill, grew up around the harbors of Montauk Point, New York. Now that he's landlocked, he flies in fresh fish daily from both coasts, as well as the water of Hawaii and the Gulf of Mexico. The area's only raw bar is stocked not only with oysters, but with clams, shrimp, and crab as well.

THE RED LION, 304 Bridge St. Tel. 476-7676.
Cuisine: STEAK/SEAFOOD.
$ Prices: $6–$17. MC, V.
Open: Daily 11am–midnight.
Established soon after the village of Vail, the Red Lion has been a popular spot for people watching for nearly three decades. Crowds may spill out into the streets at dinnertime; look up at the porch and you'll see folks staring back down at you. Food here is traditional but good and filling: hickory-smoked barbecued swordfish, baby-back ribs, and spareribs; gourmet hamburgers and chicken sandwiches; soups and specialty salads. Bar goers are drawn by the Around the World Beer Club (over 50 varieties), live entertainment nightly, and 14 TVs for sporting events.

VENDETTA'S, 291 Bridge St. Tel. 476-5070.
Cuisine: NORTHERN ITALIAN. **Reservations:** Recommended.
$ Prices: Appetizers $4.95–$12.95; main courses $13.95–$24.95; lunch $5–$8. AE, MC, V.
Open: Lunch daily 11am–3pm; dinner daily 5:30–11pm.
Located on busy Bridge Street in the heart of Vail Village, Vendetta's is a casual, friendly spot as famous for its après-ski (on a sunny deck) and nightly entertainment as it is for its outstanding Italian cuisine. Pasta lovers enjoy such dishes as manicotti Veneziana (baked with four cheeses), and lasagne pasticciate verdi (baked with beef and sausage). Osso buco (baked veal shank), bistecca alla Florentine (an Italian pepper steak), and pollo D'Angelo (chicken sautéed with artichoke hearts, garlic, mushrooms, and pimiento) are meat favorites, and seafood specials range from linguine al salmone to cioppino to fettuccine frutti di mare.

INEXPENSIVE

D. J. McCADAMS, 616 W. Lionshead Circle. Tel. 476-2336.
Cuisine: AMERICAN.
$ Prices: $4–$7.
Open: Daily 24 hours.
Got an uncontrollable urge to munch at 2am? This small, modern-day diner in Concert Hall Plaza is the place to come for a breakfast burrito, chili-cheese omelet, or perhaps a calorie-rich dessert crêpe. Be prepared to crowd in: There's not much room.

MINTURN COUNTRY CLUB, 131 Main St., Minturn. Tel. 827-4114.
Cuisine: STEAK/SEAFOOD.
$ Prices: Main courses $7.95–$14.95. MC, V.
Open: Dinner only, daily 4:30–10pm.
You won't need your putter at this spot in the old Minturn post office. Instead, be ready to have fun cooking your own dinner. Toss a steak, chicken, fish, or lobster on the large open grill, then share cooking tips with your neighbors while seasoning your

meal with teriyaki sauce, garlic powder, butter, and spices scattered around the grill's perimeter. Main-dish prices include a salad bar.

6. LEADVILLE

113 miles W of Denver, 59 miles E of Aspen

GETTING THERE **By Plane** The Lake County Airport, Road 23 off U.S. 24 South (tel. 719/486-2627), 2 miles south of downtown, at 9,927 feet elevation is said to be America's highest commercial airport. Service here is strictly air-taxi and charter, however, so most visitors must fly into Denver's International Airport and rent a vehicle there. There's no regularly scheduled shuttle service to Leadville from Denver.

By Bus Bus and van shuttles to and from Vail, Breckenridge, and other nearby communities are operated by Dee Hive Tours, 506 Harrison Ave. (tel. 486-2339), and the Leadville Transit Department, 800 Harrison Ave. (tel. 486-2090).

By Car Coming from Denver, leave I-70 at Exit 195 (Copper Mountain) and proceed south 24 miles on Colo. 91. From Grand Junction, depart I-70 at Exit 171 (Minturn) and continue south 33 miles on U.S. 24. From Aspen, take Colo. 82 east 44 miles over Independence Pass, then turn north on U.S. 24 for another 15 miles. There's also easy access from the south via U.S. 24 from Colorado Springs (139 miles), Pueblo (156 miles), Alamosa (135 miles), and Gunnison (118 miles).

SPECIAL EVENTS Leadville hosts the following annual events: the Leadville Open Golf Tournament, in mid-June; the Leadville Music Festival, in mid- to late July; the Boom Days Celebration, over the first weekend of August; Oktoberfest in early October; the International Pack Burro Race, early August; and the Victorian Christmas Homes Tour, in early December.

There was a time, not much more than a century ago, when Leadville was the most important city between St. Louis and San Francisco. Founded in 1860 on the gold that glimmered in prospectors' pans, the Oro City site quickly attracted 10,000 miners who worked $5 million in gold out of a 3-mile stretch of the California Gulch by 1865. When the riches were gone, the town was deserted. A smaller lode of gold-bearing quartz kept Oro City alive for another decade.

In 1875 prospectors Bill Stevens and Al Wood discovered that the carbonates of lead ores in the valley's heavy black soil were laden with "15 ounces of silver to the ton." They located the California Gulch's first paying silver lode. Over the next two decades, until the silver crash of 1893, "Leadville" (as it had been designated by the Post Office Department) grew to have an estimated 30,000 residents—among them Horace Tabor, who parlayed his mercantile-and-mining investments into unimaginable wealth; and "the Unsinkable" Molly Brown, whose husband made his fortune here before moving to Denver, where the family lived at the time of Molly's *Titanic* heroism. Many buildings of the silver boom (which produced $136 million between 1879 and 1889) have been preserved in what may be Colorado's most complete National Historic District. This downtown area is fascinating to explore, and the people have retained their western warmth and friendliness.

Today, though Leadville's population has dwindled, mining remains a key industry. Some 90% of the world's molybdenum, an element used to strengthen steel, is produced atop Fremont Pass at Climax, 12 miles north of Leadville en route to Copper Mountain. Gold, silver, lead, and zinc are mined at four other large deposits around Lake County.

ORIENTATION

Leadville has the highest elevation of any incorporated city in the United States: 10,152 feet, nearly 2 miles high. The population is around 3,500.

INFORMATION   You'll get the information you need from the Greater Leadville Area Chamber of Commerce, 809 Harrison Ave. (P.O. Box 861), Leadville, CO 80461 (tel. 719/486-3900 or toll free 800/933-3901).

CITY LAYOUT   U.S. 24 is Leadville's one main street. Entering from the north, the highway is known as Poplar Street; it staggers west one block at Ninth Street. Turn left at the traffic light (one of two in town) and you stay on U.S. 24, now Harrison Avenue. The next seven blocks south, to Second Street, are the heart of this historic town. Leadville's other stoplight is at the intersection of Harrison Avenue and Sixth Street, which proceeds west to civic and recreational complexes. A block north, Fifth Street climbs east to the old train depot and 13,186-foot Mosquito Pass, America's highest, open to four-wheel-drive vehicles in summer.

GETTING AROUND

Check with the Leadville Transit Department, 800 Harrison Ave. (tel. 486-2090), or Dee Hive Tours, 506 Harrison Ave. (tel. 486-2339), for local **information.**

Auto rentals are available through Leadville Leasing at the airport (tel. 486-2627).

A seven-passenger **horse-drawn surrey** tours Leadville daily, June to Labor Day, daily 10am to 4pm, from the chamber of commerce office.

Leadville Air Tours (tel. 486-2627) conducts tours of the city and surrounding Rockies, starting at $25 per person (minimum of two).

FAST FACTS

The **area code** is 719. In case of **emergency,** call 911; for regular business, call the Leadville Police (tel. 486-1365) or the Lake County Sheriff (tel. 486-1249). The sheriff's office also provides road reports. For **medical assistance,** visit 37-bed St. Vincent General Hospital, West Fourth Street and Washington Street (tel. 486-0230), or Leadville Medical Center, 825 W. Sixth St. (tel. 486-1264). The **post office** is at West Fifth Street and Pine Street, a block west of Harrison Avenue (tel. 486-1667).

WHAT TO SEE & DO
ATTRACTIONS

THE EARTH RUNS SILVER: EARLY LEADVILLE, 809 Harrison Ave. Tel. 486-3900.

This 30-minute multi-image production uses six slide projectors, music, and narration to tell the story of Leadville and many of its famous and infamous personalities. It's presented in the Old Church Arts and Humanities Center, next door to the chamber of commerce, where tickets are sold.

Admission: $3.50 adults, $3 seniors, $2 children 12–16.

Open: Summer, daily 10am–5pm (showings hourly); call for winter hours.

HEALY HOUSE AND DEXTER CABIN, 912 Harrison Ave. Tel. 486-0487.

The refined Victorian social-and-cultural life of the privileged classes of the late 19th century is reflected in these two adjacent houses, which are a state historical museum. The three-story, wood-frame Healy House was built in 1878 by mining engineer August Meyer, who made it a center of social activity. Daniel Healy purchased the house in 1897, and leased it out as a boarding house. The adjacent Dexter Cabin was built of logs in 1879 by mining magnate James Dexter, who used the building as his Leadville residence.

Admission: $3 adults, $2 children 6–16, and $2.50 seniors over 65, free for children under 6.

Open: Memorial Day weekend to Labor Day, Mon–Sat 10am–4:20pm; Sun 1–4:20pm; Sept, Sat–Sun 10am–4:30pm; the rest of the year, by appointment.

HERITAGE MUSEUM AND GALLERY, 102 E. Ninth St., at Harrison Ave. Tel. 486-1878.

Thirty miniature dioramas, along with displays of mining artifacts and a turn-of-the-century kitchen, depict various episodes of Leadville history. You can pan for gold, learn about WW II's skiing soldiers, and see a model of Leadville's famous Ice Palace. An art gallery with rotating exhibits gives a taste of the cultural present.

Admission: $2.50 adults, $1.50 seniors 60 and over, $1 children 6–16, free for children under 6.

Open: Memorial Day–Labor Day, daily 10am–6pm, plus Wed and Sat till 9pm. Labor Day–Memorial Day, Mon–Fri 1–4pm, Sat–Sun 10am–4pm.

LEADVILLE, COLORADO & SOUTHERN RAILROAD, 326 E. Seventh St., at Hazel St. Tel. 486-3936.

The scenic train ride departs the 1883 C&S Depot, three blocks east of U.S. 24, and follows the old "high line" to the headwaters of the Arkansas River. The train stops near the molybdenum mining camp of Climax, with a spectacular view of Fremont Pass, and returns past the old Round House Water Tower at French Gulch. From here, there's a dramatic look at Mount Elbert, Colorado's tallest mountain, at 14,433 feet.

Admission: $18.50 adults, $9.75 children 4–12, free for children 3 and under.

Open: 2¾-hour tours, Memorial Day to early October, call for schedule.

Closed: Early October to late May.

LEADVILLE NATIONAL FISH HATCHERY, 2844 Hwy. 300 (6 miles southwest of Leadville off Hwy. 24). Tel. 486-0189.

Operated by the U.S. Fish and Wildlife Service, this facility raises five species of trout: rainbow, brook, brown, cutthroat, and lake. Visitors can tour the original hatchery building, constructed in 1889, which contains historical displays. Also open is the hatchery building, with incubators, plus trout tanks and a display pond. During summer months, volunteers explain the workings of the hatchery and allow visitors to feed the trout in the pond. Winter tours are self-guided. Visitors can also walk a nature trail, or take off into the high country on hiking or cross-country ski trails, which leave from the property.

Admission: Free.

Open: Summer, daily 7:30am–5pm. Rest of the year, daily 7:30am–4pm.

LEADVILLE NATIONAL HISTORIC DISTRICT. Tel. 486-3900.

A great many buildings—especially brick-and-masonry structures, but also some wood-frame houses—have survived from Leadville's heyday. Most of them line seven blocks of Harrison Avenue, the main drag, or Chestnut Street, which intersects it at the south end of downtown. The chamber of commerce can provide self-guided walking-tour maps ($1.50), walking-tour tapes ($3), or self-guided driving-tour maps of the district ($2).

MATCHLESS MINE MUSEUM, 1¼ miles east up Seventh St.

Visitors can get a surface view of Horace Tabor's Matchless Mine, then take a guided tour of the cabin where Tabor's widow, Baby Doe, spent the final 36 years of her life waiting to strike it rich once more before freezing to death in 1935.

Admission: $2 adults, 50¢ for children under 12.

Open: June–Labor Day, daily 9am–5pm; or by appointment.

NATIONAL MINING HALL OF FAME AND MUSEUM, 120 W. Ninth St. Tel. 486-1229.

This fascinating museum presents what may be the finest survey of geology and the American mining industry to be found in the country. You'll find descriptions of the mining of various ores, from silver and gold to copper, zinc, lead, and coal; working models of mining machinery; and 22 sequential dioramas giving an episode-by-episode history of Colorado gold mining. There are dioramas of individual mines, including the Climax molybdenum mine, and displays of crystals and luminescent minerals. Recently opened is a life-size model of a blacksmith shop and hard-rock mine. There's a priceless collection of gold nuggets and a wonderful display of period photos. The Mining Hall of Fame honors dozens of pioneering mining engineers and other industry leaders with biographical plaques. The museum store offers interesting gifts and publications.

Admission: $4 adults and children over 12, $2 children age 6–12, free for children under 6.

Open: May–Oct, daily 9am–5pm; Nov–Apr, Mon–Fri 10am–2pm.

TABOR HOME MUSEUM, 116 E. Fifth St. Tel. 486-0551.

✪ The home of millionaire merchant Horace Tabor and his first wife, Augusta, from 1877 to 1881, is filled with period furnishings and Tabor family memorabilia. Tours include a taped narration of the era. After the Tabors' divorce, the house remained in the family with Augusta's sister and brother-in-law, the Melvin Clarks.

Admission: $2 adults, 50¢ children.

Open: Memorial Day–Labor Day, daily 9am–5:30pm; the rest of the year, Wed–Sat 10am–4pm.

TABOR OPERA HOUSE, 308 Harrison Ave. Tel. 486-1147.

Horace Tabor financed the construction of this wonderful Victorian opera house in 1879. Over the next 75 years the acoustically outstanding theater hosted the great performers of the era, from the Ziegfeld Follies to the New York Metropolitan Opera, and from prizefighter Jack Dempsey (a Colorado native) to magician Harry Houdini (whose "vanishing" square is still evident on the stage floor). Autographed photographs of many of the entertainment greats line the walls of the foyer. Guided and self-guided tours of the 880-seat theater are available; you're encouraged to wander the aisles, visit the original dressing rooms, and study many of the original sets and scenery. The Crystal Comedy Company still performs melodramas here three nights a week in summer, helping to reenact the great days of theater in Leadville.

Admission: Tours, $4 adults, $2 children 6–11, free for children under 6; melodrama, mid-June to mid-Aug, $8.

Open: Memorial Day–Oct 1, Sun–Fri 9am–5:30pm; the rest of the year, in favorable weather or by appointment.

SPORTS & RECREATION

BICYCLING Mountain-bike rentals ($4 per hour, $15 per day) and organized tours ($30 per half day) are offered by 10th Mountain Sports, 500 E. Seventh St. (tel. 486-2202).

FISHING There's good trout-and-kokanee fishing at Turquoise Lake, Twin Lakes, and other small high-mountain lakes, as well as at beaver ponds located on side streams of the Arkansas River. There's also limited stream fishing.

Licenses and information can be obtained from Buckthorn Sporting Goods, 616 Harrison Ave. (tel. 486-3944), and other local stores. Huck Finn Pond at City Park, West Fifth Street at Leiter Street, is open for free children's fishing in summer.

GOLF The Mount Massive Golf Course, 3½ miles west of Leadville at 259 County Rd. 5 (P.O. Box 312, Leadville, CO 80461; tel. 486-2176), claims to be North America's highest nine-hole golf course, at 9,700 feet. Greens fees are $12 for 9 holes, $19 for 18 holes.

HIKING & MOUNTAINEERING The U.S. Forest Service, San Isabel National Forest office, 2015 N. Poplar St. (tel. 486-0749), has detailed maps for hikers and backpackers. The more adventurous can attempt an ascent of Mount Elbert (14,433 ft.) or Mount Massive (14,421 ft.); either can be climbed in a day without technical equipment, though altitude and abruptly changing weather conditions are factors that must be weighed.

HORSEBACK RIDING There are stables at Pa and Ma's Guest Ranch, 4 miles west of Leadville on U.S. 24 at East Tennessee Road (tel. 486-3900).

RIVER RAFTING Expeditions on the Arkansas River, including thrilling Brown's Canyon, are organized by 10th Mountain Sports, 322 Harrison Ave. (tel. 719/486-2202 or toll free 800/892-6371), or by Twin Lakes Expeditions, Colo. 82, Twin Lakes (tel. 486-3928).

RUNNING   The Turquoise Lake 20K Road & Trail Run is held in early June, beginning and ending at the Matchless Boat Ramp, at the southeast corner of Turquoise Lake; and the Leadville Trail 100 Mile Ultra Race is held the third weekend of August, leading south from Leadville on trails and backroads to the abandoned mining camp of Winfield and returning along the same route.

SKIING   Ski Cooper, P.O. Box 896, Leadville, CO 80461 (tel. 719/486-3684 or 486-2277 for snow reports), began in 1942 as a training center for 10th Mountain Division troopers from Camp Hale during World War II. Located 10 miles north of Leadville on U.S. 24 near Tennessee Pass, it offers numerous intermediate-and-novice runs, and hosts backcountry Chicago Ridge Snowcat Tours for experts. The lifts—a triple chair, double chair, T-bar, and beginners' poma—serve 21 runs on a 1,200-foot vertical. Full-day tickets are $23 for adults, $15 for children 6 to 12, $14 for seniors 60 to 69, and free for seniors over 69; lessons start at $25, full-rental packages at $12. There's also a cross-country track laid out at the foot of the mountain.

SWIMMING   The Lake County Intermediate School Recreation Complex, West Sixth Street and McWethy Drive (tel. 486-0917), offers an Olympic-size pool, a 160-yard indoor track, a gymnasium, a 22-person whirlpool spa, weight training, a racquetball court, and roller skating.

EVENING ENTERTAINMENT

From mid-June to late August, the **Crystal Comedy Company** presents melodramatic revues on Wednesday, Thursday, and Saturday at 8pm at the Tabor Opera House. Titles change, but stories remain much the same, such as past hits *The Ghoul of Gabardine Gables*. Call 486-0917 for ticket prices.

Music, storytelling, and period-attired artisans help relive the spirit of an 1860s mining camp in **Oro City: The Rebirth of a Miner's Camp**, on U.S. 24 a mile south of downtown Leadville, in early June.

On weekends in July each year, the **Leadville Music Festival** brings fine classical and contemporary music to the high Rockies with visiting artists. Check with the Chamber of Commerce for times and locations.

Nightlife in Leadville is on the quiet side. If it's lively somewhere, it will be the **Pastime Saloon**, 120 W. Second St. (tel. 486-9986), with an original Chinese bar from Oro City; or the **Silver Dollar Saloon**, 315 Harrison Ave. (tel. 486-9914), an Irish-style bar decorated with pictures of "Baby Doe" Tabor.

WHERE TO STAY

APPLE BLOSSOM INN, 120 W. Fourth St., Leadville, CO 80461. Tel. 719/486-2141 or toll free 800/982-9279. 8 rms (3 with bath).
$ Rates (including breakfast): $49–$69 single; $54–$99 double. MC, V.
An 1879 Victorian structure on Leadville's "millionaires' row," this inn features the original handcrafted woodwork, detailed mantels, and crystal lights installed by its first owners. Rooms range from warm and cozy to large and sunny. Favorites are Estelle's Room, with a large fireplace, brass feather bed, and sitting area; and the Library, with a 14-foot ceiling, five stained-glass windows, and a four-poster bed. Full breakfasts are served when guests want them, and special diets can be accommodated. Children are welcome, but pets are not. Smoking is not permitted.

CLUB LEAD, 500 E. Seventh St., Leadville, CO 80461. Tel. 719/486-2202. 10 rms (5 with bath).
$ Rates (including breakfast): $18 adults, $10 children 4–6, children under 4 stay free in parents' room. AE, MC, V.
Proprietor Jay Jones, who also owns 10th Mountain Sports, caters to adventure travelers who want to tie mountain-biking or river-rafting excursions into their travel plans. Most rooms here are bunkhouse style, but there are no more than six beds to a room; some private rooms with queen-size beds have private baths. There's a games and meeting room and a hot tub.

DELAWARE HOTEL, 700 Harrison Ave., Leadville, CO 80461. Tel. 719/ 486-1418 or toll free 800/748-2004. 32 rms, 4 suites (all with bath). TV
$ Rates (including breakfast): $55–$65 single or double; $80–$90 family rooms; $90–$100 suite. AE, CB, DC, DISC, JCB, MC, V.

⭐ Built in 1886, this hotel was restored in 1985. It is once again a Victorian gem, and a "must see" on your visit to Leadville. The lobby is beautiful. In the style of grand old hotels, it has a baby grand piano, a turn-of-the-century player piano, crystal chandeliers, and magnificent Victorian furnishings. Guest rooms have brass or iron beds, quilts, lace curtains, and cable TV. Rooms have private baths with showers but no tubs; suites have full baths with tubs. The hotel also offers a Jacuzzi. Callaway's Restaurant serves three meals daily, featuring steaks and continental cuisine. There is also a full bar.

THE LEADVILLE COUNTRY INN, 127 E. Eighth St. (P.O. Box 1989), Leadville, CO 80461. Tel. 719/486-2354 or toll free 800/748-2354. 9 rms (all with bath).
$ Rates (including breakfast): $52–$77 single; $67–$127 double. AE, CB, DC, DISC, MC, V.

A stately 15-room Queen Anne Victorian built in 1893, this bed-and-breakfast inn has been restored to its past elegance with rich hand-rubbed woods and antique furnishings—including brass and iron beds, claw-foot bathtubs, and turn-of-the-century quilts. Half the rooms are in the old Carriage House, the balance in the main inn. Smoking is not permitted. A full gourmet breakfast includes frozen-fruit smoothies and cinnamon rolls. Elaborate six-course dinners, served by waiters in period costume, are offered by reservation for $35 per person.

PAN ARK LODGE, 5827 U.S. 24, Leadville, CO 80461. Tel. 719/486-1063 or toll free 800/443-1063. 48 rms (all with bath).
$ Rates: $49–$54 single or double. MC, V.

Located 9 miles south of Leadville, this comfortable motel has spacious rooms, all with natural moss-rock fireplaces, electric kitchenettes, and beautiful mountain views. Some rooms have televisions. There's a coin-operated laundry for guests. Pets are not permitted.

CAMPGROUNDS

SUGAR LOAFIN' CAMPGROUND, 303 Colo. 300, Leadville, CO 80461. Tel. 719/486-1031 or 486-1613.
$ Rates: $16.50–$20 for two. MC, V. **Closed:** Oct to mid-May.

⭐ Located 3½ miles northwest of downtown Leadville via West Sixth Street, this campground has spectacular mountain views and clean bathhouses with plenty of hot water. There are full-hookup R.V. and tent sites, along with tables and fire rings. An ice-cream social and slide show of area attractions takes place nightly, and campers are invited to try their luck panning for gold. Located at a 9,696-foot elevation, the campground provides a playground, a self-service laundry, a telephone, and a general store selling fishing tackle and Colorado fishing licenses. Pets are welcome. There's a public golf course next to the campground.

WHERE TO DINE

GARDEN CAFE, 115 W. Fourth St. Tel. 486-9917.
   Cuisine: ITALIAN/AMERICAN.
$ Prices: Breakfast $2–$6; lunch $3–$6; dinner $6–$12. No credit cards.
   Open: Breakfast/lunch daily 7am–3pm; dinner daily 5–9:30pm.

The "garden" label is a bit of a misnomer, because there's no garden at this small house west of Harrison Avenue. There are, however, healthy, filling breakfasts and lunches, and homemade Italian dinners. Beer and wine are served, and there's a children's menu.

THE GOLDEN BURRO CAFE, 710 Harrison Ave. Tel. 486-1239.
   Cuisine: AMERICAN.

$ Prices: Breakfast $2–$6.25; lunch $3.75–$7.95; dinner $5–$12. MC, V.

Open: Summer, daily 6am–10pm; winter, daily 7am–9pm.

Established in 1938, the Golden Burro serves up generous portions of old American favorites—like ribs, seafood combo, deep-fried vegetables, a half chicken or roast beef. Breakfasts, served anytime, offer home-baked cinnamon rolls; lunches include soups like those out of grandma's kitchen.

THE GRILL BAR & CAFE, 715 Elm St. Tel. 486-9930.
  Cuisine: MEXICAN.
$ Prices: $2–$9.50. MC, V.
  Open: Daily 11am–10:30pm.

Colorful sombreros and serapes cover the white-stucco walls of this south-end restaurant, which offers delicious south-of-the-border cuisine. Enjoy burritos, enchiladas, or stuffed sopaipillas (with chicken or beef, topped with green chiles). There's patio dining, imported Mexican beer, and, in the backyard, horseshoe pits!

LA CANTINA, 1942 U.S. 24 S. Tel. 486-9927.
  Cuisine: MEXICAN.
$ Prices: Lunch $3–$6; dinner $5–$8. MC, V.
  Open: Daily 11am–10pm.

What is probably Leadville's finest Mexican food is served at this large restaurant, a mile south of downtown. Lean meat and fire-roasted green chiles, along with homemade tortillas and tamales, are typical of the cuisine. The restaurant features an antique bar, large wooden booths, and music and dancing many weekends.

MOM'S PLACE, 612 Harrison Ave. Tel. 486-1108.
  Cuisine: AMERICAN.
$ Prices: Breakfast $2.50–$4; lunch and dinner $2–$4; pizzas $9–$11. MC, V.
  Open: Daily 6am–8pm.

Good, homemade fast-food is what Mom's specializes in, and does very well. No one goes away hungry—large is the only size available. Local favorites include the 6-inch bacon cheeseburger, stuffed baked potato, and the black-bean burger. There's also a made-from-scratch ground-turkey burger, grilled ham, chicken breast, pork cutlet, BLT, steak, and country-sausage sandwiches. Breakfasts include a number of mixed skillet selections plus flapjacks.

THE PROSPECTOR, 2798 Hwy. 91. Tel. 486-3955 or toll free 800/844-2828.
  Cuisine: STEAK/SEAFOOD. **Reservations:** Recommended.
$ Prices: Main courses $9–$20. MC, V.
  Open: Tues–Sat 5–10pm, Sun brunch 11am–3pm.

Lodged in a spacious log cabin with stone entrance, three miles north of town in a picturesque mountain setting, the Prospector has long been considered one of Leadville's finest restaurants. New owners Bob, Pauline, and Greg Alex vowed to continue that tradition when they took over in summer 1993. Dinners include aged prime rib, steaks, baby-back ribs, and seafood. There are daily specials, plus a salad bar. There's also a full cocktail bar.

---

7. ASPEN

172 miles W of Denver, 130 miles E of Grand Junction

GETTING THERE   By Plane   From mid-December to early April, visitors can fly directly into Aspen's Pitkin County Airport (also known as Sardy Field), 3 miles northwest of Aspen (tel. 303/920-5380). United Express (toll free 800/241-6522) offers several flights daily from Chicago's O'Hare, daily from Los Angeles, and flights from Dallas/Fort Worth about four times weekly. Most flights are nonstop during ski season.

Charters to or from Aspen, including flights from Denver and scenic trips to Crested Butte, are offered by Aspen Aviation (tel. 303/925-2522 or toll free 800/289-1369).

Most visitors fly into Denver International Airport, and continue to Vail with either United Express or Continental Express (tel. 303/925-4350 or toll free 800/525-0280). Both airlines have many flights to and from Denver each day, up to a dozen or more each during peak ski season. Courtesy vans, taxis, limousines, rental cars, and public buses are all available at the airport.

From Denver, it's possible to take the shuttle vans or taxis of either Skier Connection (toll free 800/824-1104) or Aspen Limo (tel. 303/925-2400 or toll free 800/222-2112). Connecting ground transportation is also available from the airport in Grand Junction (see Chapter 10, "The Western Slope").

By Train En route between San Francisco and Chicago, Amtrak (tel. 303/534-2812 in Denver or toll free 800/USA-RAIL) stops in Glenwood Springs, 42 miles northwest of Aspen. The Denver-Glenwood and Grand Junction–Glenwood segments are particularly scenic. Taxis and limousines, as well as rental cars, are available at the depot.

By Bus Coaches of Greyhound (tel. 625-3980 in Rifle) stop in Aspen at the Rubey Park Transportation Center, in the 400 block of East Durant Avenue (at Mill Street).

By Car Aspen is located on Colo. 82, halfway between I-70 at Glenwood Springs (42 miles northwest) and U.S. 24 south of Leadville (44 miles east). In summer, it's a scenic 3½-hour drive from Denver: Leave I-70 West at Exit 195 (Copper Mountain); follow Colo. 91 south to Leadville, where you pick up U.S. 24; then turn east on Colo. 82 through Twin Lakes and over 12,095-foot Independence Pass. In winter, the Independence Pass road is closed, so you'll have to take I-70 to Glenwood, then backtrack up Colo. 82. In optimal winter driving conditions, it'll take about four hours from Denver.

SPECIAL EVENTS The Aspen area hosts the following annual events: the Wintersköl Carnival, in the third week of January, in Aspen/Snowmass; the Snowmass Mardi Gras, in late February or early March, in Snowmass; the International Design Conference, the third week of June, in Aspen; Jazz Aspen, the last week of June, in Snowmass; the Snowmass Hot Air Balloon Festival, on the fourth weekend of June, in Snowmass; the Aspen Music Festival, from late June to late August, in Aspen; the DanceAspen Summer Festival, from July 5 to mid-August, in Aspen; the Aspen Writers Conference, in late June or July, in Aspen; the Snowmass Children's Festival, on the first weekend of August, in Snowmass; the Snowmass Oktoberfest, on Labor Day weekend, in Snowmass; and the Aspen Filmfest, in late September, in Aspen.

Silver miners established the town of Aspen in 1879, first dubbing it "Ute City" after the Native American Ute tribe, but renaming it Aspen on its incorporation in 1880. When the Smuggler Mine produced the world's largest silver nugget (1,840 lbs.), prospectors headed to Aspen in droves. The city soon had 12,000 citizens—but just as quickly the population dwindled to one-tenth that number after the 1893 silver crash. Ranching and small mining enterprises kept the town alive as a supply center.

Shortly before World War II, three investors established a small ski area on Aspen Mountain with a primitive "boat tow." During the early 1940s, 10th Mountain Division soldiers training at Camp Hale near Leadville often weekended in Aspen, and were enthralled with its possibilities. An infusion of money in 1945 by Chicago industrialist Walter Paepcke, who moved to Aspen with his wife, Elizabeth, resulted in the construction of what was then the world's longest chair lift. The Aspen Skiing Corporation (now Company) was founded the following year; in 1950 the resort's status as an international resort was confirmed when it hosted the alpine world skiing championships. Aspen's scope as a ski destination grew with the opening in 1958 of Buttermilk Mountain and Aspen Highlands, and in 1967 with the establishment of Snowmass Village and ski area. (All but Highlands, which is under independent management, are operated by the Aspen Skiing Company.)

The Paepckes perceived Aspen as a year-round cultural center as well as a resort community. In 1949 they organized the Goethe Bicentennial Convocation, which established the Aspen Institute for Humanistic Studies and the Aspen Music Festival. In 1951 they started the first International Design Conference.

ORIENTATION

Aspen has an elevation of 7,908 feet and a year-round population of about 6,000. (The city holds as many as 20,000, including visitors.)

INFORMATION   For information on Aspen, contact the Aspen Chamber Resort Association, 425 Rio Grande Place, Aspen, CO 81611, or drop by the Aspen Visitor Center at the Wheeler Opera House, Hyman Avenue and Mill Street (tel. 925-1940).

Transportation, hotel, and other reservations are handled by Aspen Central Reservations and Travel (tel. 303/925-9000 or toll free 800/262-7736) or the Snowmass Resort Association Travel Division (tel. 303/923-2010 or toll free 800/332-3245).

CITY LAYOUT   Located in the heart of White River National Forest, Aspen is in the relatively flat valley of the Roaring Fork River, a tributary of the Colorado River. It's lodged at the northern foot of Aspen Mountain, facing Smuggler Mountain to its north and the peaks of the Elk Mountain Range to its east.

Entering town from the northwest on Colo. 82, the arterial jogs right (south) two blocks on Seventh Street, then left (east) at Main Street. "East" and "West" street numbers are separated by Garmisch Street, the next cross street after First Street. Continuing east, you'll cross Aspen Street, Monarch Street (which essentially marks the western boundary of downtown Aspen), Mill Street (the town's main north-south street), Galena Street, Hunter Street, Spring Street, to Original Street (the east end of downtown). Colorado 82 turns south again on Original, crossing Hopkins Avenue and Hyman Avenue, continuing east again toward Independence Pass on Cooper Avenue. Durant Avenue, one block south of Cooper, sits at the foot of Aspen Mountain.

At this writing, there are no one-way streets in Aspen, but there are pedestrian malls on Cooper Avenue and Hyman Avenue between Mill Street and Galena Street, on Mill Street between Hyman Avenue and Durant Avenue, and on Galena Street between Cooper and Durant, which throw a curve into the downtown traffic flow.

Looking at the entire Aspen valley from an aircraft approaching from the north, you'd see the city of Aspen and Aspen Mountain on the left (east), followed in order by Aspen Highlands, Buttermilk Mountain, the Pitkin County Airport, and Snowmass Village and ski area. Main access to Snowmass, Aspen's "second city" 12 miles closer to Glenwood Springs than the more famous resort town, is off Colo. 82 via Owl Creek Road, just east of the airport, or Brush Creek Road, 3 miles northwest of the airport.

GETTING AROUND

BY BUS   The Roaring Fork Transit Agency (RFTA), 20101 W. Colo. 82, Aspen (tel. 920-1905), provides free bus service within the Aspen city limits, and connections east as far as Carbondale, for continued transport to Glenwood Springs, for prices up to $3 for adults and $2 for children 6 to 16 and seniors 65 and older (children under 6 ride free). The fare is $1.50 (50¢ for children and seniors) to Snowmass Village. Exact fare is required. Normal hours are 7:15am to 12:30am daily. Further information can be obtained at the Rubey Park Transit Center, Durant Avenue between Mill Street and Galena Street, Aspen (tel. 925-8484). Schedules, frequency, and routes vary with the seasons; services include free ski shuttles in winter, shuttles to the Aspen Music Festival, and tours to the Maroon Bells scenic area in summer.

Free shuttle transportation within Snowmass Village is offered daily during winter, and on a limited schedule in summer, by the Snowmass Transportation Department (tel. 923-2543).

BY TAXI   Taxi service is offered by Aspen Limo (tel. 925-2400) or High Mountain Taxi (tel. 925-TAXI).

BY RENTAL CAR   Auto-rental agencies include Alamo (tel. 303/925-8056 or toll free 800/327-9633), Avis (tel. 303/925-2355 or toll free 800/331-1212), Budget (tel.

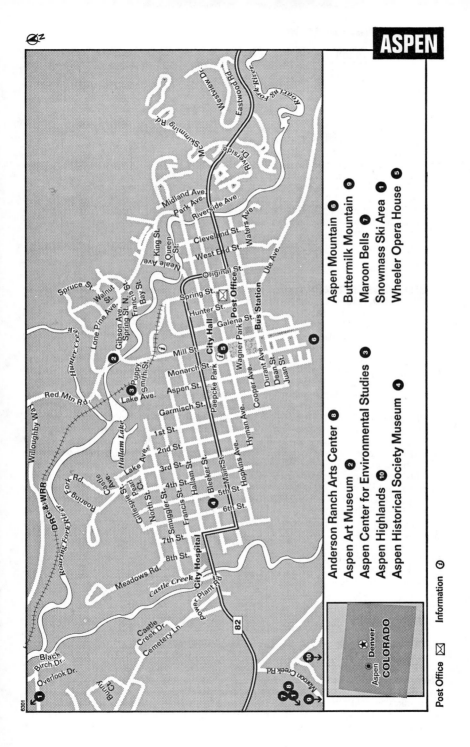

ASPEN

Anderson Ranch Arts Center **8**
Aspen Art Museum **2**
Aspen Center for Environmental Studies **3**
Aspen Highlands **10**
Aspen Historical Society Museum **4**

Aspen Mountain **6**
Buttermilk Mountain **9**
Maroon Bells **7**
Snowmass Ski Area **1**
Wheeler Opera House **5**

Post Office ⊠   Information ⓘ

303/925-2151 or toll free 800/527-0700), Eagle (toll free 800/282-2128), Hertz (toll free 800/654-3131), National (tel. 303/925-1144 or toll free 800/227-7368), and Thrifty (toll free 800/367-2277).

Mountain Express (tel. 925-2880) specializes in four-wheel-drive vehicles.

FAST FACTS

The **area code** is 303. In case of **emergency,** call 911. For regular business, contact the Aspen Police, Galena Street and Hopkins Avenue (tel. 920-5400), the Snowmass Police (tel. 923-5330), or the Pitkin County Sheriff, Main Street and Galena Street (tel. 920-5300). The **Aspen Valley Hospital** is at 401 Castle Creek Rd., near Aspen Highlands (tel. 925-1120). There are **hot lines** for mental health (tel. 920-5555) and poison center (toll free 800/332-3073). The **post office** is at 235 Puppy Smith St., off Mill Street north of Main (tel. 925-7523); there's another in the Snowmass Center (tel. 923-2497). For **road reports,** call 920-5454 (or 303/639-1234 for statewide conditions). Sales **tax** of 7.2% and a civic assessment of 4% are added to hotel bills.

WHAT TO SEE & DO

ATTRACTIONS

ASPEN MOUNTAIN, Aspen Skiing Company, Durant Ave. and Hunter St. (P.O. Box 1248), Aspen, CO 81612. Tel. 303/925-1220 or 925-1221 for snow reports.

Aspen Mountain—known to locals as "Ajax," for an old miner's claim—is not for the timid. It is the American West's original hard-core ski mountain, with no fewer than 23 of its named runs "double diamond"—for experts only. One-third of the mountain's runs are left forever ungroomed, ecstasy for bump runners. There are mountain-long runs for intermediates as well as advanced skiers, but beginners should look to one of the other Aspen areas.

From the Sundeck restaurant at the mountain's 11,212-foot summit, numerous intermediate runs extend on either side of Bell Mountain—through Copper Bowl and down Spar Gulch. To the east of the Gulch, the knob of Bell offers a mecca for mogul mashers, with bump runs down its ridge and its east-and-west faces. To the west of the Gulch, the face of Ruthie's is wonderful for intermediate cruisers, while more mogul runs drop off International. Ruthie's Run extends for over 2 miles down the west ridge of the mountain, with an extension via Magnifico Cut Off and Little Nell to the base.

Mid-mountain restaurants include Bonnie's, at Tourtelotte Park near the top of Ruthie's Lift, and Ruthie's, at the bottom of said chair lift.

Aspen Mountain has a 3,267-foot vertical, with 75 trails on 625 skiable acres. Eight lifts—the high-speed Silver Queen gondola, three quad chairs, and four double chairs—serve up to 10,775 skiers per hour. Average annual snowfall at the summit is 300 inches (25 ft.).

Snowcats deliver advanced-and-expert skiers to an additional 1,500 acres of powder skiing in back bowls.

Admission: Lift tickets, opening day through Dec 18, $37 adults; $27 children 7–12; $33 seniors 65–69. Dec 19–Jan 1, $48 adults; $27 children 7–12; $33 seniors 65–69. Jan 2–closing, $46 adults; $27 children 7–12; $33 seniors 65–69. Children 6 and under and seniors 70 and older ski free. Multiday and multiarea discounts available.

Open: Thanksgiving to mid-Apr, daily 9am–3:30pm.

ASPEN HIGHLANDS, Maroon Creek Rd. (P.O. Box T), Aspen, CO 81612. Tel. 303/925-5300.

Highlands has two major features going for it: the longest vertical drop (3,800 ft.) of any area in Colorado, and the most balanced skiable terrain—novice to expert, with lots of intermediate slopes—in the Aspen valley.

It takes four lifts to reach the 11,800-foot Loge Peak summit, where most of the advanced expert runs are found in the Steeplechase area and 65 acres of glades in the Olympic Bowl. Kandahar, Golden Horn, and Thunderbowl give the intermediate skier a long run from top to bottom, and novices are best served midmountain on trails like Red Onion and Apple Strudel. There are three **restaurants:** The Base Lodge, Merry-Go-Round at Midway, and Cloud Nine picnic hut (for groups only) atop the Cloud 9 chair.

Highlands has 78 trails on 552 acres, served by 11 lifts (nine double chairs and two Pomas). Uphill capacity is 10,000 skiers per hour.

Admission: Tickets, $30 adults (as low as $23 per day for multiday tickets), $15 children 12 and under or seniors 65–69 (as low as $14 for multiday tickets), free for seniors over 69. Full-day class lessons start at $42 per day.

Open: Thanksgiving to mid-Apr, daily 9am–4pm.

BUTTERMILK MOUNTAIN, Aspen Skiing Company, W. Buttermilk Rd. at Colo. 82 (P.O. Box 1248), Aspen, CO 81612. Tel. 303/925-1220 or 925-1221 for snow reports.

Buttermilk is nominally a beginners' mountain. In fact, *Ski* magazine has rated it the best place in North America to learn how to ski. But there's plenty of intermediate and ample advanced terrain as well.

The smallest of Aspen's four mountains has three segments: **Main Buttermilk,** rising from the Inn at Aspen, with a variety of intermediate trails and the long, easy, winding Homestead Road; **Buttermilk West,** a mountaintop (9,900 ft.) novice area; and **Tiehack,** the intermediate-advanced section where Aspen town-league races are held. The Cliffhouse restaurant is atop Main Buttermilk, and there are cafés at the foot of the other two segments.

Seven lifts (one high-speed quad, five double chairs and a platter-pull) serve 45 trails on 410 acres, with a 2,030-foot vertical. Uphill capacity is 6,600 skiers per hour; average annual snowfall at the summit is 200 inches (16 ft. 8 in.).

Special features include the Vic Braden Ski College, which offers an intensive 5-day adult learn-to-ski program; the Powder Pandas for 3- to 6-year-olds; and a 200-foot-long half-pipe for snowboarders, with a 23% grade.

Admission: Lift tickets, opening day through Dec 18, $37 adults; $27 children 7–12; $33 seniors 65–69. Dec 19–Jan 1, $48 adults; $27 children 7–12; $33 seniors 65–69. Jan 2–closing, $46 adults; $27 children 7–12; $33 seniors 65–69. Children 6 and under and seniors 70 and older ski free. Multiday and multiarea discounts available.

Open: Mid-Dec to early Apr, daily 9am–4pm.

SNOWMASS SKI AREA, Aspen Skiing Company, Snowmelt Rd. (P.O. Box 1248, Aspen, CO 81612), Snowmass. Tel. 303/925-1220 or 925-1221 for snow reports.

A huge, ostensibly intermediate mountain with something for everyone, Snowmass has 33% more skiable acreage than the other three Aspen areas combined! Actually four distinct self-contained areas, each with its own lift system and restaurant, its terrain varies from easy beginner runs to the pitches of the Cirque and the Hanging Valley Wall, the steepest in the Aspen area.

Big Burn, site of a forest fire set by 19th-century Utes to discourage settlers, boasts wide-open advanced and intermediate slopes and the expert drops of the Cirque. Atop the intermediate Alpine Springs trails is the advanced High Alpine Lift, from which experts can traverse to the formidable Hanging Valley Wall. Elk Camp is ideal for early intermediates who prefer long cruising runs. Sam's Knob has advanced upper trails diving through trees, and a variety of intermediate-and-novice runs around its northeast face and base. All areas meet in the scattered condominium developments that surround Snowmass Village Mall.

Hungry skiers head for Ullrhof restaurant at the foot of Big Burn, High Alpine atop Alpine Springs, Café Suzanne at the base of Elk Camp, and Sam's Knob at that peak's summit.

All told, there are 2,500 skiable acres at Snowmass, with a 4,087-foot vertical drop. The mountain has 72 trails served by 16 lifts (5 quad chairs, 2 triple chairs, 7 double chairs, and 2 platter-pulls), with an uphill capacity of 20,535 skiers per hour. Average annual snowfall at the 12,310-foot summit is 300 inches (25 ft.).

The renowned Snowmass ski school has hundreds of instructors, as well as Snow Cubs and Big Burn Bears programs for children 18 months and older. The area also caters to snowboarders with a "half-pipe" 545 feet long, 55 feet wide, and a 22% grade.

Admission: Lift tickets, opening day through Dec 18, $37 adults; $27 children 7–12; $33 seniors 65–69. Dec 19–Jan 1, $48 adults; $27 children 7–12; $33 seniors 65–69. Jan 2–closing, $46 adults; $27 children 7–12; $33 seniors 65–69. Children 6 and under and seniors 70 and older ski free. Multiday and multiarea discounts available.

Open: Thanksgiving to mid-Apr, daily 8:30am–3:30pm.

Natural Attractions

MAROON BELLS, Maroon Creek Rd., 10 miles west of Aspen.

These two sheer, pyramidal peaks are probably the most photographed mountains in the Rockies south of Wyoming's Grand Tetons. They're a beautiful scene in the winter, spring, or summer, but especially in the fall, when their reflection in Maroon Lake is framed by the changing colors of the aspen leaves. For a nominal fee you can take a 30 minute narrated bus tour up the Maroon Creek Valley. Call 925-8484 for more information.

Museums

ANDERSON RANCH ARTS CENTER, 5263 Owl Creek Rd., (P.O. Box 5598) Snowmass Village. Tel. 923-3181.

What was once a sheep ranch in the Brush Creek Valley is now a highly respected arts center with two nationally acclaimed programs. October to May, 20 American artists take part in an 8-month residency outside of professional or academic atmospheres, where they can create a body of work—be it ceramics, woodwork, textile art, photography, or painting—and receive critical feedback from their peers. From May to September, 81 workshops offer a wide range of artists' skills to novices and professionals in every imaginable medium. A variety of evening programs are free and open to the public, June through August. There's also a children's program of workshops for kids age 6 through teenagers. Exhibitions in the center's gallery are rotated every four weeks, year-round.

Admission: Free, gallery.
Open: Mon–Fri 9am–5pm, gallery.

ASPEN ART MUSEUM, 590 N. Mill St., Aspen. Tel. 925-8050.

Though it has no permanent exhibits, the Aspen Art Museum presents changing exhibits highlighting the work of local and nationally known contemporary artists, designers, and architects. Frequent lectures, films, discussions, and receptions are open to the Aspen community and visitors.

Admission: $3, free for children under 12, free for everyone Thurs evening after 6pm.
Open: Tues, Sun noon–6pm, plus Thurs evening until 8pm.

ASPEN HISTORICAL SOCIETY MUSEUM, Wheeler-Stallard House, 620 W. Bleeker St., Aspen. Tel. 925-3721.

Silver baron Jerome Wheeler had this three-story Victorian brick home built in 1888. Its steeply pitched roofs, dormers, and gables have made it a landmark in Aspen's West End neighborhood. As museum and archives of the Aspen Historical Society since 1969, the house has been restored to its appearance in the heady days before the silver crash, with late 19th-century furniture, photos, clothing, and toys. Exhibits describe Aspen history from the Native American Ute tribe's culture through the mining rush, from railroads and ranching to the founding of the ski industry. The Carriage House presents changing exhibits, and the gift shop offers a variety of interesting souvenirs. Inquire about information, maps, and guided walking tours of historic Aspen.

Admission: $3 adults, 50¢ children.
Open: Mid-June to Sept and mid-Dec to mid-Apr, Tues–Sat 1–4pm.

SPORTS & RECREATION

BALLOONING Aspen Balloon Adventures (tel. 923-5749) and Unicorn Balloon Company (tel. 925-5752) fly high over the Roaring Fork Valley and surrounding mountain slopes, offering spectacular bird's-eye views. Inquire about the romantic champagne flights. The annual Snowmass Balloon Festival brings the colorful vessels into the air by droves the last weekend of June.

Visitors interested in other air sports can check with Gliders of Aspen (tel. 925-3418 before 9am or 925-3694 after 10am) for sightseeing trips or instruction. Paragliding—popular in winter among adventurous skiers—is taught by the Aspen Expeditions and Paragliding (tel. 925-7625).

BICYCLING There are two bike paths of note. One connects Aspen with Snowmass Village; it begins at Seventh Street south of Hopkins Avenue, cuts through wilderness to Colo. 82, then follows Owl Creek Road and Brush Creek Road to the Snowmass Mall. Extensions link it with Aspen High School and the Aspen Business Park. The Rio Grande Trail follows the Roaring Fork River from near the Aspen Post Office, on Puppy Smith Lane, through Henry Stein Park to the community of Woody Creek, off Colo. 82 near Snowmass.

The best source of biking information is the Aspen Bicycle Club (tel. 925-7978). Backcountry mountain-biking tours and downhill road cruises from Independence Pass are offered by Aspen Bike Tours (tel. 920-4059), Blazing Pedals (tel. 925-5651 in Aspen or 923-4544 in Snowmass), and Timberline Bicycle Tours and Cycle Center (tel. 925-5773).

For rentals and service, check with Ajax Bike & Sports, 635 E. Hyman Ave. (tel. 925-7662); Aspen Sports, 408 E. Cooper Ave. (tel. 925-6331) or Snowmass Mall (tel. 923-6111); Aspen Velo Bike Shop, 465 N. Mill St. (tel. 925-1495); Hub of Aspen, 315 E. Hyman Ave. (tel. 925-7970); or Sabbatini's, 434 E. Cooper Ave. (tel. 920-1180). All shops have full information to guide bikers.

DOG SLEDDING For rides, and a kennel tour, call Krabloonik, 4250 Divide Rd., Snowmass Village (tel. 923-3953). Every day in winter, teams of 13 Alaskan sled dogs pull people and provisions on handcrafted sleds into the Snowmass–Maroon Bells Wilderness Area. Half-day trips, departing at 9am and 1:30pm, include lunch at Krabloonik's fine restaurant. Children under 3 are not permitted on the ride.

FISHING Perhaps the best of a great deal of good trout fishing in the Aspen area is to be found in the Roaring Fork and Frying Pan rivers. Both are rated "gold medal streams." The Roaring Fork follows Colo. 82 through Aspen from Independence Pass; the Frying Pan starts near Tennessee Pass, northeast of Aspen, and joins the Roaring Fork at Basalt, 18 miles down valley.

The Taylor Creek Fly Shop, next to City Market in Basalt (tel. 927-4374), is one of the nation's largest fly-fishing guide services. They also have a shop next to the gondola on Aspen Mountain (tel. 920-1128).

GOLF There are two public 18-hole championship courses in the Aspen valley, both with pro shops, driving ranges, and PGA instruction. The Aspen Golf Course, Colo. 82, 1 mile west of Aspen (tel. 925-2145), 7,125 yards, also has a restaurant and a marvelous view of the Maroon Bells. The Snowmass Lodge & Golf Course, Snowmass Club Circle, Snowmass (tel. 923-3148), is a 6,900-yard course designed by Arnold Palmer and Ed Seay. It has a putting green and snack shop, and is adjacent to the Snowmass Club's full athletic facilities.

HEALTH CLUBS Aspen's only public downtown health club is the Aspen Athletic Club, 720 E. Hyman Ave. (tel. 925-2531), with weights and exercise equipment, aerobics classes, racquetball courts, a lap pool, steam-and-suntan rooms, and a pro shop.

HIKING & BACKPACKING   Your best source of information is the U.S. Forest Service for White River National Forest (tel. 925-3445). Perhaps the favorite among many outstanding trails is the route past the Maroon Bells to Crested Butte; the trek would take 175 miles by mountain road, but it's only about 30 miles by foot—14 from the end of Aspen's Maroon Creek Road.

For maps and additional hiking information, as well as camping-and-hiking equipment, see Ute Mountaineer, 308 S. Mill St. (tel. 925-2849). Hardy outdoors-lovers can join Aspen Expeditions, P.O. Box 2432, Aspen, CO 81612 (tel. 303/925-7625), for guided adventure-travel treks and peak ascents, or its adjunct Rocky Mountain Climbing School for rock- and ice-climbing courses.

HORSEBACK RIDING   Several stables in the Aspen valley offer everything from riding lessons to day rides, overnights to Crested Butte, and week-long pack trips into the Snowmass–Maroon Bells Wilderness Area. Some outfitters even package gourmet meals and country-and-western serenades with their expeditions.

Inquire with Brush Creek Stables, 1 mile south of Colo. 82 on Brush Creek Road, Snowmass (tel. 923-4252); Snowmass Stables, 2735 Brush Creek Rd., Snowmass Village (tel. 923-3075); or T Lazy 7 Ranch, Maroon Creek Road (tel. 925-7040). The T Lazy 7 also offers winter sleigh rides and summer stagecoach rides!

ICE SKATING   There's ice skating at the indoor City of Aspen–Ice Garden, 233 W. Hyman Ave. (tel. 920-5141). Call for public skating hours, admission fees, and rental rates.

RIVER RAFTING   In summer, several outfitters have booths set up opposite the Aspen Visitor Center in the Wheeler Opera House at Mill Street and Hyman Avenue. Sharing a toll-free phone (tel. 800/282-RAFT), they include Blazing Paddles (tel. 925-5651), River Rats (tel. 925-7648), and Snowmass Whitewater (tel. 925-5651 or 923-4544 at Snowmass Village Mall).

Another local rafting firm is Colorado Riff Raft, 555 E. Durant (tel. 925-5405). The Aspen Kayak School (tel. 925-4433) offers weekend and week-long classes and a variety of kayaking trips.

RODEO   Snowmass Stables, 2735 Brush Creek Rd., Snowmass Village (tel. 923-3075), hosts a western barbecue and rodeo every Wednesday night from late June through late August. Food service starts at 6pm, followed by a 2-hour rodeo at 7:30pm with bull-and-bronc riding, calf roping, and barrel racing. Prices for the combination barbecue-rodeo are $21 for adults, $15 for kids 12 and under; for the rodeo only, $10 for adults, $7 for kids. Reservations are advised for the barbecue.

SKIING [NORDIC]   The Aspen/Snowmass Nordic Council (tel. 925-2145) oper-ates a free Nordic trail system—supported by private-and-municipal donations—with nearly 50 miles of groomed double track extending throughout the Aspen-Snowmass area, and incorporating summer bicycle paths. Instruction and rentals are offered along the trail at the Aspen Cross Country Center, Colo. 82 between Aspen and Buttermilk (tel. 925-2145), and the Snowmass Lodge & Club Touring Center, Snowmass Club Circle, Snowmass Village (tel. 923-5600).

Ashcroft Ski Touring (tel. 925-1971), has 30km (18 miles) of terrain around the old ghost town of Ashcroft in the Castle Creek Valley, 12 miles up Castle Creek Road off Colo. 82. All services from rentals, to instruction, to guided backcountry day-and-overnight trips, are available—as is the popular Pine Creek Cookhouse restaurant.

Independent backcountry skiers should consult the U.S. Forest Service, White River National Forest (tel. 925-3445), and the Avalanche Conditions Hotline (tel. 920-1664). Two hut systems are especially significant—the 14-hut 10th Mountain Trail Association (tel. 925-5775) toward Vail, and the 6-hut Alfred A. Braun Hut System (tel. 925-7345) toward Crested Butte. Call for hut reservations, or join a tour with Aspen Alpine Guides (tel. 925-6618). Aspen Expeditions and Paragliding (tel. 925-7625) offers ski-mountaineering expeditions as well as hut-to-hut tours.

SLEIGH RIDES   These could include gourmet dinner rides or simple lunch trips and are offered by Snowmass Stables, 2735 Brush Creek Rd., Snowmass Village, (tel. 923-3075); and T Lazy 7 Ranch, Maroon Creek Road (tel. 925-7040).

SNOWBOARDING Snowboarders are welcome at Aspen Highlands, Buttermilk, and Snowmass mountains (see "Attractions," above), where lessons are also offered. Buttermilk and Snowmass have "half-pipes" reserved for "shredders." For equipment rentals and information, see the Alternative Edge, 520 E. Durant Ave. (tel. 925-8272), or Hub of Aspen, 315 E. Hyman Ave. (tel. 925-7970).

SNOWMOBILING There's snowmobiling on 26 miles of groomed trails from the T Lazy 7 Ranch (above), all the way to the base of the Maroon Bells. Guided tours include a lunch tour to the ghost town of Independence, and a Gold Hill mine tour with lunch at the Sundeck Restaurant atop Aspen Mountain. Tours (including moonlight tours) are also offered by Western Adventures (tel. 923-3337).

TENNIS There are 11 public courts at the Snowmass Lodge & Club Tennis Garden, Snowmass Club Circle, Snowmass Village (tel. 923-5600, ext. 122), with pro shops with rentals and instruction.

SHOPPING

ART Aspen Grove Fine Arts (internationally recognized artists), 525 E. Cooper Ave. (tel. 925-5151); Blue Corn (Navajo and Zapotec textiles), 520 E. Durant Ave. (tel. 920-3302); Patrick Collins Gallery (wilderness photography), 520 E. Durant Ave. (tel. 920-4105); Christy Lee Fine Arts (fine 19th-and-20th century prints and originals), 205 S. Mill St. (tel. 927-4399); the Omnibus Gallery (vintage posters), 533 E. Cooper Ave. (tel. 925-5567); Shaw Gallery (antique North American Indian art), 525 E. Cooper Ave. (tel. 925-2873); and the World Collection (international folk art), 525 E. Cooper Ave. (tel. 925-8822).

FASHIONS Aspen Exotics (leather goods), 205 S. Mill St. (tel. 925-2552); Aspen Kids (children's casual), 400 E. Hyman Ave. (tel. 925-4626); the Freudian Slip (lingerie), 416 S. Hunter St. (tel. 925-4427); Mark Justin (men's and women's), 217 S. Galena St. (tel. 925-1046); Stefan Kaelin (ski-and-casual wear), 447 E. Cooper St. (tel. 925-2989); Kristan of Aspen (men's and women's), 602 E. Cooper St. (tel. 925-7409); Spurs (western), 207 S. Galena St. (tel. 925-6130); and Suzanne's (sweaters), 205 S. Mill St. (tel. 920-2535).

GIFTS Chepita (a toy store for adults) 525 E. Cooper Ave. (tel. 925-2871); the Christmas Shop (handcrafted-and-unique ornaments, nativities, nutcrackers) 616 E. Hyman Ave. (tel. 925-8142); Curious George Collectibles (western artifacts that used to belong to notorious cowboys and Indians) 410 E. Hyman Ave. (tel. 925-3315); Quilts Unlimited (quilts; regional handcrafts in glass, wood, and fiber; children's gifts), Silvertree Plaza Mall, Snowmass Village (tel. 923-5467); Solos Colorado (original creations in clay, fibers, wood, metal and stone) Mill Street Plaza, 205 S. Mill St. (tel. 925-9064).

JEWELRY Aspen Leaf Jewelers, 121 S. Galena St. (tel. 925-5693); the Golden Bough, 433 E. Hyman Ave. (tel. 925-2660); HWR Jewelry, 318 S. Galena St. (tel. 925-4610); and MacMillan, 425 E. Hopkins Ave. (tel. 925-4797).

SPORTING GOODS Aspen Sports with five locations including Snowmass Village Mall (tel. 923-6111) and 408 E. Cooper Ave., Aspen (tel. 925-6331); and Gene Taylor Sports, Snowmass Village Mall (tel. 923-4336).

EVENING ENTERTAINMENT

THE PERFORMING ARTS The focus of the performing arts in Aspen is the 1889 **Wheeler Opera House,** 320 E. Hyman Ave. (tel. 920-5770 for the box office). Built in the heyday of the mining era by silver baron Jerome B. Wheeler, this stage—meticulously restored in 1984—hosts a year-round program of music, theater, dance, film, and lectures. The box office is open Monday through Saturday from 10am to 5pm, guided tours by appointment. The Music Association of Aspen uses the theater from late June to late August for their opera productions, master classes, and chambermusic concerts.

The ✪ **Aspen Music Festival** (tel. 925-3254 or 925-9042 after May 15 for the box office) has been held annually since 1949. Lasting nine weeks from late June to late August, it offers classical music, opera, jazz, choral and children's programs. Most concerts take place in the 1,700-seat Music Tent and new 500-seat **Joan and Irving Harris Concert Hall** at Third Street and Gillespie Street, but there are free events around the Aspen area, matinees and other programs at the Wheeler Opera House, and Saturday "Music on the Mountain" concerts atop Aspen Mountain. About 100,000 music lovers visit Aspen for the festival, so plan ahead: Write P.O. Box AA, Aspen, CO 81612. Most individual event tickets are $12 to $26, with some events as high as $35. If you plan a longer stay, inquire about subscription tickets. Special packages including air, lodging, and festival tickets are offered through Aspen Music Tours (toll free 800/525-2052).

The ☯ **DanceAspen Festival** (tel. 925-7718 or 925-5770 after June 1 for the box office) has taken its place with Jacob's Pillow in the Massachusetts Berkshires and the American Dance Festival in Durham, N.C., as the nation's leading summer dance festivals. Lasting 8 weeks from July through August, it features a broad spectrum of dance forms. The festival uses the new 550-seat Aspen School District Auditorium. For tickets, write P.O. Box 8745, Aspen, CO 81612. Tickets are $10 to $30 for evening performances, $5 to $16 for matinees; subscription tickets are discounted. Running concurrently is a summer dance school for 200 teenagers selected during a 28-city winter audition tour.

The **Snowmass/Aspen Repertory Theatre** (tel. 923-3773) offers three musical comedies or mystery productions between late June and mid-August, plus a children's matinee show at the Snowmass Performing Arts Center, Snowmass Mall.

NIGHTCLUBS Ebbe's, 312 S. Galena St. (tel. 925-6200), has three floors: a piano bar in the basement, a *karaoke* (video sing-along) bar, and live music for dancing beneath a top-level skylight. **The Tippler,** 535 E. Dean St. (tel. 925-4977), near the gondola base, draws après-skiers as well as late-night dancers. Its counterpart in the Snowmass Village Mall is the **Timber Mill** (tel. 923-4774). Country music lovers appreciate **Shooters Saloon,** 220 S. Galena St. (tel. 925-4567), and **Cowboys,** at the Silvertree Hotel in Snowmass (tel. 923-3520).

THE BAR SCENE It seems the fashion to do one's drinking at a historic bar. The **Hotel Jerome Bar** (the "J Bar"), Main Street and Mill Street (tel. 920-1000), has universal appeal. **Bentley's at the Wheeler,** 328 E. Hyman Ave. (tel. 920-2240), is an elegant English-style pub. The **Red Onion,** 420 E. Cooper Ave. (tel. 925-9043), is Aspen's oldest bar. The **Ute City Banque,** 501 E. Hyman Ave. (tel. 925-4373), is a former silver miners' bank, and the **Smuggler Land Office,** Hopkins Street and Galena Street (tel. 925-8624), is just that—a 19th-century land office.

Aspen's requisite **Hard Rock Café,** 210 S. Galena St. (tel. 920-1666), opened in 1991. **Shlomo's,** in the Little Nell Hotel, 675 E. Durant Ave. (tel. 920-6333), draws scores of après-skiers, though those of better means prefer to tipple before dinner at **Mezzaluna,** 600 E. Cooper Ave. (tel. 925-5882). **Boogie's,** 534 E. Cooper Ave. (tel. 925-6610), attracts a late-night crowd.

WHERE TO STAY

Occupancy rates run 90% or higher during peak winter-and-summer seasons, so it's essential to make reservations as early as possible. The easiest way to do so is to call **Aspen Central Reservations** (toll free 800/262-7736), or if you're planning to stay in Snowmass Village, **Snowmass Central Reservations** (toll free 800/322-3245).

Most hotels and condos offer sharply differing rates according to the "season." That means more than just winter and summer. Depending upon the lodge, there are either three or four winter seasons. "Value season" (from the opening of ski season in November to the beginning of the Christmas holidays, and the last few weeks of ski season in April) is the least expensive. The Christmas–New Year holiday period is the most expensive. Relatively high "regular" or "peak" ski-season rates may be posted the entire ensuing January to March period, although many lodges reduce rates during the less-busy weeks of January and early February. Summer rates are low compared to those of ski season. Many accommodations close during the spring and fall; if they're open, rates during those months are typically the lowest of any time during the year.

ASPEN

Very Expensive

HOTEL JEROME, 330 E. Main St., Aspen, CO 81611. Tel. 303/920-1000 or toll free 800/331-7213; 800/423-0037 in Colorado. Fax 303/920-1040. 40 rms, 49 suites. TV TEL

$ Rates: Value season, $189 single; $229 double; $299–$419 suite. Jan 2–27, $229 single; $269 double; $329–$459 suite. Jan 28–Mar 26, $339 single; $439 double; $489–$689 suite; Mar 27–Dec 21, $199 single; $239 double; $239–$439 suite. AE, CB, DC, MC, V. **Parking:** Underground.

Jerome B. Wheeler, made rich by silver and anxious to tell his friends in New York (he was president of Macy's) that Aspen had a hotel the equal of the Ritz in Paris, had the Jerome built during the peak of the silver boom. It opened in 1889 as Colorado's first hotel with electricity and indoor plumbing, and the first west of the Mississippi with a hydraulic elevator. For four years the Jerome was indeed a showpiece. Then came the silver crash—but the hotel lived on. The Jerome is on the National Register of Historic Places, its Eastlake Victorian architecture lovingly preserved and furnished with $1 million in period antiques.

Each guest room is different. All are elegant, with one-of-a-kind antiques (like writing desks and settees) and objets d'art. Lace curtains adorn the tall windows, floral paper covers the walls, and the floors are fully carpeted. Ornate headboards and down comforters grace the king-size or double beds. There are concessions to modern luxury, of course: remote-control color TVs, VCRs, multiline telephones, and refrigerated minibars. Bathrooms, finished with white Carrera marble and reproduction 19th-century octagonal tiles, contain hair dryers, plush terry-cloth robes, showers, and oversize Jacuzzi tubs.

Dining/Entertainment: The Century Room offers savory American fare served in Victorian elegance. Entrées include a choice of beef, seafood, poultry, wild game, and pasta with prices ranging from $16.50 to $25.50. The mustard-crusted salmon is the chef's specialty and is offered year-round. Jacob's Corner offers more casual surroundings for breakfast-and-lunch dining. Lighter appetites can also visit the historical J-Bar where "pub grub" (sandwiches and salads) is offered.

Services: 24-hour room service, concierge, 24-hour front desk, valet laundry, complimentary shuttle van, ski concierge, daily newspaper, and business-and-secretarial services.

Facilities: Heated swimming pool with sun deck, two Jacuzzis, workout room, and 6,000 square feet of meeting space.

THE LITTLE NELL, 675 E. Durant Ave., Aspen, CO 81611. Tel. 303/920-4600 or toll free 800/525-6200 or 800/525-6200. Fax 303/920-4670. 79 rms, 13 suites. A/C MINIBAR TV TEL

$ Rates: Summer, $210–$285 single or double; $325–$1,250 suite. Spring and fall, $160–$285 single or double; $290–$1,030 suite. Pre-Christmas and early Jan to Mar, $320–$425 single or double; $475–$1,900 suite. Holiday period, $450–$540 single or double; $640–$2,650 suite. AE, CB, DISC, MC, V. **Parking:** Valet parking.

The Aspen Skiing Company opened its showcase hotel for the 1989–90 ski season, and today rooms here may be the most sought-after of any in the resort. Located 17 paces (yes, it's been measured) from the base terminal of the Silver Queen gondola, the Little Nell deserves every plaudit it receives for its location, its design, and its highly professional and friendly staff. Here's a hotel that not only has a full-time ski concierge to handle ski storage and complimentary nightly waxing, tickets, rentals, and lessons, it even has a snowmelt system built into the sidewalks.

Because of the hotel's innovative architectural design and variations in decorating, no two guest rooms are exactly alike. All have working gas fireplaces, Belgian wool carpeting, alder-wood furniture, down-filled lounge chairs and sofas, and Audubon bird prints on the walls. A remote-control television (with built-in videocassette recorder) and refrigerator are contained in a wall unit. Closets are large enough to have separate dressing-and-storage areas. Telephones have two line capability. Marble-finished bathrooms contain two vanities, hair dryers, steam irons, telephones, and Crabtree & Evelyn toiletries. Standard suites have separate Jacuzzi tubs and steam showers. Five executive apartments have all this and more, including their own fax machines.

Dining/Entertainment: The restaurant (see "Where to Dine," below) serves "American alpine cuisine" in an artsy atmosphere with large windows looking toward the hotel courtyard. The Living Room Bar is just that—a plush living room—with lots of greenery, a two-sided sandstone fireplace, and outdoor terrace seating. Shlomo's deli offers ski-in/ski-out casual dining three times a day.

Services: 24-hour room service, full-service concierge, winter ski concierge, same-day valet laundry, complimentary shuttle, full accessibility for the disabled.

Facilities: Year-round outdoor heated swimming pool and Jacuzzi; fitness club with Nautilus equipment, steam room, and spa services, including massage; ski technician on staff; specialty arcade with eight shops; meeting space for 200; temporary membership to Snowmass Lodge & Club (racquet sports, golf, cross-country skiing, etc.).

Expensive

ASPEN CLUB LODGE, 709 E. Durant Ave. (at Spring St.), Aspen, CO 81611. Tel. 303/925-6760 or toll free 800/882-2582; 800/443-2582 in Colorado. Fax 303/925-6778. 90 rms. TV TEL

$ Rates (including continental breakfast): Summer, $115–$135 single or double; $165 suite. Spring and fall, $70–$100 single or double; $100–$115 suite. Early/late ski season, $120–$145 single or double; $175 suite. Christmas, $250–$275 single or double; $305 suite. Jan–Mar, $195–$235 single or double; $260–$275 suite. Children 12 and under stay free in parents' room. AE, CB, DC, MC, V. **Parking:** Available.

The special attraction about the Aspen Club is, well, the Aspen Club. It's *the* athletic club for Aspen residents. The club's Fitness and Sports Medicine Institute is of major importance to professional athletes in rehabilitation. The club is about a mile out of town, but guests at the Aspen Club Lodge—or any of the various condominiums and private homes rented by Aspen Club Realty—become temporary members of the Aspen Club.

The lodge is adjacent to the Little Nell, near the foot of the Aspen Mountain gondola. The spacious lobby has a large central lounge with big picture windows on the slopes. Rooms are comfortable and crisply decorated, with nice use of light woods. All have a king-size or two queen-size beds, a private balcony, a TV tucked away in an armoire, and a coffee maker.

Dining/Entertainment: The restaurant menu changes nightly, but specializes in unique, international appetizers and entrées.

Services: Complimentary club privileges, concierge, valet laundry, airport shuttle.

Facilities: Heated outdoor swimming pool, Jacuzzi, meeting space for 50. The Aspen Club, 1450 Crystal Lake Rd. (tel. 925-8900), offers indoor-and-outdoor tennis, racquetball, squash, basketball, indoor golf, swimming, aerobics, weights, exercise equipment, Jacuzzis, saunas, steam rooms, cold plunges, massage rooms, and more. The Fitness and Sports Medicine Institue offers fitness evaluations, conditioning sessions, and nutritional analyses.

THE SARDY HOUSE, 128 E. Main St. (at Aspen St.), Aspen, CO 81611. Tel. 303/920-2525. 14 rms, 6 suites. TV TEL

$ Rates (including breakfast): Early/late ski season, $135–$215 single or double; $225–$350 suite. Pre-Christmas and Jan–Mar, $235–$325 single or double; $375–$550 suite. Holiday period, $335–$425 single or double; $500–$675 suite. Summer, $155–$215 single or double; $285–$425 suite. AE, DC, MC, V. **Parking:** Free.

A red-brick Victorian mansion built in 1892, the Sardy House stands opposite Paepcke Park where Colo. 82 enters downtown from the west. Majestic spruce trees rise above the inn's landscaped grounds. Inside, lace curtains, rose-filled carpets, and period antiques lend a delicate elegance. An enclosed gallery bridges a private brick mews, joining the Sardy House to its Carriage House wing.

The well-kept rooms combine antique Victorian and modern furnishings: cherry-wood beds and armoires, wicker chairs and sofas. There are Jacuzzi tubs in all but two, which have antique claw-foot tubs. Other touches include clock radios, down comforters, terry-cloth robes, and heated towel racks. All suites have entertainment centers with VCRs, stereos, dry bars, and hideaway sofas. Three have private entrances; one has a private balcony and sitting room; one has a fireplace. The Carriage House Suite features a winding, wrought-iron staircase to its second floor.

Dining/Entertainment: The Sardy House restaurant presents candlelit American dinners with silver service, in a plush fireplace room. Main courses of venison, free-range chicken, lamb, and salmon run $19.75 to $29.75. It's also open to the public for breakfast ($5.75 to $10.25). Jack's Bar is open from 4pm daily.

Services: Room service morning and evening, concierge, valet laundry.

Facilities: Heated outdoor swimming pool, hot tub, sauna; private ski storage and heated boot lockers.

Moderate

ASPEN COUNTRY INN, Colo. 82 at Tiehack Rd. (P.O. Box 1368), Aspen, CO 81612. Tel. 303/925-2700 or toll free 800/525-4012. Fax 303/925-1737. 49 rms. TV TEL

$ Rates (including breakfast): Single or double, $95–$140 winter, higher at Christmas, $67–$105 summer. AE, MC, V. **Closed:** Mid-Apr to mid-June and mid-Sept to mid-Dec. **Parking:** Free.

This delightful inn, located between the Tiehack and Buttermilk base facilities at the foot of Buttermilk Mountain, offers a touch of country elegance. It has a sitting area and library around a big stone fireplace. Rooms have a view of either the Rockies or the Roaring Fork valley. Most have a king-size or two double beds and handsome vanities; 15 poolside and fireplace rooms have Jacuzzi tubs or bidets.

Situated right on the bus line, the inn has a heated outdoor swimming pool and year-round Jacuzzi.

HEARTHSTONE HOUSE, 134 E. Hyman Ave. (at Aspen St.), Aspen, CO 81611. Tel. 303/925-7632. Fax 303/920-4450. 18 rms (all with bath). TV TEL

$ Rates (including breakfast and afternoon tea): Summer, $112–$148 single; $110–$148 double; $158–$168 suite. Winter, $178–$208 single or double; $218–$238 suite. AE, MC, V. **Parking:** Free.

Small and sophisticated in the tradition of European luxury inns, the Hearthstone House is located just two blocks west of the Wheeler Opera House. Guests share a large, elegant living room with teak-and-leather furnishings, a wood-burning fireplace, a dining room with bright flowers, and an extensive library. Most of the rooms are bright and homey but relatively small, with queen-size, double, or twin beds, original abstract art, small TVs, and vanities. Three "king" rooms feature Jacuzzi tubs, full-wall mirrors, and much more space.

Special touches include valet laundry and an Austrian herbal steam.

HOTEL ASPEN, 110 W. Main St. (at Garmisch St.), Aspen, CO 81611. Tel. 303/925-3441 or toll free 800/527-7369. Fax 303/920-1379. 45 rms (all with bath). TV TEL

$ Rates (including continental breakfast): Early/late ski season, $69–$89 single or double; $135–$155 penthouse. Holiday period, $200–$220 single or double; $275–$295 penthouse. Early Jan to early Feb, $99–$119 single or double; $155–$180 penthouse. Early Feb to late Mar, $160–$185 single or double; $225–$245 penthouse. Mid-Apr to mid-June and late Sept to late Nov, $65–$79 single or double; $100–$118 penthouse. Mid-June to late Aug, $94–$105 single or double; $130–$160 penthouse. Late Aug to late Sept, $74–$89 single or double; $105–$120 penthouse. AE, CB, DC, DISC, MC, V. **Parking:** Free.

Bridging the geographical gap between Aspen's Victorian West End neighborhood and its bustling downtown is this pleasant modern hotel, located just three blocks west of the Hotel Jerome. Above the small lobby, a second-floor living room with a fireplace and library doubles as a breakfast and après-ski party room. All rooms are upscale and well lit, making attractive use of light woods and strong pastels. Standard one-bedroom units have a king- or queen-size beds; deluxe units have a terrace or balcony. Solarium suites include enclosed sitting porches overlooking Aspen Mountain. Many rooms, including the penthouses, have private Jacuzzi tubs. All rooms have a wet bar, minirefrigerator, and coffee maker.

Services and facilities include valet laundry, an outdoor swimming pool, two outdoor Jacuzzis, and meeting space for up to 60.

INDEPENDENCE SQUARE HOTEL, 404 S. Galena St., Aspen, CO 81611. Tel. 303/920-2313 or toll free 800/633-0336. Fax 303/920-2020. 28 rms (all with bath). TV TEL

$ Rates (including continental breakfast): Single or double, $79–$210 early/late ski season, $210–$300 holiday period, $120–$235 Jan to mid-Feb, $145–$265 mid-Feb to Mar. 5-night minimum in winter. AE, MC, V. **Parking:** Free.

A renovated historic property on the downtown mall opposite the Rubey Park bus station, this hotel is one of the Aspen Club group. Light breakfasts and après-ski drinks are served in the second-floor atrium lounge with a large fireplace and the ground-floor library with books, newspapers, and board games. Colorful photographs adorn the hallways. Guest rooms can dazzle with colors alone—purple doors and peach trim—but decor is otherwise simple, with lots of light woods and good use of modern-and-historic photos. All rooms have queen beds (some of them Murphys) with down comforters, ample closet space, refrigerators, and modern but cramped bathrooms.

Services and facilities include concierge, airport shuttle, individual ski lockers, rooftop Jacuzzi and sun deck, and complimentary use of the Aspen Club.

THE INN AT ASPEN, 38750 Colo. 82, Aspen, CO 81611. Tel. 303/925-1500 or toll free 800/952-1515; 800/826-4998 in Colorado. Fax 303/925-9037. 120 rms, 4 suites (all with bath). A/C TV TEL

$ Rates: Early/late ski season, $110–$155 single or double; $200–$400 suite. Holiday period, $235–$310 single or double; $620–$800 suite. Jan to mid-Feb, $140–$190 single or double; $320–$375 suite. Mid-Feb to Mar, $165–$220 single or double; $360–$450 suite. Mid-Apr to Mid-Nov, $75–$155 single or double; $120–$240 suite. AE, CB, DC, DISC, MC, V. **Parking:** Free.

Nestled at the foot of Buttermilk Mountain, this ski-in/ski-out hotel offers views of either the slopes or the Roaring Fork valley. Studios are neat and cozy, with private balconies, queen-size Murphy beds, double sleeper sofas, easy chairs, dining tables, and vanities. Kitchenettes (stocked for four people) have microwave ovens, refrigerators, toasters, and coffee makers. Executive studios are larger but furnished the same; all rooms have mauve or pale-lilac color schemes. Most guests prefer to pay a little extra for the mountain view.

Dining facilities include: Barrington's Fireside Dining Room and Barrington's Café. The hotel lounge has a sunken section that enables indoor/outdoor Jacuzzi bathers to imbibe. The hotel also offers a heated outdoor swimming pool, fitness center, masseuse, gift shop, private ski lockers, meeting space for 225, room service, concierge, shuttle service, valet laundry, and safety-deposit boxes.

LIMELITE LODGE, 228 E. Cooper Ave. (at Monarch St.), Aspen, CO 81611. Tel. 303/925-3025 or toll free 800/433-0832. Fax 303/925-5120. 60 rms, 3 suites (all with bath). TV TEL

$ Rates (including continental breakfast): Early/late ski season, $68–$98 single or double; $130 suite. Holiday period, $148–$168 single or double; $225 suite. Jan, $102–$118 single or double; $170 suite. Feb–Mar, $138–$158 single or double; $215 suite. May–June, $58–$98 single or double; $130 suite. July–Aug, $88–

$118 single or double; $170 suite. Sept–Oct, $68–$98 single or double; $130 suite. AE, CB, DC, DISC, MC, V. **Parking:** Free.

A unique bronze sculpture stands outside this motel cater-corner from Wagner Park. The lodge has two separate buildings facing each other across Cooper Avenue—one three stories, the other two—each with its own heated outdoor swimming pool and Jacuzzi. Rooms are very well kept. Most have two double beds with down comforters, a large pinewood dresser and other furnishings, floral wallpaper, and a small private bath on the other side of a walk-through closet/vanity. Jacuzzi rooms are available.

The Columbine Room offers breakfast every morning and a warming fire every night. On Monday and Thursday nights in winter, there are hot-spiced-wine après-ski parties. Hot beverages are available 24 hours.

Services and facilities include a 24-hour desk, rooms for the disabled, two heated outdoor swimming pools, Jacuzzis, sauna, guest laundry, and ski lockers.

Inexpensive

ST. MORITZ LODGE, 334 W. Hyman Ave., Aspen, CO 81612. Tel. 303/925-3220. 12 dorm rms (shared bath), 13 standard (all with bath). TV TEL
$ Rates (including continental breakfast): Peak summer season, $29 dorm bed; $65 standard room (single or double). Peak winter season, $39 dorm bed; $125 standard room. AE, MC, V.

A friendly European-style lodge with a large fireplace in its lobby, the St. Moritz appeals to budget watchers with dorm rooms (small but sufficient) and low-priced standard rooms with cable color television and private, tiled bathrooms. There's also a heated outdoor swimming pool, Jacuzzi, and sauna. Breakfast and après-ski refreshments are served daily in the lower lounge.

THE SKIER'S CHALET, 233 Gilbert St. (P.O. Box 248), Aspen, CO 81612. Tel. 303/920-2037. 18 rms (all with bath). TV TEL
$ Rates (including continental breakfast): Summer, $55 single; $60–$75 double. Winter, $60–$105 single; $80–$140 double. MC, V. **Parking:** On street.

Howard Awrey built this lodge and restaurant at the foot of Lift 1A at Gilbert Street and Aspen Street in 1952, and he has run it ever since. He added a second building in 1965. Combining European style with old-time Aspen ambience, it's popular with folks who come to ski and don't need frills, for instance, international ski racers. Basic rooms have two double beds with down comforters, a desk/dresser, refrigerator, and ski photos on the walls. Breakfast is served in the family room, which also boasts a fireplace and piano. Adjacent, at 710 S. Aspen St., is the Skier's Chalet Steak House, serving large portions at reasonable prices. The outdoor swimming pool is heated to 104° in winter.

SNOWMASS

Snowmass lodges about 8,000 guests in seven lodges and 22 condo complexes. Call **Snowmass Central Reservations** (tel. 800/332-3245).

Very Expensive

THE SNOWMASS LODGE & CLUB, Snowmass Club Circle (P.O. Box G-2), Snowmass Village, CO 81615. Tel. 303/923-5600 or toll free 800/525-0710. Fax 303/923-6944. 76 rms, 65 suites. A/C MINIBAR TV TEL
$ Rates (including breakfast): Early/late season, $140–$210 single or double; $200–$375 villa. Pre-Christmas and Feb–Mar, $255–$325 single or double; $385–$675 villa. Holiday period, $310–$415 single or double; $460–$760 villa. Jan, $200–$250 single or double; $250–$430 villa. Spring and fall, $140–$195 single or double; $200–$375 villa. Summer, $170–$225 single or double; $225–$400 villa. Children 12 and under stay free in parents' room. AE, CB, DC, DISC, JCB, MC, V. **Parking:** Free.

A mile below the ski lifts at Snowmass Village sprawls this 567-acre sports resort and conference center. Despite this distance from the slopes, this is indeed a skiers' hotel: All room prices include lift tickets! Surrounded by a golf course that converts in winter to a Nordic ski center, and near 11 outdoor tennis courts and two swimming pools, the three-story building of stone and cedar shakes is ideal for the sports lover. Within, a massive rock fireplace dominates a living room of plush couches and pinewood floors. A reading nook has out-of-town papers and current magazines, and a handcrafted piano bar highlights an intimate cocktail lounge.

The lodge itself has 76 rooms, including nine premium units and four deluxe rooms. Each has a queen-size bed and sofa bed, reproduction antique pine furniture including a desk, cable television hidden in an armoire, direct-dial phones, radio, humidifier, terry-cloth robes, wet bar, refrigerator, coffee maker, and a private patio or balcony with mountain or poolside view. Sixty-five adjacent villas of one to three bedrooms have all these amenities and more, including full kitchens, a bath per bedroom, and full living/dining areas. Most also have wood-burning fireplaces.

Dining/Entertainment: The Four Corners dining room serves three meals daily in a two-level garden atmosphere. Gourmet American food is priced in the high moderate range. From May to September, casual lunches are served in the Summerhouse restaurant by the tennis courts. There's a snack bar in the golf/cross-country clubhouse, and a cocktail lounge/piano bar in the main lodge.

Services: 24-hour room service and valet laundry, full-service concierge, ski concierge slopeside, ski and golf equipment storage, nursery and child care, foreign exchange desk, morning newspaper and fresh coffee in room, business services, room for the disabled.

Facilities: 18-hole championship golf course converts to Nordic ski center in winter, with seasonal pro shop/ski-rental shop; two indoor and 11 outdoor tennis courts, with pro shop; racquetball-and-squash courts; heated outdoor lap pool and recreational swimming pool; bicycle rentals; full athletic club (including weights, aerobics, hot tubs, saunas, steam rooms, massage, and facials); guest laundry; games room; meeting space for up to 225.

Moderate

MOUNTAIN CHALET, 115 Daly Lane (P.O. Box 5066), Snowmass Village, CO 81615. Tel. 303/923-3900 or toll free 800/843-1579. 64 rms. TV TEL

$ Rates (including breakfast): Single or double, $89–$115 early/late ski season, $171–$215 holiday period, $140–$178 Jan, $162–$197 Feb–Mar, $80–$100 June–Sept. Minimum 7 nights in holiday period and Feb–Mar. AE, DISC, MC, V. **Closed:** Mid-Apr to May and mid-Sept to Thanksgiving. **Parking:** $6 per day in covered garage.

A small but elegant European-style ski hotel, the four-story Mountain Chalet is a ski-in/ski-out accommodation on the slopes below the Snowmass Village Mall. Rooms are simple but nicely kept, with light-wood furnishings, including a desk, plus cable TV, AM/FM radio, and small refrigerator. Many rooms have a fireplace or private balcony.

Hot beverages are available 24 hours on the third floor. Winter Sundays, there's always an après-ski party. Services and facilities include limited airport shuttle, valet laundry, heated outdoor swimming pool, hot tub, saunas, guest laundry, games room, and ski storage. Pets are not permitted.

THE WILDWOOD LODGE, 40 Elbert Lane (P.O. Box 5037), Snowmass Village, CO 81615. Tel. 303/923-3550 or toll free 800/445-1642; 800/833-1603 in Colorado. Fax 303/923-4844. 142 rms, 6 suites (all with bath). TV TEL

$ Rates (including continental breakfast): Early ski season, $106–$134. Holiday period, $225–$260. Jan, $160–$190. Feb–Mar, $120–$235. Summer and fall, $92–$115. All rates are single or double. Children 12 and under stay free in parents' room. Call for suite rates. AE, MC, V. **Parking:** Free.

Adjacent to the ski slopes, the Wildwood is an eclectic blend of mountain charm and bold Southwest colors. Rooms are decorated with framed prints and wood furnishings, and each comes with minirefrigerator and coffee maker. There is an outdoor heated pool and hot tub.

Pippin's Steak & Lobster Restaurant, located in the lodge, is open nightly for family-style dining. Children staying at the lodge receive a 50% discount off the children's menu. Après-ski drinks are served in Pippin's bar.

Services and facilities include evening room service, valet laundry, courtesy van to the airport and around Snowmass, ski lockers, and meeting rooms. The lodge is next door to Snowmass Village Mall.

Inexpensive

SNOWMASS INN, Daly Lane (P.O. Box 5640), Snowmass Village, CO 81615. Tel. 303/923-4202. 44 rms (all with bath). TV TEL

$ Rates (including continental breakfast): Single or double, $80 Thanksgiving to mid-Dec, $100 pre-Christmas period, $140 Christmas, $115 Jan, $125 Feb–Mar, $90 end of Mar to mid-Apr, $70 mid-May to mid-Oct. MC, V. **Parking:** Free.

Closed: Mid-Apr to mid-May and mid-Oct to Thanksgiving.

Located opposite the north side of the Village Mall, the Snowmass Inn has a large stone fireplace in its lobby and four floors of guest rooms. Queen-size Murphy beds lower electronically from the walls, and large sleeper sofas enable each room to sleep four. All rooms have minirefrigerators, wet bars, cable TV, full bathrooms with vanities, and coffee and tea each morning. Facilities include a year-round heated swimming pool, king-size Jacuzzi, sauna, guest laundry, and courtesy airport shuttle.

WHERE TO DINE

Most restaurants in the Aspen-Snowmass area are open nightly during the winter (Thanksgiving to early April) and summer (mid-June to mid-September) seasons. Between seasons, however, most close their doors. Call ahead if you're visiting at these times.

ASPEN

Very Expensive

PINE CREEK COOKHOUSE, 11399 Castle Creek Rd., Ashcroft. Tel. 925-1044.

Cuisine: CONTINENTAL. **Reservations:** Recommended at lunch, required at dinner.

$ Prices: Lunch $7.95–$14.95; dinner $16.95–$28.95. AE, MC, V.

Open: June 15–Oct 1 and Dec 15–Apr 15, lunch daily noon–2pm; dinner daily 6–9pm.

A cross-country ski center was established near the mining ghost town of Ashcroft, 13 miles from Aspen at the foot of the Elk Mountain Range, and this restaurant followed soon after. Surrounded by 13,000-foot peaks, the cook house can be reached by road in summer, by sleigh or cross-country skis only in winter. Skiers put on miners' headlamps and follow a guide for 20 minutes to reach the rustic restaurant, while sleigh riders huddle under fur rugs as mules pull them to dinner.

Lunch is served on an outdoor deck, weather permitting. Dinner is always an event. It starts with a steaming mug of hot mulled cider, then continues with a hearty homemade soup and a main course that might be trout, lamb, or venison. Smoking is not permitted.

PIÑONS, 105 S. Mill St. Tel. 920-2021.

Cuisine: CREATIVE REGIONAL. **Reservations:** Recommended.

$ Prices: Appetizers $8–$12; main courses $22–$34. AE, MC, V.

Open: Dinner only, daily 6–10pm.

Tremendous attention to detail went into creating the contemporary western ranch setting of Piñons, with its aged stucco walls and braided whip leather around the stairwell. Be prepared to savor foods like lobster strudel, Freddy salad, fresh fish, wild game, grilled dishes and mixed berry gratin—food for the soul as well as the body. For dessert, the chocolate macadamia-nut tart is "to die for."

RENAISSANCE, 105 S. Mill St. Tel. 920-2021.

Cuisine: MODERN FRENCH. **Reservations:** Recommended.

$ Prices: Appetizers $10–$14; main courses $24–$36; complete five-course wine-tasting dinners, $95. AE, MC, V.
Open: Daily 6–10pm. **Closed:** Late spring and fall.

Chef-owner Charles Dale has created a beautiful, intimate, and contemporary setting for his creative dishes, served as part of an elaborate wine-tasting dinner, or à la carte. The menu changes frequently, but nightly specials frequently include selections such as carpaccio of tuna, freshwater striped bass with fennel-tomato marmalade, risotto with Aspen mushrooms, curried lamb, beef tenderloin, grilled tenderloin of venison, and roast pheasant. There is an extensive selection of wine by the glass. For dessert, you might enjoy the chocolate soufflé.

Expensive

THE GOLDEN HORN, 320 S. Mill St. Tel. 925-3373.
　Cuisine: SWISS. **Reservations:** Highly recommended.
　$ Prices: Appetizers $6–$14; main courses $23–$35. AE, CB, DC, MC, V.
　Open: Dinner only, daily 5:30–10:30pm. **Closed:** Early Apr to mid-June and Labor Day–Thanksgiving.

An Aspen favorite since 1949, and the town's longest continually operating restaurant, the Golden Horn features the friendly alpine atmosphere of chef-owner Klaus Christ's native Switzerland. Named for the golden horn on the dark-paneled wall near the fireplace, it's famous for its hearty Swiss cuisine—wiener schnitzel, lamb, filet mignon, venison, and fresh fish—and more recently for "cuisine minceur."

　The latter is a low-calorie style of cooking developed in the spa town of Eugénie-les-Bains, France, that keeps three-course dinners to less than 450 calories. A serving of tomato-basil soup, a main course of free-range chicken breast sautéed with rosemary and white wine, and a dessert of fresh berries steamed in parchment paper fills the bill. All items are fat free and salt free. The Golden Horn's 260-bottle wine list has earned it a place on the *Wine Spectator*'s "top 100" list of U.S. restaurants.

THE LITTLE NELL, 675 E. Durant Ave. Tel. 920-4600.
　Cuisine: CREATIVE REGIONAL. **Reservations:** Highly recommended.
　$ Prices: Appetizers $4.50–$12.75; main courses $7.50–$15 at lunch, $21–$31 at dinner. AE, CB, DC, DISC, JCB, MC, V.
　Open: Breakfast daily 7–10am; lunch daily 11:30am–2pm; dinner daily 5:30–10:30pm.

Dinner here usually begins with a cocktail in the Living Room Bar, with its plush chairs and couches spaced around a massive, two-sided sandstone fireplace. Then it moves into the spacious restaurant, its big windows gazing toward the Little Nell hotel courtyard, its walls hung like an art gallery.

　The cuisine bears the moniker "American alpine cooking," focusing on innovative preparations of wild game and fresh seafood. Breakfast has numerous egg specialties; lunch focuses on pasta creations and one-pot dishes like black bean and venison chili pie. At dinner, you can start with a corn and wild-rice chowder or trout cakes with cabbage-and-apple slaw. Main dishes, all served à la carte, include Atlantic halibut, caribou, rainbow trout, pork chops, rack of lamb, and eggplant ratatouille.

SMUGGLER LAND OFFICE LTD., 415 E. Hopkins Ave. Tel. 925-8624.
　Cuisine: CAJUN/SEAFOOD. **Reservations:** Recommended.
　$ Prices: Appetizers $7.95–$12.95; main courses $18.95–$27.95. AE, CB, DC, MC, V.
　Open: Dinner daily 6–10:30pm; food service daily 4:30pm–midnight (bar open to 2am Mon–Sat, to midnight Sun).

The historic Brand Building, which indeed housed the company that controlled the late 19th-century Smuggler Mine, has been restored in grand Victorian style. From its casual ground-floor bar to the two upper dining levels, there's a feeling of old-time elegance. In summer, dinner is served in an outdoor sculpture garden. Rack of lamb, fresh seafood, pasta, and creole and Cajun specialties—including crawfish pie—highlight the menu.

SYZYGY, 520 E. Hyman Ave. Tel. 925-3700.

Cuisine: CREATIVE INTERNATIONAL. **Reservations:** Requested.
$ Prices: Appetizers $7–$14; main courses $18–$26.50. MC, V.
Open: Dinner only, Wed–Mon 6–10pm (lounge open to 2am Mon–Sat, to midnight Sun). **Closed:** Mid-Apr to May and Oct to mid-Nov.

In scientific terms, a "syzygy" is an alignment of heavenly bodies or a union of biological organisms. In culinary terms it's a perfect fusion of food, service, and presentation. At least that's the claim of this second-story restaurant, a casually elegant establishment with "water walls" accenting an otherwise gray decor.

The menu blends elements of French, Italian, Asian, and southwestern cuisines. This leads to such innovations as grilled ahi with red-chile pesto, roast elk with shiitake mushrooms, and curried shrimp with tempura pancakes. There's also an extensive wine list featuring California, French, and Italian wines.

Moderate

ASPEN GROVE CAFE, 525 E. Cooper Ave. Tel. 925-6162.
Cuisine: INTERNATIONAL. **Reservations:** Recommended at dinner.
$ Prices: Main courses $3.50–$8.25 at breakfast, $3.50–$6.75 at lunch, $9–$19 at dinner. AE, MC, V.
Open: Breakfast/lunch daily 7am–3pm; dinner daily 5–10pm.

This garden restaurant in the heart of downtown Aspen offers a bright, airy atmosphere during the day, a more elegant mood in the evening with pink linen and candlelight service. Luncheon specials include pastas and hot-and-cold sandwiches. For dinner, consider the Norwegian salmon, Santa Fe duck, or Greek spinach pie.

THE CHART HOUSE, 219 E. Durant Ave., at Monarch St. Tel. 925-3525.
Cuisine: STEAK/SEAFOOD. **Reservations:** Recommended.
$ Prices: Main courses $16.95–$28.95. AE, DC, MC, V.
Open: Dinner only, daily 5:30–10pm.

The first Chart House in the United States was established here in Aspen in 1961. Contemporary rustic decor—rough-hewn wood walls with sports-action photos, planter boxes beside marble-top tables, and polished brass around the incredible salad bar. The menu emphasizes steaks, prime rib, and seafood.

THE GRILL ON THE PARK, 307 S. Mill St. Tel. 920-3700.
Cuisine: AMERICAN. **Reservations:** Not accepted.
$ Prices: Breakfast $3–$6.50; lunch $3.95–$8.95; dinner $10.95–$19.95. AE, CB, DC, DISC, MC, V.
Open: Daily 11:30am–11pm.

It's not the view toward the Wagner Park soccer field across the street that makes the Grill so popular among Aspen residents. It's the open mesquite grill, generous portions, and friendly service. Barbecued ribs and chicken, fresh fish, thick steaks and chops highlight the dinner menu. Pasta is always a midday hit, along with half-pound burgers and imaginative salads.

TAKAH SUSHI, 420 E. Hyman Ave. Tel. 925-8588.
Cuisine: JAPANESE. **Reservations:** Recommended.
$ Prices: Appetizers $6–$16; main courses $16–$25. AE, CB, DC, MC, V.
Open: Dinner only, daily 5:30–11pm.

This lively sushi bar and Japanese restaurant has been praised by the *New York Times,* which called its sushi "some of the best between Malibu and Manhattan." A wide variety of sushi are sliced and rolled here, from halibut to octopus. If raw fish isn't your style, try the deep-fried soft-shell crab. Or go for more traditional steak teriyaki or tempura-fried shrimp.

UTE CITY BANQUE, 501 E. Hyman Ave., at Galena St. Tel. 925-4373.
Cuisine: AMERICAN/CONTINENTAL. **Reservations:** Recommended.
$ Prices: Appetizers $5.45–$8.95; main courses $5.95–$12.95 at lunch, $16.95–$29.95 at dinner. AE, CB, DC, MC, V.
Open: Lunch daily 11:30am–2:30pm; dinner daily 6–10pm (bar-café daily 4:30–11pm; bar open until 2am).

A financial institution (the Aspen State Bank) in the 1890s and a popular restaurant in the 1990s, the Ute City features Victorian decor and the longest solid-oak bar in town. The menu specializes in such dishes as rack of lamb, veal, and fresh fish. A light bar menu is served from 4 to 11pm daily.

WIENERSTUBE, 633 E. Hyman Ave., at Spring St. Tel. 925-3357.

Cuisine: AUSTRIAN. **Reservations:** Recommended at dinner.

$ Prices: Breakfast $2.95–$8.95; lunch $5–$16.50. AE, CB, DC, MC, V.

Open: Tues–Sun 7am–2pm.

Boyhood friends Gerhard Mayritsch and Helmut Schloffer, natives of the Austrian city of Villach, opened this restaurant in 1965. One tradition they preserved from the old country was the Stammitsch, a large community dining table that Aspen locals quickly found to their liking. Today, behind the stained glass of this beautiful garden establishment, you'll find the shakers and movers of this bustling community talking in animated tones over breakfast and lunch. There are private tables and booths for everyone else, where they enjoy Viennese pastries in the morning and Austrian sausages, Wiener Schnitzel, and other specialties at lunch.

Inexpensive

ASIA, 132 W. Main St. Tel. 925-5433.

Cuisine: CHINESE. **Reservations:** Recommended.

$ Prices: Appetizers $3.95–$7.95; main courses $8.95–$18.95. AE, CB, DC, MC, V.

Open: Daily 11:30am–10:30pm.

Lodged in an opulent century-old Victorian manor, this is probably Aspen's finest Chinese restaurant. Chef Steve Ko, who cooked for two decades in Taipei and New York before moving to the Rockies, makes Cantonese, Mandarin, Hunan, and Szechuan dishes to individual order. House specialties include Shan-tan beef, shrimp in spicy Yu-shan sauce, and Mandarin crispy duck.

BAHN THAI, 308 S. Hunter St. Tel. 925-5518.

Cuisine: THAI. **Reservations:** Recommended.

$ Prices: Appetizers $6.95–$13.95; main courses $7.95–$11.95. AE, MC, V.

Open: Mon–Fri 11:30am–10pm, Sat–Sun 5:30–10pm.

Got a taste for something spicy . . . really spicy? Start with a bowl of *tom yum goong* (hot-and-sour lemongrass soup), then follow it with a red or green chicken curry, *pahd Thai* (fried noodles with chicken and ground peanuts), or a variety of other Southeast Asian dishes. The restaurant is on the lower level of the Centennial Building, between Cooper Avenue and Hyman Avenue. Smoking is not permitted.

BENTLEY'S AT THE WHEELER, 328 E. Hyman Ave. Tel. 920-2240.

Cuisine: AMERICAN. **Reservations:** Not accepted.

$ Prices: Lunch $3.75–$7.95; dinner $8.95–$16.95. AE, DISC, MC, V.

Open: Mon–Fri 11am–11pm; Sat–Sun 10am–11pm. Bar open daily until 2am.

A Victorian pub in the 19th-century Wheeler Opera House, Bentley's has a classic bar made from an old English bank counter. Luncheon menu includes "Bentley's burger", chicken quesadillas, Caesar salad, and fish-and-chips. Generous dinners range from poached salmon to barbecued ribs and a New York strip steak.

THE CANTINA, 411 E. Main St., at Mill St. Tel. 925-FOOD.

Cuisine: MEXICAN. **Reservations:** Not accepted.

$ Prices: Lunch $5.75–$8.95; dinner $8.95–$13.95. AE, MC, V.

Open: Daily 11am–11pm (bar open to 2am Mon–Sat, to midnight Sun).

"The last time anything this enjoyable came up from Mexico, it was confiscated by the sheriff." That's the claim of this restaurant, one of Aspen's most popular taco-and-enchilada joints. The decor is simple—hardwood floors and tables—with lots of greenery around, and courtyard seating in summer. Portions are huge: They fill a plate that's a foot in diameter. Try the chimichangas, a house specialty.

LITTLE ANNIE'S EATING HOUSE, 517 E. Hyman Ave. Tel. 925-1098.

Cuisine: AMERICAN. **Reservations:** Not accepted.

$ Prices: Lunch $3.95–$8.95; dinner $9.50–$16.95. MC, V.
Open: Daily 11:30am–11:30pm (bar open to 2am).
The atmosphere here is casual, western style. Little Annie's is famous for its barbecued ribs, chicken, and outrageous burgers. But it's becoming equally popular for its newer menu items, including healthy summer salads, totally fresh pastas, vegetarian lasagne, and fish.

POUR LA FRANCE! CAFE & BISTRO, 413 E. Main St., at Mill St. Tel. 920-1151.
Cuisine: INTERNATIONAL. **Reservations:** Not accepted.
$ Prices: Breakfast $4.50–$6.95; lunch $4.50–$7.50; dinner $6.95–$13.75. MC, V.
Open: Summer, daily 7am–9pm; winter, daily 7am–10pm.
This pleasant European-style sidewalk café—known for its freshly baked croissants and pastries in the morning, its vegetarian chili and unusual sandwiches, midday—undergoes an evening metamorphosis to a quiet bistro. Nightly specials might include such dishes as chicken potpie or vegetarian pasta, or any number of interesting beef or fish dishes. Wines, including champagne, are served by the glass. Smoking is not permitted.

Budget

LA COCINA, 308 E. Hopkins Ave. Tel. 925-9714.
Cuisine: MEXICAN.
$ Prices: Main courses $6.50–$10.75. No credit cards.
Open: Dinner only, daily 5–10pm. **Closed:** Mid-Apr to May and Oct to mid-Nov.
Ski magazine calls La Cocina "one of the unmissables" in Aspen. A free basket of corn chips and spicy-hot salsa have greeted diners here for more than two decades. Start with the green-chile soup, then slide into a platter of blue-corn chicken enchiladas with a side of posole. There's no lard used for cooking here. Top it off with homemade "chocolate velvet" dessert. The bar keeps hopping until the wee hours.

MAIN STREET BAKERY & CAFE, 201 E. Main St., at Aspen St. Tel. 925-6446.
Cuisine: INTERNATIONAL.
$ Prices: $3.50–$12.95. MC, V.
Open: Daily 7am–9:30pm.
This old-time Aspen bakery beside Paepcke Park serves three meals a day to hungry locals and pastries, teas, and espresso drinks in between. Stuffed french toast is a morning favorite; homemade soups, sandwiches on fresh-baked bread, and salads set the tone at lunch. The dinner menu includes meat or vegetarian lasagne, Colorado lamb, alpine trout, and roast chicken.

THE RED ONION, 420 E. Cooper St. Tel. 925-9043.
Cuisine: AMERICAN/MEXICAN.
$ Prices: Lunch $4.95–$6.50; dinner $5.95–$9.95. AE, MC, V.
Open: Daily 11:30am–10pm (bar open until 2am Mon–Sat, to midnight Sun).
Aspen's oldest surviving bar changes with the times: It has an indoor ski "corral" for folks just off the slopes. Burgers and Philadelphia steak sandwiches are big favorites at lunchtime; Mexican cuisine holds forth at night, with the likes of burritos, fajitas, and taco salads. Daily specials feature traditional American fare.

SNOWMASS

Expensive

KRABLOONIK, 1201 Divide Rd., off Brush Creek Rd., Snowmass Village. Tel. 923-3953.
Cuisine: WILD GAME/SEAFOOD. **Reservations:** Recommended at lunch, essential at dinner.
$ Prices: Appetizers $4.25–$12.50; main courses $8.95–$28.95 at lunch, $21.75–$45 at dinner. MC, V.

Open: Winter, lunch daily 11am–2pm; dinner seatings daily at 6 and 8:30pm. Summer, dinner seatings daily at 6 and 8:30pm; brunch Sun 10am–2pm.

There's something very wild, something that hearkens to Jack London, perhaps, about sitting in a long cabin watching teams of sled dogs come and go as you bite into a caribou stew or wild-boar sandwich. That's part of the pleasure of Krabloonik. A venture of the largest dog kennel in America's lower 48 states, this rustic restaurant has huge picture windows with mountain views and seating around a sunken fire pit.

Skiers can drop into the restaurant from the Campground lift for winter lunch, or visitors can dine before or after an excursion on a dog sled. The stew and the barbecued Swedish boar are popular midday meals, as is smoked Cornish game hen. In the evening, begin with Krabloonik's wild-mushroom soup or grilled caribou. Then try moose loin, pheasant breast, or Rocky Mountain trout.

Moderate

COWBOYS, in the Silvertree Hotel, Elbert Lane, Snowmass Village Mall. Tel. 923-5249.
    Cuisine: CONTEMPORARY COLORADO. **Reservations:** Accepted only for groups of eight or more.
$ **Prices:** Appetizers $5.25–$8.95; main courses $17.95–$28.50. AE, CB, DC, DISC, MC, V.
    Open: Après-ski daily 2:30–5:30pm, dinner daily 5:30–9pm.

Country-and-western music fans, exalt: This may be your ultimate restaurant. Not only can you dance to your favorite swing when dinner is over, but you can get two-step instruction as well. That is, of course, after you've sampled the self-labeled "contemporary cowboy cuisine." The menu offers fresh wild game and pheasant, river fish, and Colorado beef and lamb.

IL POGGIO, Elbert Lane, Snowmass Village Mall. Tel. 923-4292.
    Cuisine: ITALIAN. **Reservations:** Recommended for the Ristorante.
$ **Prices:** Appetizers $5.50–$11; main courses $12–$21. Pizzas start at $8 in the Caffè. MC, V.
    Open: Dinner only, daily 5:30–10pm.

Actually two eateries in one, Il Poggio consists of the Ristorante—an elegant fine dining room with an extensive wine list—and a livelier and more casual Caffè, with its huge wood-burning pizza oven and pasta menu. The Ristorante focuses on "authentic food from Italy's small towns," with a menu that changes to reflect the particular region of the moment.

THE TOWER BAR AND RESTAURANT, Snowmass Village Mall. Tel. 923-4650.
    Cuisine: AMERICAN. **Reservations:** Recommended at dinner.
$ **Prices:** Lunch $5.50–$10.95; dinner $13.50–$20.95. AE, CB, DC, MC, V.
    Open: Lunch daily 11:30am–3pm; dinner daily 5:30–10:30pm.

Three features, besides its central location in the heart of the Snowmass Village Mall, make the Tower special. First is the tower for which it's named, a valley landmark. Second is the fact that it's owned by popular singer John Denver, an Aspen resident who frequently drops by. Third, there's no telling what its bartenders may have up their sleeves: They're amateur magicians who help maintain the food of a family-oriented restaurant. Main dishes include traditional favorites such as prime rib, New York steak, and barbecued shrimp, as well as creative dishes such as grilled raspberry-marinated chicken, and fettuccine primavera.

Inexpensive

LA PIÑATA, Daly Lane, Snowmass Village. Tel. 923-2153.
    Cuisine: MEXICAN. **Reservations:** Not accepted.
$ **Prices:** Appetizers $4.95–$7.95; main courses $7.95–$14.95. AE, CB, DC, MC, V.
    Open: Winter, dinner only, daily 5–10pm; summer, dinner only, daily 5–11pm (bar daily 3pm–2am).

Festive decor, a roaring fire, and a spacious deck make this a favorite Snowmass dining spot. Margarita specials highlight après-ski beginning at 3pm, and dinner specials such as margarita chicken and London broil, Santa Fe style, keep things hopping. Standard combination meals—chimichangas, enchiladas, and chile rellenos—are prepared Sonora style. There are nightly fresh-fish specials, such as smoked seafood enchiladas, ahi fajitas, and langoustine ravioli with pesto. Gringo dinners include steaks and chicken.

MOON DOGS, Village Shuttle Depot, Daly Lane, Snowmass Village. Tel. 923-6655.
   Cuisine: AMERICAN.
$ Prices: $1–$6.50. No credit cards.
   Open: Daily 8am–midnight.
A 100-year-old cable car beside the Snowmass shuttle depot houses this self-proclaimed "gourmet fast-food stand." Moon dogs—slow-grilled beef frankfurters—are the house favorite, but you can also get huge subs, breakfast burritos, danish, and popcorn all day long.

WOODY CREEK TAVERN, Upper River Rd., Woody Creek. Tel. 923-4585.
   Cuisine: AMERICAN. **Reservations:** Not accepted.
$ Prices: $3.50–$14.95. No credit cards.
   Open: Daily 11:30am–10pm (bar open until 2am Mon–Sat, to midnight Sun).
Woody Creek has become as much a hangout for celebrities, including maverick writer Hunter S. Thompson and actor Don Johnson, as for locals. Probably the only old-time, rustic tavern left in the Aspen area, its walls are covered with a variety of news clippings and other paraphernalia. Grilled buffalo beer sausage, barbecued pork ribs, and thick steaks are the most popular menu choices, along with burgers and Mexican food.

   To get there, drive three-quarters of a mile west of Brush Creek Road (the Snowmass Village turnoff) on Colo. 82, turn north on River Road, take a left at the first fork, and continue 1¼ miles.

CHAPTER 10

THE WESTERN SLOPE

1. GRAND JUNCTION
- **WHAT'S SPECIAL ABOUT THE WESTERN SLOPE**

2. GLENWOOD SPRINGS

3. MONTROSE

Westward-flowing rivers like the Colorado, Gunnison, and Yampa are the lifeblood of the vast, semidesert Western Slope of the Colorado Rockies. These streams support the region's largest communities (Grand Junction and Glenwood Springs on the Colorado, Montrose on the Uncompaghre, Delta on the Gunnison, Craig on the Yampa), irrigate the fertile soils for agriculture and ranching, and enable exploitation of rich mineral resources, including oil, coal, and uranium.

From the tourist standpoint, though, the rivers are much more. Over tens of thousands of years their ceaseless energy has gouged stunning canyons now encompassed by three national monuments: Colorado, Dinosaur, and Black Canyon of the Gunnison. Colorado National Monument, west of Grand Junction, is remarkable for its landforms and prehistoric petroglyphs. Dinosaur National Monument, in the state's northwestern corner, preserves a stunning wealth of fossil remains, along with the spectacular canyons of the Yampa and Green rivers. The Black Canyon, east of Montrose, is a dark, narrow, and virtually impenetrable chasm that draws adventurous rock climbers and rafters from throughout the West.

---

1. GRAND JUNCTION

251 miles W of Denver, 169 miles N of Durango

GETTING THERE   By Plane   On the north side of Grand Junction, Walker Field, 2828 H Rd. (tel. 244-9100), is less than a mile off I-70's Horizon Drive exit. Over 25 commercial flights arrive each day nonstop from Denver, Phoenix, Salt Lake City, Albuquerque, and Durango, with connections to cities nationwide.

The airport is served by American West (tel. 303/245-3460 or toll free 800/247-5692), Continental (tel. 303/241-4200 or toll free 800/525-0820), Mesa Airlines (tel. 243-3605), SkyWest (for Delta; toll free 800/453-9417), and United Express (toll free 800/241-6522).

By Train   Amtrak, First Street and Pitkin Avenue (tel. 800/USA-RAIL), is firmly established in Grand Junction. The *California Zephyr* stops once daily, in each direction, on its main route from San Francisco and Salt Lake City to Denver and Chicago.

By Bus   The coaches of Greyhound, and TNM&O, 230 S. Fifth St. (tel. 242-6012), connect Grand Junction with communities throughout the United States and Canada.

By Car   Grand Junction is located on I-70. U.S. 50 is the main artery from the south, connecting also with Montrose and Durango.

Information   Contact the Grand Junction Visitor & Convention Bureau, 360 Grand Ave., Grand Junction, CO 81501 (tel. 303/244-1480 or toll free 800/962-2547). There's a Tourist Information Center (tel. 243-1001) on Horizon Drive at I-70,

WHAT'S SPECIAL ABOUT
THE WESTERN SLOPE

Natural Spectacles
- ☐ Black Canyon of the Gunnison National Monument, a deep awe-inspiring canyon that can be seen from above, or for the adventurous, by foot.
- ☐ Colorado National Monument, an easily accessible trip into red rock canyons with towering sandstone monoliths.
- ☐ Dinosaur National Monument, a real dinosaur quarry.

Museums
- ☐ Ute Indian Museum in Montrose, showing what life for the Ute tribe was like in the mid-19th century.
- ☐ Montrose County Historical Museum, depicting pioneer life with a homesteader's cabin, a country store, and a children's room.
- ☐ Dinosaur Valley Museum in Grand Junction, with noisy, animated dinosaur replicas for kids, and exhibits on geology for adults.
- ☐ Pioneer Town Historical Museum in Cedaredge, a fun place for kids of all ages, with a re-created 1880s western town, complete with a saloon, a newspaper office, and a jail.
- ☐ Museum of Western Colorado in Grand Junction, with a historical timeline as well as guns, Native American artifacts, and pioneer exhibits.

- ☐ Frontier Historical Museum in Glenwood Springs, featuring the original bedroom furniture of Colorado legends Horace and Baby Doe Tabor, plus a walk-through coal mine.

Activities
- ☐ Glenwood Hot Springs Pool, two open-air mineral springs pools in business for more than a century.
- ☐ Wine tasting in Colorado wine country, east of Grand Junction, where local vintners like to show off their products.
- ☐ River rafting down the Colorado River through spectacular Glenwood Canyon.

The Arts
- ☐ Western Colorado Center for the Arts in Grand Junction, with works by some of Colorado's best artists, and a fantastic gift shop with one-of-a-kind creations.
- ☐ Art on the Corner, where you can walk among dozens of sculptures while checking out the downtown stores.

Exit 31, and a Colorado Welcome Center at I-70, Exit 19 (Fruita and Colorado National Monument), 12 miles west of Grand Junction.

Getting Around Sunshine Taxi (tel. 245-8294) will whisk you around town, with 24-hour service.

    Car rentals are available in the airport area from Avis (tel. 244-9170), Budget (tel. 244-9155), Hertz (tel. 243-0747), National (tel. 243-6626), and Thrifty (tel. 243-7556).

Fast Facts The **area code** is 303. In case of **emergency,** call 911; **St. Mary's Hospital** is at Patterson Road and Seventh Street (tel. 244-2273). The main **post office** is at 241 N. Fourth St. (tel. 244-3400). For **weather conditions,** call 242-2550.

SPECIAL EVENTS The Grand Junction area hosts the following annual events: Cinco de Mayo, in early May; Colorado Mountain Wine Fest the last weekend in

September; the Colorado Stampede Parade and Rodeo, on the third full weekend of June; Country Jam Music Festival, the last weekend in June; Dinosaur Days, during the fourth week of July; Junior College Baseball World Series, starting Memorial Day weekend; the Mesa County Fair, in the first full week of August; and the Peach Festival, in Palisade in mid-August.

Located at the confluence of the Gunnison and Colorado rivers, Grand Junction was founded in 1882 where the spike was driven to connect Denver and Salt Lake by rail. It quickly became the primary trade and distribution center between the two state capitals, and its mild climate, together with the fertile soil and irrigation potential of the river valleys, helped it grow into an important agricultural area. Soybeans, and later peaches and pears, were the most important crops; recently, its profile as a wine-producing region has increased. The city also was a center of the western Colorado uranium boom in the 1950s and the oil-shale boom in the late 1970s.

WHAT TO SEE & DO
ATTRACTIONS

ART ON THE CORNER, 115 N. Fifth St. Tel. 245-2926.

This outdoor sculpture exhibit, with over four-dozen works, helps make Grand Junction's Downtown Shopping Park one of the most attractive and successful in the country. Art on the Corner has placed sculptures seemingly everywhere up and down Main Street, from Second to Seventh streets. Sculptures are loaned by the artists for one year, during which time they are for sale. The shopping park also features art galleries, antique shops, restaurants, and a variety of retail stores, with wide tree-lined pedestrian walkways.

Admission: Free.

Open: Daily 24 hours, with shops and restaurants open usual business hours.

COLORADO NATIONAL MONUMENT, off Colo. 340, Fruita. Tel. 303/858-3617.

Eons of erosion by water and wind created this spectacular landscape along the northern rim of the Uncompahgre Plateau. Red-rock canyons and sandstone monoliths, some towering more than 2,000 feet above the Colorado River and its intermittent tributaries, dominate a wilderness of 32 square miles. Bighorn sheep, mountain lions, and golden eagles are among the semidesert denizens of the monument, which was established in 1911.

The east entrance is only 5 miles west of Grand Junction off Monument Road. But the best way to explore is to begin at the west entrance, following the signs off I-70 from Fruita, 15 miles west of Grand Junction. It's here that the 23-mile **Rim Rock Drive** begins, snaking up dramatic **Fruita Canyon** and offering panoramic views across the Colorado River valley to the Grand Mesa and Book Cliffs. At 7½ miles it reaches the national monument headquarters and **Visitor Center** near the Saddlehorn Campground. Exhibits on geology and history, and a slide show, introduce the park year-round; guided walks and campfire talks are frequently scheduled.

Rim Rock Drive offers access to hiking trails throughout the national monument, varying in length from 400 yards to 8½ miles. Most of the park's canyons are accessible to hikers, often following well-trodden deer trails as they crisscross north-facing slopes. Strange formations such as Window Rock, the massive rounded Coke Ovens, the boulder-strewn Devils Kitchen, the barely touching Kissing Couple, and the free-standing Independence Monument—all of which can be viewed from the road—are easily reached by foot. Ancient Native American petroglyphs are frequently seen.

Entombed within the rock layers throughout the national monument are the fossil remains of dinosaurs, fish and shellfish, early mammals, and other creatures that lived over a span of 100 million years. A combination of upward lifts, erosion, and volcanic eruptions caused the chaos of formations here. Each layer visible in the striations of

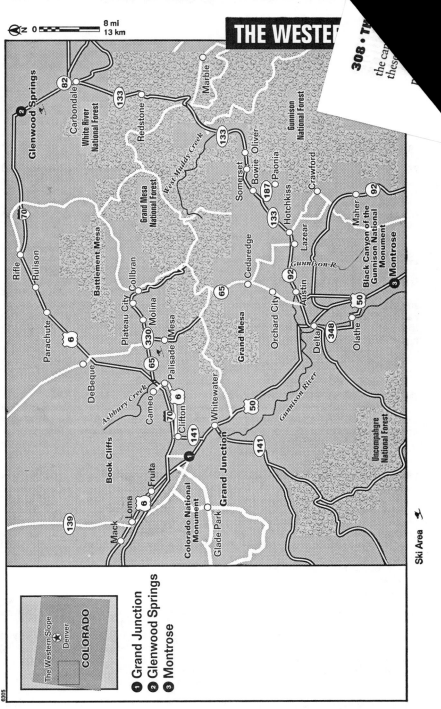

8 mi
0
13 km

N

Marble

82
Glenwood Springs

133

Carbondale

White River
National Forest

Redstone

70

Rifle

Rulison

133

Somerset
Bowie Oliver

Paonia

Gunnison
National Forest

Crawford

92

Maher

Battlement Mesa

Grand Mesa
National Forest

West Muddy Creek

133
Hotchkiss

187

Lazear

Black Canyon of the
Gunnison National
Monument

Montrose

Parachute

6

DeBeque

65

Plateau City

Collbran

330 Molina

Palisade Mesa

92
Austin

Gunnison R.

50

348

Olathe

50

Cedaredge

65

Orchard City

Grand Mesa

Delta

Asbbury Creek

Cameo

70
Clifton

141

Whitewater

50

Gunnison River

141

141

Uncompahgre
National Forest

Grand Junction

Book Cliffs

Fruita

6

139

Mack

Loma

6

Colorado National
Monument

Glade Park

Ski Area

The Western Slope

Denver

COLORADO

① Grand Junction
② Glenwood Springs
③ Montrose

6305

yon walls marks a time in the land's history. The fossils permit scientists to date rocks back through the Mesozoic Era of 225 million to 65 million years ago.

Admission: $4 per vehicle or $1 per person for cyclists, pedestrians, bus assengers, etc.

Open: Memorial Day–Labor Day, daily 8am–8pm; the rest of the year, daily 8am–4:30pm.

CROSS ORCHARDS HISTORIC SITE, 3079 F Rd. Tel. 434-9814.

Considered the finest remaining site from the early 20th-century Grand Valley agricultural boom era, Cross Orchards (a division of the Museum of Western Colorado) has re-created a life-style now usually found only in history books. On its 24.4 acres are a blacksmith shop, barn and packing shed, workers' bunkhouse, and former farm manager's residence, as well as an extensive collection of vintage farming and road-building equipment, a railway exhibit, a farm activity area, and a country store and gift shop. Living-history demonstrations are offered several times daily in summer, and various special events are held throughout the year. The original Cross Orchards Farm (1896–1923) covered 243 acres and boasted 22,000 apple trees.

Admission: $3 adults, $2.50 seniors 60 and older, $1.50 children 2–12.

Open: Mid-May to Nov 1, Tues–Sat 10am–5pm, and other days for special events.

DINOSAUR VALLEY, 362 Main St. Tel. 243-DINO or 241-9210.

The animated replicas (complete with sound effects) of such dinosaurs as stegosaurus, triceratops, and apatosaurus thrill youngsters at Dinosaur Valley. Adults can study regional paleontological history, examine a model of a dinosaur dig, and look at plaster casts of dinosaur prints. On the premises are a working "paleo lab" and a gift shop.

Admission: $4 adults, $2.50 children 2–12.

Open: Memorial Day–Sept, daily 9am–5:30pm; the rest of the year, Tues–Sat 10am–4:30pm.

DOO ZOO CHILDREN'S MUSEUM, 635 Main St. Tel. 241-5225.

Children 1 to 12 get hands-on experience in a variety of activities, from playacting a grownup profession to performing scientific experiments and testing their creative artistic horizons. The toy store here specializes in educational items.

Admission: $2 adults and children.

Open: Mon–Sat 10am–5:30pm.

MUSEUM OF WESTERN COLORADO, 248 S. Fourth St., at Ute St. Tel. 242-0971.

The geology, history, and culture of western Colorado are highlights of this very worthwhile museum. Of special interest is the Western Colorado Timeline, with photos and exhibits from every decade since the 1880s, and the Pioneer Room, which contains mining-and-ranching exhibits including a pioneer kitchen. The museum also has an extensive firearms collection, Native American artifacts, natural history, Old West-style paintings, and changing exhibits.

Admission: $2 adults, $1 children 2–17.

Open: Memorial Day–Labor Day, Mon–Sat 10am–4:45pm; the rest of the year, Tues–Sat 10am–4:45pm.

RIMROCK DEER PARK, Hwy. 340 between Fruita and the west entrance to Colorado National Monument. Tel. 858-9555.

Exotic deer from around the world are the highlight of this park/zoo, where you can also see buffalo, goats, sheep, llamas, and Roscoe the elk, who enjoys being hand-fed by visiting children.

Admission: $3.50 adults, $2.50 children 3–13, free for children under 3.

Open: May to Memorial Day, daily 8:30am–5:30pm.

WESTERN COLORADO CENTER FOR THE ARTS, 1803 N. Seventh St., at Orchard Ave. Tel. 243-7337.

This art museum has hundreds of works of art, many with western themes, as well as traveling exhibits. The collection includes lithographs by Paul Pletka and dozens of Navajo weavings dating from the turn-of-the-century.
Admission: Free, but donations accepted.
Open: Tues–Sat 10am–5pm.

SPORTS & RECREATION

BICYCLING   Grand Junction has become important to mountain bikers as the eastern terminus of Kokopelli's Trail to Moab, Utah. Winding for 128 miles through sandstone and shale canyons, it has an elevation differential of about 4,200 feet. There are primitive campsites at intervals along the trail. The Colorado gateway is at the Loma Boat Launch, 15 miles west of Grand Junction off I-70.

Another popular route is the Tabeguache Trail, running 142 miles from Shavano Valley, near Montrose, to No Thoroughfare Canyon, near the Colorado National Monument west of Grand Junction. For information on either trail, contact the Colorado Plateau Mountain-Bike Trail Association, P.O. Box 4602, Grand Junction, CO 81502 (tel. 241-9561), or the Bureau of Land Management, 2815 H Rd., Grand Junction (tel. 244-3000).

There's also a bike route through and around Colorado National Monument (see above); covering 33 miles, it follows Rim Rock Drive through the park and 10 additional miles on rural South Camp Road and South Broadway at the base of the canyons. The national monument publishes a descriptive brochure. The Four Corners Center for Experimental Learning (tel. 858-3607), offers mountain-bike tours through the monument, as does Endless Summer Tours (toll free 800/345-3389).

The Colorado Riverfront Project includes four trails that meander along the Colorado River. The trails offer opportunities to see ducks, geese, blue heron, deer, and rabbits. Audubon Trail, 1½ miles long, is accessed from Highway 340 and Dike Road; Connected Lakes Trail, 1 mile long, is reached from the west end of Dike Road; Blue Heron Trail, 2 miles long, is accessible from Redlands Parkway; and Watson Island Trail, at .87 mile, is entered at the intersection of South Seventh Street and Struthers Avenue.

GOLF   The 18-hole Tiara Rado Golf Course, 2063 S. Broadway (tel. 245-8085), is at the base of the Colorado National Monument canyons. The 9-hole Lincoln Park Golf Course, 12th Street and North Avenue (tel. 242-6394), is in the center of town. Also open to the public is the 9-hole Adobe Creek National Golf Course, in Fruita (tel. 858-0521).

HIKING   Hikers need look no further than Colorado National Monument (see above) for a wide choice of excellent day-and-overnight trips. A variety of descriptive brochures can be obtained at the park Visitors Center.

An alternative to loading yourself down with gear is using goat power. Cabra d'Oro Pack Goats, 1459 Grove Creek Rd., Collbran, CO (tel. 487-3388), offers year-round trips to Grand Mesa, Battlement Mesa, and other scenic areas. Guided trips start at $25 per person for half day; $40 for a full day.

Hikers and walkers who want to stay closer to town can explore the trails in the Colorado Riverfront Project (see "Bicycling," above).

HORSEBACK RIDING   Trail rides of one hour ($12) to a half day ($45) are available through Rimrock Adventures, on the Colorado River near the west entrance to the Colorado National Monument (tel. 858-9555). Hayrides and cookouts can also be scheduled.

RIVER RAFTING   Colorado River raft trips from 1½ hours to a full day are provided by Rimrock Adventures, Box 608, Fruita, CO 81521 (tel. 858-9555). Prices start at $13 for adults, $11 for children 13 and under, for a peaceful float, with departures every half hour. Rimrock also offers half-day trips through the Walter Walker State Wildlife Area, with some small rapids, for $25 for adults and $18 for children 13 and under. A full-day trip through the towering red Ruby and Horse Thief Canyons, including lunch, is $55 for adults and $45 for children 13 and younger.

More experienced rafters who seek remote wilderness areas can do so with Adventure Bound Expeditions, 2392 H Rd., Grand Junction, CO 81505 (tel. 241-5633 or toll free 800/423-4668), which specializes in trips lasting from two to five days through Canyonlands National Park, Dinosaur National Monument, and other remote areas.

SKIING   The Powderhorn Resort, Colo. 65, 7 miles west of Mesa (tel. 268-5700, or toll free 800/241-6997), is located 35 miles east of Grand Junction on the north face of the Grand Mesa. A favorite of powder skiers of all ability levels, it offers 255 acres of skiing, with an overnight lodge, two restaurants, a lounge, shops, and full equipment rentals. Full-day tickets are $26 for adults and $18 for children 7 to 12; kids 6 and under ski free.

The resort also offers 18km (11 miles) of groomed cross-country trails (trail pass $7), and snowmobile tours ($50 per person).

SWIMMING   The centrally located Lincoln Park, at 12th Street and North Avenue (tel. 244-1548), has an outdoor heated swimming pool with a 351-foot water slide, along with lighted tennis courts, playgrounds, picnic areas, and a nine-hole golf course. The main pool measures 25 yards by 50 meters and has a diving area. There are also two smaller children's pools.

The Orchard Mesa Community Center Pool, 2736 C Rd. (tel. 244-1485), is an indoor pool, open year-round, that also has a diving area and shallow-water section. The pool is open Monday through Saturday from 1:30 to 8pm, and Sunday from 1:30 to 6pm. General admission costs the same as the Lincoln Park pool.

WHERE TO STAY

MODERATE

GRAND JUNCTION HILTON, 743 Horizon Dr., Grand Junction, CO 81506. Tel. 303/241-8888 or toll free 800/HILTONS. Fax 303/241-8888, ext. 160. 248 rms, 16 suites (all with bath). A/C TV TEL
$ Rates: $69–$140 single or double; $135–$225 suite. Weekend rate $69 single or double. Children stay free in parents' room. AE, CB, DC, DISC, MC, V. **Parking:** Free.

A modern eight-story hotel just off I-70, the Hilton is memorable for its bright pastel decor and fine display of artwork in the lobby. The spacious guest rooms have a king-size or two double beds, full-length curtains to separate the entranceway and bathroom from the bedroom area, and contemporary furnishings like clear-glass lamps and full-mirror closet doors.

Dining-and-entertainment facilities include the Red Cliffs Restaurant, Christie's Restaurant, the Beer Garden, the Observatory Lounge off the lobby, and Cancun Saloon. There are occasional summer concerts on the lawn.

Room service, valet laundry, no-smoking rooms, and facilities for the disabled are available, as are an outdoor swimming pool and Jacuzzi, three tennis courts, weight-and-exercise room, volleyball court, horseshoe pits, children's playground, games room, travel agent, meeting space for 600; and vending machines with microwave ovens on some floors.

HOLIDAY INN, 755 Horizon Dr. (P.O. Box 1725), Grand Junction, CO 81502. Tel. 303/243-6790 or 800/HOLIDAY. Fax 303/243-6790, ext. 2233. 278 rms, 14 suites (all with bath). A/C TV TEL
$ Rates: $46–$51 single; $51–$56 double; $60–$65 suite. AE, CB, DC, DISC, JCB, MC, V. **Parking:** Free.

A spacious central garden courtyard and a skylit indoor garden-style HoliDome— both with swimming pools and other facilities—make this property a delight for recreation lovers. Most mauve-and-green floral-decorated rooms face one pool or the other. Most have two double beds, but many have queen-size or king-size beds, and some also have sofa sleepers or working desks.

Cinnamon's restaurant serves three meals daily, and the lounge has a large dance floor.

The hotel offers room service, valet laundry, courtesy shuttle, no-smoking rooms, facilities for the disabled, indoor-and-outdoor swimming pools, Jacuzzi, sauna, exercise room, games room, video arcade, guest laundries, gift shop, liquor store, and meeting space for 500.

THE ORCHARD HOUSE, 3573 E½ Rd., Palisade, CO 81526. Tel. 303/ 464-0529. 3 rms (1 with bath, 2 with shared bath). A/C
$ Rates (including breakfast): $50 single; $70 double. MC, V.
Situated in the midst of the Grand Valley orchard and wine country, this pleasant country homestead is more than just a bed-and-breakfast. Hosts Bill and Stephanie Schmid have created a true home environment, with a living room connecting to an upstairs master bedroom (complete with king-size brass bed) and a second downstairs bedroom (this one with twin beds). Guests have a private entrance and their own kitchen, available for limited use, and can use the washer and dryer. Gourmet home-cooked candlelight dinners, complete with wine, are a nightly option at $60 per couple. The scenery is spectacular.

RAMADA INN, 2790 Crossroads Blvd. (at Horizon Dr.), Grand Junction, CO 81506. Tel. 303/241-8411, or toll free 800/2-RAMADA. Fax 303/241-1077. 139 rms, 17 suites (all with bath). A/C TV TEL
$ Rates: Mon–Fri, $55 single; $60 double. Sat–Sun, $45 single or double June–Aug, $42 single or double Sept–May. Suite $110–$170. Children under 18 stay free in parents' room. AE, CB, DC, DISC, JCB, MC, V. **Parking:** Free.
There's an elegant, country-style feel to the Ramada lobby, with its parquet floors and reproduction antique furnishings. Guest rooms are more modern in appearance. Most have two double beds and standard hotel furnishings, including clock radios and vanities. Executive Choice rooms have working desks and Jacuzzi baths.

Oliver's, built to resemble a Victorian library, serves three meals daily. Bailey's Lounge features free hors d'oeuvres from 5 to 7:30pm nightly and a disc jockey playing dance music nightly. Services and facilities include room service, free shuttle van, facilities for the disabled, 24-hour heated indoor pool and whirlpool, health-club privileges, video arcade, and meeting space for 300. Nonsmoking rooms are available.

INEXPENSIVE

BEST VALUE INN, 718 Horizon Dr., Grand Junction, CO 81506. Tel. 303/243-5080. Fax 303/242-0600. 138 rms (all with bath). A/C TV TEL
$ Rates: $32–$42 single or double. Children 12 and under stay free in parents' room. AE, DC, DISC, MC, V. **Parking:** Free.
This Southwest-style motel, extensively remodeled in mid-1993, has spacious, comfortable rooms surrounding a courtyard with trees and a large grassy area. Most rooms have two sinks and queen beds, with some kings. All rooms have individual thermostats, direct-dial phones with free local calls, and cable TV with HBO. There's a heated pool and kiddie pool, open in summer; a large lobby with spiral staircase and free coffee; and a guest laundry. Nonsmoking rooms are available. Pets are not accepted.

BUDGET HOST INN, 721 Horizon Dr., Grand Junction, CO 81506. Tel. 303/243-6050 or toll free 800/888-5736. 54 rms (all with bath). A/C TV TEL
$ Rates: Summer, $30–$40 single; $34–$45 double. Winter, $28–$34 single; $32–$38 double. Children under 12 stay free in parents' room. AE, DC, DISC, ER, MC, V. **Parking:** Free.
Clean, attractive, basic rooms at a reasonable price are what you'll find at this motel.

Rooms have queen or extra-long beds, desks, and remote-controlled cable TV with HBO. There is free coffee and tea, and a microwave in the 24-hour lobby for guests' use. Fax and copier services are also available. Nonsmoking rooms are available. Pets are not permitted.

HOTEL MELROSE, 337 Colorado Ave., Grand Junction, CO 81501. Tel. 303/242-9636 or toll free 800/430-4555. Fax 303/242-5613. 26 rms (12 with bath).

$ Rates: $10 dorm bed; $16–$20 single or double with shared bath; $25–$35 single, $34 double with private bath and TV. MC, V. **Parking:** Free off street.

This centrally located historic brick building—the oldest part dates to 1908, the newest from the 1950s—has been lovingly restored, and now provides bargain-priced lodging to those seeking nostalgia and charm. Dorm rooms hold three or four, and private rooms vary considerably, but all are neat, clean, and comfortable. A common area, open to all, has a kitchen, dining room, and living room with cable TV, a VCR, videos, and books. Free pick up from the Grand Junction airport is available. Pets are not permitted.

JUNCTION COUNTRY INN, 861 Grand Ave., Grand Junction, CO 81501. Tel. 303/241-2817. 3 rms (1 with bath), 1 suite. A/C

$ Rates (including full breakfast): $34–$44 single; $35–$49 double; $54–$59 suite. AE, MC, V.

Not many bed-and-breakfasts welcome children, but this is one that does, with toys, an outdoor play area, cribs, and high chairs. One room even has a playhouse under the stairs. The 1907 Victorian home, which belonged to a pioneer physician, has bright, well-decorated rooms, with lace curtains, old-fashioned rocking chairs, and antiques. Rooms have clock radios, and the suite and one room have private sun porches. A TV is in the inn's common room. Pets and smoking are not permitted.

PEACHTREE INN, 1600 N. Ave. (at 16th St.), Grand Junction, CO 81501. Tel. 303/245-5770 or toll free 800/525-0030. 75 rms (all with bath). A/C TV TEL

$ Rates: Summer, $24.95–$37.95 single or double. Winter, $21.95–$36.95 single or double. Children under 12 stay free in parents' room. AE, DISC, MC, V.

Nice, clean rooms at a great price are the lure at this two-story motel, located right across the street from Lincoln Park, with its 9-hole golf course, tennis courts, playground, and swimming pool with huge slide. Rooms at the Peachtree aren't fancy, but they're quiet and comfortable, and have everything needed, including cable TV, available VCRs, and direct-dial phones with free local calls. There's a heated swimming pool, open in summer, and a bar and restaurant that features great breakfast specials. Nonsmoking rooms are available, and pets are welcome.

WHERE TO DINE

MODERATE

THE FEED LOT RESTAURANT AND LOUNGE, 118 Main St. Tel. 241-1360.

Cuisine: STEAK/SEAFOOD/CONTINENTAL. **Reservations:** Accepted.

$ Prices: Appetizers $2.95–$6.95; main courses $3.25–$6.25 at lunch, $4.95–$30.95 at dinner. AE, MC, V.

Open: Mon–Sat 11am–10pm.

A favorite of locals and visitors since it opened in 1977, the Feed Lot keeps bringing them back for its generous portions. The decor is Southwest, and there's live entertainment most weekends—light jazz or maybe country western. The lounge also has a happy hour from 4 to 6pm, with half-price drinks and appetizers.

Lunches include half-pound burgers, prime rib and steak sandwiches, Reubens, chicken sandwiches, burritos and chili, and several salads. Dinner choices include an excellent 12-ounce prime rib, T-bone, or a number of other steaks, all fresh and cut daily. The menu also features spaghetti, a hearty stew, Cajun red snapper, shrimp, or lobster tail. There are also steak-and-seafood combinations and a children's menu.

G. B. GLADSTONE'S, 2531 N. 12th St., at Patterson Rd. Tel. 241-6000.
   Cuisine: STEAK/SEAFOOD. **Reservations:** Recommended.
$ **Prices:** Appetizers $4–$6; main courses $4–$8 at lunch, $7–$15 at dinner. AE, DC, DISC, MC, V.
   Open: Daily 11am–10pm.
Nostalgia dominates the mood of this popular restaurant. The Croquet Room, for instance, is decorated with early 20th-century sports regalia. The Library would delight an old-book collector. The Sun Room has huge windows to let in the light of day. The sunken central bar is most nostalgic (and most packed) on Friday nights, when blues records blast patrons.

Local businesspeople enjoy the lunches here: hot-and-cold sandwiches, soups, salads, quiche, fish-and-chips, and more. Dinners include everything from pastas, teriyaki chicken, and fresh-fish specials to succulent prime rib and Australian lobster tail. Favorite appetizers are peel-and-eat shrimp and crab-stuffed wontons.

THE WINERY, 642 Main St. Tel. 242-4100.
   Cuisine: STEAK/SEAFOOD. **Reservations:** Accepted.
$ **Prices:** Appetizers $4–$7; main courses $8.50–$29.90. AE, DC, DISC, MC, V.
   Open: Dinner only, daily 4:40–10pm.
A dimly lit restaurant with a modern rustic decor of unfinished wood and brick, the Winery looks the part. Reached off an alleyway between Sixth Street and Seventh Street, it has beautiful cut-glass windows and oil paintings of regional or classical interest. The food is of *everyone's* interest. You can start with stuffed mushrooms, then dive into one of the house-special combo meals: steak or prime rib, matched with lobster or crab legs.

INEXPENSIVE

LOS REYES, 811 S. Seventh St. Tel. 245-8392.
   Cuisine: MEXICAN. **Reservations:** Not accepted.
$ **Prices:** $1.75–$7.50. No credit cards.
   Open: Daily 11am–9pm.
This authentic, family-operated Mexican restaurant is in a less attractive part of Grand Junction, near the railroad tracks—but it's definitely the right side of the tracks! The simple white-stucco building with tile floors serves diners in two large rooms; a third room, at the entrance, is a waiting room for hordes who wait patiently for tables. Most folks find it worthwhile to experiment with house variations on standard favorites like tacos, tamales, and enchiladas, such as the avocado-and-pork tortilla.

PANTUSO'S RISTORANTE, 2782 Crossroads Blvd. Tel. 243-0000.
   Cuisine: ITALIAN. **Reservations:** For large parties only.
$ **Prices:** Appetizers $4.50; main courses $3.25–$13.25 at lunch, $5.75–$14 at dinner. AE, DC, MC, V.
   Open: Lunch Mon–Fri 11:30am–1:45pm; dinner Mon–Thurs 5:30–9:30pm, Fri–Sat 5:30–10pm.
Located behind the Holiday Inn and Ramada hotels, off Horizon Drive, Pantuso's has casual garden-style decor and a simple but imaginative menu. There's pizza, pasta, and sandwiches for lunch; homemade ravioli and lasagne for dinner. House specialties include manicotti and cannolis.

PEACHTREE INN RESTAURANT, 1600 N. Ave. Tel. 245-5770.

Cuisine: AMERICAN.
$ Prices: Breakfast $2–$5.50; main courses $2–$5 at lunch, $3.30–$11.50 at dinner. AE, DISC, MC, V.
Open: Daily 6am–10pm; lounge open until about midnight.

This is a good place for visitors to stop for a quick, inexpensive meal. All the standard American breakfasts are on the menu, along with huevos rancheros and a breakfast burrito. For lunch, you can order burgers and a wide range of sandwiches and salads, and at dinner, the menu offers Mexican specialties such as beef or chicken enchiladas, red snapper, shrimp, several chicken dishes, ham, and several steaks. There's peach cobbler for dessert, and the lounge features peach daiquiris.

RIVER CITY CAFE AND BAR, 748 N. Ave., at Seventh St. Tel. 245-8040.
Cuisine: INTERNATIONAL. **Reservations:** Recommended.
$ Prices: Appetizers $1.50–$5.75; main courses $4.95–$7.95 at lunch, $4.95–$13.95 at dinner. AE, MC, V.
Open: Mon–Sat 11am–midnight.

Colorful stained glass and poster-size photos of old-time sports figures inject a party atmosphere in the restaurant. (It's considerably quieter than the bar, which has live bands—playing everything from bluegrass to infusion jazz to reggae—Wednesday through Saturday nights.) Pasta, pizza, sandwiches, and Mexican food are popular at lunch. At dinner, unusual sauces such as Thai peanut, Indian tandoori, and lemon pepper spice-up steaks, chicken, and seafood specials. The andulli sausage-and-garlic fettuccine is unique and delicious. Try the "sheep-clip" appetizer.

7TH STREET CAFE, 832 S. Seventh St. Tel. 242-7225.
Cuisine: AMERICAN.
$ Prices: Breakfast $1.50–$4.75; lunch $2.50–$5.50. MC, V.
Open: Mon–Fri 6:30am–2:30pm, Sat 7:30am–2pm.

The '50s are back at 7th Street Café, with a soda fountain (there's plenty of seating at tables also), photos of Marilyn and Elvis, and 45 rpm records. Breakfasts include bacon and eggs, pancakes, and the like, and for the more adventurous several fantastic combinations. For lunch, there are numerous sandwiches and salads, great burgers, and hot-plate specials including Italian meat loaf and hot turkey. Save room for a banana split or a hot-fudge sundae. The café also prides itself on taking care of special requests, so just ask.

SWEETWATERS UPTOWN, 336 Main St. Tel. 243-3900.
Cuisine: ITALIAN. **Reservations:** Recommended.
$ Prices: Appetizers $3.75–$6.50; main courses $4.50–$6.95 at lunch, $6.95–$12.95 at dinner. AE, MC, V.
Open: Mon–Thurs 11:30am–9pm, Fri–Sat 11:30am–10pm.

Sweetwaters offers casual dining in a street-side lounge and espresso bar, and more elegant garden-style dining in upholstered wooden booths at the rear of the restaurant. Art photography and light jazz help attract a cultured crowd. Daily luncheon specials include the likes of hamburger Italiano or vegetarian cannelloni. Dinners include pasta, meats, and fresh seafood dishes. Try veal or chicken saltimbocca, Bresciana steak, shrimp or scallops scampi.

EASY EXCURSIONS

PALISADE

Heading east from Grand Junction, take U.S. 6 about 12 miles up the Grand Valley to the farming community of **Palisade,** the self-proclaimed "Peach Capitol of Colorado," famous for its fruit orchards and vineyards. Most fruit is picked between late June and mid-September, when you'll be able to purchase it at roadside fruit stands. For a fruit directory, harvest schedule, and map, contact the Palisade Chamber of Commerce, P.O. Box 729, Palisade, CO 81526 (tel. 303/464-7458).

There are about a half-dozen wineries in the area, making good use of the grapes and other fruits grown. The state's oldest existing winery, **✪ Colorado Cellars,** 3553 E. Rd., Palisade, CO 81526 (tel. 464-7921), produces an excellent selection of red, white, blush, champagne, and even kosher wines. The winery grows its own grapes, and produces some 15,000 cases of wine annually. Most of its wines sell for $10 or less a bottle. Tours of the winery and tastings are given year-round, Monday through Saturday from noon to 4pm.

Carlson Vineyards, 461 35 Rd., Palisade, CO 81526 (tel. 303/464-5554), is a winery with a sense of humor, as well as a good product. Its wines, in the $7 to $8 range, have names such as Prairie Dog White and Tyrannosaurus Red, and are made with only Colorado grapes. From April to December, tours and tastings are given Wednesday to Sunday from noon to 6pm; from January to March, the winery is open Friday, Saturday, and Sunday only.

Other **local wineries** include Grande River Vineyards, 3708 G Rd. #2, Palisade, CO 81526 (tel. 303/464-5867); Plum Creek Cellars, 3708 G Road. #1, Palisade, CO 81526 (tel. 303/464-7586); and Vail Valley Vintners, 363 Troyer (P.O. Box 787), Palisade, CO 81526 (tel. 303/464-0559). It's best to call ahead for directions and to confirm that wineries will be open.

GRAND MESA

If you take I-70, Exit 49, 18 miles east of Grand Junction, and turn east on Colo. 65, you'll climb nearly 6,000 feet to the crest of Grand Mesa, the largest flat-top mountain in the world. Forty miles across, and averaging 10,500 feet in elevation, it is largely encompassed within Grand Mesa National Forest. Atop the mesa are more than a dozen campgrounds and countless picnic sites in rich pine forests, and more than 200 tiny lakes stocked with rainbow trout. You can follow Colo. 65 south some 70 miles through Cedaredge to Delta, or follow the all-weather gravel Land's End Road down 55 hairpin curves (it sometimes seems you're falling off the edge of the earth) to Whitewater, on U.S. 50 south of Grand Junction. A brochure on the Grand Mesa Scenic and Historic Byway can be obtained from the U.S. Forest Service, 764 Horizon Dr., Grand Junction (tel. 242-8211).

DINOSAUR NATIONAL MONUMENT

The main attraction in northwestern Colorado is **Dinosaur National Monument,** off U.S. 40, Dinosaur (tel. 303/374-2216). Straddling the Colorado-Utah border, the national monument encompasses 325 square miles of stark canyon land at the confluence of the Yampa and Green rivers.

About 145 million years ago this region was a suitable habitat for dinosaurs, including vegetarians such as diplodocus, brontosaurus, and stegosaurus, and sharp-toothed carnivores like allosaurus. Most of their skeletons decayed and disappeared, but in at least one spot, floodwater washed dinosaur carcasses onto a sandbar, where they were preserved in sand and covered with sediment. This **Dinosaur Quarry,** 7 miles north of Jensen, Utah, off U.S. 40, has revealed many long-vanished species, including fossils of sea creatures two to three times older than any land dinosaurs.

The main park headquarters and **Visitor Center** are 2 miles east of the community of Dinosaur on U.S. 40, and accessible only from the Utah side, 20 miles northwest of Rangely and 95 miles from Grand Junction. Exhibits and a short slide program provide an orientation to the canyon country, reached via the 31-mile Harpers Corner Scenic Drive. There are several turnouts en route for canyon overlooks, and a 1½-mile hike from Harpers Corner itself, at the end of the road, to an even more spectacular viewpoint. Several four-wheel-drive roads branch off Harpers Corner Drive. Also accessible by car are **Deerlodge Park,** where the Yampa River drops into its canyon, about 50 miles east of Dinosaur off U.S. 40; and the **Gates of Lodore,** at the head of the Green River's Canyon of Lodore, about 80 miles west of Craig off Colo. 318.

The National Monument is open around-the-clock, and the Visitor Center is open daily from Memorial Day to Labor Day, 8am to 4:30pm; the rest of the year, Monday through Friday from 8am to 4pm. Admission, charged at the Utah entrance, is $5 per vehicle and $3 per person for those on foot, motorcycles, or bicycles, or in buses.

2. GLENWOOD SPRINGS

169 miles W of Denver, 84 miles E of Grand Junction, 41 miles NW of Aspen

GETTING THERE   By Train   There's Amtrak (toll free 800/USA-RAIL) service to Glenwood Junction daily aboard the *California Zephyr,* direct from Denver and Salt Lake City. The depot is on South River Street at Cooper Avenue, opposite the hot springs.

By Bus   The coaches of Greyhound (tel. 945-8501) stop next to the Village Inn at Laurel Street and West Sixth Street, just off I-70.

By Car   I-70 follows the Colorado River through Glenwood Springs. Colo. 82 (the Aspen Highway) links the city with Aspen, 41 miles southeast.

ESSENTIALS   Orientation   Glenwood Springs (elevation 5,746 ft.) has a population of about 6,000. The northward-flowing Roaring Fork River joins the Colorado River at a T junction in the heart of Glenwood Springs. Streets follow the valleys carved by the two streams. Downtown Glenwood is south of the Colorado and east of the Roaring Fork, with north-south Grand Avenue (Colo. 82) its main thoroughfare. Old Glenwood, including the hot springs and Hotel Colorado, is on the north side of I-70 and the Colorado.

Information   The Glenwood Springs Chamber Resort Association, 1102 Grand Ave., Glenwood Springs, CO 81601 (tel. 303/945-6589), maintains a visitor information center on the south side of downtown, en route to Aspen.

Getting Around   There's daily commuter service to and from Aspen, and east on I-70 as far as Rifle, via Aspen Limousine, 330 Seventh St. (tel. 303/945-9400 or toll free 800/222-2112). Roaring Fork Transit Authority (RFTA) has service daily to Aspen and back (tel. 920-1905 or 925-8484). Yellow Cab (tel. 945-2225) is good for shorter hops.

Fast Facts   The **area code** is 303. In case of **emergency,** call 911. **Valley View Hospital,** providing 24-hour emergency care, is at 1906 Blake Ave. (tel. 945-6535), a block east of Colo. 82 at 19th Street. The main **post office** is on Colorado Avenue at Ninth Street.

SPECIAL EVENTS   Annual events in the Glenwood Springs area include the Ski Spree Winter Carnival, from late January to early February; Summer of Jazz, June through August; the Strawberry Days Festival, in the second full week of June; and the Fall Art Festival, in the fourth week of September.

Ute tribespeople visited the Yampah (big medicine) mineral springs on the banks of the Colorado River for centuries. They came from miles around to heal their wounds, or to use nearby vapor caves as a natural sauna. The first white party to find the springs was a geological expedition led by Capt. Richard Sopris in 1860. But it wasn't until 1882 that the springs were developed by three Devereux brothers, who had made a small fortune in silver at Aspen. They built the largest hot-springs pool in the world in 1888, added a red sandstone bathhouse, then built the Hotel Colorado in 1893, soon attracting everyone from European royalty to movie stars to President Theodore Roosevelt.

The springs supported the town until the outbreak of the Great Depression and

World War II caused a business decline. But after the war, with the growth of the ski industry at nearby Aspen, Glenwood Springs began to emerge as a tourist resort town. Today it's a popular recreational center. The hot-springs complex underwent a total renovation in the 1970s. Additional improvements were made in 1993, as it celebrated its centennial.

Also completed in 1993 was a 12-year $490-million project to build a four-lane interstate through the 18-mile Glenwood Canyon. One of the most expensive roadways ever built, the project includes a number of recreation stops and scenic view areas, for travelers to safely gaze at the Colorado River and its spectacular canyon.

WHAT TO SEE & DO

ATTRACTIONS

GLENWOOD HOT SPRINGS POOL, 401 N. River Rd. Tel. 945-7131.

In business for more than a century, this pool—created in 1888 when enterprising developers diverted the course of the Colorado River—is fed by one of the world's hottest springs. Yampah Spring flows at a rate of 3.5 million gallons per day, with temperatures measuring between 124°F and 130°F. Its content is predominantly sodium chloride, but there are significant quantities of lime, potassium, and magnesium, and traces of other therapeutic minerals.

The two open-air pools together are nearly two city blocks in length. The larger pool, 405 feet long and 100 feet wide, holds more than a million gallons of water, and is maintained between 86°F and 90°F. The smaller pool, 100 feet square, is kept between 102°F and 104°F. There's also a children's pool with a water slide and a miniature golf course.

The red-sandstone administration building overlooking the pools was the Hot Springs Lodge from 1890 to 1986, when a new hotel and bathhouse complex were built. An athletic club was also opened at that time.

Admission: $6 adults, $3.75 children 3–12, 2 and under are free; reduced night rates. Suit-and-towel rentals available. Call for athletic club nonmember use charge.

Open: Summer, daily 7:30am–10pm; Winter, daily 9am–10pm. **Closed:** Second Wed of each month, Sept–May.

YAMPAH SPA AND VAPOR CAVES, 709 E. Sixth St. Tel. 945-0667.

The hot Yampah Spring water flows through the floor of nearby caves, creating natural underground steam baths. Utes once used the chambers to take advantage of their curative powers. Today the cave has an adjacent spa where such treatments as massages, facials, herbal wraps, and body "muds" are offered.

Admission: $6.75 for caves; spa treatments start at $26.

Open: Daily 9am–9pm.

FRONTIER HISTORICAL MUSEUM, 1001 Colorado Ave. Tel. 945-4448.

The highlight of this museum, which occupies a late Victorian home, is the original bedroom furniture of Colorado legends Horace and Baby Doe Tabor, brought here from Leadville. The collection also includes other pioneer home furnishings, antique dolls and toys, historic photos and maps, Native American artifacts, minerals, and a walk-through coal mine.

Admission: $2 adults, free for children 12 and under.

Open: May–Sept, Mon–Sat 11am–4pm; the rest of the year, Thurs–Sat 1–4pm.

SPORTS & RECREATION

BICYCLING A bike trail runs from the Yampah Vapor Caves into Glenwood Canyon, and four-wheel-drive roads in the adjacent White River National Forest are ideal for mountain bikers. Rent from Alpine Bicycle, 109 Sixth St. (tel. 945-6434), or BSR Sports, 210 Seventh St. (tel. 945-7317).

FISHING   Get licenses, equipment, and advice from Roaring Fork Anglers, 2022 Grand Ave. (tel. 945-0180).

GOLF   Glenwood Springs has two nine-hole courses: Glenwood Springs Golf Club, 193 Sunny Acres Rd. (tel. 945-7086), and Westbank Ranch Golf Club, 1007 Westbank Rd. (tel. 945-7032). Some 27 miles west, near Rifle, is the championship 18-hole Battlement Mesa Golf Course, North Battlement Mesa Parkway (tel. 285-PAR-4).

The best miniature golf course in Glenwood is Johnson's Park Miniature Golf, 51579 U.S. 6 and 24, West Glenwood Springs (tel. 945-9608), with two 18-hole water-obstacle courses.

HIKING   There are many trails in the Glenwood area; ask at the White River National Forest office, Ninth Street and Grand Avenue (tel. 945-2521), for the "Hiking and Biking Trails" map. Perhaps the most convenient walk for day hikers is the Doc Holliday Trail, which climbs about half a mile from 13th Street and Bennett Street to an old cemetery that contains the grave of notorious gunslinger Doc Holliday. There's a panoramic view across the town from here.

Hikers will also find numerous trails in Glenwood Canyon, with some of the best scenery in the area. Hanging Lake Trail, nine miles east of Glenwood Springs off I-70, is especially popular. The trailhead is accessible from eastbound I-70; westbound travelers must make a U-turn and backtrack a few miles to reach the parking area. The trail climbs 1,000 feet in one mile—allow several hours for the round-trip—and just beyond Hanging Lake is Spouting Rock, with an underground spring shooting out of a hole in the limestone cliff.

The Grizzly Creek Trail Head is in Grizzly Creek Rest Area, in Glenwood Canyon, where there is also a boat-launching area for rafts and kayakers. The trail climbs along the creek, past wild flowers and dogwood trees.

HORSEBACK RIDING   Trips by the hour, day, or week, including pack expeditions and sunset barbecue rides, are offered by several outfitters and local ranches. Check with A. J. Brink Outfitters, 3406 Sweetwater Rd., Gypsum (tel. 524-9301); 7-W Guest Ranch, 3412 County Rd. 151, Gypsum (tel. 524-9328); Twin Pines Stables, 2880 County Rd. 3, Marble (tel. 963-1220); or Winterhawk Outfitters, 687 Johns Dr., Silt (tel. 876-2623).

RIVER RAFTING   Travel down the Colorado River through spectacular Glenwood Canyon in rafts or inflatable kayaks with Rock Gardens, 1308 County Rd. 129 (tel. 945-6737), Blue Sky Adventures, 319 Sixth St. (tel. 945-6605), or White Water Rafting, I-70, Exit 114, West Glenwood Springs (tel. 945-8477). Half-day trips cost about $30; $50 for a full day. Rafts can be rented from Rock Gardens.

SKIING   Ski Sunlight, 10901 County Rd. 117 (tel. 303/945-7491 or toll free 800/445-7931), is located 10 miles above Glenwood in the White River National Forest. Geared toward families and intermediate skiers, Sunlight has a 2,010-foot vertical, from the day lodge to the 9,895-foot summit of Compas Mountain. Served by three chair lifts and a ski-school surface lift, it has 460 acres of skiable terrain and 45 trails. Full-day tickets are $28 for adults, $16 for children 6 to 12 and seniors 60 to 69; under 6 and over 69 ski free. There is also a special area for snowboarders. For equipment rentals and repairs, see the Ski Sunlight Ski Shop, 1315 Grand Ave. (tel. 945-9425).

Nordic skiers can try the 14km (8¾ miles) of track laid out in the Spring Gulch Trail System by the Mount Sopris Nordic Council. There's a parking area and rest rooms 7 miles south of Carbondale (20 miles from Glenwood Springs) on County Road 108. Get directions and cross-country equipment from Summit Canyon Mountaineering, 1001 Grand Ave. (tel. 945-6994).

SNOWMOBILING   The Sunlight to Powderhorn Trail, running 120 miles from Glenwood's local ski area to Grand Junction's, on the Grand Mesa, is the longest multiuse winter recreational trail in Colorado. It is fully marked and continuously groomed. Numerous other trails—a total of 300 miles—can be accessed from the end of Country Road 11, 2 miles beyond Ski Sunlight and 12 miles south of

Glenwood Springs. For information and rentals, contact Rocky Mountain Sports, 2177 300th Rd. (tel. 945-8885).

WHERE TO STAY
MODERATE

HOTEL COLORADO, 526 Pine St., Glenwood Springs, CO 81601. Tel. 303/945-6511 or toll free 800/544-3998. Fax 303/945-7030. 101 rms, 25 suites (all with bath). TV TEL

$ Rates: $64–$85 single; $72–$95 double; $120–$250 suite. AE, CB, DC, DISC, MC, V. **Parking:** Free.

The stately Hotel Colorado, which celebrated its centennial in June 1993, is a truly remarkable building. Constructed of sandstone and Roman brick, this registered National Historic Landmark was modeled after Italy's Villa de Medici. Two American presidents—William Howard Taft and Theodore Roosevelt—spoke around the turn-of-the-century to crowds gathered beneath the orators' balcony in a lovely landscaped fountain *piazza*. In fact, this was the home of the "Teddy Bear": One story has it that when a disappointed Roosevelt returned to the hotel in May 1905 after an unsuccessful bear hunt, hotel maids made him a small bear from scraps of cloth, thereby causing a reporter to coin the phrase.

Today's guest rooms have been fully redecorated and furnished with period antiques. No two are alike. Most have double beds and the usual hotel furnishings; parlor suites are much more spacious than standard rooms, with upgraded decor and amenities. Fifth-floor penthouse suites have wet bars and refrigerators to go along with outstanding views. Two bell-tower suites, reached by stairs only, have double Jacuzzis and private dining balconies. They also have private staircases into the ancient bell towers, where 19th-century graffiti can still be deciphered!

The Devereux Room, with its vaulted ceiling, serves gourmet continental fare in a formal turn-of-the-century atmosphere. The Palm Court Bar and Grill offers casual dining in a garden atmosphere beneath the hotel's original 19th-century skylight.

Services and facilities include valet laundry, courtesy van to and from the train station, 24-hour desk; European-style health spa with sauna, Jacuzzi, massage, Nautilus and free weights; chiropractor; gift shop; sports center with rental equipment; and meeting space for up to 200.

HOT SPRINGS LODGE & POOL, 415 Sixth St., Glenwood Springs, CO 81601. Tel. 303/945-6571 or toll free 800/537-SWIM in Colorado. Fax 303/945-6683. A/C TV TEL

$ Rates: Mar 15–Sept and Christmas holidays, $57–$73 single, $62–$78 double; Oct–Mar 14 except Christmas, $46–$60 single, $51–$65 double. AE, CB, DC, DISC, MC, V. **Parking:** Free.

Heated by the springs that bubble through the hillside beneath it, this handsome modern motel overlooks the Glenwood Hot Springs Pool complex. The handsome blues and roses of the high-ceilinged lobby extend to the spacious guest rooms, 75% of which have private balconies or patios. Rooms have two queen-size or one king-size bed and light-wood furnishings, as well as coffee makers and safes for valuables. Larger rooms have hideabeds, refrigerators, and double vanities.

The poolside Hot Springs Restaurant serves coffee shop–style meals, and there's a small lounge. The hotel also offers no-smoking rooms, facilities for the disabled, guest discounts for hot-springs pool and athletic club (see "What to See & Do," above), Jacuzzi, video arcade, guest laundry, sportswear shop, and meeting space for 60.

RAMADA INN, 124 W. Sixth St., Glenwood Springs, CO 81601. Tel. 303/945-2500 or toll free 800/228-2828; 800/332-1472 in Colorado. Fax 303/945-2530. 121 rms, 4 suites (all with bath). A/C TV TEL

$ Rates: High season (Mon–Fri, Mar, mid-May to mid-Oct, Christmas holidays), $65–$79 single or double; low-season (all other times), $59–$68 single or double; high-season Sat–Sun and holidays, $74–$88 single or double. Children under 18 stay free in parents' room. AE, CB, DC, DISC, MC, V. **Parking:** Free.

The only true full-service hotel in Glenwood Springs, the Ramada offers spacious guest rooms with bright decor. All have one king-size or two queen-size beds and standard motel furnishings. Studio suites have kitchenettes and hideaway sofas to accommodate families; larger suites also have fireplaces and steam Jacuzzis.

The Rosegarden Restaurant serves three meals daily. A seafood buffet is served every Friday night. The Celebrations Lounge has live country-and-western entertainment Wednesday through Saturday nights, with free dance lessons Tuesday through Thursday. The hotel also offers room service, valet laundry, free shuttle service, no-smoking rooms, facilities for the disabled, an indoor swimming pool, hot tub, guest laundry, and meeting space for 500.

INEXPENSIVE

ADDUCCI'S INN BED & BREAKFAST, 1023 Grand Ave., Glenwood Springs, CO 81601. Tel. 303/945-9341. 5 rms.
$ Rates (including breakfast): $28–$65 single; $38–$65 double. MC, V.
A lovely turn-of-the-century Victorian on Glenwood's main street houses this bed-and-breakfast. Furnished with period antiques, it also has a games parlor, a hot tub, and complimentary pick up from train-and-bus depots. Rooms have private baths, but showers are shared.

GLENWOOD SPRINGS HOSTEL, 1021 Grand Ave., Glenwood Springs, CO 81601. Tel. 303/945-8545. 24 beds.
$ Rates: $9.50 per night; $55 per week. MC, V.
A plus for this hostel is its large record library, from which guests are encouraged to record their own cassette tapes. Otherwise, it's similar to many others: dormitory bunks, a large (modern) shared kitchen, common toilets and showers, guest laundry facilities, and other common areas. One room has been set aside for couples. Linen is provided, and bus or train pick up can be arranged with advance notice. There's also a dark room available for photo enthusiasts.

CAMPING

ROCK GARDENS CAMPER PARK, 1308 County Rd. 129 (I-70, Exit 119), Glenwood Springs, CO 81601. Tel. 303/945-6737. Fax 303/945-2413. 75 sites.
$ Rates: $14.50 tent sites; $16.50 R.V. sites, with electric-and-water hookups. MC, V. **Closed:** Nov to mid-Apr.
Right on the banks of the Colorado River in beautiful Glenwood Canyon, Rock Gardens Camper Park is a great home base for those exploring this scenic wonderland. The Glenwood Canyon Bike Trail passes the campground on its way into Glenwood Springs, and hiking trails into the White River National Forest are nearby. Bathhouses are clean, showers are hot, and there's a dump station, although no sewer hookups. In addition, a store sells groceries, firewood, and ice; rents rafts, kayaks, bikes and in-line skates; and takes raft trips down the Colorado.

WHERE TO DINE

ANDRE'S RESTAURANT, 51753 U.S. 6 & 24, West Glenwood Springs. Tel. 945-5367.
Cuisine: AMERICAN. **Reservations:** Not necessary.
$ Prices: Lunch $5–$7; dinner $5–$10. AE, DISC, MC, V.
Open: Wed–Mon 11:30am–9pm.
Model trains circle the dining room on an elaborate track system suspended from the ceiling of this family-oriented restaurant, located midway between I-70, Exits 114 and 116. Guests sit in wrought-iron chairs and enjoy home-style cooking including chicken potpie and beef stew. Portions are huge, especially the combination dinner, which includes a meatballs or Italian sausage appetizer, soup or salad, and a choice of

two pasta dishes—lasagne, ravioli, spaghetti, or gnocchi. Homemade desserts include New York–style cheesecake and ice cream home-churned in a wooden bucket. There's a children's menu, but no alcohol is served. Andre's candies and a variety of decorative items are sold in a small gift shop. Smoking is not permitted.

THE BAYOU, 52103 U.S. 6, West Glenwood Springs. Tel. 945-1047.

Cuisine: CAJUN/CREOLE. **Reservations:** Suggested for large parties.
$ Prices: Appetizers $2.75–$6; main courses $5.95–$13. AE, MC, V.
Open: Dinner only, daily 4–10pm.

Western Colorado's classic New Orleans–style eatery can't be mistaken: Frog eyes bulge from the green awning over its deck, which looks toward I-70 near Exit 114. Harlequin masks hang on the walls and Zydeco music filters through this very rustic, often rowdy restaurant. Come for down-home Cajun cuisine—including sautéed frogs' legs, deep-fried catfish, shrimp lagniappe, chicken étouffée, or swamp and moo (redfish and rib eye)—and stay for the staff-provided entertainment, including "dumb waitron tricks," birthday specials (ask if you dare), and the Frog Leg Revue. On summer Sunday afternoons there's live music on the deck.

BUFFALO VALLEY INN, Colo. 82, 1½ miles south of Glenwood Springs. Tel. 945-5297.

Cuisine: STEAK/SEAFOOD. **Reservations:** For parties of 6 or more only.
$ Prices: Appetizers $3.95–$4.95; main courses $8.95–$17.95. AE, DC, MC, V.
Open: Dinner only, daily 5–10pm.

An oversize log cabin with country-style decor, right down to the red-checkered tablecloths, the Buffalo Valley Inn specializes in steaks, seafoods, and barbecues. Diners can start with Rocky Mountain oysters, then dive into prime rib, buffalo steak, or Rocky Mountain rainbow trout. Barbecue chicken, and baby-back ribs are slow-smoked over apple wood and include soup-or-salad bar, potatoes or beans, and rolls. Ther's also a new bar, inlaid with 1,000 silver dollars, and a dance floor with live country-western music.

DELICE, 1512 Grand Ave. Tel. 945-9424.

Cuisine: DELI. **Reservations:** Not accepted.
$ Prices: $2.30–$5.25. No credit cards.
Open: Mon–Fri 10am–3pm.

Aspenites still talk about European immigrant Walter Huber's Swiss Pastry Shop, an institution for three decades after it was opened in 1957. Huber's family has continued that tradition, serving deli-style sandwiches, homemade soups, gourmet salads, Swiss sausage platters, and Black Forest cakes at this friendly downtown luncheon stop in Glenwood's Executive Plaza.

ITALIAN UNDERGROUND, 715 Grand Ave. Tel. 945-6422.

Cuisine: ITALIAN. **Reservations:** Not accepted.
$ Prices: Appetizers $3–$3.25; main courses $7.25–$9.25; pizzas $7.75–$13.75. AE, DISC, MC, V.
Open: Daily 5–10pm.

Get there early and expect to wait. The Italian Underground has some of the best Italian food you'll find in Colorado. This basement restaurant, below an antique shop, has stone walls, brick floors, red-and-white checked tablecloths, candlelight, and exceedingly generous portions of very fine food. Try the lasagne, northern Italian rotisserie chicken, or a combination plate—spaghetti, sausage, meatballs, cannoli, and lasagne. All entrées come with salad, bread, and ice cream. There's an excellent selection of Italian wines by the glass. The restaurant does not permit smoking.

19TH STREET DINER, 1908 Grand Ave. Tel. 945-9133.

Cuisine: AMERICAN. **Reservations:** Not required.
$ Prices: $1.95–$8.95. MC, V.

Open: Mon–Sat 7am–10pm, Sun 7:30am–3pm.

This local hangout has stools at a counter facing the kitchen, a black-and-white tile floor, and all the usual diner selections, done quite well. Breakfasts, served all day, include lots of omelets, french toast, and a breakfast banana split—banana, yogurt, blueberries, and granola. The lunch-and-dinner menu has hamburgers, sandwiches and salads, fajitas, southern-fried chicken, and blue-plate specials including an open-faced hot roast beef. There's also a children's menu, soda fountain, and full-service bar.

RESTAURANT SOPRIS, Colo. 82, 7 miles south of Glenwood Springs. Tel. 945-7771.
Cuisine: CONTINENTAL. **Reservations:** Recommended.
$ Prices: Appetizers $2.50–$4.95; main courses $8.95–$25.95. AE, DC, MC, V.
Open: Dinner only, daily 5–10pm.

Luzern, Switzerland, native Kurt Wigger spent 17 years as chef at Aspen's Red Onion before opening his own restaurant. In 1991 he celebrated his 17th year at the Sopris. Amid red-lit Victorian decor, accented by reproductions of classic oil paintings, Wigger serves up generous portions of veal-and-seafood dishes, as well as steaks and other meats. House specialties include wienerschnitzel, rack of lamb, filet mignon chasseur, and lobster scampi in a garlic sauce.

EASY EXCURSIONS

REDSTONE

Traveling south from Glenwood Springs, Colo. 82 follows the Roaring Fork River as far as Carbondale, an old coal-mining town. Colo. 133 branches off south from Carbondale, following the Crystal River Valley toward Paonia and Delta. And 17 miles south of Carbondale and 30 miles from Glenwood, it passes through the historic community of Redstone. In 1900, coal-and-steel baron John Cleveland Osgood, one of the wealthiest industrialists of his day, built this model company village for the men who worked in his coal mines. The brightly colored chalet-style family cottages, built for married couples, still line the streets today.

WHERE TO STAY & DINE The ✪ **Redstone Inn,** a handsome bachelors' residence with a Tudor-style clock tower, is now a hotel-restaurant. (Write 0082 Redstone Boulevard, Redstone, CO 81623; tel. 303/963-2526 or toll free 800/748-2524. Rates are $40 to $77 single or double with shared bath, $68 to $98 with private bath, and $90 to $130 for suites.)

Osgood's own ✪ **Cleveholm Manor,** 0058 Redstone Blvd., Redstone, CO 81623 (tel. 303/963-3463 or toll free 800/643-4837 outside Colorado only), was a 42-room mansion that quickly became known as "The Redstone Castle." The red sandstone walls were carved by stonecutters from Austria and Italy; the elegant interior was furnished with Tiffany chandeliers, Persian rugs, Chinese urns, and a backdrop of leather, silk, damask, and velvet wall coverings. Roosevelts, Rockefellers, Goulds, Morgans, and other turn-of-the-century notables were entertained here. The manor is now a bed-and-breakfast, with three suites ($147 to $175), five upscale rooms ($116), and eight former servants' rooms that share three bathrooms ($80). And the entire castle can be rented for 24 hours for private functions—for just $4,240. For nonguests, tours are conducted by reservation Monday through Friday from the nearby Redstone Country Store (tel. 963-3408); the cost is $10 for adults, $5 for children 5 to 12.

CRAIG

Some 47 miles north of Meeker—115 miles from Glenwood Springs—is Craig, with 10,000 people the largest town in Colorado north of I-70 and west of the Front Range. Located in the Yampa River Valley, it's a popular center for river rafters and big-game hunters. Of particular interest in town are the **Museum of Northwest Colorado,** 590 Yampa Ave. (tel. 824-6360), with colorful historical exhibits open Monday through Saturday, and the **Sand Rock Nature Trail,** Alta Vista Drive at Ninth Street, accessing prehistoric petroglyphs and a panoramic view of Craig.

WHERE TO STAY & DINE   A good place to stay is the **A Bar Z Motel,** 2690 U.S. 40, Craig, CO 81625 (tel. 303/824-7066), with rates of $30 to $40 single or double. Hungry? Try ✪ **Desperado Restaurant,** 111 W. Victory Way (tel. 824-6900). For more **information,** consult the Greater Craig Area Chamber of Commerce, 360 East Victory Way (tel. 303/824-5689).

---

3. MONTROSE

61 miles S of Grand Junction, 108 miles N of Durango

GETTING THERE   By Plane   The Montrose County Airport, 2100 Airport Rd. (tel. 303/249-3203), off U.S. 50 2 miles northwest of town, is served daily by Continental Express (tel. 303/249-1399 or toll free 800/525-0820) and United Express (tel. 303/249-8455 or toll free 800/241-6522).

By Bus   TNM&O coaches arrive and depart from the Montrose Bus Depot, 132 N. First St. (tel. 303/249-6673).

By Car   Montrose is an hour's drive southeast of Grand Junction via U.S. 50, 2½ hours' drive north of Durango via U.S. 550, and 5½ hours' drive west of Colorado Springs via U.S. 50 through Salida and Gunnison.

ESSENTIALS   Orientation   Montrose has a population of about 9,500. The city sits on the east bank of the Uncompahgre River. Its main street, Townsend Avenue (U.S. 50 North/U.S. 550 South), parallels the stream in a northwest-southeast direction. Main Street (U.S. 50 East/Colo. 90 West) crosses Townsend in the center of town. Numbered streets extend north and south from Main.

Information   Contact the Montrose Visitors & Convention Bureau (toll free 800/873-0244) or the Montrose County Chamber of Commerce (tel. 303/249-5515), both at 550 N. Townsend Ave., Montrose, CO 81401.

Getting Around   Western Express Taxi (tel. 249-8880) provides round-the-clock cab service.
Car rentals are available in the airport area from Budget (tel. 249-6083), Dollar (tel. 249-3770), Hertz (tel. 249-9447), Thrifty (tel. 249-8741), and National (tel. 249-3453).

Fast Facts   The **area code** is 303. In case of **emergency,** call 911. The **Montrose Memorial Hospital** is at 800 S. Third St. (tel. 249-2211). The main **post office** is at 321 S. First St. (tel. 249-6654). For **road conditions** or **weather,** call 249-9363.

SPECIAL EVENTS   Each year Montrose hosts the Lighter Than Air Balloon Affaire and the Ducky Derby in July, the Montrose County Fair and Shades of Bluegrass in August, the Native American Lifeways in September, Colorfest in September and October, and Tabeguache Tour de Gold and Chocolate Lovers Affaire in December.

The Montrose area was once home to the famous Ute chief Ouray and his wife Chipeta, who ranched in the Uncompahgre Valley until the government forced the

Native American tribe to migrate to Utah in 1881. Once the Utes were gone, settlers founded the town of Pomona, named for the Roman goddess of fruit. Later the town's name was changed to Montrose, for a character in a Sir Walter Scott novel.

The railroad arrived in 1882, providing relatively reliable transportation and a way of shipping out potatoes, beets, and other crops. In 1909, the 7-mile-long Gunnison Tunnel was built to bring water up the Black Canyon to the farmers in the valley.

Today, Montrose continues its agricultural heritage with ranching and farming, and has also found another way to capitalize on its scenic beauty and good climate. Surrounded by the Uncompahgre, Gunnison, and Grand Mesa national forests, and within a short drive of Black Canyon of the Gunnison National Monument and Curecanti National Recreation Area, Montrose has become a major outdoor recreation center.

WHAT TO SEE & DO

ATTRACTIONS

BLACK CANYON OF THE GUNNISON NATIONAL MONUMENT, Colo. 347, 6 miles north of U.S. 50. Tel. 303/249-7036.

"No other canyon in North America combines the depth, narrowness, sheerness, and somber countenance of the Black Canyon." These words were penned by geologist Wallace Hansen, who mapped the canyon in the 1950s and probably knew it better than anyone else. The deepest and most spectacular 12 miles of the 53-mile canyon are located within the national monument. The walls are almost always in dark shadows, the rays of sunlight penetrate to the Gunnison River at the canyon floor only for brief periods at midday.

The Black Canyon ranges in depth from 1,730 to 2,700 feet. Its width at its narrowest point ("The Narrows") is only 1,100 feet at the rim . . . and 40 feet at the river. This deep slash in the earth took two million years of erosion to form, a process that's still going on—albeit slowed by the damming of the Gunnison above the park.

The Black Canyon is one of the few remaining unspoiled areas of its kind in the United States. Although a summer-only access road winds to the bottom of the canyon at the East Portal dam, in the adjoining Curecanti National Recreation Area, only foot trails permeate the wilderness of the canyon floor through the national monument. Few visitors make that trek. Most view the canyon from the South Rim Road, site of a Visitor Center open year-round, or the less-accessible North Rim Road, open summers only. Short paths off both roads lead to viewpoints with informational signs explaining the unique geology of the canyon. Printed brochures describe several hikes.

Kayak trips are dangerous and are blocked in many places by rocks; those who have tried it agree that they spend more time scrambling over rocks than running the river. Accomplished rock climbers, however, adore the sheer canyon walls.

There are **campgrounds** on both rims, with a restricted water supply hauled in by truck. To reach the south rim, travel east 6 miles from Montrose on U.S. 50 to the well-marked turnoff. To reach the north rim from Montrose, you must drive north 21 miles on U.S. 50 to Delta, east 31 miles on Colo. 92 to Crawford, then south on a 13-mile access road. **National Park Service** headquarters are at 2233 E. Main St., Montrose, CO 81401 (tel. 303/249-7036).

Admission: $4 per vehicle.

Open: Visitor center: summer, daily 8am–7pm; shorter hours spring and fall; closed winter. Road to south rim open 24 hours per day year round; north rim road open 24 hours except when closed by snow, often between December and March.

HISTORIC WALKING TOURS, Visitor's Center, 5500 N. Townsend Ave. Tel. 249-5515 or toll free 800/873-0244.

Downtown Montrose has several dozen historic buildings, constructed between the mid-1880s and the early 20th century. Among those listed on several free self-guided walking-tour maps (available from the above address) are the 1888 Morris

Diehl home, with its Italianate bay windows; the 1895 Victorian home of brick maker Thomas Brook Townsend; the 1904 carriage works, a blacksmith shop where Jack Dempsey is said to have trained for his boxing career; and the Gothic revival–style St. Mary's Catholic Church, built in 1912, with the town's original church bell.

MONTROSE COUNTY HISTORICAL MUSEUM, W. Main St. and Rio Grande Ave. Tel. 249-2085 or 249-6135.

Pioneer life is highlighted at this museum which features an 1890s homesteader's cabin, railroad memorabilia, antique dolls and toys, a country store, Native American artifacts, and more.

Admission: $2 adults, 50¢ children 5–12, free for children under 5.
Open: May–Sept, Mon–Sat 9am–5pm.

UTE INDIAN MUSEUM, 17253 Chipeta Dr. Tel. 249-3098.

Located on the site of the final residence of southern Ute chief Ouray and his wife, Chipeta, this interesting museum—2 miles south of town off U.S. 550—offers the Colorado Historical Society's most complete exhibition of Ute traditional-and-ceremonial artifacts, including clothing. Several dioramas depict mid-19th-century life-styles. Also on the grounds are Chipeta's grave and tiny, bubbling Ouray Springs.

Admission: $2 adults, $1 seniors (over 65) and children 6–16, free for children under 6.
Open: May 15–Sept, Mon–Sat 10am–5pm, Sun 1–5pm; Sept, modified hours.

SPORTS & RECREATION

BICYCLING The Tabeguache Trail—142 miles from Shavano Valley, near Montrose, to No Thoroughfare Canyon, near the Colorado National Monument west of Grand Junction—is a popular-and-challenging route for mountain bikers. For information, contact the Colorado Plateau Mountain-Bike Trail Association, P.O. Box 4602, Grand Junction, CO 81502 (tel. 303/241-9561). Bikers can also use the Uncompahgre Riverway; it is eventually scheduled to connect Montrose with Delta (21 miles north) and Ouray (37 miles south). A free map of city bike trails is available at the Visitors Center, Chamber of Commerce, and City Hall.

BOATING Morrow Point Reservoir is 20 miles east of Montrose via U.S. 50. Boat tours lasting 1½ hours leave the Pine Creek Boat Dock near the Cimarron Visitors Center (tel. 249-4074) daily, Memorial Day to Labor Day. Boats can also be rented from the Elk Creek Marina (tel. 641-0707) and the Lake Fork Marina (tel. 641-3048) in Curecanti National Recreation Area; and at Ridgway Reservoir (tel. 626-5822) in Ridgway State Recreation Area, 20 miles south of Montrose off U.S. 550.

FISHING For starters, you can drop a line into the Uncompahgre River from Riverbottom Park, reached via Apollo Road off Rio Grande Avenue. Most anglers seek rainbow trout here and at Chipeta Lake, behind the Ute Indian Museum south of Montrose. About 20 miles east via U.S. 50 is the Gunnison River, which produces trophy-class brown-and-rainbow trout. Kokanee salmon can also be caught in Morrow Point Reservoir, 35 miles east of Montrose via U.S. 50. There are numerous other fishing spots in the region. Among outfitters leading fishing trips is Gunnison River Expeditions (tel. 249-4441).

GOLF The 18-hole Montrose Golf Course, 1350 Birch St. (tel. 249-8551), welcomes visitors. For miniature golf there's Putt-A-Round USA, half a mile east of town on Highway 50 (tel. 240-GOLF).

HIKING Important hiking trails in the area include the 4½-mile Ute Trail along the Gunnison River, 20 miles northeast of Montrose, and the 17-mile Alpine Trail from Silver Jack Reservoir in Uncompahgre National Forest, 35 miles southeast of Montrose via Cimarron on U.S. 50. For a wide choice of hiking options, consult the

U.S. Forest Service, 2505 S. Townsend Ave. (tel. 249-3711), or the Bureau of Land Management, 2505 S. Townsend Ave. (tel. 249-6047).

HORSEBACK RIDING Stables in the region include Montrose Dressage (tel. 249-4441); Needle Rock Ranch, 4345 F Rd., Crawford (tel. 921-3050); and Hyatt Guides & Outfitter (tel. 249-9733).

RIVER RAFTING Gunnison River Expeditions (tel. 249-4441) runs frequent trips down the Gunnison and other streams.

SHOPPING

There are about a dozen antique shops in the Montrose area, including **Best of the West Gallery,** 324 Main St. (tel. 249-9549), which carries furniture, glassware, books, and prints; **Black Bear Antiques,** 62281 Hwy. 90 (tel. 249-5738), specializing in depression glass, primitives, and railroad memorabilia; and **Ltd. Edition Antique Company,** 4433 E. Main St. (tel. 249-7877), which sells furniture.

If you're looking for a wide variety, **Jack's Trading Post, CO-OP,** 7086 Hwy. 550 (tel. 249-9589), has 12 vendors under one roof, offering antiques, collectibles, farm primitives, and new-and-used furniture.

For a new pair of jeans, a cowboy hat, or camping-and-sporting goods, stop at **Jeans Westerner,** 219 W. Main St. (tel. 249-3600). **Mountain Home Store,** 513 E. Main St. (tel. 240-1608), has unique gifts for sports fans, as well as a year-round Christmas room. Chocolate lovers can't leave Montrose without a stop at the **Russell Stover Candies Factory Outlet,** 2200 Stover Ave., just off Townsend Avenue on the south side of town (tel. 249-6681).

WHERE TO STAY

RED ARROW MOTOR INN, 1702 E. Main St., Montrose, CO 81402. Tel. 303/249-9641 or toll free 800/468-9323. Fax 303/249-8380. 58 rms, 2 suites (all with bath). A/C TV TEL
$ Rates: Sept–June, $64–$99 single or double; $140 suite. July–Aug, $99–$109 single or double; $160 suite. AE, CB, DC, DISC, MC, V.
A Best Western property, the Red Arrow is a large two story near the east end of town, on the way toward the Black Canyon. Rooms, most of which have queen-size beds, are very spacious. Small refrigerators, hair dryers, and makeup mirrors are found in every room. A handful of "spa rooms" have large Jacuzzi tubs and additional amenities. Motel facilities include a solarium with a hot tub and fitness center, an outdoor swimming pool, a children's playground and picnic area, a guest laundry, and conference space for up to 350 people. The adjoining Sizzler Buffet Court & Grill restaurant serves three meals daily.

RED BARN MOTEL, 1417 E. Main St., Montrose, CO 81401. Tel. 303/249-4507. 70 rms (all with bath). A/C TV TEL
$ Rates: June–Oct, $46 single; $53–$70 double. Nov–May, $30 single; $33–$40 double. AE, CB, DC, DISC, MC, V.
Clean, quiet, and comfortable, this centrally located motel offers pleasant rooms with either double or queen-size beds and cable TV with videos available. Furnishings vary, but most rooms have desks, vanities, and coffee makers. Local calls are free, and pets are welcome. There's a heated swimming pool, hot tub, sauna, and fitness center. Nonsmoking rooms are available.

WESTERN MOTEL, 1200 E. Main St. (at Stough Ave.), Montrose, CO 81401. Tel. 303/249-3481 or toll free 800/445-7301. 28 rms (all with bath). A/C TV TEL
$ Rates: Memorial Day–Labor Day, $35–$42 single; $40–$55 double. Labor Day to mid-Nov, $30–$40 single; $38–$50 double. Mid-Nov to Memorial Day,

$28–$39 single; $36–$45 double. 2- and 3-room family units $52–$80. AE, DISC, MC, V.

A one-story red-brick building with a two-story annex, this pleasant-and-inexpensive motel is ideal for budget watchers. Rooms are cozy, clean, and comfortable, with bright earth-tones decor, full baths, good-size desks, and other standard furnishings. A few family rooms and water-bed rooms are available. Facilities include a heated swimming pool, open seasonally, and a Jacuzzi.

CAMPING

THE HANGIN' TREE R.V. PARK, 17250 Hwy. 550 S., Montrose, CO 81401. Tel. 303/249-9966. 25 sites.
$ Rates: $11 tent or R.V. with no hookups; $16.50 full hookups. $1 for a third person over 6 years old. DISC, MC, V.

A conveniently located campground, open year-round, the Hangin' Tree has pull-through sites and very clean bathhouses with hot showers, but no private dressing areas. There's also a self-service laundry, a convenience store, a liquor store, an antique shop, and a gas station. The campground is just a short walk from Chipeta Lakes, which has excellent trout fishing.

WHERE TO DINE

GLENN EYRIE RESTAURANT, 2351 S. Townsend Ave. Tel. 249-9263.
Cuisine: CONTINENTAL. **Reservations:** Recommended.
$ Prices: Appetizers $3.95–$6.75; main courses $10–$19.75. AE, DC, MC, V.
Open: Dinner Tues–Sun 5–9pm; brunch Sun 10:30am–2pm.

This fine restaurant is lodged in a large colonial farmhouse on the south end of town. In summer, guests can dine outdoors in the wine garden beneath apricot trees; in winter, folks seek tables nearest the large central fireplace. Gourmet dinner choices include chateaubriand bouquetière, veal, duck, lamb, freshly made pastas, and fresh seafood. There are also vegetarian dishes, an in-house bakery, and a children's menu.

RED BARN RESTAURANT & LOUNGE, 1413 E. Main St. Tel. 249-9202.
Cuisine: AMERICAN. **Reservations:** Recommended at dinner.
$ Prices: Appetizers $2.95–$5.95; main courses $3.95–$5.95 at lunch, $7.95–$16.95 at dinner. AE, CB, DC, DISC, MC, V.
Open: Lunch Mon–Sat 11am–3pm; dinner daily 3–10:30pm; brunch Sun 9am–3pm.

A homey restaurant with a big fireplace and bigger portions, the Red Barn is a favorite of locals, serving excellent steaks (including a 16-oz. top sirloin), prime rib, jumbo shrimp, and a popular beef-stew pot. A salad bar comes with every main dish. Lighter meals and gourmet burgers are available day or night, and there are daily specials.

STARVIN' ARVINS, 1320 S. Townsend Ave. Tel. 249-7787.
Cuisine: AMERICAN. **Reservations:** Not required.
$ Prices: Breakfast $1.55–$5.95; lunch $3.50–$5.50; dinner $3.50–$12.99. DISC, MC, V.
Open: Daily 6am–10pm.

This regional chain specializes in healthy family dining, with a varied-and-extensive menu. The dining room has a large aquarium with tropical fish and walls covered with bookshelves. Breakfast, served all day, has all the usuals, plus giant, hot cinnamon rolls, and the fantastic Green Supreme—hash browns topped with scrambled eggs, chili, sausage gravy, and Cheddar cheese. For lunch, try the half-pound burgers or sandwiches. The dinner menu features steaks, chicken, and seafood. There are also children's and senior citizens' menus.

THE WHOLE ENCHILADA, 44 S. Grand Ave., near W. Main St. Tel. 249-1881.

Cuisine: MEXICAN. **Reservations:** Not necessary.
$ Prices: Appetizers $1.95–$5.50; main courses $2.50–$6.50 at lunch, $2.50–$10.75 at dinner. AE, MC, V.
Open: Mon–Sat 11am–10pm, Sun noon–9pm.

Come for the expected—burritos, tostadas, fajitas, chimichangas, and so forth—or the unexpected, such as enchiladas Acapulco (filled with chicken, olives, and almonds), crab enchiladas, or the El Paso chimichanga (filled with beef and jalapeño peppers). A full-service outdoor patio is open in summer.

EASY EXCURSIONS

DELTA

Between Montrose and Grand Junction lies Delta County, bounded on the south by the Black Canyon of the Gunnison and on the north by the Grand Mesa. Its county seat is Delta, a town of 4,000 people, 21 miles north of Montrose on U.S. 50. Delta is sometimes called "the city of murals" because many of its fine historical buildings display colorful murals on their outer walls, with themes ranging from Native American legends to wildlife to apple labels. The historic downtown area is converting their empty storefronts into factory outlets, while keeping their old-style appearance.

The highlight of a visit here is ✪ **Fort Uncompahgre,** in Confluence Park at the west end of Gunnison River Drive (tel. 874-8349), just north of Delta off U.S. 50. The original fort was built in 1826 at the confluence of the Gunnison and Uncompahgre rivers as a small fur-trading post; it was abandoned in 1844 after an attack by Utes. Today it has been replicated as a living-history museum, with four hand-hewn log buildings—a trade room, storeroom, and living quarters—facing a courtyard. Costumed traders, trappers, and laborers describe their lives, and zealous history buffs can arrange weekend stays to temporarily assume 19th-century life-styles. The fort is open year-round: Memorial Day to Labor Day, Tuesday through Saturday from 10am to 5pm; the rest of the year, Wednesday through Sunday from 10am to 5pm.

Also in Delta is the **Delta County Museum,** 251 Meeker St. (tel. 874-4483). It's best known for its world-class butterfly collection; other exhibits include the historic Delta County Jail, built in 1886, early household appliances, a Victorian room, a schoolroom, a great collection of old photos and cameras, farm machinery, and the Jones Gallery of large dinosaur bones. Call for hours.

WHERE TO STAY & DINE If you're planning to stop in Delta, a good place to stay is the **Best Western Sundance Motor Inn,** 903 Main St., Delta, CO 81416 (tel. 303/874-9781). Eat at **Davelo's,** 520 Main St. (tel. 874-8277). For more **information,** contact the Delta County Tourism Council, P.O. Box 753, Delta, CO 81416 (tel. 303/874-8616 or toll free 800/436-3041).

ON FROM DELTA

If you follow State Highway 92 four miles east from Delta, you can turn north onto State Highway 65, which takes you through Cedaredge (about 14 miles from Delta), where you can pick up the Grand Mesa Scenic and Historic Byway, which continues on Highway 65 some 55 miles over the Grand Mesa before intersecting with I-70 to the north.

However, before heading off down the scenic highway, stop in Cedaredge at **Pioneer Town,** Highway 65 (tel. 856-7554), a re-creation of an early western town, complete with jail house, saloon, bank, country store, and other period buildings. There's also a Native American museum and a country chapel that is available for weddings. It's open from Memorial Day to Labor Day, Monday through Saturday from 10am to 4pm, and Sunday from 1 to 4pm. Admission is free, although donations are welcome. There's also a visitor center.

WHERE TO STAY & DINE If you're in this neck of the woods, you might enjoy staying at the unique **Cedars' Edge Llamas Bed and Breakfast,** 2169 Colo. 65,

Cedaredge, CO 81413 (tel. 303/856-6836), whose guest rooms have private decks overlooking pastures of llamas. Farther on, atop the Grand Mesa at 10,200 feet, is the **Alexander Lake Lodge,** 2121 AA 50 Rd. (P.O. Box 93), Cedaredge, CO 81413 (tel. 303/856-6700), a turn-of-the-century log building with a full-service restaurant and lounge, cabins, an R.V. park, summer stables, and winter snowmobiling.

SOUTHWESTERN COLORADO

Southwestern Colorado is a land apart from the rest of the state. The spectacular mountain wall of the San Juan Range formed a barrier between cultural regions, with the result that residents of this area traditionally have more in common with the Native American tribes of New Mexico and Arizona than with those of the greater Rocky Mountain region. The prehistoric Anasazi cliff dwellings of Mesa Verde National Park are a case in point, and there are many more similar but less-well-known sites throughout this corner of the state, focused primarily around Cortez.

Durango is the main city of the region. Its vintage-1880 main street and narrow-gauge railroad hearken back to the Old West days of the late 19th century, when it boomed as a transportation center for the region's rich silver-and-gold mines. Telluride, at the end of a box canyon surrounded by 14,000-foot peaks, has capitalized on its highly evident mining heritage in its evolution as a major ski and summer resort. And those who drive the Million Dollar Highway—down U.S. 550 from Ouray, over 11,008-foot Red Mountain Pass, through Silverton, and on past the Purgatory resort to Durango—can't miss spotting the remains of turn-of-the-century mines scattered over the mountainsides.

---

1. DURANGO

332 miles SW of Denver; 169 miles S of Grand Junction;
50 miles N of Farmington, N. Mex.

GETTING THERE By Plane   La Plata Field, 18 miles southeast of Durango off Colo. 172 (tel. 303/247-8143), has direct daily nonstop service from Grand Junction and Denver; Phoenix, Ariz.; Albuquerque and Farmington, N.Mex.; and Dallas/Fort Worth, Tex.; with connections to cities throughout North America. The airport is served by Continental Express (tel. 303/259-3466 or toll free 800/525-0280), Mesa (tel. 303/259-5178 or toll free 800/637-2247), and United Express (tel. 303/259-5178, or toll free 800/241-6522).

By Train   There's no direct passenger service from out of town, unless you're coming in from Silverton, 47 miles north. In that event, you can ride the Durango & Silverton Narrow Gauge Railroad (tel. 247-2733). See "What to See & Do," below.

By Bus   Coaches of Greyhound/Trailways and TNM&O (Texas, New Mexico, & Oklahoma) arrive and depart from the Durango Bus Center, 275 E. Eighth Ave. (tel. 303/259-2755).

By Car   Durango is located at the crossroads of east-west U.S. 160 and north-south U.S. 550. From I-70, turn south at Grand Junction on U.S. 50, which joins U.S. 550 at Montrose. From I-25, turn west at Walsenburg on U.S. 160. The most direct route from Denver, when snow conditions allow, is via U.S. 285 south to Del Norte, then

✔

WHAT'S SPECIAL ABOUT SOUTHWESTERN COLORADO

A Train Ride
☐ Durango & Silverton Narrow Gauge Railroad, with a genuine turn-of-the-century steam locomotive that puffs its way through the scenic Animas Canyon.

Activities
☐ Mountain biking from Telluride to Moab, Utah, via the San Juan Hut System, with primitive cabins every 35 miles.
☐ Skiing at Wolf Creek, which receives almost 39 feet of snow each winter, more than any other Colorado ski resort.

Art
☐ Fred Harman Art Museum in Pagosa Springs, displaying original drawings by Fred Harman, originator of the *Red Ryder* and *Little Beaver* comic strips.

Historic Sites
☐ Mesa Verde National Park, the largest collection of ancient Anasazi Indian ruins in the country.

☐ Hovenweep National Monument, where it takes a bit more effort to see ruins similar to Mesa Verde. Usually uncrowded.
☐ Ute Mountain Tribal Park, for those who would like a personal guided tour by descendants of the ancient Anasazi.

Scenic Drives
☐ San Juan Skyway, a 236-mile drive that winds through some of the most spectacular mountain scenery on earth.

Natural Spectacles
☐ Box Canyon Falls, just outside of Ouray, among the most impressive falls in the Rockies.

Museums
☐ Anasazi Heritage Center north of Cortez, which offers a hands-on experience to learn about Anasazi life 1,000 or more years ago.

west on U.S. 160 across Wolf Creek Pass to Durango. From Santa Fe, N.Mex., follow U.S. 84 north to Pagosa Springs, Colo., and turn west on U.S. 160 to Durango. From Farmington, N.Mex., take U.S. 550 north. From the Grand Canyon area, follow U.S. 160 northeast through the "Four Corners" of Arizona, New Mexico, Utah, and Colorado.

SPECIAL EVENTS Annual events in the Durango area include Snowdown!, in Durango and Purgatory, from late January to early February; the Iron Horse Bicycle Classic in Durango, Memorial Day weekend; the Durango Fine Arts Festival and Songwriters Rendezvous, in Durango, on the first weekend of May; the Sky Ute Stampede and Rodeo, in Ignacio, on the first weekend of June; the Animas River Days, in Durango, on the last weekend of June; Music in the Mountains, in Purgatory, during the last week of July and the first week of August; Fiesta Days, in Durango, on the last weekend of July; the La Plata County Fair, in Durango, during the second week of August; and Hardrockers Holidays, in Silverton, on the second weekend of August.

Durango was founded in 1880 when the Denver & Rio Grande Railroad line was extended to Silverton to haul precious metals from high-country mines. Within a year 2,000 new residents had turned the town into a smelting-and-transportation center. Although more than $300 million worth of silver, gold, and other minerals rode along the route over the years, the unstable nature of the mining business gave the town many ups and downs. One of the "ups" occurred in 1915, when southern

Colorado boy Jack Dempsey, then 20, won $50 in a 10-round boxing match at the Central Hotel. Dempsey went on to become the world heavyweight champion.

Durango remained a small center for ranching and mining into the 1960s. With the opening in 1965 of the Purgatory ski resort, 25 miles north of Durango, a tourism boom began. When the railroad abandoned its tracks from Antonito, Colo., to Durango in the late 1960s, leaving only the Durango-Silverton spur, the town panicked. But from that potential economic disaster blossomed a savior. The Durango & Silverton Narrow Gauge Railroad is now Durango's biggest tourist attraction, hauling more than 200,000 passengers each summer.

ORIENTATION

INFORMATION   Contact the Durango Area Chamber Resort Association, 111 S. Camino del Rio (P.O. Box 2587), Durango, CO 81302 (tel. 303/247-0312 or toll free 800/525-8855), or the Durango Central Reservations, 940 Main St. (P.O. Box 3496), Durango, CO 81302 (tel. 303/247-8900 or toll free 800/525-0892). The chamber's Visitor Center is just south of downtown, on U.S. 160/550 opposite the intersection of East Eighth Avenue; it's open Monday through Friday from 8am to 7pm, on Saturday from 10am to 7pm, and on Sunday from noon to 7pm.

CITY LAYOUT   The city is situated on the banks of the Animas River, which flows south to join the San Juan River at Farmington, N.Mex. U.S. 160 brushes the south side of downtown Durango; U.S. 550 branches north at the river as Camino del Rio, turning northeast to intersect Main Avenue at 14th Street. Downtown Durango is built around Main Avenue, from Fifth Street north to 14th Street; the numbered streets continue north beyond 32nd. Sixth Street, from Camino del Rio to East Eighth Avenue, is the principal downtown cross-street. Numbered avenues parallel Main to the east and west; East Third Avenue becomes Florida Road after 15th Street, winding eventually to Vallecito Lake and Lemon Reservoir; East Eighth Avenue climbs a mesa to the campus of Fort Lewis College, a 4-year liberal-arts school.

GETTING AROUND

The Durango Lift (tel. 259-LIFT) is the **city bus,** providing transportation through-out Durango May to August, daily from 8am to 5:30pm; and September to April, daily from 7am to 6:30pm; closed major public holidays. The fare is 75¢ per ride. There are bus stops on Main Avenue at Sixth, Ninth, and 12th streets, and at Rotary Park, East Second Avenue and 15th Street; otherwise, you must "wave enthusiastically at the driver if you want him to stop," as the official route map urges.

A fun way to get around Durango in summer is the **Durango Trolley** (tel. 247-0312), which runs up and down Main Street daily, 6:30am to 10pm, from mid-June through mid-September. Although designed more for transportation than tours, trolley drivers point out landmarks and talk about historic Durango as they make their way from the railroad depot to the Days Inn, with more than a dozen stops in between. An unlimited-use daily pass costs $1, and trolleys run every 20 to 30 minutes.

Of course, if you want to travel in real style, call Carriage for Hire (tel. 247-5699), which provides **horse-drawn carriage rides** throughout the downtown area during summer.

Taxi service in Durango is provided 24 hours by Durango Transportation (tel. 259-4818).

Rental Cars   Several car-rental agencies, including Avis (tel. 247-9761), Hertz (tel. 247-3933), Budget (tel. 259-1841), and National (tel. 259-0068), have outlets at the airport; in town, you can get a vehicle from Rent-a-Wreck, 21698 U.S. 160 W. (tel. 259-5858), or Thrifty, 20541 U.S. 160 W. (tel. 259-3504).

FAST FACTS

The **area code** is 303. In case of **emergency,** call 911; for other law-enforcement business, call the Durango Police (tel. 247-3232) or the La Plata County Sheriff (tel.

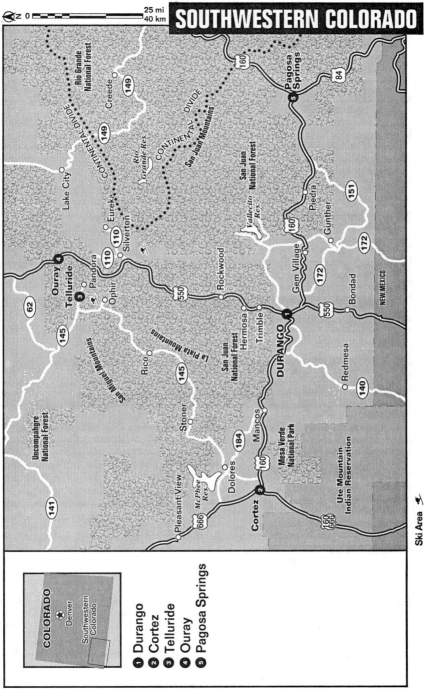

247-1155). The **hospital,** Mercy Medical Center, is at 375 E. Park Ave. (tel. 247-4311). For **road conditions,** call 259-2366. For **weather** call 247-0930.

WHAT TO SEE & DO

ATTRACTIONS

DURANGO & SILVERTON NARROW GAUGE RAILROAD, 479 Main Ave. Tel. 303/247-2733 or 247-9349.

⭐ Colorado's most famous train—and rightfully so—has been in continual operation since 1881. In all that time, its route has never varied: up the Rio de las Animas Perdidas (the River of Lost Souls) and through 45 miles of mountain and San Juan National Forest wilderness to the tiny mining town of Silverton and return. The 100% coal-fired steam locomotives pull strings of Victorian coaches on the 3,000-foot climb, past relics of mining and railroad activity from the last century.

The trip takes 3¼ hours each way, with a 2-hour stopover in Silverton (see "Easy Excursions," below) before the return trip. (It's also possible to overnight in Silverton and return to Durango the following day.) Stops are made for water, and may also be made for hikers and fishermen at trailheads inaccessible by road. Refreshments and snacks are available on all trains; there's a bar in the first-class Alamosa Parlor Car. Several private cars are available for charter, including the 1878 *Nomad*—the oldest operating private car in the world, host of U.S. presidents from Taft to Ford—and the *Railcamp.* The latter is a boxcar refurbished as a recreational vehicle; it's "spotted" on a siding in secluded Cascade Canyon each Monday and then picked up and returned to Durango each Friday. Inquire for rates and other information.

Admission: Round-trip fare, $42.70 adults and children 12 and older, $21.45 children 5–11; $73.45 parlor car (minimum age 21). Advance reservations are strongly advised. Railroad yard tours (45 minutes) $5 adults, $2.50 children 5–11.

Open: First Sat of May through last Sun of Oct. At the peak of the summer season, trains depart at 7:30, 8:30, 9:15, and 10:15am, with a shorter run to Cascade Canyon at 4:40pm, July to mid-Aug. (The 8:30 and 9:30am trains have extended seasons.) There's also a Winter Holiday Train to Cascade Canyon from Thanksgiving through Jan 1, leaving at 10am (except Dec 24 and 25). Call for fares.

ANIMAS MUSEUM, 3065 W. Second Ave., at 31st Street. Tel. 259-2402.

An old stone schoolhouse is the home of the La Plata County Historical Society museum, so it's appropriate that a turn-of-the-century classroom is one of its central displays. They've recently added a restored 1870s log home depicting the early days of Animas City (town that predated Durango). Local history, Native American prehistory, and natural history are unveiled in a variety of exhibits. There's also a museum store.

Admission: $1.75 adults, free for children under 12.

Open: Mid May through Sept, Mon–Sat 10am–6pm.

SPORTS & RECREATION

AIRBORNE SPORTS You can get a quiet, airborne look at Durango and the San Juan Mountains if you go aloft with Air Durango Hot Air Balloon Co. (tel. 385-1749) or Val Air Glider Rides, U.S. 550 (tel. 247-9037 or 247-2628), 2½ miles north of Durango.

ALPINE SLIDE The Purgatory Alpine Slide (tel. 247-9000) is open weekends, Memorial Day to mid-June, then daily to Labor Day, weather permitting. Enthusiasts ride the chair lift up, then come down the mountain in a chute, on a self-controlled sled.

BICYCLING The varied terrain and myriad trails of San Juan National Forest have made Durango a nationally important center for mountain biking. The Colorado Trail (see "Hiking," below), Hermosa Creek Trail (beginning 11 miles north of Durango off U.S. 550), and La Plata Canyon Road (beginning 11 miles west of Durango off U.S. 160) are among the favorite jaunts for locals. More enthusiastic bikers can tackle the

238-mile San Juan Skyway loop from Durango through Cortez, Telluride, Ouray, Silverton, and back to Durango.

For more complete information on routes, guided tours, and bicycle rentals in Durango and vicinity, contact Hassle Free Sports, 2615 Main Ave. (tel. 259-3874); or the Outdoorsman, 949 Main Ave. (tel. 247-4066).

BOATING There are two large lakes in the Durango area. Vallecito Lake, 22 miles east via County Roads 240 and 501, has numerous marinas with boat and fishing-equipment rentals. Marinas on the 6-mile-long lake include Angler's Wharf, 17250 County Rd. 501 (tel. 884-9477), and Mountain Marina, 14810 County Rd. 501 (tel. 884-9450), both on the lake's west shore. There's plenty of lodging (including camping) and restaurants available.

Forty miles southeast of Durango on Colo. 151, the village of Arboles is the northern gateway to Navajo Lake, a 37-mile-long reservoir that spans the Colorado–New Mexico border. The Arboles Marina (tel. 883-2343) has rental boats and a marine-equipment store.

FISHING Vallecito Lake (see "Boating," above) is a prime spot for rainbow-and-brown trout, kokanee salmon, and northern pike. The Animas River is good for trout through Durango, and it's even better 20 miles north of the city, in the Devils Falls area at Takoma power plant. Savvy anglers also recommend the Piedra River, 38 miles east of Durango via U.S. 160. Don't forget to get your Colorado fishing license first.

But you won't need a license if you drop a line in a private trout pond. Tackle and bait are provided free, and all the angler pays is $3 a pound (until inflation drives the price up) for fish caught. Try the Twin Buttes Trout Ranch, Lightner Creek, 3 miles west of Durango on County Road 207 off U.S. 160 (tel. 259-0479); or the Silver Streams Lodge, County Roads 500 and 501, Vallecito Lake (tel. 884-2770).

Fly-fishing expeditions are offered by Duranglers (tel. 385-4081).

GOLF Three 18-hole golf courses open in May, weather permitting. In Durango, there's Hillcrest Golf Course, 2300 Rim Drive (tel. 247-1499), adjacent to Fort Lewis College and Dalton Ranch and Golf Club, 435 County Rd. 252 (tel. 247-7921). Eighteen miles north on U.S. 550 is the challenging Tamarron Resort Golf Course, nationally renowned for its narrow fairways. Golfers will find that accuracy on the drive is more important than distance.

HIKING & BACKPACKING Durango is at the western end of the 469-mile Colorado Trail to Denver. The trailhead is 3½ miles up Junction Creek Road, an extension of 25th Street west of Main Avenue. There are numerous other trails in the Durango area, including paths into the Weminuche Wilderness Area reached via the Durango & Silverton railroad. For full information, contact the Animas Ranger District, San Juan National Forest, 701 Camino del Rio, Room 301 (tel. 247-4874) or the BLM, also at 701 Camino del Rio (tel. 247-4082).

"Be on top by noon." Though precipitation averages under 20 inches a year, thunderstorms are frequent on summer afternoons, when the temperatures can drop quickly.

HORSEBACK RIDING Hourly, all-day, and overnight rides, as well as hunting-and-fishing expeditions, are arranged by a variety of stables and outfitters throughout the Durango area. If you're interested only in the ride, check out Meadowlark Ranch, 19786 County Rd. 501, Vallecito Lake (tel. 884-2966). For longer expeditions, talk to Rapp Guide Service, Bear Ranch, 20 miles north of Durango on U.S. 550 (tel. 247-8923 or 247-8454); Silverado Outfitters, 7575 County Rd. 203 (tel. 247-1869); Southfork Riding Stables and Outfitters, Inc., 6 miles south of Durango on U.S. 160 E. (tel. 259-4871); or any of several guest ranches in the Vallecito Lake area.

Llama hikes with gourmet lunches, or overnight expeditions accompanied by Andean beasts of burden, are the specialty of Buckhorn Llama, 1843 County Rd. 207 (tel. 259-5965).

HOT SPRINGS Trimble Hot Springs, 6 miles north of Durango on U.S. 550 (tel. 247-0111), at the junction of County Road 203 and Trimble Lane, is a national historic site. Facilities include an Olympic-size natural hot-springs pool and therapy pool, massage-and-therapy rooms, private tubs, a snack bar, a park, and gardens. It's open daily from 7am to 10pm.

ICE SKATING   Ice skating is available at Chapman Hill and at several locations around Vallecito Lake.

MOUNTAINEERING   Guided tours and instruction in standard mountaineering, rock- and ice-climbing, backcountry skiing, avalanche awareness, and other arduous pursuits are offered by Southwest Adventures, 780 Main Ave. (tel. 259-0370).

RIVER RAFTING   The three stages of the Animas River provide excitement for rafters of all experience and ability levels. The churning Class IV and V rapids of the upper Animas mark its rapid descent from the San Juan Range. The 6 miles from Trimble Hot Springs into downtown Durango are an easy, gently rolling rush. Downstream from Durango, the river is mainly Class II and III, promising a few thrills but mostly relaxation.

Most of the many outfitters in Durango offer everything from quick 1½-hour river trips to overnight guided excursions. They include Durango Rivertrippers, 720 Main Ave. (tel. 259-0289); Flexible Flyers Rafting, Ninth Street and Roosa Avenue (tel. 247-4628); Mountain Waters Rafting, 108 W. Sixth St. (tel. 259-4191 or toll free 800/748-2507); and Southwest Adventures, 780 Main Ave. (tel. 259-0370). The Four Corners River Sports & Kayak School, 360 S. Camino del Rio (tel. 259-3893 or toll free 800/426-7637), offers daily lessons in kayaking and canoeing.

RODEO   From the second week of June through the third week of August, the Durango Pro Rodeo takes place every Tuesday and Wednesday night at the La Plata County Fairgrounds, Main Avenue and 25th Street (tel. 247-1666).

SKIING   Some 25 miles north of Durango on U.S. 550, Purgatory/Durango, operated by the Durango Ski Corporation, #1 Skier Place, P.O. Box 666, Durango, CO 81302 (tel. 303/247-9000 or toll free 800/525-0892 for reservations), has a reputation of getting more sunshine than any other Colorado resort. Surprisingly, the sun doesn't come at the expense of snowfall: More than 250 inches a year (over 20 ft.) falls here. The 675 acres of skiable terrain are predominantly intermediate, but there are ample expert runs on the mountain's Backside, and plenty of easy runs for beginners. Sixty-two trails are served by nine chair lifts (four triples and five doubles), providing an hourly uphill capacity of 12,700 skiers on a vertical of 2,029 feet (base elevation 8,793 ft.; summit elevation 10,822 ft.).

Two on-mountain restaurants—Dante's and the Powderhouse—complement the facilities of Purgatory Village, which include a hotel, condominiums, several restaurants and taverns, shops, and activity centers. All-day tickets are $36 for adults, $22 for seniors 65 and over, $19 for children 12 and under. The area usually is open from Thanksgiving to mid-April, daily from 9am to 4pm.

The Purgatory Cross-Country Ski Center offers 16km (10 miles) of trails for Nordic skiers. Trail fees are $5 for adults, $3 for children and seniors.

There are small local ski areas at Chapman Hill, adjacent to the Fort Lewis College campus overlooking Durango, with night skiing Monday through Friday from 6 to 8pm and day skiing on Saturday and Sunday, snow permitting; and at Hesperus, with one lift rising above U.S. 160, 12 miles west of Durango.

SLEIGH RIDES & SNOWMOBILING   Sleigh rides and snowmobiling from Purgatory can be arranged with a quick phone call to Purgatory/Durango Central Reservations (toll free 800/525-0892).

SWIMMING   The Durango Municipal Pool, 2400 Main Ave. (tel. 247-9999), is open summers only. Year-round indoor public swimming is available at Fort Lewis College (tel. 247-7184).

EVENING ENTERTAINMENT

During the summer season, two stage shows draw Durango visitors. The **✪ Diamond Circle Theatre,** in the Strater Hotel, 699 Main Ave. (tel. 247-4431), presents turn-of-the-century melodrama and professional vaudeville.

Dinner shows, including cowboy-style barbecues and live western-music revues, are offered by **Bar D Chuckwagon,** 8080 County Rd. 250 (tel. 247-5753), 9 miles north of Durango. Reservations are suggested, Memorial Day to Labor Day only.

Back in town, there's entertainment and dancing nightly, year-round, at many of Durango's bars and restaurants. **Farquahrts,** 725 Main Ave. (tel. 247-5440), is the top venue for live rock bands, while the **Sundance Saloon,** north side of Sixth Street between Main Avenue and East Second Avenue, is the place to dance to country-and-western music. The **Diamond Belle Saloon,** in the Strater Hotel, 699 Main Ave. (tel. 247-4431), has an unforgettable Victorian ambience, complete with honky-tonk piano player, and the Diamond Circle Melodrama in the summer—ranked one of the top-three live melodramas in the nation by *Time* magazine.

Other popular bars are the **Carvers Bakery & Brew Pub,** 1022 Main Ave. (tel. 259-2545), Durango's only commercial custom brewery; **Father Murphy's Pub and Gardens,** 636 Main Ave. (tel. 259-0334), an Irish pub; **Francisco's,** 619 Main Ave. (tel. 247-4098), a Mexican cantina with a big-screen TV for sporting events; and **Olde Tymer's,** 1000 Main Ave. (tel. 259-2990), a favorite local hangout.

WHERE TO STAY

The following selections are categorized according to their high-season rates—generally Memorial Day to Labor Day, though the mid-winter ski season is most expensive at the Purgatory ski resort. Lodging at other times of year is considerably cheaper.

VERY EXPENSIVE

THE WIT'S END GUEST RANCH & RESORT, 254 County Rd. 500, Vallecito Lake, CO 81122. Tel. 303/884-4113. 21 cabins. TV TEL
$ Rates (for two guests, including all meals and activities): $290–$335 one bedroom, $390–$485 two bedrooms. Additional adults $145; children's discounts. Rates effective Memorial Day–Labor Day, Thanksgiving and Christmas holidays, with minimum stay of 4–7 days; off-season cabin only rates available. DISC, MC, V.

What a lovely place this is! Encompassing 365 acres in a narrow valley at the head of Vallecito Lake, surrounded by the 12,000- to 14,000-foot peaks of the Weminuche Wilderness, the Wit's End offers guests a unique combination of rustic outdoors and sophisticated luxury. Its main focus is a beautiful three-story hunting lodge, a memorable structure (dating from the 1870s) of hand-hewn logs, with a huge stone fireplace and walls mirrored with cut glass from London's 1853 Crystal Palace.

Log cabins, some of them 120 years old, have retained their rustic outer appearance but have been totally renovated with knotty-pine interiors and modern luxuries. The cabins all have fully equipped kitchens, stone fireplaces, queen-size beds, full bathrooms, French doors, porches and/or decks, and invariably striking views. Largest of all is the utterly charming, two-story John Patrick Cabin, built by hand in the 1870s. Many cabins are on the ranch ponds; others are located on Vallecito Creek.

Dining/Entertainment: Dinner and drinks are served in the Old Lodge at the Lake Restaurant and Colorado Tavern. The evening meal is included in all packages for resort guests, and is open to the public as well, by reservation, from 5 to 9:30pm nightly in summer, Thursday through Saturday in winter. Filet mignon, roast duckling, or chicken Culbertson, are $20; other hearty American dishes are priced $18 to $22. The Game Room, on the second floor, has an antique billiards table; above it is a library loft. Breakfast and lunch are served daily at the Café at "D" Creek, adjacent to the Wit's End General Store; meal hours are 7am to 3pm in summer.

Services: Room service (additional charge).

Facilities: Swimming pool, four spas, tennis courts, volleyball, horseshoes, mountain bikes, children's programs, trout fishing (five spring-fed ponds); some packages also include horseback riding, cross-country skiing, ice skating, snowmobiling, and other activities. Additional charge for hunting-and-fishing packages. Facilities for large groups (up to 120) and conferences. General store, sporting-goods store.

EXPENSIVE

GENERAL PALMER HOTEL, 567 Main Ave., Durango, CO 81301. Tel. 303/247-4747 or toll free 800/523-3358. Fax 303/247-1332. 34 rms, 5 suites. TV TEL

$ Rates (including breakfast): May–Oct and Christmas holidays, $78–$135 single; $115–$145 double; $175 suite. Nov–Apr except Christmas, $75–$85 single; $70–$95 double; $125 suite. AE, CB, DC, DISC, MC, V. **Parking:** Free.

As you enter the lobby of this elegant Victorian hotel built in 1898, you'll see two rooms: a library to your left, testifying to the property's sophistication; and a Teddy Bear room to your right, indicative of its charm. In fact, guests aren't allowed to go to sleep at night without Hugs and Kisses on their beds. (They're Hershey's Kisses, and the bears are all nicknamed "Hugs.")

Staircases or old-time elevators ascend to narrow turn-of-the-century corridors. Guest rooms are all individually decorated, each with a character of its own. All have unique beds: brass, pewter, wicker, or perhaps a wooden four-poster with hand-crocheted canopies. Brass lamps and other handsome appointments add to the mood, along with Caswell & Massey amenities in the bathrooms. Specialty rooms include studios with queen-size Murphy beds, refrigerators, and wet bars; family suites with adjoining rooms; and a pair of bridal suites with Jacuzzis for two and champagne in the refrigerator.

Services: Room service, concierge, valet laundry, complimentary morning newspaper, no-smoking rooms.

PURGATORY VILLAGE HOTEL, Purgatory/Durango Resort, U.S. 550 (P.O. Box 666), Durango, CO 81302. Tel. 303/247-9000 or toll free 800/525-0892. 140 units. TV TEL

$ Rates: June–Sept, $59–$75 double; $85–$190 suite. Apr–May and Oct to mid-Nov, $49–$65 double; $75–$180 suite. Mid-Nov to early Mar except Christmas holidays, $89–$110 double; $125–$360 suite. Holiday $119–$155 double; $165–$475 suite. Weekly rates available Apr–Nov. AE, DISC, MC, V. **Parking:** Free, covered lot.

The main hotel at the Purgatory/Durango Resort, 25 miles north of the city of Durango, is located at the base of the resort. The surrounding village offers shops, bars, restaurants, and just about everything skiers want.

A variety of room types are available, both in the hotel building itself and in adjacent condominiums under resort management. Every room, regardless of size, has a kitchen, fireplace, and private deck, as well as a "snow room" with a ski locker in the entry. Standard one- and two-bedroom suites have Jacuzzi baths and/or steamer showers, classic furnishings, and microwaves and dishwashers in their kitchens. The efficiency unit makes ultimate use of space: Its Murphy bed doubles as a dining table, and its room divider is also a sleeper sofa.

Dining/Entertainment: Mesquite's restaurant offers fine continental dining, evenings during the winter-and-summer seasons. Sterling's cafeteria and lounge serves three meals daily. Farquahrt's pub, adjacent to the hotel, serves up pizza and live music for dancing.

Services: Concierge.

Facilities: Sports shop, rental shop, child care, activities desk, indoor/outdoor pool and hot tub, two rooftop hot tubs, guest laundry.

RED LION INN/DURANGO, 501 Camino del Rio, Durango, CO 81301. Tel. 303/259-6580 or toll free 800/547-8010. Fax 303/259-4398. 157 rms, 2 suites. A/C TV TEL

$ Rates: Jan–Apr and mid-Oct–Dec 24, $78–$108; May, $88–$118; June to mid-Oct, $120–$150; Christmas, $105–$135; suite $250 year-round. AE, CB, DC, DISC, MC, V. **Parking:** Free.

Not all of Durango dates from the 19th century. This expansive modern hotel, stretched along the banks of the Animas River at the intersection of U.S. 160 and U.S. 550, is a case in point. The lobby, restaurant, and lounge separate two four-story wings of guest rooms, with views of either the river or downtown Durango.

Typical rooms are handsomely appointed in earth tones with rich dark-wood furnishings. They have a king-size or two queen-size beds, a clock radio, a working desk with a telephone *or* a sofa and chair beside a coffee table, and a TV hidden away in an armoire.

Dining/Entertainment: The Edgewater Dining Room serves three meals daily overlooking the Animas River. Breakfast features an omelet bar; lunch includes sandwiches, salads, and light dishes. Steak, seafood, and pasta are the fare at dinner. In summer, the River Rat Café offers outdoor riverside dining.

Services: Room service, complimentary shuttle to airport.

Facilities: Indoor swimming pool, spa, sauna, fitness center, ski rental, meeting space for up to 300, gift shop.

STRATER HOTEL, 699 Main Ave. (P.O. Drawer E), Durango, CO 81302. Tel. 303/247-4431 or toll free 800/247-4431; 800/227-4431 in Colorado. Fax 303/259-2208. 93 rms. TV TEL

$ Rates: Jan–Apr, $48–$125 single; $59–$145 double. May to mid-Oct, $92–$127 single; $107–$147 double. Mid-Oct to Dec, $50–$130 single; $58–$150 double. AE, CB, DC, DISC, MC, V.

Durango's most famous hotel, a four-story red-brick structure, is an exceptional example of American Victorian architecture. Built in 1887 by Henry H. Strater, a prominent druggist of the mining-boom era, the hotel boasts its original ornamental brickwork and white-stone cornices. Crystal chandeliers and a variety of ornate woodworking styles can be seen in the public areas, along with intricately carved columns and anaglyptic ceiling designs. The hotel has been in the family of current general manager Rod Barker for three generations (since 1926).

Spread throughout the guest rooms is one of the world's largest collections of American Victorian walnut antiques, which assure that every room is unique and of museum quality. Even the wallpaper is authentic to the 1880s. One of the most popular rooms is Room 222, at the corner of Seventh Street and Main Avenue and directly over the Diamond Belle Saloon, where prolific author Louis L'Amour gave life to his western heroes.

Dining/Entertainment: Henry's restaurant serves local favorites and chef's specialty cuisine in an elegant atmosphere. Three meals are served daily. Henry's specializes in steak, seafood, fish, and pasta. Locals enjoy the Sunday brunch buffet. The Diamond Belle Saloon has live piano and summer melodrama (see "Evening Entertainment" in "What to See & Do," above).

Services: Room service, valet laundry, no-smoking rooms.

Facilities: Victorian-style Jacuzzi, by reservation.

TAMARRON RESORT, U.S. 550 (P.O. Drawer 3131), Durango, CO 81302. Tel. 303/259-2000 or toll free 800/678-1000. Fax 303/259-0745. 250 rms, 50 suites. A/C TV TEL

$ Rates: Apr, $85 single or double; $125 suite. May and Oct, $110 single or double; $165 suite. June–Sept, $149 single or double; $216 suite. AE, CB, DC, DISC, MC, V. **Parking:** Free.

There's no denying the commitment to nature at this quiet year-round conference resort 18 miles north of Durango. Spread across 650 acres in the midst of San Juan National Forest, Tamarron was specially designed to fit its beautiful natural setting, on a rocky cliff near the Animas River, with the least intrusion possible. The championship 18-hole golf course becomes a Nordic ski course in winter, and there's a family orientation in activities from horseback riding to fishing. The Main Lodge, on which most activities center, maintains a feeling of western elegance with its use of stone and natural woods, picture windows, cathedral ceilings, and regional artwork.

Guest rooms are in the Main Lodge or in three separate town-house clusters (Pinecone, Gamble Oak, and High Point) spread across nearly a mile of land. Most have fully equipped kitchenettes and private balconies. Many have lofts with vaulted ceilings. Guests can choose between spacious studio units; one-, two-, and three-bedroom town-house units; and executive suites.

Dining/Entertainment: Breakfast and lunch are served daily in the San Juan, with its strong southwestern decor. Afternoon-and-evening snacks can be garnered in the Caboose Café.

Services: Concierge; shuttle service (fee) between Purgatory, Durango, Mesa Verde, and La Plata airport.

Facilities: Indoor/outdoor swimming pool, hot tubs, saunas, steam rooms, fitness club, golf course/Nordic ski course, tennis courts, stables, other summer-and-winter activities; children's recreational program (includes stocked trout pond, miniature train, and mile-long nature trail); general store; gift, clothing, and sports shops; guest laundries; meeting facilities for up to 500.

MODERATE

BEST WESTERN MOUNTAIN SHADOWS, 3255 N. Main Ave., Durango, CO 81301. Tel. 303/247-5200 or toll free 800/528-1234. 63 rms, 2 suites (all with bath). A/C TV TEL

$ Rates (including continental breakfast): Jan–Mar, $45 single; $50 double. Apr–Memorial Day $52–$55 single; $54–$58 double. Memorial Day–Labor Day and Christmas holidays, $68–$83 single or double. Labor Day–Christmas Eve, $37–$58 single; $41–$63 double. AE, CB, DC, DISC, MC, V. **Parking:** Free.
You can't miss this two-story motel on the north end of town. Its geodesic Plexiglas dome, housing its swimming pool and hot tub, is one-of-a-kind in Durango. Equally unusual is the cigar-store cowboy standing at the lobby entrance. The spacious and colorful guest rooms have small refrigerators, microwave ovens, and coffee makers, and the motel also offers a guest laundry, free airport pick up, and a ski bus in winter.

COMFORT INN, 2930 N. Main Ave., Durango, CO 81301. Tel. 303/259-5373 or toll free 800/228-5150. 48 rms (all with bath). A/C TV TEL

$ Rates: Memorial Day–Labor Day, $74 single; $84 double. Christmas holidays, $55 single; $69 double. Rest of the year, $38–$74 single; $42–$84 double. Children under 18 stay free in parents' room. AE, CB, DC, DISC, MC, V. **Parking:** Free.
Built in modern pueblo style, with flat roofs and stuccoed walls, this Comfort Inn has a heated swimming pool and two hot tubs at the top of a hillside overlooking the Animas River. Bright, comfortable rooms are in three separate buildings, and feature standard furnishings as well as tiled bathrooms and vanities. Complimentary continental breakfast is served each morning.

IRON HORSE INN, 5800 N. Main Ave. (U.S. 550 N.), Durango, CO 81301. Tel. 303/259-1010 or toll free 800/748-2990. Fax 303/385-4791. 138 suites. A/C TV TEL

$ Rates: Mid-May to June, $80–$85 single; $95–$105 double; $115 deluxe. July to mid-Sept and Christmas, $85–$90 single; $100–$110 double; $120 deluxe. Oct to mid-May, $55–$60 single; $70–$80 double; $90 deluxe. AE, CB, DC, DISC, MC, V. **Parking:** Free.
Located a mile north of Durango beside the tracks of the Durango & Silverton Narrow Gauge Railroad, the Iron Horse boasts 138 bilevel suites. Upstairs is the bedroom. Downstairs, there's a fireplace, television, wet bar and sink, dining table, bathroom, and either a sleeper sofa or a queen-size bed. Buckskin Charlie's serves breakfast and dinner with a southwestern flair, the emphasis on wild game and Cajun specialties; the adjoining lounge has a big-screen TV for sporting events. The motel also features a large indoor pool and hot tub, two games rooms, two guest laundries, and meeting space for up to 600 people.

REDWOOD LODGE, 763 Animas View Dr., Durango, CO 81301. Tel. 303/247-3895. 16 rms (all with bath). A/C TV TEL

$ Rates: Summer $40–$60 single or double; winter $38–$48 single or double. AE. CB, DC, DISC, MC, V. **Parking:** Free.

This small, quiet mom-and-pop motel has clean, comfortable rooms. Smaller rooms have one queen bed and a shower only—no tub; larger rooms come with two queen-size beds and a shower-tub combination, plus convenience kitchen with sink, two-burner stove, and small refrigerator. There's also a playground, large outdoor hot tub, and a sauna. The Redwood has cable TV and direct-dial phones with free local calls. Pets are not accepted.

SILVER SPUR MOTEL, 3416 N. Main Ave., Durango, CO 81301. Tel. 303/247-5552 or toll free 800/748-1715. 34 rms, 3 suites (all with bath). A/C TV TEL

$ Rates: May–Oct, $64 single; $79 double; $125 suite. Nov–Apr, $28 single; $32 double; $42 suite. AE, CB, DC, DISC, MC, V. **Parking:** Free.

Junipers and pine trees surround this motel in the heart of Durango. The Silver Spur is one of the older hostelries along north Durango's motel row. Rooms are clean and comfortable, with standard furnishings. There's a family restaurant, lounge, and an outdoor swimming pool, open seasonally.

WHERE TO DINE

MODERATE

ARIANO'S, 150 E. Sixth St. Tel. 247-8146.
Cuisine: ITALIAN. **Reservations:** Not accepted.
$ Prices: Appetizers $3.95–$6.25; main courses $8.50–$15.95. AE, MC, V.
Open: Summer, dinner only, daily 5–10:30pm; winter, dinner only, Mon–Sat 5–10pm.

Enter this restaurant through its sports bar, with old photos and news clippings of great boxers and baseball players. Then proceed past the open kitchen into the dining room, where chains of garlic hang from the columns. Pasta is made fresh daily here; veal is hard carved and pounded. And everything is made to order, from the spicy fettuccine Napolitano to the veal Zingara to the Italian baked trout to the chicken Vincent. The wine list is dominated by Italian imports, and cappuccinos complement fine desserts.

FRANCISCO'S RESTAURANTE Y CANTINA, 619 Main Ave. Tel. 247-4098.
Cuisine: MEXICAN/AMERICAN. **Reservations:** Not accepted.
$ Prices: Breakfast $3.25–$5.95; lunch $3.75–$8.95; dinner $6.50–$15.50. AE, CB, DC, DISC, MC, V.
Open: Daily 11am–10pm; Sun breakfast 8am.

This enormous come-as-you-are family restaurant, 8,000 square feet in area, maintains a festive Mexican atmosphere. Adobe bricks, carved wooden pillars, a traditional *viga-latilla* ceiling, and the Hispanic dress of the servers make it feel like a courtyard in Guadalajara. The menu ranges from south-of-the-border specialties such as enchiladas Durango (two blue-corn tortillas over a bed of beef and green chiles) and carne adovada burritos (marinated pork in a hot chile Caribe sauce) to steaks, trout, and chicken Navajo style (roast with a cilantro-cream sauce). There's a children's menu, and the bar manufactures excellent margaritas.

ORE HOUSE, 147 E. Sixth St. Tel. 247-5707.
Cuisine: STEAK/SEAFOOD. **Reservations:** Not accepted.
$ Prices: $10–$20. AE, MC, V.
Open: Dinner only, daily 5:30–11pm.

The decor in this dimly lit restaurant is nearly equal to the food, and that's saying a lot. Everything from antique spurs to old skis to kitchen cannisters decorates the walls, along with handsome western oils and Navajo sand paintings. A full-wall mural by artist John Grow depicts turn-of-the-century Durango at the corner of Sixth and

Main, with various citizens of modern Durango and Hollywood stars in the surrealistic set. The menu, on the other hand, is *realistic*—though generous, and now includes "heart healthy" items. More than a dozen steaks are offered, including steak Ore House—a filet wrapped in bacon, stuffed with crabmeat, and topped with béarnaise sauce. Other specials include chicken Sonora and shrimp Hawaiian. All dishes come with salad bar, baked potato, and sourdough bread. The double-chocolate fudge cake has won local awards.

THE PALACE GRILL, 2 Depot Place. Tel. 247-2018.
  Cuisine: STEAK/SEAFOOD. **Reservations:** Accepted only for Sun brunch and lunch.
  $ Prices: Appetizers $4.25–$6.50; main courses $10.50–$26. AE, CB, DC, MC, V.
  Open: Lunch Mon–Fri 11:30am–2:30pm; dinner daily 5:30–10pm; Sun brunch 10am–2pm. Closed Christmas and Thanksgiving.

With its Victorian drawing-room atmosphere, adjacent to the Durango & Silverton Narrow Gauge Railroad terminal, this may be Durango's finest restaurant. Tiffany lamps hang over the tables, graciously positioned near a large fireplace, in an ambience of historical photos and classic oil paintings. The menu is noted for its mesquite grills and daily fish specials. Frequent diners rave about the duck, roasted with a honey-and-almond sauce, and steak McMahon, a New York sirloin on hash browns, with a brown sauce and sautéed onions. Fish of the day may be salmon, swordfish, ahi (Hawaiian tuna), or something entirely different. The Quiet Lady Tavern, named for the headless female sculpture at its entrance, is a beautiful lounge, complete with library.

THE RED SNAPPER, 144 E. Ninth St. Tel. 259-3417.
  Cuisine: SEAFOOD. **Reservations:** Required for parties of 7 or more.
  $ Prices: Appetizers $2.95–$5.95; main courses $12.50–$30. AE, MC, V.
  Open: Dinner only, daily 5–10pm.

The atmosphere at this fine restaurant, occupying the first floor of the 1905 Colorado Heritage Plaza, is truly exotic. Silk orchids and birds-of-paradise flowers hover over tropical aquariums, where clown fish coddle themselves in sea anemones between the smoking and no-smoking rooms. Etched-glass seashore designs separate the quiet bar from the rest of the establishment. The restaurant boasts a superb salad bar that includes fruits, nuts, and homemade dressings and breads. Other choices are fresh seafoods, fine steaks, and prime rib. Be sure to save room for "Death by Chocolate," or one of the other yummy homemade desserts.

INEXPENSIVE

CARVERS BAKERY/CAFE/BREWERY, 1022 Main Ave. Tel. 259-2545.
  Cuisine: AMERICAN. **Reservations:** Not accepted.
  $ Prices: Appetizers $1.50–$4.95; main courses $3.25–$9.95.
  Open: Mon–Sat 6:30am–10pm, Sun 6:30am–1pm, breakfast only.

A bakery in the front of this restaurant features muffins, bagels, danish, and breads, while the restaurant has a full menu with both meat-and-vegetarian dishes. Entrées include eggs Benedict on a whole wheat English muffin; there are also bowls filled with soups, stews, or salads. The restaurant also serves "brew-jitas"—fajitas panfried in tequila and salsa—which go well with the six varieties of beer that come from the brew pub in the back of the restaurant.

OLDE TYMER'S CAFE, 10th St. and Main Ave. Tel. 259-2990.
  Cuisine: AMERICAN. **Reservations:** Not accepted.
  $ Prices: $3.50–$10. DISC, MC, V.
  Open: Mon–Sat 11am–10pm, Sun 11am–9pm.

This ever-popular local hangout is packed seven nights a week. A mountain bike belonging to world-champion racer Greg Herbold, a Durango native, is suspended from the ceiling, which is the original tin, and antique bottles and tins from this early 20th-century Wall Drug store are filed away in mezzanine-high shelves. The local newspaper voted hamburgers here—seven ounces of meat in an onion roll—as the best in Durango. The menu also features homemade chili, a variety of sandwiches, hearty salads like chicken and cashews in pasta, and daily specials, including fried chicken on Tuesday and Mexican meals on weekends.

EASY EXCURSIONS
SAN JUAN SKYWAY

No visitor to southwestern Colorado should miss a drive around the ✪ **San Juan Skyway,** a 238-mile circuit that crosses five mountain passes and takes in the spectacular best of the San Juan Mountains, as well as the cities and towns of the region. It can be accomplished in a single all-day drive from Durango, or can be divided up into several days, incorporating stops in such communities as Cortez, Telluride, and Ouray—all of them subsequently discussed in this chapter. Check for closed passes in winter and early spring.

The route can be driven either clockwise (heading west from Durango on U.S. 160) or counterclockwise (heading north from Durango on U.S. 550). The former choice passes through the village of Hesperus, 11 miles west of Durango, from which a county road runs 10 miles north up the **La Plata Canyon,** with its mining ruins and ghost towns. Farther west, U.S. 160 passes the entrance road to **Mesa Verde National Park** and on into the city of Cortez, 46 miles west of Durango.

Turn north here on Colo. 145, which passes through the historic town of Dolores, site of the **Anasazi Heritage Center and Museum,** then proceeds up the Dolores River Valley, a favorite of trout fishermen. Sixty miles from Cortez, the route crosses 10,222-foot **Lizard Head Pass,** named for a startling rock spire that looms above the alpine meadows beside the road. It then descends 13 miles to the resort town of **Telluride,** set in a beautiful box canyon 4 miles off the main road.

Follow Colo. 145 west from Telluride, down the San Miguel River valley to **Placerville,** then turn north on Colo. 62, across 8,970-foot Dallas Divide, to **Ridgway,** a historic railroad town and home of a new state recreation area. Turn south here on U.S. 550 to the scenic and historic hot-springs town of **Ouray.** Here begins the remarkable Million Dollar Highway, so named for all the mineral wealth that once passed over it.

The 23 miles from Ouray over 11,008-foot ✪ **Red Mountain Pass** to Silverton is one of the most gorgeous drives anywhere on earth. It shimmies up the sheer sides of the Uncompahgre Gorge, through tunnels and past cascading waterfalls, then follows a historic toll road built in the 19th century by Otto Mears, "Pathfinder of the San Juans." Various mining apparatus and log cabins are in evidence everywhere on the slopes of the iron-colored mountains, many of them over 14,000 feet in elevation.

From Silverton, U.S. 550 climbs over Molas Divide (elevation 10,910 ft.), then more-or-less parallels the track of the Durango & Silverton Narrow Gauge Railroad as it follows the Animas River south to Durango, passing en route the **Purgatory/ Durango** ski resort (see "Skiing" in "Sports & Recreation," above) and the impressive **Tamarron Resort** complex (see "Where to Stay," above).

SILVERTON

Silverton calls itself "the mining town that never quit." Situated at an altitude of 9,318 feet, at the northern terminus of the Durango & Silverton Narrow Gauge Railroad, the town has a year-round population of 500, perhaps twice that many in summer. The entire town is a National Historic Landmark District. Founded on silver production in 1871, it boomed after the rail spur from Durango was built a decade later. Blair Street was such a notorious area of saloons and brothels a century ago that no less a character than Bat Masterson, fresh from taming Dodge City, Kans., was imported to subdue the criminal elements. Today the original false-fronted buildings remain, but they now house restaurants and galleries, and are frequently used as Old West movie sets.

WHAT TO SEE & DO The **San Juan County Historical Society Museum,** in the turn-of-the-century jail on Greene Street at 15th Street (tel. 387-5838), displays memorabilia of Silverton's boom days daily from Memorial Day weekend to mid-October. Admission is $1.50 adults, and free for children 12 and under. The adjacent San Juan County Courthouse has a gold-domed clock tower, and a Colorado Historical Society grant has helped in the restoration of the Town Hall, at 14th Street and Greene Street. An outstanding gallery is **Silverton Artworks,** 1028 Blair St. (tel. 387-5823), featuring the work of weaver-ceramicist Ruth A. Darr and watercolorist Michael Darr. They also offer prints and local area photographs.

You can get walking-tour maps of the historic commercial area, and other **information** from the Silverton Chamber of Commerce, Greene Street (Colo. 110) off U.S. 550 (P.O. Box 565), Silverton, CO 81433 (tel. 303/387-5654 or toll free 800/752-4494).

WHERE TO STAY   For overnight stays, consider the **Grand Imperial Hotel,** 1219 Greene St., Silverton, CO 81433 (tel. 303/387-5527), an opulent showcase dating from 1883 that houses the Hub Saloon, where the old song, "There'll Be a Hot Time in the Old Town Tonight," was penned. A stone facade, tin mansard roof, and pressed-tin ceilings usher guests into 40 Victorian-style rooms with private baths. Rates are $60 to $90 double, $125 to $150 suite. The hotel is open year-round, and has a dining room, saloon, and lounge.

Year-round lodging is available at the **Prospector Hotel,** 1015 Greene St., Silverton, CO 81433 (tel. 303/387-5466), with rates of $30 to $40; and the **Teller House Hotel,** 1250 Greene St., Silverton, CO 81433 (tel. 303/387-5423), a bed-and-breakfast with rates of $29 to $45.

WHERE TO DINE   Leading restaurants open year-round include **Zhivago's,** a family restaurant on Blair Street just east of the train station; and the **San Juan Café & Saloon,** 1129 Greene St. (tel. 387-5630), with lunch and dinner in an 1893 building.

---

2. CORTEZ

46 miles W of Durango, 203 miles S of Grand Junction

GETTING THERE   By Plane   Cortez Airport, off U.S. 160 and 666, southwest of town (tel. 303/565-9510), is served by Mesa Airlines (toll free 800/637-2247), with daily flights from Denver and Colorado Springs; Albuquerque and Farmington, N. Mex.; Phoenix, Ariz.; and Laramie, Wyo.

By Car   Cortez is located at the junction of U.S. 666 and U.S. 160. U.S. 666 runs north to Monticello, Utah (and on to Salt Lake City), and south to Gallup, N.Mex. (on I-40); U.S. 160 runs east through Durango to Walsenburg, on I-25, and west through the Four Corners to the Grand Canyon region of Arizona. Colo. 145, north to Telluride and Grand Junction, intersects U.S. 160 at the east end of town.

ESSENTIALS   Orientation   U.S. 160 from Durango crosses north-south Colo. 145 (Dolores Road) as it enters Cortez from the east, then runs due west through town for about 2 miles as Main Street. Easily the city's main thoroughfare, Main Street eventually intersects U.S. 666, which runs roughly southwest-northeast as Broadway at the west end of town.

Cortez has a population of about 8,000 and elevation of 6,200 feet.

Information   The best source is the Colorado Welcome Center at Cortez, Cortez City Park, 928 E. Main St., Cortez, CO 81321 (toll free 800/346-6528). Also consult the Mesa Verde–Cortez Visitor Information Bureau, P.O. Drawer HH, Cortez, CO 81321 (toll free 800/253-1616); and the Cortez Area Chamber of Commerce, P.O. Box 968, Cortez, CO 81321 (tel. 303/565-3414).

Fast Facts   The **area code** is 303. In case of **emergency,** call 911.

SPECIAL EVENTS   Cortez's annual events include the Indian Dances, at Main Street and Market Street, Monday through Thursday nights from June to August; the

Ute Mountain Tribal Bear Dance, in the American Legion Arena on the first weekend of June; the Montezuma County Fair, at the Fairgrounds on the first weekend of August.

Sometimes called "the archeological center of the United States," Cortez is surrounded by a vast complex of ancient Anasazi villages that dominated the Four Corners region—where Colorado, New Mexico, Arizona, and Utah's borders meet—1,000 years ago.

Mesa Verde National Park, 10 miles east, is certainly the most prominent nearby attraction, drawing some 800,000 visitors annually. In addition, ruins such as those of Hovenweep National Monument, Sand Canyon Pueblo, Lowry Pueblo, the Dominguez and Escalante Ruins, and the various sites of Ute Mountain Tribal Park are an easy drive from the city. And San Juan National Forest, just to the north, offers many recreational opportunities.

WHAT TO SEE & DO
THE MAJOR SITES

MESA VERDE NATIONAL PARK, P.O. Box 277, Mancos, CO 81328. Tel. 303/533-7731.

Mesa Verde is the largest archeological preserve in the United States. There are 4,000 known ruins in its canyons, dating from A.D. 600 to 1300. Many sites have never been excavated.

The area was unknown until ranchers Charles and Richard Wetherill chanced upon some of the ruins in 1888. More-or-less uncontrolled looting of artifacts followed the discovery until a Denver newspaper reporter's stories aroused national interest in protecting the site. The 52,000-acre site was declared a national park in 1906, and is the only U.S. national park devoted to the works of man.

The earliest-known inhabitants of Mesa Verde (Spanish for "green tableland") built subterranean pit houses on the mesa tops. During the 13th century they moved into shallow caves and constructed complex cliff dwellings. These homes were obviously a massive construction project. Yet the Anasazi lived in them for only about a century, and abandoned the site around A.D. 1300 for reasons that may never be determined.

The largest and most elaborate ruin in the Southwest is the ✪ **Cliff Palace,** a four-story apartment complex with stepped-back roofs forming porches for the dwellings above. Reached by a self-guided quarter-mile downhill path, its assemblage of towers, masonry facades with square windows, and *kivas* (large circular rooms used for spiritual ceremonies) are all set back beneath the rim of a cliff.

Although none of the trails to the Mesa Verde ruins is strenuous, the 7,000-foot elevation can make the treks tiring for visitors from lower climes. To reach the inside of one major ruin, Balcony House, visitors must go with a ranger and climb a 32-foot ladder. The 12-mile Ruins Road makes a number of pit houses and cliffside overlooks easily accessible by car. Two more important ruins—Step House and Long House, both on Wetherill Mesa—can be visited in summer only. Rangers lead tours to Spruce Tree House, another of the major cliff-dwelling complexes, only in winter, when other park facilities are closed. Three-hour ($10) and six-hour ($12) guided park tours are offered from Far View Lodge during the summer.

In addition to the hidden cliffside villages, the park has other treasures in the ✪ **Chapin Mesa Museum,** open daily year-round. The museum was established to house artifacts and specimens related to the history of the area, including other nearby sites such as Hovenweep National Monument. The dry climate and cliff overhangs of the canyons have preserved artifacts that would have deteriorated elsewhere.

Chapin Mesa, site of the park headquarters, the museum, and a post office, is 21 miles from the park entrance on U.S. 160. **Morefield Village,** site of Mesa Verde's 477-site campground, is 4 miles in from U.S. 160. The **Far View Visitor Center** (open in summer only), site of the 150-unit Far View Lodge (see "Where to Stay," below), a restaurant, gift shop, and other facilities, is 15 miles off U.S. 160. In summer, organize nightly campfire programs on various subjects. In winter, the Ruins and museum remain open, but other facilities are closed.

Admission: $5 per vehicle, or $2 per passenger for motor coaches; free for (62 and over), children (12 and younger), and the disabled.

Open: Park, 24 hours a day, year-round; ruins, daily 9am–6pm; museum, daily 8am–6:30pm in summer, daily 8am–5pm the rest of the year. Food, gas, and lodging available May–Oct; full interpretive services available mid-June to Labor Day.

HOVENWEEP NATIONAL MONUMENT, 43 miles west of Cortez via Colo. 10 or McElmo Canyon Rd. Tel. 303/529-4461.

Located along the Colorado-Utah border, this national monument—consisting of six separate groups of ruins (four of them in Colorado)—contains some of the area's most striking and isolated Anasazi sites. It's noted for its mysterious, 20-foot-high sandstone towers, some of them square, others oval, circular, or D-shaped.

The towers have small windows up and down their masonry sides, and remain very solid today. Archeologists have suggested their possible function as everything from guard or signal towers to celestial observatories or ceremonial structures, to water towers or granaries. The ranger on duty keeps a collection of visitors' guesses.

Headquarters are located at the **Square Tower Ruins,** the most impressive and best preserved of the sites; the Tower Point Loop Trail here winds past the ruins and identifies desert plants used by the Native Americans for food, clothing, medicine, and other purposes. Also in Colorado are the Holly Ruins, Horseshoe Ruins, and Cutthroat Castle Ruins; across the line in Utah are the Brush Arbor Ruins and the Cajon Ruins.

Hovenweep is the Ute word for "deserted valley." The Anasazi abandoned it about A.D. 1300, and even today it's often overlooked by tourists, in sharp contrast to Mesa Verde. Even the campground is nearly vacant during the peak summer season, perhaps because there are no firewood, camping supplies, gasoline, or telephone service available at the monument. Moreover, access is by graded dirt roads that become muddy—sometimes impassably so—during rainstorms.

Admission: Free.

Open: Daily 8am–sunset.

OTHER ANASAZI SITES

ANASAZI HERITAGE CENTER, 27501 Hwy. 184, Dolores. Tel. 303/882-4811.

When the Dolores River was dammed and McPhee Reservoir created in 1985, some 1,600 ancient Anasazi sites were threatened. Because the U.S. Congress acted with foresight and set aside 4% of the project costs for archeological work, many of them were saved: a stunning two million artifacts, samples, and other prehistoric records were rescued. The largest share are displayed in this museum, which opened in 1989. Located 10 miles north of Cortez, it is set into a hillside near the remains of the 12th-century Dominguez and Escalante ruins.

Operated by the Bureau of Land Management, the Anasazi Heritage Center emphasizes visitor involvement in its exhibits. Children and adults are invited to examine corn-grinding implements, a loom and other weaving materials, and a re-created pit house. There's an opportunity to touch artifacts 1,000 to 2,000 years old, to examine samples through microscopes, to research using interactive computer programs, and to engage in video lessons in archeological techniques.

A separate gallery houses temporary exhibits. The center also has a theater and a superb bookshop with a national mail-order catalog. A trail leads from the museum half a mile to the Escalante Ruin, atop a low hill with a spectacular view across the Montezuma Valley. Guided tours to the collections and conservation-and-storage area can be arranged in summer, Mon–Sat.

Admission: Free.

Open: Daily 9am–5pm. **Closed:** New Year's Day, Thanksgiving, Christmas.

CORTEZ COLORADO UNIVERSITY CENTER AND MUSEUM, 25 N. Market St., Cortez. Tel. 303/565-1151 or toll free 800/346-6528.

The center is a clearinghouse for information on various Anasazi sites and participation in Native American cultural experiences in Colorado's southwestern corner. It also features interpretive exhibits from various Anasazi sites and the modern Ute reservation. Monday to Saturday, in summer, evening programs including lectures on archeology and other cultural topics, Native American storytellers, and demonstrations are offered. The rest of the year there's about one per week offered here.

Admission: Free, donations welcome.

Open: June–Aug, Mon–Fri 10am–9pm, Sat 1–9pm; May and Sept, Mon–Sat 10am–6pm; Oct–Apr, Mon–Fri 10am–5pm.

CROW CANYON ARCHEOLOGICAL CENTER AND SCHOOL, 23390 County Rd. K, Cortez. Tel. 303/565-8975 or toll free 800/422-8975.

It's rare to find a research facility that actively encourages the participation of lay outsiders. Here, even if you've never turned a trowel of dirt, you can work side-by-side with professional archeologists in an important dig. Programs at this independent center also include laboratory analysis, artifact classification, and other insights into methods used to unravel the mysteries of the Anasazi.

Day programs are open to Cortez visitors, with a minimum 1-day advance reservation. Participants in extended programs live on site, either in the dormitory-style lodge or in one of 10 four-bed hogans.

In addition to its excavations, Crow Canyon sponsors specialized programs for teachers and students of all ages, as well as field seminars and cultural explorations.

Admission: Day programs, $40 adults, $20 children under 12 (includes lunch and 1-year membership).

Open: Last week of May through second week of Oct, Tues through Thurs 9am–4pm.

FOUR CORNERS MONUMENT, 38 miles southwest of Cortez via U.S. Hwys. 666 and 160.

This is the only place in the United States where you can stand in four states at the same time. Operated as a Navajo Tribal Park, the monument has Navajo vendors selling traditional food and handmade arts and crafts.

Admission: $2.

Open: May–Oct, daily 7am–8pm; Nov–Apr, daily 8am–5pm.

LOWRY PUEBLO RUINS, County Rd. CC, 9 miles west of Pleasant View. Tel. 303/247-4082.

An excavated 12th-century Anasazi village, 26 miles from Cortez via U.S. 666, Lowry Pueblo may have been a ritual center. A self-guided interpretive trail leads past a painted *kiva*, or circular spiritual chamber, to the remains of a great *kiva* at 54 feet in diameter, one of the largest ever found. The Bureau of Land Management, which maintains this designated National Historic Landmark, also operates a picnic area and rest-room facilities here. There's no overnight camping.

Admission: Free.

Open: Daily 8am–sunset, year-round (except when winter weather conditions close the gravel access road).

UTE MOUNTAIN CASINO, Towaoc (11 miles south of Cortez on Hwys. 160/666). Tel. 303/565-8800 or toll free 800/258-8007.

Colorado's first tribal gaming facility has more than 300 slot machines, 10 blackjack tables, four poker tables, and high-stakes bingo. The electronic slots include video poker, and bingo prizes up to $10,000 are offered Wednesday through Sunday afternoons. Like all Colorado gambling, bets are limited to $5 and gamblers must be at least 21, except for bingo where participants must be at least 18. The casino has a full-service restaurant offering southwestern cuisine. No alcoholic beverages are served or permitted in the building or on the grounds. A shuttle service connects the casino with Cortez and surrounding communities. Call the casino for schedules and fares.

Admission: Free.

Open: Daily 8am–4am.

UTE MOUNTAIN TRIBAL PARK, Towaoc. Tel. 303/565-3751, ext. 282, or toll free 800/847-5485.

If you liked Mesa Verde, but would have enjoyed the ruins more without the company of so many fellow tourists, you'll *love* the Ute Mountain Tribal Park. Set aside by the Ute Mountain Indian Reservation to preserve its Anasazi heritage, the 125,000-acre park—which abuts Mesa Verde National Park to the south and west—includes hundreds of surface ruins and cliff dwellings that compare in size and complexity with those in Mesa Verde, as well as wall paintings and ancient petroglyphs.

Accessibility to the Ute park, however, is strictly limited to guided tours by confirmed reservation. Full- and half-day tours begin at the Ute Mountain Ute Pottery factory on U.S. 666, 15 miles south of Cortez (open Monday to Saturday 9am to 6pm, and in summer also Sunday noon to 6pm; tel. 565-8548). Mountain-bike and backpacking trips are also offered. No food, lodging, gasoline, or other services are available within the park. Be sure to bring your own food and drinking water; and because you're expected to use your own vehicle for transportation within the park, make sure your gas tank is full: The main ruins are 40 miles off the paved roads. There's one primitive campground on the Mancos River for overnight stays.

Admission: Tours start at $20 half day, $30 full day.

Open: Full-day tours begin at 8:30am, half-day tours at 8am and noon, by confirmed reservation, daily, year-round.

WHERE TO STAY

ANASAZI MOTOR INN, 640 S. Broadway, Cortez, CO 81321. Tel. 303/565-3773 or toll free 800/972-6232. Fax 303/565-1027. 85 rms, 2 suites (all with bath). A/C TV TEL

$ Rates: Memorial Day–Sept. $55 single; $63–$69 double. Oct–Memorial Day, $40 single; $44–$48 double. AE, DISC, MC, V.

A large motel on U.S. 666 south out of Cortez, the Anasazi boasts rooms with queen-size or double beds and standard motel furnishings. There's a large outdoor pool, a covered hot tub, a coffee shop (open daily from 5:30am to 10pm), and a lounge with live country-and-western entertainment Thursday through Saturday nights year-round. The motel also has a gift shop.

ARROW MOTEL, 440 S. Broadway, Cortez, CO 81321. Tel. 303/565-7778 or toll free 800/524-9999. 30 rms (all with bath). A/C TV TEL

$ Rates: Memorial Day–Labor Day, $42–$48 single; $48–$58 double. Labor Day–Memorial Day, $28–$32 single; $28–$36 double. Children under 12 stay free in parents' room, $4 for children 12 and over. AE, CB, DC, DISC, MC, V.

A small Ma and Pa–style motel, the Arrow is perfect for families on a budget. Flower boxes decorate the buildings, and facilities include an outdoor swimming pool, Jacuzzi, guest laundry. Ten rooms have refrigerators and microwave ovens. Most rooms have queen-size beds, although there are a few kings. Nonsmoking and disabled-accessible rooms are available.

FAR VIEW LODGE, Mesa Verde National Park, ARA Mesa Verde Co., P.O. Box 277, Mancos, CO 81328. Tel. 303/529-4421. Fax 303/533-7831. 150 rms (all with bath).

$ Rates: Mid-Apr to Memorial Day and first 3 weeks of Oct, $72 single or double; Memorial Day–Oct 1, $88 single or double. Additional person in same room, $6.

Closed: Mid-Oct to mid-Apr. AE, DC, DISC, MC, V.

Fourteen miles from the national park entrance, in the heart of Mesa Verde National Park, this facility lodges guests in 17 separate buildings spread across a hilltop. Rooms are cozy, with private balconies and southwestern decor, including original sand paintings. There's no TV or telephone, only the spirits of the Anasazi to keep you awake at night. The views are magnificent in all directions.

Dining/Entertainment: The Metate Room serves steak, seafood, and game

specialties nightly from 5 to 9:30pm. Main courses range in price from $7.95 to
$16.50. The Far View Lounge is open from 4 to 11pm. Multimedia shows are
presented nightly at 6:30, 7:30, 8:30, and 9:30pm. The Far View Terrace, half a mile
from the lodge, serves breakfast, lunch, and dinner from 7am to 9pm daily.
   Services: 24-hour desk, complimentary morning coffee and newspaper.
   Facilities: Gift shop, tour desk.

**HOLIDAY INN EXPRESS, 2121 E. Main St., Cortez, CO 81321. Tel.
   303/565-6000** or toll free 800/626-5652. Fax 303/565-3436. 92 rms, 8 suites
   (all with bath). A/C TV TEL
$ Rates (including continental breakfast): Summer, $80 single; $86 double. Fall,
   winter, spring, $60–$69 single; $66–$75 double. Children under 17 stay free in
   parents' room. AE, DISC, MC, V.
This handsome motel on the east (Mesa Verde) side of town is among Cortez's largest.
Rooms have king- or queen-size beds, wood furnishings, cable TV with HBO, and
Southwest decor. There's a large indoor swimming pool and Jacuzzi, and guests have
complimentary use of an adjacent health spa. Locals phone calls are free, and fax and
photocopy services are available. Small pets are permitted.

**RAMADA LIMITED, 2020 E. Main St., Cortez, CO 81321. Tel. 303/565-
   3474** or toll free 800/2-RAMADA. Fax 303/565-0923. 70 rms (all with bath). A/C
   TV TEL
$ Rates (single or double): Jan–Mar, $36–$45; Apr through late May, and Oct,
   $55–$60; late May through Sept, $75–$80; Nov–Dec, $45–$50. AE, DC, DISC,
   MC, V.
A favorite of families and business travelers because of its large, well-lit rooms and
cable TV with HBO and ESPN, this Ramada has Southwest decor, with one king-size
or two queen-size beds. Rooms are very comfortable and quiet. Fax and photocopy
services are available, and disabled-accessible and nonsmoking rooms are offered.
There's an outdoor swimming pool. A limited number of rooms are designated for
travelers with pets.

WHERE TO DINE

ANTONIO'S, 104 E. Main St. Tel. 565-9066.
   Cuisine: MEXICAN.
$ Prices: Appetizers $1.50–$5.50; main courses $4.95–$9.25 at lunch, $6–
   $16.50 at dinner. AE, MC, V.
   Open: Daily 11am–10pm.
A wall-size mural of a Mexican mountain village dominates one wall, while a garden
trellis beckons diners to a rear room. Hispanic music sets the mood for hearty
portions of tacos, tostadas, enchiladas, chimichangas, "gringo burgers," or
chimeritos—fried egg-roll skins, stuffed with ground beef and topped with green
chiles. A variety of steaks are also available.

HOMESTEADERS RESTAURANT, 45 E. Main St. Tel. 565-6253.
   Cuisine: AMERICAN/MEXICAN. **Reservations:** Recommended in summer.
$ Prices: Breakfast $2.50–$6. Appetizers $2–$4.30; main courses $3–$5 at lunch,
   $5.30–$11.50 at dinner. AE, DISC, MC, V.
   Open: Breakfast/lunch Mon–Sat 7am–3pm; dinner Mon–Sat 5–9pm.
A rustic barn provides the atmosphere for this popular family restaurant. A big
waterwheel greets guests at the entrance, while throughout the dining room
hang harnesses, skillets, and other pioneer artifacts. The menu ranges from
tacos to chicken-fried steak, rainbow trout to barbecued spareribs. Their omelets start
the day right.

**M & M TRUCK STOP AND FAMILY RESTAURANT, Hwys. 160 and 660, 1
   mile south of Cortez. Tel. 565-6511.**
   Cuisine: AMERICAN.
$ Prices: Breakfast 90¢–$6; lunch-and-dinner entrées $2.50–$13. AE, DISC, MC,
   V.

Open: Daily 24 hours.

The M & M serves breakfast 24 hours a day, along with burgers, sandwiches, meat loaf, roast turkey with all the trimmings, barbecued ribs, chicken, and salads. You'll also find regional dishes, such as a Navajo taco—fry bread topped with red or green chile and cheese. Although the restaurant caters to families, with a special children's menu, you may want to heed the sign by the cash register: "Unattended or loud children will be towed away at owner's expense."

MILLWOOD JUNCTION, U.S. 160 and Main St., Mancos. Tel. 533-7338.
Cuisine: STEAK/SEAFOOD.
$ Prices: Appetizers $3.25–$10.50; main courses $8.95–$23.75.
Open: Dinner only, daily 5:30–10:30pm.

The atmosphere at this restaurant, seven miles east (toward Durango) of the Mesa Verde National Park entrance, recalls a turn-of-the-century sawmilling industry that supported the Mancos-area economy. The food, though, is decidedly modern. House specials include the likes of steak au poivre and beer-battered catfish with pecan butter; you can also get pastas, pork ribs, and a variety of other steaks and seafood. On Friday night a seafood buffet draws folks from miles around.

NERO'S, 303 W. Main St. Tel. 565-7366.
Cuisine: ITALIAN. **Reservations:** Recommended.
$ Prices: Appetizers $3.95–$5.95; main courses $5.95–$14.95. AE, MC, V.
Open: Dinner only, daily 5–10pm.

A small, quaint restaurant with a southwestern art-gallery decor, Nero's doubles its capacity in summer when its outdoor patio opens up. Main courses—which include soup or salad and garlic bread—feature chicken breast tetrazzini, veal marsala, shrimp parmesan, and a variety of homemade pastas. Creative nightly specials include the likes of fresh marlin with a spicy garlic sauce and pork tenderloin with bourbon-cream sauce.

---

3. TELLURIDE

126 miles N of Durango, 127 miles S of Grand Junction

GETTING THERE   By Plane   The Telluride Regional Airport, atop a 9,000-foot plateau 5 miles west of Telluride, is served by Continental Express (tel. 303/728-3194 or toll free 800/525-0280) year-round from Denver, Grand Junction, and Montrose; and during the winter season by United Express (tel. 303/728-4868 or toll free 800/777-3980) from Denver, and America West Airlines (tel. 303/728-4868) from Phoenix. Visitors can also fly into airports in Montrose, Grand Junction, Durango, and Cortez, and travel by ground transportation to Telluride.

Limousine service to and from all these airports is provided by reservation by Telluride Transit Company (tel. 303/728-6000).

By Car   Telluride is reached via Colo. 145. From the north (Grand Junction) or south (Durango), turn west off U.S. 550 at Ridgway, onto Colo. 62. Proceed 25 miles to Placerville, and turn left (southeast) onto Colo. 145. The road junction to Cortez is 13 miles ahead; Telluride is another 4 miles, at the end of a box canyon.

ESSENTIALS   Orientation   Telluride has a population of about 1,300 and an elevation of 8,745 feet. The city is located on the San Miguel River where it flows out of a box canyon formed by the 14,000-foot peaks of the San Juan Mountains. Colo. 145, which enters town from the west, is known as Colorado Avenue, and is Telluride's main street. The main part of historic downtown runs five blocks west from Aspen Street to Willow Street; beyond here is the Town Park, site of many summer festivals. Columbia Avenue parallels Colorado Avenue to the north, Pacific Avenue to the south.

Telluride Mountain Village, some 750 feet higher than the historical town at 9,500 feet, is reached by ski lift (a gondola is planned) or by Mountain Village Boulevard off Colo. 145, a mile south of the Telluride junction.

Information   Contact the Telluride Chamber Resort Association, 666 W. Colorado Ave. (P.O. Box 653), Telluride, CO 81435 (tel. 303/728-3041); or Telluride Central Reservations, P.O. Box 1009, Telluride, CO 81435 (toll free 800/525-3455).

Getting Around   Skip's Taxi (tel. 728-6667) and Telluride Transit (tel. 728-6000) provide **taxi service.**

Budget (tel. 303/728-4642 or toll free 800/221-2419) and Hertz (tel. 303/728-3163 or toll free 800/654-3131) have **car rentals** at the airport.

If you're out drinking late at night and realize it's best not to drive, have the bartender call the Telluride Marshal's Office for the **Tipsy Taxi** (tel. 728-3818), if you don't have the money to hire a taxi.

Fast Facts   The **area code** is 303. In case of **emergency,** call 911. The **hospital,** Telluride Medical Center, is at 500 W. Pacific Ave. (tel. 728-3848).

SPECIAL EVENTS   Telluride's annual events include Surf the Rockies Week, the first week of April; Mountainfilm, the weekend after Memorial Day; the Bluegrass Festival, the third full weekend of June; the Wine Festival at the end of June; the Jazz Celebration, the first weekend of August; the Chamber Music Festival, for 11 days in mid-August; the Mushroom Festival, the fourth weekend of August; the Film Festival, Labor Day weekend; the Hang Gliding Festival in mid-September; and Torchlight Parades, at the Telluride Ski Resort on Christmas Eve and New Year's Eve.

Incorporated in 1878 as the mining town of Columbia, Telluride took its modern name in the 1880s. This was a seriously rowdy town a century ago. In fact, Butch Cassidy robbed his first bank here. A gold boom followed on the heels of the silver crash of 1893, and lead, copper, and zinc were mined as late as 1978. But after 1930, when the Bank of Telluride closed and the town's population had dwindled to 500 from a high of 3,000, Telluride was a dying town.

Telluride became a National Historic District in 1964, and in 1968 entrepreneur Joe Zoline set to work on a "winter recreation area second to none." The Telluride Ski Company opened its first runs in 1972, and Telluride was a boom town again. Telluride's first summer festivals (bluegrass in June, film in September) were celebrated the following year. Today Telluride is a major summer and winter destination resort.

WHAT TO SEE & DO

As a National Historic District, Telluride has many fascinating historic buildings. A walking tour described in the seasonal *Telluride Vacation Guide* suggests a detailed route.

Start at the **San Miguel County Courthouse,** at Colorado Avenue at Oak Street. Built in 1887, it remains in use today. A block north and west, at Columbia Avenue and Aspen Street, is the **L. L. Nunn House,** home of the late 19th-century mining engineer who created the first high-voltage alternating-current power plant in the world. George Westinghouse provided the generators, Nikola Tesla designed the motor, and by 1894, the entire town of Telluride and most nearby mines were electrically lighted.

Two blocks east of Fir Street, on Galena Avenue at Spruce Street, is **St. Patrick's Catholic Church,** built in 1895. Its wooden Stations of the Cross figures were carved in Austria's Tyrol region. Ironically, the church wasn't far from Telluride's red-light district, known as Popcorn Alley, three blocks south around Spruce and Pacific.

Perhaps Telluride's most famous landmark is the **New Sheridan Hotel** (tel. 728-4351), and the **Sheridan Opera House** (tel. 728-5182). Located opposite the County Courthouse (the starting point of this tour) at Colorado and Oak, the hotel was built in 1895 and in its early days rivaled Denver's Brown Palace Hotel in service and cuisine. The exquisite Opera House was added in 1914, and boasted a Venetian scene painted on its roll curtain. Both establishments are still in business today.

TELLURIDE HISTORICAL MUSEUM, 317 N. Fir St. Tel. 728-3344.

This museum has some 9,000 artifacts and 1,400 historic photos that show what Telluride was like in its wild West days, when the likes of Butch Cassidy stalked the streets. Also on display are a turn-of-the-century schoolroom, antique toys, and rare Native American pottery and weavings.

Admission: $4 adults, $3 seniors, 50¢ children under 12.

Open: Mid-May to late Oct, daily 10am–5pm; Mid-Dec to mid-April, Mon–Fri noon–5pm. **Closed:** Mid-Apr to mid-May; late Oct through mid-Dec.

OTHER ATTRACTIONS

BRIDAL VEIL FALLS, Colorado Ave. (Colo. 145).

Colorado's highest waterfall (365 ft.) can be seen from the east end of Colorado Avenue. The falls freeze in winter, then slowly melt in early spring, creating a dramatic effect. Perched at the top edge of the falls is a national historic landmark, a hydroelectric power plant that served area mines at the turn-of-the-century. Accessible by hiking or driving a switchback, four-wheel-drive road, the plant is currently under restoration by a private entrepreneur who hopes to once again supply power to Telluride.

TELLURIDE SKI RESORT, 562 Mountain Village Rd. (P.O. Box 11155), Telluride, CO 81435. Tel. 303/728-3856 or 728-3614 for snow reports.

Two separate communities—Victorian Telluride at its base and the European-style Mountain Village Resort at midslope—offer an atmosphere not found elsewhere in North America. With the Doral Telluride Resort and Spa, the largest ski-resort spa on the continent, having opened in 1992, Telluride is becoming more than just an alpine look-alike.

The mountain has four divisions. The Front Face, which drops sharply from the mountain's summit to the town of Telluride, is characterized by steep moguls, tree-and-glade skiing, and challenging groomed pitches for experts and advanced intermediates. Gorrono Basin, which rises from the Mountain Village Resort, caters to intermediate skiers. The broad, gentle slopes of the Meadows stretch beneath Gorrono Basin to the foot of Sunshine Peak. This mountain, with trails over 2½ miles long devoted entirely to novice skiers, is served by the world's longest high-speed quad chair. There are seven on-mountain restaurants, including Gorrono Ranch, a historic homestead in the middle of Gorrono Basin.

In all, Telluride offers 1,050 acres of skiable terrain. The vertical drop is an impressive 3,165 feet from the 11,890-foot summit. The mountain has 62 trails served by 10 lifts (one quad chair, two triples, six doubles, and a Poma) with an uphill capacity of 10,000 skiers per hour. There are an additional 50km (30 miles) of Nordic trails, and helicopter skiing is also available. Average annual snowfall is 300 inches (25 ft.).

For summer visitors, the Coonskin Scenic Chair Lift operates mid-June through mid-September, Thursday through Sunday from 10am to 2pm. The base facility is at Mahoney Drive and Pacific Street in downtown Telluride.

Admission: $41 adults, to as low as $35 per day for multiday tickets; $23 children 6–12, $23 per day seniors 65–69, free for children under 6 and seniors over 69. Class lessons start at $35. Call toll free 800/525-3455 for information on early ski specials at participating lodges.

Open: Thanksgiving to early Apr, daily 9am–4pm.

SPORTS & RECREATION

BALLOONING You can get a lift aloft with San Juan Balloon Adventures, P.O. Box 66, Ridgway, CO 81432 (tel. 626-5495).

BICYCLING Telluride is a major mountain-biking center. The San Juan Hut System links the town with Moab, Utah, via a 215-mile-long network of backcountry dirt roads. Every 35 miles are primitive cabins, each with bunks and cooking gear. System offices are at 117 N. Willow Ave. (tel. 728-6935).

Bicycle sales, rentals, guided tours, and repairs are handled by Telluride Sports,

150 W. Colorado Ave. (tel. 728-4477), Freewheelin, 101 E. Colorado Ave. (tel. 728-4734), and Paragon Sports, 217 W. Colorado Ave. (tel. 728-4525).

FISHING   There's excellent fishing in the San Miguel River through Telluride, but even better in nearby alpine lakes, including Silver Lake, reached by foot in Bridal Veil Basin, and Trout and Priest Lakes, 12 miles south on Colo. 145.

Equipment, licenses, and fly-fishing instruction are offered by Telluride Sports, 150 W. Colorado Ave. (tel. 728-4477), and Telluride Outside, 666 W. Colorado Ave. (tel. 728-3895 or toll free 800/831-6230).

GOLF   The 18-hole par 72 Telluride Golf Club is located at Telluride Mountain Village (tel. 728-6800 or 728-6157). Greens fee with cart is $45 per person.

HIKING & MOUNTAINEERING   Sporting-goods stores and the visitors center have maps of trails in the Telluride area. Especially popular is the 1-mile San Miguel River Corridor Trail through Telluride, the Jud Wiebe 4.8 mile loop trail that begins on Oak St. and ends a block away on Aspen St., and the 1½-mile walk to the foot of Bridal Veil Falls, at the east end of Telluride Canyon.

Guided mountain expeditions can be arranged through Antoine Savelli Guides, 335 N. Willow St. (tel. 728-3705), Lizard Head Mountain Guides (tel. 728-4904), or Fantasy Ridge Mountain Guides, 205 W. Colorado Ave. (tel. 728-3546).

HORSEBACK RIDING   See Many Ponies on Silver Pick Road (tel. 728-6278) or Telluride Horseback Adventures, 9025 Hwy. 145 (tel. 728-9611).

ICE SKATING   There's ice skating daily in winter, and from 7 to 10pm on Wednesday nights, at the Town Park (tel. 728-3851). Skate rentals are available.

SKIING (NORDIC)   Nordic skiers will also find rentals and instruction at the Telluride Nordic Center in Town Park (tel. 728-3404).

SNOWMOBILING   Tours are offered by Telluride Outside, 666 W. Colorado Ave. (tel. 728-3895).

SWIMMING   There's a public children's pool, as well as tennis courts, volleyball, skateboarding ramp, and a picnic area at Telluride Town Park, Maple Street at Colorado Avenue (tel. 728-3071).

WHERE TO STAY
EXPENSIVE

PENNINGTON'S MOUNTAIN VILLAGE INN, 100 Pennington Court (P.O. Box 2428), Mountain Village Resort, Telluride, CO 81435. Tel. 303/728-5337 or toll free 800/543-1437. 12 rms (all with bath). TV TEL

$ Rates (single or double, including breakfast): Ski season, $150–$250; late spring through fall, $140–$200; suites $25 additional. AE, CB, DC, DISC, MC, V.

Located just off Colo. 145 at the entrance to Telluride Mountain Village, high above the San Miguel River valley, Pennington's is indeed a luxurious getaway. This is the ultimate in bed-and-breakfasts, with French country decor throughout. Every room has king-size or queen-size beds, private decks, and refrigerators stocked with beverages—included in the price of the room. Breakfast can be served in your room (if you so choose) from 8 to 10am. There's a daily happy hour; a library lounge with books, games, and a large fireplace; billiard room; an indoor Jacuzzi and steam room; guest laundry facilities; and lockers for ski-and-golf equipment.

MODERATE

CIMARRON LODGE, 568 W. Pacific Ave. (P.O. Box 756), Telluride, CO 81435. Tel. 303/728-3803 or 800/233-9292. Fax 303/728-5236. 52 units (40 suites). TV TEL

$ Rates: Summer season, $65–$85 single or double; $100–$115 suite. Summer festival weekends, $135–$150 single or double; $190–$220 suite. Peak winter season (Feb–Mar), $155–$200 single or double; $195–$330 suite. Christmas holidays, $195–$250 single or double; $240–$360 suite. The rest of the ski season, $110–$150 single or double; $155–$300 suite. AE, DISC, MC, V. **Parking:** Free, underground.

A luxury lodging with a premier location at the foot of the Coonskin chair, the Cimarron offers a dozen charming hotel rooms and a wide choice of one-, two-, and three-bedroom condominiums. Each suite is like a small studio apartment with a queen-size bed, sleeper sofa, and kitchenette (with microwave oven and minirefrigerator). Pets are not allowed.

Within the lodge complex is a conference center that seats 120. Facilities include ski shops and boutiques, a guest laundry, and a beautiful tile spa overlooking the San Miguel River.

ICE HOUSE LODGE, 310 S. Fir St. (P.O. Box 2909), Telluride, CO 81435. Tel. 303/728-6300 or toll free 800/544-3436. Fax 303/728-6358. 42 rms (all with bath). MINIBAR TV TEL

$ Rates (single or double, including continental breakfast): $98–$185 summer season, $100–$205 summer festival weekends, $170–$270 peak winter season (Feb–Mar), $220–$350 Christmas holidays, $130–$245 rest of the ski season. AE, CB, DC, DISC, MC, V. **Parking:** Free, covered lot.

A full-service hotel just half a block from the Oak Street chair lift, the Ice House offers casual luxury in the European alpine style. Stairs or an elevator ascend from the ground-floor entrance to the lobby, where bright furnishings and southwestern motifs prevail. The decor carries to the guest rooms, each of which has a king-size bed and sleeper sofa or two full-size beds, European comforters, a 6-foot tub, and a gorgeous mountain view from a private deck. Room service from La Marmotte French restaurant next door is available in season. There is a hot tub and a steam room on the premises.

MANITOU HOTEL, 333 S. Fir St. (P.O. Box 756), Telluride, CO 81435. Tel. 303/728-3803 or toll free 800/233-9292. Fax 303/728-5236. 11 rms (all with bath). TV TEL

$ Rates (single or double, including breakfast): $75–$110 summer season, $135–$175 summer festival weekends, $125–$195 peak winter season (Feb–Mar), $145–$225 Christmas holidays, $115–$175 the rest of the ski season. AE, MC, V.

A hideaway for devoted skiers just steps from the Oak Street chair lift, this bed-and-breakfast hotel keeps things cozy—and friendly. Rooms have queen-size beds with sleeper sofas and small refrigerators. Furnishings are basic; guests spend more time in the hotel hot tub than in their rooms when they're not sleeping. The hotel serves fresh fruit, cereal, juice, and coffee or tea in the morning and après-ski refreshments.

RIVERSIDE CONDOMINIUMS, 450–460 S. Pine St. (P.O. Box 276), Telluride, CO 81435. Tel. 303/728-4311 or toll free 800/852-0015. 70 rms.

$ Rates: Summer, $125–$215; festival weeks, $200–$385. Winter, $155–$285 early/late ski season, $280–$585 Christmas holidays, $195–$420 regular. AE, MC, V. Minimum lengths of stay may be required at busy times.

A luxury condo on the south bank of the San Miguel River, literally on the lower slopes of Telluride Mountain, rooms at the Riverside are among the best available in the town of Telluride. Decor varies, but rooms typically have gas fireplaces, entertainment centers, private ski locker, private decks or balconies, steam showers, washers and dryers, and hot-water heaters. Upper-story rooms are especially spacious, with posh furnishings and fully stocked kitchens, complete with microwave ovens and dishwashers.

THE TOMBOY INN, 619 W. Columbia Ave. (P.O. Box 2038), Telluride, CO 81435. Tel. 303/728-6621 or toll free 800/446-3192. Fax 303/728-6160. 41 units (all with bath). TV TEL

$ Rates: Summer, $55–$125 standard unit; $75–$135 with kitchen. Winter, $75–$125 standard unit; $85–$135 with kitchen. AE, DISC, MC, V.

This former Best Western motel offers clean, comfortable, affordable lodging. Most units have queen-size beds, although some have king size, and all have daybeds. Twenty-nine units are similar to basic motel rooms, and have coffee makers, clock radios, desks, and cable TV with HBO. A dozen rooms have complete kitchens and dining tables. A Jacuzzi and steam room are also at the complex. Pets are not accepted.

VIKING LODGE, 651 W. Pacific Ave. (Box 2038), Telluride, CO 81435. Tel. 303/728-6621 or toll free 800/446-3192. Fax 303/728-6160. 48 units (all with bath). TV TEL

$ Rates: Summer, $70–$150; winter, $100–$210. AE, DISC, MC, V.

Very pleasant condo-suites, with plenty of beds (including a Murphy bed on one wall), complete kitchens, and everything you need to feel right at home, including cable TV with HBO. Some deluxe units, which cost a bit extra, have upgraded furnishings, but the standard units are fine. There's a small outdoor heated pool and Jacuzzi. Pets are accepted in some units.

INEXPENSIVE

NEW SHERIDAN HOTEL, 231 W. Colorado Ave. (P.O. Box 980), Telluride, CO 81435. Tel. 303/728-4351. Fax 303/728-5024. 23 rms (about half with bath), 1 suite. TV TEL

$ Rates (single or double): Spring-and-fall seasons, $29 without bath, $49 with bath. The rest of the year, $39–$59 Memorial Day–Labor Day, $39–$69 early ski season, $79–$139 Christmas holidays, $52–$99 Jan, $89–$109 Feb to early Apr. Children under 14 stay free in parents' room. AE, MC, V.

The pride of Telluride when it was built in 1895, the New Sheridan reached the peak of its fame in 1902 when presidential candidate William Jennings Bryan delivered a famous speech from a platform outside. Just about every room has a wonderful view of the surrounding mountains. About half the rooms are without private baths. The Sheridan bar—with its Austrian-made cherry-wood bar—is on the first floor. Pets are not permitted.

THE VICTORIAN INN, 401 W. Pacific Ave. (P.O. Box 217), Telluride, CO 81435. Tel. 303/728-6601. 26 rms (20 with bath). TV TEL

$ Rates (including continental breakfast): Spring, summer, and fall, $44 single without bath, $49–$56 single with bath; $47 double without bath, $57–$64 double with bath. Festival weeks, $65–$92 single; $73–$99 double. Winter except Christmas, $47–$79 single; $55–$85 double. Christmas holidays, $84–$99 single; $91–$109 double. AE, CB, DISC, MC, V.

Built in 1976 in keeping with the turn-of-the-century flavor of the town of Telluride, the Victorian is a budget guest lodge offering rooms with either private or shared baths. Rooms are fully carpeted, with individually controlled heating. The hotel has a sauna and hot tub for sore skiers. Queen-size beds and refrigerators are standard in each room. There's no smoking and no pets allowed.

WHERE TO DINE
EXPENSIVE

CAMPAGNA, 435 W. Pacific Ave. Tel. 728-6190.
  Cuisine: ITALIAN. **Reservations:** Recommended.
$ Prices: Appetizers $6.50–$9.25; main courses $15–$26. MC, V.
  Open: Early June to early Oct and late Nov to early Apr, dinner only, daily 6–10pm.

Recalling his parents' home in Italy, chef Vincent Esposito has converted an old miner's house into an open, friendly, country-style Italian restaurant. A third generation chef, Esposito fell in love with Tuscan food while in the area studying art history. He changes the menu nightly, but it always includes wild game. Boar is a favorite, along with pheasant and quail. The *pollo e salsiccia* in *umido* (chicken and spicy sausage in broth, served over grilled polenta) is especially tasty. There's a good selection of antipasti and pastas to start, and home-cooked desserts to finish.

EXCELSIOR CAFE, 200 W. Colorado Ave. Tel. 728-4250.

Cuisine: INTERNATIONAL. **Reservations:** Recommended.

$ Prices: Breakfast $2.75–$7.50, lunch $5–$8.50; dinner appetizers $5.95–$7.50, main dishes $10.50–$23.50. MC, V.

Open: Memorial Day–Labor Day and late Nov to early Apr, breakfast/lunch daily 7:30am–2:30pm; dinner daily 5:30–9:30pm.

The building occupied by this charming restaurant was a bowling alley in the 1890s; now it's so charming with its brick walls, pressed-tin ceilings, and spiral staircase, you could still hear a pin drop. Breakfast features eggs Benedict, Florentine, and Excelsior (scrambled with smoked salmon and hollandaise); lunches include pasta Sicilia (penne with broccoli and pine nuts in a tomato sauce) and a variety of deli-style sandwiches. Dinner is more upscale: Start with venison terrine or lobster and Brie, then move on to Annamese grilled shrimp, vegetable strudel, cheese fondue, or beef tenderloin stuffed with crabmeat and vegetables. The espresso machine is always active.

LA MARMOTTE, 150 W. San Juan Ave. Tel. 728-6232.

Cuisine: FRENCH. **Reservations:** Recommended.

$ Prices: Appetizers $6–$11.75; main courses $18–$25. AE, MC, V.

Open: Dinner daily 6–10pm; closed Tues in summer.

In a tiny house of exposed brick and weathered wood beside the Ice House Lodge—in fact, this building *was* Telluride's icehouse at the turn of the century— Bertrand and Nöelle Lepel-Cointet have fashioned a memorable dining experience. This is country-style French cuisine at its finest. The hors d'oeuvres feature an array of seafood in unique settings and seasonings. Entrées range from salmon to lamb to beef to pork, and all are distinctively different from anything you'll taste anywhere else.

MODERATE

EDDIE'S, 300 W. Colorado Ave. Tel. 728-5335.

Cuisine: ITALIAN. **Reservations:** Not necessary.

$ Prices: $6.25–$23. AE, MC, V.

Open: Lunch Mon–Fri 11:30am–2pm; dinner daily 5:30–10pm.

One of the few Telluride restaurants that doesn't close during the slow periods between summer and winter visitor seasons, Eddie's specializes in New York–style pizza and gourmet pasta in a casually elegant atmosphere. And there are 12 beers on tap. The build-your-own pizza menu offers 26 different toppings; typical of the choices is the California Dreamin' blend of artichoke hearts, sun-dried and fresh tomatoes, avocado, and mozzarella and Gorgonzola cheeses. Pasta includes spinach-and-chicken canneloni, and a tortellini with smoked salmon. Take-out and delivery are available.

SILVERGLADE, 115 W. Colorado Ave. Tel. 728-4943.

Cuisine: CREATIVE AMERICAN. **Reservations:** Recommended.

$ Prices: Appetizers $6.95–$8.50; main courses $13.25–$17.50. MC, V.

Open: Late May to mid-Sept and mid-Nov to mid-Apr, dinner only, daily 6–10pm.

This new addition to the Telluride dining scene has been welcomed by locals, especially those who love fresh seafood. Sushi is an overwhelmingly popular appetizer. Main courses vary nightly, according to what seafood is available. They might include a linguine with smoked salmon, asparagus, mushrooms, and lemon cream; shrimp grilled in a garlic black-bean sauce or curried à la Thai; or veal with roasted red peppers, marsala, and mushrooms. You can also get steaks, prime rib, poultry, and pasta.

INEXPENSIVE

DELI DOWNSTAIRS, 217 W. Colorado Ave. Tel. 728-4004.

Cuisine: AMERICAN/MEXICAN/VEGETARIAN.

$ Prices: $1–$7.25. MC, V.

Open: Daily 9am–midnight.

This pleasant basement delicatessen has a loyal local following for its sandwiches, like the Logpile (German sausage and sauerkraut), the Dewdrop (crab salad), and the

Plunge (ham, roast beef, turkey, avocado, and two cheeses). It also serves a variety of burritos (including the breakfast burrito) and tacos, as well as delicious milk shakes and ice-cream sundaes. Smoking is not permitted.

FLORADORA, 103 W. Colorado Ave. Tel. 728-3888.
  Cuisine: AMERICAN. **Reservations:** Recommended.
  $ Prices: Appetizers $3.25–$5.50; main courses $4.75–$7.25 at lunch, $10.95–$14.50 at dinner. MC, V.
  Open: Daily 11am–10pm. **Closed:** Mid-Apr to mid-May and mid-Oct to mid-Nov.

A Telluride dining institution for decades, this rustic saloon was named for two "working girls" of the mining era, Flora and Dora. Their images grace the menu and other decor. House specialties, including the Floradora burger, chicken sandwich, and fajitas, are topped with grilled onions, green peppers, and cheese. Steaks and seafood, including local trout and Alaskan halibut, highlight the dinner menu. There's a soup-and-salad bar and a children's menu. Take-out available.

GREGOR'S BAKERY AND CAFE, 217 E. Colorado Ave. Tel. 728-3334.
  Cuisine: VEGETARIAN/AMERICAN. **Reservations:** Accepted.
  $ Prices: Breakfast $2.75–$5.25; lunch $3.95–$6.25; dinner $5.50–$10.25. MC, V.
  Open: Mon–Wed 6:30am–5:30pm, Thurs–Sat 6:30am–9pm, Sun 6:30am–noon.

The atmosphere here is simple, with wooden tables in a rustic building, but the cuisine is elaborate, and geared toward natural-foods lovers. Breakfast dishes include raspberry granola and macadamia-nut oatmeal pancakes. Lunches include a black-bean chile soup and a "Number Seven" sandwich—hummus, tomato, and spinach on seven-grain bread. But dinners are the real production, with dishes such as chiles rellenos (with pecans and raisins), vegetarian lasagne, and uppma bhara bandghobi (cabbage leaves stuffed with quinoa, peppers, and onions, served on zucchini pancakes, and topped with tomato sauce). Wine and beer are available. So are nonvegetarian meals and take-out.

T-RIDE COUNTRY CLUB, 333 W. Colorado Ave. Tel. 728-6344.
  Cuisine: STEAK/SEAFOOD. **Reservations:** Not necessary.
  $ Prices: Lunch $2.95–$6.95; dinner $6.95–$16.95. MC, V.
  Open: Daily, lunch 11am–4pm; dinner 5–10pm.

There's no golf course at this country club, on a second story overlooking Telluride's main street. Instead, there's a large, essentially nondescript room where diners are encouraged to cook their own steaks, chicken, or seafood and indulge themselves at the town's largest salad bar. Hungry guests order their cut from a counter, throw it on a grill, then watch and wait for it to be ready. Also on the menu are deli sandwiches, pasta, burgers, and other hot sandwiches.

---

4. OURAY

73 miles N of Durango, 96 miles S of Grand Junction

GETTING THERE By Bus Coaches of TNM&O, U.S. 550 (tel. 303/249-6673), stop in Ouray on their run between Durango and Grand Junction.

By Car U.S. 550 runs through the heart of Ouray, connecting it with Durango to the south and—via U.S. 50, which it joins at Montrose—Grand Junction (and I-70) to the north.

ESSENTIALS Orientation Ouray is basically a one-street town. As you enter from the north on U.S. 550, which parallels the Uncompahgre River, the highway passes the Ouray Hot Springs Pool and becomes known as Main Street. Most civic buildings are a block east of Main, on Sixth Avenue at Fourth Street; several motels are three blocks farther south on Third Avenue, and west on First Street. Above Third

Avenue, U.S. 550 begins its climb up switchbacks to the Million Dollar Highway. Ouray has an elevation of 7,800 feet and a population of about 700.

Information Stop in the Ouray Visitor Center beside the Hot Springs Pool, on U.S. 550 at the north end of town; or contact the Ouray Chamber Resort Association, P.O. Box 145, Ouray, CO 81427 (tel. 303/325-4746 or toll free 800/228-1876).

The Ouray Historical Museum (see "What to See & Do," below, has self-guided walking tour maps.

Getting Around Ouray is so small—about eight blocks long and five blocks wide—that the only practical way to travel around the community is on foot.

Fast Facts The **area code** is 303. In case of **emergency,** dial 911. There's a **medical clinic** on the south side of town, on Third Avenue at Second Street. The **post office** is on Main Street, between Sixth Avenue and Seventh Avenue.

SPECIAL EVENTS Annual events in Ouray include Cabin Fever Days, in mid-February; the Music in Ouray Chamber Music Festival, in early June; the Annual Fourth of July Celebration; the Ouray County Fair, the first weekend of September; and the Imogene Pass Run, in mid-September.

Named for the greatest chief of the southern Ute tribe, whose homeland was in this area, Ouray got its start in the 1870s as a gold- and silver-mining camp. Today Ouray is a major center for exploring the ghost towns of the San Juan Mountains.

WHAT TO SEE & DO

BOX CANYON FALLS, Oak St. above Third Ave. Tel. 325-4464.

Located at the southwest corner of Ouray, these falls are among the most impressive in the Rockies. The Uncompahgre River tumbles 285 feet through—not over, *through*—a solid cliff: It's easy to get a feeling of vertigo as you study the spectacle. The trail to the bottom of the falls is easy; to the top it is strenuous.

Admission: $1.25 adults, 75¢ children and seniors.

Open: Mid-May to mid-Oct.

OURAY HISTORICAL MUSEUM, Sixth Ave. at Fifth St. Tel. 325-4576.

Lodged in the original Miners' Hospital, built in 1887 by the Sisters of Mercy, this three-story museum is packed to its rafters with fascinating exhibits from Ouray's past. Displays include pioneer-and-mining-era relics, memorabilia of Chief Ouray and the Utes, turn-of-the-century hospital equipment, and photographs and other archival materials. Ask here for a walking-tour guide to the town's many historic buildings.

Admission: $2 adults; $1 children 5–12.

Open: May–June 14 and Sept–Oct 15, Mon–Sat 10am–4pm, Sun 1–4pm; June 15–Aug, Mon–Fri 9am–6pm, Sat 9am–5pm, Sun 1–5pm; Oct 16–Apr, Wed–Sun 1–4pm.

OURAY HOT SPRINGS POOL, U.S. 550, at the north end of Ouray. Tel. 325-4638.

This pool, 250 feet long and 150 feet wide, holds nearly a million gallons of odorless mineral water. Spring water is cooled from 150°; the pool here is normally 80°, but there's a hot soak of 104°.

Admission: $5 adults, $4 students 13–17, $3 children 5–12 and $4 seniors.

Open: Summer, Mon–Sat 10am–10pm, Sun 10am–8pm; winter, Wed–Mon noon–9pm.

WHERE TO STAY

THE MAIN STREET HOUSE, 334 Main St. (P.O. Box 87), Ouray, CO 81427. Tel. 303/325-4317. 3 suites.

$ Rates: $58–$70 single or double. MC, V.

A turn-of-the-century home that has been fully restored, this house offers quiet and privacy just a few steps from the center of downtown. The Hayden Mountain Suite, which occupies the entire upstairs, has private decks on both sides of the house. The Oak Creek Suite includes a greenhouse, and both it and the adjacent Cascade Suite have futon sofas that convert to second beds.

OURAY VICTORIAN INN, 50 Third Ave. (P.O. Box 1812), Ouray, CO 81427. Tel. 303/325-4064 or toll free 800/443-7361; 800/233-0392 in Colorado. 34 rms, 4 suites (all with bath). TV TEL
$ Rates: $66–$86 single or double. **Closed:** Jan 16–Mar. AE, DISC, MC, V.
A pretty two-story motel with gabled windows just below Box Canyon Falls, the Victorian also has two outdoor hot tubs and a sun deck. Rooms have a king-size bed and sofa sleeper or two queen-size beds and standard furnishings. A guest laundry and a games room are bonuses.

ST. ELMO HOTEL, 426 Main St. (P.O. Box 667), Ouray, CO 81427. Tel. 303/325-4951. 9 rms (all with bath).
$ Rates: Summer, $79–$89 single or double; winter, $58–$89 single or double. DISC, MC, V.
An 1898 town landmark that has been restored to Victorian splendor, the St. Elmo has an old-fashioned lobby that's a meeting place for locals and guests alike. Its rooms, all with private baths, contain many original furnishings. Throughout are stained glass, polished wood, and brass trim. There's a television in the parlor, and an outdoor hot tub and sauna for guests. All rooms are nonsmoking. In the basement is the Bon Ton Restaurant (see "Where to Dine," below).

WIESBADEN HOT SPRINGS SPA & LODGINGS, Sixth Ave. and Fifth St. (P.O. Box 349), Ouray, CO 81427. Tel. 303/325-4347. 18 rms, 3 suites (all with bath). TV
$ Rates: $75–$90 double; $110–$135 suite. Rates discounted Sun–Thurs in winter. JCB, MC, V.
Built over a continually flowing hot-springs vapor cave, the Wiesbaden need never worry about artificial heating. The swimming pool, though outdoors, is open year-round and heated to between 95° and 102°; massages, facials, and other spa services are always available. There's also a weight-and-exercise room, a float tank with sensory deprivation, a sauna and a "flow-through" Jacuzzi. The original structure here was built in 1879. Today's rooms have an "old country" ambience with old photographs on the walls. Some rooms with outside entrances have small refrigerators and coffee makers; the Hill Cottage has its own wood stove; and the Sun Room, built into the natural rock above the vapor cave, has a piano and fireplace.

WHERE TO DINE

BON TON RESTAURANT, in the St. Elmo Hotel, 426 Main St. Tel. 325-4951.
   Cuisine: ITALIAN. **Reservations:** Recommended.
$ Prices: Appetizers $2.75–$6.95; main courses $4.95–$6.95 at lunch, $7.50–$19 at dinner. DISC, MC, V.
   Open: Lunch Mon–Sat 11:30am–2pm; dinner daily 5–9pm; brunch Sun 9:30am–1pm.
A fixture in Ouray for more than a century—it had another location before moving into the St. Elmo Hotel basement in 1898—the Bon Ton is Ouray's finest. With stone outer walls, hardwood floors, and reproduction antique furnishings, it carries a Victorian rustic appeal. The menu includes a variety of pasta dishes, from tortellini carbonara to ravioli pesto; a "miners medley" of sautéed veal, sausage, and chicken on fettuccine; and various beef, veal, chicken, and fresh seafood dishes. There's a children's menu too.

SILVER NUGGET CAFE, 746 Main St. Tel. 325-4100.
   Cuisine: AMERICAN/MEXICAN. **Reservations:** Not necessary.
$ Prices: Breakfast $2.50–$5.95; lunch $4.25–$5.95; dinner $6.25–$13.95. No credit cards.
   Open: Daily 7am–7pm. **Closed:** Christmas Day.

A clean, contemporary eatery, the Silver Nugget occupies a historic building at the north end of Ouray. You can get a Denver omelet or huevos rancheros for breakfast, and a wide variety of deli-style sandwiches for lunch. The dinner menu runs the gamut from liver and onions to fish-and-chips, rib-eye steak to steak fajitas.

5. PAGOSA SPRINGS

55 miles E of Durango, 89 miles W of Alamosa

GETTING THERE By Car U.S. 160 connects Pagosa Springs with Durango and points west, and Alamosa and points east. It's also at the junction of U.S. 84, which runs south from here to Santa Fe, N. Mex.

ESSENTIALS Orientation Pagosa Springs has a population of about 1,200 and an elevation around 7,200 feet. The town is located on the banks of the **San Juan River,** which flows southwest from Wolf Creek Pass, eventually joining the Colorado River in Utah. Pagosa Street (U.S. 160) parallels the river through downtown until the river turns south. Hot Springs Boulevard, which crosses the river opposite the Town Park, passes the Pagosa hot springs. U.S. 84 intersects U.S. 160 at the eastern edge of the town.

Information Consult the Pagosa Springs Chamber of Commerce, P.O. Box 787, Pagosa Springs, CO 81147 (tel. 303/264-2360 or toll free 800/252-2204). The chamber has a visitor center on the south bank of the San Juan River at Hot Springs Blvd., across from the town park, which has picnic tables and a river walk.

Fast Facts The **area code** is 303. In case of **emergency,** dial 911. The police station is on Pagosa Street near Fifth Street. The **post office** is on Hot Springs Boulevard three blocks south of U.S. 160.

SPECIAL EVENTS The Red Ryder Roundup is held on the Fourth of July weekend; and the Archuleta County Fair is the first weekend in August.

Pagosa (Ute for "boiling waters") took its name from the thermal springs that spurt from the ground at 146°. There was no major white settlement here until 1878, when Fort Lewis was constructed to help control the Utes. The town was incorporated in 1891, and although the spa never became a great commercial success, Pagosa Springs grew as an important lumbering center. Today it's a major recreational center, with hiking, camping, and fishing in summer, cross-country skiing and snowmobiling at nearby Wolf Creek Pass in winter. The hot mineral baths are fast becoming a great favorite of visitors.

WHAT TO SEE & DO

CHIMNEY ROCK ARCHEOLOGICAL AREA, about 20 miles southwest of Pagosa Springs via U.S. Hwy. 160 and Colo. Hwy. 151. Tel. 883-2442 or 264-2268.

Home and sacred shrine to the Anasazi 1,000 years ago, this area, now managed by the U.S. Forest Service, is one of the most unique archeological sites in the Four Corners region. Two developed trails lead to both excavated and undisturbed ruins of an Anasazi village, perched on a high mesa. One trail is a third of a mile long, an easy walk on a relatively smooth surface. The other trail is about a half mile, but more challenging, with loose rock. A Forest Service fire lookout tower offers an excellent view of the ruins. The site is open only to those who take 2-hour guided tours, offered four times daily during the summer.

Admission: $2 adults, $1 students, free for kids under 6.
Open: May 15 to Sept 15, daily. Call for tour times.

FRED HARMAN ART MUSEUM, U.S. 160, 2 miles west of Pagosa Springs. Tel. 731-5785.

The original works of Fred Harman, creator of the "Red Ryder" and "Little Beaver" comic strips, are on display along with a great deal of rodeo and western movie art and western memorabilia.

Admission: $1 adults, 50¢ children under 6.

Open: Summer, Mon–Sat 10:30am–5pm, Sun 12:30–4pm; Winter, Mon–Fri 10:30am–5pm, weekends by appointment.

PAGOSA HOT SPRINGS, Hot Springs Blvd., south of the San Juan River.

Here's the source of those great mineral baths and pools at several local motels (see below), which for years have lured those seeking cures for a large variety of ills. Designated a state Historic Site, the springs are privately owned and fenced, but several large signs give the mineral content of the 146° water and explain the geology of the area.

PAGOSA SPRINGS HISTORIC WALKING TOUR, Downtown Pagosa Springs.

A free brochure, available at the San Juan Historical Society Pioneer Museum (see below) or Chamber of Commerce, includes a map locating and describing 16 historic buildings or sites and the hot springs.

ROCKY MOUNTAIN WILDLIFE PARK AND ART GALLERY, Colo. Hwy. 84, 6 miles south of Pagosa Springs. Tel. 264-4515.

This combination wildlife park, museum, and gallery has native wildlife, including elks, bears, cougars, and bobcats, in a natural setting. There is a wildlife museum with mounted animals, and a gallery with western-and-wildlife art. The park also arranges hunting-and-fishing trips, trail rides, and pack trips.

Admission: $4 adults, $2 children under 12.

Open: Late May to Oct, daily 9am–6pm.

SAN JUAN HISTORICAL SOCIETY PIONEER MUSEUM, First and Pagosa Sts. Tel. 264-4424.

Exhibits explain local history with a vast collection of antiques, memorabilia, and photos. There's also a replica of an old-time schoolroom and a blacksmith shop.

Admission: $1 adults, 50¢ children 6 to 18, free for children under 6 (suggested donations).

Open: Memorial Day–Labor Day, Tues–Sat 10am–5pm.

WOLF CREEK SKI AREA, U.S. 160, 25 miles east of Pagosa Springs (P.O. Box 2800, Pagosa Springs, CO 81147). Tel. 303/264-5629.

Wolf Creek is famous throughout Colorado as the area that consistently has the most snow. In fact, its annual average of 465 inches (almost 39 ft.) of powder exceeds any other resort in the Rocky Mountains. The region's topography is just right to capture cold fronts from all directions.

One of the state's oldest ski areas, Wolf Creek has terrain for skiers of all ability levels, but especially intermediates. Expert skiers often leave the lift-served slopes to dive down the powder of the Water Fall Area, then await pick up by a snow-cat shuttle that returns them to the base area. The Alberta Peak area offers extremely steep skiing and one of the most spectacular views of the peaks and pristine wilderness.

In all, the area boasts 800 acres of terrain, with a vertical drop of 1,425 feet from the 11,775-foot summit. The mountain has 50 trails served by five lifts (two triple chairs, two doubles, and a Poma). Two chairs are reserved for beginners. The Wolf Creek Lodge has restaurant and bar service and ski sales and rentals.

Admission: Tickets, $29 adults, $18 children (12 or under) and $17 seniors (65 or older); discounts for 3 or more days. Full-day class lessons start at $29; rental packages begin at $11.

Open: Thanksgiving to mid-April, daily 9am–4pm.

WHERE TO STAY

ECHO MANOR INN, 3366 Hwy. 84, Pagosa Springs, CO 81147. Tel. 303/264-5646. 9 rms (7 with bath), 2 suites.

$ Rates (including breakfast): $40–$49 with shared bath, $50–$59 with bath, $70–$125 suite. DISC, MC, V.

★ This magnificent four-story Dutch Tudor–style inn, with turrets, towers, and gables, is a delightful bed-and-breakfast, with its various rooms and suites all having very distinctive personalities. Rooms are comfortable, with country furnishings and little nooks and crannies everywhere—a good house for a game of hide-and-seek. There is one suite that can accommodate up to 12, with it's own kitchen, perfect for small family reunions. Owners Sandy and Ginny Northcutt serve delicious breakfasts that might include quiche, giant cinnamon rolls, crêpes, or breakfast burritos. There is a common Game Room and an outside deck with hot tub and Jacuzzi. The inn is not disabled accessible. Neither pets nor smoking are permitted inside.

PAGOSA LODGE, U.S. 160 (P.O. Box 2050), Pagosa Springs, CO 81147. Tel. 303/731-4141 or toll free 800/523-7704. 100 rms (all with bath). A/C TV TEL

$ Rates: Single or double, $80–$85 June–Sept; $65–$70 Oct–May; $90–$95 major holidays. AE, CB, DC, DISC, MC, V.

Located 3½ miles west of downtown Pagosa Springs, this major four-seasons resort complex not only has 27 holes of golf and seven tennis courts, but also boasts a marina (which becomes a skating rink in winter), a cross-country ski and snowmobile center, a complete health spa, and organized activities for every kind of outdoors lover. Newly remodeled with Southwest decor, the resort has a fine restaurant (the Great Divide) and lounge, and a heated indoor swimming pool, sauna, and whirlpool.

THE SPA MOTEL, 317 Hot Springs Blvd. (P.O. Box 37), Pagosa Springs, CO 81147. Tel. 303/264-5910 or toll free 800/832-5523. 18 rms and family units (all with bath). TV TEL

$ Rates: $40–$50 single; $48–$58 double; $87 family units. AE, DISC, MC, V.

If you're looking for the motel with the best pool in town, this is it. The Spa Motel gets its name from its large outdoor mineral-water swimming pool, and indoor hot-mineral baths in a recently renovated bathhouse. The water, of course, is from the nearby 146° hot springs, but is cooled to 108° in the baths, and 90° in the swimming pool. Rooms here are spacious, neat, and clean, with good lighting and simple, solid furnishings. Kitchenettes are available. Pets are welcome.

THE SPRING INN, 165 Hot Springs Blvd. (P.O. Box 1799), Pagosa Springs, CO 81147. Tel. 303/264-4168 or toll free 800/225-0934. Fax 303/264-4707. 20 rms (all with bath). A/C TV TEL

$ Rates: June–Sept, $54 single or double; Oct–May, $44 single or double. Ski packages in winter. DC, MC, V.

Six outdoor hot tubs, open year-round with mineral water from the nearby hot springs, overlook the San Juan River at this motel. Inside, the recently remodeled rooms are decorated in Southwest decor, with two double beds or one king, cable TV with HBO, and tub-shower combinations. Rooms have two entrances—to the parking area and to an inner hallway. Nonsmoking rooms are available, and small- and medium-sized pets are accepted.

WHERE TO DINE

BRANDING IRON BAR-B-Q, 3 miles east of Pagosa Springs on Colo. Hwy. 160. Tel. 264-4268.

Cuisine: BARBECUE. **Reservations:** For parties of six or more.

$ Prices: $2.25–$11.95. DISC, MC, V.

Open: Mon–Sat 11am–8pm. **Closed:** Jan–Mar.

★ You don't have to go to Texas for great barbecue. Here you'll find delicious barbecued ribs, along with barbecued chicken and brisket. This is an informal restaurant, where the toast gets branded and kids get to straddle little saddles instead of sitting in chairs. Save some room for dessert—owner Ed Campbell's chocolate-icebox pie took first place at the local county fair.

GREENHOUSE RESTAURANT & BAR, Piedra Rd. Tel. 731-2021.

Cuisine: NEW AMERICAN. **Reservations:** Recommended.
$ Prices: Appetizers $4–$7; entrées $8–$25. AE, CB, DC, MC, V.
Open: Sun–Thurs 5–9pm, Fri–Sat 5–10pm.

Creative variations on old favorites are what to expect at this upscale restaurant, with the menu including prime rib, fresh seafood, pasta, and vegetarian items. The emphasis is on fresh and natural, such as the use of organically produced beef and poultry and freshly grown herbs. The menu changes seasonally, with lighter selections in the summer, game during hunting season, and so forth.

THE MALT SHOPPE, 124 Pagosa St. Tel. 264-2784.

Cuisine: AMERICAN. **Reservations:** Not accepted.
$ Prices: $1–$6. MC, V.
Open: Daily 7am–9pm.

You can get a good, quick breakfast here—bacon and eggs, scrambled eggs in a pita-bread pocket, or an omelet—costing from $3 to $5. For lunch or dinner, there are excellent burgers and sandwiches. Save room for one of the Malt Shoppe's 14 flavors of shakes and malts.

OLE MINER'S STEAKHOUSE, U.S. 160, 3½ miles east of Pagosa Springs. Tel. 264-5981.

Cuisine: STEAK/SEAFOOD. **Reservations:** Recommended.
$ Prices: Dinner main courses $10–$25. AE, MC, V.
Open: Summer and winter high seasons, dinner only, daily 5:30–10pm; rest of the year, dinner only, Mon–Sat 5:30–10pm.

This looks like an old mine shaft beside the highway on the way to Wolf Creek Pass, but the low lighting and attentive service inside quickly convince you otherwise—as does the food. The menu lists nearly a dozen charbroiled steaks, as well as shrimp, lobster, crab, chicken teriyaki, and pork kebabs. You'll have to leave your vices behind, though: The restaurant doesn't permit smoking and doesn't serve alcohol.

ROLLING PIN BAKERY & CAFE, 214 Pagosa St. Tel. 264-2255.

Cuisine: AMERICAN. **Reservations:** Not accepted.
$ Prices: Breakfast $2–$4; lunch $3–$5. No credit cards.
Open: Mon–Fri 7am–5:30pm, Sat 7am–2:30pm.

The bakery is the king here, which you will quickly see as you sit at breakfast and watch just about everyone in Pagosa Springs stop in and walk away with a bag of buns, rolls, danish, or whatever. Of course, it won't bother you, because you'll be eating the same, while sipping some of the restaurant's gourmet coffee. Lunches are good, too, with quiches, burgers, salads, soups, and a variety of sandwiches and subs.

CHAPTER 12

THE SOUTHERN ROCKIES

1. GUNNISON
• WHAT'S SPECIAL
  ABOUT THE
  SOUTHERN ROCKIES
2. CRESTED BUTTE
3. SALIDA
4. ALAMOSA

If Colorado is the rooftop of America, then the southern Rockies region is the rooftop of Colorado. Some 30 of Colorado's "14-ers"—14,000-foot peaks—ring the area, and from Monarch Pass, at 11,312 feet, rivers flow in three directions: the Gunnison west toward the Colorado, the San Luis south toward the Rio Grande, and the Arkansas east toward the Mississippi. Isolated from the rest of Colorado by these high mountains and rugged canyons, the region developed in a way that bred proud, independent-minded people.

The Spanish took several hesitant steps north, up the Rio Grande Valley from Taos, in the late 18th century; the Hispanic influence remains stronger in the San Luis Valley than in any other part of Colorado. Capt. Zebulon Pike's party of U.S. Army explorers wandered through the mountains of this region in the winter and spring of 1807, and fur trappers knew it well in subsequent decades. San Luis was established in 1851, the first incorporated community in Colorado, and other farming settlements followed. Settlement of the northern mountains didn't begin until the 1870s.

Today the mountain-and-river towns of the north have earned a reputation as recreational capitals: Gunnison for fishing and hunting, Crested Butte for skiing and mountain biking, and Salida and Buena Vista for river rafting. Alamosa, hub of the San Luis Valley, is within easy reach of numerous scenic and historic attractions (including the Cumbres & Toltec Scenic Railway) as well as the remarkable Great Sand Dunes National Monument on the western flank of the Sangre de Cristo Range. In the foothills of the San Juan Range, which demarcates the western boundary of this region, are the fascinating old mining towns of Creede and Lake City.

1. GUNNISON

196 miles SW of Denver, 161 miles W of Pueblo, 65 miles E of Montrose

GETTING THERE   By Plane   The Gunnison County Airport, Rio Grande Avenue at 11th Street (tel. 641-0526), is just off U.S. 50, a few blocks south of downtown Gunnison. Continental Express (toll free 800/525-0280) and United Express (toll free 800/241-6522) provide daily year-round service from Denver and Grand Junction. During nearby Crested Butte's winter ski season, United (toll free 800/241-6522) flies direct from Chicago, American Airlines (toll free 800/433-7300) direct from Dallas/Fort Worth, and Delta (toll free 800/221-1212) direct from Salt Lake City.

By Bus   Buses of Greyhound (toll free 800/528-6055) and TNM&O both pass

WHAT'S SPECIAL ABOUT THE SOUTHERN ROCKIES

A Train Ride
- ☐ Cumbres & Toltec Scenic Railroad, offering narrow-gauge steam train rides through the mountains of southern Colorado and northern New Mexico.

Activities
- ☐ White water rafting on the Arkansas and Gunnison rivers.
- ☐ Mountain biking from Crested Butte, Colorado's mountain bike capital.
- ☐ Salida Hot Springs, offering Colorado's largest indoor hot spring pools, plus private hot baths.

Natural Spectacles
- ☐ Great Sand Dunes National Monument, with North America's tallest sand dunes.
- ☐ Curecanti National Recreation Area, a water sports paradise with power-boats, sailboats, guided boat tours, fishing, hiking, and camping.

Historic Drives
- ☐ Bachelor Historic Tour, from Creede, follows a 17-mile loop of dirt road past abandoned mines and 19th-century town sites.

Museums
- ☐ Pioneer Museum in Gunnison, with 19th-century Old West buildings, a narrow gauge steam locomotive, and a collection of classic cars.
- ☐ Fort Garland State Museum, a re-creation of an 1858 fort that was once commanded by Kit Carson.
- ☐ Jack Dempsey Museum, a must stop for boxing fans in the famous fighter's hometown of Manassa.
- ☐ Underground Mining Museum in Creede, where visitors wind through a 250-foot tunnel inside a mountain.

through Gunnison twice daily—once eastbound, once westbound. The station is at 303 E. Tomichi Ave. (tel. 303/641-0060).

By Car Gunnison is located on U.S. 50, midway between Montrose and Salida. From Denver, the most direct route is U.S. 285 southwest to Poncha Springs (near Salida), then west on U.S. 50. From Grand Junction, follow U.S. 50 through Montrose.

ESSENTIALS Orientation The town is built on the southeast banks of the westerly flowing Gunnison River. Tomichi Avenue (U.S. 50) runs due east-west through town; many civic buildings are on Virginia Avenue, one block north. Main Street (Colo. 135) intersects Tomichi Avenue in the center of town, and proceeds north to Crested Butte. The campus of Western State College, a 4-year liberal arts school, is three blocks north of Tomichi Avenue and four blocks east of Main Street.

Gunnison has a population of 4,700 and an elevation of 7,700 feet.

Information Contact the Gunnison County Chamber of Commerce, 500 E. Tomichi Ave. (P.O. Box 36), Gunnison, CO 81230 (tel. 303/641-1501 or toll free 800/274-7580).

Getting Around There's a Budget Rent-a-Car (tel. 641-4403) agency at the Gunnison County Airport.

Fast Facts The **area code** is 303. The **climate** in winter can become extremely cold—the average January low is −8°F, with occasional forays into the −30s—but midsummer temperatures frequently climb into the 80s. In case of **emergency,** call 911; for normal business, contact the Gunnison County Sheriff (tel.

641-1113). **Gunnison Valley Public Hospital** is at 214 E. Denver St. (tel. 641-1456), two blocks east of Main Street and six blocks north of U.S. 50. The main **post office** is at Virginia Avenue and Wisconsin Street (tel. 641-1884). For **road conditions,** call 641-8008. Total local **sales tax** is 7%.

SPECIAL EVENTS Annual events in Gunnison include the Gunnison County Airshow in mid-June; Cattlemen's Days and Rodeo, Colorado's oldest continually held rodeo, in the third week in July; the Classic Car Show in mid-August; and the Parade of Lights, in late November or early December.

Ute peoples began hunting in this area around the middle of the 17th century. Hispanic explorers probably never penetrated this isolated region, but mountain men, pursuing pelts, certainly had done so by the 1830s. It was first mapped by U.S. Army captain John Gunnison and his party of surveyors in 1853. A town platted near the confluence of Tomichi Creek and the Gunnison River in 1874 grew as a ranching center and transportation hub for nearby silver-and-gold mines. Western State College was established in 1911; now with an enrollment of 2,500, it is the only college in the United States with a certified technical-evacuation mountain-rescue team. Today ranching remains important to the region, but the leading economic stimuli are tourism and outdoor recreation: skiing, fishing, and hunting.

WHAT TO SEE & DO

ATTRACTIONS

CURECANTI NATIONAL RECREATION AREA, 102 Elk Creek Rd. (U.S. 50), west of Gunnison. Tel. 303/641-2337.

The Blue Mesa, Morrow Point, and Crystal dams on the Gunnison River, just below Gunnison, have created a series of three very different reservoirs, extending 35 miles to the mouth of the Black Canyon of the Gunnison (see "Montrose" in Chapter 10). **Blue Mesa Lake** (elevation 7,519 ft.), the easternmost of the three (beginning 9 miles west of Gunnison), is the largest lake in Colorado when filled to capacity, and is a water-sports paradise, popular for fishing, motorboating, sailboating, board sailing, and other activities. Fjordlike **Morrow Point Lake** (elevation 7,160 ft.) and **Crystal Lake** (elevation 6,755 ft.) fill long, serpentine canyons accessible only by precipitous trails, and thus are limited to use by hand-carried boats.

The **Elk Creek Visitor Center,** 15 miles west of Gunnison off U.S. 50, presents numerous exhibits and audiovisual programs, as well as maps and publications. Nature hikes and evening campground programs are presented throughout the season. A 90-minute **boat tour,** offered by Elk Creek Marina (tel. 641-0402), leaves the Pine Creek Trail boat dock on Morrow Point Lake daily, Memorial Day through Labor Day, to explore the Upper Black Canyon of the Gunnison. Call for schedules and reservations. There's a second marina at Lake Fork at the reservoir's west end. At **Cimarron,** 45 road miles west of Gunnison, there's an information center with a historic train exhibit and a road to the **Morrow Point Dam** power plant, where free public tours are offered daily from Memorial Day to Labor Day.

U.S. 50 follows the north shore of Blue Mesa Lake, crossing to the south shore on a bridge between Sapinero and Cebolla basins. At Lake Fork, Colo. 92 to Crawford crosses to the north shore of Morrow Point Lake; it traces the canyon rim west for the next 30 miles, offering numerous spectacular views of the western lakes and canyons.

Fishermen visit Curecanti year-round—there's ice fishing in winter—but the main season is May to October, when rainbow, brown, and Mackinaw trout and kokanee salmon are caught in large numbers. Hunting, especially for elk and deer, is popular in season in the adjacent West Elk Mountains. Numerous day-hike trails, including a 4-mile round-trip path to the volcanic Dillon Pinnacles, are located in the recreation area. There are 10 campgrounds in Curecanti and 21 picnic areas.

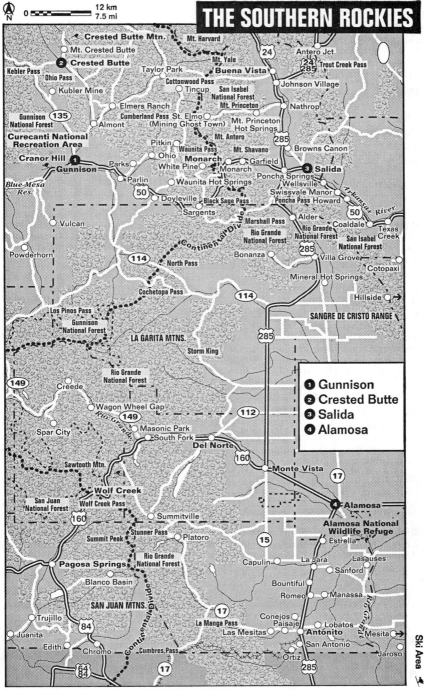

THE SOUTHERN ROCKIES

0 —— 12 km / 7.5 mi

Legend:
- ❶ Gunnison
- ❷ Crested Butte
- ❸ Salida
- ❹ Alamosa

Crested Butte Mtn.
Mt. Crested Butte
❷ Crested Butte
Kebler Pass
Ohio Pass
Kubler Mine
Gunnison National Forest (135)
Almont
Curecanti National Recreation Area
Cranor Hill
❶ Gunnison
Blue Mesa Res.
Powderhorn
Vulcan
Parks
Parlin
(50)
Doyleville
Sargents
(114)
North Pass
Cochetopa Pass
Los Pinos Pass
Gunnison National Forest
LA GARITA MTNS.
Storm King
Rio Grande National Forest
(149)
Creede
Wagon Wheel Gap
(149)
Spar City
Masonic Park
South Fork
Sawtooth Mtn.
San Juan National Forest
Wolf Creek
Wolf Creek Pass
(160)
Summit Peak
Stunner Pass
Platoro
Rio Grande National Forest
Pagosa Springs
Blanco Basin
SAN JUAN MTNS.
Trujillo
Juanita
(84)
Edith
Chromo
Cumbres Pass
(17)

Mt. Harvard
Mt. Yale
Taylor Park
Cottonwood Pass
Tincup
Elmers Ranch
Cumberland Pass St. Elmo
(Mining Ghost Town)
Pitkin
Ohio
White Pine
Waunita Pass
Monarch
Monarch
Waunita Hot Springs
Black Sage Pass
Continental Divide
Marshall Pass
Rio Grande National Forest
Bonanza
Buena Vista
San Isabel National Forest
Mt. Princeton
Mt. Princeton Hot Springs
Mt. Antero
Mt. Shavano
Garfield
Poncha Springs
Wellsville
Swissvale Manor
Poncha Pass Howard
Alder
Rio Grande National Forest
San Isabel National Forest
(285)
Villa Grove
Mineral Hot Springs
(114)
SANGRE DE CRISTO RANGE
(285)
(112)
Del Norte
(160)
Monte Vista
(17)
❹ Alamosa
Alamosa National Wildlife Refuge
Estrella
(15)
Capulin
La Jara
Lasauses
Sanford
Bountiful
Romeo
Manassa
Rio Grande
(17)
La Manga Pass
Las Mesitas
Conejos
Paisaje
Antonito
Lobatos
Mesita
San Antonio
Ortiz
Jaroso
(285)

Antero Jct.
(24)
(24)(285)
Trout Creek Pass
Johnson Village
Nathrop
(285)
Browns Canon
❸ Salida
Arkansas River
(50)
Coaldale
Texas Creek
Cotopaxi
Hillside

Ski Area

Continental Divide

Admission: Free; fee for camping ($7–$8 per night per site) and for boat tours ($7.50 adults, $6.50 seniors 62 and over, and juniors 13–17, $4 children 12 and under, by advance reservation).

Open: Recreation area, daily 24 hours. Elk Creek Visitor Center, mid-May to September, daily 8am–6pm; the rest of the year, intermittently.

PIONEER MUSEUM, S. Adams St., at Tomichi Ave. Tel. 641-9963 or 641-0943 in summer.

A narrow-gauge steam locomotive, caboose, and depot are among the machines and structures on display at this historical society museum. Other exhibits include 19th-century fashions, thousands of arrowheads, antique cameras, some scary-looking beauty-shop equipment, and about a dozen classic-and-antique cars.

Admission: $3 adults, $1 children 6–12, free for children under 6.

Open: Memorial Day to Labor Day, Mon–Sat 9am–5pm.

SPORTS & RECREATION

BOATING The lakes of Curecanti National Recreation Area (see "Attractions," above) offer some of Colorado's best boating; rentals can be arranged at the Elk Creek Marina on Blue Mesa Lake, 15 miles west of Gunnison off U.S. 50 (tel. 641-0707). There's another small marina on Taylor Reservoir, 30 miles north of Gunnison on the Taylor Canyon Road; contact the Taylor Park Boat House (tel. 641-2922).

FISHING & HUNTING The Gunnison River, both above and below town, and the tributary Taylor River, which joins the Gunnison at Almont, 11 miles north of town, are outstanding trout streams. In addition, the region's lakes are also rich in fish (see "Curecanti National Recreation Area" in "Attractions," above). Throughout the surrounding Gunnison National Forest, hunting for deer, elk, and other game animals is extremely popular. For fishing or hunting equipment, licenses, and information in Gunnison, visit Berfield's Stage Stop, 519 W. Tomichi Ave. (tel. 641-5782), or Gene Taylor's Sporting Goods, 201 W. Tomichi Ave. (tel. 641-1845). Willowfly Anglers, at the Three Rivers Resort, Almont (tel. 641-1303), offers fly-fishing instruction, rentals, and guide service. Inquire at the chamber of commerce about other guide services.

GOLF The 18-hole, par 71, 6,535-yard Dos Rios Country Club, County Road 33, off U.S. 50 southwest of town (tel. 641-1482), also has a driving range and practice facility. In addition, the Rocky Mountain Family Golf School, 2 miles east of Gunnison off U.S. 50 (tel. 641-0451), has a driving range, 9-hole putting green, and golf school.

HIKING There are endless opportunities for backcountry experiences in the Gunnison National Forest, which surrounds the town. For trail maps and other information, contact national forest headquarters at 216 N. Colorado St. (tel. 641-0471).

RIVER RAFTING For trips on the Gunnison and other rivers, check with Three Rivers Resort and Outfitting, 11 miles north of Gunnison on Taylor Canyon Road, Almont (tel. 641-1303).

SKIING The two major winter-sports centers in the area are Crested Butte Mountain Resort, 32 miles north on Colo. 135 (see "Crested Butte," below), and Monarch Ski Resort, 44 miles east on U.S. 50 (see "Salida," below).

WHERE TO STAY

BEST WESTERN TOMICHI VILLAGE INN, U.S. 50, 1½ miles east of Gunnison (P.O. Box 763), Gunnison, CO 81230. Tel. 303/641-1131 or toll free 800/528-1234. 48 rms, 1 suite (all with bath). A/C TV TEL

$ Rates (including continental breakfast): Summer, $74–$89; winter, $36–$49. AE, CB, DC, DISC, MC, V.

An alpine appearance characterizes this motel at the east end of Gunnison, across the highway from Tomichi Creek. The exterior is of wood and flagstone, with green decorative trim. The spacious guest rooms are appointed in shades of peach and slate, with rich wood furnishings; all have either two queen-size beds or a king-size bed and sleeper sofa. An outdoor swimming pool is open in summer; an indoor sauna and whirlpool are open year-round. Next door is Josef's restaurant.

MARY LAWRENCE INN, 601 N. Taylor St., Gunnison, CO 81230. Tel. 303/641-3343. 3 rms, 2 suites (all with bath).
$ Rates (including full breakfast): $63 double, $78 and up suites. MC, V.
Built in 1885 and named for its longtime owner, the Mary Lawrence Inn is located in a quiet neighborhood near Western State College. Antiques, sponge-painted and stenciled walls, along with homemade quilts and colorful artwork make each room in this two-story inn unique. Creative breakfasts are served, with an assortment of juices, hot teas, and gourmet coffees. The large outdoor deck and backyard, which includes a playhouse, is a perfect place for children to play while their parents lounge in the enclosed porch.

WILDWOOD MOTEL, 1312 W. Tomichi Ave., Gunnison, CO 81230. Tel. 303/641-1663. 18 units (all with bath). TV
$ Rates: $36–$48 single or double; $60–$85 3 bedroom unit. Fishing-and-hunting packages available. MC, V.
Built in 1928 as a summer refuge for members of the Chicago underworld, the Wildwood today is a favorite hideaway for budget-conscious outdoor sports lovers. Rooms here aren't fancy, but they're very quiet, very clean, and well maintained, and all include a kitchen nook with refrigerator. Decor varies from regional art to nature themes; furnishings range from two queen-size beds, to one queen size plus a table and chairs, to a double and two singles. All rooms have cable TV, but there are no phones except the pay phone beside the fish-cleaning station. The grounds contain a playground area, horseshoe pit, picnic tables, and two duck ponds, where Tasmanian rainbow trout are raised for release into the Gunnison River. Pets may be accepted by prior arrangement.

CAMPING

MESA CAMPGROUND, 36128 W. Hwy. 50, Gunnison, CO 81230. Tel. 303/641-3186. 135 sites.
$ Rates: $15 tent, $16.50 full R.V. hookup. DISC, MC, V. **Closed:** Nov–Apr.
A great base camp for fishing, hunting, or sightseeing trips, this campground and R.V. park four miles west of Gunnison has grassy, shaded sites, and clean bathhouses with plenty of hot water. A store supplies gasoline, propane, groceries, and some R.V. supplies. Pets are welcome.

WHERE TO DINE

CATTLEMEN INN, 301 W. Tomichi Ave. Tel. 641-1061.
   Cuisine: AMERICAN. **Reservations:** Accepted.
$ Prices: Breakfast $1.50–$7; lunch $3–$6; dinner $4–$15. CB, DC, MC, V.
   Open: Daily, breakfast 6:30–11am; lunch 11:30am–3pm; dinner 5–9pm.

Beef is the specialty here—only the best hand-cut steer beef—so you can bet you'll thoroughly enjoy your steak, prime rib, or even burger. There are two dining rooms; the downstairs one with attached bar has the look of a western steak house, with lots of rough wood, while the upstairs restaurant appears more family oriented. For breakfast, you can get all the standard selections, plus Southwest variations. Lunches include lots of sandwiches, fish-and-chips, burritos, pinto bean soup, and a salad bar. And at dinner, in addition to the great steaks, you can get many of the lunch items, plus trout, broiled chicken breast, and breaded deep-fried shrimp.

EPICUREAN RESTAURANT, 110 N. Main St. Tel. 641-2964.
   Cuisine: EUROPEAN DELI. **Reservations:** Not necessary.
$ Prices: Breakfast $3.25–$7.50; lunch $3.95–$7.50.

Open: Mon–Sat 7am–5pm, Sun 7am–2pm.

Proprietress Ina Gerkey, a native of East Prussia, has created a tranquil island of continental culture in the wild West. Classical music, oil paintings, and fresh flowers on every table have established a little bit of Europe between the rough-hewn log walls of this downtown café. If you're here for breakfast, don't miss the *ebelskiver*— 2-inch ball-size Danish apple pancakes. You can also get soufflés, omelets, and wild-rice pancakes. For lunch, consider the Reuben (with sauerkraut and Swiss cheese on rye, of course) or the homemade soup with muffins. Catered continental-style dinners are served to large groups by reservation only.

JOSEF'S, U.S. 50, 1½ miles east of Gunnison. Tel. 641-5032.
   Cuisine: CONTINENTAL/AMERICAN. **Reservations:** Recommended at dinner.
$ Prices: Appetizers $4.95–$6.95; main courses $9.95–$16.95; lunch $4.95–$7.95. AE, CB, DC, DISC, MC, V.
   Open: Lunch Mon–Fri 11am–2pm; dinner Sun–Thurs 5–9pm, Fri–Sat 5–10pm.

An Old World atmosphere pervades this fine restaurant adjacent to the Best Western Tomichi Village at the east end of town. The menu features a variety of steaks, chops, poultry, and fresh seafood dishes, but the house specialties are German: beef Rouladen, served with egg noodles and red cabbage; Jäegerschnitzel champignons, a rich preparation of traditional wienerschnitzel; Kässler Ribchen, a pork loin charbroiled with an apple, brandy, and honey glaze; and more. Lunch visitors enjoy Josef's burger, on a homemade Kaiser roll, or a lighter meal of coffee with Austrian pastries.

RAMBLE II, Colo. 135, 2 miles north of Gunnison. Tel. 641-1207.
   Cuisine: STEAK/SEAFOOD.
$ Prices: Appetizers $1.50–$4.95; main courses $4.95–$19.45. MC, V.
   Open: Lunch, daily 11:30am–2pm; dinner Sun–Thurs 4:30–9pm, Fri–Sat 4:30–10pm.

You can't miss this turquoise-painted building beside the road north toward Crested Butte. A family restaurant, it has pleasant tavern-style decor, with stained-glass windows casting a touch of elegance across the booths and tables. The menu features a variety of steaks, from chopped sirloin to a 20-ounce T-bone, and tasty local catches, including trout and walleye. Early-bird specials (starting at $4.95) are served from 5 to 6pm nightly; the restaurant also features excellent burgers and a good dessert menu. Patio riverfront dining is delightful, weather permitting.

EASY EXCURSION

LAKE CITY

The most interesting day trip for visitors to Gunnison is to the historic mining town of ✪ **Lake City,** 55 miles southwest via Colo. 149 (turn south off U.S. 50, 9 miles west of Gunnison). Founded in 1874, this former silver-and-gold town is set against a backdrop of 14,000-foot peaks in three different national forests—the Gunnison, Uncompahgre, and Rio Grande.

Today Lake City is Colorado's largest national historic district, with more than 75 buildings that date from the 19th century. Tour the **Hinsdale County Courthouse** (1877), site of the trial of the notorious Alferd Packer, who allegedly killed and ate five members of his mining party. Packer was sentenced to hang, but a technicality commuted his crime to manslaughter, and he wound up serving only five years. The fascinating geological area north of Lake City is known as the Cannibal Plateau (and in an instance of bad taste that can only be ascribed to college students, the University of Colorado has named its student cafeteria in honor of Packer).

Lake City is an important recreational center, especially for hiking and fishing in summer, cross-country skiing and snowmobiling in winter. Lake San Cristobal, just south of town, is Colorado's second-largest natural lake.

For information, contact the Lake City Chamber of Commerce, P.O. Box 430, Lake City, CO 81235 (tel. 303/944-2527 or toll free 800/569-1874).

2. CRESTED BUTTE

224 miles SW of Denver, 28 miles N of Gunnison

GETTING THERE   By Plane   The Gunnison County Airport (see "Gunnison," above) serves Crested Butte. Continental Express and United Express provide year-round service; American Airlines and Delta fly during winter ski season.

By Bus   The Alpine Express (tel. 303/641-5074 or toll free 800/822-4844) provides transportation between Gunnison Airport and Crested Butte hotels. The charge is $32 round-trip, with children 12 and under $22.

By Car   Crested Butte is 28 miles north of Gunnison on Colo. 135. The only year-round access is via Gunnison (see "Gunnison" above). In summer, the gravel-surface Kebler Pass Road links Crested Butte with Colo. 133 at Paonia Reservoir, to the west; and four-wheel-drive vehicles can negotiate a difficult route south from Aspen, around the Maroon Bells.

SPECIAL EVENTS   Crested Butte's annual events include the Wildflower Festival, in early July; the Fat Tire Bike Week, the second week of July; the Mountain Man Rendezvous, in late July; Aerial Weekend, in late July; the Festival of the Arts, in early August; the Chamber Music Festival, in mid-August; and the Vinotok Slavic Fall Festival, in mid-September.

The town of Crested Butte was born in 1880 as the Denver & Rio Grande line laid a narrow-gauge rail track from Gunnison to serve the gold-and-silver mines in the area. But coal, not the more "precious" minerals, sustained the town for six decades after its discovery in the late 1880s. Only in 1952 was the last of the mines operated by the Colorado Fuel and Iron Company forced to close. The economy languished until the Mount Crested Butte ski area was developed in 1961. The resort community followed in 1976.

Throughout the 1970s and 1980s young people moved to the town and renovated the old buildings as homes and businesses. An architectural review board ensured that all construction was true to the town's heritage, with the result that Crested Butte is one of the most authentic Victorian towns in Colorado today. You won't find any rich miners' mansions here: This was and is a working-man's town, without the ostentation seen elsewhere in the state.

Crested Butte has a permanent population of about 1,100 residents; Mount Crested Butte has another 350. The town is located at an elevation of 8,885 feet, with the resort village at 9,350 feet.

ORIENTATION

INFORMATION   Consult the Crested Butte–Mount Crested Butte Chamber of Commerce, P.O. Box 1288, Crested Butte, CO 81224 (tel. 303/349-6438 or toll free 800/545-4505). For specific resort information, contact Crested Butte Mountain Resort, 12 Snowmass Road (P.O. Box A), Mount Crested Butte, CO 81225 (tel. 303/349-2333 or toll free 800/544-8448; fax 303/349-2250).

TOWN LAYOUT   There are actually two separate communities here: the old mining town of Crested Butte and the modern resort village of Mount Crested Butte, 3½ miles away. Colo. 135 enters Crested Butte from the south and is intersected by Elk Avenue, which runs west-east as the town's main street. Numbered streets run north-south beginning with Fifth Street to the west of the highway. Beyond Elk Avenue, the highway is known as Gothic Road, which leads to the winding condominium-speckled roads surrounding the Mount Crested Butte village.

GETTING AROUND

Mountain Express (tel. 349-5616) provides **free shuttle-bus** service between Crested Butte, Mount Crested Butte, and area condominiums, in winter daily from

7:15am to midnight, with shorter hours in summer. Local **taxi** service is also available from Town Taxi (tel. 349-5543).

FAST FACTS

The **area code** is 303. In an **emergency,** dial 911. The **Crested Butte Medical Clinic,** Gothic Road at Emmons Road, Mount Crested Butte (tel. 349-6651), can handle most health needs; emergency service evacuates patients to **Gunnison Valley Public Hospital,** 214 E. Denver Ave., Gunnison (tel. 641-1456). The **post office** (tel. 349-5568) is on the north side of Elk Avenue between Second Street and Third Street. Local **sales tax** is 8%.

WHAT TO SEE & DO

CRESTED BUTTE MOUNTAIN RESORT, 12 Snowmass Rd. (P.O. Box A), Mount Crested Butte, CO 81225. Tel. 303/349-2222 or toll free **800/544-8448; 303/349-2323** for snow reports. Fax 303/349-2250.

Crested Butte may be Colorado's best-kept secret. Situated at the intersection of two overlapping winter storm tracks, it's guaranteed outstanding snow. More than one-quarter of its terrain is devoted to beginners, yet it has what many experts consider the most challenging runs—"Extreme Limits" skiing—in the Rockies. Couple that with a town rich in Victorian heritage, and with "more fine restaurants per capita than any other town in America," according to the *Denver Post,* and you're left with a remarkable resort community.

From the Grand Butte Hotel at the foot of the mountain, the **Silver Queen Quad** ascends to the top of the skiable peak, serving a series of advanced runs. The **Keystone Lift** departs from the same location and serves an expansive beginner area off Keystone Ridge. Over the backside of the ridge, the **Teocalli and Paradise Lifts** serve a predominantly intermediate series of trails. The **North Face Poma,** which climbs above Paradise Bowl near the top of the mountain, offers access to the extreme skiing of the North Face, the Glades, and Phoenix Bowl, which *Skiing* magazine has called "Expert skiing with a capital E."

The resort has 1,160 acres of skiable terrain, not including an additional 395 acres of "Extreme Limits." The vertical drop is 3,062 feet from a summit of 11,400 feet. Mount Crested Butte has 85 trails served by 13 lifts (3 triples, 1 quad, 5 doubles, and 4 surface lifts) with an uphill capacity of 13,550 skiers per hour. Average annual snowfall is 229 inches (19 ft.) at the base, 300 inches (25 ft.) at the summit.

Admission: Lift tickets, $39 adults ($28 in early and late season), $24 children 12 and under ($17 early and late), $19.50 seniors 65–69 ($14 early and late), free for seniors 70 and over, and free for children 12 and under when an adult buys a lift ticket, except during the Christmas holidays and the last half of March. Class lessons start at $28; adult rental packages, at $12.

Open: Thanksgiving to early Apr, daily 9am–4pm.

SPORTS & RECREATION

BALLOONING   The highest-altitude balloon company in North America is Bighorn Balloon (tel. 349-6335), offering year-round flights over the Rockies surrounding Crested Butte.

BICYCLING   Crested Butte has established a firm reputation as the mountain-biking capital of Colorado. From Jeep roads to hiking trails, there's something here to please every ability level. Popular rides include the challenging 25-mile ride over 10,707-foot Schofield Pass to the village of Marble, off Colo. 133; and the shorter Cement Creek Trail to the base of Italian Mountain.

For information on rentals or guided tours, contact Flatiron Sports, Treasury Center, Emmons Road, Mount Crested Butte (tel. 349-6656), or other sporting-goods stores. There's even a Mountain Bike Hall of Fame Museum, 126 Elk Ave. (tel. 349-7482), open summer, daily from 10am to 5pm.

GOLF   Robert Trent Jones II designed the 7,200-yard, 18-hole Skyland Mountain

Golf Resort course, 385 Country Club Lane (tel. 349-6131), 2½ miles south of Crested Butte. Considered one of Colorado's best, the course has water hazards on each of the first 9 holes, rolling hills and knolls on the back 9.

HIKING   There are rich opportunities for hiking and backpacking in the Crested Butte area. Ask the chamber of commerce for trail suggestions, or contact the Gunnison National Forest office, 216 N. Colorado St., Gunnison (tel. 641-0471).

HORSEBACK RIDING   Guided rides are offered year-round by Fantasy Ranch (tel. 349-5425) and Teocalli Outfitters (tel. 349-5675). Perhaps the most popular trips are into the Irwin Lodge (tel. 349-5308) or Lost Lake Lodge, a pair of wilderness hideaways that prepare gourmet home-cooked lunches for riders.

RIVER RAFTING   Crested Butte Rafting (tel. 349-7423) leads trips down the Gunnison or Taylor rivers, or for the more adventurous, the Arkansas.

SKIING   The Crested Butte Nordic Center, based at the Crested Butte Athletic Club, 512 Second St. (tel. 349-6201), is open in winter daily, from 9am to 4pm. The center maintains 30km (18½ miles) of groomed trails and organizes backcountry tours into more than 100 miles of wilderness trail. Tickets for track skiing are $6 per day for adults, $3 for children; rentals are $12 per day; all-day tours run $40 per person, with a two-person minimum.

TENNIS   There are more than 20 outdoor tennis courts between Crested Butte and Mount Crested Butte, including several in Town Park on Seventh Street at Elk Avenue. Inquire at the chamber of commerce about others.

WHERE TO STAY

GRANDE BUTTE HOTEL, Emmons Rd. (P.O. Box 1639), Mount Crested Butte, CO 81225. Tel. 303/349-4000 or toll free 800/642-4422. Fax 303/349-6332. 210 rms, 52 suites (all with bath). TV TEL
$ Rates: Thanksgiving to pre-Christmas, $110–$140 single or double; $165–$300 suite. Christmas holidays $180–$220 single or double; $280–$550 suite. Jan 2–Feb 16, $140–$180 single or double; $220–$400 suite. Feb–Mar, $165–$195 single or double; $240–$500 suite. Last week of season, $110–$140 single or double; $180–$300 suite. Early June to late Sept, $75–$90 single or double; $130–$300 suite. Children 17 or under stay free with parent. **Closed:** Early Apr to early June and late Sept to late Nov. AE, CB, DC, DISC, MC, V. **Parking:** Free valet service.

A luxurious property at the foot of the Silver Queen and Keystone lifts, this is the Crested Butte Mountain Resort's showcase hotel. Some 40,000 square feet of red cedar went into its construction, and an impressive collection of original oil paintings is hung throughout the hotel. Every guest room has a private balcony, wet bar and refrigerator, Jacuzzi bath, cable TV with in-house movies, and direct-dial phone. Standard rooms have a queen-size bed and sleeper sofa or two double beds.

Dining/Entertainment: Fine continental dinners are served in the Grande Café, which boasts a 160° wall of windows facing the ski slopes. The Roaring Elk coffee shop serves three meals daily; its outdoor barbecue deck is especially popular with skiers. In the evening, the Roaring Elk becomes an après-ski saloon with live dance music. Quieter conversations take place at the Fireside Lounge.

Services: Room service, concierge, valet laundry, complimentary shuttle service, ski valet and storage, no-smoking rooms, facilities for the disabled.

Facilities: Indoor swimming pool, 2 outdoor Jacuzzis, sauna, games room, guest laundry, ski shop, ice-skating rink (with rentals), meeting space for 400.

THE CLAIM JUMPER, 704 Whiterock Ave. (P.O. Box 1181), Crested Butte, CO 81224. Tel. 303/349-6471. 6 rms (all with private baths). TV
$ Rates (including full breakfast): $69–$99 double (discount for singles). No credit cards.
A huge log home packed with a museum full of eclectic antiques and family

heirlooms, this bed-and-breakfast inn easily qualifies as Crested Butte's most unusual accommodation. Each of the guest rooms has a particular theme, and is decorated accordingly. The Rough and Ready Room, of course, is dedicated to cowboys; Prospector's Gulch, to miners; and Commodore Corrigan's Cabin, to seafarers. The Sportsfan Attic is packed with baseball-and-football memorabilia. Fifties nostalgia buffs will enjoy Ethyl's Room (complete with restored gas pump) and Soda Creek ("Things go better with Coke"). The common living room has a turn-of-the-century hunting-lodge motif, complete with wood-burning stove; and the inn also features a redwood hot tub, full sauna, and antique gaming parlor. A VCR and movies are also available.

CRESTED BUTTE CLUB, 512 Second St. (P.O. Drawer 309), Crested Butte, CO 81224. Tel. 303/349-6655 or toll free 800/782-6037. 7 suites (all with bath). TV TEL

$ Rates (including continental breakfast): Single or double, spring and fall, $70–$95; summer and winter, $125–$165. AE, DISC, MC, V.

This is perhaps Crested Butte's most elegant lodging. The building, a national historic landmark that houses the town's athletic club, dates from 1886—though it didn't become an "inn" until 1989. The guest suites have captured the Victorian era and moved it into the late 20th century. All rooms have rich antique furnishings of oak, walnut, or cherry; four-poster king- or queen-size beds; gas fireplaces; copper-and-brass claw-foot bathtubs; his-and-hers pedestal sinks; and other 19th-century touches. The inn is entirely smoke free, by the way. Guests have full athletic club access, including use of the lap pool, weight-and-exercise room, Jacuzzis, steam rooms, and aerobics studio. The sophisticated Club Pub, a turn-of-the-century establishment with a marble-top piano bar is located here.

ELK MOUNTAIN LODGE, Second and Gothic Sts. (P.O. Box 148), Crested Butte, CO 81224. Tel. 303/349-7533 or toll free 800/374-6521. 16 rms (all with bath). TV TEL

$ Rates (including full breakfast): Single or double, $65–$75 summer; $96–$103 winter. AE, DC, DISC, MC, V.

Built in 1919 as a miners' hotel, this historic lodge has been beautifully renovated by new owners John and Patty Vermillion. Located two blocks north of Elk Avenue, near the center of town, the lodge offers rooms with twin-, queen-, or king-size beds. Third-floor rooms have balconies, and spectacular views of the town and surrounding mountains. There's also an indoor hot tub, lobby bar, and free ski storage.

THE NORDIC INN, Emmons and Treasury Rds. (P.O. Box 939), Mount Crested Butte, CO 81225. Tel. 303/349-5542. 24 rms, 2 suites, 2 chalets (all with bath). TV

$ Rates (including continental breakfast): $67–$216. Children stay free in parents' room. AE, MC, V.

When the Nordic Inn was built in 1970, it was the only overnight accommodation at the foot of the Crested Butte ski slopes. The charming Norwegian-style inn is still going strong, its big fireplace the focus of attention for breakfasts and late-afternoon hot-wine and cider gatherings. Each guest room has two double beds, cable TV, and a private bath. A sun deck and outdoor Jacuzzi hot tub are shared by everyone. Some kitchen units are available. Families are especially welcome.

WHERE TO DINE

THE BAKERY CAFE, Elk Ave. and Third St. Tel. 349-7280.
Cuisine: DELI. **Reservations:** Not accepted.
$ Prices: $2.70–$5. MC, V.
Open: Mid-June to Sept and Thanksgiving to early Apr, daily 7am–9pm; off-season, daily 7:30am–3:30pm.

Large picture windows and a sun room give this popular café a bright, spacious atmosphere. All food is made fresh daily, including savory pastries, creative deli-style sandwiches, soups, salads, and desserts. You can also fill up on pizza or a complete bakery selection. Espresso coffees and juices are always available.

KAROLINA'S KITCHEN, 127 Elk Ave. Tel. 349-6756.

Cuisine: AMERICAN. **Reservations:** Not accepted.
$ Prices: Appetizers $3–$7; main courses $4.50–$12. No credit cards.
Open: Daily 11:30am–10pm.

A former blacksmith's shop has been transformed into one of Crested Butte's most popular budget restaurants. Come for genuine home cooking like pork chops with applesauce, T-bone steak, Appalachian turkey melt sandwiches, chili, or fish-and-chips. There are blue-plate specials daily, and breakfasts are served until 4pm. At night, Karolina's preparations are served in the adjoining Kochevar's Saloon and Gaming Hall, a popular tavern that displays a roulette wheel and slot machine from the Butte's rowdier days.

LE BOSQUET, Elk Ave. and Second St. Tel. 349-5808.

Cuisine: FRENCH. **Reservations:** Recommended.
$ Prices: Dinner, appetizers $6.50–$9; main courses $11–$29; lunch $5–$8. AE, CB, DC, MC, V.
Open: Lunch Mon–Fri 11:30am–2pm, dinner daily 5:30–9pm. Call about spring-and-fall closures.

Green plants peek through the lace curtains of this popular garden-style restaurant, well known for its imaginative menu. Choices change weekly, but always include fresh seafood dishes and a chateaubriand. You might also find Colorado lamb shank, grilled duck breast, tournedos au Bosquet, hazelnut chicken, or any number of other hearty meals.

OSCAR'S BAR & CAFE, 229 Elk Ave. Tel. 349-6107.

Cuisine: INTERNATIONAL. **Reservations:** Accepted.
$ Prices: Appetizers $1.95–$7.50; main courses $4.95–$8.50 at lunch, $8.95–$16.95 at dinner. AE, MC, V.
Open: May 15–Oct, lunch daily 11:30am–4pm; dinner daily 5–10pm. Thanksgiving–Apr, lunch daily 11am–3pm; dinner daily 5–10pm. **Closed:** Early Oct to late Nov and early Apr to mid-May.

This old building has had more incarnations than Crested Butte itself: Once a bank, it was later a drugstore, then a funeral parlor, before taking shape as this popular family restaurant. Prime rib, hand-cut steaks, and half-pound hamburgers are specialties, but you can also find a choice of southwestern fare and pastas, as well as a handful of Asian and continental preparations. Kids have their own menu.

THE SLOGAR BAR & RESTAURANT, Second St. at Whiterock Ave. Tel. 349-5765.

Cuisine: AMERICAN. **Reservations:** Recommended.
$ Prices: Fixed-price dinner $10.95. MC, V.
Open: Dinner only, daily 5–9pm.

If you do something right, why mess around with anything else? That's the way the Slogar feels about its skillet-fried chicken. Bird highlights the fixed-price menu every night, accompanied by tangy coleslaw, mashed potatoes and gravy, biscuits with honey butter, creamed corn, and ice cream. Also offered is a family-style steak dinner, but most folks come for the chicken—it may be the best you've ever had! The atmosphere here, incidentally, is 1880s Victorian. The Slogar was the Slogar then, too, but nowhere near as elegant as it is today.

SOUPÇON, in the alley off Second St. between Elk and Maroon Aves. Tel. 349-5448.

Cuisine: CONTINENTAL. **Reservations:** Highly recommended.
$ Prices: Appetizers $7.50–$10; main courses $18–$24. AE, MC, V.
Open: Dinner only, daily 6–10pm.

This tiny log cabin with rough-hewn log benches, hidden in an alley behind Kochevar's Saloon, is hardly a place you'd expect to find candlelit, white-linen service and gourmet cuisine. But many big-city folks consider Soupçon to be Crested Butte's finest restaurant. In a casual, smoke-free atmosphere, diners pick their menu choices off a chalkboard that's changed nightly. You might start with scallops in caviar cream or duckling mousse, followed by a main dish of fresh swordfish with béarnaise sauce, roasted tenderloin of beef with green peppercorn sauce, or perhaps a colonial-style chicken curry. Desserts are sinful.

3. SALIDA

138 miles SW of Denver, 96 miles W of Pueblo, 82 miles N of Alamosa

GETTING THERE By Plane Small planes and charters can land at Harriet Alexander Airport (tel. 539-3720), 2 miles west of downtown off Monarch Avenue. The nearest airport with commercial service is at Gunnison, 65 miles west (see "Gunnison," above).

By Bus Coaches of Greyhound (toll free 800/528-6055) and TNM&O, 731 Blake St. (tel. 719/539-7474), serve Salida.

By Car U.S. 50 connects Salida with Grand Junction, 193 miles west on I-70, and Pueblo, 96 miles east on I-25. U.S. 285 runs north-south 5 miles west of Salida (through Poncha Springs); it extends northeast 138 miles to Denver, and south 255 miles to Santa Fe, N.Mex. Colo. 291 provides a vital 9-mile link through Salida, completing a triangle that ties the two U.S. highways together. About 23 miles north of Salida, and 2 miles south of Buena Vista, U.S. 24 branches north off U.S. 285, connecting Salida with I-70 at Vail, via Leadville.

SPECIAL EVENTS Annually, Salida sponsors the FIBArk Festival ("First in Boating on the Arkansas"), in mid-June; the Chaffee County Fair, in early August; and the River Rendezvous, the third week of September.

With a strategic location on the upper Arkansas River, near the headwaters of the Colorado River and Rio Grande tributaries, it was natural that Salida should become an important farming and transportation center for the central Rockies. Various Native Americans made it a part of their annual migration routes for millennia before Spanish explorers breached the wilderness in the early 18th century. Zebulon Pike opened the area for Americans 100 years later, and trappers and miners followed, the latter after the discovery of gold in 1859. When Leadville boomed on silver in the late 1870s, the Denver & Rio Grande Railway built a line up the Arkansas from Pueblo, and the town of Salida was founded at a key point on the line. The downtown core has kept its historic ambience alive to the present day. The railway no longer carries passengers, but it still operates up the Arkansas today as a freight line.

With the recreation boom of the past two decades, Salida and the neighboring community of Buena Vista, 25 miles north, have emerged as the white-water-rafting capitals of the Rockies. They're the principal centers of the **Arkansas Headwaters Recreation Area,** a 148-mile stretch of river from Leadville to Pueblo Reservoir. No fewer than 11 different rafting outfitters operate in the greater Salida area, and all have more business than they can handle during the May-to-September season.

Salida has a population of about 4,700 and an elevation of 7,036 feet.

ORIENTATION

INFORMATION Consult the Heart of the Rockies Chamber of Commerce, 406 W. Hwy. S., Salida, CO 81201 (tel. 719/539-2068).

TOWN LAYOUT Salida sits on the southwestern bank of the Arkansas River, just above its confluence with the South Arkansas. U.S. 50 (Rainbow Boulevard), which follows the north bank of the South Arkansas, marks the southern edge of the town. At the eastern city limit, Colo. 291 (Oak Street) turns north off U.S. 50, and six blocks later, turns northwest as First Street through the historic downtown area. Though the southeastern quadrant of the city is platted north-south, most of Salida is oriented at a 45° angle: lettered streets (A through O) run southwest-northeast, and numbered streets (First through 17th) run northwest-southeast. The heart of town is around First through Third Street, where they are intersected by D Street and E Street.

GETTING AROUND

Chaffee County Transit, 132 W. First St. (tel. 539-3935), provides low-cost **public transportation** throughout the Salida-Buena Vista-Monarch area. Call for schedules.

Ford **rental cars** are available at Salida Motors, 6250 U.S. 50 (tel. 539-6633).

FAST FACTS

The **area code** is 719. The **climate** ranges in temperature from an average July high of 84° to an average January low of 12°. In case of **emergency,** call 911, or contact the Chaffee County Sheriff, Crestone Avenue off Third Street (tel. 539-2596). Health care is provided by the **Heart of the Rockies Regional Medical Center,** 448 E. First St. (tel. 539-6661). The main **post office** is at 310 D St. (tel. 539-2548). For **road conditions,** call 539-6688.

WHAT TO SEE & DO
ATTRACTIONS

THE ANGEL OF SHAVANO, Mount Shavano, 15 miles west of Salida on the Continental Divide.

In May and early June, this unusual feature is easily discerned on the slopes of 14,239-foot Mount Shavano. Created by spring snow lingering in open meadows, it resembles a woman, her arms outstretched, guarding the Arkansas Valley below her. Native American legend says her body melts away to nourish arid farmlands in the summer months, only to reappear the following spring.

MONARCH AERIAL TRAMWAY, Monarch Pass, U.S. 50, 22 miles west of Salida. Tel. 539-4789.

Open in summer only, this scenic tramway climbs from 11,312-foot Monarch Pass to the Continental Divide Observatory at an altitude of 11,921 feet, where there is a spectacular 360° view of the southern Colorado Rockies. When visibility is perfect, you can see for about 75 miles in any direction. The tram consists of six four-passenger gondolas.

Admission: $5 adults, $2.50 children.
Open: May 15–Oct 15, daily 9am–4pm.

SALIDA HOT SPRINGS, 410 W. Rainbow Blvd. Tel. 539-6738.

Colorado's largest indoor hot springs have been in commercial operation since 1937, when the Works Progress Administration built the pools as a depression-era project. Ute tribes considered the mineral waters, rich in bicarbonate, sodium, and sulphate, to be sacred and medicinal. Today, a lap pool is kept at 90°, shallow pool between 100 to 102°, and wading pool between 96 to 98° year-round; European style private hot baths, at 114 to 120°, are also available. In adjacent Centennial Park are tennis-and-volleyball courts and other recreational facilities.

Admission: $4 adults, $2 students 6–17, $1 children 5 and under, $1.50 seniors (60 and older).
Open: Memorial Day–Labor Day, daily 1–9pm (noon–1pm is adult lap swimming); Labor Day–Memorial Day, Tues–Fri 4–9pm, Fri–Sun 1:30–9pm.

SPORTS & RECREATION

BICYCLING The Colorado Cyclery, 111 N. E St. (tel. 539-BIKE), has information on bicycling throughout the region. The shop itself specializes in custom work and unusual bicycles. For rentals try the Pedal Pusher, 513 E. Rainbow Blvd. (tel. 539-7498).

FISHING The Arkansas River is considered by many as the finest fishing river in Colorado. There's also trout fishing in numerous alpine lakes, including Cottonwood Lake, Twin Lakes, Rainbow Lake, and O'Haver Lake.

GOLF The Salida Golf Club, an 18-hole, par-70 municipal course at Crestone

Avenue and Grant Street (tel. 539-6373), and the Collegiate Golf Course, an 18-hole, par-72 course at 28775 Fairway Dr., Buena Vista (tel. 395-8189), are popular among Chaffee County residents and visitors.

HIKING There are outstanding trails for all experience levels throughout the region, particularly in the San Isabel National Forest, along the eastern slope of the Continental Divide west of Salida. Of particular interest are hikes into the Collegiate Range (Mounts Harvard, Columbia, Yale, Princeton, and Oxford) off the Cottonwood Creek road west of Buena Vista, and trips from the ghost town of St. Elmo up the Chalk Creek road from Mount Princeton Hot Springs.

For maps and other information, visit the offices of the U.S. Forest Service, 325 W. Rainbow Blvd., Salida (tel. 539-3591).

RIVER RAFTING As previously mentioned, this region is the white-water-rafting center of the Rockies. The biggest reason is the ✪ Arkansas Headwaters Recreation Area, with headquarters on Colo. 291 (P.O. Box 126, Salida, CO 81201; tel. 539-7289). The recreation area has created 14 new sites along the river—4 of them above Salida, 10 below—offering everything from raft and kayak access to fishing, hiking, camping, and picnicking. The busiest stretch of the river is Browns Canyon, a pink-granite wilderness between Buena Vista and Salida, with Class III to IV rapids focused on an 8-mile stretch from Nathrop to Hecla Junction.

For a full listing of all rafting companies operating in the Chaffee County area, check with the Heart of the Rockies Chamber of Commerce. Leading outfitters include Canyon Marine, 129 W. Rainbow Blvd., Salida (tel. 539-7476 or toll free 800/643-0707); Dvorak's Kayak & Rafting Expeditions, 17921 U.S. 285, Nathrop (tel. 539-6851 or toll free 800/824-3795); Moondance River Expeditions, Ltd., 310 W. First St., Salida (tel. 539-2113); Rocky Mountain Outdoor, 10281 Hwy. 50, Howard (tel. 942-3214 or toll free 800/255-5784); and Wilderness Aware, P.O. Box 1550, Buena Vista, CO 81211 (tel. 395-2112 or toll free 800/462-7238). Half-day excursions can run as low as $26 per person.

ROCKHOUNDING The richest mineral-and-gem beds in Colorado are found in the upper Arkansas River valley and the eastern slope of the Continental Divide, just west of Salida. For information, contact the Columbine Gem and Mineral Society, 525 W. 16th St., Salida (tel. 539-6196).

SKIING The Monarch Ski Resort, 20 miles west of Salida at Monarch Pass on U.S. 50, is among the finest of Colorado's smaller ski areas. It not only serves all levels of skiers, but also boasts the 100-room overnight Monarch Mountain Lodge (with very moderate prices) and family-priced restaurant. For information on either, write 1 Powder Place, Monarch, CO 81227 (tel. 719/539-2581 or toll free 800/332-3668).

Monarch's four chair lifts serve distinctly different areas. The short Tumbelina Lift is ideal for beginners and early intermediates. The Breeze Way Lift serves predominantly intermediate terrain. The Garfield Lift is popular among advanced skiers, who can tango down the Kanonen and Cleanzer runs, but the long, winding Sleepy Hollow and Roundabout trails are ideal for novices. Less adept skiers can also take the Panorama Lift to the mountaintop and return to the bottom via Ticaboo or Sky Walker, but head-wall runs like High Anxiety appeal to experts, and a recent expansion has added 30 acres of upper-level glade and powder skiing in the Curecanti Bowl.

All-day tickets cost $27 for adults, $16 for juniors (age 7 to 12) and seniors (age 62 to 69), with discounts for multiday tickets and free skiing for all those under 7 or over 69. Group ski lessons cost $25. The area is open from Thanksgiving to early April, daily from 9am to 4pm.

WHERE TO STAY

ASPEN LEAF LODGE, 7350 W. U.S. 50, Salida, CO 81201. Tel. 719/ 539-6733 or toll free 800/759-0338. 17 rms (all with bath). A/C TV TEL

$ Rates: June to mid Sept and holiday, $44.50–$50.50; spring and fall, $26.50–$44.50. AE, CB, DC, DISC, MC, V.

A central park strip with paths through a forest of small evergreens and aspens, focused around a hot-tub pavilion, gives this small budget motel a friendly feel right from the start. Besides, coffee is always on in the office in the morning. Single rooms have a king-size bed, desk with a phone, nightstand, table and chairs, and large bathroom. Doubles are more spacious, and contain two queen-size beds. No-smoking rooms are available.

THE POOR FARM COUNTRY INN, 8495 County Rd. 160, Salida, CO 81201. Tel. 719/539-3818. 5 rms (2 with bath), 14 dormitory beds (shared bath).

$ Rates (including full breakfast): $45 single or double without bath, $55 single or double with bath. Children under 5 stay free in parents' room. JCB, MC, V.

Built by Chaffee County in 1892 as a home for the indigent, this building—about 2 miles northwest of town—served that purpose for half a century. Since 1983, however, it has been a charming bed-and-breakfast, and is listed on the National Register of Historic Places. The grounds cover 11 acres, including a quarter-mile stretch along the Arkansas River, as well as a fishing pond and play area for children. The downstairs contains a TV and games parlor with a piano, a large dining room, and an open kitchen. Guest rooms, appointed in country-style floral decor, are furnished with turn-of-the-century antiques. Two rooms have private baths; three rooms share two baths. A dormitory loft sleeps another 14.

RED WOOD LODGE, 7310 U.S. 50, Salida, CO 81201. Tel. 719/539-2528 or toll free 800/234-1077. 25 rms, 3 suites. A/C TV TEL

$ Rates: May 15–Sept 15 and holiday periods, $48–$58 single; $58–$70 double or suite. Other times, $42–$44 single; $44–$58 double, $52–$58 suite. AE, CB, DC, DISC, MC, V.

Red cedar is used throughout this very nice property, from construction to custom furnishings to the two outdoor hot tubs. Every room is different, but each typically has king-size or queen-size beds, original artwork on the walls, a desk with phone, a TV on a credenza or tucked away in an armoire, pedestal sinks, clock radios, and other touches. Family suites have two full bedrooms, each with its own remote-control TV and phone. No-smoking rooms and facilities for the disabled are available; complimentary coffee and newspaper are offered in the lobby each morning. Besides the hot tubs, there's a heated outdoor pool, and a changing room, also heated, for those cold winter nights.

WHERE TO DINE

COUNTRY BOUNTY RESTAURANT & GIFT SHOPPE, 413 W. Rainbow Blvd. (U.S. 50). Tel. 539-3546.

   Cuisine: AMERICAN/MEXICAN. **Reservations:** Not accepted.

$ Prices: Breakfast $2.25–$6.75; lunch $3.25–$7.95; dinner $6.95–$11.95. DISC, MC, V.

   Open: Daily 6am–9pm.

It's hard to determine if this is more a gift shop than a restaurant or vice versa. Each seems to pervade the other, with all manner of country-style crafts, southwestern Native American jewelry, books, postcards, and more items on display almost spilling over into the dining booths. The fare on the menu is equally traditional: hotcakes, Denver omelets, and ham and eggs for breakfast; cheeseburgers, hot turkey sandwiches, a variety of salads, and homemade soups for lunch; chicken-fried steak, pork chops, chicken, and Rocky Mountain trout for dinner. There's also a Mexican menu and a variety of salads, along with locally famous pies for dessert. A children's menu is priced $2.65 to $3.50.

FIRST ST. CAFE, 137 E. First St. Tel. 539-4759.

   Cuisine: AMERICAN. **Reservations:** Not accepted.

$ Prices: Breakfast $1.25–$5.95; lunch $2.95–$8.95; dinner $6.25–$17.95. AE, DISC, MC, V.

   Open: May 15–Sept, Mon–Sat 8am–10pm, Sun 11am–4pm; Oct–May 14, Mon–Sat 8am–8pm.

A brick building dating from 1883, in the heart of historic downtown Salida, is the home of one of the city's most popular restaurants. The hardwood floor and many tables were once part of the stage at the Red Rocks Amphitheater west of Denver; less historic are the regional paintings and photographs on the walls, which give the café a gallery feel. Indeed, the establishment is a focal point for the artists, musicians, and social activists of the central Rockies. The kitchen turns out gourmet home cooking; meals such as french toast, stuffed with cream cheese and walnuts, for breakfast; vegetarian casseroles and Monte Cristo sandwiches for lunch; steak Gardenier, barbecued ribs, and halibut filets for dinner. There are daily specials, and beer and wine.

---

4. ALAMOSA

216 miles SW of Denver; 149 miles E of Durango;
173 miles N of Santa Fe, N. Mex.

GETTING THERE **By Plane** The Alamosa Municipal Airport, 3 miles off U.S. 285 South (tel. 589-6444), has daily service to and from Denver via United Express (tel. 719/589-9446).

By Bus SLV Van Lines, 8480 Stockton St. (tel. 719/589-4948), connects Alamosa with TNM&O lines at Walsenburg.

By Car Alamosa is at the junction of U.S. 160, which runs east 73 miles to I-25 at Walsenburg and west to Durango and beyond; and U.S. 285, which extends south to Santa Fe, N. Mex., and north to Denver via Monte Vista and the upper Arkansas River valley. Because of a jog in U.S. 285, however, a more direct route into the city from the north is to take Colo. 17 the last 50 miles.

SPECIAL EVENTS Annual area events include Cabin Fever Daze, in mid-February, in Creede; the Crane Festival, in mid-March, in Monte Vista; the Rendezvous of Cultures in Fort Garland on Memorial Day weekend; the Sunshine Festival, on the first weekend of June, in Cole Park, Alamosa; the Sunshine Festival, and the Pro Rodeo, Dance and Parade, in June, in Alamosa; the Colorado State Mining Championships, on the Fourth of July weekend, in Creede; Fiesta Days, on the last weekend of July, in San Luis; and Covered Wagon Days, on the first weekend of August, in Del Norte.

Founded in 1878 with the extension of the Denver & Rio Grande Railroad into the San Luis Valley, the town was named for the cottonwood (*alamosa*) trees that lined the banks of the Rio Grande. Soon rails spread out in all directions from the community, and it became a thriving transportation center for farmers and supply depot for miners. Today, with a population of about 7,500, Alamosa remains a center for farming, especially of vegetables. It is also the tourism hub for south-central Colorado, and an educational center: Adams State College, a 4-year institution, was founded here in 1921.

ORIENTATION

INFORMATION The Alamosa County Chamber of Commerce, Cole Park (Chamber Drive at Third Street), Alamosa, CO 81101 (tel. 719/589-3681 or toll free 800/BLU-SKYS), can provide information on the entire six-county San Luis Valley region.

TOWN LAYOUT Located on the southwestern bank of the Rio Grande River, Alamosa is the center of the San Luis Valley—a vast basin, 7,500 feet in elevation, surrounded on the west by the San Juan Mountains and on the east by the sharp-ridged Sangre de Cristo Range. As you enter by car from the east, U.S. 160

crosses a bridge over the Rio Grande; immediately ahead, on Fourth Street at Chamber Drive, are the city hall, police station, and chamber of commerce office. The arterial, however, runs south a block, then extends west as Main Street. Two blocks farther, Main is crossed by State Avenue, the principal north-south byway. Another six blocks ahead is the intersection of West Avenue, which runs south as U.S. 285. U.S. 160 continues in a northwesterly direction. First Street, four blocks north of Main, bisects the campus of Adams State College on the west side of town; numbered streets parallel First all the way south through 20th Street.

FAST FACTS

The **area code** is 719. The **climate** averages in temperature from about 65°F in summer to 0°F in winter. In case of **emergency,** call 589-5807, or contact the Colorado State Patrol (tel. 589-2939). **San Luis Valley Regional Medical Center** is at 106 Blanca St., at First Street (tel. 589-2511). The **post office** is at 505 Third St., just off State Avenue (tel. 589-4908). Local **sales tax** is 7%.

WHAT TO SEE & DO

ATTRACTIONS

GREAT SAND DUNES NATIONAL MONUMENT, Colo. 150, 38 miles northeast of Alamosa (Mosca, CO 81146). Tel. 719/378-2312.

One of the most startling sights in North America is this 39-square-mile expanse of sand, piled nearly 700 feet high against the western edge of the Sangre de Cristo Mountains. The tallest sand dunes on the continent, they seem totally incongruous in this location, far from any sea or major desert. Explore them on foot: Although the surrounding mountain ranges are within view, it's easy to feel as if you are in the middle of nowhere.

The dunes were formed over thousands of years by winds blowing southwesterly across the San Luis Valley. They began forming at the end of the last Ice Age, when streams of water from melting glaciers carried rocks, gravel, and silt down from the mountains into the valley. In addition, as the Rio Grande changed its course, it left behind sand, silt, and debris. Even today the winds are changing the face of the dunes, returning to the monument the sands that Medano Creek takes from the dunes' leading edge and carries into the valley.

So-called "reversing winds" from the mountains pile the dunes back upon themselves, building them higher and higher. Though it's physically impossible for sand to be piled steeper than 34°, they often seem more sheer because of deceptive shadows and colors that change with the light: gold, pink, tan, sometimes even bluish. Climbing dunes is fun, but it can be tiring at this 8,200 foot altitude. The sand can get as hot as 140°F in summer, so visitors must wear shoes to protect their feet.

Among the specialized animals that survive in this weird environment are the Ord kangaroo rat, a creature that never drinks water; and two insects found nowhere else on earth, the Great Sand Dunes tiger beetle and one type of darkling beetle. These animals and the flora of the adjacent mountain foothills are discussed in evening programs and guided walks during the summer season. Pinyon Flats Campground is open year-round.

From Alamosa, there are two main routes to the national monument: east 14 miles on U.S. 160, then north on Colo. 150; or north 14 miles on Colo. 17 to Mosca, then east on Six Mile Lane to the junction of Colo. 150.

Admission: $4 per car.

Open: Monument, daily 24 hours. Visitor center, Memorial Day–Labor Day, daily 8am–7pm; the rest of the year, daily 8am–5pm, except winter holidays.

ADAMS STATE COLLEGE MUSEUM, Richardson and Third Sts. Tel. 589-7121.

The **Luther E. Bean Museum,** on the second floor of Richardson Hall, has one of the Southwest's most complete collections of Hispanic *santos* (carved or painted images of saints), plus Anasazi artifacts, Rio Grande weavings, western art, and a priceless collection of European porcelains and furniture.

Admission: Free.
Open: Mon–Fri 1–4:30pm.

ALAMOSA–MONTE VISTA NATIONAL WILDLIFE REFUGE COMPLEX, El Rancho Lane, 6 miles southeast of Alamosa (9383 El Rancho Lane, Alamosa, CO 81101). Tel. 589-4021.

At a time when wetlands conservation is a leading cause of environmentalists, these refuges have conserved nearly 25,000 acres of vital land for a variety of marsh birds and waterfowl, including many migrating-and-wintering species. Sandhill and whooping cranes visit in October and March; at other times of the year there may be egrets, herons, avocets, bitterns, and other avian species. A wide variety of ducks are year-round residents. Check at the refuge office about the hiking-and-biking trails. The Alamosa unit, east of Alamosa via U.S. 160, straddles the Rio Grande and is the site of the refuge office; there's excellent wildlife viewing from the Bluff Overlook Road. The Monte Vista unit, 6 miles south of Monte Vista (22 miles west of Alamosa) off Colo. 15, has an auto tour.

Admission: Free.
Open: Refuge, daily sunrise–sunset; refuge office, Mon–Fri 7:30am–4pm.

FIREDWORKS GALLERY, 608 Main St. Tel. 589-6064.

The works of local artists are on display here. You'll find pottery, jewelry, art photography, weavings, handmade note cards, sculpture, candles, and furniture.

Admission: Free.
Open: Mon–Sat 10am–6pm.

SAN LUIS VALLEY ALLIGATOR FARM, Two Mile Creek. Tel. 589-3032.

Geothermal wells keep the temperature at a cozy 87° at this alligator farm and wildlife habitat, located 18 miles north of Alamosa off Colo. Highway 17.

Admission: $2 adults, $1.50 children 6–12, free children under 6 and adults over 80.
Open: Daily 9am–5pm.

SPORTS & RECREATION

BICYCLING   Rentals, repairs, and full information on mountain biking in the San Luis Valley can be obtained from Kristi Mountain Sports, Villa Mall, U.S. 160 (tel. 589-9759).

FISHING   The Rio Grande is an outstanding stream for trout, walleye, and catfish, and there are numerous reservoirs around the San Luis Valley. For licenses, tackle, and advice, visit Spencer Sporting Goods, 616 Main St. (tel. 589-4361), or Alamosa Sporting Goods, 1114 Main St. (tel. 589-3006).

GOLF   The Cattails Golf Club, on Country Club Circle off State Avenue (tel. 589-9515), is an 18-hole, par 72, course on the north side of Alamosa. The Great Sand Dunes Country Club, at Zapata Ranch, 5303 Colo. 150 (tel. 378-2356), is a championship 18-hole course, 26 miles northeast of Alamosa. There are two 9-hole courses in the San Luis Valley: the Monte Vista Golf Course, Monte Vista (tel. 852-4906), 17 miles west of Alamosa, and the Los Cumbres Golf Course, Crestone (tel. 256-4856), 50 miles northeast of Alamosa.

HIKING   The best opportunities in the region are found in the surrounding Rio Grande National Forest, with district offices at 1803 W. U.S. 160, Monte Vista (tel. 852-5941). One of the most popular hikes with easy access is Zapata Falls, reached off Colo. 150 about 20 miles northeast of Alamosa. This cavernous waterfall on the northwest flank of 14,345-foot Mount Blanca freezes in the winter, turning its cave into a natural icebox that often remains so past July 4. You can also reach it by car, ask for directions at the forest service office.

HUNTING   The national forest and surrounding public lands welcome hunters seeking deer and elk, upland game birds and waterfowl. Many enjoy stays at Mt. Blanca Game Bird & Trout, Inc., P.O. Box 236, Blanca, CO 81123 (tel. 719/379-

DUCK). This full-board lodge, reached by traveling 21 miles east from Alamosa on U.S. 160 and southwest about 5 miles on well-marked county roads, requires no license for guided bird hunting and fishing from February to December. Half-day expeditions for upland game and waterfowl start at $125, with other packages available that include lodging and meals. Trout fishing is offered in two fully stocked lakes at $45 for a full day, catch and release. Sporting clays target shooting is available on a 10-station course, with rounds starting at $20 for 50 targets. Rod-and-gun rentals and sales are also available. Rooms run $68, double occupancy, with three full meals an additional $29 per person.

SWIMMING Splashland Hot Springs, Colo. 17 (tel. 589-6307 summer, 589-5772 winter), 1½ miles north of Alamosa, has a geothermally heated outdoor pool and wading pool; it's open Memorial Day to Labor Day, Thursday through Tuesday.

WHERE TO STAY

ALAMOSA LAMPLIGHTER MOTEL, 425 Main St., Alamosa, CO 81101. Tel. 719/589-6636 or 800/359-2138. Fax 719/589-3831. 70 rms (all with bath). A/C TV TEL

$ Rates: May–Labor Day, $38–$48 single; $42–$54 double. Early Sept to Apr. $32–$42 single; $36–$48 double. AE, CB, DC, DISC, MC, V.

This downtown motel actually consists of two separate properties: the original building and an annex four blocks west. Guest rooms have queen-size or double beds, with a desk, table and chairs, and vanity outside the bathroom area. No-smoking rooms are available. There's shuttle service to the Alamosa Airport, and valet laundry service at the desk. The motel has an indoor swimming pool and sauna, as well as a Jacuzzi at the annex. The restaurant is open from 6am to 9pm, serving standard American cuisine.

BEST WESTERN ALAMOSA INN, 1919 Main St., Alamosa, CO 81101. Tel. 719/589-2567 or toll free 800/528-1234. Fax 719/528-0767. 119 rms, 2 suites (all with bath). AC TV TEL

$ Rates: $50–$80 single or double; $100–$150 suite. Slightly lower in winter. AE, CB, DC, DISC, ER, MC, V.

This comfortable, modern motel has clean, quiet rooms along with an enclosed pool you can swim in year-round and a restaurant (see "Where to Dine," below) open from 6am to 9pm. Most rooms have two double beds, and there are some kings and queens. The motel has cable TV with HBO and nonsmoking rooms are available. Small pets are welcome.

THE COTTONWOOD INN, 123 San Juan Ave., Alamosa, CO 81101. Tel. 719/589-3882. 5 rms (3 with bath).

$ Rates (including breakfast): $52–$71 single; $56–$75 double. MC, V.

This 1908 bungalow, three blocks north of Main Street, has a distinct arts-and-crafts orientation. Julie Mordecai has decorated the common areas and guest bedrooms as a gallery of regional art, much of which is for sale. Each room is a little bit different: The Rosa Room, for instance, has queen-size and single beds to accommodate small families, along with children's books and stuffed animals. The Blanca Room weds southwestern decor with art-deco motifs, while the Verde Room features old prints and a hand-loomed coverlet. A television and video library are located in the living room. They've redecorated the apartment suites in the neighboring bungalow: Sarah's Suite and the Pueblo Suite. Smoking is not permitted in any of the units.

GREAT SAND DUNES COUNTRY CLUB & INN, Zapata Ranch, 5303 Colo. 150, Mosca, CO 81146. Tel. 719/378-2356 or toll free 800/284-9213. Fax 719/378-2428. 14 rms, 1 suite (all with bath).

$ Rates (including breakfast): May–Labor Day, $170 single or double; $210 suite. Labor Day–Oct. $130 single or double; $160 suite. AE, DISC, MC, V. **Closed:** Nov–Apr.

Beautiful cottonwood trees surround and shade this lovely resort, which occupies the grounds of a former cattle ranch established by Spanish land grant in the early 19th century. The cattle aren't there anymore, but buffalo are raised on the ranch, and mule deer frequently browse the fairways of the 18-hole championship golf course. Guest rooms are intentionally rustic, with furnishings made by hand right on the ranch; but private baths, individually controlled heating, and quilted comforters take much of the raw edge off. This is a getaway spot: There's no smoking in the rooms, and the only phone is one shared by all guests. A gourmet restaurant specializes in "harvest cooking," emphasizing local San Luis Valley produce and products, with lunches priced at $6 to $7 and dinner dishes running $11 to $17. Besides the golf course, facilities include a swimming pool, sauna and Jacuzzi, exercise-and-massage room, and horseback-riding stables.

The inn is located 26 miles northeast of Alamosa: Take U.S. 160 14 miles east; turn north on Colo. 150 as if going to Grand Sand Dunes National Monument. Then 4 miles before the monument gate, turn onto a gravel road (signposted ZAPATA RANCH) and proceed three quarters of a mile to the inn.

WHERE TO DINE

BEST WESTERN ALAMOSA INN RESTAURANT, 1919 Main St. Tel. 589-2567.
   Cuisine: AMERICAN. **Reservations:** Not required.
$ **Prices:** Breakfast $2–$6.50; lunch $3.50–$6.50; dinner $5–$16. AE, CB, DC, DISC, ER, MC, V.
   Open: Daily 6am–9pm.

This restaurant features a wide variety of basic American dishes plus some Mexican items. A house specialty is the half-pound burger on an onion roll, and there are nightly specials such as prime rib or fresh seafood Fridays and Saturdays. Children's and senior citizen's menus are offered.

LARA'S SOFT-SPOKEN RESTAURANT, 801 State Ave. Tel. 589-6769.
   Cuisine: MEXICAN/ITALIAN/AMERICAN. **Reservations:** Not necessary.
$ **Prices:** Appetizers $2.25–$3.25; main courses $2.50–$6 at lunch, $3.95–$12.50 at dinner. Breakfast (summer only) $2–$6. No credit cards.
   Open: Mon–Sat 11am–8pm. In the summer they open for breakfast at 7am.
As the name would suggest, the decor here is subdued and simple: white plastic chairs at wooden tables, local artwork on the walls, classical music piped through. The food, however, is worth shouting about. The Mexican American dishes are particularly good, including chicken-breast quesadilla and steak-and-enchilada combination plate. Mark and Marian Lara serve a wide-ranging menu of steaks and ribs, crab legs and baked fish, Italian pastas, chicken parmesan, and standard Mexican favorites such as enchiladas, burritos, and fajitas.

OSCAR'S RESTAURANT, 710 Main St. Tel. 589-9230.
   Cuisine: MEXICAN/AMERICAN. **Reservations:** Not required.
$ **Prices:** $3.50–$9. MC, V.
   Open: Summer, Tues–Sun 11am–9pm; winter, Tues–Sun 11am–8pm.
Locals say this is the place to come for Mexican food, particularly the fajitas and carne adovada. The large dining room looks like a Mexican restaurant should, very Southwest, with rough plaster and chile ristras hanging on the walls. In addition to more than three dozen Mexican dishes and numerous side orders, Oscar's offers several steaks, shrimp, hamburgers, and sandwiches.

ST. IVES PUB & EATERY, 719 Main St. Tel. 589-0711.
   Cuisine: DELI. **Reservations:** Not accepted.
$ **Prices:** Appetizers $2.35–$4.95; lunch/dinner $2.75–$6.95. MC, V.
   Open: Mon–Sat 11am–midnight.

You'll find the "eatery" in front, with plants hanging above green-cloaked tables and big windows gazing upon pedestrians on Main Street; the "pub" in the rear, with a jukebox, sports TV, and simple wooden tables. The fare focuses on New York deli sandwiches, like the Reuben and the Empire State: roast beef, ham, turkey, corned beef, Swiss cheese, and coleslaw wedged between three slices of rye bread. Soups, salads, and hamburgers satisfy most other visitors.

TRUE GRITS STEAK HOUSE, 100 Santa Fe Ave. Tel. 589-9954.
   Cuisine: STEAK/SEAFOOD. **Reservations:** Recommended summer nights.
$ Prices: Appetizers $1.50–$4.50; main courses $6–$16; lunch $3.95–$5.95.
DISC, MC, V.
   Open: Daily 11am–10pm.

Actor John Wayne is, beyond question, the star of this popular local restaurant just off U.S. 160 on the east side of the Rio Grande bridge. A movie poster of his Oscar-winning *True Grit* greets visitors near the entrance, while various photos and paintings of the Duke are interspersed with contemporary western decor elsewhere in the restaurant. Most folks come here for the mesquite-grilled steaks, like the Big Jake (a 20-ounce sirloin) or the Sons of Katy Elder (a tender filet mignon). You can also order a Rio Lobo (jumbo fantail shrimp) or other movies, *er,* meals by name. There's a children's menu and a large soup-and-salad bar, as well as a full lounge.

EASY EXCURSIONS

Each of the other counties (besides Alamosa County) that make up the San Luis Valley has interesting attractions of its own.

SAN LUIS

In the heart of Costilla County lies **San Luis,** the oldest town in Colorado. Located 42 miles southeast of Alamosa via U.S. 160 east and Colo. 159 south, the community (pop. 850) was founded in 1851 by Hispanic settlers moving north from Taos, N. Mex. Today the Spanish influence is still strong in the area. For information, contact the Sangre de Cristo Chamber of Commerce, P.O. Box 9, San Luis, CO 81152 (tel. 672-3355).

   A leading attraction is the **Shrine of the Stations of the Cross,** consisting of 15 Huberto Maestas bronzes that recount the story of Christ's death and resurrection, along a three-quarter-mile trail that winds around a hillside in the center of town. Also in San Luis are the **Sangre de Cristo Church** (Church of the Most Precious Blood), on Church Place, in continuous use as a place of worship since the early 1860s; the **San Luis Museum, Cultural and Commercial Center,** 402 Church Place (tel. 672-3611), with memorabilia of the area's rich Hispanic heritage; and the **Centro Artesano,** 512 Church Place (tel. 672-4223), a cooperative venture of some 70 San Luis Valley artisans.

   Sixteen miles north of San Luis and 26 miles east of Alamosa, on Colo. 159 just south of its junction with U.S. 160, is **Fort Garland State Museum** (tel. 719/379-3512), a re-creation of the 1858 fort that protected settlers in the San Luis Valley from attacks by Indians and outlaws for 25 years. Col. Kit Carson was among the commandants of the fort, which consists of six flat-roofed adobe buildings. Exhibits portray life at the frontier post. There's also a visitor center, a bookstore, and souvenir shop. From April to October the complex is open daily 9am to 5pm; the rest of the year it's open Thursday to Monday 8am to 4pm. Call for admission fees.

WHERE TO STAY & DINE The Centro Artesan in San Luis is a part of **El Convento Bed and Breakfast,** 512 Church Place, San Luis, CO 81152 (tel. 672-4223). Built as a school in 1905, it now houses four handsome guest rooms with handcrafted furnishings and southwestern motifs. Rates, including breakfast, are $50 first person, $10 each additional person, $5 for children under 12. Good Mexican food is available at Emma's Hacienda, Main Street (tel. 672-9902).

ANTONITO

South from Alamosa, U.S. 285 cuts a nearly straight line through the heart of Conejos County. The best-known attraction in this part of the state is the ✪ **Cumbres & Toltec Scenic Railroad,** P.O. Box 668, Antonito, CO 81120 (tel. 376-5483). The depot is 28 miles south of Alamosa, just off the highway. Built in 1880 to serve remote mining camps, the train follows a spectacular 64-mile narrow-gauge track through the San Juan Mountains from Antonito (pop. 875, elevation 7888 ft.) to Chama, N. Mex., and is considered the finest remaining example of a once-vast Rocky Mountain rail network. The *Colorado Limited* weaves through groves of pine and aspen, and past strange rock formations, before ascending through the spectacular Toltec Gorge of the Los Piños River. At the rail junction community of Osier, passengers picnic or have a catered lunch while the *Limited* stops to change engines with the *New Mexico Express.* Then round-trip passengers return to their starting point in Antonito, while onward passengers continue a climb through tunnels and trestles to the summit of 10,015-foot Cumbres Pass, then drop down a precipitous 4% grade to Chama.

A through trip from Antonito to Chama (or vice versa), traveling one-way by van, runs $50 for adults, $26 for children 11 and under. A regular round-trip, without transfers, is $32 adults, $16 children 11 and under, but this omits either the gorge or the pass. Either way, it's an all-day adventure, leaving between 8 and 10:30am, and returning between 4:30 and 6:30pm. Write or phone ahead for reservations: The train operates daily from Memorial Day weekend to mid-October. Jointly owned by the states of Colorado and New Mexico, it's a registered National Historic Site.

In the nearby community of Conejos is **Our Lady of Guadalupe Church,** the oldest church in the state of Colorado, built in the late 1850s.

MANASSA

Seven miles north of Antonito on the highway back toward Alamosa, and 3 miles east on Colo. 142, is the village of Manassa (pop. 950), best known as the hometown of heavyweight boxing great Jack Dempsey. The former world champion (1919–26) was born here in 1895 and began his fighting career at the age of 14, earning $1 a bout in mining camps. He went on to international acclaim and was an elder statesman of the sport until his death in 1983. The **Jack Dempsey Museum,** on Main Street in the town park across from Town Hall (tel. 843-5207), open from Memorial Day to Labor Day, Monday through Saturday from 9am to 5pm, has many photographs and memorabilia of Dempsey and his family.

CREEDE

Another 17 miles beyond Del Norte (48 miles west of Alamosa), Colo. 149 forks north off U.S. 160 at South Fork and follows the Rio Grande nearly to its source in the San Juan Mountains. It's 23 miles from the junction to ✪ **Creede** (pop. 600, elevation 8,852 ft.), one of the best preserved of all 19th-century Colorado silver-mining towns. Founded in 1889, it had a population of 10,000 by 1892, when a balladeer wrote, "It's day all day in the daytime, and there is no night in Creede." Over $1 million in silver was mined *every day.* But the Silver Panic of 1893 eclipsed Creede's rising star. For most of the next century area mines produced just enough silver and other minerals to sustain the community, until the 1960s when tourism and outdoor recreation became paramount.

WHAT TO SEE & DO The former Denver & Rio Grande Railroad depot is now the **Creede Museum,** behind City Park, which tells the story of the town's wild-and-woolly heyday. There were dozens of saloons and gambling tables, and shootouts were not uncommon: Bob Ford, the killer of Jesse James, was murdered in his own saloon. Bat Masterson and "Poker Alice" Tubbs were other notorious early residents. Photographs and exhibits on gambling and other activities are among the museum's collection. It's open Memorial Day to Labor Day, Monday through Saturday from 10am to 4pm; off-season, by appointment.

You can obtain a walking-tour map of historic Creede from the **Creede–Mineral County Chamber of Commerce,** north of the county courthouse at the north end of Main Street (P.O. Box 580), Creede, CO 81130 (tel. 658-2374 or toll free 800/327-2102). The chamber will also give intrepid travelers directions to the **Wheeler Geologic Area,** a region of volcanic rock formations accessible only by Jeep, horseback, or 5-hour hike; and **North Creede Canyon,** where remnants of the old town of Creede still stand near the **Commodore Mine,** whose workings seem to keep a ghostly vigil over the canyon. Don't miss the **Creede Firehouse,** hewn out of solid rock; tours are offered, Monday through Friday, in summer (tel. 658-2374). Next to the firehouse, the **Underground Mining Museum** (tel.

658-2374) takes visitors on a winding trip through a 250-foot tunnel inside a mountain, as they explore the history of mining. Open seven days a week; call for hours and admission fees.

The 17-mile ✪ **Bachelor Historic Tour** is described in a booklet available from the Chamber of Commerce for $1. The route follows a U.S. Forest Service road through the mountains past abandoned mines, mining equipment, the original Creede cemetery, and 19th-century town sites. The road is fine for passenger cars in dry weather, but may be closed by winter snow.

Of special interest is the ✪ **Creede Repertory Theatre,** P.O. Box 269, Creede, CO 81130 (tel. 658-2540), established in 1966 by a small troupe of young actors from the University of Kansas. Now a nationally acclaimed repertory company, it will celebrate its 29th year in 1994, with performances from mid-June through Labor Day in its theater on Creede Avenue at North First Street. Tickets for most performances run $10 to $12.

WHERE TO STAY & DINE Next door to the Rep Theatre is the **Creede Hotel & Restaurant,** Creede Avenue, Creede, CO 81130 (tel. 658-2608). A bed-and-breakfast establishment, open May to October, it has four rooms, each with private bath, priced at $59 to $69 double, $10 for each additional person; full breakfast included. Reservations are suggested for the gourmet dinners served here.

Outside of Creede, the **Wason Ranch,** excellent for hunting and fishing, 2 miles southeast on Colo. 149 (P.O. Box 220, Creede, CO 81130; tel. 658-2413), has modern, two-bedroom log cabins available for $45 per day, for up to four people. Three bedroom riverside cottages are available for $115.

LA GARITA

Saguache County, north of Alamosa and Del Norte, is nearly as large as the other five San Luis Valley counties combined. One of its most interesting communities is La Garita, a quaint hamlet 43 miles northwest of Alamosa, 8 miles west of U.S. 285. Located here is the historical **San Juan Art Center** (tel. 719/734-3191 or 589-4769), where you may see Hispanic artisans turning out works of traditional design in the old La Sapilla de San Juan Bautista Church. Built in 1923, the church has an unusual six-arm cross on top, and is on the National Register of Historic Sites. The craftspeople include weavers, potters, sculptors, and *colcha* embroiderers, all members of the Artes del Valle cooperative. The center is open from Memorial Day to Labor Day, Monday through Friday from 10am to 5pm and on Saturday from 1 to 5pm; call for winter hours.

West of La Garita in the Rio Grande National Forest are several interesting sites, including **La Ventana Natural Arch** and the sheer cliffs of **Penitente Canyon,** internationally famed among rock climbers. Both are reached via County Road 38A. Inquire locally for directions.

CHAPTER 13

SOUTHEASTERN COLORADO

1. PUEBLO
- **WHAT'S SPECIAL ABOUT SOUTHEASTERN COLORADO**

2. TRINIDAD

3. LA JUNTA

Colorado's southeastern quadrant is dominated by the Arkansas River system. This mighty stream forges one of the world's most spectacular canyons—the deep, narrow Royal Gorge—as it wends its way down from the Rocky Mountain foothills. As it runs through Pueblo, the state's third-largest city, it supplies water for a major steel industry. Then it rolls across the Great Plains, providing life-giving water to an arid but soil-rich region that produces a wide variety of vegetables and fruits. Bent's Old Fort, a national historic site that has re-created the west's most important trading post of the 1830s and 1840s, also rests beside the river on the plains. South of Pueblo down I-25, the towns of Trinidad and Walsenburg are the centers of a century-old coal-mining district.

---

1. PUEBLO

111 miles S of Denver; 42 miles S of Colorado Springs;
317 miles N of Albuquerque, N. Mex.

GETTING THERE   By Plane   The Pueblo Memorial Airport, Keeler Parkway off U.S. 50 East (tel. 948-3355), is served daily by America West (toll free 800/247-5692), Continental Express (tel. 948-2254 or toll free 800/525-0280), and Trans World Airlines (tel. 543-6100).

By Bus   Buses of Greyhound serve Pueblo several times daily. The station is at 116 N. Main St. (tel. 719/544-6295).

By Car   I-25 links Pueblo directly with Colorado Springs, Denver, and points north; and Santa Fe, Albuquerque, and other New Mexico cities to the south. U.S. 50 runs east to La Junta and west to Cañon City, Gunnison, and Montrose.

SPECIAL EVENTS   Major annual events include the Fiesta del Rio Bluegrass Festival, at the Greenway and Nature Center; the Governor's Cup Regatta, at Pueblo Reservoir, in May; the Rolling River Raft Race, in July; the Colorado State Fair, in late August; the Christmas Posada, in December; and the Yule Log Festival, in Beulah, in December. The chamber of commerce has a recorded listing of weekly events (tel. 542-1776).

Although Zebulon Pike and his U.S. Army exploratory expedition camped at the future site of Pueblo (elevation 4,695 ft.) in 1806, there was no white settlement here until 1842, when Fort El Pueblo was constructed as a fur-trading outpost. It was abandoned following a Ute massacre in late 1854, but when the Colorado gold rush began in 1859, the town of Pueblo was laid out on the north side of the Arkansas River, at the site of the former fort. Other towns were platted in close proximity. Four communities—Pueblo, Central Pueblo, South Pueblo, and Bessemer (Minnequa)—grew together, each with its own street configuration, to become the modern city of Pueblo.

✔ WHAT'S SPECIAL ABOUT SOUTHEASTERN COLORADO

Natural Spectacles

☐ Royal Gorge, a 1,000-foot-deep canyon that is one of the most impressive natural attractions in the state.

☐ Comanche National Grassland, where visitors can see dinosaur tracks 150 million years old.

Historic Sites

☐ Bent's Old Fort National Historic Site, showing what this fort was like when it was a busy trade center in the early 19th-century.

☐ Baca and Bloom Houses in Trinidad, historic homes depicting life in southeast Colorado in the late 19th-century.

☐ Rosemount Victorian House Museum in Pueblo, a magnificent mansion considered to be one of the finest examples of Victorian architecture and furnishings in North America.

Zoos

☐ Pueblo Zoo, with more than 85 species.

For the Kids

☐ Buckskin Joe Park & Railway, a western movie set where *The Cowboys, Cat Ballou,* and dozens of other films were shot.

☐ Old Firehouse No. 1 Children's Museum in Trinidad, with two historic fire trucks and a restored turn-of-the-century schoolroom.

The Arts

☐ Sangre de Cristo Arts and Conference Center in Pueblo, with an excellent display of Western art, plus a hands-on participatory art museum for children.

☐ A.R. Mitchell Memorial Museum of Western Art in Trinidad, with a vast collection of western art.

☐ Koshare Indian Museum and Kiva, in La Junta, a superb collection of Native American art.

Museums

☐ Aultman Museum of Photography in Trinidad, displaying late-19th- and early-20th-century photographs of southern Colorado.

☐ Fred E. Weisbrod/International B-24 Memorial Museum, in Pueblo, with about two dozen military planes from the 1940s and 1950s on display.

In the early 20th century the city grew as a major center for coal mining and steel production. Although its importance has waned somewhat, the CF&I Steel Corporation remains Pueblo's single largest employer. Job opportunities drew large immigrant populations, especially from Mexico and eastern Europe. Modern Pueblo has diversified, with many high-technology industries based here, as well as the University of Southern Colorado. As the largest city in southeastern Colorado, Pueblo is the market center for a 15-county region extending to the borders of New Mexico, Oklahoma, and Kansas. It's population is just under 100,000.

ORIENTATION

INFORMATION Contact the Pueblo Chamber of Commerce Convention and Visitors Council, 302 N. Santa Fe Ave. (P.O. Box 697), Pueblo, CO 81002 (tel. 719/542-1704 or toll free 800/233-3446), for most tourism needs. A Visitor Information Center is located in a modular unit adjacent to the caboose off I-25, Exit 101, in the K-Mart parking lot on Elizabeth Street at U.S. 50 West (tel. 719/543-1742); it's open daily from 8am to 6pm, and is disabled accessible.

CITY LAYOUT The city of Pueblo is situated on the eastward-flowing Arkansas River at its confluence with Fountain Creek. The downtown core is located north of the Arkansas and west of the Fountain, immediately west of I-25. Santa Fe Avenue and

Main Street, one block to its west, are the principal north-south thoroughfares; the cross streets are numbered (counting northward), with Fourth Street and Eighth Street the most important. Paralleling Main Street four blocks to its west is Elizabeth Street, another arterial that intersects U.S. 50 at I-25, opposite Pueblo Mall, at the north end of the city. U.S. 50 runs west from here toward Cañon City; U.S. 50 East exits I-25 about a mile farther south, and proceeds past the airport toward La Junta. Main and Fourth both cross the Arkansas to the Mesa Junction residential district, where several fine restaurants and bed-and-breakfasts are located. Pueblo Boulevard circles the city on its south-and-west sides, with spurs leading to the Nature Center and Pueblo Reservoir.

GETTING AROUND

Public transportation is provided on a citywide network by **City Bus** (tel. 542-4306). For taxi service, call **City Cab** (tel. 543-2525).

Car rentals are available at the airport from Budget (tel. 948-3363), Hertz (tel. 948-3345), and Enterprise (tel. 542-6100).

FAST FACTS

The **area code** is 719. In case of **emergency,** dial 911. Medical services are provided downtown by **Parkview Episcopal Medical Center,** 400 W. 16th St. (tel. 584-4000), or on the south side by **St. Mary–Corwin Regional Medical Center,** 1008 Minnequa Ave. (tel. 560-4000). The main **post office** is downtown at 421 N. Main St. For **road conditions,** call 545-8520. State and local **taxes** on rooms total 11.2%.

WHAT TO SEE & DO

ATTRACTIONS

EL PUEBLO MUSEUM, First and Main Sts. Tel. 583-0453.

This downtown museum presents a full-size reproduction of the original 1842 fort after which Pueblo was named. Previously occupying a former airport hangar at 905 S. Prairie St., its new location is where the El Pueblo fur-trading post stood for 12 years. Other permanent historical exhibits include artifacts from Native American tribes of the region and a description of the steel-making process.

Admission: $2.50 adults, $2 ages 6–16 and over 65.
Open: Mon–Sat 10am–4:30pm, Sun noon–3pm.

FRED E. WEISBROD/INTERNATIONAL B-24 MEMORIAL MUSEUM, 568 S. Bayfield Ave., Pueblo West. Tel. 948-9217.

About two-dozen aircraft are on display here, as well as numerous exhibits on the B-24 and its role in World War II.

Admission: Free, but donations welcome.
Open: Mon–Fri 10am–4pm, Sat 10am–2pm, Sun 1–4pm.

THE GREENWAY AND NATURE CENTER, 5200 Nature Center Rd. Tel. 545-9114.

A major recreational center, this park area comprises more than 20 miles of biking-and-hiking trails along the Arkansas River, along with a fishing dock, volleyball courts, horseshoe pits, an amphitheater, tepees, reptile exhibit room, picnic areas, and a restaurant, the Café del Rio. Located here is the **Raptor Center of Pueblo,** where injured eagles, owls, hawks, and other birds of prey are nursed back to health and released to the wild.

Admission: Free to the park; Raptor Center suggested donation $1 adults, 25¢ ages 6–12.
Open: Daily 9am–5pm. Call for hours at the Raptor Center.

HISTORIC WALKING TOUR, Union Ave. Tel. 542-1704.

Historic Pueblo runs along Union Avenue north from the Arkansas River to First Street, a distance of about five blocks. More than 40 buildings here are listed on the

National Register of Historic Places, including the **Vail Hotel,** headquarters of the Pueblo County Historical Society museum and library (open Tuesday through Saturday from 1 to 4pm), and **Union Depot,** which still serves freight lines although passenger service ended in 1971. Walking-tour maps can be obtained from the chamber of commerce, 302 N. Santa Fe Ave.

Admission: Free.
Open: Daily 24 hours.

PUEBLO ZOO, City Park, 3455 Nuckolls Ave. Tel. 561-9664 or 561-1452.

More than 85 species of animals are exhibited at this zoo, which includes a tropical rain forest. You'll find reptiles, insects, and all sorts of cold-blooded creatures in the herpetarium; plus kangaroos, camels, leopards, lions, crocodiles, ostriches, emus, and numerous other animals. In the Ranch-at-the-Zoo, visitors can feed a variety of animals. The Discovery Room is a hands-on exhibit room for kids, and there's also a souvenir shop.

Admission: $2 ages 13 and over, 50¢ children 3–12, free children 2 and under.
Open: Daily 9am–4pm; later closing hours May–Sept.

ROSEMOUNT MUSEUM, 419 W. 14th St. Tel. 545-5290.

Pueblo's single leading historic attraction is this 37-room mansion, considered one of the finest surviving examples of turn-of-the-century architecture and decoration in North America. Built in 1891 for the pioneer Thatcher family, the three-story, 24,000-square-foot home is entirely of pink rhyolite stone in Richardsonian Romanesque style. Inside are exquisite oak, maple, and mahogany woodwork; remarkable works of stained glass; hand-decorated ceilings; exquisite Tiffany lighting fixtures; and 10 fireplaces, each with a unique character. Nearly all the furnishings are original to the mansion.

Admission: $4–$10.
Open: June–Aug, Tues–Sat 10am–4pm, Sun 2–4pm; Sept–Dec and Feb–May, Tues–Sat 1–4pm, Sun 2–4pm. **Closed:** Jan.

SANGRE DE CRISTO ARTS AND CONFERENCE CENTER, 210 N. Santa Fe Ave. Tel. 543-0130.

Pueblo's cultural hub is a two-building complex that contains a 500-seat theater; two dance studios; four art galleries, one of which houses the Francis King Collection of Western Art; a spacious conference room, gift shop, and the Pueblo Art Works Children's Museum, a hands-on participatory museum.

Admission: Free to galleries; Chidren's Museum, $1 adults, 50¢ children.
Open: Times vary; children's museum, Mon–Sat 11am–5pm; arts center, Mon–Sat 9am–5pm; galleries, Mon–Sat 11am–4pm; shop, Mon–Sat 11am–5pm.

SPORTS & RECREATION

BICYCLING The Greenway and Nature Center (see "Attractions," above) includes more than 30 miles of bicycle paths along the Arkansas River.

BOATING The Pueblo Reservoir, also known as Lake Pueblo, is just minutes from downtown Pueblo. It features more than 60 miles of shoreline, and is one of Colorado's most popular water sports areas. Boat rentals are available both from the North Shore Marina, off McCulloch Boulevard, Pueblo West, or the South Shore Marina, off Colo. 96, west of Pueblo Boulevard via Thatcher Avenue. Call 561-9320 for information. Waterskiing, sailing, board sailing, and jet sailing are among the popular activities. Boats and canoes can also be put into the Arkansas River at the Greenway and Nature Center, 5200 Nature Center Rd. (tel. 545-9114).

DOG RACING There's live and simulcast dog racing and simulcast horse racing at Pueblo Greyhound Park, Colorado's oldest dog track, Lake Avenue at Pueblo Boulevard (I-25, Exit 94; tel. 566-0370). Grandstand admission is $1. Call ahead for schedules.

FISHING The Greenway and Nature Center, 5200 Nature Center Rd. (tel. 545-9114), boasts a 150-foot dock on the Arkansas River for fishing. Angling for rainbow trout, brown trout, kokanee salmon, and other fish is popular from shore or boat at Pueblo Reservoir.

HIKING   Pueblo is the headquarters of the Pike and San Isabel National Forest, Comanche and Cimarron National Grasslands, 1920 Valley Dr. (tel. 545-8737). Information on hiking-and-backpacking opportunities throughout central and southern Colorado and southwestern Kansas is available from its U.S. Forest Service office there (see the address and telephone number above).

ICE SKATING   Public skating, lessons, hockey, figure skating, broomball, curling, and other rink activities take place at the Pueblo Plaza Ice Arena, 100 N. Grand Ave. (tel. 542-8784). Admission costs $2 for adults, $1.50 for children 12 and under. The rink is open during the summer, Monday through Friday from 10am to 3pm, and from mid-September through May, it is open the same weekday hours plus Saturdays from 1 to 3pm and Sundays from 3 to 6pm. Skate rentals and sharpening are available at the arena's shop.

MOTOR SPORTS   Nationally sanctioned drag racing, motocross, quarter scale, quarter midget racing, and Sportscar Club of America competitions take place early spring through September at the Pueblo Motorsports Park, U.S. 50 and Pueblo Boulevard (tel. 547-9921).

Top stock-car races are held at the Beacon Hill Speedway, 400 Gobatti Place (tel. 545-6104).

SWIMMING   The most popular area locally is the Rock Canyon Recreation Area at the east end of Lake Pueblo, 640 Pueblo Reservoir Rd. (tel. 561-9320). The area has a beach (50¢ admission), a water slide ($7 for all day), and bumper boats ($1 for five minutes).

There are also several public swimming pools in Pueblo, including Mineral Palace Pool, 1600 N. Santa Fe Ave. (tel. 545-5319); City Park Pool, City Park (tel. 564-2373); Minnequa Park Pool, 1708 E. Orman Ave. (tel. 564-2847); Eagleridge Pool, 4650 Ridge Dr. (tel. 545-8362); and Mitchell Park Pool, 1300 E. 12th St. (tel. 543-3119).

WHERE TO STAY

ABRIENDO INN, 300 W. Abriendo Ave., Pueblo, CO 81004. Tel. 719/ 544-2703. Fax 719/542-1806. 7 rms (all with bath). A/C TV TEL

$ Rates (including breakfast): $49–$80 single; $54–$85 double. AE, DC, MC, V. Built in 1906 as the mansion of brewing magnate Martin Walter, his wife, and his eight children, this house—built in traditional Foursquare architectural style—is Pueblo's finest bed-and-breakfast establishment. Located in the Mesa Junction neighborhood, just three blocks north of historic Union Avenue at the corner of Jackson Street, it has seven guest rooms, each decorated with antique furniture, quilts, armoires, and crocheted bedspreads on brass or four-poster beds. All rooms have TVs and Touch-Tone telephones with modem jacks. A gourmet breakfast is served in the oak-wainscoted dining room or on an outside patio in summer. Complimentary drinks are served daily from 5:30 to 7pm. Smoking is permitted only on the veranda.

DAYS INN, 4201 N. Elizabeth, Pueblo, CO 81006. Tel. 719/543-8031 or toll free 800/325-2525. Fax 719/546-1317. 34 rms (all with bath), 3 suites. A/C TV TEL

$ Rates (including free continental breakfast): $46–$65 single; $52–$85 double; $55–$135 suite. Higher rates during special events such as State Fair. AE, CB, DC, DISC, MC, V.

Southwest decor and clean, comfortable rooms are what you'll find at this Day's Inn, which has a small, heated indoor pool and hot tub and cable TV with HBO. Nonsmoking and disabled-accessible rooms are available. Local phone calls are free, and computer modem hookups are available. Pets are not permitted.

HAMPTON INN, 4703 N. I-25 (at Eagle Ridge Rd.), Pueblo, CO 81008. Tel. 719/544-4700 or toll free 800/972-0165 or 800/HAMPTON. Fax 719/ 544-6526, ext. 155. 112 rms (all with bath). A/C TV TEL

$ Rates (including continental breakfast): $49–$65 single; $57–$75 double. During the State Fair, $65 single; $75 double. AE, CB, DC, DISC, MC, V.

A two-story beige concrete structure just off I-25, this motel at the north end of Pueblo is a solid representative of this reputable national chain. About half the guest rooms are geared for business travelers, with a king-size bed, sofa sleeper, and desk; the others have two double beds and a table and chairs. All rooms have remote-control cable TVs with in-house movies, clock radios, and hair dryers. No-smoking rooms and facilities for the disabled are available. There's a guest laundry and an outdoor swimming pool (open seasonally). Local calls are free.

WHERE TO DINE

IRISH PUB & GRILLE, 108 W. Third St. Tel. 542-9974.

Cuisine: ITALIAN/AMERICAN. **Reservations:** Not required.

$ Prices: Appetizers $2–$5; main courses $5.25–$13.95. AE, MC, V.

Open: Mon–Sat 10am–11pm (bar open to 2am), Sun 10am–2pm.

If you want to meet everybody who's anybody in Pueblo, squeeze into the Irish Pub and Grille any evening after work. Have a drink, hobnob with the locals, then head for a table for a great meal. The Calantino family, which opened the pub in 1944, is still at it, serving everything from traditional bar food such as Philly cheese steak, buffalo burgers, and chicken club, to exotic and delicious pasta specialties, lamb, chicken, beef, and wild game.

IANNE'S WHISKEY RIDGE, 4333 Thatcher Ave. Tel. 564-8551.

Cuisine: ITALIAN/STEAKS/SEAFOOD. **Reservations:** Recommended for dinner.

$ Prices: Appetizers $5–$6; main courses $3.50–$7 at lunch, $7–$20 at dinner. MC, V.

Open: Daily 11am–10pm.

Serving food in Pueblo for over 50 years, this family-owned and -operated restaurant prepares everything from scratch and warns evening diners that because each meal is cooked to order, there may be a wait for some items. Pasta dishes are a specialty here. Particular favorites are the lasagne and the ravioli. There is also a large selection of fresh seafood dishes, chicken, veal, and superb steaks from certified Angus beef.

LA RENAISSANCE, 217 E. Routt Ave., Mesa Junction. Tel. 543-6367.

Cuisine: STEAK/SEAFOOD. **Reservations:** Recommended.

$ Prices: $4.95–$7.95, three-course lunch; $9.75–$25, five-course dinner. AE, CB, DC, DISC, MC, V.

Open: Lunch Mon–Fri 11am–2pm; dinner Mon–Sat 5–9pm.

Housed in an old Presbyterian church building that dates from the 1880s, La Renaissance has stubbornly refused to make any major structural changes in becoming a restaurant. Instead, the pews are still used for seating, and the sanctuary, chapel, and parish hall have become separate dining rooms—albeit with revamped decor! Dining here is an all-inclusive experience. A three-course lunch and five-course dinner begin with a tureen of soup and finish with a dessert, served at the table from a wooden cart. Pasta contrapuntal (with mushrooms and onions) and baked asparagus Virginia (wrapped in ham) are popular lunches; prime rib, New Zealand deep-sea filet, and chicken Kalgoorlie are delicious dinners. The restaurant features a wide selection of domestic and imported wine and beer. It's in Mesa Junction, two blocks southwest of Abriendo Avenue at the corner of Michigan Street.

AN EASY EXCURSION

ROYAL GORGE

One of the most impressive natural attractions in the entire state—albeit a bit overwhelmed these days by commercialism—is the ✪ **Royal Gorge,** 50 miles west of Pueblo (tel. 719/275-7507). This narrow-and-spectacular canyon on the Arkansas

River, 1,055 feet deep, was cut through solid granite by three million years of water-and-wind erosion. It is spanned by the world's highest bridge and by an aerial tramway, built for no other reason than to thrill tourists. And more than half a million of them visit every year.

When Zebulon Pike encountered the gorge in 1806, he predicted that man would never conquer it. But by 1877 the Denver & Rio Grande Railroad had laid a route through the canyon, and it became a major national tourist attraction. The quarter-mile-long bridge was built in 1929, suspended from two 300-ton cables; it was reinforced in 1983. A funicular railway, the world's steepest, was completed in 1931; it plunges from the rim of the gorge to the floor at a 45° angle. The tram opened in 1969. Owned by the city of Cañon City, the 160-acre park also includes a multimedia theater, miniature railway, children's play area, four restaurants, six gift shops, craft village, entertainment gazebo, trolley shuttle service, and herds of tame mule deer.

The gorge is open every day, year-round, from dawn to dusk. Admission—$8.50 for adults, $7.50 seniors, $6.50 for children 4 to 11—includes crossing the bridge and a choice of a funicular or tram ride or theater show.

Royal Gorge raft trips are organized over varying lengths of the river, some involving rough white-water passages. Trips vary in length from a quarter of a day to three days, and adult rates range from $13.75 to $80 per day. A major outfitter is **River Runners Ltd.,** 8 miles west of Cañon City on U.S. 50 (toll free 800/525-2081).

Near the entrance to the park is ♦ **Buckskin Joe Park & Railway,** a living western movie set that opened in 1958 and has since provided the scene for some two dozen films, including *How the West Was Won* and *The Cowboys.* Built on 30 acres, Buckskin Joe is a realistic re-creation of a frontier town of the late 1860s. A population of 70, all in period costume, play the roles of citizens of the day—most of them law abiding, some of them not. (Watch out for the gunslingers!) The scenic railway skirts the edge of the Royal Gorge. There's also a huge gift shop, a stagecoach, a museum, and stables for horseback riding. An all-inclusive ticket costs $14, or pay $7 for Buckskin Joe alone, $5.50 for the train. Open Memorial Day to Labor Day, daily 9am to 7:30pm (Railway 8am to 8pm). Shorter hours in off-season.

---

2. TRINIDAD

197 miles S of Denver; 192 miles N of Santa Fe, N. Mex.

GETTING THERE   By Plane   The Trinidad Municipal Airport, 10 miles east off U.S. 350 (tel. 719/846-6271), handles private planes and charters, but no commercial flights.

By Train   The Amtrak *Southwest Chief* passes through Trinidad twice daily—once eastbound, once westbound—on the main line between Chicago and Los Angeles. The depot is on Nevada Street north of College Street, beneath I-25 (toll free 800/872-7245).

By Bus   Coaches of Greyhound (toll free 800/528-6055) serve Trinidad. The bus station is on State Street north of College Street (tel. 846-7271), a block west of the rail depot.

By Car   If you're traveling from north or south, take I-25: Trinidad sits astride the interstate, halfway between Denver and Santa Fe, N. Mex. From the east, you can take U.S. 50 into La Junta, then turn southwest for 80 miles on U.S. 350. From Durango and points west, take U.S. 160 to Walsenburg, then travel south 37 miles on I-25.

SPECIAL EVENTS   Area annual events include the Spanish Peaks Fiesta, in Walsenburg, the first weekend of June; the Santa Fe Trail Festival, in Trinidad, the second weekend of June; Concerts in the Park, in Kit Carson Park, Trinidad, on Sunday from June to August; Cowboy Days, in Trinidad, in early September; the Trinidad Roundup, in Trinidad, on Labor Day weekend; Plaza de los Leones, in

Walsenburg, the third weekend of September; and Fallfest in Trinidad, in October.

Trinidad has a long-and-colorful history. The longest single trail of dinosaur tracks in the world was found just southeast of the city; Plains tribes roamed the area for centuries before the first 17th- and 18th-century forays by Spanish explorers and settlers. Traders and trappers made this location an important stop on the northern branch of the Santa Fe Trail between Bent's Old Fort and Fort Union. It was incorporated in 1876, and the Atchison, Topeka, & Santa Fe Railway soon followed. Bat Masterson was sheriff in the 1880s, Wyatt Earp drove the stage, Kit Carson helped open the trade routes, and even Billy the Kid passed through. Many historic buildings—handsome structures of brick and sandstone—survive from this era.

German, Irish, Italian, Jewish, Polish, and Slavic immigrants were drawn to the area around the turn-of-the-century by extensive coal mining just west of town and large cattle companies on the plains to the east. Mining—along with agriculture and railroading—sustained the town for decades. But in 1982 the coal mines closed, sending unemployment in the region to a staggering level. Trinidad has never completely recovered, but an economic-development effort, strong on tourism, has helped the town of about 8,600 survive. The coal mines recently reopened on a reduced level.

ORIENTATION

INFORMATION The **Trinidad Visitor Center,** 135 N. Animas St. (I-25, Exit 14A), Trinidad, CO 81082 (tel. 719/846-7244), is housed in an old Colorado & Southern Railroad caboose. It's open Monday through Saturday from 9am to 5pm. A free trolley ride around historic downtown Trinidad begins here, Memorial Day to Labor Day.

The Colorado Welcome Center, 309 N. Nevada Ave. (I-25, Exit 14A), Trinidad, CO 81082 (tel. 719/846-9512 or toll free 800/748-1970), open daily, has information not only on southeastern Colorado, but on the entire state. The Trinidad Chamber of Commerce is in the same building (tel. 719/846-9285).

TOWN LAYOUT Trinidad is nestled in the foothills of the Rocky Mountains. To its west is the Sangre de Cristo Range; to its east, the Great Plains. El Rio de Las Animas en Purgatorio (the river of lost souls in Purgatory), better known as the Purgatoire River, an Arkansas River tributary, flows from southwest to northeast through the center of town, paralleling Main Street (U.S. 160/350). The historic downtown area is focused around Main and Commercial Street on the south side of the river. Main joins I-25 on the west side of downtown.

GETTING AROUND

If you haven't your own car, the best way to get around is by **Yellow Cab** (tel. 846-2237).

You can **rent a car** from National, Hadad Motor Sales, 723 N. Commercial St. (tel. 719/846-3318 or toll free 800/748-2277).

FAST FACTS

The **area code** is 719. In case of **emergency,** dial 0 (zero) for the operator or 846-2227 for the Colorado State Patrol. Medical services are rendered at **Mt. San Rafael Hospital,** 410 Benedicta Ave. off Main Street (tel. 846-9213). For **road conditions,** call 846-9262.

WHAT TO SEE & DO

ATTRACTIONS

AULTMAN MUSEUM OF PHOTOGRAPHY, 136 E. Main St. Tel. 846-3881.

★ In 1889, Oliver E. Aultman moved to Trinidad and established the Aultman Photography Studio. For the rest of the 19th century and much of the 20th, he and his son Glenn recorded southern Colorado history through their camera lenses. Their photographic record is exhibited at this museum, which also features displays of early cameras, darkroom equipment, hand-painted backdrops, and other studio props. The studio, incidentally, is still operated by Glenn Aultman himself—unretired at age 90 (he was born December 14, 1904). There are also changing exhibits.

Admission: Free.

Open: Early May to Sept, Mon–Sat 10am–4pm; off-season, by appointment.

BACA HOUSE, BLOOM HOUSE, AND PIONEER MUSEUM, 300 E. Main St. Tel. 846-7217.

★ Standing together overlooking the old Santa Fe Trail, these buildings rank as Trinidad's principal tourist attraction. The Baca House, built in 1870, is a two-story adobe in Greek revival style, owned by sheep rancher Felipe Baca. His descendants lived here until the 1920s, and the house still has many of its original furnishings. Nearby stands the Bloom House, a Second Empire–style Victorian manor embellished with fancy wood carving and ornate ironwork. Built in 1882 for cattleman Frank G. Bloom and his family, it also contains fascinating period decor. Both are Certified Sites on the Santa Fe National Historic Trail; and the Denver Historical Society has named Felipe Baca one of the 100 most influential Coloradans. The Colorado Historical Society operates both homes and the Pioneer Museum in outbuildings of the Baca House, with 19th-century ranch implements and transportation, and exhibits on the era.

Admission: $2.50 adults, $1.25 children 6–16 and seniors, under 6 are free.

Open: Mid-May to mid-Sept, Mon–Sat 10am–4pm, Sun 1–4pm; off-season, by appointment.

CORAZON DE TRINIDAD NATIONAL HISTORIC DISTRICT, Main St.

Main Street was once part of the Mountain Branch of the Santa Fe Trail, and many of the streets that cross it are paved with red brick. The Trinidad Historical Society distributes a booklet titled "A Walk Through the History of Trinidad," available (for $1.50) at the visitor center and elsewhere. Among the buildings it singles out for special attention are the Trinidad Opera House (1883), Columbian Hotel (1879), across from each other on Main Street, and the Trinidad Water Works (1879) on Cedar Street at the Purgatoire River.

A. R. MITCHELL MEMORIAL MUSEUM OF WESTERN ART, 150 E. Main St. Tel. 846-4224.

★ More than 250 paintings and illustrations by western artist Arthur Roy Mitchell (1889–1977) are displayed here, along with works by other nationally recognized artists and a collection of early Hispanic religious folk art. The building is 1906 western style with the original tin ceiling, wood floors, and a horseshoe-shaped mezzanine.

Admission: Free.

Open: Apr–Sept, Mon–Sat 10am–4pm; off-season, by appointment.

OLD FIREHOUSE NO. 1 CHILDREN'S MUSEUM, 314 N. Commercial St. Tel. 846-8220 or 846-7721.

A historic fire truck, Trinidad's original 1930s-era alarm system, and a restored turn-of-the-century schoolroom are exhibited. Another section of the museum has hands-on displays for children, including Grandma's trunk for dress up.

Admission: Free.

Open: June–Aug, Mon–Fri 10am–2pm.

SPORTS & RECREATION

BOATING Located 3 miles west of town on Colo. 12, Trinidad State Recreation Area (tel. 846-6951) features a 700-acre reservoir on the Purgatoire River. Powerboating and sailing, as well as waterskiing and board sailing, are popular.

There's a boat ramp, and swimming is prohibited. There's also a 62-unit campground. About 40 miles west of Trinidad on Colo. 12, Monument Lake Resort (tel. 868-2226) also offers a marina and boating.

FISHING   Largemouth bass, rainbow-and-brown trout, channel catfish, and wall-eye are caught in Trinidad Reservoir (see "Boating," above). Blue Lake, 5 miles from Cuchara, is disabled accessible. Crystal Spring Lakes, 28 miles west of Trinidad, offers family fishing on private property, so no license is needed (tel. 868-2219). Fishing is also good in the Purgatoire River and other area streams.

GOLF   The 9-hole, par-36 Trinidad Municipal Golf Club, off the Santa Fe Trail adjacent to I-25 (tel. 846-9918), has a driving range and pro shop. Some 60 miles northwest of Trinidad, on Colo. 12 near La Veta, is the 18-hole, par-72 Grandote Golf and Country Club (tel. 742-3123), a championship course designed by pro golfer Tom Weiskopf. The pro shop is fully stocked, and there's a snack bar with a grill and sandwiches. They offer a stay-and-play package (call toll free 800/886-2833).

HIKING   There are numerous fine trails in the San Isabel National Forest (tel. 275-4119) around Cuchara, off Colo. 12 some 50 miles west of Trinidad. Nearer town, the Levsa Canyon Trail extends 5 miles from Trinidad State Recreation Area (see "Boating," above) to historic Cokedale (see "Easy Excursions," below).

SKIING   The Cuchara Valley Resort, P.O. Box 3, Cuchara, CO 81055 (tel. 742-3163 or toll free 800/227-4436), is one of Colorado's newest winter destinations. Located 54 miles west of Trinidad on Colo. 12, the ski area has a vertical drop of 1,562 feet from the summit of 10,810-foot Baker Mountain. Four lifts, including three double chairs and one triple chair, serve 25 trails of all ability levels. The mountain also has a ski shop, restaurant, and other facilities.

WHERE TO STAY

BEST WESTERN COUNTRY CLUB INN, 900 W. Adams St., I-25, Exit 13A, Trinidad, CO 81082. Tel. 719/846-2215 or toll free 800/955-2215. Fax 719/846-2215, ext. 308. 55 rms (all with bath). A/C TV TEL

$ Rates: Nov–Apr, $45 single; $49 double. May, Sept, and Oct, $55 single; $59 double. Memorial Day–Labor Day, $65–$69 single or double. AE, DC, DISC, MC, V.

Situated on a hillside overlooking I-25, adjacent to the municipal golf course, the Country Club Inn offers a splendid view of Trinidad, as well as elegance at reasonable prices. The spacious guest rooms have one king or two queen-size beds, table and chairs, dresser, and double vanity. Facilities and services include a restaurant, a seasonal outdoor swimming pool, a Jacuzzi, a fitness room, a guest laundry, a 24-hour front desk, and courtesy shuttle service.

HOLIDAY INN, Rte. 1, I-25 at Exit 11, Trinidad, CO 81082. Tel. 719/846-4491 or toll free 800-HOLIDAY. Fax 719/846-2440. 110 rms, 3 suites (all with bath). A/C TV TEL

$ Rates: Summer, $58–$69 single; $66–$78 double. Winter, $39–$66 single; $47–$74 double. Suites $86–$96. AE, CB, DC, DISC, JCB, MC, V.

This fine motel was recently renovated. It offers attractive and very comfortable rooms, an indoor heated pool, a hot tub, an exercise room, plus room service, a 24-hour front desk, and security-coded room keys. There are wonderful views of the Sangre de Cristo Mountains, a good restaurant serving three meals daily, and a lounge. Fax service is available, and pets are accepted.

TRINIDAD MOTOR INN, 702 W. Main St., Trinidad, CO 81082. Tel. 719/846-2271. 60 rms. A/C TV TEL

$ Rates: Oct–May $30 single; $36–$38 double. June–Sept, $36 single; $45–$51 double. AE, CB, DC, DISC, MC, V.

The downtown historic district is only a short walk away from this property, located just off I-25 at Exit 13B. Rooms are spacious and have all standard furnishings, including queen-size beds in most units. There's a heated outdoor swimming pool and guest laundry; the Stagecoach Dining Room serves three meals daily, and has an adjoining lounge.

WHERE TO DINE

NANA & NANO'S PASTA HOUSE, 415 University St. Tel. 846-2696.
Cuisine: ITALIAN. **Reservations:** Accepted.
$ Prices: Lunch $2.75–$4.50; dinner $5.25–$10.50. AE, MC, V.
Open: Memorial Day–Labor Day, lunch Tues–Fri 11:30am–2pm; dinner Tues–Fri 4:30–8:30pm, Sat 4:30–9pm. Close half hour earlier in winter.

The decor is simple here with red-checked tablecloths, but that doesn't stop crowds from waiting outside the door for a table. Enjoy a variety of sandwiches for lunch; a choice of steak, pasta, or the daily special (such as rigatoni or lasagne) for dinner.

THE YELLOW ROSE FOOD AND SPIRITS, 229 W. Main St. Tel. 846-8611.
Cuisine: MEXICAN/AMERICAN. **Reservations:** Not required.
$ Prices: Lunch $2.50–$5; dinner $4.50–$8. MC, V.
Open: Mon–Sat 11am–9pm, Sun 11am–8pm.

Homemade Mexican food from family recipes is the fare at Yellow Rose, also known locally as Maria's. Neon cactuses adorn the walls in the simply decorated dining room. Mexican combination plates, tacos, tamales, chile rellenos, carne adovada, and burritos are served, along with burgers and a variety of American-style sandwiches.

EASY EXCURSIONS

SCENIC HIGHWAY OF LEGENDS

Unquestionably the most interesting day trip from Trinidad is the 77-mile **۞ Scenic Highway of Legends.** Colo. 12 runs west, north, then northeast to Walsenburg, via Cuchara and La Veta, en route passing numerous historic locations and many points of great natural beauty.

Traveling west, the first site of special note is **Cokedale,** just off the highway 7 miles west of Trinidad. The best example of an intact coal camp in Colorado, Cokedale was built in 1907 by the American Smelting and Refining Co. as a self-contained company town. When the mine closed in 1947, it was home to 1,500 people. Many of today's handful of residents are descendants of those miners, or are retired miners themselves. The town and surrounding area are listed on the National Register of Historic Places.

As you proceed west, you'll pass several old coal towns, including Segundo, Weston, and Vigil, and two coal mines, the Golden Eagle Mine, where underground mining is still done, and New Elk Mine, now a processing plant, before entering the **Stonewall Valley,** 32 miles west of Trinidad. Named for a striking rock formation, a vertical bed of lithified sandstone, Stonewall is both the site of a small timber industry and the location of many summerhomes. Lodging and camping are available at Stonewall. The highway turns north past the Monument Lake Resort and across 9,941-foot Cucharas Pass into Huerfano County.

Overlooking the pass are the **Spanish Peaks,** eroded remnants of a 20-million-year-old volcano. The native Arapahoe believed them to be the home of the gods, and they served as guideposts to early travelers. Legends persist about the existence of a treasure of gold in this area, but none has ever been found.

EN ROUTE TO WALSENBURG

Numerous fascinating geologic features become prominent as the road descends toward Walsenburg. Among them are the **Devils Stairsteps,** one of a series of erosion-resistant igneous dikes that radiate out like spokes from the Spanish Peaks; **Dakota Wall,** a layer of pressed sandstone thrust vertically from the earth; and

Goemmer Butte, sometimes called "Sore Thumb Butte," a volcanic plug rising 500 feet from the valley floor.

Fourteen miles west of Walsenburg is the foothills village of **La Veta** (pop. 725), founded as a ranching center in 1862. Its **Fort Francisco Museum,** on Francisco Street at Colo. 12 (tel. 738-1107), occupies that original plaza building and incorporates a saloon, schoolhouse, blacksmith shop, Presbyterian church, and mining museum to depict frontier life. It's open from Memorial Day to Labor Day daily from 9am to 5pm; admission is $2 for adults, $1 for children. You can stay in La Veta at the **1899 Bed and Breakfast Inn,** 314 S. Main St., P.O. Box 372, La Veta, CO 81955 (tel. 719/742-3576).

FARTHER AFIELD

Northwest of Walsenburg, Colo. 69 winds through the Sangre de Cristo foothills 65 miles to Westcliffe before proceeding another 25 miles to join U.S. 50 west of Cañon City. En route, it passes through **Gardner,** 27 miles from Walsenburg, a growing artists' community and home of **Mission Wolf,** a sanctuary and refuge for some 30 pure and hybrid wolves. **Westcliffe** (pop. 350) is a popular summer and winter recreational center and the seat of Custer County.

At the eastern edge of the county, on Colo. 165 near Rye, 29 miles east of Westcliffe and 33 miles southwest of Pueblo, is the unique **Bishop Castle,** a three-story-high medieval castle singlehandedly built by laborer Jim Bishop, who has gathered and set more than 2,000 tons of rocks per year since 1969. Bishop, now 50, calls it a monument "to hard-working poor people everywhere." Admission is by donation only.

3. LA JUNTA

64 miles E of Pueblo; 80 miles NE of Trinidad; 274 miles NW of Amarillo, Tex.

GETTING THERE   By Plane The La Junta Municipal Airport is 4 miles north of town off Colo. 109 (tel. 384-8407). It handles private-and-charter flights, but has no commercial service. Pueblo is the nearest commercial airport.

By Train Passenger service is available aboard Amtrak, with a depot on First Street at Colorado Avenue (tel. 719/384-2275 or toll free 800/872-7245). The *Southwest Chief* passes through twice daily—once eastbound, once westbound—on the main line between Chicago and Los Angeles.

By Bus Buses of Greyhound serve the town several times daily from all directions. Coaches stop at My Car Wash, 619 E. Third St. (tel. 719/384-9288).

By Car La Junta is easily reached via U.S. 50. The highway, which runs east into Kansas, is linked in the west to I-25 at Pueblo. From New Mexico, exit I-25 at Trinidad and take U.S. 350; from Durango and southwestern Colorado, take U.S. 160 to Walsenburg, and continue on Colo. 10 to La Junta.

SPECIAL EVENTS Area annual events include Fiesta Days, in La Junta, the second weekend of June; Kid's Rodeo in La Junta, in August; the Arkansas Valley Fair, in Rocky Ford, the third week of August; the Fur Trade Encampment, at Bent's Old Fort, in July; Early Settlers Day, in La Junta, the Saturday after Labor Day; Oktoberfest, in Rocky Ford, in October; and 1846 Christmas, at Bent's Old Fort, in mid-December.

Arapahoe, Cheyenne, and Ute tribes once made the Arkansas River Valley their hunting-and-fishing grounds. Spanish soldiers passed through in the 17th and 18th centuries, but not until Zebulon Pike led his exploratory expedition up the river in 1806 did it become known to white Americans. Trappers and traders followed, creating the Santa Fe Trail; brothers William and Charles Bent built Bent's Fort in 1833 as a trading post, the first American settlement in the region. As settlers moved in, and with them the railroad, Fort Wise and Fort Lyon were built in the 1860s to house cavalry troops and put down tribal uprisings.

La Junta was founded in 1875 as a railroad camp. First called Manszaneras, then Otero, it was renamed La Junta—Spanish for "the junction"—on completion of rail links to Pueblo and Trinidad in 1877. The town flourished as a farming-and-ranching center. Today, with a population of about 8,500, its highly irrigated land produces a wide variety of fruits, vegetables, and wheat.

ORIENTATION

INFORMATION The best source is the La Junta Chamber of Commerce, 110 Santa Fe Ave. (P.O. Box 408), La Junta, CO 81050 (tel. 719/384-7411).

TOWN LAYOUT La Junta is located on the Arkansas River at an elevation of 4,100 feet. U.S. 50, which runs through town as First Street, follows the river's south bank. The highways from Trinidad and Walsenburg join it just west of town. The downtown core focuses around First Street, Second Street, and Third Street, crossed by north-south Colorado Avenue and Santa Fe Avenue. At the east edge of town, Colo. 109 (Adams Avenue) crosses the Arkansas into North La Junta (where it becomes Main Street); six blocks past the river, Colo. 194 (Trail Road) forks to the right and leads 5 miles to Bent's Old Fort.

FAST FACTS

The **area code** is 719. In case of **emergency,** dial "0" (zero) for the operator, or call 384-2525 for police, 384-2323 for ambulance or fire. Health services are rendered by the **Arkansas Valley Regional Medical Center,** 1100 Carson Ave. at 10th Street (tel. 384-5412). The **post office** is located at Fourth Street and Colorado Avenue. For **road conditions,** call 336-4326.

WHAT TO SEE & DO
ATTRACTIONS

BENT'S OLD FORT NATIONAL HISTORIC SITE, 35110 Colo. 194 E. Tel. 384-2596.

✪ Once the most important settlement on the Santa Fe Trail between Missouri and New Mexico, Bent's Old Fort has been reconstructed exactly as it was during its reign as a major trading post, from 1833 to 1849. Located 7 miles east of modern La Junta, this adobe fort on the Arkansas River was built by brothers Charles and William Bent and partner Ceran St. Vrain. It was the hub of trade between eastern U.S. merchants, Rocky Mountain fur trappers, Hispanics and Navajos from New Mexico, and Plains tribes (mainly Cheyenne, but including Arapahoe, Ute, Apache, Kiowa, and Comanche).

A description written by a traveler in 1840 is still apt today:

Although built of the simple prairie soil, made to hold together by a rude mixture with straw and the plain grass itself, the fort is constructed with all the defensive capacities of a complete fortification. The dwellings, kitchens, the arrangements for comfort, are all such as to strike the wanderer with the liveliest surprise, as though an 'air-built castle' had dropped to earth before him in the midst of the vast desert.

As American settlement increased and drove off the buffalo that were the lifeblood of the Plains tribes, the Bents were caught between two cultures. Serious hostilities began in 1847 and trade rapidly declined. The fort burned to the ground in 1849 and was not rebuilt until modern times. But it is as faithful as possible to the original design. Reproductions furnish the 33 rooms, which include a kitchen with an adjoining pantry, a cook's room, and a dining room; a trade room with robes, pelts, and blankets in stock; blacksmith-and-carpenter shops; William Bent's office and bedroom; quarters for Mexican laborers, trappers, and soldiers; a billiard room; and the quarters of a merchant's wife who kept a meticulous diary during her stay here in 1846, en route to Santa Fe.

It's a quarter-mile walk on a paved path from the historic site's contact station to the fort itself, where hosts in period costume greet visitors year-round. Start your visit by viewing a 22-minute video, *Castle on the Plains,* which describes the rise and fall of the Bent empire. Then wander through the fort, pausing to watch demonstrations of frontier ways—blacksmithing, adobe making, trapping, cooking, medicine, and survival skills. In summer, 45-minute guided tours begin on the hour daily. Books on the Santa Fe Trail and fur-trade era are for sale at the fort, along with period goods in the trade room.

Admission: $2 per person.

Open: Memorial Day–Labor Day, daily 8am–6pm; the rest of the year, daily 8am–4:30pm.

COMANCHE NATIONAL GRASSLAND, south of La Junta around several highways. Tel. 384-2181.

Dinosaur tracks from the Jurassic period, about 150 million years ago, are a highlight of this 419,000-acre national grassland, which is also a favorite of bird-watchers, hunters, anglers, and hikers. Access to Picket Wire Canyonlands, where the dinosaur tracks are located, is limited to those hiking or on mountain bicycles or horseback.

The tracks are believed to be from dinosaurs in the Sauropodmorpha "reptile-type feet" and Theropoda "beast feet" families, who lived in the area when the climate was warm and wet, with forests of ferns, pines, sequoias, and other vegetation. This produced plenty of food for the Sauropods, who were plant-eaters, and made them more tempting to their enemies, the meat-eating Theropods. The Sauropods, particularly the Brontosaurus, grew to about 14 ½ feet tall, and weighed up to 33 tons. Theropods grew to about 16 ½ feet tall, but were not as long, and weighed only about four tons. Still, with their sharp claws, they would attack the Sauropods whenever given the chance.

A high-clearance vehicle or four-wheel drive is needed to get to a parking area, and from there it's at least a 10.6-mile round-trip hike to the dinosaur tracks. Maps to the area are available from the Comanche National Grasslands office at 1321 E. Third St. (P.O. Box 817), La Junta, CO 81050 (tel. 719/384-2181). This office can also provide information on the other attractions in the grasslands, including the wildlife, which includes the lesser prairie chicken, a threatened species, and Native American rock art that's close to 5,000 years old.

KOSHARE INDIAN MUSEUM AND KIVA, Otero Junior College, 115 W. 18th St. Tel. 384-4411.

✪ A $10-million collection of Native American art—featuring tribal members both as artists and as the subject of works of art—is the focus of this excellent museum. Clothing, jewelry, basketry, and other crafts are presented, along with western paintings and sculptures. One of the finest collections of works by early Taos artists is on display here. The museum itself is an adobe-style building that resembles a Taos-area pueblo, one block west of Colorado Avenue.

But the highlight of a visit, if at all possible, is to view a performance by the Koshare Dancers. This nationally acclaimed troop of Boy Scout Explorers performs an average of 50 times a year, primarily in their own great *kiva,* a circular chamber traditionally used for religious rites. Dances are held at least weekly in summer, and the Koshare Winter Ceremonial Dances are a December tradition.

Admission: Museum, free; dances, $4 adults, $2 students and children.

Open: Memorial Day–Labor Day, daily 10am–5pm; the rest of the year, Tues–Sun 12:30–4:30pm. Dancers perform mid-June to mid-Aug, Sat at 8:15pm, and other times; call for schedule. **Closed:** Major holidays.

OTERO MUSEUM, Third and Anderson Sts. Tel. 384-7406 or 384-7500.

This museum will give you insight into what life was like for folks in eastern Colorado between the 1870s and 1930s. There's a complete grocery store, several early La Junta homes, a replica of the community's first school, a doctor's office, railroad equipment and memorabilia, classic cars, and more.

Admission: Free. Donations welcome.

Open: June–Sept, daily 1–5pm; off-season, tours by appointment.

WHERE TO STAY

**QUALITY INN, 1325 E. Third St. (P.O. Box 1180), La Junta, CO 81050.
   Tel. 719/384-2571.** 56 rms, 4 suites (all with bath). A/C TV TEL
$ Rates: $44–$53 single; $42–$57 double; $64 suite. AE, CB, DC, DISC, JCB, MC, V.

All guest rooms have king-size or double beds, satellite TVs, desk/dressers, and other standard furnishings. The property has an outdoor swimming pool and separate children's pool, a hot tub, meeting rooms, and shuttle service. The Capri Restaurant serves three meals daily, with room service available, and there's an adjoining lounge. Nonsmoking rooms are available, and pets are accepted. The motel is situated at the junction of Colo. 109, on the principal route to Bent's Old Fort.

**MID-TOWN MOTEL, 215 E. Third St., La Junta, CO 81050. Tel. 719/
   384-7741.** 26 rms (all with bath). A/C TV TEL
$ Rates: $24 single; $32 double. AE, DC, DISC, MC, V.

 A great little mom-and-pop motel off the main highway, the Mid-Town offers a clean, very quiet room with good-quality sheets and towels and cable television with HBO. Single rooms have recliners, and owners Jack and P. J. Culp are an invaluable source of information for visitors to the area. Pets are welcome.

WHERE TO DINE

**THE KIT CARSON HOTEL RESTAURANT AND LOUNGE, 123 Colorado
   Ave. Tel. 384-4471.**
   Cuisine: AMERICAN/MEXICAN. **Reservations:** Accepted.
$ Prices: Breakfast $2.25–$5, lunch $2–$5, dinner $5–$11. DISC, MC, V.
   Open: Mon–Thurs 6am–8pm, Fri–Sat 6am–8:30pm, Sun 6am–2pm.

Although the Kit Carson Hotel is closed, the restaurant is going strong. Many La Junta residents say it serves the best food in the area. Specializing in home-style cooking, with everything made from scratch, popular items include chicken-fried steak, fried chicken, the Sunday-only leg of lamb, prime rib, or any steak. Beef is aged on site and cut fresh; burgers are ground fresh. There are also daily specials, such as ribs or corned beef and cabbage. For dessert try the peach or apple cobbler.

NEARBY EXCURSION
LAS ANIMAS

Las Animas (pop. 2,800) is 20 miles east of La Junta on U.S. 50. Just two miles south on Colo. 101 is **Boggsville,** one of Colorado's earliest permanent settlements, now being restored. Among its historical buildings is the last home of famed frontier scout Kit Carson. **Fort Lyon** (built 1867), six miles east on U.S. 50, is now a veteran's hospital; but it includes the Kit Carson Chapel, which occupies the building in which Carson died in 1868. The **Kit Carson Museum,** Bent Avenue and Ninth Street in Las Animas (tel. 456-2005), tells his story and that of the area's history, Memorial Day to Labor Day, daily from 1 to 5pm.

Nearby, the 1887 Bent County Courthouse, the oldest operating courthouse in Colorado, is being restored. Visitors to the area can also stop at the **Las Animas Fish Hatchery and Rearing Unit,** 33128 County Rd. 5.5 (tel. 456-0499), for self-guided tours and an opportunity to feed the fish; and the **John Martin Reservoir,** east of Las Animas on the Arkansas River, just off Highway 50 (tel. 336-3476), with boating, water skiing, swimming, fishing, hunting, picnicking, and camping. For **information,** contact the Las Animas/Bent County Chamber of Commerce, 511 Ambassador Thompson Blvd., Las Animas, CO 81054 (tel. 719/456-0453).

A good place for a bite to eat or a warm bed is the **Best Western Bent's Fort Inn,** 10950 U.S. 50, Las Animas, CO 81054 (tel. 456-0011).

INDEX

Now Save Money on All Your Travels by Joining
FROMMER'S ™ TRAVEL BOOK CLUB
The World's Best Travel Guides at Membership Prices

FROMMER'S TRAVEL BOOK CLUB is your ticket to successful travel! Open up a world of travel information and simplify your travel planning when you join ranks with thousands of value-conscious travelers who are members of the FROMMER'S TRAVEL BOOK CLUB. Join today and you'll be entitled to all the privileges that come from belonging to the club that offers you travel guides for less to more than 100 destinations worldwide. Annual membership is only $25 (U.S.) or $35 (Canada and foreign).

The Advantages of Membership

1. Your choice of *three* free FROMMER'S TRAVEL GUIDES (any *two* FROMMER'S COMPREHENSIVE GUIDES, FROMMER'S $-A-DAY GUIDES, FROMMER'S WALKING TOURS *or* FROMMER'S FAMILY GUIDES—plus *one* FROMMER'S CITY GUIDE, FROMMER'S CITY $-A-DAY GUIDE *or* FROMMER'S TOURING GUIDE).
2. Your own subscription to **TRIPS AND TRAVEL** quarterly newsletter.
3. You're entitled to a **30% discount** on your order of any additional books offered by FROMMER'S TRAVEL BOOK CLUB.
4. You're offered (at a small additional fee) our **Domestic Trip-Routing Kits.**

Our quarterly newsletter **TRIPS AND TRAVEL** offers practical information on the best buys in travel, the "hottest" vacation spots, the latest travel trends, world-class events and much, much more.

Our **Domestic Trip-Routing Kits** are available for any North American destination. We'll send you a detailed map highlighting the best route to take to your destination—you can request direct or scenic routes.

Here's all you have to do to join:

Send in your membership fee of $25 ($35 Canada and foreign) with your name and address on the form below along with your selections as part of your membership package to **FROMMER'S TRAVEL BOOK CLUB, P.O. Box 473, Mt. Morris, IL 61054-0473.** Remember to check off your *three* free books.

If you would like to order additional books, please select the books you would like and send a check for the total amount (please add sales tax in the states noted below), plus $2 per book for shipping and handling ($3 per book for foreign orders) to:

> **FROMMER'S TRAVEL BOOK CLUB**
> P.O. Box 473
> Mt. Morris, IL 61054-0473
> (815) 734-1104

[ ] **YES.** I want to take advantage of this opportunity to join FROMMER'S TRAVEL BOOK CLUB.

[ ] **My check is enclosed.** Dollar amount enclosed_____*
(all payments in U.S. funds only)

Name_____
Address_____
City_____ State_____ Zip_____
All orders must be prepaid.

To ensure that all orders are processed efficiently, please apply sales tax in the following areas: CA, CT, FL, IL, NJ, NY, TN, WA and CANADA.

*With membership, shipping and handling will be paid by FROMMER'S TRAVEL BOOK CLUB for the three free books you select as part of your membership. Please add $2 per book for shipping and handling for any additional books purchased ($3 per book for foreign orders).

Allow 4–6 weeks for delivery. Prices of books, membership fee, and publication dates are subject to change without notice. Prices are subject to acceptance and availability.

AC1

Please Send Me the Books Checked Below:

FROMMER'S COMPREHENSIVE GUIDES
(Guides listing facilities from budget to deluxe,
with emphasis on the medium-priced)

	Retail Price	Code		Retail Price	Code
☐ Acapulco/Ixtapa/Taxco 1993–94	$15.00	C120	☐ Japan 1994–95 (Avail. 3/94)	$19.00	C144
☐ Alaska 1994–95	$17.00	C131	☐ Morocco 1992–93	$18.00	C021
☐ Arizona 1993–94	$18.00	C101	☐ Nepal 1994–95	$18.00	C126
☐ Australia 1992–93	$18.00	C002	☐ New England 1994 (Avail. 1/94)	$16.00	C137
☐ Austria 1993–94	$19.00	C119	☐ New Mexico 1993–94	$15.00	C117
☐ Bahamas 1994–95	$17.00	C121	☐ New York State 1994–95	$19.00	C133
☐ Belgium/Holland/ Luxembourg 1993–94	$18.00	C106	☐ Northwest 1994–95 (Avail. 2/94)	$17.00	C140
☐ Bermuda 1994–95	$15.00	C122	☐ Portugal 1994–95 (Avail. 2/94)	$17.00	C141
☐ Brazil 1993–94	$20.00	C111	☐ Puerto Rico 1993–94	$15.00	C103
☐ California 1994	$15.00	C134	☐ Puerto Vallarta/Manzanillo/ Guadalajara 1994–95 (Avail. 1/94)	$14.00	C028
☐ Canada 1994–95 (Avail. 4/94)	$19.00	C145	☐ Scandinavia 1993–94	$19.00	C135
☐ Caribbean 1994	$18.00	C123	☐ Scotland 1994–95 (Avail. 4/94)	$17.00	C146
☐ Carolinas/Georgia 1994–95	$17.00	C128	☐ South Pacific 1994–95 (Avail. 1/94)	$20.00	C138
☐ Colorado 1994–95 (Avail. 3/94)	$16.00	C143	☐ Spain 1993–94	$19.00	C115
☐ Cruises 1993–94	$19.00	C107	☐ Switzerland/Liechtenstein 1994–95 (Avail. 1/94)	$19.00	C139
☐ Delaware/Maryland 1994–95 (Avail. 1/94)	$15.00	C136	☐ Thailand 1992–93	$20.00	C033
☐ England 1994	$18.00	C129	☐ U.S.A. 1993–94	$19.00	C116
☐ Florida 1994	$18.00	C124	☐ Virgin Islands 1994–95	$13.00	C127
☐ France 1994–95	$20.00	C132	☐ Virginia 1994–95 (Avail. 2/94)	$14.00	C142
☐ Germany 1994	$19.00	C125	☐ Yucatán 1993–94	$18.00	C110
☐ Italy 1994	$19.00	C130			
☐ Jamaica/Barbados 1993–94	$15.00	C105			

FROMMER'S $-A-DAY GUIDES
(Guides to low-cost tourist accommodations and facilities)

	Retail Price	Code		Retail Price	Code
☐ Australia on $45 1993–94	$18.00	D102	☐ Israel on $45 1993–94	$18.00	D101
☐ Costa Rica/Guatemala/ Belize on $35 1993–94	$17.00	D108	☐ Mexico on $45 1994	$19.00	D116
☐ Eastern Europe on $30 1993–94	$18.00	D110	☐ New York on $70 1994–95 (Avail. 4/94)	$16.00	D120
☐ England on $60 1994	$18.00	D112	☐ New Zealand on $45 1993–94	$18.00	D103
☐ Europe on $50 1994	$19.00	D115	☐ Scotland/Wales on $50 1992–93	$18.00	D019
☐ Greece on $45 1993–94	$19.00	D100	☐ South America on $40 1993–94	$19.00	D109
☐ Hawaii on $75 1994	$19.00	D113	☐ Turkey on $40 1992–93	$22.00	D023
☐ India on $40 1992–93	$20.00	D010	☐ Washington, D.C. on $40 1994–95 (Avail. 2/94)	$17.00	D119
☐ Ireland on $45 1994–95 (Avail. 1/94)	$17.00	D117			

FROMMER'S CITY $-A-DAY GUIDES
(Pocket-size guides to low-cost tourist accommodations
and facilities)

	Retail Price	Code		Retail Price	Code
☐ Berlin on $40 1994–95	$12.00	D111	☐ Madrid on $50 1994–95 (Avail. 1/94)	$13.00	D118
☐ Copenhagen on $50 1992–93	$12.00	D003	☐ Paris on $50 1994–95	$12.00	D117
☐ London on $45 1994–95	$12.00	D114	☐ Stockholm on $50 1992–93	$13.00	D022

FROMMER'S WALKING TOURS
(With routes and detailed maps, these companion guides point out
the places and pleasures that make a city unique)

	Retail Price	Code		Retail Price	Code
☐ Berlin	$12.00	W100	☐ Paris	$12.00	W103
☐ London	$12.00	W101	☐ San Francisco	$12.00	W104
☐ New York	$12.00	W102	☐ Washington, D.C.	$12.00	W105

FROMMER'S TOURING GUIDES
(Color-illustrated guides that include walking tours, cultural and historic
sights, and practical information)

	Retail Price	Code		Retail Price	Code
☐ Amsterdam	$11.00	T001	☐ New York	$11.00	T008
☐ Barcelona	$14.00	T015	☐ Rome	$11.00	T010
☐ Brazil	$11.00	T003	☐ Scotland	$10.00	T011
☐ Florence	$ 9.00	T005	☐ Sicily	$15.00	T017
☐ Hong Kong/Singapore/			☐ Tokyo	$15.00	T016
Macau	$11.00	T006	☐ Turkey	$11.00	T013
☐ Kenya	$14.00	T018	☐ Venice	$ 9.00	T014
☐ London	$13.00	T007			

FROMMER'S FAMILY GUIDES

	Retail Price	Code		Retail Price	Code
☐ California with Kids	$18.00	F100	☐ San Francisco with Kids		
☐ Los Angeles with Kids			(Avail. 4/94)	$17.00	F104
(Avail. 4/94)	$17.00	F103	☐ Washington, D.C. with Kids		
☐ New York City with Kids			(Avail. 2/94)	$17.00	F102
(Avail. 2/94)	$18.00	F101			

FROMMER'S CITY GUIDES
(Pocket-size guides to sightseeing and tourist accommodations and
facilities in all price ranges)

	Retail Price	Code		Retail Price	Code
☐ Amsterdam 1993–94	$13.00	S110	☐ Montréal/Québec		
☐ Athens 1993–94	$13.00	S114	City 1993–94	$13.00	S125
☐ Atlanta 1993–94	$13.00	S112	☐ Nashville/Memphis		
☐ Atlantic City/Cape			1994–95 (Avail. 4/94)	$13.00	S141
May 1993–94	$13.00	S130	☐ New Orleans 1993–94	$13.00	S103
☐ Bangkok 1992–93	$13.00	S005	☐ New York 1994 (Avail.		
☐ Barcelona/Majorca/Minorca/			1/94)	$13.00	S138
Ibiza 1993–94	$13.00	S115	☐ Orlando 1994	$13.00	S135
☐ Berlin 1993–94	$13.00	S116	☐ Paris 1993–94	$13.00	S109
☐ Boston 1993–94	$13.00	S117	☐ Philadelphia 1993–94	$13.00	S113
☐ Budapest 1994–95 (Avail.			☐ San Diego 1993–94	$13.00	S107
2/94)	$13.00	S139	☐ San Francisco 1994	$13.00	S133
☐ Chicago 1993–94	$13.00	S122	☐ Santa Fe/Taos/		
☐ Denver/Boulder/Colorado			Albuquerque 1993–94	$13.00	S108
Springs 1993–94	$13.00	S131	☐ Seattle/Portland 1994–95	$13.00	S137
☐ Dublin 1993–94	$13.00	S128	☐ St. Louis/Kansas		
☐ Hong Kong 1994–95			City 1993–94	$13.00	S127
(Avail. 4/94)	$13.00	S140	☐ Sydney 1993–94	$13.00	S129
☐ Honolulu/Oahu 1994	$13.00	S134	☐ Tampa/St.		
☐ Las Vegas 1993–94	$13.00	S121	Petersburg 1993–94	$13.00	S105
☐ London 1994	$13.00	S132	☐ Tokyo 1992–93	$13.00	S039
☐ Los Angeles 1993–94	$13.00	S123	☐ Toronto 1993–94	$13.00	S126
☐ Madrid/Costa del			☐ Vancouver/Victoria 1994–		
Sol 1993–94	$13.00	S124	95 (Avail. 1/94)	$13.00	S142
☐ Miami 1993–94	$13.00	S118	☐ Washington, D.C. 1994		
☐ Minneapolis/St.			(Avail. 1/94)	$13.00	S136
Paul 1993–94	$13.00	S119			

SPECIAL EDITIONS

	Retail Price	Code		Retail Price	Code
☐ Bed & Breakfast Southwest	$16.00	P100	☐ Caribbean Hideaways	$16.00	P103
☐ Bed & Breakfast Great American Cities (Avail. 1/94)	$16.00	P104	☐ National Park Guide 1994 (avail. 3/94)	$16.00	P105
			☐ Where to Stay U.S.A.	$15.00	P102

Please note: if the availability of a book is several months away, we may have back issues of guides to that particular destination. Call customer service at (815) 734-1104.